Marketing Strategies

'An excellent book for any marketing student or practitioner needing to be prepared for the future. Professors Ranchhod and Gurău have taken the 21st Century "bite-sized chunks" approach and produced a valuable resource for the student of marketing, whether new to the field or seasoned professional.'

Charles Jennings, Global Head of Learning, Reuters Group

'The authors navigate through environmental analysis, marketing ethics, market segmentation and strategic positioning through discussing underpinning resources that support value creation yet never losing sight of the need for sustainability, which is all too often a missing component within many marketing strategies. This book is essential reading for those wishing to better understand the challenges and opportunities facing those competing for success and growth in the 21st Century.'

Professor Zahir Irani, Head of Brunel Business School, UK

'This book provides very important insights into the challenges facing marketers today. It has well developed sections on sustainability issues and new perspectives in marketing. It is a must for marketers looking beyond standard textbooks.'

Professor Naval Bhargava, Dean of International Relations, Senior Professor in Marketing, Mudra Institute of Communications Ahmedabad (MICA), India

'Professors Ranchhod and Gurău not only explain the key concepts and tools for effective marketing in today's changing business environment, but also put forward what's next in the marketing world. This is a well written text by authors with vision and insight.'

Birgi Martin, Ph.D. (Research Development Director, USA), and Sharon Albert, Ph.D. (SVP, Marketing and Product Development), Lightspeed Research (WPP Group)

Visit the *Marketing Strategies, second edition* Companion Website at **www.pearsoned.co.uk/ranchhod** to find valuable **student** learning material including links to relevant sites on the web.

Second Edition

Marketing Strategies
A Contemporary Approach

Ashok Ranchhod

and

Călin Gurău

Prentice Hall
FINANCIAL TIMES

An imprint of **Pearson Education**
Harlow, England • London • New York • Boston • San Francisco • Toronto • Sydney • Singapore • Hong Kong
Tokyo • Seoul • Taipei • New Delhi • Cape Town • Madrid • Mexico City • Amsterdam • Munich • Paris • Milan

Pearson Education Limited

Edinburgh Gate
Harlow
Essex CM20 2JE
England

and Associated Companies throughout the world

Visit us on the World Wide Web at:
www.pearsoned.co.uk

———————————

First published 2004
Second edition published 2007

ISBN: 978-0-273-70674-8

British Library Cataloguing-in-Publication Data
A catalogue record for this book is available from the British Library

10 9 8 7 6 5 4 3 2 1
10 09 08 07

Typeset in 9.5/13pt Stone Serif by 30
Printed by Ashford Colour Press Ltd, Gosport

The publisher's policy is to use paper manufactured from sustainable forests.

Contents

Preface   xiii
Acknowledgements   xvii
Publisher's acknowledgements   xvii

1 From structure to chaos? Understanding marketing strategy   1

Introduction   1
Technological advances   2
The marketing concept   4
Marketing as a business process   5
The role of market orientation   6
   Case study: Apple and the iPod   9
   Loyalty   11
Strategic planning to deliver the marketing concept   12
Environmental factors   14
Creating a sense of identity   15
   Limitations   17
Time as an issue in planning   18
   Time and first mover advantages   19
   Time-cycle for products   19
   Time and consumers' perceptions   20
   Case study: Slow coaching *and* The Official Slow Food Manifesto   21
   Time and experiential advantages   22
   Time and technological advantages   22
Ethics as a marketing issue   24
Towards a new strategic marketing planning model   24
   Case study: Internet banking: quick to adapt to technology   25
   Case study: Banco Bradesco trials Fujitsu palm vein authentication
   technology   26
Summary   27
Chapter questions   28

2 Opening up analysis and positioning — 29

Introduction	29
Internal analysis	29
The analysis of tangible and intangible resources	29
Operant and operand resources	30
Organisational strengths and weaknesses	30
Product portfolio analysis	33
The value added chain approach	38
Internal resources (competitive advantage) and corporate objectives (strategic mission)	39
External analysis	40
Market threats and opportunities	40
Porter's model of industry attractiveness	42
Case study: Eminem's CD sales impressive despite music sharing	45
Overview of analysing the industry	47
The industry attractiveness/business'competitive strength matrix	48
Key issues to consider when using portfolio matrices	52
The marketing information system	52
Market segmentation	53
Segmentation criteria	55
Geographic segmentation	56
Demographic segmentation	57
Case study: The power behind PlayStation: going for old	59
Case study: Lifestyle snapshots	62
The segmentation process	69
Strategic positioning	71
Case study: Little Dyson cleaner finds a niche in the smaller Japanese home	73
The Internet, postmodern marketing and globalisation	75
Summary	78
Chapter questions	78

3 Stakeholder concerns and solutions — 79

Introduction	79
Case study: Slow decline of high-street champion	79
Case study: M&S sales surge stuns city	81
Stakeholder theory	82
Stakeholder interactions	82
Case study: Image in the balance	91
Case study: Customers as stakeholders of Nestlé	97
Case study: Bhatia v. Sterlite Industries (2001)	100
Developing competitive marketing strategies	101
Narrow view	103

Broad view   104
Understanding stakeholder evolution and management   107
Case study: British Biotechnology   108
Competitive positioning   109
Summary   112
Chapter questions   112

4 A sustainable Earth matters   113

Introduction   113
Understanding environmental marketing   115
Energy and the climate   116
Chemicals and the biological boomerang   117
Commerce and the oceans   117
Case study: Nike Corporation   126
The lifecycle analysis (LCA) concept–lifecycle thinking   126
Case study: APRIL takes a leaf out of the green book   129
Implications for organisations   134
Green consumer behaviour   139
Green marketing strategies   142
Case study: Green marketing: lessons from the leaders   143
Responsible marketing   145
Green marketing   146
Social marketing   147
Summary   149
Chapter questions   149

5 Communicating effectively   150

Introduction   150
Case study: The ad revolution will not be televised   153
Corporate image and corporate identity   155
Defining the IMC concept   157
Organisational challenges to implementing the IMC concept   159
Lack of horizontal communication   160
Functional specialisation   160
Decentralisation   160
Lack of IMC planning and expertise   160
Lack of budget   161
Lack of a database and the accompanying technology   161
Culture   162
Fear of change   162
One size does *not* fit all   163

Implementing the IMC concept   163
   The seven evolutionary steps model   163
   The three-dimensional model   165
   The eight-step process   166
IMC in an online environment   170
   Internet-based communication synergies   170
   Internet-based communication challenges   171
   A model for implementing an IOMC strategy   172
Brands   175
   Case study: Why British shoppers are sniffing at everyday low prices   176
   Brand strategies   178
   Brand management   180
   Case study: Morgan Motor Company Limited   181
   Brand values   184
   Case study: How Philips got brand buzz   185
   Brand equity   188
Summary   189
Chapter questions   189

6 Implementation is the key   190

Introduction   190
Planned versus emergent implementation   190
   Case study: Dark days for Guinness   193
The main factors influencing strategy implementation   195
   Internal factors   196
   Case study: 'Do your homework', French professor tells small firms   197
   External factors   204
The impact of technology on marketing implementation   213
   Case study: What makes a business more agile?   214
   IT-related organisational benefits   216
Customer relationships   220
Summary   226
Chapter questions   226

7 Understanding and creating effective marketing cultures   227

Introduction   227
The visible and invisible parts of an organisation   228
   The visible parts of an organisation   228
   Case study: Setting off a chain reaction   232
   The roles of the invisible parts of an organisation   234
The transition from focusing on products to a customer orientation 241

The learning organisation   242
   What are learning processes?   243
   From individual to organisational learning   246
Keeping the benefits of a learning orientation   250
   Organisational memory and mental models   250
   The culture of learning   251
   Case study: Adapt or die …   251
   Learning is not straightforward   254
   Developing a learning, market-orientated organisation   256
Summary   261
Chapter questions   262

8 Globalising marketing efforts   263

Introduction   263
The main factors influencing international marketing operations   264
The internationalisation of firms   265
   Case study: Sabon cleans up in America   267
   Case study: Success for Tasmanian 'born global'   270
Offshoring and globalisation of suppliers   272
International marketing orientations   276
Standardisation versus adaptation   277
Selecting which foreign markets to target   278
   Evaluate and understand the assets and strategic objectives of the firm   279
   Define the main criteria for selecting a country   280
   Apply the selection criteria and select the country or countries   280
   Case study: Establishing countries'attractiveness for exporting opportunities   281
   Study the profile of the selected foreign market(s)   283
   Develop the strategic marketing plan   283
Market entry strategies   284
   Exporting   284
   Licensing   285
   Franchising   285
   Strategic alliances   286
   Joint ventures   287
   Subsidiaries   288
   Case study: When big business bites   289
Managing international operations   291
   Multinational   292
   International   292
   Global   293
   Transnational   294
Summary   294
Chapter questions   295

9 Measuring for effectiveness in marketing — 296

Introduction	296
Measuring marketing performance	296
The role of financial analysis	297
Profit ratios	298
Gross profit margin	298
Net profit margin	298
Return on total assets	299
Net income	299
Return on shareholders' equity	299
Liquidity ratios	299
Leverage ratios	300
Activity ratios	300
Marketing metrics	301
Adaptability or innovativeness	302
Effectiveness	302
Efficiency	303
Measuring the major marketing attributes	304
What we have learned	309
Understanding measurement within the global context	312
Case study: Sweet ambitions to tempt more takers	313
Measuring environmental effectiveness	315
Case study: The Co-operative Bank	319
Case study: Novo Nordisk: TakeAction! – make the triple bottom line your business	320
Developing individual measures	324
Strategic	324
Tactical	324
Suitability	325
Acceptability	325
Feasibility	325
Using the measures and the TBL	326
Summary	327
Chapter questions	327

10 New perspectives in marketing and the way forward — 328

Introduction	328
Moving away form the 4 Ps	328
Price	329
Product	330
Place	330

Promotion 330
Consumer behaviour 331
 Case study: The cultural melting pot 333
Value co-creation 335
 The service-dominant logic in marketing 335
 Marketing flexibility 337
 Flexibility regarding customers' participation 337
 Flexibility of interaction 338
 Flexibility of implementation 338
 Open innovation 340
 Case study: Open-source biotech 342
The dynamic environment 346
 Structure of markets 347
 Speed 349
 The future impact of technology 350
Digital marketing 351
 Introduction 351
 What is happening to the individual? 352
 Case study: My virtual life 354
 Blog marketing 358
 Mobile marketing 362
 Case study: Digital marketing – flying higher and higher via mobile platforms 364
 Marketing on the Internet 364
 What next in the digital age? 365
Social marketing 369
 Previous studies 371
 Theories and models of social change 372
 The role of social marketing campaigns 375
 Online social marketing 376
 Case study: Jamie Oliver in talks over campaign for family meals 377
 Case study: Diet industry will be winner in battle of the bulge as
 Europe goes to fat 382
Rural marketing 383
 Develop products that meet market needs 384
 Understand the informal economy 384
 Understand the role of second-generation émigrés to countries in
 Europe, the USA, Canada and Japan 384
 Case study: Act local, think global 386
Towards a new strategic marketing model 388
Summary and final observations 390

References and further reading 392
Index 408

Supporting resources

Visit **www.pearsoned.co.uk/ranchhod** to find valuable online resources

Companion Website for students
- Links to relevant sites on the web

For instructors
- Complete, downloadable Instructor's Manual
- PowerPoint slides that can be downloaded and used for presentations

For more information please contact your local Pearson Education sales representative or visit **www.pearsoned.co.uk/ranchhod**

Preface

In launching into the second edition of *Marketing Strategies*, it became apparent to the authors that much had changed quite dramatically in the world since the last edition. We have therefore retitled this edition *Marketing Strategies: A Contemporary Approach*. A marketing textbook has to be contemporary in order to absorb and reflect new ideas and processes, at the same time reflecting the changing needs and desires of the society at large. Social norms have changed and are continually changing, with technology making ever greater inroads into the marketing process. Markets, too, are becoming more global in nature than before. At the same time, issues such as global warming, discussed in the first edition, are now taking the main stage in many political and marketing debates.

Most practising marketers realise that the practice of marketing can be quite messy and difficult to define. In order to understand the rather untidy and chaotic nature of marketing, this book does not follow a linear format. The chapters consider some of the major issues that impact on marketing strategy development and can be read in any order. The book also aims to close the gap in understanding cultural issues by offering case studies that have been drawn from various parts of the world. It shows different views on marketing and their impact on the discipline. It is also a mix of the practical and theoretical. Exercises in many chapters can be used practically by readers to assess their companies' marketing stances. The book takes an international perspective rather than the conventional North American approach. The underlying theme of the book addresses issues such as sustainability and ethics. In many ways, the book tries to explain the holistic and rather organic nature of marketing. In fact, in line with the way in which marketing is evolving and the growing interest in market orientation, there is little discussion of the 4 Ps in the book. This may come as bit of a disappointment to those looking for hard and fast rules when developing marketing strategies. Strategies are often context- and company-specific. This becomes apparent as you read the book.

This edition retains the radical nature of the first because it expands five of the main contemporary factors affecting marketing in the twenty-first century – sustainability, ethics, market orientation, the impact of technology and globalisation. In addition, there are several new sections, which are described and discussed below. There is an emphasis on understanding the role of branding and the development of customer relationships. This book develops the role of marketing and gives it a thought-provoking stance. It shows the types of questions that marketing managers and students should consider. The philosophy of marketing is as important as its application and implementation.

Structure

This book is divided into ten chapters, each with a distinctive theme. The chapters are interlinked and support each other. Chapter 1 considers the key impacts on strategy making and how a range of crucial factors should be considered when developing a marketing strategy. The impact of new factors is taken into account. This chapter has been enlarged with a new case study featuring Apple and a discussion of time in marketing strategy development.

Chapter 2, on understanding analysis, has been greatly expanded with new cases and even more useful analytical techniques that take a better view of the internal and external forces driving a company.

Chapter 3 is still mainly concerned with the role that stakeholders play in the development of strategies. The difference between the UK's and Continental models of corporate governance is taken into consideration. Ethical and moral dimensions are also emphasised. This chapter has a new section on corporate social responsibility.

Chapter 4 largely follows on from Chapter 3 and develops the theme of sustainability and ways in which marketing could and should contribute to the development of sustainable strategies. This chapter has new sections on understanding the current issues that are being debated regarding climate change and also indicates marketing strategies for developing responsible customer behaviour. The chapter ends with a practical example of how to formulate ethical and sustainable strategies, given the changing nature of the consumer profile.

Chapter 5 is a new chapter looking at integrated marketing communications and understanding the role of branding in a company's strategy.

Chapter 6 looks at how marketing strategies can be implemented in this technological age. It also discusses the interplay between technology and people when implementing marketing strategies. This chapter contains new case studies with a newer and wider range of implementation issues that marketers need to consider.

Chapter 7 is now much more about organising for marketing success, together with an emphasis on organisational learning. There is a new section on corporate culture with a questionnaire that can be used to gauge organisational culture.

Chapter 8 is another new chapter and takes an in-depth view of globalisation, which is touching the lives of consumers and organisations. The international strategies that a company could adopt are fully discussed.

Chapter 9 looks at the increasing importance of marketing metrics. Marketers are constantly having to justify their positions in companies and so developing good metrics that take into account both financial and marketing aspects is important. It is a way of monitoring whether or not objectives have been met. This chapter also has a new element on the marketing audit and marketing performance measures. Not only does it consider ecological and ethical measures in its approach but it also has a new section on the triple bottom line.

Chapter 10, the final chapter, considers new perspectives in marketing that offer ways forward for developing new kinds of strategies. Many new ideas with regard to becoming customercentric, understanding the future impact of technology and the growing importance of rural marketing are considered. There are new sections on social marketing, value co-creation and digital marketing, encompassing up-to-the-minute ideas and views.

As marketing enters the twenty-first century, the consumer base is changing, the world of consumption is changing and marketers need to become more ethical and accountable in their approach to business. At the same time, they need to understand social and technology issues as never before. Communications are now not only instantaneous but also can be recorded and stored for posterity be means of Internet and mobile technology. Marketers need to embrace these changes to build better and longer-lasting relationships with their customers.

Key features

The text offers both philosophical and practical approaches to marketing and has the following key features:

- it discusses the changing nature of marketing and impact of technology
- the fragmentation of markets
- it analyses the stakeholder perspective and offers insights into how to work with stakeholders
- it takes a comprehensive look at how analysis and segmentation are practised and some of the pitfalls associated with this
- the arguments for sustainability and ethics are developed and practical ways of implementing these types of marketing strategies are explained
- globalisation is discussed extensively
- marketing communications, in the form of integrated marketing strategies and branding, are discussed
- the impact of digital marketing is discussed comprehensively
- numerous examples of different strategies are offered
- a range of case studies is used to illustrate the arguments put forward in each chapter
- examples are drawn from all over the world
- the holistic nature of marketing is stressed
- the book illustrates why it is important for marketers to be wide open to ideas when developing marketing strategies
- the book attempts to portray how marketing is likely to develop in the future and the key issues that marketers should consider
- the book's radical approach offers readers the opportunity to understand each chapter independently
- the book emphasises the need to understand cultural dynamics when implementing marketing strategies.

Figure P.1 illustrates how the chapters relate to each other in the book.

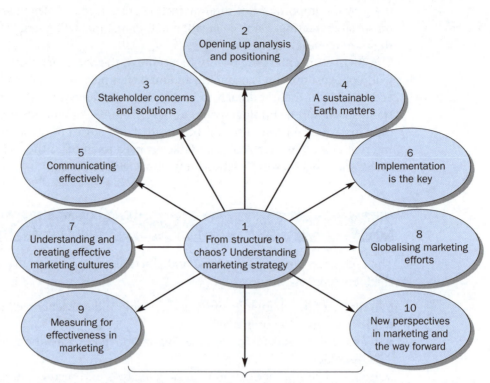

Figure P.1 How the chapters relate to each other

When developing strategies, it is important that marketers take into consideration the range of issues discussed in this book and keep an eye on how marketing is likely to change in the future. This book provides guideposts, not solutions.

Professor Ashok Ranchhod and Professor Călin Gurău

Acknowledgements

I would like to thank a range of people who made this project feasible. First of all, I would like to thank my co-author, Dr Călin Gurău who has made a strong impact on the new edition. His encouragement and support were invaluable in producing this text on time. I would also like to thank the contributors to the first edition, Dr Julie Tinson and Dr Claire Gauzente as their work helped to provide some building blocks for the new edition.

A person who made this possible in the dim and distant past is my older brother, Kantilal, who awakened my curiosity about the written word at a very early age, as well as Mrs Fynn, my first tutor at the age of three in Zambia.

Finally, I would like to thank my wife, Nilanta, and my children, Jaimini, Chintan and Reshma, for putting up with my disappearances into the study and piles of paper all over the house.

Professor Ashok Ranchhod

Publisher's Acknowledgements

We are grateful to the following for permission to reproduce copyright material:

Figure CS1.1 from www.applematters.com/index.php/section/comments/apples-q2-numbers-a-closer-look, Chris Seibold/Apple Matters; Figure CS1.2 from http://maddogfog.blogspot.com/2006/02/itunes-song-purchases-plotted-on-graph.html, Michael Doeff; Figure 1.2 from Measuring market orientation: a multi-factor, multi-item approach, *Journal of Marketing Management*, Vol. 10, pp. 725–42 (Deng, S. and Dart, J. 1994), Westburn Publishers Ltd; Figure 1.3 from Market-driving organizations: a framework, *Academy of Marketing Science Review*, Vol. 5, pp. 1–14 (Carrillat, F. A., Jaramillo, F. and Locander, W. B. 2004), Academy of Marketing Science; Figure 1.5 from *Exploring Corporate Strategy,* 5th edition, Prentice Hall (Johnson, G. and Scholes, K. 2000); Figure 1.7 from Creating a sense of mission, *Long Range Planning*, Vol. 24 No. 4, pp. 10–20 (Campbell, A. and Yeung, S 1991), copyright 1991, with permission from Elsevier; Figure 2.10 from The directional policy matrix-tools for strategic planning, *Long Range Planning*, June, (Robinson, S. J. Q., Hitchen, R. E. and Wade, D. P. 1978), copyright 1978, with permission from Elsevier; Figure 2.11 from *Strategic Management*, Addison Wesley (Rowe, A.J., Mason, R.O. and Dickel, K.E. 1986), with permission from Professor Alan J. Rowe; Table 2.4 from *Contemporary Perspectives on Strategic Market Planning,*

Allyn and Bacon (Kerin, R. A., Mahajan, V. and Varadarajan, P. R. 1990), with permission from Roger A Kerin; Table 2.7 from *Consumer Behavior, 9th edition* (Hawkins, D. I., Best, R. J. and Coney, K. A. 2004), reproduced with permission of The McGraw-Hill Companies; Table 2.8 from Life cycle concept in marketing research, *Journal of Marketing Research*, Vol. 3, November, pp. 355–363 (Wells, W. and Gubar, G. 1966), reprinted with permission from the American Marketing Association; Tables 2.9 and 2.10 from Measuring customer satisfaction: a platform for calculating, predicting and increasing customer profitability, *Journal of Targeting, Measurement and Analysis for Marketing*, Vol. 10 No. 3, pp. 203–19 (Gurău, C. and Ranchhod, A. 2002), reproduced with permission of Palgrave Macmillan; Figure 3.2 and Table 3.1 from *Criteria for Board Construction in the Entrepreneurial Firm*, paper presented to RENT XI Conference – Research in Entrepreneurship and Small Business, Mannheim, 26–29 November (Watkins, D. 1997); Table 3.3 from Stakeholder excellence? Framing the evolution and complexity of a stakeholder perspective of the firm, *Corporate Social Responsibility and Environmental Management*, Vol. 9 No. 4, pp. 187–95 (Jonker, J. and Foster, D. 2002), copyright John Wiley & Sons Limited, reproduced with permission; Figures 4.1 (WWF) and 4.18 (ADE) from *Talk the Walk: Advancing Sustainable Lifestyles through Marketing and Communications*, www.uneptie.org/pc/sustain/reports/advertising/Talk_the_Walk.pdf (UNEP 2005, WWF, ADE) and Figures 4.5, 4.6, 4.7 and 4.8 from *GEO-3, Global Environment Outlook 3*, www.unep.org/geo/geo3, (UNEP 2002), United Nations Environment Programme; Figures 4.2, 4.3 and 4.4 from *World Watch* March/April 2000, Worldwatch Institute, www.worldwatch.org; Figure 4.9 from *Environmental Marketing Management*, Pitman Publishing (Peattie, K. 1995); Figures 4.12 and 4.13 from *The Greenpeace Guide to Greener Electronics*, Greenpeace (25 August 2006); Table 4.1 from *Green Marketing and Management: a Global Perspective*, Blackwell Publishing (Wasik, J.F. 1996); Table 4.2 from www.naturalbusiness.com/market.html, Conscious Media Inc. (2000); Table 5.1 from Marketing opportunities in the digital world, *Internet Research: Networking Applications and Policy*, Vol. 8 No. 2, pp. 185–94, Emerald Group Publishing Limited (Kiani, R. G. 1998); Figure 5.3 from The concept, process and evolution of integrated marketing communications (Duncan, T. and Caywood, C.) in *Integrated Communications: Synergy of Persuasive Voices*, Lawrence Erlbaum Associates, Inc. (Thorson, E. and Moore, J., eds 1996); Figure 5.5 from *Communicating Globally: An Integrated Marketing Approach* (Schultz, D.E. and Kitchen, P.J. 2000), reproduced with permission of The McGraw-Hill Companies; Figure 5.13 from Cultivating service brand equity, *Academy of Marketing Science Journal*, Vol. 28 No. 1, pp. 128–37 (Berry, L.L. 2000), copyright 2000, reprinted by permission of Sage Publications; Figure 6.8 from *Value Co-creation in Industrial Buyer–Seller Partnerships: Creating and Exploiting Interdependencies*, Doctoral Thesis, Åbo Akademi University Press (Forsström, B. 2005); Figure 6.16 from IT: know thyself, *Intelligent Enterprise*, Vol. 3 No. 8, CMP Technology (Flohr, T. 2000); Figure 6.17 from www.dc.com/obx, Deloitte Consulting; Table 6.1 from The strategic market planning – implementation interface in small and midsized industrial firms: an exploratory study, *Journal of Marketing*, Vol. 5 Summer, pp. 77–92 (Sashittal, H.C. and Tankersley, C. 1997), American Marketing Association; Table 6.2 from

Prioritising target markets, *Marketing Intelligence & Planning*, Vol. 16 No. 7, pp. 407–17 (Simkin, L. and Dibb, S. 1998), with permission from MCB UP Ltd; Table 6.4 from *Information Masters: Secrets of the Customer Race* (McKean, J. 1999), © John Wiley and Sons Inc., reproduced with permission; Figure 7.8 from Marketing department organisational chart, WH Smith plc; Figure 7.9 from *Organizational Culture and Leadership, 2nd edition*, John Wiley & Sons, Inc. (Schein, E.H. 1992); Table 7.1 from Measuring organizational cultures: a qualitative and quantitative study across twenty cases, *Administrative Science Quarterly*, Vol. 35 No. 2, pp. 286–316 (Hofstede, G., Neuijen, B., Ohayv, D.D. and Sanders, G. 1990), Cornell University; Figure 7.12 from Les facteurs de complexité des schémas cognitifs des dirigeants, *Revue Française de Gestion*, March–May, pp. 86–93 (Calori, R. and Sarnin, P. 1993), © 1993 Hermes Science Publications; Figure 7.22 from Knowledge-based organization, *Business Review*, November–December, Vol. 41 No. 1, pp. 59–73 (Nonaka, I. and Konno, N. 1993); Table 7.2 from La mémoire organisationnelle, *Revue Française de Gestion*, September–October, pp. 30–42, Lavoisier SAS (Girod, M. 1995); Table 7.4 from Network learning: exploring learning by interorganizational networks, *Human Relations*, Vol. 55 No. 4, pp. 427–54 (Knight, L. 2002), reproduced with permission, copyright © The Tavistock Institute, London, UK, 2002, by permission of Sage Publications Ltd and Dr L. Knight; Table 8.2 from www.oecd.org/daf/governance/principles.htm, *Principles of Corporate Governance*, p. 23 © 1997 OECD; Figure 9.3 from *Customer Lifetime Value: Powerful Insights into a Company's Business and Activities*, Booz Allen Hamilton (Bacuvier, G., Peladeau, P., Trichet, A. and Zerbib, P. 2001); Table 9.1 from *Promotion des ventes et action commerciale*, Librarie Vuibert (Ingold, P. 1995); Table 9.2 from Selecting environmental performance indicators, *Greener Management International*, Vol. 33 Spring, pp. 97–114 (Scherpereel, C., Koppen, V. and Heering, G. B. F. 2001), Greenleaf Publishing Limited, and *WBCSD Project on Eco-efficiency Metrics and Reporting: State-of-play Report,* World Business Council for Sustainable Development (Lehni, M. 1998); Table 9.3 from *WBCSD Project on Eco-efficiency Metrics and Reporting: State-of-play Report,* World Business Council for Sustainable Development (Lehni, M. 1998); Figure 10.1 from The antecedents and consequences of customer-centric marketing, *Journal of the Academy of Marketing Science*, Vol. 28 No. 1, pp. 55–66 (Sheth, J.N., Sisodia, R.S. and Sharma, A. 2000), copyright 2000, reprinted by permission of Sage Publications; Figure 10.3 from Feeling the heat: making marketing more productive, *Marketing Management*, Vol. 4 No. 2, pp. 8–23 (Sheth, J. and Sisodia, R.S. 1995), American Marketing Association; Figure 10.4 from Strategic marketing models for a dynamic competitive environment, *Journal of General Management*, Vol. 24 No. 4, pp. 63–78 (Karin, I. and Preiss, K. 2002), The Braybrooke Press; Figures 10.8 and 10.9 from *Open Innovation: The New Imperative for Creating and Capturing Value*, Harvard Business School Press (Chesbrough, H. 2003); Figure 10.10 from *Science and Engineering Indicators 2006*, Volume 1, courtesy: National Science Board; Figures 10.11 and 10.12 from *Innovation, Social Capital, and the New Economy: New Federal Policies to Support Collaborative Research*, Progressive Policy Institute, PPI Briefing, 1st July (Fountain, J.E. and Atkinson, R.D. 1998); Figures 10.13, 10.14, 10.15 and 10.18 from Ofcom research; Figures 10.19 and 10.20 from

Ethical marketing for competitive advantage on the Internet, *Academy of Marketing Science Review*, Vol. 10 (Gauzente, C. and Ranchhod, A. 2001), © Academy of Marketing Science; Figure 10.24 from www.census.gov/prod/3/98pubs/p23-194.pdf, *Population Profile of the United States: 1997*, US Census Bureau, Washington DC; Table 10.3 from Arieanna Foley in *Blog Marketing: The Revolutionary New Way to Increase Sales, Profits and Growth* (Wright, J. 2006), reproduced with permission of The McGraw-Hill Companies; Table 10.4 from Marketing social marketing in the social change marketplace, *Journal of Public Policy and Marketing*, Vol. 21 No. 1, pp. 3–13 (Andreasen, A.R. 2002), American Marketing Association; Table 10.9 from the United Nations Population Division, http://esa.un.org/unpp/

Finextra for the article 'Banco Bradesco trials Fujitsu palm vein authentication technology', published on www.finextra.com; The Associated Press for the article 'Eminem's CD sales impressive despite music sharing', published in *USA Today*, 31st May 2002, www.usatoday.com; TBWA, London Ltd for 'The power behind Playstation: Going for Old' by Carl Radcliffe; The Guardian News and Media Group for the extracts from 'Little Dyson cleaner finds niche in the smaller Japanese home' by Terry Macalister published in *The Guardian* 24th May 2006, the article 'The ad revolution will not be televised' by Owen Gibson published in *The Guardian* 20th March 2006, the article 'Dark Days for Guinness' by Owen Bowcott and Simon Bowers, published in *The Guardian*, 29th August 2006, the article ' "Do your homework" French professor tells small firms' by John Dunn, published in *The Guardian*, 8th June 1999, the article 'When big business bites', by Fiona Walsh, published in *The Guardian*, 8th June 2006, the article 'Jamie Oliver in talks over campaign for family meals' by David Brindle and Jacqueline Maley published in *The Guardian*, 27th June 2006, and 'Diet industry will be winner in battle of the bulge as Europe goes to fat', by John Carvel, published in *The Guardian*, 31st May 2002; Justin Hunt for his article 'What makes a business more agile?', published in *The Guardian*, 9th May 2002; Press Holdings Media Group for the article 'Slow decline of high-street champion' by Richard Northedge published in *The Business* (previously *Sunday Business*), 30th September 2001; Associated Newspapers for an extract from 'M&S sales surge stuns City', by Jim Armitage published in *The Evening Standard*, 11th April 2006; Andrew Pharoah for 'Inside track: image in the balance' published in the *Financial Times* 16th September 2002; Express Newspapers for the article 'Losses cut as Martin wins back M&S deals' published in *The Daily Express* 29th September 2001; Public Concern at Work for the article 'Bhatia v Sterlite Industries', published on www.pcaw.co.uk, 2001; Macmillan Ltd for an extract from the article 'Looking good: Public Relation strategies for biotechnology' by Ranchhod and Gurău, published in the *Nature Biotechnology Summer Supplement*, (Europroduct Focus) 1999; Simon & Schuster for the extract 'Nike Corporation' from *Beyond the Bottom Line: Putting Social Responsibility to work for your Business and the World* by Joel Makower, 1994; RISI for the article 'APRIL takes a leaf out of the green book', by Anna Jenkinson, published in *Pulp And Paper International* 2001; Joel Makower for the extract 'Green marketing: lessons from the leaders' from www.worldchanging.com/archives/003502.html, J. Makower, 18 September 2005;

The Economist Newspapers Ltd for the article 'Why British shoppers are sniffing at everyday low prices', published in *The Economist* 28th September 2006; Mike Wilman for the article 'Morgan Motor Company Limited: Retaining traditional brand values to become a long-term niche player', by Mike Wilman (with additional material by Donna Goodwin), 2007; Business in the Community for the article 'The Co-operative Bank', 2004; the World Business Council for Sustainable Development (WBCSD) for the article 'Novo Nordisk: Take action! Make the triple bottom line your business', 1st April 2004; Yasmin Sekhon for her article 'The Cultural Melting Pot' 2002; and *Fast Company* for the article 'Act local, think global' by Rekha Balu, June 2001, *Fast Company*.

We are grateful to the Financial Times Limited for permission to reprint the following material:

Internet banking: quick to adapt to technology, © *Financial Times*, 20 December 2000; Sweet ambitions to tempt more takers, © *Financial Times*, 16 July 2002.

In some instances we have been unable to trace the owners of copyright material, and we would appreciate any information that would enable us to do so.

1 From structure to chaos? Understanding marketing strategy

Introduction

Marketing as a subject is continually evolving and the recent impact of ideas and technology need to be assessed carefully as the new century gets underway. This book attempts to give some insights into the way in which marketing is evolving and progressing. The basic premise of marketing revolves around matching companies' offerings with consumers' needs. While this basic premise is still the same, the ways in which companies' offerings are matched to customers' needs are constantly in a state of flux. With advancing technologies such as the Internet and mobile communications, several paradoxical situations are set up. Although customers may be given a faster, more cohesive service, it can become depersonalised. Customers can become 'spoilt' and demand a one-to-one relationship even though companies may not have the resources to cope with this.

Strategy in marketing involves harnessing a company's resources to meet customers' needs via market analysis, an understanding of competitors' actions, governmental actions and globalisation, together with a consideration of technological issues and other environmental changes. The management of these complex interrelationships needs a more lateral approach than the linear approach often applied in conventional strategic marketing thinking.

This book attempts to unravel the difficulties associated with changes in marketing, juxtaposing them with some of the more conventional approaches. The book therefore uses many of the latest marketing theories as well as a range of case studies to help readers improve their marketing thinking and skills. As ever, it is the authors' view that good marketers need both practical experience and a good knowledge of academic approaches to solving marketing problems. Given the rapid changes that are taking place in marketing, academics are often left behind by the groups of individuals or companies that can see gaps in the market offered by the new technologies. Many marketing techniques are developed quickly and 'on the hoof' as new applications of technology emerge. This book dynamically embraces these changes and attempts to make sense of the bewildering changes taking place in the marketing landscape in terms of technology, environment and society. Finally, the book tries to develop new academic frameworks to understand the impact of these changes and provide new avenues for marketers to engage with their consumers and customers.

Technological advances

Marketing has evolved over the last two centuries as the systems of production and consumption have changed owing to the unprecedented rate of development of technology. This rate of development in technology has seen the advent of mass manufacturing, near instantaneous communication systems and the development of rapid transport systems. In this context, marketing progressively moved from fragmentation to mass marketing, then to segmentation marketing (Tedlow 1993). There is now another technological drive, owing to powerful computing techniques (Patron 1996). The increasing ease of communication for the average person (Cronin 1996) and the development of technologies for flexible manufacturing (Yasumuro 1993) is leading marketers to consider the absolute dislocation of time and space when undertaking marketing transactions. The Internet, in turn, offers a virtual 24-hour shopping experience in any market sector for any person in the world who is able to access it. At the same time, traditional retailers, such as Tesco, are offering a 24-hour shopping experience without the Internet. These changes are now accelerating with even more sophisticated targeting of customers via various media. Consumers are used to a range of ways in which companies can build relationships with them via:

- the Internet
- interactive television
- mobile phones (though this is still nascent)
- 'active' billboards
- microchips embedded in products.

In many ways, the exciting range of digital media means that the days of mass marketing are numbered and consumers themselves are *choosing* to opt in or out of marketing messages and advertising. Gradually, consumers are beginning to take control of what they want, when they want it and how they want it. The era of personalised marketing is here.

Figure 1.1 shows the development of different marketing phases and indicates that markets are not only fragmenting (Ranchhod and Hackney 1997) because of the ease and variety and speed of communication on offer but also being driven to offer more personal experiences. Paradoxically this contrasts with the situation in the early part of the nineteenth century, when markets were fragmented as a result of *poor* communications and transport systems.

Fragmentation is occurring now as market segments cannot be clearly defined, with consumers continuously rearranging their preferences as a result of greater

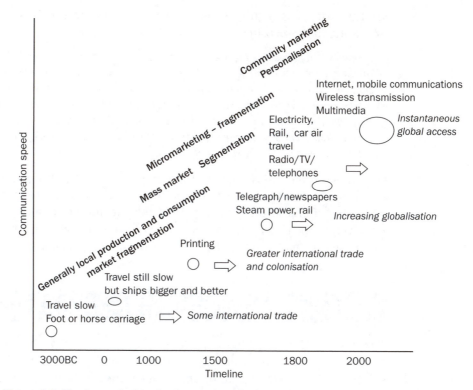

Figure 1.1 The impact of technology on marketing

product choice. Allied to this, rapid and continuous communication allows consumers infinite choices of products and scattered markets that can be accessed globally. Certainly, much of the literature on postmodernism seems to point towards fragmentation. The fragmentation of society, made possible and fostered by the developments of industry and commerce, is one of the most visible consequences of postmodern individualism (Cova 1996). This fragmentation is encouraged by the ability of the individual to maintain 'virtual' contact with the world, electronically, freeing the individual from social interaction, but at the same time increasing the concentration of the ego, placing demands for 'tailored' products and services in the marketplace. This heralds the era of personalised products and permission-based marketing. There are indications that some of the demographic and lifestyle changes in society are just beginning to offer such a scenario. This scenario has been taken even further by the development of a hyperreal world, such as Second Life (www.secondlife.com). There, a worldwide community can be built and transactions take place in a virtual currency (Linden dollars) that can be converted into US dollars. Second Life is a virtual world where over 300,000 individuals 'live', work, play and create and sell products. They can buy land, build houses or just follow their own fantasies. There are no real objectives and no tasks – it is not a game. Many individuals create art, have discussions, fly around the different locations, make friends and generally just browse. Some 'netrepreneurs' even set up businesses selling services that then become mainstream businesses. According to the website:

> *Shopping is a big part of the Second Life experience for many Residents. You can buy and sell anything that can be made in-world, from clothes, skins, wigs, jewelry, and custom animations for avatars, to furniture, buildings, weapons, vehicles, games, and more. Once you're ready to bring your products to the market, it's simply a matter of buying or sub-renting property, for opening up a shop. There are also Resident-owned malls which charge rental fees, or take a cut of your proceeds. As in the real world, the challenge is to build up a reputation that earns a steady stream of customers.*

Given such profound changes in the way people are beginning to market products and services, marketers have be able to understand, explore and galvanise their marketing efforts so that they are more flexible and personalised than previously. However, at the other end are the 'digital have nots' who also have to be catered for in the vast marketing landscape and this is explored later in the book.

The marketing concept

The marketing concept has been discussed at great length by a range of authors (Kotler 2000). The main premise of the concept is linking production and consumption. A company has to be able to meet the needs of customers. This meeting of needs should be within the company's ability and the range of resources available. Meeting customers' needs is a multifaceted activity, needing the full range of a company's resources – ranging from sales activities to final delivery and after sales service. In service industries, although the range of activities differs, their success still depends on satisfying customers.

Charities, too, have begun to embrace the marketing concept. However, defining customer satisfaction is more nebulous and complex than it is in other sectors. Satisfaction in relation to charities often resides with the recipients of food, money or training.

In all cases, however, the marketing concept relies on the creation of *value* for the consumers. The connection between value creation and marketing is not new. The marketing concept is considered as a process of achieving organisational goals by determining the needs and wants of target markets and delivering the desired satisfactions more effectively and efficiently than competitors do (Kotler 1996, 1997). This definition suggests that the companies most likely to succeed in the increasingly dynamic and competitive markets are those that take into account the expectations of their customers and gear themselves to satisfying them better than do their rivals. It recognises that the process of marketing consists of understanding, learning and developing values as a result of marketing activities. Similar ideas can also be recognised in the definition of marketing given by the American Marketing Association (AMA) in 1985, which holds that marketing is the process of planning and executing activities to create exchanges that satisfy individual and organisational objectives. However, in line with modern thinking, the marketing concept ought to take a much broader view and so the definition should also include the satisfaction of a whole range of stakeholders. Thus, it is defined here as:

> *Marketing is the process of planning and executing activities that satisfy individual, ecological and social needs ethically and sincerely, while also satisfying organisational objectives.*

Within this definition, it is clear that marketing objectives are not always financial in nature. Ecological and social needs are becoming increasingly important in the context of marketing strategies. Marketing strategies are defined by the overall corporate vision of an organisation and constitute the actions taken to satisfy customers and their needs. In doing this, it is important that an organisation understands the competitive situation, the general environment, as well as its role and obligations within it, when developing and executing marketing strategies. Out of this understanding, an organisation can develop segmentation and performance criteria by choosing to follow particular options that may present themselves. It is interesting note, therefore, that on 15 September 2005, the AMA changed the definition to:

> *Marketing is an organisational function and a set of processes for creating, communicating and delivering value to customers and for managing customer relationships in ways that benefit the organisation and its stakeholders.*

This definition is more in line with that adopted in this book and the emphasis now is on stakeholders and delivering value to customers. Customers of organisations can be varied in nature. For charities and NFPs the greater number would be the recipients and donors, whereas for business organisations they would be the consumers. In any case, some benefit has to be expected from marketing activities for both the organisation and its stakeholders. The stakeholders can be quite varied, ranging from shareholders, employees and NGOs to the environment. Stakeholder interaction is explored in Chapter 3.

Marketing as a business process

That marketing should be thought of as the design and management of all the business processes necessary to define, develop and deliver value to target customers has often been the cornerstone of marketing thinking (Webster 1997). He suggests that the marketing process should include the following.

- *Value-defining processes* Processes that enable an organisation to understand the environment in which it operates better, understand its own resources and capabilities more clearly, determine its own position in the overall value chain and assess the value it creates by analysing its target customers.
- *Value-developing processes* Processes that create value throughout the value chain, such as the procurement strategy, new product and service development, design of distribution channels, strategic partnership with service providers and, ultimately, the development of the value proposition for customers.

■ *Value-delivering processes* Processes that enable the delivering of value to customers, including service delivery, customer relationship management, distribution and logistical management, marketing communications management (such as advertising and sales promotion), product and service enhancement and customer support services.

The role of market orientation

As a result of the discussions directly or indirectly associated with the marketing concept, pioneering work undertaken by Narver and Slater (1990) attempted to bring together the various elements that together make up the marketing concept. These elements were put together as the market orientation scale, which could be empirically tested, allowing companies to measure their degree of market orientation and this could then be compared to their corporate performance (see Figure 1.2).

Different authors have developed different market orientation scales (Deng and Dart 1994; Jaworski and Kohli 1993; Kohli and Jaworski 1990; Narver and Slater 1990; Ruekert 1992). However, the essence of all the arguments lies in the following.

■ *Information generation* This is the generation of customer-, market- and competitor-related information as a result of a company's intelligence-gathering activities. The information is either from internal or external sources.
■ *Information dissemination* Having obtained the necessary information, a company needs to disseminate this information effectively to all the individuals operating within its confines. If information dissemination is poor, it can be difficult for a company to develop the correct strategy for a given market or set of customers.
■ *Implementation and response to the information received* A company needs to act on the information received in a clear and precise manner. Therefore, the *type* of information gathered and the *speed* with which it is disseminated within a company play an important role in the development and implementation of marketing strategies.

Figure 1.2 Components of market orientation
Source: After Deng and Dart 1994

Figure 1.2 encapsulates the key components of market orientation and how they affect the success of a company in the marketplace. In general, there are three main themes that relate to the marketing concept:

- *Customer orientation* information generation pertaining to customers
- *Competitor orientation*
- *Interfunctional coordination* dissemination of information obtained pertaining to customers across the functional departments.

The main purpose of this approach is to meet customers' needs as quickly as possible by having good interfunctional coordination between the departments. Market orientation is usually implemented in the form of market-driven strategies (Jaworski et al. 2000) that often rely on how a firm reacts to changes in the marketplace. Frequently discussions address the impact of environmental turbulence and intelligence dissemination. Once this is known, a company can develop strategies to become more market orientated. However, successful companies are often *market-driving* – that is, they actually make a difference in the marketplace and change parts of it. It is argued that when a market orientation philosophy is effected by means of a market-driven strategy, there is no guarantee that a sustainable competitive advantage can be achieved (Johnston et al. 2003). These authors state that if every actor in the market follows a market-driven strategy and every firm adapts to competitors' strategic moves and stays aligned with consumers' requirements, then no actor will be able to offer a value proposition superior to that of the competition. This could be a recipe for a 'stalemate' position in the marketplace. In this situation, competitors with ground-breaking ideas that actually change the rules of the game can become highly successful. Discussions on how to create *market-driving* organisations centre on the following issues.

- The possibility of creating sustainable competitive advantage by changing the structure or composition of a market and possibly the behaviour of the major players in the market (Jaworski et al. 2000). This works by using the following possible mechanisms.
    - *Deconstruction* by eliminating links within the value chain (suppliers, wholesalers and so on). In this manner, better value is provided to customers. Many of the financial services on offer via the Internet are classic examples of this.
    - *Construction* In this stage, new links or alliances can be added to the value chain. For instance, Starbucks has introduced music retailing to its stores and Google has introduced Google Pack as an add-on service to the browsing tool that it provides on the Internet.
    - *Functional* This is when companies provide additional advantages by creating or removing constraints, either for customers or competitors. For example, Microsoft products may or may not be compatible with other competitors and e-Bay allows consumers to effectively see transparent pricing for products.
- The possibility of offering to consumers products and services that they truly value.
- The possibility of exploiting opportunities that competitors cannot access or use (Hamel and Prahalad 1994).
- The reliance on innovation and creativity (Kumar et al. 2000).

The model for market-driving organisations has much to do with transformational leadership, a visionary approach and a flexible organisation (usually an adhocracy, discussed in detail in Chapter 7), as shown in Figure 1.3. (An adhocracy is an organisation that is managed using visionary leadership and individuals are allowed to grow by being flexible. The general gist of this type of approach to business is more organic than mechanistic.)

The model proposed by Carrillat et al. (2004) is quite comprehensive in nature, but does not explicitly take into account the role of technology in opening up possibilities for creating market-driving opportunities, so this has been considered in the modified picture presented in Figure 1.3. For instance, when Sony first began mass production of the Sony Walkman, it was in a market-driving position. However, this was only possible because of changes in technology and the miniaturisation of electronic components. Certain applications and transactions are only possible because of the growth of the World Wide Web. Indeed, companies such as e-Bay and Google have been created from start-up situations within the last five to ten years. However, they are already major global players in the online marketplace. The key aspects of organisational transformation and the implementation of marketing strategies will be considered in Chapter 6.

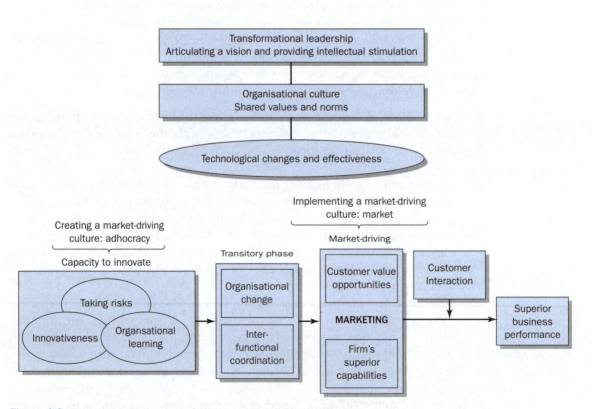

Figure 1.3 **A conceptual framework for a market-driving strategy**
Source: Carrillat et al. 2004, modified

The following case study explores the way in which Steve Jobs has developed an organisation that not only understands the demands of its market but has also been flexible and innovative in its approach to satisfying these demands.

Apple and the iPod

Apple is a quintessentially modern company, embracing wave after wave of new developments in technology since the 1970s. This has largely been due to the vision of Steve Jobs, the founder.

Apple Computers, Inc. was launched with great fanfare in the late 1970s. By all accounts Apple had an excellent operating system and many customers became life-long devotees. In those early days, Apple was a fantastically innovative, off-beat company with a counter-cultural corporate ethic. A celebrated Silicon Valley joke asked, 'What's the difference between Apple and the Boy Scouts?' The answer was, 'The Boy Scouts have adult supervision.' However, as the company began to make its mark in the computer world and became well known for good-quality computers and operating sytems, it failed to capture its share of the market growth and Microsoft became the major operating system in the world, largely as a result of Apple not making its system available to third parties. Thus, the Apple product, though better, became a niche player. Nonetheless, the company prospered and Job's hired John Sculley from Pepsico. He changed the company from being technology and 'fun' driven to becoming more market driven. Subsequently, Jobs left and set up his own companies NeXt and Pixar, both becoming multi-billion dollar companies in their own right. Pixar was sold to Disney for $7.4 billion. Pixar pioneered the use of digital cartooning and one of the first films it made using it was *Toy Story*.

In the meantime, Apple was struggling under various marketing executives. In 1996, Apple bought NeXt, its operating system OSX and offered Jobs the position of CEO. Within the last ten years, the company has again become very innovative, embracing the digital revolution and being the first one to offer desktop publishing and storage of multimedia data. It appears that Apple has an innovation lead in these areas that is indomitable.

Around 2000, Tony Fadell approached Jobs with idea of the iPod, having been turned down by Philips and funding organisations. Jobs quickly saw the potential and asked Fadell to oversee the launch of the first two generations of iPod as a consultant to Apple. Before the launch of the iPod, iTunes software was made available for Mac users as a music jukebox on the computer, to organise music. The first-generation iPod held 5Gb and had a scroll wheel. It was for Mac users only, handling 1000 songs. In 2002, the next iPod was compatible with Windows software, had a 10Gb hard disk and was capable of storing 2000 songs. In July 2002, the second-generation iPod was launched and it had a solid-state touch wheel – an innovation credited to Jonathan Ives. It was available in 5, 10 and 20Gb versions. The third-generation iPod – and, some would say, this was the model that really caught the public's mainstream attention – came out in April 2003. It looked different from the first- and second-generation models and the buttons had moved from the outside of the wheel to just below the display. There were now three sizes available: 10Gb (2000 songs), 15Gb (3750 songs) and 30Gb (7500 songs). Another major upgrade this time was the fact that there were no separate Mac or Windows PC models – any iPod would work on either type of computer – and USB functionality was built in for the first time. In September of 2003, a 20Gb model replaced the 15Gb one (holding 5000 rather than 3750 songs) and a 40Gb model replaced the 30Gb one (holding 10,000 rather than 7500 songs). The innovation continued with the launch of the the iPod mini, released in January 2004. This was a smaller version of the iPod that could easily slip into a pocket and hold up to 1000 songs. It was

▶

available in five colours – silver, pink, green, blue and gold – rather than just white and the buttons were replaced with a click wheel. At the same time, the 10Gb iPod was replaced by a 15Gb model.

In June 2004, the iTunes music store was launched in the UK and, in September of that year, the fourth-generation iPods were launched with 30 and 40Gb capacities. Also available were the iPod Photo and the limited edition U2 iPod in black with a red wheel and the band's signatures engraved on the back. In January 2005, the cheaper iPod shuffle appeared (like a memory stick for music). The iPod nano was introduced in September 2005 and at the same time, the iPod Video was launched both to great acclaim. The revamped nano appeared in September 2006 and was available in several colours – purple, silver, blue and green. It is now possible to watch music videos, short films and some TV programmes (in the USA) on an iPod. Apple has also innovated with the development of Podcasting and the term has become synonymous with Apple, although, of course, Podcasting is used as a generic term and broadcasts or films can be downloaded on to Sony and any other MP3 players. However, the term is unlikely to change to 'Walkmancasting'!

It was widely expected that Apple would lead the convergence between iPod and mobile telephone technologies, but the alliance between Sony and Ericsson managed to make this leap first, with a mobile that is a phone, camera, MP3 player, radio, video recorder and a mini Internet browser, capable of downloading video clips. However, a 'revolutionary' device from Apple is due to be launched in June 2007, as the following article (AOL, 10 January 2007) elaborates.

Apple unveils 'revolutionary' iPhone

Apple has ended months of speculation as it unveiled a mobile phone that offers music. Internet access, email and a camera.

The iPhone will 'reinvent' telecommunications, the technology giant's chief executive Steve Jobs promised.

It will go on sale in the US in June . . . and should hit Europe late this year.

Just 11.6 millimetres thick, the handset has no conventional buttons but instead uses a large touch-screen.

'iPhone is a revolutionary and magical production that is literally five years ahead of any other mobile phone', Mr Jobs said.

'We are all born with the ultimate pointing device – our fingers – and iPhone uses them to create the most revolutionary user interface since the mouse.'

As well as functioning as a music and video iPod it offers new services such as 'visual voicemail', which shows users a list of their messages so they can go straight to the ones they want to listen to most.

A full touch keyboard is available for text messaging and there is a built in 2 megapixel camera.

The phone, which runs the Mac OSX operating system, will display album artwork on its 3.5in screen when it is being used for music.

Special sensors automatically deactivate the screen and turn off the touch pad when the device is raised to the ear.

Mr Jobs, who offered a sneak preview of the iPhone as he gave his annual address to Mac fanatics at the Macworld Conference Expo in San Francisco, said it would 'leap frog' over harder-to-use devices which currently offer Internet and email.

[There will be] a 4Gb model . . . or punters can splash out on . . . an 8Gb model.

Source: AOL (UK) Limited, www.news.aol.co.uk accessed 10 January 2007

The figures given in Figure CS 1.1 indicate how iPod sales have grown over the years.

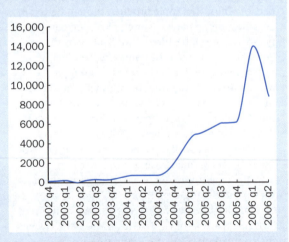

Figure CS 1.1 iPod unit sales per quarter

Source: www.applematters.com/index.php/section/comments/ apples-q2-numbers-a-closer-look   Chris Seibold/Apple Matters

Case study *continued*

An even more interesting statistic is the growth in the purchase of iTunes. In January 2006, Apple announced that customers had purchased 1 billion songs on iTunes. This trend is likely to accelerate in spite of illegal downloads and the increasing sales of pirated CDs. The downloads will be related to the increasing sales of iPods. As record companies crack down on the illegal dispersal of copyright material, providers such as iTunes will be seen more and more as safe havens for downloading music.

Sources: www.geofftech.co.uk/obsessions/ipod/ipod_history.htm, www.daringfireball.net/2005/07/podcast_pocket and J. Naughton and N. Mathiason 'Will Job's departure cut Apple to the Core?' *The Observer*, 30 July 2006

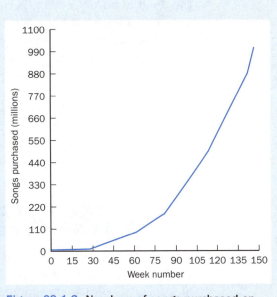

Figure CS 1.2 Numbers of songs purchased on iTunes

Source: http://maddogfog.blogspot.com/2006/02/itunes-song-purchases-plotted-on-graph.html

The case study illustrates how a company such as Apple started out being a market-driving organisation and ended up being market-driven in the 1980s and 1990s, until Steve Jobs took the helm again and the ground-breaking developments of the iPod and iTunes were launched. The existence of these two products enabled a major revolution in the recording industry, the shock waves of which are likely to continue reverberating for some time to come.

Loyalty

For some companies, such as Apple, loyal customers are paramount (Davis et al. 1991). Retaining customers can have a significant positive impact on the profitability of companies. Studies have shown that retaining an additional 2–5 per cent of customers can improve profits significantly – as much as cutting costs by 10 per cent (Power et al. 1992; Reichheld 1990). Large organisations, such as Procter & Gamble, are studying how and why customers contribute to profitability. Most researchers and practitioners (Oliver and Swann 1989; Wilkie 1990) agree that satisfaction occurs when purchase expectations are met and even exceeded – that is, when the product's attributes are the ones desired by customers. This implies that companies should be – in addition to being customer- and competitor-orientated –

satisfaction-orientated in order to meet purchase expectations. Dissatisfaction is the result of unconfirmed expectations. Herein also lies a problem for marketers as it is not always easy to ascertain exactly what customers' expectations are. Nevertheless, marketers who understand the impact of customer satisfaction on business performance will attempt to secure future sales orders on the basis of the recommendations given by currently satisfied end users of their products because what happens around the current buying decision will affect future purchase decisions (Tanner 1996).

Given all these factors that enlarge and elaborate the notion of the marketing concept, over the years, marketers have spent considerable time and effort on developing marketing planning.

Strategic planning to deliver the marketing concept

Countless authors have written about strategic planning in marketing (Ackoff 1981; Grant 2002; Johnson and Scholes 2000; McDonald 1993) and many companies spend a considerable amount of time and energy developing and executing strategic plans. All these plans largely contain marketing stances and positioning strategies that enable an organisation to be placed in a winning position vis-à-vis its competitors. A definition of strategic market planning, therefore, could be as follows:

> Strategic marketing planning involves careful analysis of an organisation's environment, its competitors and its internal strengths in order to develop a sustainable plan of action that will develop the organisation's competitive advantage and maximise is performance within given availability of resources.

Often these planning systems are quite systematic and designed to help organisations work through a strategic plan step by step. These steps guide an organisation towards a deliberate strategy (Mintzberg 1987). This process is often top management-driven and based on complex deliberations between different functions within an organisation. Much of the marketing literature is preoccupied with this linear, rational approach to strategic planning. Mintzberg (1994) calls this the rationalist approach. A proponent of this type of deliberate planning is McDonald (1993), who discusses the marketing planning process in detail. The essential steps surrounding this process are outlined in Figure 1.4.

The analytical part of such plans often begins with an audit to ascertain the current position of an organisation in relation to its marketplace. This is followed by a SWOT (strengths, weaknesses, opportunities and threats) analysis. The SWOT analysis lays the foundations for developing strategies for the organisation. The SWOT analysis and audit are nearly always incomplete because the information required to make perfect strategies is often hidden or not available. As a result, a series of informed assumptions have to be made on the basis of available data. Following this exercise, the objectives are set as measurable outcomes. The feed-

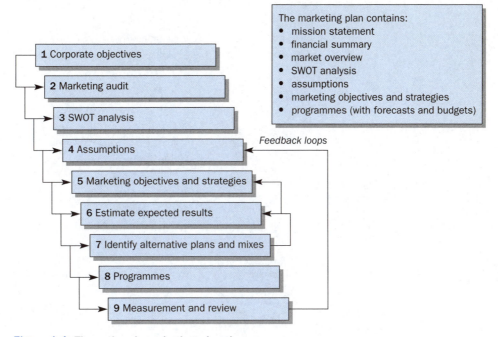

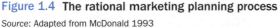

Figure 1.4 The rational marketing planning process

Source: Adapted from McDonald 1993

back loops are designed to create an iterative process of planning. Mintzberg argues that in a planned strategy:

> *Leaders at the centre of authority formulate their intentions as precisely as possible and then strive for their implementation – their translation into collective action – with a minimum of distortion, 'surprise free'. To ensure this, the leaders must first articulate their intentions in the form of a plan in as much detail as possible, to minimise confusion, and then elaborate this plan in as much detail as possible, in the form of budgets, schedules and so on, to pre-empt discretion that might impede its realisation. Those outside the planning process may act, but to the extent possible they are not allowed to decide. Programmes that guide their behaviour are built into the plan, and formal controls are instituted to ensure pursuit of the plan and the programmes.*

Other models take a more general strategic point of view (Johnson and Scholes 2000), many of the human and cultural issues being taken into account. Johnson and Scholes' model is much more comprehensive than McDonald's and Mintzberg's and based on analysis, choice and implementation (see Figure 1.5). Within this comprehensive framework, marketing strategies are developed from comprehensive portfolio analyses.

Many forms of strategy are possible. If one takes the view that the environment is uncontrollable, then it is quite possible that a company will have to be adaptive to the environment. However, a definition of the 'environment' is not straightforward. For some, the environment means the physical environment, encompassing

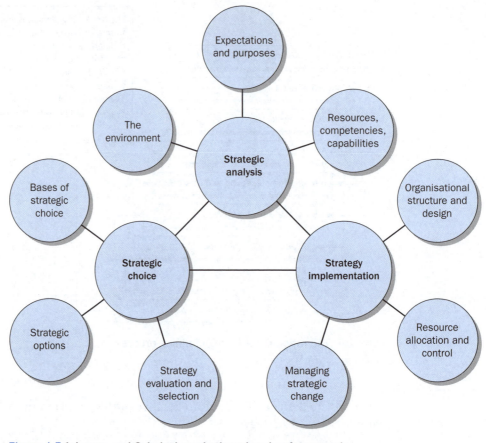

Figure 1.5 Johnson and Scholes' marketing planning framework
Source: Johnson and Scholes 2000

weather, politics and war. For others, the environment means the 'near' environment encompassing competitors and the general market environment. In most cases, organisations are rarely immune to environmental pressures and therefore environmental turbulence has to be taken into account.

Environmental factors

Studies into market orientation often utilise an environmental turbulence scale to understand its effect on the level of market orientation practised by organisations. However, this environmental turbulence only measures the impact of technology and competitors within a given market. For a greater understanding, companies need to analyse the role played by the general environment, including global climate and political issues, as shown in Figure 1.6.

Within this environment, organisations may follow a range of strategies that are planned, entrepreneurial, ideological, umbrella-type, process-driven, unconnected

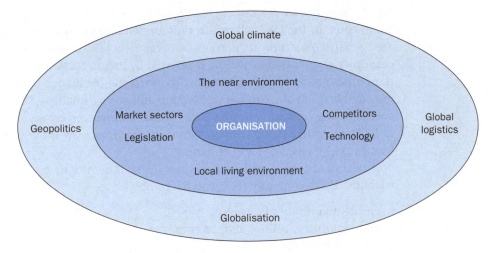

Figure 1.6 Environmental factors affecting strategy

(different strategies in different areas of an organisation), consensus-driven or imposed (Mintzberg 1987).

Others argue that strategy has to be developed in a way that stretches and leverages a company (Hamel and Prahalad 1989). Market analysis and then strategy formulation as practised by many marketers is not enough to position a company for sustainable growth and help it to gain competitive advantage over its rivals. A company needs to understand and leverage its core competencies to the full. For instance, they feel that many companies are competent at diagnostics but not at actually breaking down managerial mindsets. For instance, to quote from Hamel and Prahalad's paper:

> *Driven by the need to understand the dynamics of battles (GM vs Toyota, CGS vs CNN, Pan Am vs British Airways, RCA vs Sony), we have turned competitiveness into a growth industry. Companies and industries have been analysed in mind-numbing detail, autopsies performed, and verdicts rendered. Yet when it comes to understanding where competitiveness comes from and where it goes, we are like doctors who have diagnosed a problem – and have found ways to treat some of its symptoms – but who still don't know how to keep from getting sick in the first place.*

Thus, the views of Hamel and Prahalad open the door for a greater analysis of the underlying managerial issues when analysing markets and competition.

Creating a sense of identity

The importance of creating a sense of mission within an organisation is important for many companies (Yeung and Campbell 1991). Many marketers would contend that a marketing plan is incomplete without reference to a company's mission. The proposed Ashridge model shown in Figure 1.7 takes into account the purpose, values and behaviour standards of an organisation. The purpose of a company often determines the markets that it will target. For instance, the Co-operative Bank, based in the UK, believes in only undertaking ethical investments. This creates a particular type of market opportunity, which determines the types of consumer segments that will be interested in its products. Corporate values drive the purpose and strategy of a company, with the behaviour being actionable and measurable (such as customer satisfaction and service quality). The distinctive competencies of a company may be constrained or enhanced by the resources available to it. The resource-based theory of strategy discusses how these distinctive competencies can be leveraged and enhanced.

It is argued that a well-crafted mission statement can provide the following advantages to a company (Bart and Baetz 1998):

- ensure unanimity of purpose
- arouse positive feelings about a firm
- provide direction
- provide a basis for objectives and strategies
- serve as a focal point
- resolve divergent views among managers.

In order to achieve this, Pearce and David (1987) suggested that a mission statement should contain the following aspects:

1 customers (the target market)
2 products/services (offerings and value provided to customers)
3 geographic markets (where the firm seeks customers)
4 technology (the technology used to produce and market products)
5 concern for survival/growth/profits (the firm's concern for being financially sound)
6 philosophy (the firm's values, ethics, beliefs)
7 public image (contributions the firm makes to communities)

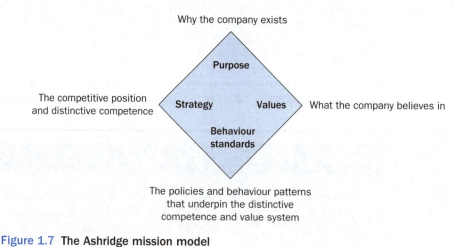

Figure 1.7 The Ashridge mission model

Source: Yeung and Campbell 1991

8 employees (the importance of managers and employees)
9 distinctive competence (how the firm is better than or different from its competitors).

In one study (David and David 2003), it was found that many companies fail to include six of the nine recommended components in their mission statements, these being market, technology, survival/growth, philosophy, public image and employees.

This is interesting and disturbing as stakeholders are given scant consideration and technology is not given the prominence it deserves, given the dramatic changes wrought by the Internet and database systems. Clear mission statements play an important part in helping to frame marketing strategies. However, a wrongly defined mission statement can determine strategic limitations and loss of competitiveness.

Limitations

Tightly defined mission statements are potential sources of problems. For instance, as present markets are constantly evolving with even greater rapidity than before, how rigid can a firm's mission statement be?

The Dixons Group is essentially an electrical and electronics-based retailer. In 1999, it launched Freeserve, an Internet service. This was a diversification from its normal business. However, Dixons saw the opportunity offered by the growth of the Internet and began to broaden its target market (Levitt 1960). At the same time, it developed the capabilities to meet its customers' requirements. The resources were leveraged accordingly.

Doing this is not necessarily a clear-cut process as profits have to be earned in the new market. Grant (2002) maintains that companies ought to look at the resources that they can leverage before thinking about positioning in the market-place. Having identifed these resources, they can then be utilised to position the core competencies accordingly in order to exploit existing market opportunities. A company's resources may comprise brands, financial assets, key personnel, R&D and distribution systems, among others. Grant contends that companies are in the business of maximising rents from these resources on a long-term basis. Resource-based strategy builds on an individual company's strengths and weaknesses (in terms of resources) and how it can leverage these internal assets compared to its competitors. The approach it takes is then unique to the firm itself and exploits the competencies that it possesses. The effective utilisation of these resources enables a company to meet its customers' needs more quickly and more efficiently than would otherwise be the case (Barney 1996).

The discussion above illustrates the complexities involved in developing marketing strategies. Despite these challenges, strategy development, by its very nature, peers into the future. Strategies are created and executed within given time periods. Thus, in addition to the many issues presented above, time, fragmentation and technological developments need to be addressed before developing a new guide to planning.

Time as an issue in planning

Time is an important aspect of planning. Many companies succeed or fail depending on:

- their speed of entry into a market with a new product
- the length of time a particular organisation has been operating within its market – may endow it with market knowledge and distribution strengths
- the length of time that a company has been operating within a market as it may prevent it from taking advantage of new opportunities in new markets
- the speed with which a company can harness its resources to meet competitive challenges
- the time and place of the formation of a company
- consumers' perceptions of the value of time.

Some management authors indicate that the moment when a firm is founded impacts on its structure and strategy (Stinchcombe 1965). Hence, the age of the firm constitutes a determining variable in the firm's strategic choices and ability to change. In the strategic management field, Boeker (1989 demonstrates that both the age of the firm and its history constrain the available strategic spectrum. He also shows that when firms have one specific dominant strategy, they are not likely to change it, even if poor performance is encountered. This type of analysis matches the notion of organisational inertia identified by Hannan and Freeman (1984). Schein (1983, 1992) also discusses the predominant role of the founder in developing a firm's culture and strategy. He or she may also be a product of a particular age and time. We propose taking a new look at time from different angles so that companies can incorporate this into their marketing strategies. From the points made above, we propose the time pentagon shown in (Figure 1.8).

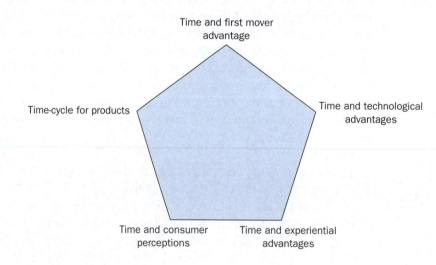

Figure 1.8 The time pentagon

Time and first mover advantages

For many companies, being the first to the market is highly significant as they can often, as a result, become market leaders and enjoy superior profits and returns to those that came along after them. Examples of this are companies such as Coca-Cola and Levis, which really took advantage of the dislocation of production and consumption in the 1880s and are still reputable international brand names. More recently, companies such as Amazon have garnered a large market share in the online sales of books by being first to the Internet market. Several authors have studied the impact of the order of entry on market share and business performance (Szymanski et al. 1995). First movers are supposed to have competitive advantage with regard to mastering technology, developing distribution systems and creating a brand image (Tellis and Golder 1996).

Although there has been much discussion about first mover advantages, empirical research indicates that, on average, being first to market leads to a long-term profit *disadvantage* relative to later entrants (Boulding and Christen 2003). In general, first movers have an initial profit advantage that erodes over time. The advantage lasts for 12 to 14 years. Often, as customers learn about a new product or service and as the patent protection expires, a first mover can experience erosion of its competitive advantage. However, if there is limited customer learning or if the patent protection is strong and lengthy, the advantages can continue. Often, second movers can reap profits in the form of experiential learning that can not only help to lower costs but also provide a better understanding of the market dynamics created by the first mover. Again, timing the launch of a new product or service is an important strategic decision and the level and availability of resources may determine a first mover or a second mover marketing strategy. In some cases, late entry into the market may foster better market orientation. This is because the competitive intensity (Porter 1985) is likely to be stronger over time, therefore newcomers are bound to demonstrate higher market orientation levels in order to reach a profitable place in the market. Hence, from a competitive point of view, time could reinforce the necessity of strong market orientation for young firms or firms entering new markets.

Time-cycle for products

The ability to compete on time has paid huge dividends for companies that can outsmart and outmanoeuvre their rivals. Often this time-based activity relates to the ways in which companies can reduce the length of the cycle before products are available to buy. For instance, by adapting to the communications revolution, Dell has managed to recalibrate time in terms of the processes required to get the product to market. In utilising the Internet, Dell has managed both informational time and logistical time efficiently and effectively. The company has recalibrated the time required for *global supply planning* by speeding up the exchange of information between Dell, its customers and its suppliers (Fields 2006). It also speeded up *demand fulfilment* by instituting quick logistics regarding the movement of materials from procurement to assembly line and to distribution. All in all, this has resulted in lower inventory (see Table 1.1). Other research (Dibrell et al. 2005) indicates that, when internationalising, a firm should emphasise time as a source of advantage in the international arena.

Table **1.1** **Number of days supply of inventory at Dell**

1994	1995	1996	1997	1998	1999	2000	2001	2002
32	21	16	13	8	6	5	4	3

Source: Field 2006

Time and consumers' perceptions

Consumers behave in different ways depending on their perceptions of time. In the Western world, a great deal of emphasis is placed on the value of time, leading to a string of inventions that have created more time for individuals. Witness the amazing growth of labour-saving devices, such as vacuum cleaners, microwave ovens and speedy communication tools, such as mobile phones. Consumers are also delineated as monochromic or polychromic (Kaufman-Scarborough and Lindquist 1999). Monochromic and polychromic individuals are assessed by posing the following kinds of statements with which they express their agreement or disagreement; their responses are then measured on a Likert scale to gauge their behaviour patterns.

1 I do not like to juggle several activities at the same time.
2 People should not try to do many things at once.
3 When I sit down at my desk, I work on one project at a time.
4 I am comfortable doing several things at the same time.

By measuring these attitudes, individuals are placed in a particular position on the Polychromic Attitude Index (PAI). According to Kaufman-Scarborough and Lindquist, this can lead to a better understanding of what products and services will suit each consumer group. Monochromic individuals tend to follow regular patterns and schedules try to do activities within strict time limits and rarely deviate from patterned behaviour. Polychromics, on the other hand, deliberately combine activities, prefer a flexible schedule, enjoy doing several things at a time and break their projects down into parts. This clearly has implications for developing products and services that meet the needs of these differing time styles.

The Slow Food movement encapsulates how important time may be for consumers in the future in terms of regulating consumption. The current marketing models all try to look at the value of time, saving as much of it as possible, whereas there is a growing number of consumers who wish to integrate ecologically sound practices into food production and eating – in essence, slowing down the time for products to get to the market in order to reintegrate the consumption process with the more natural rhythm of the year, determined by seasons.

CASE STUDY

Slow coaching

From multi-tasking to speed-dating, we seem to be living our lives on constant fast-forward. Time to press the pause button, says Lucy Siegle

When I say that the residents of Ludlow in Shropshire and Aylsham in Norfolk are slow, I mean it very kindly. Both places have been awarded Slow City status by the international Slow Food organisation (slowfood.com). Instead of falling prey to the identikit supermarkets and chain stores that make up 'clone-town Britain', as described by the New Economics Foundation, they have preserved their unique identity, supported local suppliers and producers, cut traffic pollution and protected green spaces.

Carlo Petrini, author of *Slow Food* (Grub Street Publishing), founded the Slow Food Movement in 1989 after McDonald's moved on to Rome's historic Piazza di Spagna. The aim was to 'rediscover the flavours of regional cooking and banish the degrading effects of fast food' – a rude awakening for those who considered the Pot Noodle to be the greatest thing since sliced bread. However, the Slow Food movement has, ironically, gathered a lot of pace recently, not to mention more than 60,000 members across the world. Now there's 'slow' activism, education and consumption, all pertaining to a more holistic, sustainable way of life. 'The rhythm of life is ever faster,' explains Petrini. 'We don't want to lose the capacity to give pleasure and to reason. Let's be a little calmer.'

He has a good point. From multitasking to speed dating, increasingly we're 'speedaholics'. By next year there will be 1.6bn cellphone users on the planet, and the top 10 fast-food chains have 100,000 outlets across the globe. Meanwhile the average 'lunch hour' has shrunk to just 27 minutes, far too low to ensure productivity, according to unions, but luxurious compared to the average mealtime in a fast-food joint: 11 minutes.

And not only is fast food bad for you, it's bad for the planet, and very definitely Not Slow. As a result of industrialised food production, which revolves around monocultures, we are losing species. One hundred years ago we ate more than 100 different species; now 75 per cent of the global food supply comes from just 12 crop species. We are losing varieties within those species – British examples include hundreds of varieties of English strawberries and apples. A variety of vegetable is lost every six hours. Animals are fed growth hormones to get them to slaughter quicker, the world's aquifers are drained to feed commercial agriculture, and 13 of the world's 15 fishing grounds are now in decline, largely thanks to industrial fishing. It's enough to make you yell: 'Stop, I want to get off!'

If that is the case, then *In Praise of Slow* by Carl Honore (Orion) is essential reading. He discovered all sorts of things are on fast forward, even his favourite Mozart sonata – it should take 22 minutes, but orchestras get through it in 14. Then there's consumption patterns: slow these by buying fewer, higher-quality items that will last and can be reused. Protect your right to a work/life balance by joining a union – or read Tom Hodgkinson's *How To Be Idle* (Hamish Hamilton) and resolve to do very little indeed.

The Slowfood Manifesto (from slowfood.com)

Source: Lucy Siegle, 'Slow coaching', *The Observer*, 12 December 2004

The Official Slow Food Manifesto

Endorsed and approved in 1989 by delegates from 20 countries

Our century, which began and has developed under the insignia of industrial civilization, first invented the machine and then took it as its life model.

We are enslaved by speed and have all succumbed to the same insidious virus: Fast Life, which disrupts our habits, pervades the privacy of our homes and forces us to eat Fast Foods.

To be worthy of the name, Homo Sapiens should rid himself of speed before it reduces him to a species in danger of extinction.

A firm defence of quiet material pleasure is the only way to oppose the universal folly of Fast Life.

May suitable doses of guaranteed sensual pleasure and slow, long-lasting enjoyment preserve us from the contagion of the multitude who mistake frenzy for efficiency.

Our defence should begin at the table with Slow Food. Let us rediscover the flavours and savours of regional cooking and banish the degrading effects of Fast Food.

In the name of productivity, Fast Life has changed our way of being and threatens our environment and our landscapes. So Slow Food is now the only truly progressive answer.

This is what real culture is all about: developing taste rather than demeaning it. And what better way to set about this than an international exchange of experiences, knowledge, projects?

Slow Food guarantees a better future. Slow Food is an idea that needs plenty of qualified supporters who can help turn this (slow) motion into an international movement, with the little snail as its symbol

Source: www.slowfoodludlow.org.uk/docs/manifesto.html

Time and experiential advantages

As a firm ages, history is created. This history enables a company to draw on its previous successes and failures. For instance, once Stelios Haji-Ioannou created the easyJet company, he leveraged the brand 'easy' in many ways to create easyCar, easyInternetcafe, easyCinema, easyHotel and, the latest venture, easyCruises. The name 'easy' is now synonymous with value and simplicity and this has been garnered when setting up a range of businesses within the easyGroup. Similarly, Richard Branson has leveraged the Virgin brand into new areas, such as airlines and rail transport, when the brand began its life within the record retail sector. Other possible ways in which company history and experience can help to increase competitiveness are:

- better knowledge of the market than other companies, which can be efficiently used to launch new products or services
- a known brand identity can ease the launch of a new product or service compared with an unknown company doing so
- an established supply chain and distribution system
- an established customer base
- established networks and alliances.

A classic example of this is the Philips group, which has excellent capabilities in innovation and uses them effectively to launch products and services successfully, based on the points made above.

Time and technological advantages

Technological innovations can create opportunities for existing firms as they can develop new products and services based on their experiential advantages, as described above. Often, companies in this situation will have proprietary knowledge or have access to patents. For instance, the juxtaposition of chip technology and knowledge of electronics allowed Sony to enter successfully the Japanese games console market in 1994. At that time, the games market was dominated by Nintendo and success was not guaranteed, but the PlayStation sold more than 1 million units, with the initial 100,000 units being sold out within a day (www.sony.net/Fun/SH/1-34 /h5.html). In May 1996, Sony PlayStation had reached a worldwide sales record of 5 million units. The games platform has now become one of the strongest and newest areas of business within the Sony portfolio.

The growth of the Internet has spawned new companies such as Amazon books, eBay and Google. These companies are household names and international brands, yet they have achieved this status in less than ten years. As technology develops and new companies seize and exploit quickly the new opportunities, they are fully utilising the possibilities afforded by technological advances. Biotechnology companies are benefiting from the work carried out by the Human Genome Project, mapping human genetic codes. Many companies are starting to specialise in autoimmune diseases and targeted cancer treatments. These companies are often new and do not have established positions within the marketplace.

In some instances, companies that are old in the marketplace cannot survive the onslaught of new ideas and new possibilities as they may not be very fleet of foot. In fact, their very 'experience' could be detrimental to their survival. For instance, five years ago, Kodak was one of the strongest brands in the world. However, as photos have moved from being chemically processed to being digital, their monopoly – represented by 100,000 film development outlets – has been seriously challenged by the 100 million 'outlets available to digital cameras – that is, the computers on every desk and in every home – not to mention mobile phone cameras, which are also ubiquitous.

Kodak did not embrace the digital revolution as quickly as it should have done. One reason may have been that its long previous experience of producing, selling and developing photographic films and papers within its served market (Lindstrom 2006) prevented it – on the level of the company's mindset – from moving into the new digital formats for images. Another reason may have been the purely practical one that, as technology creates disruptions, it is difficult for companies such as Kodak to respond swiftly to the resulting market changes because it already has established global factories, retail outlets and distribution systems and these have to be modified or dismantled in order to reach digital consumers. This cannot be achieved overnight. The company is now attempting to regain leadership via Kodak PhotoNet, which offers digital copies of photo prints delivered to a personalised online album.

Another example provided by Lindstrom (2006) is Lego, which saw its worldwide dominance of the toy market slashed by 30 per cent in 1994 by the introduction of online games puzzles and challenges.

Therefore, time and technology can provide advantages for some companies and problems for others. In this context, companies need to incorporate time and technological analysis into the development of their marketing strategies. With the growth in technological developments, companies' strategies are becoming more transparent and the issue of ethics is playing an increasingly important role in company development. The next section introduces this area.

Ethics as a marketing issue

Many companies are now becoming acutely aware that their marketing strategies are either hampered or enhanced by their ethical stances. For instance, Nike found to its cost that many consumers were not only refusing to buy its products but were also ready to actively campaign against its activities. The reasons for this were the poor conditions and pay it offered to workers in its factories in Indonesia.

Nike is primarily a design and marketing company that subcontracts much of the manufacturing to smaller outfits. In 1998, the company was associated with offering unfair pay and poor working conditions to employees. The company has gone to great lengths to improve the situation, but the stigma still remains, with the company having to deal with the long-term effects and consequences of this image for years to come.

Prolonged bad publicity can have a critical impact on a brand. Other companies are taking a more proactive stance and creating ethical alliances (Andreasen and Drumwright 2001) with non-profit organisations. These ethical alliances initially begin with donations and then extend to cause-related marketing, event sponsorship, employee exchange and the provision of services. Reebok, for instance is actively involved with Amnesty International, while Visa – the credit card company – is associated with literacy programmes in developing countries. Markets are now less local and more globalised as products traverse the world. Such cause-related marketing strategies may become ways in which companies can distinguish themselves in the marketplace.

Towards a new strategic marketing planning model

The previous sections have highlighted and discussed the various factors that are dynamic in nature and impinge on marketing planning. It is obvious that a linear and iterative approach to the strategic planning and implementation of marketing may be too restrictive and not dynamic enough when companies need to consider and integrate the complex influences of various internal and external factors. Companies need to consider how best to leverage their resources and understand their level of market orientation. A rethink – in terms of planning using a new interactive model – is replacing the linear approach. For instance, during the strategic planning stage, many companies still follow tried and tested models with the requisite audits and SWOT analyses. However, rarely do they analyse or understand their level of market orientation, resource activity levels and the requisite time horizons, which may be quite short or relatively long.

The following case study illustrates the speed with which Bradesco exploited a window of opportunity. These strategic windows are not always available indefinitely (Abell 1978), yet Bradesco successfully manoeuvred its resources and knowledge within a short timespan to build a better and cheaper customer service. Of course, a situation such as this means that Bradesco can now also take maximum advantage of the new digital age and incorporate mobile technology into its business.

CASE STUDY FT

Internet banking: quick to adapt to technology

Bradesco's embrace of IT puts it among the world's leading online institutions and earns high plaudits

A couple of years ago, Jean Phillipe Leroy was met by disbelief when he told international fund managers about how Bradesco, Brazil's biggest bank, was taking advantage of the Internet.

'They know now. But it was a big shock for them at first to see us among the biggest Internet banks in the world', says Mr Leroy, who is head of corporate relations at Bradesco's São Paolo headquarters. A study published earlier this year by Cluster Consulting of Barcelona that rated Bradesco as the third biggest Internet bank in the world – behind Bank of America and Wells Fargo – has been extensively reported. Last year, Bradesco gained an honorary mention in Bill Gates' best-selling *Business at the Speed of Thought*. In a chapter called 'Get to markets first', Mr Gates writes, that 'almost since its inception, this [bank] has made "time to market" practically a mantra'. Last December Bradesco's first free Internet service led to a sharp rise in the share price and was widely noted. Growth this year has been impressive. By October, Bradesco had 1,530,000 clients for its Internet banking service, more than twice as many as in the same month of the previous year. A total of 9.2m transactions were conducted online during the same month, and of the 486,000 Brazilians who opened new accounts with Bradesco during the third quarter, more than half of the new customers – 51 per cent – were banking by Internet. Bradesco – and other big Brazilian banks such as Itau, Unibanco and Banco de Brasil – have been quick to adapt technology for a range of reasons. The Brazilian government's industrial policy is one. Until the late 1980s, Brazil protected its domestic computer industry by making it prohibitively expensive to import the machines. One of the byproducts was that many companies researched and developed their own inhouse technology. Bradesco was particularly quick off the mark, being the first Brazilian bank to introduce computers.'It has always been a bank that has been on top of the technology', says Luiz Carlos Trabuco Cappi, an executive vice-president who is responsible for Internet banking. At the same time, during the 1970s and 1980s Brazilian banks developed their systems to a much greater degree than elsewhere in Latin America in order to accommodate the effect of permanent levels of very high inflation. Because a bank needs to conduct financial transactions quickly if it is to make money in an environment where monetary values are rapidly eroded, sysems to clear cheques within 24 hours were introduced, for example. In his book, Mr Gates describes how Bradesco developed a cash-management software application to assist with payables and receivables, which it then sold to about 4100 businesses. For another customer Bradesco developed a salary card that enabled employees to be paid directly from ATM machines without being required to have a bank account. Again, the system was quickly generalised. 'The bank focuses on short development cycles – weeks and months; no longer', writes Mr Gates.

Its management accustomed to innovation, Bradesco was able to react quickly to the opportunity of the Internet. Initially it developed a system that depended on customers using a CD-ROM on which they entered details before

▶

transmitting by a modem. Subsequently a full online service has been introduced. Bradesco has been clever about introducing innovation to allow customers to personalise their access to the site, in order to defeat hackers and reduce the risk of fraud. The hours during which the site is open can be restricted, for example says Mr Cappi. The big advantage is efficiency. Mr Cappi says that the average cost of an Internet transaction is just 11 centavos, compared with 54 centavos for a transaction conducted over the telephone and R1.20 for one conducted at a branch. But unlike many of its counterparts in the developed world, Bradesco is not seeking to replace its network of 2500 branches with a cyber network.

Fearing that such a course might make it less easy to grow among the sector of the market which is just beginning to open bank accounts, Bradesco is developing a strategy which is designed to increase the efficiency of the network. At least one Internet terminal has been placed inside each branch and a series of incentives offered to make both its customers and its staff more computer-friendly.

Special lines of credit have been made available to allow its staff to buy computers. More than 17,000 of its workers have taken advantage in the last 4 months or so. Bradesco has also begun to install computers inside shopping centres and supermarkets, allowing even wider Internet banking access.

Source: Richard Lapper, *Financial Times*, 20 December 2000

The next case study shows how Bradesco has used time and technology to its advantage once again – especially to counteract fraud.

Figure 1.9 illustrates the key issues that an organisation should take into account when developing marketing strategies. Instead of a linear approach, a more dynamic and holistic model needs to be undertaken and each of the factors should be considered in a general environmental context. This level of importance associated with each factor could then be utilised to ascertain the speed with which the strategy should be undertaken and the levels of resources that are required within given constraints. The values, purposes and ethical stance of the organisation should be fairly explicit in order to create positive links with the social community. Some organisations enshrine these within their mission statement; others neglect the importance of clearly presenting their corporate values and objectives.

CASE STUDY

Banco Bradesco trials Fujitsu palm vein authentication technology

Brazil's Banco Bradesco, the largest private bank in Latin America, is to begin using Fujitsu's PalmSecure biometric authentication application to verify customers using its ATMs.

The PalmSecure application features a sensor that captures the palm vein pattern of the user and compares it with preregistered data to authenticate the customer's identity. Fujitsu says the sensor is compact and can be safely used in a wide range of

applications, such as in PCs, ATMs and for building and room access. The bank is currently testing the application internally, with general roll out scheduled to start soon. The vendor says, after researching various biometric technologies, Bradesco chose PalmSecure for its high levels of verification accuracy and for being non-invasive and hygienic, making it easier to be accepted by customers.

Source: www.finextra.com/fullstory.asp?id=15575

Figure 1.9 Strategic 'marketing' planning

Summary

The above discussions and examples illustrate the view that marketing strategy is closely related to corporate strategy. However, the process of developing a plan is not always straightforward. A model for considering the key points of developing a marketing strategy is shown in Figure 1.10.

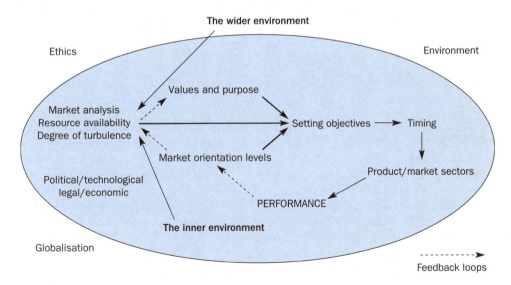

Figure 1.10 Key components for strategic planning

Companies and organisations have to consider a wide range of issues before they develop particular strategies. There are many schools of thought on how strategy actually develops and how it should develop. In this chapter, some of the complexities that are involved in the strategic planning process have been illustrated and the major issues that need to be taken into account by organisations have been highlighted. With the advent of new technology, the shape and nature of markets are changing. The old maxims are no longer true. One could argue that almost every product, media and location offer new marketing possibilities. The markets are becoming both global and local. The new technologies and the Internet are helping to fragment markets into continually smaller segments and niches. The idea of satisfying a customer is no longer a linear process. A customer has to be approached and involved simultaneously on several dimensions. These dimensions could include, among others, service, quality, speed of communication, quality of communication, product quality and brand image. The challenge for marketing strategists is to be able to blend some of the old ideas with new thinking and forge coherent marketing strategies that can work effectively in the twenty-first century.

Chapter questions

1 Discuss why developing marketing strategy is a complex task.

2 What role does time play in the development of strategies?

3 How can a strong market orientation help an organisation develop an effective marketing strategy?

2 Opening up analysis and positioning

Introduction

Strategic positioning represents one of the most important endeavours in strategic marketing. The positioning process is long and complex, including an analysis of the internal and external environment, the definition and segmentation of the targeted market, together with the evaluation of the present and future marketing strategies of competing firms. The information processed and analysed during this process comes from many sources, with various departments being involved in data collection and evaluation. As a result, it is essential that there is good cooperation between the marketing department and other corporate divisions. The representation of the marketing strategic vision at top management level is essential for achieving effective strategic positioning.

Internal analysis

Marketing activities are realised on the basis of existing resources and corporate capabilities. Some of these resources are owned by the firm, while others can be attracted from outside collaborators and suppliers in exchange for other resources. For example, market data can be collected and processed by consulting organisations or additional production capacity can be subcontracted from other companies.

The design of an effective strategic marketing plan requires an in-depth knowledge of the company's resources and capabilities. This knowledge is the result of a complex internal analysis.

The analysis of tangible and intangible resources

At any given moment a firm controls both tangible and intangible resources. Tangible resources include raw materials, equipment and installations, machinery, buildings and furniture. These assets are usually evaluated using specific accounting principles and methods, to assess their market value.

The company's intangible resources are much more difficult to assess as they include the personal capabilities of its staff, professional expertise and experience of its managers and employees, its brand name and corporate reputation, intellectual property portfolio and existing partnerships. Some authors have even argued that loyal customers represent the most important asset of a business organisation. However, this precious resource is, rather, the relationships developed with each customer as a person rather than a number. Most of these assets are unique and their proper use depends on specific organisational and environmental circumstances. That is why they are often considered irreplaceable. The intangible assets represent the dynamic element of an organisation, which exploits more or less effectively the existing tangible resources for achieving specific strategic objectives.

Money represents a resource with an ambiguous status. Although in day-to-day life money is often tangible, in reality it is often represented by a flow through a company's accounts. It is often information about this flow that is more important than the actual materiality of a company's assets.

Operant and operand resources

In their revolutionary paper on the predominance of the service paradigm in modern marketing, Vargo and Lusch (2004) have developed the distinction between *operand* and *operant* resources. Operand resources are the assets on which various actions are performed in order to create value, such as raw materials or machinery, which are almost synonymous with the category of tangible resources. On the other hand, operant resources are usually intangible and unique, such as knowledge, skills, competencies, capabilities and experience, which are applied to operand resources for value creation. Vargo and Lusch also emphasise that, in the present-day marketplace, it is the operant resources that are more important for an organisation whereas, traditionally, operand resources have been considered the basis for calculating national wealth and the value of goods.

Operant resources have a unique and qualitative nature, their development requiring time and investment. In today's marketplace, information has truly become one of the most important operant resources, allowing firms to assess correctly their internal capabilities, evaluate the risks and opportunities present in the market and understand consumers' needs. Figure 2.1 shows how operant and operand resources work together to create value.

Organisational strengths and weaknesses

To understand correctly the capabilities of a firm, its internal resources should be considered in relation to their value for customers and with the resources controlled by competitors. This kind of analysis can indicate the areas of strength and

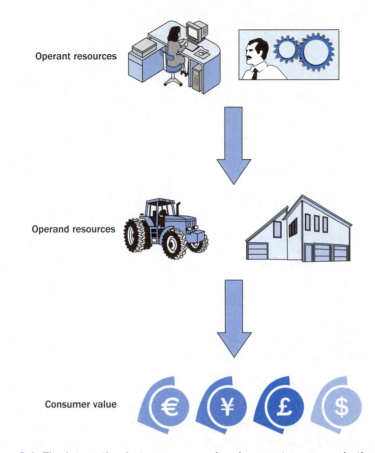

Operant resources

Operand resources

Consumer value

Figure 2.1 The interaction between operand and operant resources in the value-creation process

weakness of the company and permit the decision makers to take corrective actions in order to protect and nurture the strengths, while trying to reduce or even eliminate the organisational weaknesses.

In order to categorise and represent firm's resources from this dual perspective, every internal resource can be represented in a system of coordinates, as in Figure 2.2.

Every internal resource of the firm is represented as a circle in the dual system of coordinates proposed in Figure 2.2. The radius of each circle is proportional to the cost required to maintain and control a specific resource. Obviously, the best resources are those represented in the top right-hand corner. These are the 'crown jewels', which should be nurtured and maintained by the firm in their current status. However, the diagram indicates that some of these resources are extremely expensive for the firm. In these circumstances, the management team can try to identify cost-reduction methods or replace the present sources of these resources with cheaper ones. These resources can be successfully used by the firm to differentiate their competitive image from other competitors.

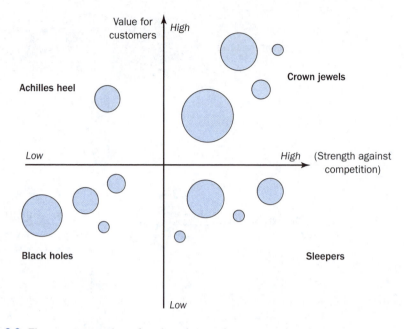

Figure 2.2 **The representation of various internal resources in relation to their value for customers and strength against competition**

The internal resources that have high value for customers, but are weak in comparison with competitors' resources, should be further developed in order to reduce this competitive gap. These resources can be labelled as 'Achilles heels' because they represent a weak element in the organisational structure.

The resources located in the area characterised by low customer value and low strength against competitors are the 'black holes' as they do not provide any particular advantage to the firm, but consume money. However, it is not advisable to eliminate such resources, because some of them might be essential for the good functioning of the organisation. However, an important line of action can be the reduction of costs related to this category of resources.

Finally, the resources that are strong against competition but hold a low value for customers can be called 'sleepers'. The analysis of these resources can eventually determine a reorientation of the company's mission and the implementation of procedures for better exploiting these resources for the benefit of the market.

This framework of analysis has the advantage of providing a clear image of the existing values of various internal resources. However, because in most cases, the firm is targeting various market segments and has multiple competitors, a representation of internal resources has to be made for each specific market segment, as both the value for consumers and strength against competition may differ from segment to segment.

Product portfolio analysis

The existing product portfolio of a firm is one of the most important organisational assets, because it represents the basis of the company's profitability.

One way in which to assess the diversity of the product portfolio is simply to list all the product families with their components. This representation provides a general view of the existing product portfolio, but its static nature reduces its importance for strategic marketing planning. For example, the product portfolio used by Hyundai for the French market can be represented as shown in Table 2.1.

Table 2.1 The product portfolio of Hyundai for the French market

Product lines	Mono-space	Berlines	Professional	4X4	Sport et Luxury
	Atos	Accent	H1 (van)	Tucson	Coupé
	Getz	Elantra	SR (plateau)	Santa Fe	Sonata
	Matrix			Terracan	XG
	Trajet				
	Satellite				

Source: Hyundai, www.hyundai.fr

On the other hand, the product portfolio and its evolution has to be linked with the product lifecycle (PLC) model. The PLC has been used for many decades and continues to be discussed in marketing theory. Depending on which of the various stages of the lifecycle a product is in, various strategic alternatives are available to companies. These are summarised in Table 2.2, the strategies presented being taken from the classic paper by Day (1986).

Table 2.2 Product lifecycle stages and their potential strategies

	Embryonic	Growing	Mature	Ageing
Dominance	All-out push for share	Hold position	Hold position	Hold position
	Hold position	Hold share	Grow with industry	
Strong	Attempt to improve position	Attempt to improve position	Hold position	Hold position or harvest
	All-out push for share	Push for share	Grow with industry	Harvest
Favourable	Selective or all-out push for share	Attempt to improve position	Custodial or maintenance	
	Selectively attempt to improve position	Selectively push for share	Find niche and attempt to protect	Phased withdrawal
Tenable	Selectively push for position	Find niche and protect it	Find niche and hang on or phased withdrawal	Phased withdrawal or abandon
Weak	Up or out	Turn around or abandon	Turn around or phased withdrawal	Abandon

The characteristics of each stage of industry maturity are as follows (Hax and Majluf 1984).

■ *The embryonic industry* is characterised by rapid growth, changes in technology, vigorous pursuit of new customers and fragmented, unstable market share.
■ *The growth industry* exhibits rapid growth, clear trends in customer purchase patterns, a growth in competitors' market shares, technological developments and increasing barriers to entry.
■ *The mature industry* presents stable purchase patterns, technology and market shares (however the industries themselves may be highly competitive).
■ *The ageing industry* is characterised by falling demand, a declining number of competitors and a narrowing product line.

As a result of these stages, the following competitive positions could be adopted.

■ *Dominant* In any industry, only one firm can dominate. For instance, Boeing in the aircraft industry and Microsoft in computer software (with its Windows products.
■ *Strong* This includes firms that are leaders within their sector of industry, but do not exhibit absolute dominance. They have large market shares and are strong competitors. Examples of such companies are Unilever in the toiletries market and Volkswagen in the car sector.
■ *Favourable* This describes a particular competitive position reached by a company in a fragmented industry, achieved by pursuing a differentiation strategy or exploiting a particular market niche in which the company excels. An example of this is Dell Computers which has created a highly differentiated product in the PC market by means of its just-in-time, customised, direct marketing strategies.
■ *Tenable* This describes a position that can be maintained profitably via geographic or product specialisation in a narrow or protected market niche. Examples of this are localised organic farmers in Europe who supply local markets. Another example is the Morgan car, for which there is a waiting list.
■ *Weak* This describes a position that cannot be sustained by a company, given the competitive economics of the industry. In such a situation, the firm can strive to improve its position or decide to exit the sector.

The BCG matrix

For a dynamic analysis of the product portfolio, most companies use the growth-share matrix developed by the Boston Consulting Group in the 1970s. This matrix provides a representation of the product portfolio in relation to the growth rate of the market and the relative market share of each product in comparison with its most important competitor.

The matrix involes placing each of the firm's products into one of four categories: Hungry dogs, Problem children, Stars and Cash cows, although the names of the categories vary in the academic and professional literature (see Figure 2.3).

The products are represented in this matrix as circles, the radius of each being proportional to the revenue it provides. The analysis of these products can be

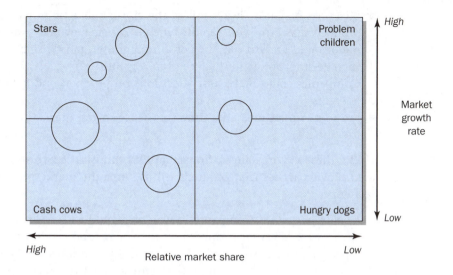

Figure 2.3 **The BCG product portfolio matrix**

related to their positions and evolutionary stage within the PLC. Usually, any new product starts as a Hungry dog because of the investments required for its technological development and market launch. After this, in the growth phase, the product should adopt the role of a Problem child and then a Star. At maturity, the healthy products must become Cash cows that feed the process of developing and launching new products. Finally, in the decline stage, the moribund products again become Hungry dogs that fight to resist in a regressing market. Any mismatch between a product that has reached a specific phase in its product lifecycle and the corresponding category in the BCG matrix can indicate serious problems in the performance and management of that product. On the other hand, it is important to differentiate between various types of products, even if they are included in the same category. For example, the marketing strategies applied to new and declining products must be obviously different from each other, even if they are both included in the Hungry dogs category.

Finally, preserving a healthy equilibrium for the various categories of products is essential to a firm's long-term success. A high number of Problem childen and Stars can indicate a promising future for a company, but only if there are enough Cash cows to support this ongoing development.

Despite its capacity to provide a clear representation of the product portfolio, there are some problems associated with using the BCG matrix for analysis.

■ Determining a particular market share. In industry sectors such as automobiles and pharmaceuticals, market share data is available and, as the number of players is known, market shares can be determined. However, in many other sectors, it is difficult to determine actual market shares.
■ It is not easily to use it in the service sector, where services and clients can be varied (for instance, in accountancy firms). The value of the clients, rather than absolute market shares, may make more sense in this sector.

- Lifecycles may not always follow the classic shape of growth and decline. Some products may grow very rapidly whereas others may take time to grow. An example of rapid growth may be certain computer games, such as *Tombraider*, that then decline rapidly in the face of new games.
- Companies could make hasty decisions on products and fail to invest in potential Stars.
- Products sometimes take time to diffuse in the marketplace and need initial investment.

Under these circumstances, Rogers' (1995) diffusion curve should also be considered. Rogers argues that products diffuse into the marketplace according to five factors.

- *Relative advantage* Companies developing products or services need to consider the relative advantages offered by their new products. Economic factors, status aspects and incentives can all add to an innovation's perceived advantage. For instance, the Dyson vacuum cleaner offers a relative advantage over conventional vacuum cleaners with its innovative technology and the elimination of the need for bags that periodically have to be removed and replaced and reduce suction.
- *Compatibility* A new product or service needs to be compatible with consumers' values and beliefs, needs and previously adopted innovations. For instance, a consumer familiar with a Windows machine is more likely to upgrade to a computer that will offer compatibility with his or her previous experience of PCs and also with the old files that have been generated.
- *Complexity* The complexity of an innovation is generally negatively related to an innovation's rate of adoption. Complex products are less likely to be adopted by consumers. Consider the case of the new mobile technology.
- *Trialability and observability* Trialability and observability are usually positively related to adoption. Trialability is of particular importance to early adopters as they do not usually have peers to ask for advice. If individuals can trial a product or observe the way it works and benefits their lives, they are more likely to adopt it. Company's such as Microsoft often bring out beta versions of their new software so that consumers can observe and trial the software.

Figure 2.4 shows the typology of consumers who are willing to adopt new products or services. They tend to fall into the following categories.

- *Innovators* Individuals who are venturesome and may also have the financial clout to try out new inventions and innovations. When new products are introduced, they are often priced at a premium rate as companies are aware that a new product may not always diffuse into a marketplace. They represent only 3.5 per cent of the market.
- *Early adopters* This group of consumers are willing to observe and trial a new product. As new, similar products enter the market, they will start purchasing, following the innovators' example. Often, once a product or service reaches this stage, further progress can be achieved. The early adopters represent 13.5 per cent of the market. In the graphical representation of the adoption

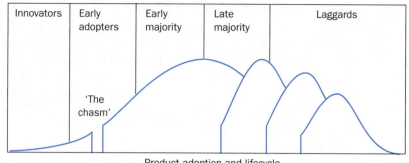

Product adoption and lifecycle

Figure 2.4 **The typology of new product users**

process, there is a gap at the beginning of the early adopters group. This 'chasm' represents a critical moment in the adoption process of a product. If the new product passes this stage, it means that the product concept is good enough to convince a critical mass of consumers of its utility and value. Otherwise, the new product will have an early decline, as is the case with most gadgets and fashion products, the novelty of which is the most valuable appeal for customers.

– *Early majority* This segment of the population is value-driven and tends to make a deliberate choice when purchasing a product. It is likely that economies of scale have made the new product cheaper and more accessible via the distribution network. This set of consumers will wait for this to happen before making their decision to purchase.

– *Late majority* By the time the product reaches this segment of the population it will have matured. The late majority (or sceptical consumers) are not easily convinced by the advertised advantages of a new product or service. They may or may not adopt it. If they do, it may be grudgingly as everyone else already has the product. Mobile phones were resisted for a long time by a section of the population, but, ultimately, they were forced to adopt them as friends and relatives already possessed and used this new device as the only means of communication when travelling. The early and late majority segments each account for 34 per cent of the market, thus together making up 68 per cent of the total market. These are both very important segments for marketers, each requiring different strategies.

– *Laggards* The laggards comprise a section of the population that never seems to move in line with popular opinion. They are usually the last to adopt an innovation, usually grudgingly. Laggards can, however, be quite numerous. The existing studies consider that their proportion of the total market is 16 per cent.

As a product diffuses through the marketplace, from the innovators to the laggards, it also moves through the lifecycle of its existence. It is important to remember that not all products follow a smooth bell-shaped curve. Some products may take a long time to reach maturity and some may never reach the early majority stage. So, caution should be exercised when using this model in conjunction with the PLC.

The value added chain approach

Porter introduced the concept of the value added chain, defining it as the succession of various operations that progressively incorporate new value elements into the product, ending with the commercialisation of the final product on the market. Usually, a company is responsible for only a limited number of specific value operations, although large corporations might be able to control all the stages of product development.

The integration of a firm within the value added chain of activities is determined by its particular competitive advantage. The competitive advantage can be defined as the resource or capability the firm has that gives it absolute strength in comparison with other competitors. The competitive advantage can be, for example, a cheaper production process, a good-quality final product or a highly responsive customer support service. Every firm should identify its particular competitive advantage, making a thorough inventory of its resources and carrying out a competitive benchmarking analysis of other companies.

Using the knowledge about the structure of the value-added chain of activities specific to the company, it is possible to draw a diagram like that in Figure 2.5. It shows the succession of activities, the specific resources required for each stage, the levels of each resource controlled by the organisation and the possible sources of complementary resources.

In Figure 2.5, on the horizontal axis are represented, in the successive order of their use in the value added chain of activities, the various resources required for

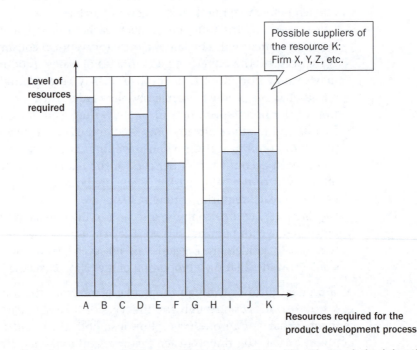

Figure 2.5 A possible model for identifying, evaluating, allocating and obtaining the necessary resources for the product development process

the completion of a product development project. On the vertical axis the level of each of these resources required is represented. The shaded area indicates the resources controlled by the firm, while the white area shows the complementary resources required to successfully complete the project.

For each type of resource, the firm can also indicate the source of the complementary resources required, such as internal development, outsourcing or collaboration. The level of complementary resources required can be communicated to the firm's management, helping to create a clear view of resources needed for the entire project. Without this level of information, new product development should proceed on an ad hoc basis and stage by stage, without a clear image of the entire process and of the level of resources required to complete the project.

The competitive advantage is the most profitable specialisation of the firm in the context of the existing market conditions. Figure 2.6 indicates, on the one hand, the vertical positioning of the firm in relation to its competitors, and, on the other hand, its horizontal positioning in the value added chain.

Internal resources (competitive advantage) and corporate objectives (strategic mission)

The internal resources of the firm show their significance only in relation to the strategic objectives of the firm: they are the means that permit the enterprise to successfully reach its established strategic objectives. Equally, the definition of specific strategic objectives should always be based on the levels of internal resources and capabilities controlled by the organisation. Setting up of overly ambitious projects, while neglecting the real levels of internal assets, can create significant difficulties for the implementation and success of any strategic marketing plan. For example, the process of defining the corporate mission – which can be considered as the general, long-term strategic objective of the firm – is significantly influenced by the levels of resources controlled by the organisation and, more specifically, by its specific competitive advantage.

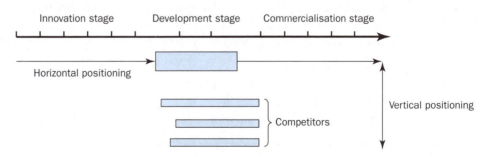

Figure 2.6 **The process of horizontal/vertical positioning of a firm in the value added chain of activities**

The relationship between these two elements can determine three possible situations.

Corporate mission > Competitive advantage

In this situation, the company tries to achieve more than it is able to realise in the existing competitive conditions. The corporate mission should be adjusted accordingly, reflecting the existing levels of differentiating resources.

Corporate mission = Competitive advantage

The firm is well focused on its specific capabilities and has established a realistic strategic objective.

Corporate mission < Competitive advantage

The firm is not fully exploiting its competitive advantage and will be offering market opportunities to other companies that have a similar organisational profile.

The management team should also consider the dynamic aspect of this relationship. On a long-term basis, both corporate mission and competitive advantage might change, creating the need for a strategic adjustment in order to re-establish the balance between these two terms.

External analysis

Business organisations do not exist in a void. On the contrary, their strategic and tactical actions are dictated by the need to continuously adapt to a dynamic market environment. Therefore, the internal analysis of the organisational environment needs to be complemented by an assessment of the main elements of the competitive market environment.

Market threats and opportunities

The first level of external analysis should take into account the specific profile of the target market in terms of its specific threats and opportunities. These two elements are general categories that include various elements. Among the possible threats that can be encountered in the competitive environment are:

- new competitors
- a change in consumption patterns
- the evolution of technology
- new governmental regulations.

Opportunities are also varied and can include:

- the development of a new market niche
- governmental intervention for business development in specific industrial sectors
- changes in consumption patterns or the evolution of technology.

An interesting fact to note is that some events can represent both a threat and an opportunity depending on the firm's competitive strength and on its capacity to favourably exploit, or be threatened by, these changes. A strong company, using flexible structures and procedures, will have a positive perspective on market changes, perceiving them as opportunities and creative challenges rather than negative threats. On the other hand, any perceived threat can be considered as an indication of various organisational weaknesses that should be identified and corrected in order to strengthen the organisation's capacity to compete in a dynamic market.

Modern markets are highly dynamic and the combination of threats and opportunities can change rapidly. The online market is a good example in this respect as the barriers to entry are very low and every online company potentially competes not only with domestic but also overseas firms. The solution to this problem is an increase in flexibility and adaptability of the company structure and processes, combined with effective procedures for identifying market changes and competitive threats.

Porter's model of industry attractiveness

In his seminal work, Porter (1985) considers the main forces that shape the competitive environment of a specific industry. However, the large variety of activities developed by some corporations requires, in the first instance, the identification of the industrial sector(s) in which the company is participating. The definition and classification of various industrial sectors can be made in many ways. A company can choose to develop its own classification or use the classification followed by some governments for statistical or financial purposes.

A very restrictive definition of an industrial sector can be beneficial for identifying the specific competencies of a firm and driving an increased specialisation. However, on the other hand, it can also cause the phenomenon of 'marketing myopia', which is when the company loses potential business opportunities because of its extremely tight focus.

The premise for analysing the competitive environment is that attractive industry sectors offer higher levels of profitability than less attractive ones. This means that market *sectors* rather than market *segments* determine the profitability of a company. However, as the profile of any industrial sector is complex, its attractiveness will be determined by the following elements.

The threat of new entrants

If a sector is attractive, it is going to bring new players into the marketplace. In time, the new entrants will increase competition intensity and slowly reduce the attractiveness of the industry. For instance, currently, the computer games sector is very attractive to software games writers as well as console providers. The growth exhibited in the games industry has been extraordinary and the sector now rivals Hollywood in terms of the size of its revenue and turnover. It is therefore not too surprising that it has attracted a major new entrant into its marketplace – Microsoft with its Xbox.

Companies protect a profitable sector by creating considerable barriers to entry, such as the following.

■ *Brand image* A strong brand image can be a major deterrent to companies wishing to enter a sector. For instance, Coca-Cola presents a formidable barrier to entry for many cola makers as it has a strong worldwide brand image. The brand also creates a differentiated image for Coca-Cola, making it easier for consumers to identify the product and adhere to the set of values expressed by the brand.

■ *Distribution* Companies that develop and maintain their distribution channels effectively offer another potential barrier to entry for new entrants. The example of Coca-Cola is again relevant here in that its aim is to be able to provide a Coke within 100 yards for every consumer. This type of statement shows that the company has strong distribution channels, making it very difficult for new entrants to emulate this.

■ *Patents or know-how* For many companies, patenting offers an effective barrier to entry. Many of the large pharmaceutical companies rely on patents to protect their new drugs. This prevents others from entering the market for certain periods of time. When the patent protection elapses, then other companies can enter the market. For other companies, such as Cisco Systems, the know-how developed with regard to maintaining IT networks provides a barrier to entry for other players in the market.

■ *Cost advantages* Being the lowest-cost producer in a particular sector may deter potential competitors as they could not match or beat the costs of production. For instance, Colgate-Palmolive can produce toothpaste at the lowest possible cost owing to its experience in the sector and the economies of scale of its production of toothpaste. This type of experience can be difficult to develop overnight and presents a significant barrier to entry for other companies.

■ *Government regulations* Government regulations, such as those for drug approval, may be time-consuming and very costly to adhere to, deterring new companies from challenging older, more established companies.

Given these barriers to entry, companies often have to consider whether or not it is possible for them to enter markets by using specific segmentation strategies.

Industry rivalry

Competition within a sector can determine the level of profitability a company achieves. Some sectors of industry are intensely competitive, driving prices below industry cost levels, making the entire industry unprofitable (perhaps on a global basis). An example of this is the global airline industry, which has seen spectacular collapses, such as Swissair. However, companies such as Ryanair and easyJet have shown remarkable growth as low-cost airlines. They have cut costs by using more remote airports and offering nofrills services. Some of the main factors determining competition (Grant 2002) are:

■ industry concentration
■ range and diversity of competitors

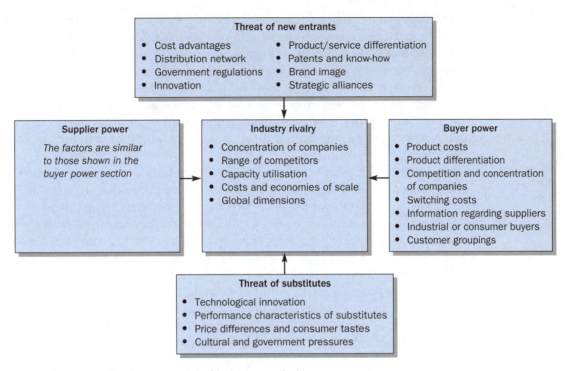

Figure 2.7 Porter's five forces model of industry analysis

Source: Adapted from Porter 1985

- product differentiation
- capacity utilisation and exit barriers
- cost advantages or disadvantages.

Industry concentration

One or two major players dominate some industry sectors, creating a situation of oligopoly. For instance, the software industry is dominated by Microsoft, giving it considerable power in its pricing decisions regarding its range of Windows products. However, when the company entered the new games console market that was previously dominated by Sony, Sega and Nintendo, it faced price competition and had to drop the price of its Xbox. Coca-Cola and Pepsi Cola, generally set the prices in the cola market and there are few challengers to this strategy. The revenue earned is used for advertising (building further barriers to entry) and new product development. In the airline industry, where the competition is global and there are many carriers, the price competition increases dramatically, with substantial variations within the different segments, such as economy, premium, business class and first class.

Range and diversity of competitors

Often companies can do well in certain sectors, if they can agree on industrywide pricing strategies. Where sectors determine to operate on a 'closed shop' basis, such as OPEC, this can be possible. However, experience shows that such cartels are now becoming difficult to operate, with one or two players often breaking agreed parameters (such as Russia in its willingness to expand its oil production).

In many cases, the exhaustive evaluation of an entire industrial sector is costly and unnecessary as, in many cases, a company competes with only a few other firms, deals with a limited number of suppliers and sells to only selected market segments. Thus, only the main strategic group needs to be analysed. A strategic group can be defined as the main institutions and organisations that directly influence the activity of a company.

On the other hand, it has been argued that many companies are now confronted by a bewildering array of competitors that may or may not be within their traditional industry sector. An example of this is the recent growth of digital music, offered on the Web. Traditionally, record companies would compete against each other in a well-defined sector. More recently, however, artists have realised that they can reach a global audience via webcasts. Thus, the computer-mediated environment has created a different form of competition as a result of the development of specific Internet applications (see the case study on Eminem). Another example is the pharmaceutical industry, which was challenged by the producers of food supplements and alternative therapies. In many instances, industry sectors are blurring so that, for instance, television broadcasting appears not only via TV sets but also via computers and mobile phones.

Considering the importance of technological innovation in relation to creating new competitive challenges and altering existing ones, the technological factor should be added to Porter's five forces model. However, in comparison with the first five forces, technology acts not only on general industry rivalry but also on the remaining four forces.

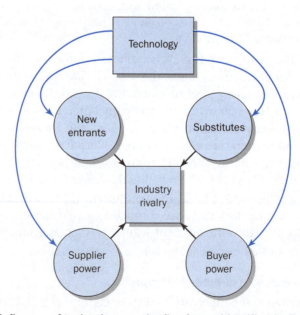

Figure 2.8 The influence of technology on the five forces identified by Porter

Analysing industry sectors in the digital age becomes quite a complicated task. The case study on Eminem's CD sales illustrates how technology was used effectively to mitigate some of the adverse effects of consumer power and the growth of substitutes to conventional sources of music in the music industry.

CASE STUDY

Eminem's CD sales impressive despite music sharing

Eminem's record label was so nervous about music pirates cannibalising sales of the rapper's latest CD that it released *The Eminem Show* nine days early, disrupting well-laid marketing plans.

But when the CD hit stores Memorial Day weekend, it still managed to debut at number 1 in record time. Some industry observers say the CD's success in the face of widespread bootlegging proves that online music swapping doesn't crush legitimate retail sales and can actually generate better buzz for a new release. 'The jury is still out on how significantly file-sharing actually effects record label revenues,' said Michael Goodman, a senior music analyst with Forrester Research in Boston. 'But to a certain extent, file-sharing can actually prime the pump for sales.' SoundScan, which gathers sales data from more than 17,000 retailers across the United States, said that 284,534 copies of *The Eminem Show* were sold nationally during the long weekend.

'We've never had a record debut at number 1 on the SoundScan chart that hasn't had the benefit of a full six days of sales behind it', said Mike Shalett, chief executive of SoundScan, but Interscope Geffen A&M, the label behind Eminem, insists that illegal copies, made from one of three closely guarded master copies sent to manufacturers, hurt the release: 'I absolutely believe that the bootlegs and downloads have a huge negative effect on sales', said Steve Berman, head of sales and marketing at Interscope, a division of Universal Music Group.

Individual songs from the CD became widely available online in mid-May and bootlegged copies of the entire CD began appearing on street corners around the same time. It's impossible to calculate how many sales were lost in the process, Berman said. Interscope took a number of steps to counter the impact of the downloads, beyond moving up the release date.

Two million of the three million copies of *The Eminem Show* were shipped with a complimentary DVD that featured interviews and live footage of Eminem. The record label also pursued websites posting the CD, persuading some of them to remove it, Berman said. But some analysts said the music industry continues to take the wrong approach to counter online downloads. Web surfers downloading music files are the same people who go out and buy the CDs and music companies need to treat them like customers, not criminals, said Sean Baenen, managing director of Odyssey, a market research firm in San Francisco.

'It's not a group of pirates looking to steal,' Baenen said. 'It's a group of people who want more choice and control over the music they receive.' The early success of *The Eminem Show* in the wake of widespread file-sharing and bootlegging provides some understanding to an industry trying to come to terms with a new marketplace. 'What's happened to Eminem is going to be a real learning point for the industry and artists,' said Michael Bracy, a Washington lobbyist with the Future of Music Coalition, which represents artists' interests. 'Part of the puzzle is offering consumers some entertainment value that they're not going to get through file-sharing', he said.

Note: Since the article, it is clear that file-sharing is now common on the Internet, with the growth of locations such as MySpace and Bebo and, at the same time, iTunes (as shown in Chapter 1) has become a significant player.

Source: 'CD sales impressive despite music sharing', *USA Today*, 31 May 2002 (available at: www.usatoday.com/life/cyber/tech/2002/05/31/eminem.htm)

Product differentiation

Companies often use product differentiation to create a distinctive image for their products. Often this is based on branding and pricing. In commodity markets, product differentiation is difficult, but, in luxury goods markets, such as perfumes or designer clothes, differentiation offers certain segments of consumers a specific image and they are then unwilling to purchase different products even if the price differential is slightly higher or lower.

Capacity utilisation and exit barriers

In some industries, there may be overcapacity in terms of the production of particular goods. This is true of the automobile industry and the personal computer market. When this occurs, prices tend to drop. In large industry sectors, such as the automobile industry, it is difficult for companies to exit the sector as the exit costs may be prohibitive. Under these conditions, mergers and acquisitions often ensue.

Cost advantages or disadvantages

Some of the profit impact of marketing strategies (PIMS) studies show that companies that have a high market share often show better rates of return than those that have smaller shares. In part, this may be because they achieve cost advantages as a result of high production levels, creating better economies of scale than their competitors. However, in other areas, excess capacity may mean that companies are forced to sell at cost to cover their overheads.

Buyer power

Porter regards the bargaining power of buyers as an important factor in determining the attractiveness of an industry sector. Buyers come in all shapes and sizes. Sometimes they are powerful; at other times they are weak. Their relative strength or weakness depends on the desirability of the product and/or its utility to the buyer. They can be either industrial or consumer buyers.

Industrial buyers

Industrial buyers tend to differ from each other according to the sectors that they are operating in. The forces acting on them may also vary. In fact, the whole area can be extremely complex and it is impossible to illustrate all the possibilities. However, listed below are some examples of forces that act on industrial buyers.

- Car manufacturers rely on tyre manufacturers for building cars. There are many tyre manufacturers and so there is overcapacity. This gives car manufacturers strong buying power and the ability to switch suppliers if they wish. The tyre manufacturers are mutually dependent on the car industry. If their sales go up, so do the tyre sales. If intense competition exists among buyers, as in the electric cable industry, they in turn will put pressure on the suppliers, such as Pirelli.
- In the computer industry, processors and their quality is of vital importance to computer manufacturers. They therefore have less bargaining power with the suppliers as they rely on specialist devices and quality. In the biotechnology industry, certain companies such as Biocatalyst provide specialist enzymes for producing olive oil. The farmers who need this enzyme are in a weak position when bargaining about price.

- Industrial buyers can also decide to vertically integrate along the chain, thereby purchasing companies that supply their raw materials. Companies such as Coca-Cola and Pepsi Cola own their own bottling plants in various countries, for example.

Consumer buyers

Compared to industrial buyers, consumers are many and varied. Companies grapple with the different ways of understanding segments of consumers so that some sense can be made of behaviour patterns and the forces that they can create within industry sectors and exert on companies.

- Consumers can exhibit collective buyer power when they group together to purchase items from manufacturers.
- Consumers carry considerable power as they can choose to buy or not buy a product. They can also decide to switch from one product or brand to another. Aware of this power, marketers are forever trying to understand the segments of buyers that exist and their buying motives, so that companies can position themselves sensibly in the marketplace.
- Consumers may or may not be price sensitive, depending on their make up as a segment. Consumers are also increasingly sophisticated and ready to search for information regarding the best prices and quality for a range of products and services. With the Internet this has become both possible and easy to do.

Supplier power

The debate surrounding supplier power covers areas similar to those discussed above, as one company will be a buyer and the other a supplier. Suppliers are often smaller companies, manufacturing and selling components or raw materials to larger corporations. The factors that are pertinent to suppliers are therefore the same or similar to the ones discussed in the previous section.

Threat of substitutes

As technology advances, it becomes increasingly difficult for companies to predict the changes that could take place within their own industry sectors. For instance, the new biotechnology companies, which offer more effective treatments to combat diseases such as cancer and Alzheimers, are challenging the establshed pharmaceutical companies. Equally, many individuals are searching for alternative methods for curing ailments rather than relying on drugs. The Swiss watch industry was initially decimated in the 1970s as a result of the advent of digital technology. However, it is now the leading supplier of watches in the world as a result of its development of quality watches and branding strategies.

Overview of analysing the industry

Industry analysis enables a company to understand how market forces are driving the sector it is competing in. At the same time it helps to highlight the significant ways in which the company can target and segment its consumer base, understanding the power it wields in the marketplace. The following section discusses a range of other analyses that can be performed by companies. It is important to remember that there are links between these and industry analysis.

The competitive attractiveness of an industry cannot be considered objectively without an assessment of the company's capabilities. In order to be applicable in specific situations, the sector's attractiveness must be related to the competitive strength of the firm. This bidimensional evaluation can be done using an Industry attractiveness/Business' competitive strength matrix.

The Industry attractiveness/Business' competitive strength matrix

The Industry attractiveness/Business' competitive strength matrix was developed by General Electric and refined by McKinsey Consulting Group. This matrix, as shown in Figure 2.9, is composed of two main axes, depicting, respectively, Industry attractiveness and Business strength. The two dimensions considered in the matrix are complex indicators that combine many different aspects related to the industrial sector and the competitive profile of the organisation. In addition, the management team has to con-

Determinants of business' competitive strength

- Size
- Growth
- Market share
- People
- Information systems

- Profitability
- Margins
- Technology position
- Distribution

- Strengths/weaknesses
- Image
- Ethical stance
- Innovation

Determinants of industry attractiveness

- Size
- Market growth
- Market diversity
- Competitive structure
- Degree of change
- Industry profitability
- Inflation effects
- Role of technology
- Social environmental
- Legal environment
- Human factors

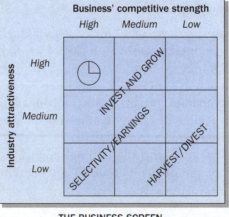

THE BUSINESS SCREEN

McKinsey's checklist of factors for developing a multifactorial portfolio matrix

- Market size – domestic – global
- Market growth – domestic – global
- Price trends
- Captive market
- Cyclical demand
- Degree of concentration
- Competitive characteristics
- Top group strength
- Possibility of substitutes
- Market leader's profit trend
- Sociopolitical and economic environment
- Labour situation
- Legal issues
- Cultural trends
- Impact of technology
- Environmental issues

Figure 2.9 The GE/McKinsey business screen portfolio matrix

Source: Adapted from Kerin et al. 1990

sider the fact that these elements might have different levels of importance, requiring the application of various weights in the assessment of their effects (see Table 2.3.).

Depending on what strengths a company exhibits in terms of either its products or strategic business units, particular strategies can be followed. The various portfolios can be plotted on the grid in circles, indicating the market shares within particular sectors. The direction in which a company could decide to move are indicative. In using matrices such as these, factors that are most important to a company within a particular sector are considered and analysed.

Factors contributing to market attractiveness and business position

Table 2.3 Factors contributing to market attractiveness and business position

Attractiveness of your market	*Status of your business*
Market factors	
Size ($, £, Euros, Yen or units or both)	Your share in equivalent terms
Sizes of key segments	Your share of key segments
Growth rate per year: Total segments	Your annual growth rate: Total segments
Diversity of market	Diversity of your participation
Sensitivity to price, service features and	Your influence on the market
external factors: cyclical demand, seasonality	Lags or leads in your sales
Bargaining power of upstream suppliers	Bargaining power of your suppliers
Bargaining power of downstream suppliers	Bargaining power of your customers
Competition	
Types of competitors	Where you fit, how you compare in terms of products, marketing capability, service
	Production, financial, management strength
Entries and exits	Segments you have entered or left
Changes in share	Your relative share change
Substitution with new technology	Your vulnerability to new technology
Degrees and type of integration	Your own level of integration
Financial and economic factors	
Contribution margins	Your margins
Leveraging factors, such as economies of scale and experience	Your scale and experience
Barriers to entry or exit (financial and non-financial)	Barriers to your entry or exit (financial and non-financial)
General capacity utilisation	Your capacity utilisation
Technological factors	
Maturity and volatility	Your ability to cope with change
Complexity	Depth of your skills
Differentiation	Types of your technological skills
Patents and copyrights	Your patent protection
Manufacturing process technology required	Your manufacturing technology
Sociopolitical factors in your environment	
Social attitudes and trends	Your company's responsiveness and flexibility
Laws and government agency regulations	
Influence with pressure groups and human factors, such as unionisation	Your company's ability to cope
	Your company's relationship and influence
	Your company's relationships and stakeholder acceptance

Source: Adapted from Abell and Hammond 1979

The directional policy matrix

The directional policy matrix (DPM) is useful for analysing a company's prospects in particular markets. It was originally conceived and used by Shell Chemicals UK (Hughes 1981). The matrix (see Figure 2.10) is based on:

- business sector prospects – the possible profitability and growth potential of the sector within which the company operates
- the competitive position of the business in that sector.

The DPM offers a flexible and sensible way in which to analyse a company's competitive strengths and prospects within markets. The key points made in the matrix show the directions in which a company could proceed as it may be either making money (Cash generation) or losing it (Disinvest). On the other hand, it may wish to invest in potentially lucrative markets (Double or quit). Again, these possible directions are not meant to be prescriptive – they are suggestions and a final decision needs to be based on various other factors that a company needs to consider.

Factors underlying analysis of business-sector prospects and a company's competitive capabilities

Table 2.4 encompasses the range of other factors that are important to consider when positioning a company in its marketplace.

Growth vector analysis

Figure 2.11 is a modified version of the more commonly used Ansoff matrix for segmenting products and services within companies. A company has to determine how attractive or poor a company's products or services are in matching certain consumer segments' needs. It can then make a decision as to whether or not it would like to extend its product/service offerings.

The directions of the arrows in Figure 2.11 show the level of risk a company may be committing itself to as it moves away from familiar segments and markets. The numbers indicate how the level of risk increases. Each case has to be taken on its own merits as a high-risk situation may also produce high returns.

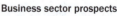

	Business sector prospects		
Company's competitive advantage	Unattractive	Average	Attractive
Weak	Disinvest	Phased withdrawal / Custodial	Double or quit
Average	Phased withdrawal	Custodial / Growth	Try harder
Strong	Cash generation	Growth / Leader	Leader

Figure 2.10 **The directional policy matrix**
Source: Robinson et al. 1978

Table 2.4 Segmenting business based on positioning and capabilities

Factors relevant to analysis of business-sector prospects	*Factors relevant to analysis of company's competitive capabilities*
1 Market growth 2 Market quality 3 Environmental aspects	1 Market position 2 Production capability 3 Product R&D
Guidelines for assessing market quality	**Guidelines for assessing market position**
A sector to which the answers to all or most of the following questions are yes would attract a four or five point quality rating. The following questions are more relevant for manufacturing companies and will need modification for other sectors. 1 Has the sector a record of high, stable profitability? 2 Can margins be maintained when manufacturing capacity exceeds demand? 3 Is the product resistant to commodity pricing behaviour? 4 Is the technology of production freely available or is it proprietary and specialist? 5 Is the market free from domination by a small group of powerful customers? 6 Has the product a high added value when converted by the customer? 7 In the case of a new product, is the market likely to remain small enough, being unattractive to other producers? 8 Is the product such that the customer has to change formulation or even machinery if he changes suppliers? 9 Is the product free from the risk of substitution by an alternative supplier?	Primary factor: percentage share of total market. Secondary factor: degree to which market share is secured. Ratings associated with alternative competitive positions: *current position negligible **minor market share, less than adequate to support R&D and other departments ***a company with a strong viable stake in the market, but below the top league; usually, when one producer is a leader, the next level of competition will comprise producers meriting a 3-star rating **** major producer – situation when two to four companies are equally strong, will all merit a 4-star rating. ***** leader – a company in a pre-eminent market position, likely to be followed by others and also the acknowledged technological leader (the market share associated with this position is likely to vary from case to case, so, for instance, in a field of 10, a company with a 25% share may be a leader, whereas, a 50% share in a field of 2 competitors may not confer market leadership).

Source: Kerin et al. 1990

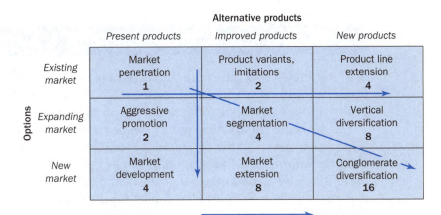

Level of risk increases

Figure 2.11 Growth vector analysis

Source: Rowe et al. 1986

Key issues to consider when using portfolio matrices

Portfolio matrices have evolved and become significant tools in helping to understand the macro environment in developing segments. They also enable a company to understand and develop its positioning strategies. However, there are caveats that need to be mentioned.

- A high growth market may offer opportunities, but will also demand high investments.
- A large proportion of portfolio matrices are geared to understanding product markets and based on manufacturing companies, so need to be modified for the non-profit and services sectors. For instance, factors such as the experience curve may not have direct relevance. Also, market share may not be a critical issue. Service levels may be more important.
- Portfolio matrices largely focus on the current capabilities of a company rather than stressing future possibilities.
- A blinkered approach to the use of portfolio matrices may result in narrowly defined strategies (invest, harvest, divest, for example), based on a limited range of considerations. It also prevents innovation and creativity being applied to developing segments and strategies.
- New products and services could attract funding from venture capital markets and therefore there should not be an automatic assumption that strategies are constrained by resources (Wensley 1981).
- It is not always easy to define product/market segments.
- The judgements are largely subjective, but appear to be scientific when plotted in two dimensions.

The above section has highlighted some of the key points that need to be considered when a macro analysis of the environment is coordinated with a particular portfolio that exists within a company.

The marketing information system

Both the internal and the external analysis of the competitive environment require up-to-date information, which should be collected, archived, processed and analysed by the marketing information system of the organisation.

The marketing information system can be considered to be a part of the general information system of the organisation. However, its function cannot be isolated from the information flows and databases of other departments. First of all, in order to realise a good internal analysis, the information from many different departments has to be treated as inputs for the marketing information system – information from human resources, accounts, finance, supply, production, distribution and so on. On the other hand, the information analysed and processed by

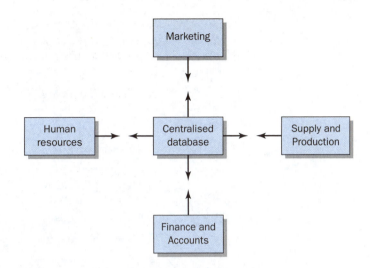

Figure 2.12 **The centralised information system implemented by customer-focused organisations**

the marketing information system has to be available to the managers of various departments, for strategic coordination.

At present, the change of focus from product to consumers has determined that many companies now develop multifunctional and centralised databases in which all relevant information is introduced, organised and accessed in a flexible way. The creation of such a database is not always easy, especially when traditionally the organisation and storage of information was handled at departmental level.

On the other hand, the sophistication of the marketing information system depends also on the importance of the marketing function and size of the firm. Large companies usually have a highly developed information system, organised in hierarchical levels of access and with highly structured information flows. In small firms, the information system can be hosted on a computer or even a laptop used by the manager entrepreneur and the main information flows are represented by interpersonal, informal communication.

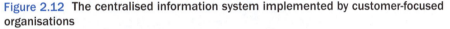

Market segmentation

No company can satisfy the needs and wants of all consumers. This reality is even more obvious in the modern competitive environment, which is characterised by a fragmentation/atomisation of markets and intense competition. Market segmentation is now one of the most important activities marketing undertakes.

Market segmentation is a selection process in which the company attempts to identify the categories of consumers whose needs and wants it is capable to satisfying better than its competitors (see Figure 2.13). During this process, the marketing specialist first needs to understand very well the resources and the capabilities of the

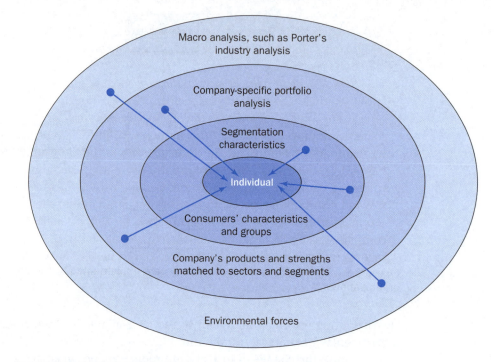

Figure 2.13 Segmenting markets

firm. This is achieved by undertaking an internal analysis. Second, the marketer must have a clear picture of the competitive situation in the market environment and its future evolution. That requires an in-depth external analysis. On the basis of this internal and external knowledge, the specialist can then match the needs and wants of a specific segment of the market to the capabilities of the firm.

Many authors argue that the following factors have to be taken into account when segmenting a market.

- *The market has to be well defined* This is not as easy as it seems because a specific need or combination of needs has to be related to a product or service. For example, the consumers' need for entertainment cannot be considered a good basis for defining a market – it is so multidimensional. Focusing on one aspect of entertainment instead – music, for example – can represent a good approach to defining the target market.
- *The market segment has to be measurable* Has the company gathered enough market research data to ascertain the size, buying power and profiles of the segments that they are targeting? This is a difficult issue as certain measures and statistics are not always readily available. Also, it may be costly to undertake specific market research. Under these circumstances, firms often buy research from specialist market research companies.
- *The market segment must be accessible* Most companies would be anxious to know whether or not they can reach and serve their designated market segments effectively. In order to access certain markets, issues of distribution, advertising and

branding need to be considered. Access to particular segments may be dependent on advertising that is backed up by adequate distribution strategies. The designated segments have to be accessible to a company so that it can sell and market its products.

■ *The market segment must be substantial* For most companies, it is important to know whether or not a particular segment is large enough or profitable enough to service. For some companies, a large market segment may be important for market share development, while for others, the profitability of a niche segment may be more important. For instance, a company such as the Morgan Motor Company is happy to serve a small but substantially profitable segment of car enthusiasts, whereas a company such as Procter & Gamble will be interested primarily in the size and distribution aspects of a segment for anti-dandruff shampoos.

■ *Can marketing strategies be actioned to serve the selected market segments?* Every company has limited resources and it may not always be possible to serve all segments effectively. A company therefore has to be certain that it can implement marketing and targeting strategies for its chosen segments.

Segmentation criteria

There is no single way to segment a market. For both personal and business customers, there is a plethora of criteria that may be considered when trying to segment the total market. The possible classification variables/criteria are as widely varied as are the ways in which different researchers classify them into groups. A classification by Frank et al. (1972) is shown in Table 2.5.

Frank et al. (1972) and Wilkie and Cohen (1976) also indicate the distinction in terms of:

■ *general customer characteristics*, such as demographic, socio-economic, personality, and lifestyle factors that represent relatively enduring characteristics

■ more *market-dependent* or *situation-specific customer characteristics*, such as tendencies towards brand loyalty or basic consumption patterns, as well as attitudes, perceptions and preferences (in undertaking market research, general lifestyle and attitudes can be overlaid with product specific attributes to gauge consumer behaviour patterns).

Table 2.5 Segmentation criteria

	Customer-specific	Product-specific
Observable	Cultural, geographic, demographic and socio-economic variables	User status, usage frequency, brand loyalty, store loyalty and patronage, usage situation
Unobservable	Psychographics: personality and lifestyle	Psychographics, benefits, perceptions, attitudes, preferences and intentions

Source: Adapted from Frank et al. 1972

A categorisation based on behavioural measures as classifiers linked to other factors can also be used (Van Raaij 1982). The variables closely related to behaviour here are behavioural intention, attitudes, lifestyle and so on that could be linked to socio-demographics, personality and neighbourhood characteristics.

Variables can be classified as being quantitative or qualitative:

- *quantitative* variables include geodemographic and economic factors, size and type of customer
- *qualitative* variables are, for example, psychographic and behavioural factors, and benefit sought; they may be used singly or in some combination.

Another classification scheme relies on factors being divided into two large groups (Cahill 1997), those based on *physical attributes* (geographic, demographics and the combination of the two, geodemographics) and *behavioural attributes* of customers (lifestyle, life stage, psychographics, and usage). A marketer should try different segmentation variables, alone and in combination, to find the best way to view the market structure.

It is important to consider a range of variables when segmenting consumers. Some of the key characteristics used for this purpose are explained below.

Geographic segmentation

Historically, geographic schemes are probably the oldest segmentation method. Small manufacturers that wished to limit their investments or had distribution channels that were not large enough to cover the entire country segmented the market by selling their products only in certain areas. Geographic segmentation assumes that people from a certain location have needs that are different from those of people living elsewhere. Usunier (1998) has written a whole treatise trying to understand how cultural attributes resulting from geographic locations may determine different individuals' propensity to purchase a range of goods.

Geographic segmentation calls for dividing the market into different geographical units, such as nations, regions, cities or neighbourhoods. A company may decide to operate in one or a few geographical areas or to cover all areas, but paying attention to geographical differences in needs and wants (Kotler et al. 2001). Many companies today are 'regionalising' their marketing programmes – localising their products, advertising, promotion and sales efforts to fit the needs of individual regions, cities and even neighbourhoods. Geographical segmentation has many advantages: it is simple to understand, simple to perform and implement, and simple to manage (Cahill 1997).

Sometimes, the type of neighbourhood facilitates or hinders the diffusion of an innovation. Lunn (1982) described the ACORN approach (see Table 2.6) in the UK, based on census data. Webber conceived ACORN when he was working at the Centre for Environmental Studies. ACORN is based on the government's Census of Great Britain, conducted in 1981. It represents a radical departure from previous types of geographical classification. These groupings, with their 38 neighbourhood

Table 2.6 ACORN – a classification of residential neighbourhoods (commonly used in the UK)

ACORN group	Description
A	Agricultural areas
B	Modern family housing, higher incomes
C	Older housing of intermediate status
D	Poor-quality older terraced housing
E	Better-off council estates
F	Less well-off council estates
G	Poorest council estates
H	Multiracial areas
I	High-status, non-family areas
J	Affluent suburban housing
K	Better-off retirement areas

Source: CACI Limited, www.caci.co.uk/acorn/default.asp

type subgroupings, have the advantage of being very easy to measure and relate to. In particular, it has been possible to give each postcode in the UK an ACORN classification, which is a descriptor of the predominant type of household to be found in that postcode. By relating financial services behaviour to type of household, the propensity of each postcode to respond to a given financial services offer can be, in part, determined (Palmer and Lucas 1994). This type of segmentation can be helpful for locating retail outlets such as supermarkets, banks and other services. It can also be used to identify groups of customers who may have similar lifestyle patterns as a result of where they live.

Demographic segmentation

The demographic approach represents an alternative method of segmentation. This methodology relies on age and lifestyle. Using this basis, targets are defined as young people, men or families with children. Unfortunately, a number of recent studies have shown that demographic variables such as age, sex, income, occupation and race are, in general, poor predictors of behaviour and, consequently, less than optimum bases for segmentation strategies. However, when market segments are first defined using other bases, such as personality or behaviour, their demographic characteristics must be known in order to assess the size of the target market and reach it efficiently. Age is, probably, the demographic variable that most lends itself to credible, useful segmentation and targeting. Consumer needs and wants change with age. Income is related to ability to buy; family size to quantity of purchases. Social class is a concept built up from age, the level of education and occupation. As the new century progresses, it may be easiest to use social class and income as explanatory variables. However, demographic variables that can be used for segmentation and targeting purposes include more than just age. Height and/or weight can work for some products, such as clothing. Race works for other products, as does religion in specific cases.

Sex segmentation has long been used in clothing, hairdressing, cosmetics and magazines. For products and services such as automobiles, boats, clothing, cosmetics and travel, the marketers have also used income segmentation. Some companies target affluent consumers, with luxury goods and convenience services, but many other companies profitably target low-income consumes, such as discount shop chains. Handled properly, with a great deal of discretion and understanding, any demographic variable is usable.

A set of demographic variables that has been around in social science research and the popular press for decades is 'social class'. The concept of a social class is constantly changing and what was once a particular social category is now no longer appropriate. Also, the previous assumptions about age and consumption have had to be drastically altered with the growth of the 'grey' market. Even this 'grey' market is now so large and complex that only psychographics can be used to break it down into the smaller segments necessary to market to the different sub-markets. For example, in the United States, the most widely adopted social classification is the Warner index (see Table 2.7).

The demographic attributes used in segmentation may include dozens of elements, but the basic elements include age, income, home ownership, length of residence and occupation. Customer demographics are important because industry trends indicate that markets need to be carefully designated and they are continually fragmenting. The following case study concerning the PlayStation illuminates the issues raised above.

Table 2.7 The Warner index of social classification

Class name	Description	Consumption patterns
Upper-upper	Elite social class with inherited social position	Expansive, irrelevant, but purchase decisions are not meant to impress; conservative
Lower-upper	Highly successful in business and profession; position acquired as result of wealth	Conspicuous consumption to demonstrate wealth, luxury cars, large estates, etc.
Upper-middle	Successful business and professional	Purchases directed at projecting a successful image
Lower-middle	White-collar workers, small businesspeople	Concerned with social approval; purchase decisions conservative; home and family orientated
Upper-lower	Blue-collar workers, technicians, skilled workers	Satisfaction of family roles
Lower-lower	Unskilled labour, poorly educated, poorly off	Attraction to cheap, low-quality items; heavy exposure to TV

Source: Adapted from Hawkins, Best and Coney 2004. Reproduced with permission of The McGraw-Hill Companies.

The power behind PlayStation: going for old

Everyone's getting younger, older. Apparently. Thirty-plus-somethings continue on in the vein of teenage-somethings: coffee-table hip hop, Nike Shox, G Star Denim, the odd, wayward spliff, a desire to spend money rather than save – all manifestations of your average 35 year old. Youth 'lifestyle' has become everyman's mantra. And included within this, is video gaming's 'massification'. You're as likely to find a PlayStation2 console in a 50-year-old architect's office as you are within a 13-year-old's bedroom. PlayStation has managed gaming – aggressively at times – into an age profile that extends way beyond the conventional tween (early teen) territory.

Five years ago, gaming resided in male, teenagers' bedrooms. Gaming was nerdy. Masturbatory. An embarrassment. Something you wouldn't admit to. Today it enjoys mainstream acceptance; its aesthetic or artistic appeal is widely recognised and debated. Gaming has become a serious, mass-market leisure pursuit. And PlayStation, in particular, has helped to accelerate this societal change.

How?

Back in 1995, Sony sought to command and conquer older individuals' leisure time, not just their gaming time, with their 32-bit console. 'Micro' disruption of the category was sought through a four-fold strategy:

- 'older' communication targeting
- 'older' technology (CDs not cartridges)
- launch of 'older', adult-themed games versus childish, platform titles
- investment in 'serious' role-playing icons – like Lara Croft – rather than cartoon 'heroes', such as Mario or Sonic.

Consistently, the brand was marketed over and above the product's technical capacity. The reward in gaming, communication reasoned, rested within the benefit of experiential output, not the console's input, as previous hardware manufacturers had iterated. Powerful gaming experiences could change you, move you, reshape you.

Feeding off this desire to own leisure time ran a media strategy, which *understood* the requirements for 'meeting points' between PlayStation and an older consumer. Building a skate park meant developing a touch point with skate fans in their late teens who were, simultaneously, gaming fans, too (the Tony Hawkes franchise continues to sell impressively). A roach card magazine insert delivered an acknowledgement of what older gamers did when they gamed, with their mates, in each other's homes. Further, an 'intelligent' brand voice told these audiences they could 'quote themselves', could 'be their own hero 'or 'land on their own moon'.

The power of play, through PlayStation, was dramatically and compellingly told. Gaming was much more than gaming. It was a sport. An art form. An interaction that could terrify, fascinate and frustrate. More significantly, you – the gamer – decided on how your gaming 'escape' should manifest. You might choose to be David Beckham in one moment or fly a jet fighter plane in another. If not these, then you might prefer to role-play God or at least a superhero, to become a deadly assassin or a triple-a-snowboarder; why not a streetfighter or a DJ? The choice – the possibilities – were infinite. An infinity made practical by the largest library of games. Games that were – and continue to be – uniquely positioned and marketed.

When we consider the consumer profile of PS2 and PSOne today, we see a brand that enjoys an almost unnatural span of age profile. Where the junior console drops off – around the age of 14 – the senior, second-generation console picks up and enjoys its largest number of gamers between the ages of 20 and 25. A healthy penetration continues, afterward, beyond the age of 40, however, and well into the grey market of 50, 60 and 70.

Breaking the targeting and brand rules of this category has, ultimately, changed the status of gaming. In six short years, PlayStation has evolved and grown the gaming category out of the kid's bedroom, into all of our lives. Let's give this some perspective. In terms of money, gaming now generates more cash than that of the American film industry. In fact, Datamonitor suggests that sales of games consoles and software in Europe and the USA will generate over $20 billion-worth of business by 2003. Not bad for a category that was – according to 1995 business forecasts – rasping its way into extinction.

Source: Carl Radcliffe, TBWA personal communication

Life-stage segmentation

Life-stage segmentation, also called the 'family lifecycle' is the recognition that a family's needs and expenditure change over time as people leave their parents' home, marry, have children and grow up to repeat the cycle. In a sense, life-stage segmentation represents family demographics, particularly regarding ages and income levels. The focus on longitudinal changes in purchasing behaviour is valuable for predicting macro-demand for specific product categories, such as houses, education, household appliances, services and so on.

Examining the demographic makeup of customers enables an understanding of the types of customers and whether it is in a company's interest to pursue similar segments or not (Coffey and Palm 1999). Andreasen (1984) explored the effects of life status change on attitudes, needs, wants and behaviour. He notes that 'for many people, the break with the past that is inherent in the occasion of a status change can represent an opportunity to rethink and organise their lives' and concluded that the transition from one stage of life to the next causes much stress in individuals. It is this stress that can make customers become more susceptible to seeking the suggestions of others (particularly marketers) and could result in them being prime targets for products and services that are viewed as necessary requirements for the next life stage. The greater the change in the life pattern, the greater will be the lifecycle change.

Table 2.8 The stages of the family life lifecycle

Stage	Financial and purchasing characteristics
Bachelor – young, single, not living at parental home	Few financial burdens, recreation-orientated; holidays, entertainments outside home
Newlywed – young couple, no children	Better off financially, two incomes; purchase home, some consumer durables
Full nest I – youngest child under 6	Home purchasing peak; increasing financial pressure, may have only one income earner; purchase of household products
Full nest II – youngest child over 6	Financial position improving; some working spouses
Full nest III – older married couples with dependent children	Financial position even better; update household products and furnishings
Empty nest I – older married couples, no children at home	Home ownership peak; renewed interest in travel and leisure activities; buy luxuries
Empty nest II – older couples, no children at home, retired	Drastic cut in income, medical services bought
Solitary survivor – still in labour force	Income good, but likely to sell home
Solitary survivor – retired	Special needs for medical care, affection and security

Source: Wells and Gubar 1966

Geodemographic segmentation

By combining geographic and demographic to form *geodemographics*, marketers have built a strong analytical tool. Geodemographics are based on an understanding that people with similar needs and lifestyles tend to live close together. As Weiss (1994) states, 'where we live affects our attitudes toward what we buy'. Although this may be true, it reverses the direction of major causality – that is, the statement should read 'what we think influences where we live', at least at the micro level (Cahill 1997).

Other developments in this area of geodemographic segmentation include FINPIN coding (PinPoint analysis) and MOSAIC (CCN). In both cases, the approach was to cross-reference other research-based data on the uptake of financial services to the original geodemographic descriptor. For example, PinPoint analysis cross-tabulated their PIN code against the usage pattern of financial services established by the Financial Research Survey (FRS is a national regular survey of respondents' usage of financial products). From this cross-tabulation, a more industry-specific classification was produced of FINPIN types (Palmer and Lucas 1994).

Psychographic segmentation

Psychographic segmentation became an important aspect of advertising and marketing research in the 1960s. Understanding psychographics is important as it is difficult to develop demographic categories for many product categories (such as clothes, cars). The difficulties associated with the use of demographic and socio-economic characteristics as bases for segmentation have led to various attempts to segment markets based on psychographic characteristics. Often, demographic data is collected routinely and marketers are comfortable with this (Wells 1975). However, the reality is that even consumers categorised in the same demographic group can have very different psychographic characteristics. People tend to have differing behaviour patterns.

According to Ziff (1971), 'Some have used the term to refer to basic *personality* characteristics – aggression, anxiety, extroversion, masculinity; some have applied it to *lifestyle* variables – community involvement, home entertainment, leisure activities, etc.' However, social class, lifestyle and personality traits constitute psychographics (Kotler 1988, and see Figure 2.14 overleaf). The clearest and most complete definition is the following (Gunter and Furnham 1992):

> *psychographics seek to describe the human characteristics of consumers that may have a bearing on their responses to products, packaging, advertising and public relations efforts. Such variables may span a spectrum from self-concept and lifestyle to attitudes, interests and opinions, as well as perceptions of product attributes.*

The case study overleaf is an example of lifestyle segmentation being used in mobile communications applications.

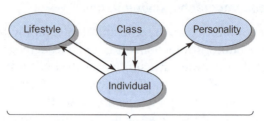

Figure 2.14 **Psychographic segmentation**

CASE STUDY

Lifestyle snapshots

Solving the context problem for wireless design

Introduction

In her recent interview with uidesign.net, Laura Arlov, author of *GUI Design for Dummies*, IDG Books, 1997, stated that one of her biggest design problems, when considering wireless Internet design, was the lack of context understanding. Optimising a design is best done when the context of the user's interaction with the software, device or machine is understood. Context is a description or understanding of the actual interaction event.

For example, in a banking application, the user may be a clerk, the context may be that the clerk is working at the counter with a customer on the other side of the counter who wishes to deposit money into their savings account. Various interactions with the bank's computer system need to occur in order to complete the transaction. However, they are all occurring within the same context – a single customer, at the counter, with money to deposit.

Laura Arlov was merely pointing out that, with wireless Internet devices, it is so much more difficult to predict the context for an interaction.

I have had some success with a technique I am calling, 'lifestyle snapshots'. A lifestyle snapshot is an addition to existing techniques for defining personas (or user roles) and usage scenarios. A lifestyle snapshot helps us to better understand the context of a particular usage scenario. Lifestyle snapshots are particularly useful when designing for consumer wireless Internet.

An airport application

Recently, John M. Thompson of IBM, revealed that they had implemented a system for Swiss Air which automatically checks in a passenger when they arrive at the airport. The system works by using their passenger's cellular phone and the local telephone carrier's transceiver or cellsite. When a phone is detected on the airport cellsite, the IBM system checks to see if the phone is owned by a person who is also registered as a passenger on Swiss Air for that day. If so, then the system proceeds to check the passenger in, receiving any confirmations required over the cell phone.

This is a classic WAP application. The airline can deliver increased passenger service with faster check-in. The passenger doesn't have to stand in line and can probably afford to turn up a little bit later than normal (providing the system is reliable and is working properly).

It is impossible for me to talk about any wireless Internet work I might be doing, so we will explore a design approach which includes lifestyle snapshots using this IBM/Swiss Air example. Imagine for a moment that this system did not yet exist. An executive at Swiss Air has just asked you to improve customer service by reducing check-in time for loyal, regular customers using new technology. Where do you start?

Persona definitions

You start by trying to understand who the passengers are. These people will be the users. The client will doubtless have market research, demographic studies, perhaps actual passenger surveys. You start with these. However, as Laura Arlov pointed out, 'demographics don't buy products, people buy products'. So you must invent some real people who match the demographics. Alan Cooper has called these invented people, personas (Cooper 1999). Cooper's observation was that you should not try to design a product for all of the target audience. You should design it for just one of them (or perhaps three or four specific people). This profound counter-intuitive observation works because people are not unique. However much we pride our individuality, the truth is that there is always someone very similar not far away.

Lifestyle snapshots

Lifestyle snapshots work in a similar fashion to Cooper's personas. The principle is that you should not try to design a wireless Internet application for every possible situation when it might be used, but instead design it well for at least one situation when it *will* be used. By making the application precisely what is needed, and as easy, intuitive and usable as it can be for just that one situation, then you are designing a great product.

So for that 'just one persona', we are going to pick that 'just one lifestyle snapshot'. A lifestyle snapshot gives us a context for a design. We are going to design the feature or set of features for the wireless application for that one persona in one context. If we get that right then the chances are that the design will provide good to excellent operation for most of the people, most of the time.

A lifestyle snapshot describes a 'day in the life of' a persona, or simply a period of time. A long enough period of time to give us a context for usage of their wireless application.

Usage scenarios and use cases

We use lifestyle snapshots to determine the usage scenarios for an application. From the lifestyle snapshot ask yourself, 'At what points in this scene could the main characters have benefited from use of the technology?', 'Where can the technology fit into their lifestyle in order to make it better, easier, faster, simpler, more informed?'

With each lifestyle snapshot a number of candidate usage scenarios will emerge. Usage scenarios describe precise, exact occasions where a device or application is being used. The development of usage scenarios is the first stage in a usage-centred design approach which leads to the development of essential use cases (Constantine & Lockwood 2000). Essential use cases can be mapped and abstracted. There is an opportunity when doing this to make a design which delivers suitable interaction for several usage scenarios, hence several lifestyle snapshots and perhaps for several personas.

In other words, we start with very specific descriptions of the user, the context and the usage, and later we use our analysis phase to examine the similarities in the requirements for different users and deliver a good, well-balanced design which is suitable for a broader audience.

Let us take an imaginary exploration of the Swiss Air requirements.

Example: Zurich airport system

So imagine for the purposes of this paper that we have been asked to design the system for Swiss Air. For brevity we will consider only one persona, and only one lifestyle snapshot. In a real design you would expect to develop up to five personas and perhaps five to 10 lifestyle snapshots for each persona.

Persona definition: Hans, senior partner of a Zurich law firm

Hans is 45 years of age. He is a lawyer in a major firm in Zurich providing legal services to the banking community and major industrial concerns in Switzerland and the predominantly German speaking business community. Hans studied law at college and has been with the same firm since receiving his practising certificate around 20 years ago. He has a wife and two children all of whom are very costly. He lives in luxury by Swiss standards, in a large house, around 20km from the city, nestled in the low mountains, with a nice view. He drives an S Class Mercedes. Hans has all the trappings of success and in order to be successful he has to be competitive.

Hans has become dependent on his cell phone and his laptop computer. He uses his laptop for email, presentations, word processing and financial calculations with spreadsheet software.

He regularly flies around central Europe negotiating mergers and acquisitions for his clients. It's high value business and he needs to get around Europe quickly and easily in order to be in the right meetings at the right time.

Hans relies on Swiss Air to get him there. He is a frequent flyer who flies business class and gets upgraded into first class often. He expects first class service from the airline just as his clients expect first class service from him.

Now, let us consider a lifestyle snapshot for Hans.

Lifestyle snapshot: Monday morning business in Munich

Hans is flying to Munich to close a deal. His client is buying a small Bavarian ISP as part of their expansion of Internet services in the German-speaking world.

Hans is woken at 4.30am by his alarm clock. He gets up and checks that his phone has recharged. He fires up his laptop and checks for any last minute e-mail. While the machine is working, he darts back and forth getting ready. It's a one-day trip so he doesn't need to pack much.

By 5.30 he is dressed, has had his first coffee of the day, has his laptop packed in its leather briefcase and his phone in his pocket. He also has a Psion Organizer with his diary for the day and week ahead. His colleagues have been tempting him with gentle nudges to buy a Palm Pilot but so far he has stuck with the Psion.

All the technology was preloaded with the information he was going to need the previous Friday afternoon by Hans' private secretary.

He gets into his car, the ever-reliable Mercedes, and sets off for the airport.

It becomes apparent that the weather has turned poor overnight and there has been a late spring snowfall. The roads are difficult but not impossible. His journey, nevertheless, is slower than it might be and he gets stuck behind some snowploughs on the Autobahn.

He parks in the one-day parking at the airport and walks to the terminal, quickly. Although not too late, he is close to the closing time for the flight. The airport is still quiet at this time. Luckily

as a business class passenger he doesn't have to wait in line. There is only one passenger ahead of him. However, he finds that there are no window seats left and he will need to take an aisle seat. He checks to see if his frequent flyer miles have been credited to his account. Seemingly not. Some mistake. A few more minutes are wasted as the check-in clerk checks his details and amends the error. Just a little bit of stress that he might have done without.

He proceeds to the business lounge which he knows well and enjoys another coffee. Breakfast will be served on the plane.

The flight leaves a few minutes later than expected with no real danger to Hans' schedule for the day. He eats breakfast, rereads his client notes on his laptop and sleeps a little. The flight arrives in Munich.

As he proceeds off the airliner, Hans realizes that he is short of euro currency and will need to change some money. He has prebooked a rental car and will afterward make his way to the underground garage to collect his car. The car rental company is affiliated with the airline and he wants to ensure that his airmiles are credited to his frequent flyer account. He discovers when he reaches the desk that the company is making a special offer today. He can drive a Mercedes for a small upgrade fee and earn double airmiles on his account. Slightly more time is wasted while he takes advantage of this offer. Accumulating maximum airmiles is important for family vacations . . .

We could continue to explore the rest of Hans' day. For example, the weather at Munich could worsen and the airport might be closed in the late afternoon. Hans would then need to book into a hotel and would need to acquire some toiletries and essential clothes for the following day.

We might choose to call the whole day a single lifestyle snapshot or we may choose to break the day into three distinct sections. The first would be the journey from home to the prospective acquisition in Bavaria. The second would be the session at the prospect site, including all the negotiations. The third would be the return journey with its subsequent overnight stay due to bad weather.

There are lots of opportunities for usage scenarios from this lifestyle snapshot. Let's look at just a small number.

Usage scenario: auto check-in for flight

On arrival at the airport, the Swiss Air system is alerted that a mobile phone belonging to Hans is now transceiving with a local cell site. The system pushes a welcome message (probably via SMS) asking if he would like to check-in by WAP Internet service.

At this point Hans has probably not yet left his car or he may be already walking with his luggage towards the check-in area.

Hans accesses the Swiss Air site through a bookmark and is given an easy-to-find navigation link to the check-in service. The system already knows why he is logging in. This is a key point for improved usability – we have a context for the interaction. He is asked to confirm his flight number and is prompted for his seat preference. Perhaps the system already knows that he prefers window seats rather than aisles.

Usage scenario: boarding notification

Hans has already checked in. He is now waiting in the business lounge but the phone system does not necessarily know this. He could be shopping in the airport, drinking in the bar. It sends him alerts (probably by SMS) that the flight will begin boarding in ten minutes, then later that boarding has commenced.

Usage scenario: rental car 'Push' advertising

As the system already knows that Hans has checked in and will be flying to Munich, it should also know that he has a rental car booked and with which company. There is an opportunity to advise Hans that there is a special offer available today and perhaps allow him to confirm that he wants the upgrade and it should be billed to his credit card. Assuming that the system knows his credit card details.

Summary

Lifestyle snapshots provide a context for an interaction. They help us to understand a persona and they give us a tangible situation into which we can apply a design. They act as a 'halfway house' between personas and usage scenarios.

Lifestyle snapshots have proven particularly useful when designing for wireless devices because they allow us to understand the context of use for a product which is ultimately aimed at a broad mass market and can conceivably be used in almost any location at any time. Lifestyle snapshots help us to guess the most likely locations and the most likely times for a particular feature or set of features to be used.

A lifestyle snapshot gives us clues as to which features will be needed at or around the same time, which features are needed to work together and should be tightly integrated.

For example, in our airline example, we can see that check-in and frequent flyer miles enquiries need to happen together. Rental car and related information would be useful. There are advertising opportunities too, based on what we know about the persona's life. It might also have been useful to offer weather and driving conditions.

The better we can understand the user and how that user lives, the more likely we are to design an information age appliance which provides what he needs when he needs it. Personas and lifestyle snapshots help us to do that. They are tools which help to produce great, compelling design.

References

Constantine & Lockwood (2000) 'Essential use case style and structure', Constantine & Lockwood Ltd (www.foruse.com).

Cooper, Alan (1999) *The inmates are running the asylum*, SAMS.

Notes: What is described above is an imaginary requirements analysis for an airline check-in system using WAP technology. This is being used as design exercise to demonstrate best practice when approaching such a design challenge, and in no way reflects the actual IBM implementation of the Swiss Air system.

Source: David Anderson, 'Lifestyle snapshots', White Paper, *uidesign.net*, 3 April 2000

Customer lifetime value segmentation

One of the most important objectives of any firm is to maintain and increase its profitability. From this perspective, the firm will attempt to service its most profitable customers. In a transaction-based approach, the most profitable customer is the one who has most spending power at the present moment. However, as nowadays marketing focuses rather more on long-term relationships than on-off transactions, a possible segmentation criteria is the customer lifetime value (CLTV).

In mathematical terms, the CLTV consists of taking into account the total financial contribution – revenue minus costs – of a customer over the entire life of his or her business relationship with the company. Despite its simplicity, the measurement of CLTV requires great care. All cash flows involved in the process have to be identified and measured on a very detailed level and allocated precisely to each customer or type of customer. Figure 2.15 represents a concise, seven-step approach to measuring CLTV.

Translating Figure 2.15 into mathematical formulae, we obtain:

$$CLTV = (RR - RC)\, Y - AC \tag{1}$$

$$P = CLTV \times C \tag{2}$$

$$P = [(RR - RC) \times Y - AC] \times C \tag{3}$$

CLTV = customer lifetime value (profitability)
RR = recurring revenues
RC = recurring costs
Y = lifespan of a customer relationship or number of transactions
AC = acquisition costs
P = total profits
C = number of customers

The mathematical expression of the customer lifetime value can represent a sound basis for analysing the existing situation and identifying the possible strategies to increase customer profitability. Analysing formula 3 given above, five levers of cus-

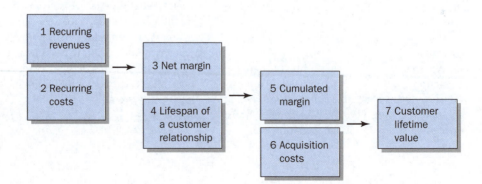

Figure 2.15   Seven-step process for measuring customer lifetime value

Table 2.9 The operational requirements for implementing customer-orientated strategies based on customer lifetime value analysis

Strategy	Tactics	Operation	Requirements
Conquer – increase C – (number of customers)	Improve existing offer in order to attract potential customers close to existing customer segments	Improve: • product • price • distribution • promotion	Research Segmentation Investment
	Diversify offer in order to attract new segments of customers	Increase product/service portfolio	Research Segmentation Investment
Increase RR (recurring revenues)	Increase volume of sales	Diversification Stimulate demand	Research Segmentation Investment
	Increase value of sales	Upgrade offer	Research Segmentation Investment
	Increase both volume and value of sales	Diversification Stimulate demand Upgrade offer	Research Segmentation Investment
Reduce RC (recurring costs)	Reduce general costs (administration, maintenance, etc.)	Increased efficiency	Research Segmentation Investment
	Reduce costs of: • product/service • distribution • communication	Cheaper supplies Cheaper outsourcing Increased efficiency	Research Segmentation Investment
Retain, increase Y (lifespan of customer relationship)	Increase customers' loyalty, maintaining and/or increasing customer satisfaction	Improve present offer Better targeting Score better than competition	Research Segmentation Investment
Reduce AC (acquisition costs)	Better targeting of potential customers	Improve offer Improve targeting Use same resources more efficiently	Research Segmentation Investment

Source: Gurău and Ranchhod 2002

tomer value creation can be identified (Gurău and Ranchhod 2002). These strategies represent only the starting point of a company-wide operational effort. Table 2.9 shows the complexity of implementing customer-oriented strategies based on the analysis of the customer lifetime value.

Problems with calculating the customer lifetime value

The calculation of the customer lifetime value is not a problem-free process. However, most of the problems can be successfully solved by taking into consideration two main issues:

■ the company applying this method has to clearly define from the beginning the purpose of using customer lifetime value analysis and the expected benefits

■ the problems raised by the customer lifetime value analysis are often industry- and company-specific and as a result, the company has to select the most appropriate way to apply this concept in its particular situation

Defining a 'customer'

The first challenge is to define the customer unit. Is it an individual, an account, a household or a business address? A second challenge is linking customer information to create a single customer record of when they leave and return multiple times during the lifespan of his or her relationship with the company.

The answers to these questions are industry-specific. The business organisation has to identify the characteristics of its customer relationship and, on this basis, define the customer unit and the customer lifetime cycle. In the present marketplace, a company can be confronted with the situations set out in Table 2.10.

Table 2.10 shows the possible combinations (27) of customer relationship characteristics as they differ for various industrial sectors and even for companies within the same industry. For example, a company with a small number of customers, making a small number of transactions that require a high level of company–customer involvement, will probably define the customer unit as being single customers (individuals or organisations) and the customer lifecycle as depending on the business cycles specific for the industry (production, investment and consumption cycles). Equally, for a company dealing with a large number of clients, a large number of transactions and low involvement, it might be more appropriate to aggregate the individual customers into particular segments with homogeneous profiles and behaviour.

Evaluating costs

Measuring cost at the customer level poses the greatest challenge to customer lifetime value measurement. While the revenue per customer can usually be collected from the appropriate billing system, cost information is aggregated into general accounts and requires a good deal of analysis before it can meaningfully be attached to individual customers or customer segments. The indirect costs are especially difficult to divide and allocate.

In solving these problems, three key principles about costing should be applied by the company:

■ customer costs must be related to the revenues they generate

Table 2.10 The characteristics of customer relationships in different industrial markets

Number of customers	Number of transactions	Level of involvement
Large	Large	High
Medium	Medium	Medium
Small	Small	Low

Source: Gurău and Ranchhod 2002

- not all costs within the organisation should be attributed down to a customer level
- it should be made absolutely clear who can influence different types of cost and revenues.

Evaluating the length of the customer relationship

The length of the customer–business relationship is difficult to measure in the present economic environment as it is characterised by unpredictability and rapid change. Many companies are using as the main tool for this prediction the analysis of historical data about the past behaviour of its customers, identifying specific segments and extrapolating the behaviour of these segments into the future. This method can be used successfully only in relatively stable market environments because it assumes that:

- the customers will repeat their past behaviour in the future
- the market conditions will not change significantly.

It is therefore completely useless in a dynamic, fast-changing market environment, such as the high-tech industries. In such sectors, the customers' needs and perceptions are changing fast, competition is intensive and market conditions are hugely variable. Thus, it is important to connect these predictions with the external market environment.

Many models for calculating customer lifetime value/profitability neglect the external environment of the firm, concentrating only on the relationship between the organisation and its customers. However, it is dangerous to think that this relation takes place in a marketing void. The market conditions might, and indeed do, change over time, impacting an organisation's policies, and customers' needs and perceptions.

The segmentation process

The segmentation process involves several stages that must be applied in a specific order.

1 Defining the market

The market is defined by considering the consumers' needs that can be successfully satisfied by using the company's resources and capabilities. The main area of a firm's competitive advantage can be used to indicate such a market.

2 Identifying the best market segmentation criteria

These criteria are the ones that succeed best in explaining the specific behaviour of different categories of clients when they are trying to satisfy their needs. For example, when segmenting the market of music, the criteria of age and level of education can indicate very effectively the specific preferences of different categories of consumers. On the other hand, for luxury products, such as sports cars, lifestyle and spending power can be used successfully to segment such a market.

If the company wants to identify very clearly the targeted market segments, it will use a large number of segmentation criteria, starting with the most general ones – for example, age or gender – and finishing with very specific ones – such as level of education, lifestyle or personality. The application of additional segmentation criteria can refine the market segment already defined. For example, the market segmentation process can be repeatedly applied, selecting finer and finer consumer segments (see Figure 2.16).

The segmentation criteria selected in every new phase can address different aspects of the company's strategic approach. For example, in the first instance, the firm might select a segmentation criteria based on its expertise, so a car manufacturer will select the consumers interested in owning their own car or institutions that need transportation. In the second stage, the firm might try to identify the consumer segments with a high growth rate, using a segmentation criteria based on its sales volume objective. Finally, in the third stage, the firm can consider segmentation on the basis of spending power, in order to be in line with its profitability targets.

Good segmentation criteria have the following characteristics:

■ easy to define
■ easy to measure – data about the market is easily available in relation to the criteria
■ relevant to the market – the application of the segmentation criteria must allow the firm to identify substantial variations in the customer purchasing and consumption behaviour in relation to a specific product or service

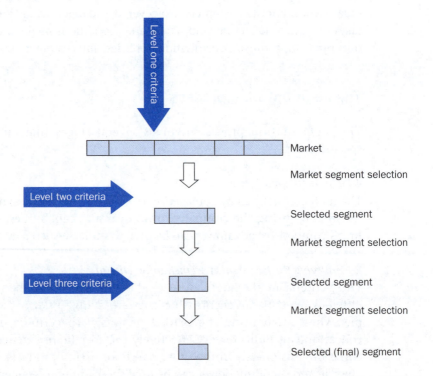

Figure 2.16 **The successive application of different levels of segmentation criteria**

■ permits a clear discrimination of various categories of consumers on the basis of their purchasing and consumption behaviour.

3 Applying the segmentation criteria and dividing the market
The market defined in the first stage has to be divided using the values of the selected segmentation criteria. These values must represent critical points that determine a behavioural change in the consumers' attitude towards a product or service. For example, familial situation is a possible criteria that can be applied to tourist services. The values taken by this segmentation variable can indicate a change in the specific preferences of consumers for different types of summer holiday destinations during their lifetime.

After splitting the defined market into segments, the firm must choose one or more customer segments as priority targets. This choice can be made considering the specific expertise of the firm in serving one particular category of consumers or identifying the most profitable segments in the present and future market conditions.

4 Analysing and understanding the profile of the priority consumer segment
Often firms do not carry out extensive market research before undertaking the segmentation process. Because of the large costs of collecting and processing secondary and primary data, they might decide to investigate only the variation of the selected segmentation criteria, postponing the in-depth analysis of consumers' profile until after the priority segment has been selected. The advantage of this method is obvious – the chosen segment is much smaller and better defined than the entire market. At this stage, the firm can initiate a comprehensive process of data collection, processing and analysis to develop a thorough understanding of consumers' characteristics and behaviour. This detailed profile will later represent the basis for designing and implementing the functional marketing strategy of the firm – the marketing mix.

Strategic positioning

Even if market segmentation is well realised, the organisation cannot yet be sure of success. This is because the same market segment might be targeted by many companies, all competing for consumers' money and loyalty. In order to attract customers, every company will try to differentiate its strategy from those of competing firms, choosing a specific strategic position. The choice and implementation of this strategic position is the result of the positioning process.

In essence, *strategic positioning* is about differentiating your company from competitors, in order to attract and maintain a specific customer segment. Strategic positioning has both a subjective and an objective basis, which influence and complement each other. The objective element of positioning comes from the product's characteristics and the specific marketing activities attached to it. In fact, every element of the marketing mix contributes to positioning, which creates a strong need for the coherence of all the marketing activities implemented by a firm at product, price, distribution and communication levels. The subjective part of positioning is determined by consumers' perceptions of the product or service. This perception is developed and maintained by the explicit and implicit messages sent by the firm through its marketing activities. Finally, these two sides of strategic positioning should be continuously related to the positions of competing firms because consumers always use, consciously or unconsciously, comparisons with the various competitive offers available on the market to inform their buying decisions.

On the basis of this analysis, it is possible to construct the trinome of consumer, marketing mix and competitors that, together, determine the strategic positioning of the firm's offer (see Figure 2.17). The neglect of one dimension, or any imbalance of the three elements has a direct effect on the offer, creating a fragile, unrealistic market position. For example, the strategic position of a product can be artificially improved for a short period of time using aggressive communication methods. However, if the other elements of the marketing mix do not correspond with the message transmitted to the market (in terms of, for example, product characteristics, quality, price, distribution channel), the boost will be only temporary and the final effect on consumers' perceptions will be very negative.

The strategic position of a firm can be represented in visual terms using perceptual maps. The process of positioning the product on a perceptual map involves a number of stages that must be followed in strict order.

1 Identifying the salient features of the product/service
Usually, consumers position products using mental evaluations of a limited number of characteristics that they consider essential for satisfying their needs and wants. For example, some customers might position cars in relation to their design and price, while others might consider that reliability and fuel consumption represent the most important features. The salient elements therefore vary from one consumer segment to another. In order to identify the salient features of a product/service for the consumers included in a target market segment, market research is necessary. Once identified, the salient features will represent the coordinates of the axes used in the perceptual map.

Figure 2.17 The interrelatedness of the three determinants of strategic positioning

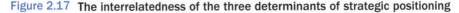

2 Finding the ideal value of the salient features for the targeted consumer segment

Even consumers who agree on the salient features that determine the value position of a product might have different perceptions of the ideal values of these features. That is why, in the second stage of the strategic positioning process, targeted customers should be asked to indicate the values of the salient features that can best satisfy their needs. Using the example of a car, the ideal values selected by a homogeneous group of consumers might be modern design and moderate price.

3 Investigating consumers' perceptions of the values of the salient features
   of competitors' products

The market research should continue, asking consumers to express their perceptions of the value of the salient features of competitors' products. Using their responses, the positions of competitors can be represented in the perceptual map as well as the area indicating the ideal values that were identified in the second stage. The representation of ideal values will most often be an area than a specific point, because the opinions of different customers may well vary. However, as long as the values are concentrated in a relatively small area, it means that consumers' perceptions are homogeneous and, therefore, their inclusion in a market segment is valid.

The Dyson case study indicates the key issues surrounding product positioning within a marketplace that has a need for a small vacuum cleaner.

CASE STUDY

Little Dyson cleaner finds niche in the smaller Japanese home

by Terry Macalister

James Dyson has beaten the Japanese at their own game by taking top slot in Japan's competitive vacuum cleaner market with a product specially designed for smaller homes. The miniaturised DC12, designed in Wiltshire for the Far East market, has increased Dyson sales in Japan by 177 per cent year-on-year and helped the company raise overall pre-tax profits in 2005 by 32 per cent to £103 million. After two years of exporting to Japan, Dyson's market share in the country is now 12 per cent, ahead of home brands such as Sharp, Sanyo and Mitsubishi. 'It seemed like we were taking coals to Newcastle when we first entered Japan's crowded vacuum cleaner market. The Japanese demand the best in electronics and they have recognised our technological benefits', Mr Dyson said. The British entrepreneur said he had increased the research and development budget by 28 per cent to £50 million during 2005 and was proceeding with plans to launch two new products in the course of this year. Criticised in the past for taking his manufacturing overseas to reduce costs, Mr Dyson says he has increased the numbers of scientists, engineers and technicians employed on R&D to 450. The DC12 uses a microchip to help produce a smaller and lighter motor. The motor runs at 100,000 revolutions per minute, which compares with 19,000 rpm in a Ferrari at full throttle, Mr Dyson said. He is in talks with motor manufacturers and aerospace companies about the possibility of using the vacuum cleaner technology for other purposes. Mr Dyson was not willing to say what new products would be launched this year, but admitted he was again working on a washing machine design. A previous design proved too expensive for commercial application. Mr Dyson is still developing – ten years on – a domestic carpet-cleaning robot, but the product has no official start date. Dyson's total export sales during 2005 rose by 44 per cent while overall group turnover was up 18 per cent to £470 million.

Source: Terry Macalister, *The Guardian*, 24 May 2006. Copyright Guardian News & Media Ltd 2006.

In Figure 2.18, the competitors' perceived position is indicated by the letters A, B, C, D, which represent product brands. It is easy to observe that, for this consumer segment, no competitor offer is located in the area of ideal values for the two salient features. Knowing this, a firm can position its offer in order to better answer the specific needs of this market segment.

The perceptual map is a powerful tool, permitting a clear image of customers' perceptions at a specific moment in time. If necessary, it can even be used for segmentation purposes, when various segments of consumers can be investigated to see what the salient features of the product and their ideal values are.

If, for the sake of simplicity, we consider that all consumer groups have identified the same two salient features for cars, the positions of the ideal values can be represented as areas of ideal values that are specific to each consumer segment. In the new representation, in Figure 2.19, it is easy to observe that, in the overall car market, the brands A and D are well positioned in specific areas of ideal values and, therefore, both of them are targeting their specific consumer segments successfully.

The representation of strategic positions on the perceptual map also has a series of disadvantages.

- There should be no major contradictions between the salient features indicated by consumers. If this happens, it might be an indication that the segmentation process was not well realised – the investigated consumer group possibly including two separate consumer segments. On the other hand, a certain variability in consumers' perceptions regarding the salient features of a product may be normal, due to personal preferences.
- The number of salient features identified should be relatively small (ideally two or three) in order to permit a clear visual representation of the market position.
- The ideal values indicated by each of the investigated consumer segments should be homogeneous. A large dispersion or a multiple polarisation of the ideal values indicates a lack of homogeneity of the consumer group.

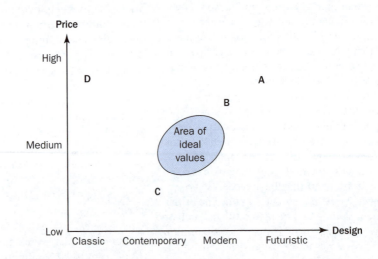

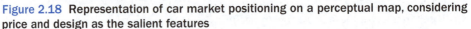

Figure 2.18 Representation of car market positioning on a perceptual map, considering price and design as the salient features

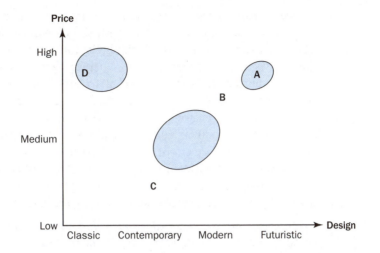

Figure 2.19 Representation of car market positioning on a perceptual map, considering the perceptions of different consumer groups

■ All the elements used for representing the market position are dynamic, changing over in time, and their evolution can be highly unpredictable. Thus, when perceptual maps are used for long-term planning horizons, the present position for ideal values might be of limited use, so the market research should also identify the future trends in consumers' perceptions. The future evolution of the ideal values can be indicated on the perceptual map by using small arrows. Ideally, the evolution of consumers' perceptions and/or of competitor's strategic positions should be identified in real time by means of repeated or continuous market investigation in order to permit the quick adaptation of the company's offer to the changing consumption trends.

The Internet, postmodern marketing and globalisation

Much of the discussion on postmodern marketing emphasises the growing importance of digital/telecommunication technologies, media, consumption, images/symbols and hyperreality (Venkatesh et al. 1993). According to Cova (1996), postmodernism champions individuality and the modern quest for liberation from social bonds. The fragmentation of society shows the consequence of postmodern individualism. Cova argues that:

> *Paradoxically, the postmodern individual is both isolated and in virtual contact with the whole world electronically. Postmodern daily life is characterised by ego concentration, encouraged by the spread of computers.*

Figure 2.20, adapted from Cova's article, shows the juxtaposition of opposites in the postmodern world. Cova goes on to say that, in postmodern marketing, one has to offer the following.

- *One-to-one marketing with the use of IT* Unpredictable and individualistic customers could be retained this way. In fact, with the growth of areas such as MySpace and Bebo, the Internet is now spawning behaviour that is both individual- and community-driven at the same time (see Chapter 10 for a fuller discussion).
- *Image* Hyperreality is the potential to offer an experience similar to Euro-Disney's theme parks. Technology offers the postmodern consumer the ability to be a participant in customising his or her own world. This is now truly happening with areas such as Second Life (again see Chapter 10 for a fuller discussion).
- *Marketing images* The era of postmodern marketing relies on image marketing (Venkatesh et al. 1993), emphasising cultural meanings and images. Cova (1996) feels that image marketing and brand management are closely related. Rather controversially, he argues that we are witnessing *the obsolescence of advertising*:

  In post-modern markets, advertising simply misses the fundamental point: to be an interactive experience of co-creation of meaning for the customer.

- *Fragmentation* Market and technology shifts in and since the 1990s are pointing towards market fragmentation and mass communication (Meuller-Heumann 1992). The fragmentation of markets is likely to herald a greater emphasis on smaller and unstable segments.

In many respects it could be argued that this type of postmodern world is not quite a reality for many people, though areas such as Second Life grew exponentially in 2006. Authors such as Clegg (1991) would argue that we are seeing signs of modernity, with seamless societal changes taking place in different cultural contexts rather than complete paradigm changes. It is impossible to tackle this contentious issue thoroughly in this book, but we mention it as some of the arguments put forward have relevance to this new world of almost instant global communications.

Ironically, much of the postmodern emphasis on fragmentation and individualism seems to be borne out by the experience of companies on the Internet. Initially, for instance, companies such as Tripod and Geocities (Hof et al. 1997) made a virtue out of helping to build community-type discussion areas, allowing communication over

Figure 2.20 Postmodern marketing as a juxtaposition of opposites
Source: Adapted from Cova 1996

large geographical areas. Tripod offered editorial content and discussions grouped into fields such as politics, health and money. The target audience was the 'twenty-somethings'. Individuals were encouraged to design and build their own web pages. In these locations, larger companies such as Ford, Visa, Sony and Microsoft took banner advertising space. This activity has now been largely superseded by blogs and areas such as MySpace. The demographics of the various communities play a large part in segmenting the advertising spend for larger companies as those in the target group are mainly aged 18–34, living in the USA and 75 per cent male.

Armstrong and Hagel (1996) discuss the merits of online communities and explain how the 'GardenWeb' area has evolved into a very successful community, where ideas are shared, plants are exchanged and links with related businesses and resources are forged. In this sense, such an online community is a powerful area for an advertiser to be in and offers much more than a simple site that only allows transactions.

These discussions show the way in which technology is creating virtual communities and determining the way in which consumers are reacting to marketing propositions. These developments make segmentation increasingly difficult and also mean that new ways of segmenting markets need to evolve constantly. Chapter 4 on sustainability, discusses how consumers are being segmented according to their concern for the environment. In order to understand this in the new millennium, Firat and Schultz (1997) argue that, in the future, work life, domestic life and life outside the home, spent in recreation and leisure, far from being delineated, will form each other and begin to merge. This will either create new configurations of life spheres or a life that cannot be differentiated into distinct spheres, but is completely fragmented into dispersed moments. They also argue that there will be a merger of the consumer and the producer. Production and consumption are likely to be insepera-ble. The consumer will also be the producer (see Figure 2.21).

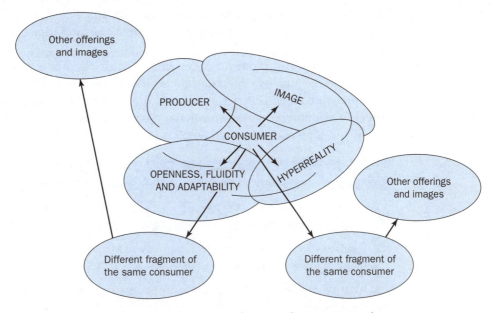

Figure 2.21 **The postmodern consumer and postmodern segmentation**

Marketers have to transform their focus from product to process. In other words, companies have to grasp the changing markets by embracing new technologies and creating both real and virtual images. They also have to move from product marketing to marketing a process and image. Processes can then be offered to customers to enable them to participate in the designing of the final product in order to customise it in line with the image they seek. This requires a fundamental shift in thinking and demands a great deal of flexibility from organisations.

Summary

This chapter has offered an insight into the complexity of the environmental analysis and considered its importance for the process of strategic segmentation and positioning. As new markets appear and develop, and the old markets permanently change, environmental scanning and analysis becomes an essential basis for the success of any company.

An environmental analysis should be well balanced between the internal and external environments of the organisation. Ultimately, the entire strategic marketing process can be considered to be a solution to the tensions that rise between the uncontrollable elements of the external market environment and the internal structure of an organisation. The first step towards positively solving these contradictions is knowing both the internal and external elements that determine, shape and limit the corporate way of doing business.

Environmental analysis on its own is not enough, however. A better understanding of the market context allows the firm to properly identify, define and segment its target market and choose the most profitable market segments. At the same time, the segmentation process should be accompanied by clear positioning in relation to other competing firms on the basis of the organisation's main competitive advantage.

The methods and procedures described in this chapter are not only practical tools for market analysis and strategic positioning but also represent a philosophical approach that considers the business organisation as only an element among others in a highly complex and dynamic environment, that has to be properly known and understood by both employees and decision makers.

Chapter questions

1 In your opinion, what is the long-term effect of environmental analysis on a company's performance? Provide supporting arguments and develop your answer.

2 What, in your opinion, is the relation between market orientation, market segmentation and strategic positioning?

3 What are the main advantages and challenges of an environmental analysis for a company?

3 Stakeholder concerns and solutions

Introduction

Organisational stakeholders are many and varied in nature. Stakeholders are any groups of individuals that are in some way either affected by a company's actions or can affect a company's actions. In many ways, understanding stakeholder interests and concerns and translating them into effective marketing strategies and company positioning within a marketplace is one of the great challenges facing organisations. It is no longer enough to take into account only products, segments and markets. Nowadays, it is necessary to consider not only customer–company interactions, but also company–shareholder, company–community, company–environment and a host of the other interactions. Consumers are becoming more knowledgeable and may want to consider not only the products on offer, but also a company's record on ethical issues and its image in the marketplace.

The following case study of an article describing M&S between 1998 and 1999 helps to illustrate how stakeholder relationships contribute to either the success or failure of marketing strategies.

CASE STUDY

Slow decline of high-street champion

Some people bought everything at Marks & Spencer and some would buy nothing, but everyone has their theory about the retailer. When the rise and fall of Marconi or Invensys is written, few will care, but for M&S – Marks to its former fans – it is like reading the obituary of a once-great statesman. Judi Bevan is thus unpicking a rich seam in detailing the hubris and nemesis of the nation's favourite clothes shop. Michael Marks' arrival in Britain from Russia in 1882 and his progress from hawking penny goods to creating the national chain by which Middle England swore – then swore against – lends itself perfectly to a former City journalist and novelist. In 1997, *The Times* pointed out that the empire's new clothes were no longer smart. Suddenly everyone joined the critical bandwagon

▶

and sales slipped – but the seeds of the decline had been sown years earlier.

M&S was a paternalistic employer with a customer base as loyal as its staff. Richard Greenbury had joined at 17, became chief executive in 1988 and chairman three years later. His retailing skills were legend: he would walk the shop floors asking what was selling and telling staff what to do. But by the 1990s, this physically big man preferred lecturing to listening and not only did sales staff no longer dare answer back, neither did directors. His own deputy, Keith Oates, started plotting a coup to take Greenbury's seat. As Bevan writes, just talking to the press was as alien as wearing an Asda shirt. But Oates was allowed to stay and lead a policy of expanding out of trouble, increasing overseas exposure and paying GBP192m for 19 Littlewoods stores that eventually cost GBP450m.

But in dashing for profits to cover its problems – even considering mergers with GUS and Safeway – Marks forgot its basic formula and a public that could once find nothing wrong with the shops could now find nothing right. Belatedly introducing fitting rooms and credit cards did not help. Greenbury's answer was to cut costs and ranges. The non-executives' wives complained that Marks no longer had the right garments in the right place – nor assistants to assist. Oates waited until his chairman was in India to make his bid for power, but Greenbury returned unexpectedly to confront him at the regular Monday meeting, forcing the non-execs to choose who ran M&S. Bevan is at her best detailing the failed compromise of firing Oates and giving Greenbury's executive duties to another long-server, Peter Salsbury. But the overbearing Greenbury, retaining his office and a GBP450,000 chairman's salary, thought he still ran Marks and fired intolerant Rickograms at his many critics. Salsbury turned on his former mentor, refusing to talk to Greenbury or even have his portrait in the boardroom with the other chairman. Bevan paints Salsbury as a weak man who sacked staff and suppliers without compassion, paying consultants GBP40m to devise one restructuring after another.

Greenbury quit rather than be insulted and Salsbury was replaced by outsider Luc Vandevelde, but sales and profits have continued the fall that began in 1998. Simon Marks, who built the chain before and after the war, had a philosophy of product, people and property. Having let the product and the people go, the company is now selling the property – and undoing its overseas expansion.

Bevan compares Greenbury with Thatcher – leaders who hung on too long, pushed out by loyal lieutenants. Both possessed towering egos. Both failed to nurture a worthy successor. Their increasingly irrational behaviour was tolerated by their acolytes, she writes. Oates did for his chairman what Heseltine did for his prime minister. Both were great leaders whose tragedy was that they failed entirely to appreciate the impact of their personalities on those around them. It is a case study that should be read by any organisation – from Coke to the BBC – with a market share so big it can only fall.

Source: Richard Northedge, 'Slow decline of high-street champion', *The Business* (previously *Sunday Business*), 30 September 2001

From the case study we can see that the marketing strategies at Marks & Spencer failed because:

- customer choices and preferences were ignored
- stakeholders, such as suppliers, were treated poorly
- the poor management of customers spilled over into poor staff management
- the original philosophy of product, people and property was not respected.

This resulted in poor assessments by shareholders and the stock market. Would Marks & Spencer have got into this state if it had managed its stakeholders better over a long period? Was the power base accorded to the managing director (a stakeholder) by the shareholders (another set of stakeholders) too great? Current news shows that the company has experienced a renaissance.

This second case study on Marks & Spencer illustrates the way in which attention to key stakeholders and astute marketing campaigns have revived the company. The key stakeholders that were brought back to the fold in increasing numbers were the different customer segments. Ladies and men's wear was priced reasonably and fashion trends have been observed. Food has become innovative and creative, with more customers enticed by the company's offers. At the same time, unlike Greenbury, Rose has given staff (one of the key stakeholder groups) a share of the profits. Another stakeholder group that has been helped is composed of the overseas food suppliers, which have benefited from Fairtrade policies.

CASE STUDY

M&S sales surge stuns City

Marks & Spencer today smashed City forecasts for sales and profits as its revitalised clothing ranges and high-quality foods brought in the shoppers. Overall sales from stores a year or more old surged 6.8% in the three months to 1 April – more than doubling analysts' expectations – as strong sales of clothing and food were boosted by product improvements and an advertising blitz. General merchandise, which includes fashion and homewares, saw sales jump a huge 8.2%, while food sales surged 5.6%. The figures were for the final quarter of the financial year and M&S said they meant full-year profits would come in at between £745 million and £755m – about £10m or £15m better than City forecasts. *That comes despite today's decision to pay an extra £20m one-off bonus to shop-floor staff on top of the £50m staff incentives already agreed.* Chief executive Stuart Rose said: 'Ladies wear really led the charge, with better product, better styling and better values.' *Big-selling womenswear lines included linen outfits, pencil skirts and casual knitwear. Men's suits were also big sellers but Rose was hoping for a big push on sales of summer casuals.*

Food sales were also strong, as M&S focused on promoting its high-quality image with the *'This is no ordinary...' campaign and a marketing push around Fairtrade products.* Despite the strong figures, Rose continued to downplay the extent of M&S's resurgence. In the successive improvement in sales figures in the past year, he has refused to claim that M&S has recovered. Today he stressed that the comparative periods from the year before were still fairly weak, making sales improvements easier to achieve. Comparatives do not start getting tough until July. However, he added: 'It is clear we are pinching market share from competitors, which is great. It shows we're back in the game.'

M&S' figures looked especially strong when compared with rival retailers, who have all suffered from the tough economic environment and the cold spring weather. Next's sales are down more than 8% in recent weeks, while others on the High Street have all been suffering. M&S sales figures are also flattened by the fact that Easter weekend fell in the same weeks last year. Had Easter been in the fourth quarter, sales would have been up by a further 0.8%, M&S said. Meanwhile, it emerged today that Rose is sitting on a potential £5m paper profit from his shares and options in the business.

But few investors will begrudge him the wealth after his performance in improving ranges and turning the screw on M&S suppliers. M&S shares were expected to jump by 19p to 580p today, according to City bookmaker Cantor Index

Source: Jim Armitage, 'M&S sales sales surge stuns City', *Evening Standard*, 11 April 2006

Stakeholder theory

Stakeholder theory has many facets to it. Some theorists take a corporate governance view (Bailey and Clancey 1997), while others take a socio-economic perspective (Hutton 1996). A more operational view argues that stakeholding issues should be considered at company level, where people work, rather than just at national level or welfare policy level (MacDougall 1995). A simple view of stakeholding would be that of just considering the key actors that affect a company's well-being. A more complex view would consider the interaction between a company and various players. This type of view considers stakeholding from the point of view of dynamic interrelationships. Availability of resource, power and environmental turbulence can mediate these interrelationships.

Stakeholder interactions

In order to begin to understand the multiple relationships that interact in a complex manner, affecting both a company and its various stakeholders, it is perhaps important to go back to Freeman's (1984) seminal work in this area and consider the definition of a stakeholder:

> *any group or individual who can affect or is affected by the achievement of the organisation's objectives.*

The Organisation for Economic Cooperation and Development (OECD) starts from the perspective of corporate governance and mentions that it is a key element in improving economic efficiency as it involves a set of relationships between a company's management, its board, shareholders and other stakeholders.
The OECD goes on to say:

> *Corporate governance also provides the structure through which the objectives of the company are set, and the means of attaining those objectives and monitoring performance are determined. Good corporate governance should provide proper incentives for the board and management to pursue objectives that are in the interests of the company and shareholders and should facilitate effective monitoring, thereby encouraging firms to use resources more efficiently.*

Obviously these corporate governance issues cannot be separated from the greater macroeconomic issues within and outside national boundaries. These issues affect the nature of markets and the levels of competition within them. Legislation and regulation (usually governmental) also affect them. Business ethics and the social and economic interests of the communities directly affected by its actions have a considerable impact on the well-being of a company.

In order to make sense of the various interactions of stakeholders, it is useful to consider the various constituencies and their influences on the company. The relative inputs and outputs of various stakeholders determine the level and power of the interactions taking place (Donaldson and Preston 1995). This, in turn, allows us to understand the relative impacts of the strategies of a company on other stakeholders. Figure 3.1 shows the key constituents at play.

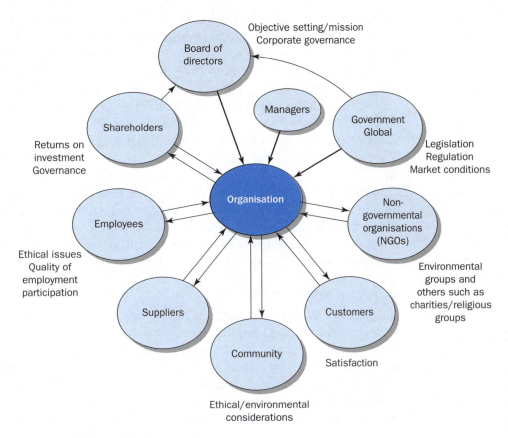

Figure 3.1 **Stakeholder components**

Board of directors

One could argue that this is the single most influential set of stakeholders in an organisation. The members of the board of directors of a company are both internal and external stakeholders. They generally determine the strategic direction that an organisation will take and how it will impact various other stakeholders. According to the OECD framework, board members need to act on a fully informed basis, with due care and diligence, in the best interests of the company and the shareholders. It also states that the board should ensure compliance with applicable law and take into account the interests of stakeholders. Some of the key functions of the board should be to:

> *Review and guide corporate strategy, major plans of action, risk policy, annual budgets and business plans; setting performance objectives; monitoring implementation and corporate performance; and overseeing major capital expenditures, acquisitions and divestitures.*

The board is also responsible for the hiring of key executives and setting their remuneration levels. Undoubtedly, this gives the board a great deal of vested power. However, board members themselves could wield disparate levels of power. There are also arguments that the chief executive officer (CEO) may carry a disproportionate level of power compared to other board members (Pettigrew and McNulty 1995), though the level of power may be contextual, reflecting particular circumstances. In one survey (Stiles 2001), it was found that strategy is typically developed at the business unit level (by managers) (Bower 1970; Burgelman 1983, 1991). The board, therefore, is largely responsible for setting the strategic parameters within which the strategic activity can take place. It is ultimately responsible for the vision and mission of the organisation, as well as its strategic focus and acts as a gatekeeper and confidence-builder. Interestingly, given the primacy of the board, Stiles' research, conducted in the UK, showed that a large proportion of the directors interviewed felt that their main roles were developing strategies and assuming responsibility for monitoring the health of the firm. Only a few responses covered dialogue with shareholders/stakeholders, responsibility for an ethical framework or a review of social responsibilities. Within a company, a board is a powerful stakeholder. At the same time, this power is tempered by its interaction with managers and the CEO.

The roles of board members

The previous case study on Marks & Spencer helped to illustrate the interaction that occurs between the CEO and managers. What is not clear is how much of a role the board played in this instance in tempering the CEO's management of the various stakeholders. To a large extent, the way in which a company is managed depends on corporate governance and the way this governance impacts stakeholders.

There are three main models for the roles of the board of directors (see Figure 3.2 and Table 3.1).

■ *The control role* The board of directors is considered as a mechanism for preventing deviant behaviour on the part of the main managerial team (Fama and Jensen 1983; Williamson 1984). This role is especially evident when financing institutions impose a person on the boards of directors in the firms in which they invest, his or her task being to monitor its evolution and assess its capacity to repay debts and/or provide a return on investments by the established deadline (Kelly 1997; Wright and Robbie 1997).

Figure 3.2 The roles of boards of directors in managing SMEs
Source: Watkins 1997

Table 3.1 Key board roles *versus* director characteristics under three models of boards' functions

Directors' characteristics	Key theoretical role		
	Control role	*Internal service role*	*External resource building role*
Dominant theoretical paradigms/relevant literatures	Agency theory; institutional theory; general governance literature	Partly within resource dependency theory, but underdeveloped; networking literature	Resource dependency theory; stakeholder theory; networking literature
Numbers of directors	Small – members cannot be played off against one another	Moderate – range of views but limited scope for internal conflict	Large – within limits, bigger equals better. Diseconomies set in with costs/complexity of coordinating large board
Executive responsibilities	Tacit or explicit knowledge regarding control issues; may be 'captured' by management	Indistinguishable from managerial role	Role may be broader than managerial role; board's status empowers this
Investor status	Classical position; absence of agency issues	Probably neutral in impact; may enhance care exercised (trend to conservatism?), but director anyway has duty of care	May be essence of involvement; can be a constraint of future financing rounds
Representative responsibilities, such as nominee of particular stakeholder interest	Focus on control issues of specific interest to stakeholder, such as shareholder value; employee welfare; cover for debt repayments, etc.	Suboptimal. Objectivity compromised by uni-dimensional interests of nominating stakeholder	May be best way of cementing/maximising benefit from stakeholder relationships; alliance creation, etc. Likely to be of greater significance as size of firm increases
Business expertise in common with CEO	Familiarity with 'custom and practice'; knows where skeletons can be buried	Missed opportunity to extend range of operational expertise available to the firm	As for service role, unless recognised industry leader
Prior personal relationship with CEO	Counterproductive; risk of 'capture' high	Personal knowledge may enhance credibility of advice	Unlikely to be strong in most effective appointments; therefore issues of trust; pre-validation through existing trust networks
Technical expertise in common with CEO	Audit/control function may extend to technical sphere	Commonality of language useful, but scope for NIH conflicts	May represent missed strategic opportunity to extend range of expertise and contacts available to the firm
Term of service	Continuity benefit in conflict with danger of 'capture'	Value may *increase* in short/medium term as knowledge of firm expands	Value may *decrease* in medium to long term as personal networks become those of the firm
Surrogate for director in role	Auditors, even if not legally required. Audit can extend beyond financial. Usually private sector	Public-sector small business advisory networks; counsellors; public- or private-sector consultants and trainers	Underdeveloped on a formal basis, particularly in public sector. Usually ad hoc rather than strategic. Scope for considerable expansion

Source: Watkins 1997

- *The internal service role* The function of the board that is most emphasised, which is to provide advice and counsel to the main managerial team of the firm. In this case, the competences of the directors complement or amplify the competences of the managerial team (O'Neal and Thomas 1996).
- *The external resource-building role* In this case, the board of directors is considered to be a vital instrument for obtaining access to external resources that are critical to the firm's success (Pfeffer 1972; Pfeffer and Salancik 1978). This is probably the most important role played by boards for companies that need to access and attract external resources for their survival and/or development. This is because it facilitates access to funds, the creation of strategic alliances and attracts complementary resources (O'Neal and Thomas 1995 and 1996; Zajac 1988).

The international dimension of todays' markets increases the complexity of directors' function. For many companies, for example, the penetration of international markets is an essential prerequisite for their survival and, therefore, the directors need to expand their role in overseas markets and operations.

Government and global pressures on corporate governance

Corporate governance has increasingly become a governmental and global issue. This is due to the increasing globalisation of capital flows and shareholding. The UK, USA and Australia are characterised by the Anglo-Saxon model of share ownership. Often, large institutional investors, such as pension funds or unit trust funds, hold the shares in companies. These, then, are the largest sets of stakeholders in many organisations. As a result, there is continued pressure to achieve the best performance possible and individuals hold fewer shares than the institutions.

Fundamental differences in the shareholding structure in European countries are the key to explaining the variations in the importance of their stock markets (Lannoo 1995). Table 3.2 shows that the largest shareowners of quoted companies in the UK are institutional investors (pension funds, insurance companies, banks

Table 3.2 **The structure of shareholding in selected countries (% of total)**

(As at end of year)	Germany 1990	France 1992	Italy 1993	UK 1993	USA 1992	Japan 1992
Financial institutions, of which:	22.0	23.0	11.3	59.3	31.2	48.0
banks	10	–	9.9	0.6	0.3	26.7
pension funds/insurers	12.0	–	0.8	51.5	23.9	17.2
others (unit trusts)	–	–	0.6	7.2	7.0	4.1
Households	17.0	34.0	33.9	19.3	48.1	22.1
Private companies	42.0	21.0	23.0	4.0	14.1	24.8
Public authorities	5.0	2.0	27.0	1.3	–	0.7
Foreign investors	14.0	20.0	4.8	16.3	6.6	3.9

Note: The comparability of data is affected by differences in definition used by the providers of the data and differences in regulatory structures when comparing data. For example, a bank is a universal bank in Germany and a high street bank in the UK.

Source: Lannoo 1995

and unit trusts). These possess an average equity of 59 per cent. Households are the second largest group in the UK, with 19 per cent, and industry (including unit trusts) owns 4 per cent. In Germany, on the other hand, the situation is reversed: industry is the largest owner of quoted companies at 42 per cent, institutional investors possess a much smaller part, only 22 per cent (of which banks hold 10 per cent), and households possess 17 per cent. Unlike the UK and Germany, households or families are the most important stockholders in France, Italy and the USA. In Italy, the government is a major stockholder, with 27 per cent ownership.

Protection for stakeholders

Traditional structures in Europe are designed to protect the stakeholders from hostile takeovers. The firm, as a coalition of both internal and external stakeholders, needs to have control over its environment in order to protect them (Groenewegen 2000). The protection is often country-specific. For instance, in the Netherlands, the legal aspects of the corporate structure are organised in a manner that creates a control mechanism over shareholders. The structure tends to favour other stakeholders, especially the employees. In Germany, close ties between banks and industry provide stability and protection against takeovers. In France, control is in the hands of the président directeur général (PDG). He or she is often elected by a board (conseil d'administration), which is appointed by the shareholders. Often, the PDG is the only one who represents the firm externally and so can be isolated from the other stakeholders in the firm. The PDG usually has good connections at his or her level in the government and industrial sectors. Shares are often sold to friendly banks and industrial firms, reflecting cross-stockholding. This creates the core shareholders (noyau dur). Sometimes shareholders in companies in France and the Netherlands enjoy multiple voting rights.

As can be seen, the different structures in different countries are complex and therefore any company analysis of stakeholders has to take the corporate governance, board structures and shareholding structures into account. Often these are country-specific rather than universal. However, the growth of globalisation is changing the nature of stakeholders, largely as a result of increased shareholder activism. The key developments are:

- the growing role of institutional investors as more companies are privatised in Europe and around the world
- the integration of financial markets and the global movement of capital
- increased shareholder activism.

Stakeholders and corporate social responsibility

Following on from the discussion above, it is clear that corporate governance is becoming the defining business issue of the twenty-first century as many companies, such as Enron, have fallen foul of their normal obligations to shareholders and society in general. Given new federal legislation and new rules from the Securities and Exchange Commission (SEC) and its financial arm, the Financial Accounting Standards Board, governments in the UK and USA are determined to legislate for some of the recommendations for a new code of governance in the Higgs Report to become a set of regulations during the next Parliament so as to force companies on both sides of the Atlantic to reassess their positions.

In Germany, the new German Corporate Governance Kodex applies to stock corporations that are listed on the German stock exchange and is expected to set standards for corporate conduct that will be applied by German courts in the future.

Notwithstanding the new legislative atmosphere, a growing number of companies have themselves recognised the business benefits of well-defined corporate social responsibilites, policies and practices. This recognition is supported by a body of empirical studies, which demonstrates that developing corporate social responsibility strategies has a positive impact on business' economic performance, enhancing shareholder value. This, in turn, can be translated into a marketing tool to benefit the future performance of the company.

Corporate social responsibility and the law

In 1970, Milton Friedman wrote that the social responsibility of business is to increase its profits. He went on to say that the most appropriate social goal for a corporate executive is 'to make as much money as possible while conforming to the basic rules of society, both those embodied in law and those embodied in ethical custom.' Further, that seeking any goal other than making money, subject to law and ethical custom, was illegitimate.

However, the law is made by the legislature in response to public and political concerns. Policy goals evolve from public dialogue (Posner 1995). Once a consensus has been achieved, legislation is drafted to achieve those policy goals. The law incorporates democratically determined values, which have been discovered as a result of creative reflection, empirical enquiry and open dialogue with stakeholders (Posner 1995). Some values may be procedural in nature, indicating that notice is given to affected parties and an opportunity to be heard. Other values may be utilitarian in nature, determining the weighing of effects to all involved parties. Such values are context-dependent and subject to re-evaluation, but still provide a value-based (as distinct from a power-based) reference to corporate social responsibility.

The new regulatory atmosphere

The USA

A new era of corporate governance and oversight began the moment President Bush signed the Sarbanes-Oxley Act in 2002, with chief executive officers (CEOs) and chief financial officers (CFOs) becoming personally responsible for their companies' disclosures. Many of the provisions of the Act became effective immediately and the new rulemaking initiatives were combined to lay the foundations for a developing new corporate order of required internal procedures, checks, oversight and standards, as well as expanded external liability when companies are not complying.

The corporate board structure is now a combination of both federal and state law, in which CEOs and CFOs are exposed to significantly increased personal liability, including long prison sentences for intentional non-compliance.

The Sarbanes-Oxley Act has been called the most significant securities legislation in more than a generation. One of the stated objectives of this change is to provide markets with more timely and transparent information, in addition to increased protection for shareholders. The first series of new rules became effective on 5 September 2002 and many senior executives recognised this as an opportunity to raise shareholder confidence by filing their statements early.

The effects of the Sarbanes-Oxley Act (SOX) beyond the USA

The directors of the former Worldcom organisation are to face criminal charges for their alleged role in providing false information to investors. Although directors of any overseas company listed in the USA are already exposed to this area of potential liability, including, indirectly, directors of overseas subsidiaries of American companies, the new Act extends to include these companies and, more particularly, to individual directors, to impose criminal liability and financial penalties on those in breach of the new regime.

Directors are required to certify, personally, the accuracy of the financial statements of the company in addition to certifying that the company has established and maintained internal financial and disclosure controls that they have evaluated within 90 days of giving that certification. Failure to give a true certification is a criminal offence under the USA's law. Fleeing the USA's jurisdiction will not protect the director of a foreign company as the long arm of the Sarbanes-Oxley Act provides for extradition proceedings, if certain criteria are fulfilled.

The Act also extends the restrictions under UK law on company loans to directors or senior executive officers, with no exception for loans of low value. Officers and directors could also face penalties for financial misstatements, including forfeiture of bonuses or other rewards. In addition, the USA's Stock Exchange Commission has new powers to require a company to disclose its code of ethics for its senior financial officers (Ranchhod and Park 2004).

Many of the USA's regulations differ from and, in some respects, conflict with the UK's corporate governance and audit codes, but directors need to be aware of these differences as it may soon be a requirement for them to explain how the UK's rules differ from those in the USA. Directors of UK-based subsidiaries of US corporations need to introduce more rigorous internal procedures and sign internal audit certificates in order to assist their main board in the USA in complying with their new obligations. This may have an effect on plans for listings on the stock exchange in New York. For example, Porsche abandoned such plans three years ago on the grounds that the liability imposed on individual directors was incompatible with the German concept of collective responsibility of the board.

The UK's proposals

The 'Review of the role and effectiveness of non-executive directors' (the Higgs Report), published in the UK in January 2003, produced proposals in relation to the roles and responsibilities of non-executive directors (NEDs) in public limited companies. The proposals give a much higher profile to NEDs, giving them greater powers and authority with regard to corporate governance, but also greater personal liability. To ensure that greater care is taken of corporate governance matters, it is advised that generally, the senior independent director and NEDs meet regularly with both management and major shareholders.

The general approach proposed by the Higgs Report is 'comply or explain'. In order to do this, a company's annual report must outline the approach taken by the company to the various guidelines set out in the code.

In the same month, a Financial Reporting Council group chaired by Sir Robert Smith produced the 'Combined code guidance for audit committees'. They referred to the Higgs Report and aimed to produce an integrated approach to corporate governance within the UK, but also highlighted where the UK system may differ from those of other jurisdictions.

The European approach

There is growing evidence of a new approach to company law harmonisation in the European Union in the wake of the Enron and Worldcom scandals in the USA. In September 2001, the European Commission established the High Level Group of Company Law Experts 'to define new priorities for the broader future development of company law in the EU'. The committee's mandate was extended further after the Enron scandal, to cover corporate governance and auditing issues, such as the role of NEDs.

The final report – 'A modern regulatory framework for company law in Europe' – is known as the Winter Report after the group's chairman, Jaap Winter, and was published in November 2002. The corporate governance issues it identifies begin with disclosure, which is described as having 'a pivotal role in company law'. Central to the report's recommendations on corporate governance is the belief that listed companies should be required to include a corporate governance statement in their annual report and accounts. This must be a coherent and descriptive statement of the governance rules that are being applied, but the key input for corporate governance codes should continue to come from the markets and their participants.

Despite its general reliance on disclosure in place of direct regulation, in some areas the Winter Report seeks to increase the number of sanctions available against directors and accordingly proposes that all board members should be made legally responsible for the 'probity' of financial statements, a Europe-wide rule imposing liability on directors for wrongful trading should be introduced and a Europe-wide director's disqualification regime should be considered.

While the proposal to increase the responsibility of board members for statements represents a potential increase in liability, the governance recommendations might present potential opportunities. As a response to the Enron and Worldcom scandals, the Winter Report is generally considered to be mature and responsible.

The roles of shareholders

Shareholder activism is encouraged in the UK and USA. As key stakeholders, shareholders are urged to exercise their voting rights. Shareholders can join forces to strengthen their position against company management. As companies are privatised, more shareholders in the USA with overseas shareholdings are demanding a greater say in the governance of companies in Europe. The advent of the euro and the Single Market is expected to hasten the move towards a more Anglo-Saxon model of open shareholding and transparency of disclosure.

In reality, there are strong national interests at play. The tussle is between globalisation and national interests. In this sense, the government and key shareholders should be seen as major stakeholders wielding a great deal of power. Many of the systems in Europe favour a slow, stable form of organisation rather than the rapidly changing, market-led, entrepreneurial systems that exist in the UK and USA. In any study of organisations, this area of stakeholding should be considered carefully.

Read the following case study and consider which key stakeholders are important in different countries. How can marketing be affected by poor stakeholder management?

CASE STUDY

Image in the balance

The past year has seen a serious run on business reputations. Uncertainties after September 11, corporate scandals such as the collapse of Enron and the decline in economies across the world have all had an impact on the image of business and of CEOs. In spite of this, a survey in Europe and North America shows that chief executives still believe their own reputation is vitally important to their company's image. Hill and Knowlton's Corporate Reputation Watch 2002, conducted by Harris Interactive, examined the views of more than 800 CEOs and senior managers in nine countries. Eighty per cent of US business leaders see their reputation as a significant influence, compared with 56 per cent in the UK and 50 per cent in Europe as a whole. Of course, it is not just about the boss. Nine out of 10 CEOs said the customer's opinion was the most important factor in shaping reputation. Employees' attitudes were rated as the second most important determinant.

For business leaders, reputation is not an abstract concern. The survey showed there is a growing tendency for CEOs to be at least partly remunerated according to their ability to affect corporate reputation, ranging from 13 per cent of CEOs in Germany to 44 per cent of those in Italy; in the UK and the US, the figures were 26 per cent and 29 per cent respectively. Where CEOs do receive cash for corporate kudos, the proportion of compensation can be significant. In the UK and Germany it was more than 40 per cent and in the US just over a third.

Furthermore, reputation management increasingly has a place at the boardroom table. The UK and Belgium led the pack on this, with 62 per cent and 69 per cent respectively reporting that the board was involved in monitoring corporate reputation. In the US the figure was just over a third. But here is the challenge. Reputation, rather like beauty, is something that largely exists in the eye of the beholder. For corporations, that beholder is the myriad stakeholders whose perceptions combine across interests and geographies to create a corporate reputation. So while companies may be remunerating chief executives on the basis of their ability to affect reputation, how are they measuring something that exists in a million different minds?

Well, measuring it they are. According to the survey, more than 75 per cent of international companies have corporate reputation measurement systems in place. For those based in the UK and the US, the figure is at 80 per cent or above. These systems are a mix of formal and informal metrics, although a significant number of companies measure only on the basis of informal systems such as word of mouth. And here is a potential problem: word of mouth is one of the most powerful marketing and communications tools but to measure reputation purely by what the corporate ear picks up suggests that reputation management may not, after all, be receiving the attention it deserves.

There is no denying that word of mouth has an important place in the measurement of corporate reputation. But it alone cannot provide the balanced view that international companies in particular need. Sensibly, most companies go beyond word of mouth, opting for formal research such as financial performance, media coverage, industry rankings, analyst commentary and even price/earnings ratio (the higher the p/e, the more positive the market). But across different markets, different measurement techniques enjoy different priorities. Formal customised research is undertaken by 50 per cent of international companies and is, on average, the second most popular technique. In Italy and the Netherlands it tops the bill.

In Germany and the UK financial performance ranks as the second most important measurement. German companies are more likely than others to use media coverage and published rankings to measure corporate reputation. With the exception of those in Belgium, international CEOs are more likely than those in the US to use p/e ratios to measure corporate reputation. Despite the plethora of measurement techniques, the survey reveals some gaps. CEOs in all countries appear to pay more attention to influences on reputation with which they have most personal contact, such as customers, employees and print media. They are less concerned by those with which they have less personal contact, such as the Internet and campaign groups. Nevertheless, there is grave danger for them in underestimating the power of such groups. The survey shows the continuing ways in which CEOs are attempting to manage their reputation. What the data cannot reveal is how long it will take for those techniques to reverse the damage done by corporate scandals.

Source: Andrew Pharoah, 'Inside track: image in the balance', *Financial Times*, 16 September 2002

(The writer is the Managing Director, Public and Corporate Affairs, at Hill and Knowlton.)

Non-governmental organisations (NGOs)

For most profit-orientated organisations, non-governmental organisations or NGOs are a real force to be reckoned with and represent key stakeholders who often determine the success or failure of particular marketing strategies. Examples of this are the pressures put on business organisations by groups such as Greenpeace, Friends of the Earth and charities such as Oxfam or Christian Aid. Such organisations play a key role in pushing the agenda of social responsibility firmly into the courts of the companies involved in profit-seeking activities, in any corner of the world. For instance, recently, Monsanto's very public foray into publicising genetically modified (GM) foods, and even setting up an expensive website for this purpose, ended in a public relations disaster. The [company's] demise was hastened by very public denunciations of their activities by groups such as Friends of the Earth and also by their graphical portrayals on their website. The Friends of the Earth developed a web page featuring a ripe tomato with a blue eye, which rotates, and a leaf tail, which wiggles. This grotesque, Frankenstein image captures the notion of the introduction of a fish gene into the vegetable. Another powerful and emotive argument that is also used by opponents of GMOs is that modified genes introduced into particular foods, such as oil seed rape, could 'migrate' to other species of wild plants. They argue that, in the case of a mistake, the danger will be spread to all flora and fauna. Paul Moroney, Hampshire spokesman for Friends of the Earth environmental organisation, said, 'Genetic pollution is irretrievable and, unlike an oil spill, cannot be cleaned up' (Simpson 1998).

The pressure applied by the NGOs can turn around company policies. For example, see the following case study from a Greenpeace article.

CASE STUDY

Novartis buckles as Greenpeace reveals GE soya in its baby products

Dear Mr Heinzer,

With respect to today's demonstration at the St Johann, Basel, headquarters of Novartis AG, we understand that representatives of Greenpeace allege that our affiliate Gerber is selling in the Philippines products intended for consumption by infants which contain genetically modified ingredients.

We will investigate these serious allegations without delay and, once we have a full understanding of all the facts, we will take appropriate actions.

Very truly yours Felix Raebe Head media relations Novartis International

Basel, Switzerland, 21 August 2001

Gerber/ Novartis will investigate its products sold in the Philippines after Greenpeace revealed scientific evidence showing that the company's baby food products contained massive amounts of GE soya, despite its promise a year ago to stop using GE ingredients worldwide.

The company's decision follows a Greenpeace action earlier today in front of the Novartis headquarters in Switzerland where activists blocked the main entrance of the building with hundreds of baby puppets. The puppets were holding protest signs saying, 'Novartis/Gerber, keep your promise!' and 'Novartis/Gerber, stop genetically modified baby food!'

Earlier, Greenpeace sent three products to the internationally certified Hong Kong laboratory, DNA Chips, where very high levels of GE contamination was found. In the products Green Monggo's, 66.7 per cent, Cream of Brown Rice, 52.2 per cent and Mixed Fruit, 34.3 per cent of the soya was found to be genetically engineered.

These levels of contamination demonstrate Novartis' deliberate intention to use GMOs in its Gerber baby food products, which are manufactured in Indonesia, in the Philippines.

'Are Novartis' promises only valid in rich countries and not in poor ones such as the Philippines?' asked Greenpeace Southeast Asia campaigner in the Philippines Beau Baconguis while presenting the test results at a press conference in Manila (Philippines) this morning. The Philippine Congress filed a bill on 15 August 2001 requiring the labelling of GMO-derived food and food products under which the penalty for failing to label would be 6 to 12 years in jail.

Food products in Europe are mostly GE free but unlabelled GE food is sold to consumers in other parts of the world. 'We demand an immediate stop to Novartis' double standards policy,' said Bruno Heinzer of Greenpeace Switzerland in front of the Novartis building.

On 11 June 1999, Novartis' Consumer Health head Martin Stefani wrote in a letter to Greenpeace 'Our consumers can be sure that our baby food does not contain any GMOs or parts derived thereof.' This was reiterated by Novartis US spokesperson Al Piergallini, who was quoted in the *Wall Street Journal Europe* of 30 July 1999 saying: 'I want our mothers to be comfortable'.

In a letter to Greenpeace dated 2 August 2000, Novartis declared it would not use any more GMOs in its food products worldwide.

Greenpeace is now urging Novartis to respect its own pledges not only in rich nations but in all countries.

▶

Case study *continued*

Scientific understanding of the impacts of genetic engineering on the environment and human health is extremely limited. Greenpeace believes that citizens and consumers worldwide have the right to know how their food is produced and to refuse to eat genetically engineered food.

Source: http://archive.greenpeace.org/geneng/highlights/food/Aug21–2001.htm

In other instances, organisations such as the World Wildlife Fund (see below) exert pressure on companies to improve their products so that the worlds' energy resources are not wasted. These and other examples illustrate the way in which NGOs need to be considered as serious stakeholders when developing and executing company's marketing strategies, as adverse publicity will not only harm the company' image but also deter future streams of money coming from concerned consumers. The results of these activities impinge on the whole range of stakeholders – from suppliers and the community to actual consumers. Consumers want eco-friendly and low-energy-use equipment, the surrounding community wants lower levels of pollution and suppliers having to manufacture the requisite components to meet these demands make their own demands in return.

The following case study considers the impact of company strategies on a range of stakeholders. Identify the key stakeholders affected and the level and power of the interactions.

CASE STUDY

Keep cool, keep clean – a deal to save the climate

Most of us try to do what we can to fight global climate change, but a deal between WWF and AEG, the German appliance manufacturer, aims to show how companies can use energy-saving technology to work towards the goals of cleaner power and efficient energy use.

Innovative and environmentally friendly products are now part of our daily lives. We use fuel-efficient cars, better housing insulation, energy-saving lightbulbs and domestic appliances. This is all helping to achieve the targets for cleaner power production and more efficient use of energy proposed by the conservation organisation WWF.

Germany has ambitious goals in the fight against climate change. It aims to reduce carbon dioxide, the main global warming gas, by 25 per cent by 2005. At the same time, however, it wants to phase out carbon-free nuclear power production, which accounts for a third of domestic electricity. So if a dramatic increase in carbon dioxide emissions caused by new coal-fired power stations is to be avoided, an improvement in energy efficiency is needed. That is why WWF-Germany has been working with selected companies to commit themselves to less and greener power consumption.

'It was clear that if we wanted to have an effect on power consumption, it was not enough just to target the consumer,' says Dr Stephan Singer, Head of the Energy and Climate Department at WWF-Germany. 'It was vital to get the manufacturers on board.'

In 1997 WWF struck a deal known as Consensus 25 with AEG, the German maker of domestic appliances, which has an overall market share of 10 per cent and is already well known for its green policies, its transparency and its openness. Publicly support-

▶

ive of WWF's climate and energy policy objectives, AEG was also in favour of an ecology tax. So it was no surprise that, unlike more conservative companies, AEG committed itself to reducing the energy consumption of five of its leading products between 1995 and 1999. Its commitment has been recognised by making Consensus 25 a Gift to the Earth in WWF's Living Planet Campaign.

'It was calculated that if these appliances sold as preceding models had, the energy equivalent of the annual electricity consumption of a small city in Germany of up to 10,000 inhabitants would be saved', said Dr Singer.

Two years later most of AEG's new 'green line' appliances have proved to be both energy efficient and successful, saving 20–50 per cent of the usual consumption of electricity. The limits of energy efficiency for some products, however, were demonstrated by cookers, which, while saving electricity, took ten hours to bake a cake. This suggests that the logical next step is to increase the availability of renewable energy sources, which is why improving the supply side of energy is the second target of the WWF campaign.

Meanwhile, AEG has committed itself to an even more ambitious target after negotiation with WWF. Within the next four years the company has undertaken to sell only fridges and freezers classified 'A' under the compulsory European Union labelling scheme. This means that products are classified from 'A' to 'G' based on their power consumption, with 'A' products consuming at least 45 per cent less electricity than average.

'The AEG agreement is a very good indication of what the domestic appliance industry can do if it has a mind to,' says Dr Singer. 'It also supports moves towards an EU-wide ban on inefficient appliances and will set strong energy efficiency standards.'

AEG is now marketing efficient, environmentally sound cooling appliances. Currently neither ozone-depleting substances nor fluorinated super warming gases (HFCs) are used for cooling or insulation in the EU. About half of AEG products are already labelled 'A', and some of these consume 70–80 per cent less energy than average.

It is estimated that if all new new technology is category 'A' from 2003 onwards, the annual saving will be in the region of 16 million kilowatt hours of electricity. Careful calculation of Germany's energy consumption reveals that if all German producers marketed only the 'A' models, one coal-fired power station of a capacity of at least 50 megawatts, the amount of energy consumed by at least 100,000 people, could be closed.

'If other appliances, such as dishwashers, washing machines, televisions, computers, videos and so on made similar technological improvements, the international debate on shutting down nuclear power plants and complying with climate targets would be much easier,' said Dr Singer. 'WWF is very excited by the possibilities that this kind of deal offers, and we hope it will show the way for other companies.'

Source: Kyla Evans, www.panda.org/news_facts WWF International, Gland, Switzerland

Customers

Customers are the lifeblood of any organisation. Organisations not only have to be receptive to their needs and wants but also understand them (see Chapter 1). Customers as stakeholders are in a powerful position to either accept or reject a company's offering. It could be argued that companies spend vast amounts of money on this stakeholder group in order to cajole and coerce them to purchase their goods. Generally, this takes place through branding strategies. Customers are often attracted to companies with a good brand image, that can offer long-lasting and good-quality products. Increasingly, customers are also loosely connected to NGOs and, in many ways, can direct company strategy towards developing environmentally sound processes and products.

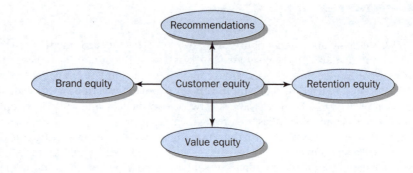

Figure 3.3 **Factors driving customer equity**

Source: Adapted from Rust et al. 2000

Classical marketing theory regards customers as supreme entities, whose needs should be profitably satisfied by a company. For many years, companies have tried to follow this philosophy. However, many companies realise now that customers could be their best marketing ambassadors, as long as they are loyal to their products and values. Increasingly, therefore, companies think in terms of relationship marketing, attempting to create a lifetime association with customers. As a philosophy for the future, it could be argued that customers should not only be satisfied but also retained (Rust et al. 2000). Firms should maximise customer equity by addressing its three key drivers.

- *Value* This covers aspects of a customer's objective assessment of the utility of a brand, based on perceptions of the value of the exchange process (money for goods/services).
- *Brand* This is the customer's subjective and intangible assessment of the brand above and beyond its objectively perceived value (see Chapter 5).
- *Retention* This is a measure of the tendency of a customer to stick with the brand above and beyond his or her objective and subjective assessments of the brand.

In addition to this, a much neglected facet of a company's operations is that of developing satisfied customers who recommend their brands to other potential clients. This helps customers to decide what and how to purchase, but also enhances the image of a brand, driving up customer equity.

In the twenty-first century, the marketing focus is increasingly moving away from brand management and transactions between companies and customers and towards actually understanding their interrelationships. A company's value lies in the lifetime value of its customers rather than just its brands.

The following case study reflects the importance of customers as stakeholders in an organisation. Increasingly important to these stakeholders is the growth of the Internet and a situation where information and product exchange processes can be undertaken in a virtual setting. Customers are also able to post their feelings about companies and their products in discussion areas, thereby either enhancing or degrading a company's image. The case study illustrates how globalisation and the free flow of information means that large multinationals following country-specific policies that may discriminate against differing groups do so at their peril.

Customers as stakeholders of Nestlé

Chinese consumer, Eileen Zhu Yanling, is suing Nestlé for not labelling Nesquik to indicate inclusion of GE ingredients in China under consumer rights law.

What motivated a mother from Shanghai to travel halfway around the world to global food giant Nestlé's HQ in Switzerland? In March 2003 Eileen Zhu Yanling was shocked to discover from the Internet that Nestlé's Nesquik milk powder, a product she had been buying regularly for her three-year-old son, contained GE ingredients without this being indicated on the label.

Zhu's shock turned to anger as the thought of unknowingly feeding her son GE food preyed on her mind and she decided to sue the company for violation of her consumer rights. Zhu wrote to Nestlé's headquarters in September last year about inconsistencies in their labelling policy but was not satisfied with their reply.

Zhu's anger was compounded by her previous trust in Nestlé's products. Nestlé was one of the first foreign food companies to become established in China and Zhu grew up with Nestlé products. She had also studied in Switzerland and was even taken on a tour of Nestlé's Vevey headquarters by a friend. Zhu is aware of the strict GE labelling regulations in Europe and feels very strongly that large global companies like Nestlé, irrespective of national variances in these regulations, should give the same information about ingredients to consumers whether they're in Europe or China.

'I am angry because Nestlé has not been truthful. This is disrespectful to Chinese consumers. I believe Chinese consumers have the right to know and to choose what they are buying for their families', said Zhu in a letter she delivered personally on her visit to Nestlé's Swiss headquarters on 16 December last year.

In June 2003, Shanghai 2 People's Intermediate court accepted Zhu's case and in August, with Nestlé China's agreement, the court commissioned a laboratory to test Nesquik for the presence of GE ingredients. The test was positive and was accepted as evidence by the court. Nestlé subsequently commissioned another laboratory independently without notifying the court. The results this time were predictably negative. The court has refused to accept the results of the second test as evidence. The date for the court hearing has yet to be set. Zhu is demanding compensation of 13.6 yuan (about US$ 1.6) – twice the price of the product.

Greenpeace has been campaigning globally to eradicate GE ingredients from food products for many years. Many food products already contain GE ingredients, so until these can be phased out and replaced by natural ingredients we have been pushing for those products containing GE to be labelled so that consumers can make an informed choice.

We heard about Eileen Zhu Yanling's case in September and committed to helping her take her concerns directly to Nestlé's top management on 16 December last year. At the meeting a Nestlé representative told Zhu that they would continue to sell GE products worldwide with the exception of Europe where consumer rejection is strong. Nestlé's response has only strengthened her resolve to continue her fight. 'I am very disappointed by Nestlé's response. I have travelled to Switzerland to tell them the concerns of Chinese consumers, but Nestlé does not seem to care.' Zhu said after the meeting.

The meeting was conducted after Zhu gave a press conference in Lausanne. She demanded that Nestlé adopt the same policy in China as in European countries and eliminate GE ingredients from its products. She is also calling on the company to respect consumers' rights to an informed choice by properly labelling its GE products during the process of phasing out of GMOs. Nestlé rejected both demands during her meeting.

'My demands were met with outright rejection. Nestlé is unconvinced that Chinese consumers are as concerned as European consumers on food safety and consumer rights. I will continue my fight and I will also ask more Chinese consumers to support me. Only a concerted voice from Chinese consumers will make their voices heard by Nestlé', said Zhu.

Zhu's battle against Nestlé has been receiving blanket coverage in all of China's main media markets and was also well covered in Switzerland.

▶

Many Chinese consumers are very well aware of Zhu's fight against Nestlé with many of them venting their anger on China's leading Internet sites. This is clearly a story that Nestlé wish would go away but interest in the case continued at a press conference held in Shanghai today with over 30 media in attendance, including Chinese state broadcaster CCTV.

Eileen Zhu Yanling is a very impressive character and we are sure that she will eventually get a satisfactory response from Nestlé. She does not see herself as a 'consumer champion': 'As a member of society I have a duty to promote individual rights within China's business environment. The rules for business practice must be fair to everybody'.

Since March last year, Zhu has consciously avoided buying Nestlé products, whenever there is a choice so if Nestlé want to maintain a stake in the huge Chinese market we strongly advise them to listen to Zhu and the many Chinese consumers rallying behind her.

Zhu´s case, the first of its kind in China, exemplifies the growing concern about food safety and consumer rights among urban Chinese consumers. On 6 December 2002, Greenpeace released news about Nestlé selling unlabelled GE products in China. Within two days, more than 5000 people cast their vote on www.sina.com.cn, one of China's most popular websites, to denounce Nestlé's double standards. Many angry Chinese consumers followed up their virtual action with real action – newspapers reported that products were being returned to Nestlé's offices.

On the apparent double standards that Nestlé seem to be applying to its operations in different parts of the world, and their claim that loopholes in labelling regulations in the 'developing' world are not their fault, Zhu has this to say: 'Nestle and other large companies should help develop rules, not exploit them [if they want consumers to continue buying their products]'.

Eileen Zhu Yanling is ready to regain her trust in Nestlé if her demands are met with action and thinks that they could be a model company in China if they respect consumer rights. She is willing, along with other consumers, to work closely with companies to try and effect change and to realise their corporate responsibility.

'I am making these demands because there are millions of mothers in the world who trust Nestlé to provide their kids with nutritious food. Please do not abuse the trust of these mothers and their children!'

Source: 'Zhu Yanling's long march for consumer rights: Chinese consumer challenges Nestlé', 7 January 2004, available at: www.greenpeace.org/international/news/chinese-consumer-challenges-ne

Suppliers

Suppliers generally have a symbiotic relationship with a company. They are major stakeholders who help in the production processes by supplying components or systems. The way in which a supplier can affect a company's well-being is dependent on its power (Porter 1985). Suppliers can influence production costs. If there are only a few suppliers in a marketplace, then they can be powerful. If the supplier's products are necessary for production, this also means that they can wield considerable power. Suppliers, in most cases, are a complex set of stakeholders. Some may have a great deal of power; others may be much less powerful. A quick overview of a company's suppliers shows the complexities. For example, a clothing manufacturer is often dependent on:

- electricity companies
- water companies
- machine suppliers
- textile manufacturers

- packaging companies
- designers
- thread manufacturers
- gas suppliers (for heating)
- vehicle dealers (for transportation)
- computer suppliers
- robot designers and suppliers.

This is just an illustrative list and is by no means exhaustive. Nonetheless, it underlines the fact that, when we consider the word 'supplier' for a company, we usually mean a range of suppliers with differing inputs into the company's products. A company is also dependent on advertising agencies, for example, to supply them with their branding and advertising strategies. Without this complex web of supplier interactions most companies would not be able to survive. In any strategy, therefore, the power of the key suppliers needs to be assessed and understood. Companies today are often based on networks of alliances, and the suppliers are an integral part of these networks and value chains. As stakeholders and suppliers value these networks, they look for long-term relationships that are not frequently disrupted.

The following case study gives an example of the kinds of factors that affect these relationships.

CASE STUDY

Losses cut as Martin wins back M&S deals

Shares in Martin International received a boost yesterday when the clothes maker announced it had regained its Marks & Spencer knitwear contract. Martin also reported that half-year pre-tax losses to June had fallen from GBP1.85 million to GBP236,000. The shares rose 1p. The company cited heavy knitwear losses and restructuring costs as reasons for the previous year's poor performance. It spent GBP1.27 million downsizing the knitwear arm in the first half of 2000. First-half sales dropped by 10 per cent to GBP46.7 million, blamed on the lack of a spring knitwear order from M&S, its major customer.

But the retailer is reinstating its knitwear deal with Martin this autumn and will use the company as a menswear supplier from 2002. Martin currently supplies M&S with lingerie, nightwear and ladies' leisurewear. Finance director David Sadler said: 'We're not pleased to be reporting a first-half loss but we are encouraged by the reinstated contract and are looking for a profit of about GBP250,000 at year end. Analysts said that, despite difficult market conditions, a small profit might be realistic now that Martin had regained the important knitwear contract. Martin is not supplying materials for the new M&S womenswear range Per Una launched yesterday.

Source: Jessica Brown, *The Daily Express*, 29 September 2001

The article shows the power of the relationships between suppliers and buyers. In this instance, the interaction between the buyer and the supplier, in their positions of stakeholders, is the crucial factor. The power of the buyer (Marks & Spencer) nearly brought Martin to its knees and, paradoxically, also looks likely to revive its fortunes. The article illustrates the evolving nature of stakeholder management and the importance of power and time in understanding relationships.

Employees

Employees are important stakeholders in any organisation. They are individuals who have made a commitment to work for a particular company and devote their time and skills to it for monetary reward and satisfaction. Employees are rarely homogeneous and every organisation requires a range of skills that adds to its market value (Doyle 2000). A good mix of key skills sets a company aside from its competitors. Employees are also board members in many companies in Europe, as we saw earlier. Employees range from management to secretarial support to shop floor workers, each operating in a complex web of interactions. A particular and unique web of interactions also helps to create competitive advantage for a company and, because of this, companies are often defensive about public exposure of their work systems.

In many cases, employees are also shareholders in their companies, either by design (company share options as bonuses or rewards) or by choice (individuals purchase shares). In each case, as shareholders, employees will be looking for long-term growth in their shares. As shareholders, they also play an important role in determining this potential growth (or decline) of the shares' value. As Hamel (2000) says, 'Entrepreneurs won't work for peanuts, but they will work for a share of the action.' Research by Strategic Compensation Research Associates found that the average Internet company had issued enough share options to employees to dilute normal shareholders by 24 per cent (if exercised) (Krantz 1999). All this shows that employees are an important, but complex group of stakeholders.

Employees, under various legislative acts in different countries, are able to individually raise and follow up issues that bother them under the general umbrella of corporate social responsibility. The case study below illustrates how an employee can complain about dubious practices within a company. However, in this case, as the interests of other stakeholders were threatened, he was ostracised.

CASE STUDY

Bhatia v. Sterlite Industries (2001)

PIDA's (Public Interest Disclosure Act) application overseas; Detriment: threat to destroy the whistleblower was a detriment; £800,000 award

Bhatia, when visiting family in India, saw a job ad for a senior post at Sterlite Industries, working on mergers and acquisitions for its chairman in London and paid in US dollars. Bhatia applied and was appointed. ET accepted jurisdiction and found that, within two months, Bhatia had raised concerns about breaches of US and Australian stock exchange rules. He had raised these concerns internally and to the relevant investment bank that the information Sterlite Industries was supplying about a $5 million initiative for a proposed listing on NYSE was misleading and would breach its legal rules. This concern was then properly addressed. Bhatia subsequently raised a concern internally that the proposed dilution of equity in an Australian company, contrary to an understanding, would breach Australian legal rules. As a result of these concerns, ET found that the chairman threw his digital diary at Bhatia and threatened to destroy him, prompting Bhatia to leave. Bhatia was awarded £805,000.

Source: Public Concern at Work
www.pcaw.co.uk/policy_pub/case_summaries.html

Shareholders

Shareholders are often the key stakeholders within an organisation as they are the institutions and individuals who actually risk their funds in supporting it. The shareholders' interests vary, as do their goals and investment horizons. In almost all OECD countries, basic shareholder rights include those to:

- secure methods of ownership registration
- convey or transfer shares
- obtain relevant information on the corporation on a timely and regular basis
- participate and vote in general shareholder meetings
- elect members of the board
- share in the profits of the corporation.

In addition to this, shareholders are entitled to vote in general meetings and have to be consulted when any fundamental corporate changes are undertaken. Shareholders may have different voting rights according to what class of shares they hold. In return for risking their funds, shareholders are looking for economic and profit growth and can influence a company's chances of success by building on their shares or by withdrawing them. As stakeholders, they are generally quiet when the returns on their holdings are reasonable. Doyle (2000) argues that the shareholder value principle is that a business should be run to maximise the return on shareholders' investments.

The most powerful group of stakeholders in any organisation, shareholders are increasingly moving their capital around within a global environment. They can be fickle and can look for short run equity growth within companies. For this reason, shareholder communications is an important part of most companies' marketing communications strategies.

Community

Communities are stakeholders as they are affected by the economic impact of companies within their locality. In many cases, business organisations also affect the local environment. The issue of communities as stakeholders is discussed in more detail in Chapter 4 on sustainability.

Developing competitive marketing strategies

This section is concerned with understanding how the interactions between stakeholders can help a company to gain a degree of competitive advantage in the marketplace.

The management of the different stakeholders' interests is a potential source of competitive advantage (Jones, 1995; Donaldson and Preston 1995) in part because managing them well reduces (Dyer and Singh 1998; Preston and Donaldson 1999). There are also arguments that stakeholder management is a condition for long-term survival, given its moral dimension (Jones 1995). Proper management of the different stakeholders, therefore helps a company to

■ reduce the costs of managing relationships
■ add a social and ethical dimension
■ take a long-term view
■ develop a competitive advantage over its rivals
■ enhance and develop marketing relationships.

Conti (2004) feels that organisations need to begin to regard stakeholders as a strategic asset. In order to do this, it makes sense to take a systematic approach to the interactions between the company and its stakeholders. Within a systematic view, it may be possible to ascertain certain problems that may arise in such a system. For instance, in Figure 3.4, stakeholders are shown to be either in the inner ring or on the outer ring. Problems can arise when there are power conflicts in the inner circle or if a stakeholder from the outer circle wishes to move into the inner circle in order to be a part of the centre of the company.

Examples of the kinds of conflicts that could arise are as follows.

■ *Pressure from the stockmarket demanding short-term profitability* In the USA, such pressure is common as quarterly results are posted, while, in the UK, there is an equal pressure on companies regarding their six-monthly disclosures. In these

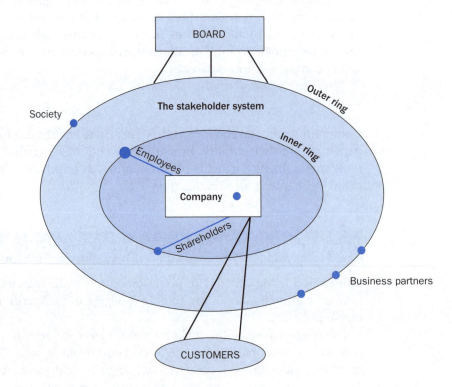

Figure 3.4 The company stakeholder system

circumstances, there could be an excessive pressure on CEOs to perform, making them both more powerful and more vulnerable, as the two case studies on Marks & Spencer illustrate. A CEO could become despotic, creating an imbalance among the key stakeholders – represented in Figure 3.4.

- *Conflict between employers and employees*. Historically, especially in Europe this has been a flashpoint. However, more recently, arbitration takes place and companies value more their human resources, so a balance between the stakeholders is created and maintained.

- *State intervention* Imbalances between stakeholders can arise when there is excessive stakeholder intervention. Many of the previously communist-run economies had this problem and companies under these regimes were simply not market-orientated, struggling with economic reform. Interestingly, there has been controversy related to stem cell research in the USA, with President Bush speaking out against embryo cloning. This is having a direct impact on companies and scientists that rely on government-sponsored research. California, a state that has one of the largest economies in the USA, supports such research and is likely to go ahead on its own (Weise 2006). However, further problems may arise when it is not possible to clearly separate state and federal funding. Whether right or wrong, interventions of this sort can have a major impact on a company's employees and shareholders, not to mention the wider community that may eventually benefit from the products of such research. This has led to some scientists and companies relocating to the EU, where the legislation is more accommodating.

Most organisations are parts of networks and have to manage these networks effectively. The following discussion attempts to outline a logical manner in which stakeholders could be managed by an organisation.

There are three steps to take when developing a management strategy for stakeholders:

1 identify a company's stakeholders as fully and as clearly as possible
2 understand and examine the relationships between how stakeholders are managed and an organisation's goals and objectives
3 incorporate the interests of the various stakeholders into the development of a corporate and marketing strategy.

The key question here is the *level* of involvement of each stakeholder in corporate processes and decisions. 'Involvement, also means that companies have to be prepared to spend money or time and lavish attention on the stakeholders. Therefore, the question of which groups will/should receive more attention is important. Companies could use either a narrow or a broad definition of 'stakeholders'.

Narrow view

Only select stakeholders that have a direct relevance to the firm's core economic interests.

These can be defined as business stakeholders – that is, those that are task-related. In general, companies are likely to shower more attention on these task-related stakeholders than on other kinds as they are central to their economic activity (Mitchell et al. 1997; Steger, 1998; see also the recent empirical work of Berman et al. 1999).

Broad view

Consider the full range of stakeholders and their likely impacts on the company from either an economic or an ethical point of view, on a long-term basis.

Research (Greenley and Foxall 1997) suggests that management orientation towards the varied and diverse interests of stakeholder groups is central to strategic planning. In many cases, failure to address multiple stakeholder groups may be detrimental to a company's performance. However, most organisations are not only constrained by resource availability but also subject to the external environment, which includes competitor hostility and general economic activity, such as market growth. The research showed that the external environment moderates the impact of multiple stakeholder orientation. Therefore, the following factors should also be considered:

- competitive hostility
- market turbulence
- market growth
- technological change
- ease of market entry.

The argument, therefore, is that the Miller and Lewis (1991) model of achieving a balance when addressing stakeholder interests is important, that this is more effective than selectively directing attention and resources at only particular stakeholders. Interestingly, the research shows that simply orientating attention towards particular groups, such as consumers per se, and giving priority to their interests does not appear to determine an enhanced company performance.

The managerial implication of this is that managers should try to map their task-related stakeholders and then go further and integrate other institutional stakeholders. This is linked to the idea that each group might interact with the others. Certain writers (Rowley 1997) advocate a network theory of stakeholders' influence:

'firms do not simply respond to each stakeholder individually; they respond, rather, to the interaction of multiple influences from the entire stakeholder set'.

Organisations, therefore, have to carefully consider the effect of the level of attention paid to different stakeholders, as stakeholders themselves are likely to interact with each other.

Jonker and Foster (2002) discuss the key elements influencing the outcome of stakeholder relations.

Legitimacy

Legitimacy is often cited as a criteria in stakeholder management. However, it is clear that legitimacy depends on particular interpretations of the law and the historical context in which particular laws are applied. Legitimacy can create problems. These issues surfaced when decisions were being made regarding Jabulika Uranium Mine in Kakadu National Park, Australia. In many cases, legitimacy is determined by the economic system and the government (Bannerjee 2000). The traditional owners of the land, the Aborigines, were regarded as stakeholders in the *debate*, but their interests or stakes were not regarded as legitimate. A similar point could be made about stem cell research, where legitimacy is determined by the government in the USA. Although the scientists doing this research can debate their interests, they do not possess legitimate rights to undertake the research, so their stake is pretty useless. In fact, if they were to carry out certain research, they could be branded as criminals.

Power

Managing stakeholder relationships is often about managing power and how to respond to power exerted by various stakeholders. The power could be resource-based (financial), legal or environmental. The case study on British Biotechnology a bit later in this chapter demonstrates this aspect of stakeholder managment.

Criticality

This is defined as a moment when a particular event causes a stakeholder to become important. Passing certain thresholds means that organisations have to engage in stakeholder relationships with lobby or pressure groups. Most of the time, these groups may not be interested in the day-to-day activities of the organisation. An example of this would be the USA's business lobby group, which has watered down the proposed legislation by the Committee for Foreign Investment in the United States (CFIUS) and it is likely to make the national security process tougher for foreign companies buying sensitive assets in the USA. A side-effect of this could be that other businesses based in the USA or in other countries would slow down investment in the country (Kirchgaessner 2006).

Rationality

This is based on Habermas's theory of 'communicative action', which is that reaching an understanding requires 'a cooperative interpretation aimed at attaining intersubjectively recognised definitions of a situation'. Essentially, this means that each party has to interpret objective, social and subjective 'worlds' in a rational way. Each party can reach 'communicative rationality (coordination through reason) and/or 'goal rationality' (egoistic calculations of success). The resultant action is 'strategic action' and the influence on a party is via incentives, sanctions and force, not necessarily reason.

This is an interesting view as some stakeholders often have relationships that are structured like a game of poker, with moves guided by incentives, sanctions and force. For instance, Mittal Steel finally won the backing of the directors of rival Arcelor in June 2006 for a merger that will create the world's largest steelmaker, five months after first announcing its interest and only after protracted negotiations that were guided by a whole range of incentives, sanctions and force.

'We have always sought a recommended merger in the interests of all stakeholders – we are delighted that is what we have now achieved', a Mittal spokesman said in a statement. The company added that it had paid a 'fair price for what is a very good business' (Milner 2006). Based on the arguments above, Jonker and Foster (2002) propose a model that is based on power, criticality and rationality. This model is summarised in Table 3.3.

Table 3.3 Basic structure of the stakeholder model

Components of the relationship

		Stake	Parties	Process	Connections
Elements influencing the outcomes of the relationship		What are the key issues in the relationship?	Who or what is involved	What processes are involved in managing the relationship?	What forms do the connections between the organisation and the stakeholder take?
	Power	Does the nature of the claim or stake have implications for the type of power involved?	What types of power do the parties involved use (if required) to obtain a result?	Do some processes result in different types of power being exercised?	What effects does the form of connections have on the form of power used? Is power exercised directly or indirectly?
	Criticality	Why is the interest or stake worth investing time and effort in?	What is it about the activities, behaviour, attributes of the parties that makes the issue critical (i.e. important enough to engage in)?	Are the processes important to the ongoing life (operations) of the parties? Is it central to the decision-making process?	How critical or important are the connections regarded by each party?
	Rationality	How is the interest or stake expressed (cognitive, social or personal)?	What are the epistemological and ontological perspectives of the parties and how do they influence their view of the issue or interest?	Do the processes and procedures affect the opportunity for the understanding based on a broad or narrow conceptualisation of rationality?	Does the form of the connection encourage or discourage dialogue rather than egocentric claims?

Source: Jonker and Foster 2002

Understanding stakeholder evolution and management

As discussed in Chapter 1, time is important in any issue relating to stakeholder management for competitive positioning. Neither organisations nor stakeholders stand still, but, equally, stakeholder patterns may also change as a result of the evolution of an organisation. Understanding an organisation's approach to its multiple stakeholders through the stages of its formation, growth and maturity, decline, revival or death may help to foster a better understanding of its strategies (Jawahar and McLaughlin 2001). A corporation's survival and continued success depends on the ability of its management to satisfy a large and diversified range of stakeholders, giving them wealth, value for money or the satisfaction of incorporating their concerns into strategy development and implementation. This has to be achieved without favouring one group over another (Clarkson 1995; Jones and Wicks 1999). However, this is a rather static view and the stakeholder strategies of any organisation are likely to evolve over time. The management of stakeholders is likely to be dependent on the following.

■ *Resources* Organisations are dependent on resources for their survival. As an organisation grows and prospers, its need for resources will change and so will the range of stakeholders providing it with particular resources. The organisation is therefore likely to expend more energy on the group of stakeholders necessary for its survival and growth than others (Kreiner and Bhambri 1991; Pfeffer and Salanick 1978). In many cases, the power exercised by the key stakeholders, such as equity providers, will be considerable (Frooman 1999).
■ *Opportunities and threats* There are many opportunities and threats involved in the process of managing stakeholders. The way they are handled often creates situations of loss or gain for an organisation.

Organisations can have different style regarding their approach to stakeholder relationships.

■ *Proactive* This means that they actively work with stakeholders and address their concerns. This includes anticipating and understanding the key issues involved.
■ *Accommodating* Having a less active approach to dealing with stakeholder concerns. This strategy involves general interaction with stakeholders, with little extra activity or anticipation of needs. An example of this approach would be the generally accommodating attention of a company to the community, without attempting a detailed anticipation of its needs.
■ *Defensive* This strategy involves doing the minimum required to keep a stakeholder happy. For example, a company may do only what is required of it to address environmental concerns, often only as a result of complying with legislation.
■ *Reactive* This strategy involves fighting particular stakeholders or ignoring them completely.

Companies may need to consider using different strategies for different stakeholders, depending on their stages of evolution (see Figure 3.5).

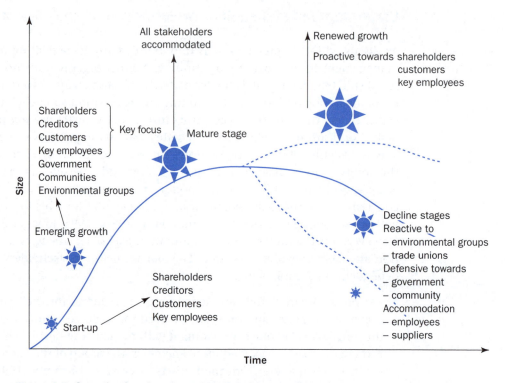

Figure 3.5 **Organisational cycle and stakeholder strategies**

Looking at the following case study, consider the evolution of British Biotech and how it should have dealt with the various stakeholders.

CASE STUDY

British Biotechnology

British Biotechnology began life in Oxford, approximately 13 years ago. As the share chart in Figure CS 3.1 shows, the company shot to prominence in the biotechnology sector as a company to watch and was even predicted to join some of the top companies in share value. However, the share price, from a high of 326p in 1996, is now languishing at around 20p. The company was the darling of the stockmarket in 1996 when it released a statement that was bullish about the prospects for Marismastat, an anti-cancer wonder drug. The potential market was enormous and this led to a wave of optimistic

buying, sending the shares to dizzy heights. The euphoria settled down on 12 May 1997 when the press release in the *Financial Times* announced 'British Biotech set for first drug launch'. Senior managers including Dr Millar, were concerned that the *Financial Times* article would lead the European Agency for the Evaluation of Medicinal Products shareholders (EMEA) to believe that the company would be seeking product approval imminently. This was not the case. The company, at this stage, sought and received assurance that media coverage would not affect the progress of its Marketing Authorisation Approval (MAA).

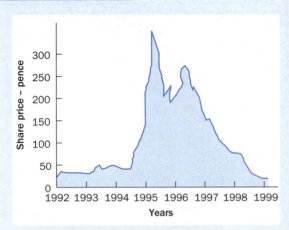

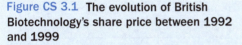

Figure CS 3.1 **The evolution of British Biotechnology's share price between 1992 and 1999**

Products can only be marketed in Europe once the EMEA extends an MAA. A similar set-up exists in America and marketing is controlled by the Division of Drug Marketing Advertising and Communications (DDMAC) within the Food and Drug Administration (FDA).

By this time, the genie had been let out of the bag. In 1998, the Head of Clinical Research, Dr Millar, was sacked for opening the debate on how valuable Marismastat could be. He expressed his concerns to Perpetual, the leading fundholder. This created a rift between him and Dr McCullagh, the founder, who remained bullish about the drug's prospects. With the rift becoming public, it was inevitable that investors would be nervous about the effects this would have.

Dr McCullagh was forced to leave by worried shareholders as trials of the drug did not show significant advances over existing treatments. The company now has a new Chief Executive, Dr Goldstein, who is to continue the Marismastat trials and trials for a new drug, Zacutex. Dr Millar felt that the original team was too enthusiastic about the prospects for the drugs. The New York and London stock exchanges are investigating share dealings.

From a PR point of view, it is not uncommon for many companies to offer possible positive progress reports to the press. The problems with the stock market arise when the positive press reports do not match the promised results. For some biotechnology companies, there is only the *promise* of products and any adverse publicity can affect their standing in the market. Consumers generally do not understand the intricacies of drug delivery systems, only their efficacy. They only want news that clearly states the prospects or the time frame in which products could be reasonably be expected to be on market. Many private investors are now sophisticated enough not to jump when they hear such stories but wait for greater returns in the future. However, institutional investors may press for shorter-term growth. There are often pressures on the management to divulge only good news, as owners may be worried that any neutral or negative news would mean falling share prices and money is desperately needed for research. Such news could also be wrongly interpreted as lack of competence on the part of the management. The key managers themselves may also own a considerable number of shares and so their levels of motivation could also be affected.

Source: Ranchhod and Gurău 1999

Competitive positioning

It is important when considering developing a comprehensive strategy to try and understand both a company's stakeholder strategy and the power exercised by each stakeholder. To help with this, it useful to consider the following set of questions and plot the answers on the matrix shown in Figure 3.6 to point up the existing situation and, therefore, where improvements could be made.

The analysis in the matrix in Figure 3.6 shows the various ways in which British Biotech had been communicating and dealing with key stakeholders. An improve-

Stakeholder	Power			Strategy			
	High	Medium	Low	Proactive	Accommodating	Defensive	Reactive
Consumers			*		*		
Shareholders	*					*	
Employees	*					*	
Press	*						*
Marketing Authorisation Authority (MAA)	*				*		

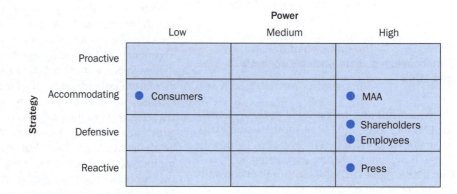

Figure 3.6 Stakeholder strategy/power analysis for British Biotechnology

ment would be for stakeholders to be approached in a proactive manner. The problems that had arisen as a result of poor stakeholder management had led to a lack of stakeholders' trust in the company's management. The company actually underinvested in trust. There is always a range of interdependence between firms and specific stakeholder groups that has to be properly considred by managers (Wicks et al. 1999). Therefore, in addition to considering the power/strategy matrix, the level of trust offered or generated should be considered as well. The lack of trust in this case was likely to hamper the company's strategic positioning and marketing activities for many years to come.

Positioning products in markets

As can be seen, competitively positioning a company in the marketplace is dependent on many factors. These factors have to be considered over short-, medium- and long-term time frames. Only by undertaking a detailed analysis of these issues can the proper positioning of a company be achieved. Success at this corporate level lays the foundations for strategic marketing.

The key factors that have to be considered in conjunction with the strategy/ power matrix are the following:

- competitor hostility
- market turbulence
- technological change
- ease of market entry.

As a result of undertaking the stakeholder analysis and assessment of the key factors shown in Figure 3.6, companies can develop clear competitive positioning strategies that *evolve over time*. Figure 3.7 illustrates the ways in which the various stakeholder and environmental factors interact and how they should be considered while developing products and markets.

The various ways in which power is handled and trust developed with stakeholders contributes to the overall brand image of a company. In considering competitive positioning and developing market advantage, it is also useful to remember that stakeholder interests will change over time. Companies that are aware of these main factors will have a clear understanding of the windows of opportunity available in a specific moment as a result of certain favourable factors and sensible management of stakeholders. These companies are the ones most likely to succeed during this century by taking advantage of flexible product/ market strategies.

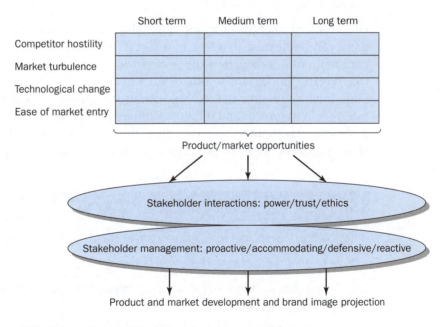

Figure 3.7 **Competitive positioning and environmental factors**

Summary

This chapter has taken a stakeholder approach to understanding how companies can position themselves in the marketplace. Simple product/market strategies do not do justice to a company. When dealing in markets, companies have to work on a range of issues that have an impact on the products or services they offer. Stakeholders have a major impact, as we have shown in this chapter, and can be dealt with by being proactive, accommodating or reactive. The turbulence of the surrounding environment offers both opportunities and threats to companies. Being successful in the marketplace results from grasping these opportunities, together with a clear stakeholder management strategy, because this has a direct impact on the brand image of the company. A positive corporate image helps, in turn, with the development of sound product positioning strategies within particular market segments. The competitive advantages of a stakeholder-based strategy, according to Conti (2004), are that it:

- creates team spirit – a crucial factor in excellence
- creates synergy and a win-win attitude as a result of networking with organisations that cooperate with an enterprise to achieve particular objectives
- allows smaller companies to accelerate learning if their customers include demanding and/or supportive larger companies
- helps to create the conditions for an organisation to become a good citizen in an increasingly global market.

However, any analysis of stakeholders should take a systems approach as a company can be likened to a tree in a forest. The firm is part of a system and any perturbations in one part of the system will affect all the other parts. In a forest, a tree has to compete for resources such as nutrients, light and water, but, at the same time, environmental factors, such as rain, wind and sunshine, play a significant role in its growth and stability. Similarly, a company has to work with its inner and outer stakeholders to create an equilibrium that benefits the *whole* system, leaving it in the optimum position to tackle environmental turbulence.

Chapter questions

1 How can stakeholder management affect customer relationships?

2 What are the limitations of a power/strategy matrix?

3 Discuss the ways in which stakeholder management can improve the brand equity of a company.

4 A sustainable Earth matters

Introduction

As the world's population grows, with some 90 million individuals being added to the planet each year, many marketers are questioning some of the basic tenets of marketing. Is it right to expect continued growth? Should we be marketing goods that are likely to harm the planet? Should marketing concentrate on products that are 'green' instead? These and many other questions are being asked not just by marketers but also by consumers generally.

In surveys that have been carried out in the last few years, it has been shown that consumers are concerned about the products that they purchase, although cost may be a factor in choosing products as well. In Germany, 88 per cent of consumers are ready to switch brands to greener products, while the corresponding figures in Italy and Spain were 84 and 82 per cent respectively (Wasik 1996). In the USA, the green market is estimated to include 52 million households (Ottman 1993). In 1996, MORI categorised 36 per cent of its British polls respondents as 'green consumers', on the basis that they 'selected one product over another because of its environmentally friendly packaging, formulation or advertising' (Worcester, 1997). This compares favourably with only 19 per cent of consumers in 1988 (although it continued the steady decline from a peak of 50 per cent in 1990).

All this makes it important that marketers actually understand and respond to customers' needs. Although marketers may attempt to do this, studies seem to indicate that there is a big difference between intent and execution in the marketplace. Figure 4.1 illustrates how human consumption patterns are now beyond the Earth's ability to sustain itself. It appears that consumers do not really wish to slow down consumption and, even if they have good intentions, most of them do not seem to be particularly inclined to purchase green products.

This trend is regarded as the 4:40 effect. Most green products struggle to get to a 1–4 per cent market share because, although around 40 per cent of adults believe in the value of purchasing green products, only around 4 per cent actually

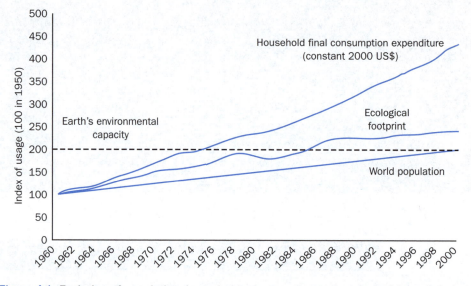

Figure 4.1 Evolution of population, household consumption and ecological footprint of the world (1960–2000)

Source: UNEP 2005a, WWF. 'Talk the Walk: Advancing sustainable lifestyles through marketing and communications' www.uneptie.org/pc/sustain/reports/advertising/Talk_the_Walk.pdf United Nations Environment Programme

translate this into reality. Promoting sustainable consumption within the general populace is a real challenge to marketers. In its report 'Talk the walk' (UNEP 2005a) Monique Barbut, a director of UNEP DTIE argues that marketing may actually hold the key to changing consumer attitudes by incorporating sustainability into the marketing mix:

> *Sustainable production, sustainable service and product design, sustainable procurement, green marketing . . . these programmes are all good for the environment, but they are also good for the economy (saving costs, developing domestic markets, seizing export opportunities) and they are also good for social progress (helping to spread good labour conditions, helping to create decent jobs).*

This area is discussed in detail towards the end of the chapter.

A further question to ask is: is the provision of certain products and services sustainable? Sustainability is about understanding the interactions of various stakeholders in an organisation. Maximising profits and looking for short-term gains in market share may, in the long run, be so harmful to certain groups of stakeholders that the company itself may suffer bad publicity. These stakeholders are the employees, local community and government agencies. The main stakeholder here, though, is probably the planet itself and increasingly, the public feels that firms should take responsibility for environmental damage inflicted on parts of the Earth in the pursuit of profit. An example of this is the cost paid by General Electric Company in the USA for removing 2 million cubic metres of contaminated sludge from the Hudson River (Anonymous 2001). For 35 years, the company poured some 500,000 kg of polychlorinated biphenyls (PCBs) into the river, before they were banned in 1977. Residents living near the riverbank claim to have suffered from a variety of PCB-related illnesses, ranging from cancer to physical deformities. As a result of this, the USA'a Environmental Protection Agency has decided to remove the sludge and asked GEC to foot the $500 million bill.

In a situation like this, when the factors are complex, the fact remains that the consumers actually bought electrical equipment that was manufactured by GEC during all this period and were generally unaware of the pollution problems. The onus, therefore, remains on companies to ensure that their products, services, and practices are environmentally friendly and sustainable or not. This information also needs to filter through to consumers.

In this chapter, we explore various notions of sustainability, ranging from 'green' products to sustainable and ethical production. The aim of this chapter is to understand the implications of being environmentally friendly and how, by taking such a stance, a company could create a sustainable competitive advantage in marketing. The consumer paradox and short-termism promoted via stock markets sometimes does not help companies that are trying to be ethical in their approach. For example, consider Gap Inc. as discussed by Vogel (2006).

> *A few years ago the company, like many other apparel retailers, Gap Inc., found itself criticised for the labour practises of its suppliers. It has responded in an exemplary fashion and arguably now has one of the most responsible and effective programmes to help ensure that the workers who produce its products are treated fairly. These policies made business sense in that they prevented its brand from being tarnished by continued activist pressures, and assured its current and prospective employees that the firm had strong social commitments.*
>
> *More recently, the Gap has experienced financial difficulties. These difficulties are completely unrelated to its social performance. Rather they are entirely due to the fact that its fickle consumers now regard its products as less attractive or appealing than those of other brands. Not surprisingly, many financial analysts have become less sanguine about its future earnings and its share price has become depressed. In short, whatever the business implications of the Gap's responsible outsourcing policies, investors are either unaware or uninterested in them. All that matters to them are Gap's future sales.*
>
> *This does not mean that the Gap should not have adopted responsible procurement policies or that it should now abandon them. Nor does it mean that other highly visible companies should avoid similar policies in order to protect their reputations. What it does imply is that we should not expect the financial markets to appreciate or reward these efforts. Instead of bemoaning the unwillingness of the financial markets and the media to reward CSR [corporate social responsibility] policies, perhaps we should be grateful that they do not penalise them.*

Understanding environmental marketing

For many consumers, the term 'green' may evoke a range of different emotions and understanding. For some, it may mean products that do not harm the environment, while for others it may mean products that have been made without harming the environment. Many may include ethical and moral considerations, such as fair trade with developing nations. For some, it could be charitable ventures, such as Oxfam. From these examples, it can be seen that the term 'environmentally-friendly', encompasses a myriad of meanings for individuals, depending on their range of experiences and perspectives. The main issue here, however, is the merging of social concerns with ecological concerns.

Many marketing specialists would argue that such concerns are now inseparable (Peattie 1995). Other people consider that simply being green is not enough and ethical issues also need to be taken into account. This is backed up by research into the notion of 'environmental justice' within the USA (Oyewole 2001). The main contention is that many companies site chemical plants and dump toxic waste near poor or deprived communities. This is also part of a global concern where some products are cheaply made by communities that are too poor to complain about environmental issues, needing jobs and money to sustain themselves. Sometimes pollution is exported from the rich countries to the poor countries, as noted by UNEP (2005c):

> Every year, 20 to 50 million tonnes of electrical and electronic equipment waste ('e-waste') are generated worldwide, which could bring serious risks to human health and the environment. While 4 million PCs are discarded per year in China alone.

The key pollutants – e-waste – presently discarded among many are lead, tin, antimony, cadmium, mercury, polychlorinated biphenyls (PCBs), polybrominated diphenyl ethers (PBDEs), polychlorinated napthalenes (PCNs), nonyl phenols (NP) and triphenyl phosphate (TPP). All these substances are toxic and create problems for humans, interfering with their metabolic systems in harmful ways and causing cancers, bone diseases, internal organ damage and weakening of the immune system. At the same time, pollutants released into the soil and water systems contaminate the ecosystem, with devastating effects on plant and animal life, affecting the whole food chain.

The main countries accepting e-waste are India and China. As their economies grow, they will be producing significant amounts of e-waste themselves, an example of which is already happening, as mentioned in the quote above. Hand in hand with this, crisis-ridden governments, such as Indonesia, the Philippines, South Korea and Thailand, cut back on environmental spending (French 2000). For instance, in Russia, the budget for protected areas was cut by 40 per cent.

The globalisation of commerce is intensifying the environmental agenda, with many countries being increasingly concerned about the effects of global consumption trends on the environment. This is shown in Figures 4.2 and 4.3 from the Worldwatch Institute (2000), which provided the information.

Energy and the climate

As our growing population has intensified the burning of coal and oil to produce power, the carbon locked in millions of years' worth of ancient plant growth has been released into the air, laying a heat-retaining blanket of carbon dioxide over the planet. As a result, the Earth's temperature has increased significantly. Climate scientists have predicted that this increase will disrupt weather. Indeed, annual damages from weather disasters have already increased over 40-fold.

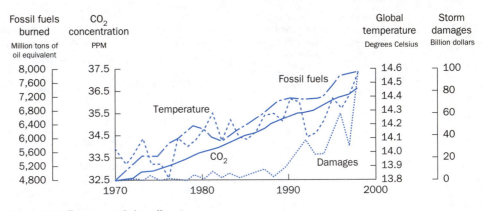

Figure 4.2 Energy and the climate

Source: Worldwatch Institute 2000

Chemicals and the biological boomerang

Our consumption of chemicals has exploded, with about three new synthetic chemicals being introduced each day. Almost nothing is known about the long-term health and environmental effects of new synthetics, so we have been ambushed again and again by belated discoveries. One of the most ominous signs of this is the evolution of pesticide-resistant pests as the use of pesticides increases.

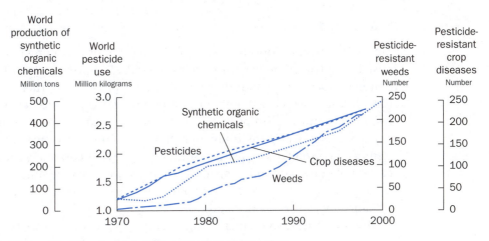

Figure 4.3 Chemicals and the biological boomerang

Source: Worldwatch Institute 2000

Commerce and the oceans

The global economy has more than doubled in the past 30 years, putting pressure on most countries to increase export income. Many have tried to increase revenues by selling more ocean fish, for which there is growing demand, as the increase in crop yields no longer keeps pace with population growth. Result: overfishing is decimating one stock after another and the catch is getting thinner and thinner (see Figure 4.4).

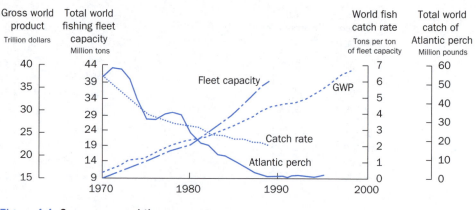

Figure 4.4 Commerce and the oceans

Source: Worldwatch Institute 2000

As the world's population expands, placing ever-increasing pressures on the environment, many major institutions are researching the likely impacts of certain scenarios on the planet. UNEP produced an excellent and very detailed report, named GEO-3 (UNEP 2002), and it outlines the various ways in which the Earth would evolve depending on differing policy initiatives. UNEP acknowledges the fact that all these initiatives are probably in progress, but in sustainability terms, the most important initiatives must attempt to save the planet. The key scenarios are as follows.

Markets first

Most of the world adopts the values and expectations prevailing in today's industrialised countries. The wealth of nations and the optimal play of market forces dominate social and political agendas. Trust is placed in further globalisation and liberalisation, which will enhance corporate wealth, create new enterprises and livelihoods and so help people and communities to afford to insure against – or pay to fix – social and environmental problems. Ethical investors, together with citizens and consumer groups, try to exercise growing corrective influence, but are undermined by economic imperatives. The powers of state officials, planners and lawmakers to regulate society, economy and the environment continue to be overwhelmed by expanding demands.

Much of the current marketing literature focuses on this type of scenario. Emphasis is placed on increasing consumption and expanding markets. Strategies proposed rarely take into account human, social and environmental costs.

Policy first

Decisive initiatives are taken by governments in an attempt to reach specific social and environmental goals. A coordinated pro-environment and anti-poverty drive balances the momentum for economic development at any cost. Environmental and social costs and gains are factored into policy measures, regulatory frameworks and planning processes. All these are reinforced by fiscal levers or incentives, such as carbon taxes and tax breaks. International 'soft law' treaties and binding instruments affecting environment and development are integrated into unified blueprints and their status in law is upgraded, though fresh provision is made for open consultation processes to allow for regional and local variants.

There are already attempts being made in this direction by governments. Such a major initiative is the Kyoto Protocol, limiting the emission of greenhouse gases, primarily carbon dioxide. The protocol, which became legally binding at midnight New York time (0500 GMT) on 16 February, demands a 5.2 per cent cut in greenhouse gas emissions from the industrialised world as a whole by 2012. However, it is clear that not all nations are willing to sign this agreement – the USA, India and China being some very important examples. The USA's government feels that the arguments are flawed, though an increasing number of states are following their own agenda on limiting CO_2 and greenhouse gas emissions. However, some 41 countries, accounting for 55 per cent of greenhouse gas emissions, have ratified the treaty, pledging to cut these emissions by 5.2 per cent by 2012.

Security first

This scenario assumes a world of striking disparities where inequality and conflict prevail. Socio-economic and environmental stresses give rise to waves of protest and counteraction. As such troubles become increasingly prevalent, the more powerful and wealthy groups focus on self-protection, creating enclaves akin to the present-day 'gated communities'. Such islands of advantage provide a degree of enhanced security and economic benefits for dependent communities in their immediate surroundings, but they exclude the disadvantaged mass of outsiders. Welfare and regulatory services fall into disuse, but market forces continue to operate outside the walls.

Such security first scenarios can occur today in regions within countries and between countries. Within countries, we have rich and poor localities, with people generally living in differing economic environments. Increasingly, some areas are 'gated' and privileged. Some countries also have very strict border controls to prevent labour movement from the poor to the rich regions. One could argue that the failure of the last round of Doha talks on trade still favours the rich nations, maintaining such 'gated communities' around a sea of poorer nations.

Sustainability first

A new environment and development paradigm emerges in response to the challenge of sustainability, supported by new, more equitable values and institutions. A more visionary state of affairs prevails, where radical shifts in the way people interact with one another and with the world around them, stimulate and support sustainable policy measures and accountable corporate behaviour. There is much fuller collaboration between governments, citizens and other stakeholder groups in decision-making on issues of close common concern. A consensus is reached on what needs to be done to satisfy basic needs and realise personal goals without beggaring others or spoiling the outlook for posterity.

This is happening now in patches around the world. However, much of the world is poor and sustainability often gives way to making money first as an option. However, environmental groups, charity organisations and certain governments are going for sustainability first as an option. Countries such as Austria and Germany are leading the way. Regional pockets in other countries are also pursuing this option, but, in general, consumer awareness about environmental issues is poor in both rich and poor countries.

Next steps

What is interesting is that the UNEP (2002) has followed these scenarios up with scientific analysis of how each one would affect the way in which the planet will evolve as a result in terms of pollution, poverty eradication and land degradation. Figure 4.5 depicts what would happen between 2002 and 2032 for each scenario.

Markets first	Policy first
Most of the world adopts the values and expectations prevailing in today's industrialised countries. The wealth of nations and the optimal play of market forces dominate social and political agendas. Trust is placed in further globalisation and liberisation, which will enhance corporate wealth, create new enterprises and livelihoods and so help people and communities to afford to insure against – or pay to fix – social and environmental problems. Ethical investors, together with citizens' and consumer groups, try to exercise growing corrective influence, but are undermined by economic imperatives. The powers of state officials, planners and lawmakers to regulate society, economy and the environment continue to be overwhelmed by expanding demands.	Decisive initiatives are taken by governments in an attempt to reach specific social and environmental goals. A coordinated pro-environment and anti-poverty drive balances the momentum for economic development at any cost. Environmental and social costs and gains are factored into policy measures, regulatory frameworks and planning processes. All these are reinforced by fiscal levers or incentives, such as carbon taxes and tax breaks. International 'soft law' treaties and binding instruments affecting environment and development are integrated into unified blueprints and their status in law is upgraded, though fresh provision is made for open consultation processes to allow for regional and local variants.
Security first	**Sustainability first**
This scenario assumes a world of striking disparities where inequality and conflict prevail. Socio-economic and environmental stresses give rise to waves of protest and counteraction. As such troubles become increasingly prevalent, the more powerful and wealthy groups focus self-protection, creating enclaves akin to the present-day 'gated communities'. Such islands of advantage provide a degree of enhanced security and economic benefits for dependent communities in their immediate surroundings, but they exclude the disadvantaged mass of outsiders. Welfare and regulatory services fall into disuse, but market forces continue to operate outside the walls.	A new environment and development paradigm emerges in response to the challenge of sustainability, supported by new, more equitable values and institutions. A more visionary state of affairs prevails, where radical shifts in the way people interact with one another and with the world around them stimulate and support sustainable policy measures and accountable corporate behaviour. There is much fuller collaboration between governments, citizens and other stakeholder groups in decision-making on issues of close common concern. A consensus is reached on what needs to be done to satisfy basic needs and realise personal goals without beggaring others or spoiling the outlook for posterity.

Figure 4.5 **Outcomes for different scenarios of world economics 2000–2032**

Source: UNEP 2002 *GEO-3: Global Environment Outlook 3* www.unep.org/geo/geo3 United Nations Environment Programme

At the sametime, some calculations have been made for global CO_2 generation (see Figures 4.6, 4.7 and 4.8).

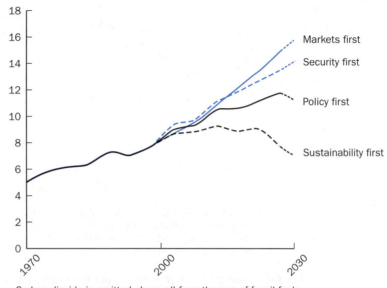

Carbon dioxide is emitted above all from the use of fossil fuels. For all four scenarios, it is assumed that stabilisation of primary energy use is first reached at the end of the 21st century.

Figure 4.6 Carbon dioxide emissions from all sources (billion tonnes carbon/year) 1970–2030

Source: Image 2.2 in UNEP 2002 *GEO-3: Global Environment Outlook 3* www.unep.org/geo/geo3 United Nations Environment Programme

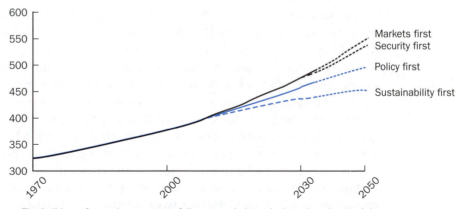

The build-up of greenhouse gases follows trends in emissions, but the stock has a long lifespan once in the atmosphere. Only the *Sustainability first* scenario is on a trajectory to stabilise at 450 parts per million carbon dioxide equivalent.

Figure 4.7 Atmospheric concentrations of carbon dioxide (parts per million by volume) 1970–2050

Source: Image 2.2 in UNEP 2002 *GEO-3: Global Environment Outlook 3* www.unep.org/geo/geo3 United Nations Environment Programme

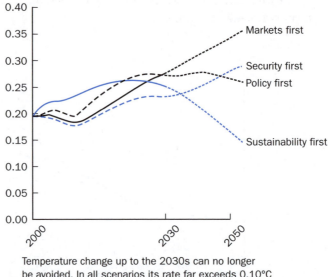

Temperature change up to the 2030s can no longer
be avoided. In all scenarios its rate far exceeds 0.10°C
per ten years – the level above which damage to
ecosystems is likely.

Figure 4.8 **Global temperature change (°C per ten years) 2000–2050**

Source: Image 2.2 in UNEP 2002 *GEO-3: Global Environment Outlook 3* www.unep.org/geo/geo3 United Nations
Environment Programme

These scenarios show how fragile the whole ecosystem has become. Further pressures
on the environment will seriously affect the lives of every single individual on the
planet. Even communities that feel they live in gated, secure areas are not immune
from land degradation and pollution. Therefore, as production, marketing and consumption become increasingly global, environmental issues affect every one of us.

For marketers – who are often concerned with single products or brands – it is
often difficult to disentangle the various interconnecting strands affecting the manufacturing of a single product. A complex piece of machinery, such as a car, may
well have certain components that are neither ethically nor environmentally produced. Some marketers would even say that the production and use of a car itself is
environmentally unfriendly, as each car in use adds to local and global pollution.

Given this range of views, we need to understand the different ways in which
green marketing is perceived (see Figure 4.9). Marketers may also have a significant
role to play in enlightening consumers and bringing about positive change.

In many ways, to be totally green means that the human population must
eschew any luxuries beyond self-sufficiency. As the history of marketing shows,
consumption has always played a large part in human existence. For this reason,
many marketers feel that being totally green is unattainable and therefore the term
'greener' should be used (Charter and Polonsky 1999). Figure 4.10 shows that
many products are global and, therefore, the ways in which they are consumed at
the local level also has global implications.

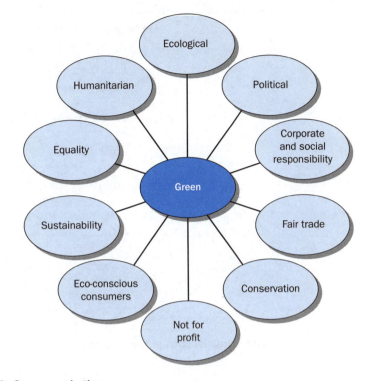

Figure 4.9 Green marketing
Source: Peattie 1995

Interestingly, for example, our demand for water has turned us into water vampires, draining the world of its lifeblood. 'What can we do to prevent mass global drought and starvation?' asks Pearce (2006) in the *New Scientist*. He argues that some of our consumption patterns actually put immense pressure on the Earth's resources. For instance, it takes 20,000 litres of water to grow 1 kilogramme of coffee, 11,000 litres of water to make a quarter pounder and 5,000 litres of water to make a kilo of cheese.

By conventional measures of greenness, Jitubhai Chowdhury is a model farmer. He uses organic manure and natural pesticides. He grows fruit trees around the edge of his alfalfa fields and tends his dairy cattle with care. Every day he produces 25 litres of milk, which he sends to a collection point in the nearby village of Kushkal in Gujarat, India, for delivery to the state dairy. It's because of people like him that India isn't starving. For all its virtues, however, Chowdhury's 2-hectare farm is sowing the seeds of a global disaster.

To grow the fodder that he needs to feed his cows, he is entirely dependent on irrigation water pumped from deep underground. Over the course of a year, his small electric pump sucks twice as much water from beneath his fields as falls on the land as rain. No wonder the water table in the village is 150 metres down.

This kind of complexity is only now beginning to be understood and, in the future, will need to be incorporated into the marketing of products so that

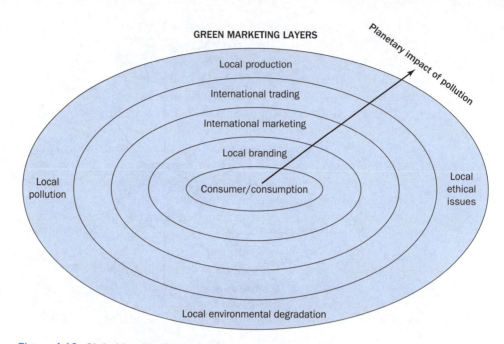

Figure 4.10 **Global implications of green marketing**

consumers can make informed choices about the depth of the ecological footprint that they are making on the Earth.

In order to understand how products can be defined as green, many complicated analytical systems have evolved over the years. As a result, many multinationals are taking green issues more seriously. McDonald's, for instance, has spent a great deal of money on improving its ability to recycle its materials, but has been quiet about discussing the impact the company has on the environment as a result of the mass production of beef. It has instituted a number of programmes in order to combat energy wastage (Wasik 1996).

- *McRecycle USA programme* The company claims to purchase over $100 million of recycled packaging. Also, switching from white to brown bags has saved bleaching costs and so prevented the resulting chemical pollution.
- *Recycled materials in construction* The company sets aside 25 per cent of its construction budget for recycled materials to use in its construction.
- *Energy efficiency* In partnering with the Environmental Protection Agency in the USA, the company instituted a 'Green Lights' programme. Eco-efficient lighting is used in stores. The stores themselves have been made more energy efficient as a result. The energy saved has meant that over 30 tons of carbon dioxide is no longer being released into the air each year.
- *Waste reduction action plan (WRAP)* The focus of this programme is on cutting down on the amount of waste materials going to landfill sites by using recycled materials and paper.

Interestingly, the biggest failure of all these various programmes has been that of recycling within the shop environment. Consumers were generally oblivious to this issue!

So, the final question is, is McDonald's offering a green product? This a difficult question to answer because the company has obviously tried hard to improve its products and services by means of such ecological efficiency programmes, yet the morality of mass-producing beef remains unresolved. Some would argue that even this brings necessary employment in poorer areas, while others would consider such farming harmful to the environment.

On the plus side, an unlikely alliance was formed between Greenpeace and McDonald's when Greenpeace highlighted the fact that many of the chickens sold at McDonald's were fed on soya imported from newly deforested areas in the Amazon. Not only did McDonald's impose a two-year moratorium on the use of such feed but it also formed an alliance with other high street retailers to stop using soya produced in the Amazon area. Greenpeace is demanding that the moratorium continue until proper procedures for legality and governance are in place and asking for the creation of an agreement with the Brazilian government and key stakeholders on the long-term protection of the Amazon rainforest (Sauven 2006).

In the light of these fundamental questions, we can only argue for greener marketing. It may well colour different companies different shades of green (see Figure 4.11) depending on individual circumstances, but it is important to try to be as green as possible. It is important to note that social and ecological issues are inextricably intertwined and a truly green company should address both issues simultaneously. This approach is the correct route to creating sustainable businesses and environments. The Nike case study illustrates the particular problems faced by an organisation caught exploiting workers and then, as a result of public pressure, attempting to set things right.

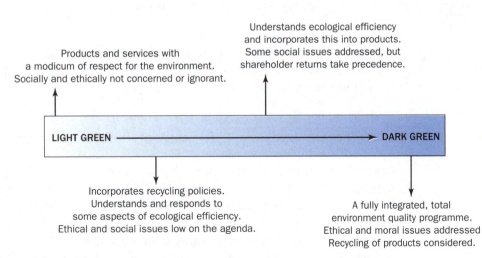

Figure 4.11 Measuring the green policies of organisations

Source: Ranchhod 2001

CASE STUDY

Nike Corporation

Consider Nike, the $8 billion footwear and apparel company that has become a lightning rod for activists, consumers, the media and others who have taken aim at the company's workplace, environmental and human rights practices. According to its critics, Nike has engaged in a variety of practices that have exploited workers in the developing world and the communities where they live. The images proffered by Nike's critics are vivid: women and young children toiling for long hours for low pay in squalid conditions, breathing the fumes of toxic chemicals, unable to protest for fear of losing their jobs, manufacturing goods the price tags of which exceed their monthly pay.

Nike acknowledges that, in the past, it was less than vigilant in monitoring the practices of its factories, although nearly all of them are contracted to independent manufacturers. It has now launched an aggressive and ambitious effort not only to correct such situations, but also to set a shining example for its industry. The company has begun to use sustainability as a design criterion, to reduce the use of toxic materials and generation of waste in its manufacturing process. Nike cut the use of solvents in its adhesives by 800,000 gallons in one year and achieved its goal of reducing its use of volatile organic compounds per unit of production by 90 per cent by 2001. The company also supports organic cotton farming by providing incentives for farmers to switch to organic production.

None of this seems to have stemmed the tide of criticism, though Nike has been named among the ten 'worst' international corporations by *Multinational Monitor* magazine. It had an Indonesian factory looted and burned by protesters and suffered criticisms by women's groups in the USA, who pilloried the company for commercials that call for women to be empowered while paying its predominantly female overseas workers poorly. Its home town of Portland, Oregon, adopted a resolution urging its troubled school district to 'respectfully decline' a $500,000 cash donation because of the company's alleged human rights abuses.

The experiences of Nike and other companies that have come under intense public scrutiny because of perceived wrongdoings suggest that consumers' expectations of brands are changing. It is no longer enough that a company delivers good-quality products. In the search for differentiation, the battleground shifts from the tangible – pounds of chemicals and other wastes released into the environment – to the intangible – ethics, values and corporate culture.

Source: Makower 1994

This last case study illustrates the part ethics plays in understanding sustainable marketing strategies. Another way to consider sustainability is to take a different view of the commonly quoted 'product lifecycle'.

The lifecycle analysis (LCA) concept–lifecycle thinking

One way to consider the creation and utilisation of environmentally friendly products and services is the LCA concept. It is recognised as both a concept and an analytical environmental management tool (SPOLD 1995). This concept – sometimes termed lifecycle thinking – helps everyone (consumers and producers alike) to understand the overall environmental implications of the services required by society. The analysis based on this concept promotes consideration of the cradle-to-grave implications of any actions taken, forcing managers to move beyond the supply chain and sector-based considerations of the environment and onwards to thinking about the wider implications of economic activities.

Greenpeace has advocated the use of a similar dial to the one adopted in this book. Here is an example of it being used for consumer electronics (see Figure 4.12).

Greenpeace scores the companies on the electronics scorecard as follows.

■ *Chemicals policy and practice (5 criteria):*
   – a chemicals policy based on the precautionary principle
   – chemicals management – that is, supply chain management of chemicals via, for example, banned/restricted substance lists, policy to identify problematic substances for future elimination/substitution
   – timeline for phasing out all use of vinyl plastic (PVC)
   – timeline for phasing out all use of brominated flame retardants (not just those banned by EU's RoHS Directive)
   – PVC- and BFR-free models of electronic products on the market.
■ *Policy and practice for producer responsibility for taking back their discarded products and recycling (4 criteria):*
   – support for individual (financial) producer responsibility – producers should finance the end-of-life management of their products, taking back and reusing/recycling their own brand discarded products

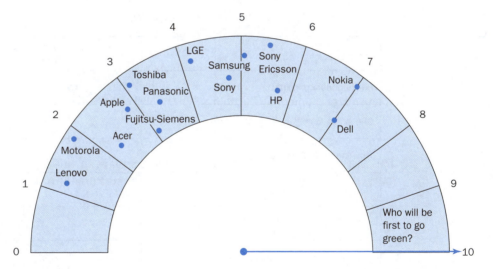

The criteria reflect the demands of the Toxic Tech campaign to the electronic companies. Our two demands are that companies should:
 • clean up their products by eliminating hazardous substances
 • take back and recycle their products once they become obsolete.
The two issues are connected. The use of harmful chemicals in electronics prevents them from being recycled safely when products are discarded. Each company was given a score out of 30 which was then divided by 3 to give a mark out of 10 for simplicity.

Figure 4.12 The Greenpeace guide to greener electronics

Source: Greenpeace 25 August 2006, *The Greenpeace Guide to Greener Electronics* www.greenpeace.org.uk

- provide voluntary take-back and recycling in every country where it sells its products, even in the absence of national laws requiring producer responsibility for electronic waste
- provide clear information for individual customers on take-back policies and recycling services in all countries where there are sales of its products
- report on amount of waste electrical and electronic equipment (WEEE) collected and recycled.

Nokia leads the way when it comes to eliminating toxic chemicals. Since the end of 2005, all new models of mobiles have been free of polyvinyl chloride (PVC) and all new models from the start of 2007 will also be free of brominated flame retardents (BFRs). Nokia loses points, though, for failing to provide an adequate definition of what 'precautionary principle' means in practice for Nokia. On the other hand, the company scores well on producer responsibility for its electronic waste. The company actively supports and lobbies for individual producer responsibility, which means that each company should take care of the electronic waste from its own brand of products. However, Nokia also loses points for not providing data on the numbers of actual mobiles recycled. Further detailed analysis for each company is provided by Greenpeace on its website (at www.greenpeace.org/international/news/green-electronics-guide-ewaste250806).

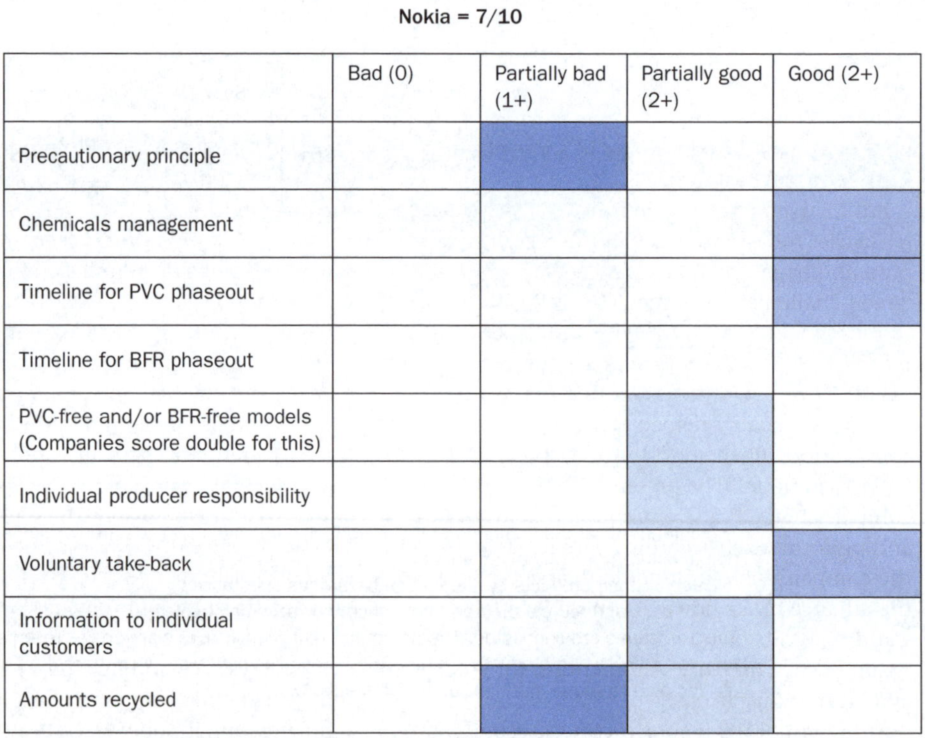

Nokia = 7/10

	Bad (0)	Partially bad (1+)	Partially good (2+)	Good (2+)
Precautionary principle		X		
Chemicals management				X
Timeline for PVC phaseout				X
Timeline for BFR phaseout				
PVC-free and/or BFR-free models (Companies score double for this)			X	
Individual producer responsibility			X	
Voluntary take-back				X
Information to individual customers			X	
Amounts recycled		X		

Figure 4.13 Nokia's electronics scorecard

Source: Greenpeace 25 August 2006, *The Greenpeace Guide to Greener Electronics* www.greenpeace.org.uk

This type of classification is important as companies produce huge amounts of e-waste globally, some of which goes for recycling in places such as India and China, where it contributes to environmental degradation and endangering human health. Any positive inputs into the ways in which products are made, commercialised and consumed are important for both consumers and recyclers.

The following case study illustrates the various factors that need to be considered by a company striving to be green. The chain to the final consumer, however, can be quite long:

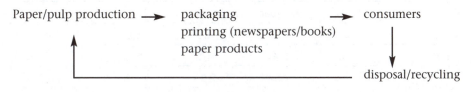

Consider the lifecycles of various products, taking into account responsibilities at various stages.

CASE STUDY

APRIL takes a leaf out of the green book

Asia is not renowned for being the most advanced region as far as environmental awareness goes. Just think of the car-clogged, highly polluted streets of many of Asia's big cities, the lack of paper recycling systems throughout much of the region or even the poor quality of drinking water in some places further off the beaten track.

But a mixed track record is no excuse for Asian industries today and many of the region's major pulp and paper manufacturers are facing up to the 'green challenge'. One such company is Indonesia's Riau Andalan Pulp and Paper (RAPP), part of the Asia Pacific Resources International (APRIL) group. On the environmental front, RAPP was arguably helped along by its cooperation, albeit short lived, with Finland's UPM-Kymmene. 'The presence of a European company helped raise environmental awareness and performance', according to Canesio P. Munoz, the company's Environmental Manager. But since the alliance broke down and RAPP was left standing on its own two feet, there has been no let-up in the company's momentum for greener and cleaner operations.

At present, RAPP is constructing a second pulp line at its Kerinci mill in the Riau province on the Indonesian island of Sumatra. As the company starts to expand towards a 2 million tonnes/year pulp capacity target, the mill is becoming increasingly aware of the need to meet stringent environmental targets to satisfy both local and international demands. The company is targeting a first quarter 2001 startup date for the new line at the Riau mill.

As part of its environmental commitment, APRIL is working on its first annual environmental report. But it is not just a moral sense of concern for the mill's surroundings which is driving APRIL – pressure is coming from many quarters. Local people have lodged complaints about skin-related diseases and fish depletion in the nearby Kampar river. As a result of these allegations, non-governmental organisations (NGOs) have levelled criticisms at the pulp and paper mill. There have also been some critical voices from overseas, for example in Europe.

In an attempt to put these fears and accusations to rest, APRIL has appointed independent bodies to carry out research and help prove that the Indonesian mill operates in line with international standards, and in some cases, beats these targets (Table CS 4.1).

Table CS 4.1 **RAPP effluent load as compared to international standards (kg/ton)**

Parameter	Indonesian (early 2000)	Canada (BC)	Sweden	Cluster rules Existing mills	Cluster rules New mills	RAPP (October 1999)
BOD5	8.5	4.5	8.7	8.05	5.5	2.93
COD	29.75	No spec	31.00	No spec	No spec	11.22
TSS	8.5	7.0	4.0	16.4	9.5	4.41
pH	6–9	5–9	5–9	5–9	5–9	7.1–8.2
AOX	No spec	1.5	0.23	0.623	0.272	0.12

Note: No spec = No specification

Source: Jenkinson 2001

Outside approval

One independent body that RAPP selected was the Finnish Environmental Research Group, which carried out an environmental impact assessment at the mill. The report was published last September and concluded that RAPP's industrial complex contained low levels of pollutants and that the external treatment seemed to work efficiently, although improvements in nutrient dosage could be carried out. The Finnish group also came to the conclusion that the risk for humans coming into contact with the Kampar river water was 'negligible or non-existent'. As for the river's fish life, investigations suggested that the level of pulp mill effluent contaminants was low enough not to have any serious effect on the animals.

Soon after the Finnish report, RAPP launched a one-year programme with local NGOs to carry out further studies into the effects of the pulp and paper operations on the quality of the local river. The gist of these investigations is to sample biodata from the Kampar river every three months and compare examples taken from upstream, downstream and at the point of effluent discharge from the pulp mill.

The research is a three-pronged effort, with local NGO Riau Mandiri assessing the water quality, the Fisheries Department of the University of Riau in charge of the river biology/ecology and the University of Singapore investigating health-related matters.

The preliminary results are good news for RAPP, with no strong condemnations being thrown in its direction. The water quality is described as 'generally good', although Riau Mandiri is looking further into the COD (chemical oxygen demand) and BOD (biological oxygen demand) readings, which have recently started to rise. The University of Riau has not noticed any significant difference to the natural river life either. In fact, fish stocks actually increased due to higher nitrogen and phosphorous levels in the effluent treatment. The university team continues to assess the quality of the fish stocks as it seems that sulphur levels are slightly higher than normal, though.

On top of that, the reports from local people about skin irritations are not being blamed on RAPP and it is thought that plants may be the problem. The findings of one Riau University study suggest that it is 'unlikely' that river water is a cause of inflammatory skin problems among villagers. Monitoring will continue, though, until a more conclusive verdict is reached.

It is certainly in RAPP's interests to cooperate with the NGOs and prove the mill's case wherever possible as the NGOs can act as a powerful lobbyist. As Riau Mandiri spokesperson Anny Hardiyanti says, 'After a year's monitoring, if we find negative results, we will urge the company to address the problem. And if the problem is not addressed, we will launch a campaign against the company responsible.' Added to that, the NGO is not afraid of carrying out threats of action. It has already launched several campaigns against other companies, which were found to be polluting another nearby river in the region.

Forest sustenance

A key tenet of APRIL's environmental policy is striving towards fully sustainable forest management. The Indonesian mill's long-term goal is to achieve sustainable forest management certification. But, as an interim step, the mill is focusing on an ISO 14001 certificate for its forestry operations, which it hopes to receive by the end of this year. If the company sticks to the timetable, certification would come just a few months after RAPP was awarded ISO 9002 for its pulp and paper operations.

ISO 14001 is an environmental management system, which provides criteria for assessing a company's use of air, water, soil and resources. The drive towards this certification comes from RAPP's customers around the globe, and particularly from European consumers.

Part of the company's efforts towards full sustainability is the development of its acacia plantations. Planting started back in 1993 and some of the plantations are already mature, but the company is waiting until next year before harvesting the area, for strategic reasons. RAPP aims to make a full switch from mixed tropical hardwood to acacia plantations by 2008.

The company has also carried out extensive tests on the plantations and is extremely pleased with the yield and quality results. The plantations are expected to yield 210 m^3/ha at harvest and achieve a wood to pulp conversion rate of 4.5 m^3/ton/ib. As a result, RAPP hopes to gain the double advantage of higher yields and limiting any adverse effects on the environment.

By RAPP's calculations, the mill will need 127,500 ha of plantations to supply pulp line #1, which has an 850,000 ton/yr capacity (Table CS 4.2). Pulp line #2A is due to come on line by the first quarter of 2001, bringing total capacity up to 1.3 million tons/year. RAPP calculates that it will need 195,000 ha/yr of acacia plantations to meet this pulp capacity, and it is no surprise perhaps that the company happens to have exactly this amount available. Originally the government allocated 280,000 ha of land to RAPP for conversion into plantations. The area chosen by the government was so-called 'non-productive land' – in other words, the land had already been logged over and exploited. Some of this area must be maintained as a greenbelt area to protect wildlife and ensure biodiversity in the area, leaving the company with the magic number of 195,000 ha/yr for converting into plantations.

Indonesia's social scene

On paper, the land transfer sounds like a relatively simple procedure – the government allocates land and the company decides to convert the area into plantations. In practice, though, there are many more hurdles to be cleared. For example, some of the allocated land is next to local settlements and the communities claim that the ground is theirs in accordance with 'community rights'. Companies such as RAPP are only able to operate effectively by avoiding conflicts with these local communities. This involves talking with the people, suggesting alternative sources of income and convincing them that they will not lose out. As Environmental Manager Munoz says, 'We don't drive people out. Resolutions are always reached by consensus.'

Of the total area allocated to RAPP, some 60,000 ha of land were termed so-called 'problem areas'. So far, the company has resolved approximately half of the issues. RAPP is all too aware of the need to work with the local people to avoid potentially serious problems. For example, last December the Kerinci mill was brought to a standstill as demonstrators took to the streets in protest over a labour dispute. And in the new era of 'reformation' which is flourishing in Indonesia, local communities are becoming increasingly aware of their rights and companies such as RAPP clearly want to avoid conflicts wherever possible.

To date, RAPP has employed a host of community development (CD) projects to try and keep the peace with the locals. The CD programmes have existed since 1993, although the initiative was significantly expanded in 1998. Last year alone, the company implemented programmes in six local villages. RAPP has carried out initiatives such as building a mosque, providing drinking water, building bridges to overcome transportation difficulties and training the villagers to cultivate unused land for productive and profitable uses.

RAPP's budget for CD programmes in 2000 is $2 million and the company's management believes that it is money well spent. Not only does it

▶

benefit the local people but it also promotes good relations with neighbouring communities and improves the skills of potential employees for the pulp and paper mill.

One village called Gunung Sahilan chose to develop oil palm plantations with the company's CD programme funds. As a result, APRIL teamed up with an associated company, Asian Agri, which is active in the palm oil industry. The alliance has worked well and the villagers seem extremely pleased with the project's success. But when asked if he was satisfied, the village chief replied, 'We don't need more, but we want more.' A note of warning to RAPP, perhaps, that it cannot sit back and relax. The company must constantly remain attentive to the demands of the local people just as much as, if not more than, those of the international community.

Table CS 4.2 Plantation supplies at RAPP

		Line 1	Line 1+2A	Line 1+2A+2B
Pulp mill capacity		850,000	1,300,000	2,000,000
Acacia growth rate mean annual increment	m^3/ha/a	30	30	30
Rotation	Yr	7	7	7
Yield at harvest	m^3/ha	210	210	210
Wood to pulp conversion – acacia species	m^3/t/ib	4.5	4.5	4.5
Wood and HTI requirement				
Annual acacia input	m^3/yr	3,825,000	5,850,000	9,000,000
Total net HTI area required	ha	127,500	195,000	300,000
Land resources for tree plantation development				
RAPP HTI concessions area	ha	195,000	195,000	195,000
Associated companies/joint ventures	ha	0	0	85,000
Tree farms	ha	0	0	20,000
Total area	ha	195,000	195,000	300,000

Note: HTI = hutan tanaman industri (local industry requirement)

Source: Jenkinson 2001

According to the Society for the Promotion of Lifecycle Development (SPOLD), life-cycle thinking reflects an acceptance of the fact that key company stakeholders cannot strictly limit their responsibilities to only those phases of the product life-cycle, process or activity in which they are actively involved. This approach expands the scope of their responsibility to include environmental implications for the entire lifecycle of the product, process or activity. The direct effect of this type of thinking is that all processors, manufacturers, distributors, retailers, users and waste managers involved the product lifecycle share responsibility for its effects on the environment.

The individual share of responsibility for each of these actors will be greatest in the parts of the lifecycle under their direct control and least in the other stages of the cycle. Lifecycle thinking has been applied to much of the legislation emanating from the European Commission, especially with regard to products and waste policies. The concept of producer responsibility is at the heart of a waste strategy and it follows from lifecycle thinking. An example of this is given in Figure 4.14.

There are various concepts that are related to developing ecologically sound products. Some of these are as follows.

■ *Design for the environment* There are many initiatives for reducing the negative impacts that a product may unleash on the environment. These effects could be concentrated at the production, usage or disposal stages. In designing for the environment, technologists are concerned with reducing energy consumption (both in the production of an item and when it is in use) and generally conserving resources. The main trends are:
  – the incorporation of information from lifecycle analysis into the designs of products
  – the definition of environmental objectives
  – a focus on the relationship between the product and the consumer and how the design can encourage environmentally responsible behaviour in the consumer.

According to the EPA in the USA (1992), lifecycle design (LCD) is:

A systems-oriented approach for designing more ecologically and economically sustainable product systems, which integrates environmental requirements into the earliest stages of design. In LCD, environmental performance, cost, cultural and legal requirements are balanced.

■ *Clean technology* Clean technology is the means of providing a human benefit that, overall, uses fewer resources and causes less environmental damage than alternative means with which it is in a direct economic competition (Clift 1995).

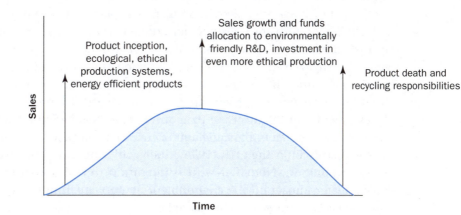

Figure 4.14 **Green lifecycle analysis**
Source: Ranchhod 2001

■ *Industrial ecology* This is generally concerned with the evolution of technology and economic systems in such a way that human activities mimic mature biological systems with regard to being self-contained in their use of materials and resources (Allenby 1994). Governments and non-governmental organisations often use this idea when they assess the sustainability of industrial processes.

■ *Total quality environment management* (TQEM) This concept synthesises environmental management and total quality management (TQM) (GEMI 1993). TQEM relies on the following basic elements:

  – *Identify customers* The definition of quality is dependent on what the customers want (a broad definition of 'customers' is used that includes consumers, legislators, environmental groups and society at large).

  – *Continuous improvement* A systematic approach directed towards continuously improving organisational processes and activities.

  – *Do the job right the first time* In terms of the environment, eliminate problems at the outset. Quality failures may be detrimental to the environment and also incur financial costs, without providing benefits to the consumer.

  – *Take a systems approach* Each part of environmental management is considered to be a 'system'. This includes people, equipment and processes. Weak links in the system should be addressed.

In general, the 'plan-do-check-act' (PDCA) cycle is followed in parallel with typical TQM programmes. All these concepts are interlinked and there is now a concerted approach to take a holistic view by incorporating them into a general framework for sustainable development (SETAC 1998).

Implications for organisations

For organisations, it is becoming increasingly important to incorporate green thinking into their processes and products. Organisations need to consider very carefully how much their activities impact the planet. Any improvement creates a net benefit for both the consumer and the environment. There are many charges against companies that they embrace a green attitude at a superficial level and are generally engaged in 'greenwashing' the public by clever advertising and public relations activities. In fact, even companies such as The Body Shop have been criticised for exaggerating their claims with regard to promoting sustainable development and the purity of their ingredients (Stauber and Rampton 1995). In many cases, companies pursuing a modicum of green policies are not rewarded in the marketplace (Wong et al. 1996). Such criticisms could be levelled at almost every corporation. Nonetheless, it is important to realise that corporations can have a major impact on the environment by implementing some of the concepts discussed above. Here are some examples.

- Anheuser-Busch has developed an aluminium can that is 33 per cent lighter. This reduction in the use of aluminium, combined with an overall recycling plan, saves the company $200 million a year.
- The Ford Motor Company has used more than 60 million two-litre plastic soft drinks bottles in the manufacturing of grille reinforcements, window frames, engine covers and boot carpets. In 1999, this effort accounted for 7.5 million pounds of plastic.
- Kellogg's plant in Bremen, Germany, employs a waste water recycling operation that reduces its water consumption and waste water effluent. In India, a Kellogg vapour absorption system is used to provide the plant's air conditioning, eliminating the use of ozone-depleting substances. Fluorescent bulbs discarded from Kellogg's plant in New Jersey are sent for recycling, removing potentially hazardous materials from landfill sites (Rand Corporation 2000).

Cynical views aside, these efforts not only save the companies concerned millions but also save resources. These types of savings are not easily obtainable from changes to the behaviour of customers, so it is important that companies pursue such strategies. This is evident when you consider that, of the 100 largest economies in the world, 51 are global corporations and only 49 are countries (Anderson and Cavanagh 1996). Mitsubishi was larger than the fourth most populous nation on Earth, Indonesia. General Motors was bigger than Denmark, and Toyota bigger than Norway. Often, large chunks of world trade are actually transactions between different parts of organisations. Companies, therefore, have to be proactive in pursuing ecologically friendly processes and introducing 'green' products. In addition to their moral obligation, they are also under pressure from consumers and NGOs, such as Greenpeace. In the last 20 years, companies have become much more sensitive to such pressures (Bennet and James 1999) due to factors such as the following.

- The growing economic value of a good corporate reputation and a strong, positively regarded brand. These can be put at risk by adverse criticism of environmental and social performance (Fomburn 1996).
- The growing number of customers who are becoming more 'green conscious', taking social and environmental criteria into account when purchasing goods or services.
- The tremendous flow of information, exchanged at unprecedented levels, via satellite TV stations, such as CNN, and the Internet. In the near future, it is likely that information will also be transferred more and more 'on the move' via mobile communication devices such as mobile phones and personal digital assistants (PDAs) that interface with the Internet. This flow of information increases the visibility of any enterprise, all over the world.
- Companies are also dependent on their members of staff who are often more highly educated and environmentally literate than their older counterparts.

Interestingly, a survey of ethical funds shows that they have performed strongly over the past three years. Many funds have shown growth ranging from 73 to 50 per cent (Bien 2001). These are early days, but the current results bode well for ethical and green investments.

What, then, should companies strive to achieve? Some of the key questions that companies should be addressing are given at the end of the chapter, but it should be said here that, in many ways, companies should attempt to get into a virtuous circle and constantly look forward to the future of their R&D (see Figure 4.15).

In addition to the environmental benefits of this type of virtuous way in which companies could operate, the competitive advantages that could also be gained are considerable. Various authors have tried different types of categorisations. For instance, Hart (2000) has developed a sustainability model that can be used by companies to rate themselves on the following scale for each quadrant:

1 non-existent
2 emerging
3 established
4 institutionalised.

Based on this assessment, each individual organisation can look for environmental policy gaps, analyse them to understand their sustainability credentials, and begin to plan both internal and external strategies for the future.

Another way in which to assess the total commitment of a company to sustainability and ethical considerations is to utilise the matrix shown in Figure 4.16.

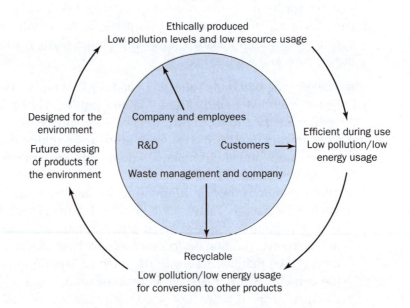

Figure 4.15 The virtuous, sustainable green circle for product management

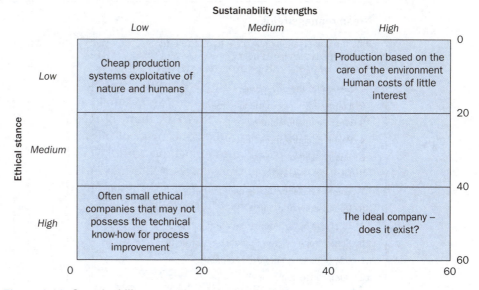

Figure 4.16 **Sustainability strengths and ethical stance matrix**

The questionnaire shown in Figure 4.17 was formulated by analysing various greener organisations (Crosbie and Knight 1995; Peattie and Charter 1997; Piasecki et al. 1999). Companies scoring 12 points in both sets of condsiderations would be put into the top left-hand box of the matrix in Figure 4.16. Companies scoring 60 in both sets of considerations would be placed in the bottom right-hand box. The set of questions is designed to show which box a company fits into and also points the way for future improvement and the opportunities that may be available.

Companies with neither high nor low scores (in the middle of the matrix) can be prone to resorting to strong advertising campaigns and PR in order to 'greenwash' the public. Consumers often have to rely on specialist journals or articles in newspapers for true indications of companies' policies. There is a great danger of companies paying lip-service to green strategies and not necessarily addressing the key issues involved. These issues are explored in detail in the hard-hitting book by Stauber and Rampton (1995). As discussed before, a company that is truly following sustainable principles has to be both ethically and environmentally sound. Customers are realising that we do not live in a world with infinite resources. In fact, the new worldview reflects the fact that we are *a part* of nature and not *apart* from it (Wasik 1996). The postmodern consumer is concerned about nature and likely to look at issues holistically. Table 4.1 sets out old and new worldviews.

Green management

Rate the organisation on a scale from 1 to 5 for each of the issues listed below.

	Very poor 1	Poor 2	Adequate 3	Good 4	Very good 5
1 Design for the environment	☐	☐	☐	☐	☐
2 Energy efficiency in manufacturing	☐	☐	☐	☐	☐
3 Waste in manufacturing	☐	☐	☐	☐	☐
4 Pollution during manufacturing	☐	☐	☐	☐	☐
5 Recyclability of packaging	☐	☐	☐	☐	☐
6 Lifespan of product	☐	☐	☐	☐	☐
7 Energy efficiency during use	☐	☐	☐	☐	☐
8 Recyclability of product	☐	☐	☐	☐	☐
9 Total quality environmental management	☐	☐	☐	☐	☐
10 Search for new green product opportunities	☐	☐	☐	☐	☐
11 Use of pollution control equipment	☐	☐	☐	☐	☐
12 Compliance consulting	☐	☐	☐	☐	☐

Total points ☐

Ethical considerations

Rate the organisation on a scale from 1 to 5 for each of the issues listed below.

	Very poor 1	Poor 2	Adequate 3	Good 4	Very good 5
1 Working conditions	☐	☐	☐	☐	☐
2 Staff welfare and healthcare	☐	☐	☐	☐	☐
3 Limitation of exposure to pollutants	☐	☐	☐	☐	☐
4 Sustainability of operations within local ecology	☐	☐	☐	☐	☐
5 Involvement of stakeholders in evironmental issues	☐	☐	☐	☐	☐
6 Continuous pollution monitoring	☐	☐	☐	☐	☐
7 Management of the end of the lifecycle without affecting others (prevention of dumping in poor areas)	☐	☐	☐	☐	☐
8 Respect for fauna and flora	☐	☐	☐	☐	☐
9 Adequate compensation to local suppliers	☐	☐	☐	☐	☐
10 Honesty in advertising	☐	☐	☐	☐	☐
11 Discussions with NGOs	☐	☐	☐	☐	☐
12 Environment restoration post production	☐	☐	☐	☐	☐

Total points ☐

Figure 4.17 Green management analysis and ethical considerations

Table 4.1 Old versus new paradigms

Old worldview	New worldview
Continuous unbridled growth	Sustainable, green economics
Conquer nature, reap resources	Biophilia (affinity for nature)
Environmental compliance	Eco-auditing
Marketing to fill needs	Marketing to sustain life
Materialism	Personalism
Industrial production	Industrial ecology
Design for obsolescence, disposal	Design for environment
Cost accounting (profit/loss statements)	Full cost accounting
Departmentalism, reductionism	Holism

Source: Wasik 1996

Green consumer behaviour

According to a survey carried out by the Wirthlin Institue (2000), two thirds of American consumers agreed that 'environmental standards cannot be too high and continuing improvements must be made regardless of the costs.' In 1999, a Gallup poll survey found that 68 per cent of Americans worried a great deal about the pollution of drinking water and 53 per cent about the contamination of soil and water by toxic waste. Understanding the complexity of the human–ecological interface requires a degree of scientific knowledge, yet surveys conducted by the National Science Foundation suggest that, even using lenient standards, only about 11 per cent of citizens understand enough of the vocabulary and concepts of science in general to be considered scientifically literate (National Science Foundation 1998).

This is an especially important issue when companies are advertising the green benefits of their products. How many consumers will actually understand the claims made? Are they likely to understand the scientific reasoning behind particular policies or be emotively manipulated by the press in a simplistic manner? Quite often, people are very likely to understand only simple cause-and-effect relationships. According to Coyle, the President of the National Environmental Education & Training Foundation(NEETF) (NEETF/Roper 2000):

> *People understand that cars pollute, or that species become extinct when habitat is destroyed. But when there are two or more steps involved . . . such as energy production from fossil-fuelled power stations contributing to climate change, thereby warming ocean waters sufficiently to inhibit the production of plankton for fish, thus impairing the survival of marine life . . . public understanding drops precipitously.*

Each year, the NEETF issues a ten-question survey on environmental awareness. In a typical year, Americans averaged fewer than 25 per cent correct answers to basic environmental literacy questions. Furthermore, myths and misconceptions persist. Surveys indicate that many Americans still believe that rubbish bags can be made to biodegrade in landfills (virtually nothing degrades in landfills). Many people still believe that aerosol cans contain ozone-destroying ingredients (chlorofluorocarbons (CFCs) were banned from aerosols in 1978) and that landfills are brimming with plastic (plastic accounts for just 9 per cent of municipal solid waste – paper and cardboard make up four times as much).

This can be illustrated by the 'Energy and environmental profile analysis of children's single-use and reusable cloth diapers' carried out by Franklin Associates in 1992 and explained in Fuller (1999). For many consumers, the intuitive understanding is that plastic/paper nappies are vastly energy consuming and polluting. The comparative scientific analysis, however, shows that the environmental answers are not clear cut. The results show that:

- reusable cloth nappies consume 33 per cent more energy than single-use disposables and 12 per cent more energy than cloth nappies from nappy laundering services.
- disposable single-use nappies produce about twice the total solid waste by volume of reusable or cloth nappies from nappy laundering services.
- reusable cloth napppies produce nearly twice the total atmospheric emissions in comparison with single-use disposables or cloth nappies from nappy laundering services.
- reusable or nappies from laundering services produce about seven times the total water-borne waste of single-use disposables.
- the manufacture of reusable or cloth nappies from laundering services consumes more than twice the water volume used for single-use disposables.

Many criticisms can be levelled at such an analysis and, indeed, some authors argue that single-use disposables also contribute to air pollution, via incineration. They may also be the cause of allergic skin reactions. Nonetheless, this example illustrates the complexity of the issues involved when undertaking a lifecycle analysis for a product. In these circumstances, consumers should also be able to follow complex arguments in order to make valid judgements.

Roper-Starch Worldwide (Rand Corporation 2000), which publishes the 'Green Gauge Report' each year on the environment and environmentally conscious purchase decisions, showed how consumer attitudes broke down in its 2000 survey.

- *11 per cent true blue greens* The recyclers, composters, letter-writers and volunteers of the world – the ones most likely to go out of their way to buy organic foods, recycled paper products, rechargeable batteries, less toxic paints and other goods with environmentally preferable attributes.
- *5 per cent greenback greens* Those who will contribute to environmental organisations or spend more to buy green products, but not consider changes in lifestyles or housekeeping due to environmental concerns.
- *33 per cent sprouts* Those who care about the environment, but will only spend slightly more for environmentally sensitive products.
- *18 per cent grousers* These are people who care about the environment, but view it as someone else's problem. Grousers don't seek environmentally sensitive goods or consider green-minded lifestyle changes.
- *33 per cent basic browns* People who are essentially unconcerned about the environment.

There is another, more traditional, way of categorising consumers.

- *Traditionalists* Those who believe in the nostalgic image of small towns and conservative churches.
- *Moderns* These are individuals who are more materialistic and consumption orientated. They are generally individuals who see life through the same filters as *Time* magazine.
- *The cultural creatives* This is a new category, discussed by Dr Paul Ray (Rand Corporation 2000) as a result of market research studies in consumer behaviour. The cultural creatives (CCs) have often been involved in, or care about, three to six social movements, including:
  - very strong concern about the environment
  - concern for the condition of the whole planet
  - civil rights
  - peace
  - social justice
  - new spiritualities
  - organic food
  - holistic health.

Many follow personal paths and spiritual goals. These individuals account for a high proportion of people using alternative healthcare products and other lifestyles of health and sustainability (LOHAS) products and services. These individuals are very good at putting their own big picture together from a diverse range of sources of information. They compare and contrast, attempting to understand the real issues. They are the least likely to be 'greenwashed' by aggressive advertising. In addition to this, to fully appreciate the sustainable lifestyle, the Natural Business Communications and the Natural Marketing Institute believe that the premier paradigm of such an existence is LOHAS. The LOHAS market comprises five core market segments – sustainable economy, healthy lifestyles, personal development, alternative healthcare and ecological lifestyles. The five segments combined represented a $226.8 billion market in the USA and an estimated $546 billion global market in 2000. Within each of these five segments there are many specific categories of products and services across a vast array of businesses and industries. Table 4.2 shows the total sizes for the five key LOHAS segments and the associated industry categories.

Table 4.2 Key LOHAS segments and industries

LOHAS market segment	Total (in $ millions)
Sustainable economy	76,470
Healthy lifestyles	27,811
Alternative healthcare	30,698
Personal development (mind, body, spirit)	10,628
Ecological lifestyles	81,178
Total LOHAS market in USA	226.8 billion

Source: Rand Corporation 2000 and www.naturalbusiness.com

The 'ecological lifestyles' and 'sustainable economy' segments represent nearly 75 per cent of the global market, if the USA's figures are emulated around the world. Considering the complexity of the green consumer profile, several interrelated factors have to be taken into account, as shown later in Figure 4.18. However, the examples and discussions presented above show that a new breed of consumers is indeed emerging. These new consumers are characterised by their need to protect the environment and lead an ethically correct lifestyle. The market trends show that these consumers are growing in numbers. Companies wishing to understand this new segment of potential customers need to address their marketing offer in a sensible and honest manner. They also need to consider the ways in which markets may move in the future.

Green marketing strategies

In many cases, companies take reactive stances to green issues. The lack of proactive initiatives often damages the credibility of a company and the profitability of products that are sold. It is therefore important for companies that are seriously concerned about green issues to be more proactive and pursue a market orientation that is green in its design. In order to gain competitive advantage, companies have to exhibit that they are:

- offering products that address the ethical, moral and sustainability issues described above.
- producing goods that are not only commercially viable but also meet consumers' needs
- using some of the profits for environmental and social improvement at the source of production
- segmenting markets effectively, so that the complexity of niche markets and these 'new' consumers are understood and targeted accordingly
- communicating honest and credible messages to customers, which should be transparent and understood by internal and external stakeholders, as well as consumers
- ensuring that their transportation and logistics systems are mirroring the company's aims and objectives of lessening pollution, being environmentally friendly and so on
- developing a marketing perspective that takes a cradle-to-grave ecological approach for products
- offering certain levels of educational marketing literature where products are complex
- presenting advertising in a clear and concise manner
- understanding the *future* needs of customers and stakeholders.

The case studies that follow are examples of how companies are dealing with green issues and facing consumer reluctance to purchase green goods in spite of good intentions. They are taken from Makower (2005).

CASE STUDY

Green marketing: lessons from the leaders

Electrolux: efficiency = green

The Swedish appliance giant doesn't go out of its way to market its products as environmental, says Karl Edsjö, Project Manager, Electrolux Sustainability Department in Stockholm. The company promotes products' energy-saving advantages on labels, but that is required in both Europe and the USA. However, the company does play up its products' efficiency. 'It's worked very well to educate people about energy', says Edsjö. 'If they choose the most efficient product, that's the most important thing for us.'

Promoting 'efficiency' has unwittingly translated into 'green' for Electrolux, leading consumers to 'assume our products are environmentally friendly,' Edsjö told me. That reputation also reduces pressure on Electrolux when new environmental concerns arise. For example, there is growing concern in some European countries over the health and environmental impacts of some flame retardants. 'It's a small concern at the moment, but we're pretty sure this will be a bigger issue in the future,' says Edsjö. He believes that Electrolux's reputation for environmental proactivity will make the company immune from consumer activism on this issue. 'They know that as soon as there is a solution, we will apply it to all our products.'

'To inform consumers is tricky,' says Edjsö. 'We'd like them to be more environmentally aware. We have a principle of both delivering the best technology, but also marketing it well to promote it well.' But despite its green image and its holistic thinking, even Electrolux can get frustrated by consumers' less than willingness to embrace some company efforts aimed at aligning environmental sustainability with business success. For example, it piloted an initiative in Sweden in which consumers were given a washing machine (for a small installation fee), then charged on a per use basis of 10 Swedish kronor (about US$1). One objective was that the consumer didn't have to worry about the appliance, relying on Electrolux to keep the most efficient machines in operation, thereby minimising their energy and water needs.

The programme was met with a decisive yawn by consumers, who apparently didn't want to change the way that they paid for doing their washing at home. Edsjö believes the experiment may have been doomed by flawed methodology and hopes it will be revived some day. As he puts it, 'It's resting – but there's still some big interest.'

Philips: durability trumps green

Netherlands-based Philips' flagship environmental consumer products are compact fluorescent lightbulbs (CFLs), which it has marketed since 1978. For years, energy-saving and longer-lasting CFLs languished in the US market, despite their success in Europe, which experiences much higher energy costs. (The penetration rate for CFLs in Holland, where Philips is based, is around 50 per cent, compared with less than 10 per cent in the USA). Among other things, US consumers didn't care for the quality of CFLs' light output and the fact that they didn't fit many existing lighting fixtures.

Things changed as the bulbs got cheaper, the quality of their light better and their adaptability into various fixtures increased. Equally important was a key name change that reflected some green-marketing realities: Philips stopped calling the bulb 'Earth Light' and changed the name to 'Marathon'.

'After sales flattened, we went out and did primary research to find out why and whether we were reaching the hearts and minds of the audience with the name Earth Light,' explains Steve Goldmacher, Director, Corporate Communications for Philips Lighting in the USA.

In its research, Philips found a great deal of sympathy (50 per cent positive, 25 per cent neutral) for green issues, combined with outright fear (60 per cent positive, 10 per cent neutral). And almost half (45 per cent) appear to be quite sympathetic to green marketing efforts, requiring additional information about the environmental benefits of the products they buy. Nevertheless, a much lower percentage are willing to change their lifestyles (20 per cent) or pay more (25 per cent).

'It turned out the environment wasn't their primary need,' says Goldmacher. 'Environmental responsibility was the number four or five purchase criterion. Number one is that they wanted the bulb to last longer. The longer a lightbulb lasted was the most important criteria. Being green is wonderful, but no one wants to pay the extra nickel.'

Toyota: green without compromise

Toyota's Prius may be the first major consumer product that fits nearly all of the criteria for success in the green consumer marketplace. it comes from a trusted company and can be bought wherever the company's products are sold; it looks and feels like a 'conventional' product and doesn't require consumers to change their habits to use it; it is (almost) comparably priced to purchase and can save consumers money to operate; and it has added benefits – it both saves money and it's stylishly cool. But when the Prius was launched in the USA market in 2000, Toyota didn't play up its environmental attributes, according to Ed La Roque, National Advanced Technology Vehicle Manager. The emphasis was on saving petrol and money. Those early marketing efforts were aimed at early adapters – the technology buffs who want the latest, coolest thing – today's iPod crowd. Environmentalists were a relatively small subset of that population. The product's original tagline was 'Prius/genius', showing 'not only the intelligence of the new technology but also the creative Web-based marketing approach'. The first 2000 or so vehicles were sold online – a key medium for early adopters.

Before rolling out the Prius, Toyota embarked on a two-year effort to develop a dialogue with consumers. That resulted in a pool of more than 40,000 interested consumers – or 'hand-raisers', in industry-speak. These prospects were given early access to a Prius website and its special order feature. 'Our focus groups and studies confirmed that people want an environmentally friendly product at a fair price, but that they didn't want any compromises,' says La Roque.

Of course, Toyota turned to an increasingly green message, says La Roque: 'We are really talking about gallons saved and the positive impact on the environment. I think a lot of it has to do with the Middle East situation and global warming. The whole environmental focus has come more to the forefront.' One key ally has been celebrities: 'The Hollywood community really embraced Prius,' says La Roque. 'There are a number of celebrity owners. It's their way of making a statement. And it's been a great benefit for us to have that unsolicited testimonial.' Example: Cameron Diaz appeared on the '*Tonight Show*' the day she picked up her Prius and made it part of the interview.

Toyota has since transitioned to the current phase – what it calls the 'early majority buyer – sort of in between early adopter and mainstream,' explains La Roque. Success – in the form of months-long waiting lists for the Prius and the rush to market by Toyota's competitors with other hybrid models – shows the strategy's success.

In the end, however, the Prius' success was all about quality: 'It's very important that companies interested in promoting environmental products deliver,' says La Roque. 'We think we've delivered a great product for the market. We like to think we set a good example for other companies selling hybrids. There's no doubt that we get a good halo effect on the overall Toyota brand.'

Source: Makower, 18 September 2005

A UNEP report (2005a) discusses how marketing could help to change social attitudes towards consumption. In essence, as discussed above, consumer behaviour results from a range of interactions between factors such as public policy, cultural identity, media coverage of sustainability issues and corporate marketing, not to mention cultural imprints, as well as societal and family influences. This complexity increases the difficulty of assessing the impact of marketing efforts on consumer behaviour, as the range of variables can be extremely high. The variables can range from product features, service augmentation, pricing, promotion, retail strategy, distribution or credit offers, to name just a few. Within this context, it is instructive to look at these interactions as set out in Figure 4.18.

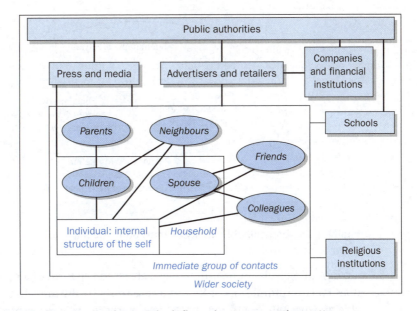

Figure 4.18 Structure and networks influencing consumption patterns

Source: UNEP 2005a, ADE. 'Talk the Walk: Advancing sustainable lifestyles through marketing and communications' www.uneptie.org/pc/sustain/reports/advertising/Talk_the_Walk.pdf United Nations Environment Programme

Companies sometimes feel that they are blamed for unsustainable consumption, even though they make efforts to inform consumers, and this is encapsulated in the following quote (Procter & Gamble 2003):

> *Despite contributions to sustainable development, advertising's role and effects have been questioned. Advertising has been blamed for spreading Western lifestyles around the world and for promoting excessive consumption in developed countries.*

This is an interesting proposition, as the model in Figure 4.18 shows multiple influences on consumption patterns. According to MORI (2003), 74 per cent of the UK's public surveyed would purchase from companies that promulgated an ethical and green policy if they had the information available to them. This offers a golden opportunity to companies to market and advertise their products and services accordingly.

One of the key arguments put forward in UNEP's report is a model that incorporates three different areas of marketing to encourage sustainable lifestyles marketing. As explained earlier, according to the LOHAS segmentation criteria, large segments of the population are interested in sustainable lifestyles encompassing a range of different products and services. This model incorporates the following types of marketing (see Figure 4.19).

Responsible marketing

Some companies are beginning to embrace policies and strategies to promote sustainable behaviour to consumers, especially regarding overconsumption of food or

Figure 4.19 A sustainable lifestyles marketing model

alcohol that results in health damage, either in the form of alcohol-related diseases or obesity. For example, according to a case study by Business in the Community (available at: www.bitc.org.uk/resources/case_studies/cola_market.html):

> *Coca-Cola Great Britain is responding to the challenge through a total business approach led by a cross-functional senior management team. Four key areas of strategic focus are actively being addressed. (1) Providing and raising awareness of a widening choice of products, particularly making diet and low-sugar choices more attractive through continuing taste enhancement. (2) Helping consumers make a more informed choice. Their consumer research showed that around 43 per cent of consumers did not know that diet Coke is 'sugar-free' and it suggested that a 'sugar-free' message is more motivating to consumers than the actual number of calories listed. The 'sugar-free' message now features on all diet Coke packs. (3) Ensure responsible sales and marketing, by reinforcing their 50-year policy of not targeting under 12s in any media, upholding their Schools Code of Practice including its commitment to not place vending machines in primary schools and give secondary schools the opportunity to provide a wide choice of products from water, 100 per cent juice, a variety of diet, low-sugar as well as regular carbonated drinks, and as well as offering unbranded machines. (4) Encouraging physical activity amongst young people and thereby challenge the rise in sedentary lifestyles.*

Green marketing

This area of marketing is largely concerned with environmental value-added propositions related to the product that is being sold to the consumer. Such value addition could consist of many of the points previously discussed, such as packaging, environmentally safe production techniques, recyclability, reusability, environmentally friendly sourcing and so on. Good examples of this have been provided in the form of the e-goods dial diagram produced by Greenpeace (see Figure 4.12).

Social marketing

This area of marketing is regarded by many authors as related to advertising and public relations. Its main application is linked to programmes aimed at raising awareness and promoting sustainable behaviour (McKenzie-Mohr and Smith 1999). Often, these programmes are promoted by local councils or government information offices and attempt to increase the adoption of positive social behaviour, such as recycling, sensible eating, low energy usage or low car usage, among many other initiatives. For instance, a 'buy recycled' campaign was launched by the King County Commission staff in 1993, in Washington State. The programme was essentially a partnership with retailers to boost sales of recycled products. Every element of the campaign strategy was designed to do one of three things:

- show consumers the importance of buying recycled
- tell them where they could buy recycled content products
- show them existing product choices.

In the end, the campaign produced good results with sales of recycled paper towels, napkins, and toilet tissue increasing by 74 per cent (see www.toolsofchange.com/English/firstsplit.asp).

As marketing evolves in the future, these areas of importance will need to overlap regularly when companies develop and execute their strategies. Understanding green consumer behaviour is a difficult and complex matter because of all the factors that influence decision-making and consumption in this area. In order to embrace all the complexity of this process, the model represented in Figure 4.19 has to be cross-related with the key points highlighted in Figure 4.20).

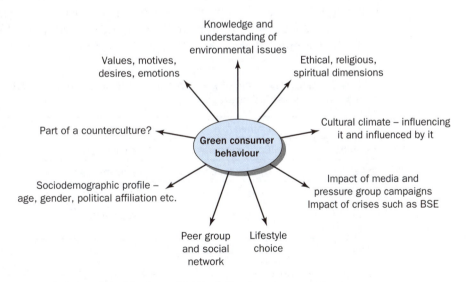

Figure 4.20 Interrelated factors affecting green consumer behaviour
Source: Adapted from Wagner 1997

As the environment is a pivotal point to the survival of the human race, marketers have a duty to not only anticipate consumers' needs but also form them, so that better consumption decisions are made. Companies are beginning to take cognisance of this, but, unfortunately, the majority of consumers are lagging behind. Future technological and biotechnological advances could spell either triumphs or disasters for the environment. Already there is considerable disquiet over the introduction of GM foods. The way in which foods are produced, distributed, commercialised and perceived has radically changed in the last 20 years as a result of the advent of new technologies such as genetic engineering.

The creation of genetically modified foods (GM) and organisms (GMO) has increased the general public's awareness of the production and quality of foods. The main concern over GM foods centres on the fact that they have not been tested conclusively in people's diets using rigorous standards (Cottrill 1998). The negative perceptions surrounding GM foods lie deep in the myths and fears of modern civilisation – the expression 'Frankenstein foods' is a good example (MacMillan 2000). Given these negative and, in many cases, serious concerns about the possible consequences of the environmental spread of 'rogue' genes via cross-pollination, the public are concerned about clarity of messages and product labelling. As a reaction against GM foods and continuing health scares, organic food sales have grown rapidly. The growing consumption of organic foods is seen, by many, as ecologically friendly and sustainable. Therefore, developing marketing strategies that entice, educate and excite consumers in favour of products and services that are sustainable is crucial. Table 4.3 illustrates the possible strategies that companies should adopt when attempting to expand sustainable consumption.

According to Datamonitor, organic sales in the USA reached $5.4 billion in 1998 and were estimated at $6.4 billion in 1999. Datamonitor (1999) projected that sales will continue to grow at approximately 20 per cent per year, reaching $7.76 billion in the year 2000, $9.35 billion in 2001, slightly more than $11 billion in 2002 and slightly more than $13 billion in 2003. Sales during the 1990s grew by

Table 4.3 The evolving role of green products and sustainable lifestyles marketing in mainstream companies' strategies

	Limited role	Reactive role	Proactive role
Inspiration	Copy poineers	Acquire pioneers	Be pioneer
Target	Opinion leaders	Niche market	Mass market
Attribute to brands	None	Differentiating	Entry stake
Claims backed by	No evidence	Green labels	Green labels + Product reporting
Connection with lobbying	Supports defensive lobbying	Disconnected	Supported by positive lobbying
Other marketing practices	Opposed/disconnected	Compliance-driven	Aligned with sustainability goals

Source: Utopies 2005, www.utopies.com/docs/UtopiesRapport_fr.pdf

20–24 per cent per year and organic produce sales in the UK now top £1.6 billion (Lawrence 2006). Organic produce still remains the leading category, although such categories as organic frozen foods, organic dairy, organic bakery items/cereals, organic baby food and organic ready meals are growing at a faster rate. Another aspect of future consumer trends may be the need for convenience, access to products and a desire to be free from material possessions.

It is quite possible that, in the future, companies may have to design products that can be shared between different individuals. For instance, cars could be pooled within cities and individuals could subscribe to leasing and using cars as and when necessary, picking them up and dropping them at their destination. Many other items, including recreation products such as surfboards, could be leased in such a manner. This type of consumption points the way towards a shared existence, away from the individualistic pursuit of gathering material goods.

Summary

This chapter has outlined the major environmental threats to the planet stemming from the consumption patterns of organisations and consumers. It has also shown the way in which companies can look at what being green means and how they can translate this into effective action and competitive advantage. It is clear that consumption patterns and consumer actions are going to change as we move further into the twenty-first century.

Marketing has a key role to play in the greening of companies and issues relating to the environment and in developing consumer tastes that benefit and protect the natural environment. At the same time, it offers a chance to improve the social status of poorer and less well-endowed sections of the developing world. Sustainability issues and ethics go hand in hand and the opportunities that exist are immense for companies that can think and act holistically in meeting the growing demand for greener products. At the same time, there is a great onus on and opportunity for marketers to begin to change consumer behaviour to create a sustainable future for the world.

Chapter questions

1 How difficult is it for companies to embrace green marketing strategies?

2 How is consumer behaviour likely to change in the future?

3 How can companies develop strategies for implementing green consumer behaviour?

5 Communicating effectively

Introduction

Since the 1990s, integrated marketing communications (IMC) has influenced both the theory and practice of communication management. The complex shift from the nineteenth-century 'product'-centred approach to that of the twentieth century's 'customer' approach and twenty-first century's 'stakeholder' model, have determined the rapid evolution of the marketing communication concept.

The emergence and the development of IMC has been facilitated by a number of evolutionary trends in various marketing areas. These include the increased fragmentation and segmentation of markets, relationship marketing and direct marketing (Durkin and Lawlor 2001; Eagle and Kitchen 2000), information technology – the development of new communication technologies and database applications (Kitchen and Schultz 1999; McKim 2002) and communication – increased fragmentation of media audiences, multiplicity and saturation of media channels (Hackley and Kitchen 1998). From this perspective, the new paradigm of IMC can be represented as a strategic answer to the social and business conditions of postmodern society (Proctor and Kitchen 2002).

The IMC approach received almost instant recognition as a result of the trend at the end of the 1990s for companies to reduce budgets allocated to mass advertising campaigns and concentrate on segmented or personalised communication with final consumers. The increased fragmentation of media and customers, as well as the revolution introduced in mass communication by the new communication channels – the Internet and mobile communication technologies – has created the need for a new approach to marketing communication, one that can ensure centralised management and consistency of corporate messages sent to various audiences.

In the traditional marketplace, business organisations had almost total control over the communication process. They dictated the messages to be transmitted via selected channels and the pace of communication, treating their audiences as passive receptors. This environment allowed the application of an 'inside out' organisational philosophy, in which business organisations attempted to reach annual targets in terms of sales volume and market share without considering the customers or prospects as the key to their success. The traditional marketplace has therefore been built on reaching short-term goals and returns, and not necessarily looking at long-term sustainability.

The evolution of information and communication technology (ICT) and the rapid development of the Internet in the last ten years have had a profound impact on traditional marketing paradigms and practices (see Table 5.1). Most importantly, though, the Internet has fundamentally changed the classical communication procedures, because of three specific and coexistent characteristics that differentiate it from any other communication channel. These are its:

- *interactivity* the Internet offers multiple possibilities for interactive communication, acting not only as an interface but also as a communication agent (allowing direct interaction between individuals and software applications)
- *transparency* the information published online can be accessed and viewed by any Internet user, unless it is specifically protected
- *memory* the Web is a channel not only for transmitting information but also for storing it – in other words, the information published on the Web remains in the memory of the network until it is erased.

These options are transforming the profile and behaviour of online audiences. Marketing communication practitioners should therefore adapt to the new realities of how audiences get and use information.

- *The audience is connected to the organisation* Detachment was one of the characteristics of the old communication model. Practitioners issued messages that were distributed via various communication channels and published in the media's outlets. Any challenge to the facts or conclusions of the communication surfaced via other channels and came to the practitioner's attention, leaving plenty of time to craft an appropriate response.

Table 5.1 The new marketing paradigm shift determined by the Internet

From	*To*	*Sources*
One-to-many communication	Many-to-many communication	Hoffman and Novak 1996
Mass marketing	Individualised marketing	Martin 1996
Monologue	Dialogue	Blattberg and Deighton 1996
Branding	Communication	Martin 1996
Supply-side thinking	Demand-side thinking	Rayport and Sviokla 1995
Megabrand	Diversity	Martin 1996
Centralised market	Decentralised market	Blattberg et al. 1994
Customer as a target	Customer as a partner	McKenna 1995
Segmentations	Communities	Armstrong and Hagel III 1996

Source: Kiani (1998)

The traditional communication channels were uni-directional – the institutions communicated and the audiences consumed the information in newspapers or on TV or radio. Even when communication was considered a two-way process, the institutions had the resources to send information through a very wide pipeline, while the audiences had only a minuscule pipeline for communicating back to institutions (letters or phone calls).

Now, however, the communication channel is a network, not a pipeline. This network has closed the gap between institution and audience. Everybody involved in sending the message – the company, its CEO, its communication manager, the external communication agency – are only a click away from the audience. To some extent, communicators have grasped and even embraced this new proximity – a fact demonstrated by the vast number of websites that display 'Contact us' buttons and links. Unfortunately, in most cases, these new facilities are not fully used. The ease of instant communication for the general public has led to an exponential increase in the number of incoming messages, but organisations have not increased the resources needed to deal with them. Many companies simply do not respond at all to most of the queries. Such neglect of the new proximity of the audience is risky because the cultural expectation attached to an e-mail enquiry is that there will be a near-instantaneous response. In the new model, communicators have to engage members of the audience on a one-to-one basis.

- *The audience is interconnected* Considering the nature of the network, if the audience is one click away from the institution, it is also one click away from other members of the audience. The communicator has to take into consideration this interconnectedness and, if possible, control its effects. Today, a company's activity can be discussed and debated on the Internet without the knowledge of that organisation. In the new environment, everybody is a communicator and the institution is just part of the network.

- *The audience has access to other information* In the past, because of the slowness and difficulty of accessing information, the communicator was able to make a statement and be reasonably certain that it would be impossible for the average audience member to challenge it. Today, the situation is different. It takes a matter of minutes to access multiple sources of information on the Internet. Any statement made can be dissected, analysed, discussed and challenged within hours by interested individuals. In the connected world, information does not exist in a vacuum.

- *Audiences pull information* Until relatively recently, television offered only a few channels. People communicated with one another by post and phone. In these conditions, it was easy for a marketing communication practitioner to emphasise and highlight a specific message. However, the networked world has increased exponentially the number of available channels of communication. Now we can get simultaneous messages from various media – e-mail, voice mail, faxes, web pages, mobile phones, interoffice memos, overnight courier packages, television (with hundreds of channels), traditional and Internet radio . . . As a result, the media that used to provide efficient channels of communication for practitioners have become noise that most the audiences have learned to filter out. The networked environment provides audiences with a new model in which they are no longer forced to accept every message a communicator wants to push at them, but, instead, they pull the information that suits their interests and needs. In the networked environment, information has to be available where audiences can find it and it needs to be customised or customisable.

Therefore, in comparison with the traditional customer, the Internet user has more control over the communication process and can adopt a more proactive attitude, expressed by the capacity to:

- easily search, select and access information using search and meta-search engines, intelligent agents and so on
- contact online organisations or other individuals using e-mail, chat or discussion forums
- express their opinions/views in a visible and lasting manner by creating and storing online content.

As consumers gain more and more access to information, knowledge and technology, the power is shifting from marketer and channel to consumer. In addition, the organisation needs to embrace a broader perspective that includes in its communication plan various categories of stakeholders. In the twenty-first century marketplace, stakeholders are not only the individuals or the institutions contacted by the organisation but also whoever the organisation listens and responds to. In these conditions, the company is no longer the supreme controller and coordinator of business communication, so the traditional inside-out approach has to be replaced by an outside-in philosophy. Organisations are forced more than ever to establish closer social relationships with various categories of stakeholders in order to preserve and develop their corporate brand equity. In these circumstances, IMC has moved on from being simply a method of coordinating and aligning external messages sent to relevant customers towards a more holistic view of communication as the backbone of the entire business strategy.

The following case study presents the challenges of communicating a coherent message via multiple media channels while at the same time targeting various audiences.

CASE STUDY

The ad revolution will not be televised *(Owen Gibson)*

After years of tiresome doomsday predictions, we're finally starting to see evidence of the old broadcast models of advertising being challenged by the advance of technology. A seismic shift is under way.

Predictions of the demise of television advertising have been around so long the doomsayers were starting to look rather like the men bearing sandwich boards at Speaker's Corner.

But all the signs are that those predictions are starting to come true, albeit in a far more complex and subtle way than originally envisaged during the first stirrings of the dotcom boom.

▶

Among most advertisers, agencies and media companies there is a growing consensus that the old broadcast models of advertising are being eroded by the march of technology and that new models will have to be found to promote their products.

Consider the growing ubiquity of broadband access and the impending switch to digital television by 2012 that will accelerate the ongoing fragmentation of television viewing across hundreds of channels.

Then combine those trends with the upsurge in personal video recorder technology and the tendency for younger viewers to watch less TV in favour of sharing their own words, pictures, music and movies online and you can see why the behemoths of the media world are being forced into action by their advertising paymasters.

These trends were borne out by a recent study from media regulator Ofcom, showing that it is among younger consumers that have grown up with the Internet and mobile phones that these shifts in media consumption are most pronounced.

It showed that television viewing had fallen for the first time in the medium's history. The decline was most pronounced among those aged 16 to 24. In the US, where broadband penetration is even more widespread, those under 25 now spend more time on the Internet than watching television – and a recent survey by Google on this side of the Atlantic suggests that we now do the same in the UK.

The effect of these changing media habits is now having a material effect on advertising spending, with knock-on consequences for everything from the future of ITV to product placement in programmes to the way in which independent producers operate.

Carat UK's Managing Director Neil Jones is head of a media agency that spends more than £600m a year buying advertising space on behalf of clients including Guinness and Renault. For him, the effect of these trends is clear.

The potency of television is definitely decreasing but it will remain a major factor for years to come. For owners of big multinational brands like Coca-Cola, Unilever and Procter & Gamble it's still the most powerful way of building and launching a brand.

Viral ads

But according to Jones and others at the sharp end, those companies are also actively reducing the amount they spend on television in favour of boosting their Internet budgets and so-called 'direct response' advertising – anything from online viral ads to traditional mail campaigns.

Unilever, the consumer goods giant, has said that during the last five years around a fifth of its £300m ad budget was shifted out of television and into outdoor posters, online and sponsorship, such as Flora's long-running association with the London Marathon.

Meanwhile, the PVR effect is starting to make its presence felt now that the devices, which allow viewers to easily record shows as well as pause and rewind live TV, are in a meaningful number of homes. Over 1.3 million people now use the technology, with the majority fast forwarding through the adverts on recorded shows.

Already advertisers are looking to combat the trend – a recent KFC advert in the US challenged viewers to slow down rather than speed up the footage in order to uncover a special offer hidden in one of the frames. And the next generation of PVR technology is likely to mark the first steps towards delivering adverts, as well as programmes, on demand based on viewer's needs and preferences.

As the boom in search-based advertising on the Internet has proved, if advertisers are sure that they are accurately targeting a receptive audience they will pay a huge premium. Meanwhile event television, that viewers will tune in to watch live, which could be anything from the World Cup to Dancing on Ice, will become increasingly vital.

Increased broadband penetration and download speeds are only likely to accelerate the trend for on-demand viewing, with its attendant implications for advertisers, and all major broadcasters are investing heavily in their broadband strategies.

Channel 4's Chief Executive Andy Duncan recently forecast that by 2016, 'the majority of all programmes will be consumed in an on-demand way, whether through personal video recorders or video-on-demand over the Internet'.

As a result of these trends the amount spent on traditional television advertising on the main channels such as ITV1 is declining, while the amount spent on the Web is booming. But it's not simply a case of television money flowing into the Internet.

Advertising experts are agreed that the impact is much more complicated but that one net effect is that brands will increasingly have to engage with individual consumers rather than hoping to catch their attention with traditional catch-all ads.

The response among traditional media giants has not quite been the outright panic-buying spree that characterised the late 1990s, but has again been heavily reliant on opening the chequebook. Rupert Murdoch's News Corp. splashed out $400m on social networking phenomenon MySpace.com, while NBC paid $600m for women's community site iVillage.com.

Holistic view

Advertisers are demanding a more holistic view from their agencies, asking them to consider how to tap into younger consumers via blogs, social networking sites, advertiser-funded content and viral advertising.

The latter, which involves making branded messages so engaging and interesting that Web users feel compelled to send them on to friends, has come of age during the past two years and its proponents say it is now an established part of the advertising world.

'We're seeing a new wave of interest because brands are looking for new forms of media and new marketing techniques,' says Will Jeffery, Managing Director of viral advertising agency Maverick.

The sector has its own awards ceremonies, has been utilised by many of the world's biggest brands and is integrated more tightly into overall campaigns.

'You're not talking to someone who thinks you're talking in Martian,' says Chris Hassell, a director at digital agency Ralph, which has worked for clients including Sky, Nickelodeon, Orange and Nintendo. 'There's more respect. Digital agencies have been established for five to ten years. They no longer think we're a bunch of guys in a shed banging out websites and so they involve us much earlier in the process.'

But it is no coincidence that the most downloaded ads tend to be those, such as Volkswagen's recreation of 'Singing in the Rain', that work creatively in any medium.

In the short term, Hassell believes that advertisers will increasingly release adverts on the Internet first as a means of creating a buzz around a particular clip. Many industry experts believe that the tumultuous next five years will be looked back on as a seismic shift in the way that advertisers reach their customers.

But far from the doomsday scenario originally predicted, for savvy advertisers the explosion in media choice and the new age of user-generated content could prove as much of an opportunity as a threat. And as the computer in the study and the television in the living room increasingly merge, they will be afforded new routes into the lives of consumers if they can come up with new ways to tap into them.

Source: Owen Gibson, *The Guardian*, 20 March 2006. Copyright Guardian News and Media Ltd 2006.

The multiplicity of media and alternative sources of information raise important challenges for the effective management of corporate image and corporate identity.

Corporate image and corporate identity

Previous research into understanding the process of corporate image formation has concentrated both on the process of creating and projecting the corporate image by the organisation and the process of reception of the corporate image by the members of the audience (Kazoleas et al. 2001).

The research orientated towards marketing, advertising and consumer behaviour has suggested that commercial organisations create images in order to foster increased sales. One of the main findings of the consumer behaviour orientation is that multiple images are used by various segments of customers and these images are variable and subject to constant change (Ackerman 1990; Knoll and Tankersley 1991).

Business management research, compared to the multiple images that individuals have, seems to favour the term 'corporate identity' and argues that this identity is primarily a form of social identification and association between the employees and organisation (Carlivati 1990; Pratt and Foreman 2000).

Public relations research, on the other hand, has argued that image is created by interaction between the organisation and the organisation's audiences during a complex communication process (Alvesson 1990; Fombrun and Shanley 1990). One particular conceptualisation of image formation is built on the cultural model of meaning, which acknowledges that meanings (images) are generated not only by multiple kinds of factors, but also through the intersection or struggle among these factors. This vision emphasises the dynamic, flexible and conflictual nature of corporate image formation (Williams and Moffitt 1997).

This conflictual model for corporate image formation (see Figure 5.1) encompasses the way in which organisations are having to create their corporate image, especially in an age where communication is possible irrespective of time and space, covering a myriad of instantaneous views. Each of these views could be different from the one that the company is trying to portray. Reaching the 'best fit' model for the corporate image is therefore crucial.

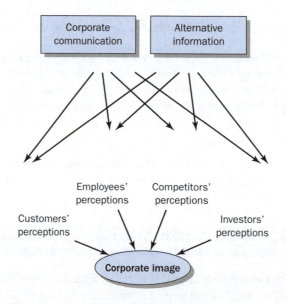

Figure 5.1 The 'conflictual' process of image formation

Defining the IMC concept

The concept of IMC has been defined in many different, often contradictory, ways (Duncan 2002; Kitchen 1999; Schultz et al. 1993; Shimp 2000; Smith et al. 1997). The integration of marketing communication procedures was considered a result of centralised management, centralised budgeting or message similarity across all communication channels.

The American Association of Advertising Agencies (AAAA) defined IMC as follows:

> *IMC is a concept of marketing communications planning that recognises the added value of a comprehensive plan, that evaluates the strategic roles of a variety of communication disciplines – for example, general advertising, direct response, sales promotion, and PR – and combines these disciplines to provide clarity, consistency, and maximum communications impact.*

According to Pickton and Broderick (2001), marketing communications tools that were traditionally separated and specialised into 'above-the-line' and 'below-the-line' activities have been challenged by the IMC concept. The definition highlights that an alignment of various communication functions increases communication efficiency, based on the premise of synergy. Pickton and Broderick (2001) claim that synergy is the principal benefit of bringing together the various facets of marketing communications in a mutually supportive way. The IMC concept fosters the so-called 'zero-based' thinking for choosing the most cost-effective communication solutions. From this perspective, marketing communication decisions should focus on which marketing communications tool offers the greatest benefit for all the stakeholders involved in this process rather than on the medium that appears the most attractive to the planner. The focus of this definition is still very much on communication functions (tactics) rather than taking a broad view and establishing close relationships with multiple stakeholders.

However, many other definitions emphasise that the integration of marketing communications should not be understood as a simple uniformity of the message transmitted across different channels (Kitchen et al. 2004), but, rather, as the complex coordination and management of the information transmitted via complementary channels in order to effectively present a coherent image of the organisation to the targeted audiences. A good example is the definition proposed by Keegan et al. (1992: 63):

> *Integrated marketing communications is the strategic coordination of all messages and media used by an organisation to collectively influence its perceived brand value.*

This definition focuses on the concept of 'strategic co-ordination', indicating the evolution from tactical coordination towards a more strategic approach to marketing communication in order to realise synergies. In addition, the definition considers 'all messages', highlighting that both internal and external activities contribute to marketing communications efforts, and stresses the focus on brand value that requires a change of marketing and communication perspective. At the heart of this definition is the assumption that when multiple messages of a company to its audiences become consistent across time and targets, the credibility and value of both the company and its brand(s) will increase.

Another definition proposed by Duncan (2002: 8) demonstrates the current conceptual perception of IMC:

> *A cross-functional process for creating and nourishing profitable relationships with customers and other stakeholders by strategically controlling or influencing all messages sent to these groups and encouraging data-driven, purposeful dialogue with them.*

An important contribution of this definition is the emphasis on 'profitable relationships'. Moreover, Duncan acknowledges that integrated marketing communications involves a cross-functional process. This indicates that all organisational departments that interact with customers and strategic stakeholders must share a common understanding and work collectively to develop long-term brand relationships. Furthermore, the notion of stakeholders implies a shift in the IMC concept from target customer audiences to the inclusion of key stakeholder groups, such as employees, investors, suppliers, distributors, the media and the social community. Additionally, Duncan concentrates on data-driven, two-way communication with customers and other stakeholders. Thus, this definition provides the three main aspects of IMC:

- strategically consistent brand communication to stakeholders using a zero-based approach (*evaluation of previous activities and questioning planned activities*)
- cross-functional planning and monitoring
- data-driven targeting and communication to achieve sustainable competitive advantage.

Duncan's (2002) definition provides a basis for examining and understanding the advantages of the IMC concept. The development of the interactive marketplace has indicated that creativity is no longer sufficient to achieve communication effectiveness. In a cluttered and overloaded marketplace, coherent images and messages have a greater impact on targeted audiences. It is therefore the IMC effort that ensures brand messages are strategically consistent and new communication technologies are used to facilitate profitable interactions with customers and other stakeholders. Duncan's (2002) notion of 'creating and nourishing profitable relationships with customers and other stakeholders' implies that the value of brand equity has become a critical issue for organisations' profitability.

Kitchen and Proctor (2002) add that there has been a significant move away from product line branding and towards the corporate brand. The main reason is, obviously, the desire to *amortise communication across the entire portfolio* as the cost of designing and supporting individual brands continues its upward curve. However, board members and executives have come to realise that a major portion of shareholder value is brand equity and so it must be managed better. IMC provides a way to identify and prioritise brand contact points and preferences. 'Contact points' are all the situations in which customers and prospects are in touch with the organisation. Such situations can be the brand, employees, channel partners, service groups or any other people associated directly with the brand. 'Contact preferences' are those means that are preferred by present and potential customers for receiving information from the organisation. Consequently, an analysis of the contact points and preferences will ensure that organisations' resources are optimised and generate the greatest synergy and return on investment.

According to Beverland and Luxton (2005), an additional advantage of IMC is the creation of brand trust and credibility. Brand trust has been challenged by a series of corporate (Enron, AIG, Tyco, Worldcom, for example) and media credibility issues (such as Dan Rather/CBS). The use of interactivity and customer feedback data in the context of IMC can help to counter consumers' scepticism.

Conceptually, IMC provides an opportunity for organisations to enhance the relationship their brands have with customers and other stakeholders. The strategic coordination of all marketing and communication tools leads to a consistent brand message being directed towards targeted audiences, using zero-based media planning. This strategy fosters an ongoing consumer-brand relationship dialogue, while also generating enhanced consumer appeal. In the rapidly changing and highly competitive world of the twenty-first century, organisations could add value to their brand equity if they successfully create and nurture these types of relationships.

Organisational challenges to implementing the IMC concept

Despite the recognised importance of implementing IMC procedures, the organisational structure of many companies prevents or restricts its effective implementation (see Figure 5.2). In reality, IMC do not fit easily into the organisational structure adopted by most firms. Percy (1997) argues that the theory of IMC,

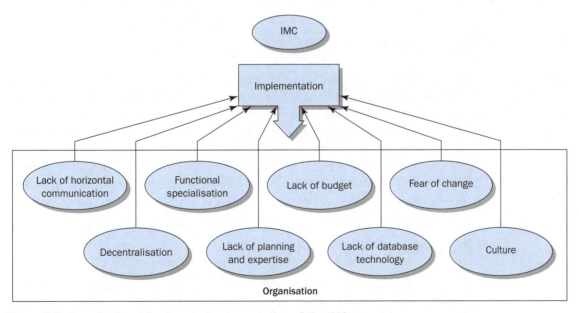

Figure 5.2 **Organisational barriers to implementation of the IMC concept**

while theoretically pragmatic, ultimately fails because of significant structural functional barriers to its implementation. The most significant organisational barriers to the implementation of the IMC concept are the following.

Lack of horizontal communication

For IMC to work, communication needs to be organised across functional disciplines, brands and separate business units (Schultz 1993). However, almost all organisations tend to establish vertical hierarchies, such as top to bottom or bottom to top (Pickton and Broderick 2001) – only a few have tried to develop horizontal communication programmes (Schultz 1999). As a result, most organisations encounter great difficulties in communicating across groups, divisions, units or even functional disciplines.

Functional specialisation

Functional specialisation of employees creates structural barriers for managing integrated marketing communications effectively. According to the IMC theory, the top management team of an organisation should be, ideally, communication generalists (Pickton and Broderick 2001). IMC requires a broad view of customers, the marketplace, competition and communication. Yet, in today's organisations, employees are trained to become specialists in a particular area. Unfortunately, these specialists rarely communicate with each other across various functional divisions. Each functional division has its own budget, objectives and procedures, tending to create, maintain and strongly defend its particular 'territory'.

Decentralisation

Decentralisation corresponds to the current trend to empower the workforce by decentralising decision making. Some theories of management advocate replacing the present decision making system, in which the top management decides and then transmits the new directives from the top down through all the hierarchical levels of the organisation, with more democratically orientated decision making methods. Although there is a need to empower the employees, preparing them to respond immediately to consumers' needs, such decentralisation can also cause fragmentation, discouraging the implementation of integrated IMC procedures.

Lack of IMC planning and expertise

These are additional organisational barriers to the implementation of IMC. According to Percy (1997), most organisations tend to have a short-term planning focus. One of the major targets of IMC, however, is to influence customers and stakeholders by using a long-term strategic planning approach. In addition, the misguided focus of many managers on financial rather than consumer-centred objectives supports short-term planning.

Research on marketers reported by Cleland (1995) identifies also a lack of expertise as a significant factor undermining the implementation of IMC by organisations. The skills required to manage IMC span across functional specialisation, but, in reality, there are very few people who have the skills and vision to integrate communication initiatives at organisational level. The special education of IMC experts could represent a solution for the future improvement of IMC planning and implementation.

Lack of budget

According to Cleland (1995), this represents the second most significant reason for not adopting IMC. In most organisations, there is constant interdepartmental competition for resources and, consequently, the level of cooperation required for successfully implementing IMC is practically impossible to achieve. In the case of mergers and acquisitions, budget allocations only intensify the competition between departments. In addition, setting the budgets for IMC activities is more difficult than for traditional approaches, due to their longer-term implications and the specific effects of various marketing communications tools. For example, not all communication activities can be easily assessed and controlled. Sales promotion activities deliver immediate returns figures and so their cost versus returns figures may be easily assessed. However, in areas such as advertising, corporate promotions, sponsorship and public relations, the effects may not be so immediate and measurable. Therefore, one of the difficulties that arises for the budgeting process is the complexity of allocating the budget for the whole range of marketing communications activities, not just advertising or public relations.

Lack of a database and the accompanying technology

The difficulty in tracking and profiling customers and other key stakeholders is a challenge to the implementation of ICM. According to Pickton and Broderick (2001), databases are vital to successful IMC. Duncan and Moriarty (1997) claim that databases are no longer just the basis for tactical activities that an organisation desires to execute, but also now constitute the primary management tool that drives the organisation's business strategy. Unfortunately, there are still significant organisational barriers that limit the straightforward use of these databases to integrate all marketing communications activities, either related to the protocols of database access and processing or the existence of multiple departmental databases with different structures and rules that prevent their integration at central level.

Culture

The culture of an organisation is the set of beliefs, values, norms or symbols (such as dramatised events and personalities) that help its members to understand the value of the organisation and provide the context for their day-to-day actions. From this perspective, the organisational culture represents the personality of an organisation.

Organisational culture is the foundation of the internal environment and plays a major role in shaping managerial behaviour and ways of thinking. Consequently, managers from different organisations are likely to have different ideas of what makes effective marketing communications. According to Percy (1997), these different visions result in organisational feelings such as 'this is the way we do it', 'we have always done it this way' and 'it works for us'. In these conditions, an attempt to introduce the IMC concept might be received with hostility by employees, who will fight to preserve the existing organisational culture. It is therefore important to realise that, despite the best-laid plans, IMC adaptation must include not only the transformation of organisational structures and processes, but also steps that lead to changes in the corporate culture.

Fear of change

As with many other innovative concepts, an important barrier for IMC implementation might be resistance to change. The complexity of IMC implementation is likely to impinge on all the functional areas of the firm, as any change in an organisation may have effects extending beyond the actual area where the change is implemented. There are various reasons that are associated with a resistance to change, such as uncertainty, threatened self-interest and feelings of loss. The biggest fear concerning IMC implementation is probably uncertainty. In the face of impending IMC, employees may become anxious and nervous, fearing that the manager responsible for its implementation might not fully appreciate their roles and areas of expertise. Such feelings easily cause resistance to the implementation of IMC.

Regarding feelings of threatened self-interest, organisational change may potentially diminish the power or influence of some managers within the corporation, causing them to resist the new organisational framework. This attitude is also referred to as ego and turf battles between individuals and departments.

A major motivation for resistance that has not yet been fully considered in IMC literature is the feeling of loss employees experience while implementing IMC. Griffin (1999) reasons that change might modify work arrangements in ways that disrupt the existing social networks. As social relationships are highly important in any organisation, most people will resist any change that might adversely affect those relationships.

One size does not fit all

As presented above, organisational barriers are a series of complex challenges that need to be assessed and properly understood in order to facilitate IMC implementation within an organisation. However, each corporation has different marketing communications structures already in place and must deal with a distinctive organisational culture that is embodied in an individual organisational design. Consequently, it is impossible to design an implementation model that generally fits all firms. The in-depth analysis of each organisation will provide a specific combination of barriers and possible synergies that have to be taken into account when planning and implementing the IMC concept.

Implementing the IMC concept

The seven evolutionary steps model

Duncan and Caywood's (1996) evolutionary model presents seven progressive steps for integrating marketing and communication within an organisation (see Figure 5.3). Duncan and Caywood prescribe this process for considering the interconnectedness of marketing communications issues, which is translated into cross-functional coordination and interaction between communication disciplines.

The first stage, labelled 'awareness integration', refers to the motivation to change in organisations. This step requires managers to evaluate the changes in the twenty-first century marketplace, which provide clear evidence for the need for a more integrated marketing communications approach. As employees' readiness for change depends on creating a rationale and a need for it, this stage is crucial to IMC implementation.

The second stage – 'image integration' – outlines the value of having a strategically consistent corporate message, image and identity. Duncan and Moriarty (1997) describe strategic consistency as the coordination of all messages that create and transmit images, positions and reputations in the minds of customers and other stakeholders. During this stage, the decision makers should therefore assess if all the messages sent to stakeholders are consistent and coherent with the overall business and marketing communications strategy.

The third stage of 'functional integration' reflects the integration process by emphasising a greater degree of cross-functional collaboration and coordination of marketing communications activities as, traditionally, they have been separated in various other communication methods. The process of integration starts with a strategic SWOT analysis of every functional communication method, which attempts to identify a more systematic form of organising data and increasing the effectiveness of various marketing communications tools.

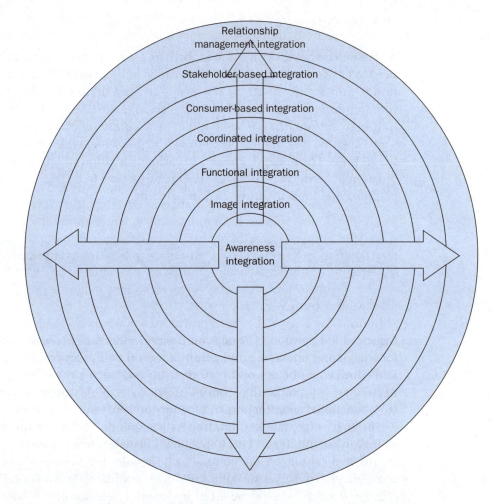

Figure 5.3 Implementing the IMC concept using the seven evolutionary steps
Source: Adapted from Duncan and Caywood 1996. Reproduced by permission of Lawrence Erlbaum Associates Inc., a division of Taylor & Francis Group.

The 'coordinated integration stage' – the fourth level of the model – aims to address barriers of effective IMC adaptation within an organisation. To overcome potential barriers, all marketing communications functions are addressed as being equal in importance. This process is guided by shared budgets, performance measurements and strategic outcomes. In some cases, at organisational level, the outcome of this stage is the creation of a centralised database.

The fifth stage, named 'consumer-based', attempts to integrate customers into the communication process of the company. In a fully mastered marketing communications process, only the most profitable customers are approached with the strongest and most effective media. The company therefore changes from an inside-out to an outside-in approach. In the new structure, organisations emphasise frequent, in-depth interactions with customers in order to quickly detect their changing wants and needs. Duncan and Moriarty (1997) argue that the facilitation of feedback and dialogue will directly contribute to integrating customers into the organisational processes of marketing communications planning and operations. In addition, these company–customer interactions should be supported by continuous quantitative and qualitative research.

The sixth stage, labelled 'stakeholder-based', claims that companies should focus on stakeholders rather than just on customers. Duncan and Moriarty (1997) agree with this view, by stating that profitability is determined by the actions of *all* stakeholders, not just customers. In other words, the stakeholders' support of the organisation translates into the value of the company's brand equity. The strategic stakeholders should be identified first, and then specific communication objectives and strategies should be developed in order to strengthen the relationships with each stakeholder category in terms of their specific needs and expectations.

The last stage is 'relationship management integration'. Nowadays, the main source of business value is not product-driven but relationship-driven. As relationships are communication-driven, there is a strong need to implement relationship management in the context of integrated marketing communications. On the other hand, the increased importance of integrated relationship management requires the inclusion of IMC decisions among the main responsibilities of the top management team.

Duncan and Caywood's model provides a useful framework for integrating marketing and communications management within the organisation. By realising the need for IMC implementation, employees will more readily accept the need for the organisational changes that go with it. The progressive transition towards total integration will allow employees to slowly adapt to the planned organisational change. The relationship management integration stage interlinks the organisation's functional departments and improves the effectiveness of IMC efforts by establishing strategic consistency. Duncan and Caywood provide further practical advice for how to establish a zero-based planning approach, proposing a SWOT analysis and aligning the public relations and marketing functions as equal partners in one department. Another important contribution of the model is the focus on various stakeholders rather than customers alone. It is evident that customers remain the most important group of stakeholders, but the value of other stakeholders to the organisation is also explicitly mentioned and emphasised. The model could be further improved by merging the fifth and the sixth stages into one as the consumer is an integral part of the stakeholder group. Another possible approach is discussed below.

The three-dimensional model

Based on a nine-year analysis of marketing and communications management at 14 leading organisations in America and Europe, Gronstedt (2000) developed a three-dimensional model of IMC implementation. The model outlines the shift from a production approach, emphasising inside out thinking in organisations, to a customer-centred organisation, focusing on outside in thinking for developing long-term customer relationships. To satisfy customers and other stakeholders, Gronstedt suggests the integration of marketing and communications management throughout the entire organisation.

The model proposes the integration of marketing communications along three dimensions: externally, with key customers and stakeholders; vertically, between senior management and frontline workers; and horizontally, across departments, business units and geographical boundaries.

The first dimension is the integration of external communication flows within the organisation. The customers and other stakeholders must be engaged by all the firm's employees in a permanent communication process, which can provide real-time information about market trends and consumption needs. The organisation itself has to become more transparent and approachable in order to stimulate the exchange of information with various categories of stakeholders. The collected information can increase the operational efficiency of the firm and help it to maximise the value for customers.

The second dimension recognises the need to develop interactive communication flows between senior management, middle management and other employees. According to Gronstedt, the essential point of vertical integration is to align top-down communicators around a clear corporate vision. Once a consensus has been reached on the strategic mission of an organisation, top management will consistently communicate it to the lower levels of the organisation. The vertical integration will therefore provide an essential management tool to implement this mission, while maintaining strategic consistency.

The third dimension, horizontal integration, involves the process of opening communication flows between work units, departments and countries. Gronstedt suggests that true integration comes from cross-business, cross-function and cross-region alignment. To effectively approach customers and other stakeholders, the organisation has to develop functional groups and project teams that are committed to sharing knowledge and expertise. One way to create an open communication environment is to eliminate the 'caste system', as evidenced by corner offices, specially assigned parking spaces, titles and dress codes. In addition, companies can use an employee rotation system, which facilitates better communication and understanding between the various work units.

The major contribution of this model is the analytical approach that is used to identify the three separate levels of integration: external, horizontal and vertical (see Figure 5.4). Gronstedt also states that the brand and stakeholder orientation is the guiding principle for maximising a company's profitability. The company should therefore analyse and approach its key stakeholder groups more effectively, using an integrated communications approach that must be realised along the three specified dimensions.

The following model builds on the two described so far.

The eight-step process

Schultz and Kitchen (2000) suggest a circular approach to IMC implementation. Their eight-step system is a tool for organisations resulting in logical outcomes and

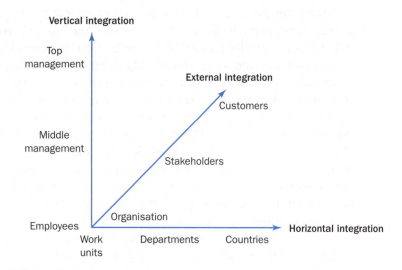

Figure 5.4 The three-dimensional application of the IMC concept
Source: Adapted from Gronstedt 2000

successful IMC programmes by using closed-loop planning (see Figure 5.5). Each step in the process is integrated and combined with the previously collected data, which is analysed to provide a foundation for the next level of the IMC effort.

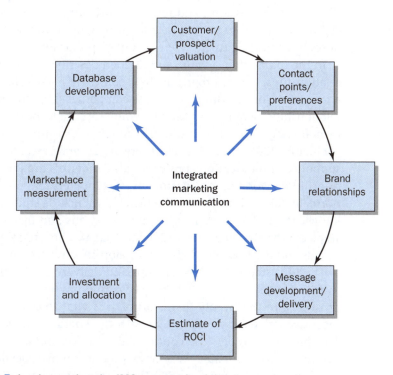

Figure 5.5 Implementing the IMC concept in eight steps
Source: Adapted from Schultz and Kitchen 2000. Reproduced with permission of The McGraw-Hill Companies.

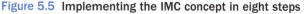

During this process, the company is constantly learning from its market experience and improving its approach to, and relationship with, its customers and other stakeholders. Schultz and Kitchen emphasise the need for continuously testing organisational assumptions and relating them to the marketplace reality.

Step one stresses the importance of a continuously updated database. Personalised communications must be based on a database that is continuously renewing its knowledge of customers, prospects and other stakeholders. To develop a purposeful dialogue with customers and other stakeholders, data must be collected by the entire organisation by means of advanced data-mining techniques and concentrated in a centralised database. Schultz and Kitchen state that the collection and analysis of reliable information is the key to developing successful IMC programmes. The organisation is therefore engaged in a continuous learning process that facilitates a closer relationship with customers and other stakeholders.

Step two involves the value segmentation of customers and prospects by means of customer databases. The purpose of this valuation is to effectively target the most profitable customers with the organisation's IMC efforts. Schultz and Kitchen argue that the best way to evaluate customers and prospects is to analyse income flows. By using the data about past transactions, the organisation can determine how much it needs to invest in order to retain and further motivate profitable customers.

Step three is the effective analysis of contact points and contact preferences. Traditionally, companies have tried to establish their communication plans by taking into account performance measures such as cost per thousand, total audience, gross impressions, and return on investment. However, Schultz and Kitchen claim that *customers* should decide on which are the best communication procedures by indicating their preferred contact points and communication methods.

In the fourth step, Schultz and Kitchen describe the process of identifying brand relationships, which progressively become the most valuable assets controlled by an organisation. Traditionally, most companies have focused on transactions, not relationships. Schultz and Kitchen emphasise that, today, the brand represents the primary support of a mutually beneficial company–customer relationship. Niemann (2005) indicates that there are several research techniques available to support communications professionals in identifying and developing brand relationship networks among customers, stakeholders and prospects. These techniques normally fall under attitudinal research and include studies of customer awareness, knowledge and feelings about corporate brands and images. Consequently, in this step, companies need to understand customers' relationships with corporate brands and use this knowledge to develop effective IMC programmes.

The fifth step is the development and delivery of effective messages and incentives, using the accumulated knowledge that has been gathered about customers or prospects. In the twenty-first century, it is vital to customise the messages or the incentive delivery system in line with the characteristics of the target audiences. This process considers the contact points and communication preferences identified in step four and aims to achieve a successful message delivery.

Schultz and Kitchen also add that chosen delivery systems must be associated with a performance measurement system that can indicate the effectiveness and impact of IMC methods. Learning progressively from this feedback loop, organisations can continuously improve their IMC approach.

After establishing the message and its delivery system, in step six, the organisation needs to estimate the return on its marketing communication activities. Schultz and Kitchen label this evaluation 'return on customer investment' (ROCI). Niemann (2005) argues that this step determines the financial value of the entire communication effort and converts marketing results into financial terms by using various measurement techniques. Whereas in step two the focus is on the general valuation of company–customer relationships and their importance for the IMC, the ROCI is associated with financial results alone. The company needs to know the current value of targeted customers in order to estimate the level of future marketing investments. This indicates that the better the process of segmenting and evaluating customers or prospects, the better the results – the ROCI. Thus, step six provides a foundation for connecting the IMC strategy with measurable performance benchmarks.

In the seventh stage, the organisation determines the financial investment and resource allocation by a process of mixing and matching various marketing communication activities and testing them in relation to their estimated return. During this stage, a series of decisions have to be made based on the information contained in the organisational database and the existing experience of the marketplace. Naturally, the final choice must include only those marketing communications tools that provide the best return on investment, reflecting the outside-in approach. At the same time, this model implies the idea of media neutrality associated with a zero-based approach. Consequently, decisions will be focused on what method offers the highest benefit, rather than on what seems most attractive to the planner.

The final step of this closed-loop system is to establish a measurement system in order to assess the communication outcome in the real marketplace. This last step evaluates whether or not all the steps have been carried out correctly and connects them to the expected returns on investments. In addition, as part of the closed-loop approach, the organisation stores all evaluated results in its database, preferably interlinking the findings with each individual customer. Even though this appears to be the last step, in reality it is just the beginning of an ongoing process that allows the organisation to continuously learn and improve its future IMC programme.

The Schultz and Kitchen (2000) model provides an effective action plan to practice an IMC strategy. By analysing the value of its customers and prospects, a company can successfully invest in its marketing communications tools while considering the return on customer investments. Another significant contribution of Schultz and Kitchen's model is that it promotes the concept of a learning company. In a continuously changing environment, companies must be able to adapt, change, develop and transform themselves to effectively meet market requirements. The closed-loop planning approach provides a method that enables organisations to learn and continuously improve their IMC approach and further facilitate changes in their structure and processes.

Unfortunately, however, the model does not offer any advice on how to implement the IMC concept within various departments of the organisation. Another point of criticism relates to the appraisal of all stakeholders. Schultz and Kitchen recognise the significance of the customer to the organisation's success, but the model still lacks an understanding of the vital role of stakeholders in the twenty-first century marketplace.

IMC in an online environment

Many studies have emphasised the lack of a unifying definition for IMC. One possible explanation of this theoretical crisis is the multitude of possible coexistent meanings for it. This assumption might also be true in the case of Internet communication.

In the specific context of the online environment, IMC can have the following meanings:

- the combination of communication modes (one-to-one, one-to-many, many-to-many)
- the integration of information types (text, sound, image)
- the consistency of messages transmitted via the online communication mix (coherent meaning)
- the integration of marketing and PR communication functions in the messages provided online
- the coordination of the process: message conception, then transmission, then feedback reception and analysis, in a closed loop
- the direct connection between the corporate information system and the Internet
- the coordination of internal, external and internal–external flows of information
- the integration of online marketing communications with the communications conducted via traditional channels
- the consistency of the corporate message at international/global level.

Integrated online marketing communications (IOMC) represent a multifaceted phenomenon that combines issues related to the message, communication function, management of information and specific mix of channels used for corporate communication. On the basis of these meanings, a series of synergies and challenges can be considered in relation to the specific characteristics of the Internet.

Internet-based communication synergies

Internet technologies allow organisations that are active online to implement three main communication synergies.

- *The integration and coordination of communication modes* The organisation can combine one-to-one (e-mail), one-to-many (list-based e-mail messages, web pages) and many-to-many (discussion forums) communications in the online environment. This synergy increases the flexibility of the ICM approach, providing opportunities for both the personalisation and integration of messages.

■ *The integration and coordination of various types of information* Advances in ICT (broadband) allow organisations to transmit or receive complex combinations of information in the forms of text, sound and images (static and/or dynamic). This synergy has a direct effect on the complexity and clarity of the communication, enhancing the capacity of the organisation to tailor its messages to the specific needs and requirements of various audiences.

■ *The integration and coordination of complex information flows between an organisation's intranet and the Internet* Organisations are now able to implement advanced software applications that connect marketing and management information systems with the online environment, and coordinate communications with various audiences automatically. This capability has a powerful impact on multiple aspects of the communication process:

  – customer data (demographic or behavioural) and customer feedback can be captured and registered automatically;
  – the information collected about audiences can be analysed, to a level of segmentation and detail that allows the implementation of one-to-one marketing communication – all automatically
  – the existing databases can automatically launch and coordinate highly targeted communication campaigns (automatic e-mail responses, automatic e-mail campaigns, personalised event marketing, promotional news and newsletters).

Internet-based communication challenges

The online environment creates not only opportunities but also challenges for the marketing communication process. The transparency of the Web makes online information available to all audiences, which reinforces the need for consistency in the planning, design, implementation and control of online marketing communications.

The marketing and PR messages published on organisations' websites are becoming more integrated than they have been in the past as they share the same channel and audiences. The corporate website is usually structured according to various information categories, such as organisational profile, activities, products and services, financial reports and other information for investors, job vacancies, contact details, and related links. A study of online communication in the UK biotechnology sector has identified the tendency of these online information categories to share both marketing and PR communication functions, although for each category there is usually a primary and secondary communication function (Ranchhod et al. 2002). This tendency is in line with the predictions made by Kotler and Mindak (1978) concerning the progressive integration of marketing and PR communications, and reinforces the benefits of the application of the IMC concept.

The variety and multiplicity of information, sources and interpretations available online raises an important challenge relating to the management of corporate image and identity. The voice of the corporation cannot be considered any more as the dominant message – it is only one component in a mosaic of communication activities. The construction of the online corporate identity needs to strike a balance between proactivity and reactivity, continuity and flexibility. The meaning is not simply transmitted, but has to be negotiated separately with each online audience. The message needs to be adapted to the specific levels of understanding and interpretation of each audience, but, on the other hand, it has to still express the same core organisational values in order to display a coherent image. The various competing messages transmitted by other organisations, pressure groups, government agencies or individuals also have to be taken into account and accommodated in such a way that the resultant effect is favourable for the company.

The international dimension of the Internet creates another specific problem for communication practitioners. Complex choices have to be made and implemented in terms of the communication strategy and tactics. If the company attempts to reach foreign audiences as well as its home ones, the message needs to be adapted to reflect the cultural specifics of each of these publics. This raises important questions regarding the possibility of integrated online marketing communication in the global context.

The specific characteristics of the Internet therefore create two conflicting tendencies:

■ the fragmentation of audiences and communication contexts, requiring customisation of online marketing messages
■ the interactivity, transparency and memory of the Web, necessitating consistency of communication and coherence of the transmitted meaning.

A new strategic model has to be adopted by any organisation that attempts to present a coherent corporate identity in the online environment. IMC is the primary instrument for achieving this objective. However, the implementation of the IMC concept has to accommodate the specific characteristics of the Internet, using the technological capabilities of the new medium to solve the specific challenges raised by the online environment and audiences.

A model for implementing an IOMC strategy

Based on the analysis of the specific characteristics of the Internet, IT applications and audiences, the implementation of IMC in the online environment has to follow a complex multilevel model that takes into account the corporate values and strategic objectives of the firm, as well as the specificities of online communication channels and audiences (see Figure 5.6).

The message sent by a company to its online audiences needs to be transformed/adapted in a three-stage process. First, the message should respect and integrate the core corporate values of the organisation. Second, the message has to be adapted to reflect to strategic and tactical objectives being pursued via the online communication campaign. Third, the message should be transformed in

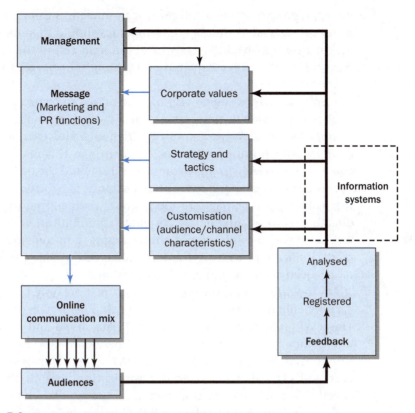

Figure 5.6 **Model for implementing an IOMC strategy**

line with the specific characteristics of the targeted audience/channel. In the case of online communication, although the Internet is the main channel, there are, in fact, various online applications or modalities of communication that can be combined and used as an online communication mix, including e-mail, chat, website, discussion forums and so on. The online communication channels vary in terms of their transparency, interactivity, memory and selectivity, and these dimensions should be taken into account when establishing the proper communication mix for each targeted audience. This process of adapting the message preserves a flexible balance between continuity and customisation, the consistency of the adapted communication being determined by the integration of the corporate core values in the structure of each message.

The interactive dimension of the Internet forces firms to adopt a more proactive attitude regarding searching, registering and analysing the direct and indirect feedback transmitted by the targeted audiences – or even, in some cases, by all categories of relevant audiences connected to the Internet. Due to the transparency and memory of the Internet, even untargeted audiences can read and react to some online corporate messages.

The use made of the feedback information collected and analysed by the firm should be speedy. The online environment is very dynamic and any delay in reacting appropriately to the messages sent by audiences can represent missed opportunities or aggravated situations. Companies should therefore use the conclusions drawn from feedback analysis to define and refine the strategic objectives of their communication campaigns and customise messages to fit audience/channel characteristics.

Feedback analysis should also be transmitted to companies' management teams so they can decide, if necessary, to modify the corporate core values in order to respond better to the market's requirements. However, a caveat to this is that changes should not be made too frequently as this may damage the long-term coherence between corporate communications and the desired corporate image.

It is essential to emphasise the importance of an efficient information system that collects, selects, registers and analyses online input (feedback) and then acts directly on any adaptations to corporate communication strategies and tactics, as well as on the customisation of online messages. In some cases, campaign management applications can use the feedback received directly and automatically for more effective online message customisation.

On the other hand, the corporate information system represents the necessary basis for enhancing the customer relationship management capabilities of the firm. The level of detail of customer-related data stored and analysed by the internal information system defines the level of personalisation that can be applied by the firm to its online communication and marketing campaigns. In fact, modern database and campaign management applications permit the implementation of effective one-to-one marketing communications in the online environment.

Figure 5.7 presents the place of IOMC in the online CRM processes of firms. The customer data/feedback collected online is used directly to improve and implement IOMC, targeting selected online audiences. Correctly implemented, the IOMC programme is a continuous cycle of gathering data and implementing response-generating marketing communication that is based on previously gathered consumer data. An effective flow of continuous information between these three components of the online CRM process can bring about increased transaction value and satisfaction for both customers and organisations.

Figure 5.7 **The place of IOMC in the online CRM process**

The issues surrounding IMC and IOMC, in the end, are all aimed at building and sustaining brands. Therefore, strategies have to be developed that take into account IMC within the concepts of brand building.

Brands

The brand is one of the most important focal points when designing and implementing IMC. A brand integrates all the disparate forms of communication about a product, service or company, providing a valuable asset for the corporation. A brand also unifies consumers' perceptions, attitudes and preferences about a specific product, service or company, translating its tangible and intangible elements into a consumption experience and lifestyle symbol. Therefore, the brand represents a useful interface between the company and its market (see Figure 5.8).

The roles and meanings of brands have evolved substantially over the last 150 years. For a long period, a brand was only a name that was used by producers, marketers and consumers to identify a specific product and service. When market competition was generally weak (during and after the Industrial Revolution), often the product name and the brand name became synonymous with one another (Hoover, for example). A similar phenomenon can be identified even today, when a popular product is newly launched on the market. If the product is highly successful, its brand name can become the generic name for the product, as has happened with Xerox photocopiers so that the name Xerox is used as a synonym for photocopiers, whether or not that particular photocopier has been made by Xerox. This situation has advantages and disadvantages for the companies whose brands are used as generic product names. The repeated use of the brand name increases the 'share of voice' of the firm, but if the brand is associated with low-quality products, the market image of the firm and its products can be damaged. This is clearly illustrated by the case study overleaf.

From the end of the nineteenth century, competition started to intensify in all market areas and the brand started to be used not only for identification but also for competitive differentiation. The brand name singularised not only a product or service, but also a specific producer or vendor. The differentiation function was intensified by using brand-centred promotion and comparative advertising. In this situation, the brand became a useful market positioning tool. Companies also started producing multiple brands and managing complex portfolios.

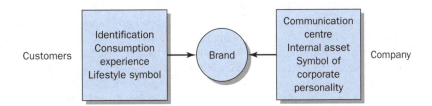

Figure 5.8 **The brand as an interface between a company and its customers**

Why British shoppers are sniffing at everyday low prices

Even at 10 pm, vehicles cluster on the damp tarmac of a car park on the fringe of London's East End. Under a vast roof, children skip through wide supermarket aisles in their pyjamas while young couples wrestle with trolleys laden with mountains of shopping. A battalion of packers stocks the shelves. It looks a picture of rude corporate health.

But look more closely at the feeble selection of fresh vegetables and the paltry few feet of shelving given to organic products (many near their sell by date); look at how far from the entrance shoppers must walk to find the ready meals that are so loved by London's professionals, and these aisles tell a different story. They help explain why the shoppers thronging this store are younger and poorer than the average and why Asda, a supermarket owned by Wal-Mart, the world's biggest retailer, is struggling in Britain.

Asda's performance is of no small consequence to Wal-Mart, which bought it in 1999 for $10.8 billion (£6.7 billion). The company is by far Wal-Mart's largest business outside America, accounting for about half its international income and roughly a tenth of its overall sales. More important, though, Asda is a litmus test for whether Wal-Mart can export its model of wooing shoppers with little more than keen pricing.

Wal-Mart's other international adventures have met with limited success. This year it pulled out of two countries: South Korea – where it failed to decode the shopping habits of the nation's housewives – and Germany, where it could not beat incumbent discount stores on price.

But Britain was always Wal-Mart's great hope. Here was a country with an established supermarket culture. The natives shopped in similar ways to Americans (who tend to prefer large, one-stop excursions, unlike Germans, for example, who buy their ham from one store, their toilet paper from another). Moreover, in Asda, Wal-Mart found a fellow traveller. The British firm was growing fast by using many of the same strategies that had enabled Wal-Mart to leave behind its humble beginnings in Bentonville, Arkansas.

After Wal-Mart bought it, Asda continued to prosper for a few years. By 2003 it had managed to seize market share and overtake J. Sainsbury, long the supermarket of Britain's middle classes, to become the country's second-largest retailer behind Tesco, which commands almost a third of the market.

But even as Asda grew, British shopping habits were changing. Low prices, Asda's main appeal, were becoming less important. Whereas four decades ago almost a quarter of household expenditure went on groceries, just 9 per cent does now. All Britain's supermarkets have relentlessly pushed their suppliers to cut costs; as a result, price differences between chains have narrowed.

A trolley of 100 common items bought at Tesco for £173.97 ($330.26) would cost just 74p less at Asda, according to *The Grocer*, which compiles a weekly price index. Comparing bigger shopping baskets of 10,000 items yields a similar result, with Asda and Tesco charging the same for almost three-quarters of their goods. Such differences as remain are too small to be noticed by most shoppers.

A 2006 study by IGD, a grocery industry think tank, found that just 42 per cent of shoppers consider cost when choosing which foods to buy, down from 46 per cent in 2003. Yet until recently Asda continued to tout its low prices, running adverts with shoppers tapping their pockets to suggest they are leaving the stores with spare change. (Its current campaign features Coleen McLoughlin, fiancée of Wayne Rooney, a pugilistic footballer and working-class hero.) 'They talk more about cheap prices than about quality food,' says Nick Harrison of Mercer Management Consulting. 'That just reinforces a perception that the quality may not be as good.'

A second trend missed by Asda was a change in British culinary habits, signalled by the rise of the celebrity chef. More people now cook meals from scratch, eat out and try new foods, helping to boost the popularity of posh cuisine. According to IGD, premium brands, distinguished by the use of words such as 'finest' or 'select', which cost more than cheaper 'value-branded' cousins, now account for almost 10 per cent of grocery sales.

So too with organic foods. Although they represent just 1.5 per cent of the market, sales are growing rapidly. TNS Worldpanel, a research firm, reckons that sales of organic milk, for instance, have doubled in two years. 'Organic has taken off dramatically and we've ignored it until recently,' says Asda's Chief Executive, Andy Bond. 'These trends are affecting everyone, not just the affluent.'

Stores such as Tesco, Sainsbury's and Waitrose (a fast-growing supermarket chain catering for people too refined to shop at Sainsbury's) have gained a double benefit from selling classier brands. Not only do such foods yield juicier margins, but they also attract the customers that retailers most want in their shops: rich people who don't look at prices. Just 2 per cent of Sainsbury's customers say they chose the store because of price, while 31 per cent cite good-quality products.

Tesco and Sainsbury's are now increasing their sales faster than Asda, according to TNS Worldpanel. Following almost ten years' growth, Asda's market share has slipped slightly to 16.7 per cent. It was the only big supermarket to lose ground in the past year other than Morrisons, which botched a takeover in 2003 and has been forced to close stores. Wal-Mart executives have said that the company, which does not disclose its profits separately from its parent's, has missed both profit and sales targets in the past year.

Mr Bond has been cutting prices aggressively, opening separate clothing and home stores and widening Asda's range of premium and organic foods. He is also paying more attention to customers' health concerns by copying rivals who are cutting salt, fat and sugar from ready meals. But none of this will be readily apparent to older and more affluent shoppers who have already departed for rivals' more verdant aisles.

Asda is now in a bind. Stocking its shelves with posh foods its existing customers don't particularly fancy will lead to costly increases in waste. Failing to do so means Asda will never be able to win back the high-spenders it really needs to increase sales. More missed targets and grumbles from the folks back in Bentonville may be in store.

Source: 'Why British shoppers are sniffing at everyday low prices', *The Economist*, 28 September 2006

After the Second World War, the emphasis in marketing communication shifted from products and companies to consumer benefits and so brands have been reformulated to represent consumption experiences. At the same time, brand names have continued to be used as identification and differentiation tools. In the historical evolution of brands, the new communication functions did not replace the old ones, but were simply added to the previous brand symbolism.

In the 1970s and 1980s, when customer power was on the rise and marketing started to concentrate on relationships rather than atomised transactions, brands were transformed into lifestyle symbols by means of an intensive process of personalisation. For the first time, brands started to be perceived as more important than products, becoming independent symbols of a certain personality type. This situation has permitted the development of umbrella brands. These use the same brand name for multiple products and services that are only linked by specific lifestyle consumption patterns. (Figure 5.9 shows how brands have evolved over time.)

For a modern firm, brands have multiple aspects that complement and enrich each other (see Figure 5.10).

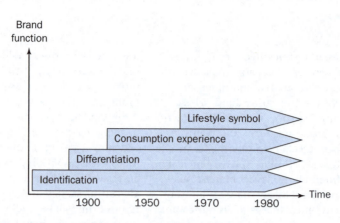

Figure 5.9 **The historical evolution of brand function**

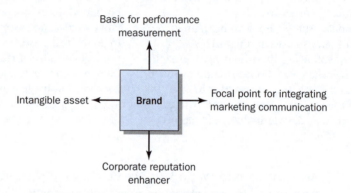

Figure 5.10 **The multiple aspects of brands that are useful to the modern company**

Brand strategies

The design and implementation of an effective brand strategy can be considered in relation to the characteristics of the brand and the product or service that is offered (see Figure 5.11)

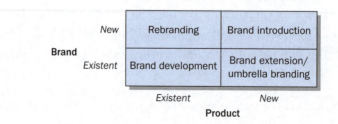

Figure 5.11 **Brand strategy matrix**

Existent brand/Existent product – brand development strategy

In this situation, both the product and the brand already exist in the strategic portfolio of the firm. However, the brand has to be continually developed as both the internal conditions of the organisation and the competitive environment are dynamic elements that change over time.

New brand/Existent product – Rebranding

In some competitive situations, the existent products have to be rebranded in line with a change in market segmentation and/or competitive positioning strategy. In these conditions, not only the name but also the other identification elements of the brand might change. The new brand package should be coherent and consistent with the new strategic orientation and an intensive communication strategy should support and enhance its introduction.

New brand/New product – brand introduction

The launch of a new brand or product requires the creation and use of a new brand name. Brand introduction, as in the case of product introduction, is a complex process, shaped by the strategic approach of the organisation in terms of market research, objective setting, segmentation, positioning, planning, implementation, performance measurement and control. The brand strategy needs to be consistent with the tangible and intangible characteristics of the newly introduced brand or product in order to create a clear, powerful image in consumers' minds.

Existing brand/New product – brand extension/umbrella branding

This combination of brand and product has two possible alternatives, depending on what type of product is being introduced. In the case of new products that represent only extensions of existing product lines, we have a situation of brand extension, whereas in the case of an innovative product that is unrelated to the existing product portfolio, an umbrella branding strategy is used. However, for umbrella branding, the profile of the innovative product has to be consistent with the main values and lifestyle represented by the umbrella brand.

The importance of brand strategies

A brand strategy is part of the overall marketing strategy of the firm, requiring consistency at the level of the marketing mix – product, price, place and promotion – but also between the various stages of the strategic process – objective setting, planning implementation and control. The dynamism of the market environment requires the use of a closed-loop of the various stages of the strategic process – the effect of controlling and performance measurement in one stage having a direct impact on objective setting for the next strategic period (see Figure 5.12).

Figure 5.12 **The centrality of brand strategy to the overall marketing strategy**

Brand management

If branding, and the associated communication approaches, are the 'last stand' of marketing, the design and implementation of effective branding strategies represent a priority for any company. Coca-Cola, Marlboro, Pepsi, Budweiser and Campbell's began the millennium as the top five brands, having a billion dollar presence in world markets (ACNielsen 2001). The image and quality of each of these brands matched the expectations and perceptions of the consumer and evolved dynamically in relation to the changing environment. There is also a strong argument for asserting that strong brands can be created within services, by integrating the message and achieving consistency of delivery (Berry, 2000).

Figure 5.13 shows four complementary approaches that have to be combined and applied by service companies in order to build strong brand equity. Service

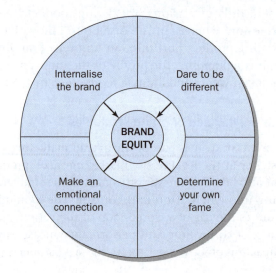

Figure 5.13 **How to enhance brand equity**
Source: Berry 2000

firms with the strongest brands (Starbucks, McDonald's and Disneyworld are a few examples) typically use all four approaches.

Leading brand companies must dare to be different using creative advertising strategies and matching their messages with services that are of a consistent quality. Emotional connections can be made using cause-related marketing (helping communities or good causes, for example) and communicating a strong message of corporate social responsibility. Emotional connections can also be made by considering issues such as heritage, nostalgia and design in relation to a product. An interesting approach in this respect is provided by the following case study which is based on Morgan Motor Company Limited.

CASE STUDY

Morgan Motor Company Limited

Retaining traditional brand values to become a long-term niche player

Morgan Motor Company Limited, based in the town of Malvern in Worcestershire, is a private family-owned company that has defied the forces of car manufacturing logic to survive as probably the only company in the world still making traditional, hand-built motor cars with an eighteen-month delivery time that is part of the proposition.

On the one hand, the company has found a niche market to survive among the giants as a non-threatening manufacturer, riding out many decades of the global hi-tech, just-in-time lean car mass manufacturing which produces the sophisticated vehicles of today. On the other hand, the company has kept going with a full order book when many other small-scale manufacturers of specialist cars have either disappeared from view or been the subject of numerous take-overs by enthusiastic multi-millionaire entrepreneurs, but never been successful long-term businesses.

The company's core products are based on two-seater, open sports cars styled in the fashion of the 1920s and '30s, built on conventional chassis compared with the monocoque integral body/chassis design of modern cars. A range of engines, varying in size from a 1.6 litre and 2.5 litre V6 Ford unit to the ultra-sophisticated V12 BMW engine in the Aero 8 model, are bought in, as are seats, transmissions and axles.

Most other components are made at the factory. Chassis members, made from ash wood and

finished with a galvanized steel overlay, are now bought-in. A wooden framework is made for each car by craftsmen, and hand-formed aluminium body parts attached. Few power tools are used in the construction of the body parts even today and hand tools are still used for many aspects of metal and wood forming and trimming. Craftsmen and women serve a traditional apprenticeship before becoming qualified to work unsupervised.

The company was criticised for inefficient working practices and costly production techniques by Sir John Harvey-Jones at the end of the 1980s for the first series of the BBC TV programme *Troubleshooter*. Since then, the company has raised production from nine to fourteen cars per working week and made production changes whilst retaining the important values of craftsmanship and individuality. Customers can specify a wide range of options which give the cars a personalised appeal. The Japanese 'kanban' system of matching components to be delivered at the right moment to the production 'line' has been implemented.

Morgan cars have one of the highest proportions of vehicles manufactured still in use in roadworthy condition of any manufacturer. Typical buyers of Morgan cars are people who have a liking for traditional cars with a sporty feel and performance which require 'real driving'. The typical customer is 46 years old with discretionary disposable income and the purchase of a Morgan is as an additional vehicle for a lifestyle choice. The British market accounts for 30 per cent of sales.

Of growing importance is the number of women who are wealthy in their own right and potential customers. The top-of-the-range Aero 8 model with its emphasis on power, luxury, style and practicality meets the needs of this segment. In North America, where the number of Morgan distributors has doubled in the past few years, women represent 39 per cent of the top wealth holders with gross assets of more than $625,000 (*Source*: IRS) and in the UK there are now a quarter more women millionaires than men in the age group 18–44 (*Source*: CEBR).

Morgan buyers are not necessarily terribly wealthy and the cars represent exceptional value for money, with the base 1.6 model costing just over £25,000 in the UK. The BMW-engined Aero costs over three times this amount, indicating successful product line and brand stretch. Many owners keep their cars for a long period of time. Digby Smith, Vice President of the Morgan Sports Car Club, has owned his Morgan for over 40 years.

It is this Morgan owners' club which represents owners in many countries of the world and provides a sense of identity and community for many of the buyers. It has strong links and influences with the factory and is often consulted for advice on product and brand development. The club is a powerful, though informal, symbol and promoter of the Morgan core brand proposition. There is a very active agenda of meetings and social gatherings, not to mention racing events, all of which create a strong relational bond between owners and the factory. It represents a classic example of customer relationship and permission marketing.

The core brand values of the product are tradition, quality, nostalgia, exclusivity, craftsmanship, fun and a sense of participating in something which is special and unchanging amidst a world of turmoil and constant change. These core values are augmented by opportunities for a personal relationship with the factory. Purchasers and prospects are able to tour the factory, inspect their car as it moves along the production line, and sometimes take delivery of their new car directly from the factory rather than from the premises of their local Morgan dealer.

Such values are often found amongst owners of vintage and veteran cars which are no longer in production, but a key differentiator for Morgan is continuity. Many features of the cars made today can be traced back directly to cars of the 1920s and '30s, and it takes an expert eye to determine whether a particular model was made last week or twenty years ago. Morgan owners also tend to be loyal and are unlikely to indulge in brand-switching, exhibiting extremely long-term commitment to the product.

However, one of the frustrations experienced by Morgan Marketing Director Matthew Parkin is that many motoring journalists believe that Morgans are old-fashioned with a very hard ride, heavy steering and poor brakes. 'Journalists quite often have pre-conceived ideas and may even have written their article before they come for a test drive, and hence won't change their mind even after a driving experience' comments Parkin. Yet nothing could be further from the truth. Today, Morgans are subject to safety and emissions testing to meet every global standard, including those in the EU, the US and the emerging Chinese market. The cars have updated suspension and braking systems and provide a modern package of reliability, ride comfort, ease of handling and regulation approval.

The brand strength, identity and continuity is such that little advertising or promotion is required. Word-of-mouth via the Morgan Sports Car Club and other Morgan owners is very important. Whilst public relations does not have to be pro-actively managed in the way it does for volume production cars, Managing Director Charles Morgan and the Morgan family place great importance on the maintenance of good public relations and other aspects of marketing communications. They are highly skilled at managing the whole promotional mix in an understated and subtle manner which results in high-profile but non-aggressive promotion of the key brand values, identity, image and attributes.

It is probably not an exaggeration to say that no other car manufacturer has achieved such consistent branding over such a long period of time for such little communications expenditure, surviving against the odds in a world of competitive auto manufacturing and yet having excellent relationships with major players such as Ford and BMW.

Source: Mike Wilman, 2007, Southampton Business School, Southampton Solent University (with additional material by Donna Goodwin)

'Internalising the brand' means that every individual within the company adopts the main values of the brand and provides an excellent service to the customer. In order to do this, employees need to fully understand and accept the brand values and make them their own.

The model presented in Figure 5.13 could be equally applicable to a range of products as well. As brands come under growing threats from a range of different factors, they cannot remain static but need to be transformed and kept in step with consumers' needs, perceptions, attitudes and consumption styles. For example, while 1999 saw the spectacular success of Proctor & Gamble's Sunny Delight drinks, the year 2000 brought an upsurge in organic products, including drinks and dairy products, so it is clear that a brand cannot remain the same forever if it is to remain successful (Dru, 1997). If branding and communications are so fundamental to the strategic success of an organisation, how can a company maintain brand identity and improve brand equity in a climate of change?

Taking a long-term view

If brands are to be successful, a long-term view of marketing decisions must be taken in order to ensure consistency and clarity. While innovation in brand management is part of a brand's dynamism, consistency of the marketing support (Bridges et al. 2000) is essential to provide uniformity and focus. Coca-Cola, for instance, truly created a global brand 30 years ago by gathering 200 multi-ethnic young people on a hilltop in Italy and asking them to sing, 'I'd like to buy the world a Coke'. However, Coca-Cola has downgraded this ambition as it has had to face challenges from local brands, such as Thumbs Up in India. It is becoming increasingly difficult for companies such as Coca-Cola to keep up with the changes in fragmenting markets (Tomkins 2000). The company is presently trying to react to market changes by launching a range of other soft drinks and bottled water, often not bearing the Coca-Cola brand at all.

A frequently used example of how *not* to manage brand and brand innovation is epitomised by the case of Intel. A rare flaw in a Pentium chip was known to cause miscalculation problems with data on infrequent occasions. Instead of replacing the chip, for many weeks Intel maintained that the fault was extremely unusual and refused to publicise the problem or provide a replacement chip. When Intel did finally offer replacements to customers, only an estimated 1 to 3 per cent of them actually requested an alternative. However, the brand image of Intel products' 'power' and 'safety' has been dented.

In order to make their purchasing choices, consumers tend to retrieve brand-related information from memory and compute a brand-related rating on the basis of external information available at a specific moment in time or, alternatively, undertake a type of mixed retrieval–deduction process in which some information is retrieved and some is deducted. This process is likely to depend on previous brand-related experiences (Alba and Hutchinson 1987). Therefore, in the above case, the lack of a PR campaign by Intel has provided an opportunity for other sources of information to influence the perceptions and attitudes of consumers, negatively.

Brand values

The apparent matching of brand promise with brand reality has been demonstrated by the top brands. Consistency in the approach towards brand management is critical for shaping the desired brand values and having them accepted by targeted customers. Freshness, quality, longevity, simplicity and social acceptability are values associated with a given brand and, once established, provide a platform for further developing, growing and strengthening of the brand's equity.

Brand 'meddling' described by Mazur (2000), is the ineffective management of a brand and its values. Levis is cited, among others, as a significant offender. Branding, Mazur asserts, is more than a catchy phrase and quirky advertising.

Brands are complex constructs that have both tangible and intangible elements. The interactions between these elements determine, in the long run, the value and reputation of brands (see Figure 5.14).

The following case study outlines the kind of interplay between tangible and intangible elements that creates and develops effective brands.

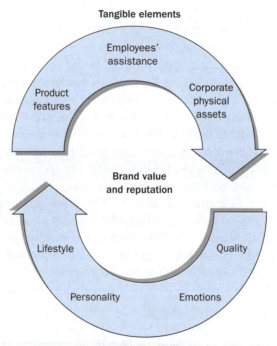

Figure 5.14 The interactions between various tangible and intangible elements that create a brand's value and reputation

How Philips got brand buzz

CEO Gerard Kleisterlee introduced the Sense and Simplicity brand to warm up the Dutch conglomerate's techie image and make it more consumer-friendly

When Gerard Kleisterlee took the helm at Royal Philips Electronics in 2001, the Dutch conglomerate's vast empire spanned sectors from TVs and lightbulbs to semiconductors and medical devices. But one important thing was missing: a coherent brand. For years, Philips (PHG) had focused on the different technologies behind each of its five major businesses instead of what unified them in the market.

'It was clear the missing link between Philips' great technology and business success was marketing,' Kleisterlee says. 'We had to choose whether Philips was a company built around its core technologies or one built around its core brand.'

Kleisterlee wisely chose the latter. Countless focus groups across the company's divisions – medical, lighting, consumer electronics, domestic appliances and semiconductors – all led to the same conclusion: new technology was often just too complex. So Philips stopped talking tech and started speaking the language of its customers. Instead of trumpeting the benefits of, say, liquid crystal displays or light-emitting diodes, Philips now talks about the better picture quality of its flat-screen TVs or how lighting can change a room's mood.

Top gainer

It's all part of a new branding effort launched two years ago called Sense and Simplicity. The idea is to create a 'healthcare, lifestyle and technology' company whose products promise innovation but are easy to use and designed around consumers. Kleisterlee hired a new marketing boss and quickly moved to ensure the company's strategy filtered down to the troops.

As branding initiatives go, it has been remarkably successful. In the 2006 annual *BusinessWeek/* Interbrand global brand study, Philips was one of the top gainers, registering a 14 per cent increase in the value of its brand, to $6.73 billion, and jumping five places in the rankings, to no. 48 (see BusinessWeek.com, 8/7/06, 'The World's Best Brands').

The company hatched a variety of strategies to pull this off. For instance, looking for new sources of creativity and innovation, Philips turned to outsiders and formed a think tank known as the Simplicity Advisory Board. Made up of an unlikely coalition of a British fashion designer, a Chinese architect, a US radiologist, a Japanese auto designer and an MIT professor, the group is an informal sounding board for management.

Home brew

Last year, Philips copied a longstanding practice from the auto industry and launched a road show for investors, suppliers, customers and media aimed at highlighting future Philips products. The tour visited Paris, Amsterdam and New York in 2005 and will swing through London, Hong Kong, and Brazil this fall (see BusinessWeek.com, 10/26/05, 'The New Simplicity').

Kleisterlee points to a few new products that best exemplify the simplicity brand. For instance, any layperson can operate Philips' Heart Start defibrillators to shock a stopped heart back into action, thanks to simple audio guided instructions. There's also the Perfect Draft beer dispenser, a twist on Philips' hugely successful Senseo coffee makers, which allows you to 'enjoy the same cooling, pressure and foam at home that you do in the pub,' Kleisterlee says.

Another recent change is the creation of consumer test centres around the world. Here, products are extensively reviewed and critiqued by consumers, sometimes leading Philips to delay a product's release in order to make suggested changes. Before Philips launched its new WACS7000 Wireless Music Centre, for instance, it ran the product through eight months of rigorous tests at its Consumer Experience Centre in Singapore.

Subjects had complained that the system was difficult to instal and lost patience with the complexity of the technology. So Philips rewrote the product software and reintroduced all the

▶

manuals with improved quick instal guides before launching the product in August 2005.

Universal control

Philips is also working on two of consumers' biggest pet peeves: complicated remote controls and incomprehensible instruction manuals. Philips' latest range of flat-screen TVs now show users a split screen image and ask them which one they like best. After doing this a few times, the TV automatically adjusts the picture quality to the preferences of the viewer.

There are also now simplified instruction cards designed to get Philips' consumer products up and running in eight to ten easy-to-follow steps. And for those tired of countless remote controls littering the living room, Philips is bringing out a range of universal remotes for all your audio and video devices.

At the same time, Kleisterlee is trying to boost brand awareness in markets – including the US – where many of Philips' products are marketed under other brand names, such as Norelco razors, Sonicare toothbrushes and Magnavox audio and video systems.

Bulking up

Philips is working with focus groups to find the best brand positioning. The company recently decided to market its Norelco shavers as Philips Norelco, with Philips as the 'endorsement' brand and Norelco as the 'category' brand. 'Everyone in the US knows Norelco shavers but few realise they are a Philips product,' says Kleisterlee. 'The brand repositioning addresses this.'

Under Kleisterlee, the structure of Philips is also changing. At the time he became CEO five years ago, the medical division was the laggard, accounting for 8 per cent of Philips' revenue and less than 4 per cent of its operating income. Without the huge range of products and services offered by rivals General Electric (GE) and Siemens (SI), Philips was

losing ground to the giants (see BusinessWeek.com, 12/1/2005, 'The New Face of Philips').

Kleisterlee decided the only way to compete was to bulk up, and spent billions on acquisitions over the last five years, adding medical companies such as Witt Biomedical and Stentor. Last year, medical systems accounted for 21 per cent of Philips' revenue and 38 per cent of operating income.

Ditch the chips

Other divisions are also getting the Kleisterlee treatment. In the past year alone, he has spent more than $4 billion on acquisitions to spur earnings growth in the appliances and lighting divisions, as well as medical systems. And by the end of this year, Philips will spin off its semiconductor division, Europe's third-largest chipmaker. Recent reports claim a number of private equity firms are eyeing the business, although Philips won't comment on the speculation.

Ditching semiconductors, analysts say, is a smart move. That's because the cyclical nature of the business has been a drag on the company's share price, which is intrinsically linked to the chip industry. 'Semiconductors is Philips' worst-performing business and the only thing moving their stock,' says Scott Geels, a senior research analyst at Sanford C. Bernstein in London.

Thanks to the roller-coaster nature of chips, Philips' share price rose throughout 2005, then fell 20 per cent in the first half of this year, and is now up 7.7 per cent for the year. Investors are undoubtedly reacting to an 11.7 per cent first-half revenue increase and near doubling in operating income, to €702 million ($895 million). But they're also cheered that one of the world's great consumer products companies has finally got some fresh brand buzz.

Source: Kerry Capell, 'How Philips got brand buzz', *BusinessWeek*, 31 July 2006. Capell is a senior writer at *BusinessWeek*'s London bureau

A mismatch between brand personality and social trends can prove catastrophic for a brand's reputation if proper strategic corrections are not implemented. Levis – a company that had clearly differentiated itself in the marketplace for a number of years – became 'uncool' to the younger generation after being associated with Tony Blair and Jeremy Clarkson. Clearly the younger generation closely associated with the brand felt that these men did not represent the Levis brand values. More importantly, Levis had failed to take notice of the recent changes in the market-place, including the rise of denim alternatives (as delineated by Gap) and the higher-priced/positioned brand extensions by Calvin Klein and Armani, to name but a few.

Understanding brand positioning and perceptual maps is an integral part of brand research. An example of this understanding is provided by Dillon et al. (2001), who undertook research on fast-moving consumer goods in the USA. The work looked at brand salient attributes (BSAs), which are general features, attributes or benefits that consumers link to a brand, thereby differentiating it from its com-petitors. The general brand impressions (GBIs) are general impressions of a brand, based on a holistic view. As brand perceptions depend on product attributes and impressions are derived from memory, this is a useful way to measure positioning.

In this instance, Colgate's brand-building activities feature *hedonic* benefits, such as good taste and breath freshening. Crest, however, concentrates on *preventative* benefits such as cavity prevention, anti-plaque and anti-gum disease actions. The interesting fact is that there is an existing variation between those consumers who have high brand knowledge (those more driven by brand attributes – BSAs – for positioning) and those with low brand knowledge (who tend to be more driven by brand impressions – GBIs). Thus, there are positioning differences between panel A and panel B, as depicted in Figure 5.15, that outline the importance of developing consistent branding strategies in direct relation to target markets (whether aiming for hedonistically driven or attribute-driven consumers).

To manage a brand effectively, it is necessary to support the brand with market-ing knowledge and targeted communication, permanently monitoring the difference between its identity and its changing external image. Also permanently

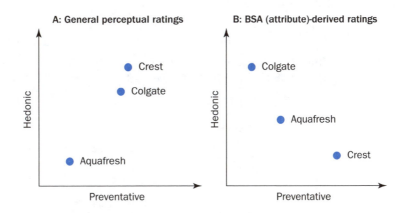

Figure 5.15 Examples of perceptual maps for brand analysis and evaluation of toothpaste brands

Source: Adapted from Dillon et al. 2001

observing the internal climate and the external competitive conditions, the organi-sation must monitor the relationship between the brand's values and its associations, and continuously develop the brand, but make changes only when appropriate (see Figure 5.16).

Brand equity

Widespread public knowledge of a brand is not the only measure of true brand equity (Knapp 1999). Awareness, loyalty, perceived quality and identity – all represent essential and complementary parts of brand equity. However, ineffective brand management can adversely affect a brand as, merely weakening a brand's impact by brand extension/stretching, its equity can decrease. Before any major change in brand strategy, risk managers must identify the drivers of brand value, define consumer perceptions of the company and its products and scrutinise corporate decisions for their impacts on the brand's power.

Brands, therefore, are both risks and assets. However, as brands are rarely sold, value for insurance is not the same as value for sale. A number of methods are used to evaluate brand equity, but the principal ones involve discounting future cash flows. These are explored to a greater extent in Chapter 9. Interestingly, Ambler (1998) observes that there is an allocation of brand equity responsibilities and each segment (consumer, employee and so on) has a duty to contribute to the brand's perception, loyalty and awareness. This can be done, for example, by means of marketing and human resources for the aforementioned segments. The brand, then, is driven, developed and enhanced by the company's employees and stakeholders.

Brands have unique emotional and functional benefits for consumers – often expressed in their names. Take, for example, the sweeping changes made to the names of confectionery products in the early 1990s. To the dismay of a number of consumers, Mars Marathons became Snickers and Opal Fruits became Starbursts. The fate of a popular cereal may also have followed a similar course, but, with

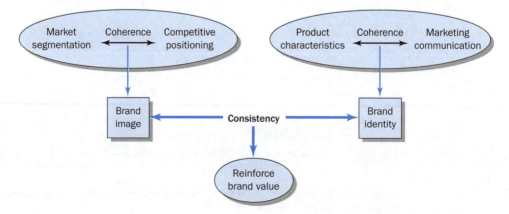

Figure 5.16 **The importance of consistency between brand image and brand identity**

competent brand management, Kellogg's Coco Pops did not permanently become Choco Krispies. Loyal consumers who phoned to vote for the Coco Pops name to remain were rewarded, as thousands decided that the name Coco Pops reflected the true nature of the product. Perhaps this was a cynical exercise, but it shows that awareness without differentiation is marginally profitable and brands with little loyalty are more prone to decline than those with a faithful following.

Summary

In the complex market environment of the twenty-first century, the customer and other categories of stakeholders were empowered by the evolution of information and communication technology applications. The multiplication of communication channels and information sources has reduced the control of the firm on its corporate communication process with various targeted audiences. The multiplication of information exchange capabilities and the fragmentation of key audiences forces modern corporations to implement an integrated marketing communications (IMC) approach.

In this era of information saturation, a company has to be aware that its corporate voice is only one among many other sources of information. The 'transmit and control' strategy is no longer effective and should be replaced by procedures based on market knowledge and proactive communication. Various corporate messages and the media used for their diffusion must be considered from the perspective of a long-term strategy of building a reputable corporate image and enhancing brand equity, even though short-term pressures are more prevalent than before.

Brands have become one of the most valuable assets firms possess. The process of brand management cannot be disconnected from market realities. The value of a brand depends on considering it as a flexible interface between a company and its customers and as a communication platform for corporate values and identity. Only by matching the brand's personality with the perceptions and attitudes of consumers can a company maintain the value and success of its branding strategies.

Chapter questions

1 Develop your own definition of integrated marketing communications (IMC). Discuss and present arguments to support your view.

2 Discuss the following statement: 'Marketing communication has to enhance brand relationships with customers and other stakeholders'.

3 What are the main strategic elements that enhance brand equity in a company?

6 Implementation is the key

Introduction

The design and implementation of marketing strategies are important aspects of a company's long-term plans. Often, however, marketing strategy objectives fail to materialise. Is this because the strategy was unsound in the first place or the implementation ineffective or both (Sashittal and Tankersley 1997)? Companies tend to spend a great deal of time planning strategies and, despite this, they sometimes fail to take into account the full implications of implementing them. Several authors have highlighted the fact that much emphasis is placed on strategy formulation and little thought is given to implementation issues, even by marketers. Strategy may or may not drive actual marketing practice (Crittenden and Bonoma 1988).

With the explosion of new forms of communications that have a global reach, it is incumbent on marketers to consider implementation as an important issue in marketing and, at the same time, find the relevant speed at which implementation should take place. Technology drivers have become increasingly important over the last ten years as the pace of information exchange increases rapidly. This has, in many ways, destroyed the luxury of developing strategies over a long period of time. Shorter periods are now available for strategy formulation and development. Even shorter periods are available for the implementation of these strategies. This chapter considers the often neglected area of marketing implementation, taking into account organisational impediments, the utilisation of new technology and issues surrounding the relative power of the marketing function in companies.

Planned versus emergent implementation

Many authors have argued that marketing strategies only result in superior returns for an organisation if and when they are implemented successfully (Bonoma 1984). Marketing implementation relies on people, first and foremost, and on the way in which they adapt to the market environment. Much of the literature tends to take a linear approach to strategy formulation and implementation, often regarding each area as a distinct step. Noble and Mokwa (1999) define marketing strategy implementation as:

the communication, interpretation, adoption and enactment of a marketing strategy or strategic market initiative.

Many authors (Cespedes 1991; Piercy 1989) argue that strategy formulation does not necessarily precede implementation. The relationship between these two is reflexive and iterative. As the environment is constantly shifting and changing, it is hard to consider formulation and implementation separately. If these processes are interrelated, then marketers must be prepared to deal with the intricacies of this relationship in order to create strategic success. From research carried out by Sashittal and Tankersley (1997), the following key factors emerged.

■ Marketing planning and implementation are closely related, with managers making improvisations in nearly all elements of their marketing plans (including objectives, targeted customers and the marketing mix) and in their implementation actions. Plans are continually improvised to fit day-to-day marketing changes and implementation procedures are adapted to fit with changing marketing plans.
■ Marketers' responses to modified strategic plans often trigger further changes in planning and implementation processes.
■ The implementation process is fraught with uncertainty as few outcomes are reached as originally intended.
■ The constant need to improvise means that strategic issues are often emergent and adaptations occur in real time, without being predetermined (Mintzberg and Waters 1985).
■ Marketing plans and implementation procedures often lack a rational approach and are determined by 'gut' feel. This point was also made by Simkin and Dibb (1998) who found that short-term priorities were often followed by many marketing managers.
■ Interactive communication within organisations is important in volatile and changing environments so as to enhance the capacity of employees to respond quickly and effectively to existing market threats and/or opportunities.
■ Competitors' activities can trigger changes in strategy formulation and implementation.

The emergent strategic perspective (Mintzberg and Waters 1985) indicates a situation where a pattern of actions emerges without any prior plan. However, the actions may show a coherent pattern with an emerging strategic purpose (see Figure 6.1). In many marketing situations, it appears that implementation occurs as a result of incremental changes and emergent issues rather than on the basis of formal objectives and planning.

Table 6.1, sourced from the study carried out by Sashittal and Tankersley (1997), shows important differences between the literature and actual research findings concerning the planning and implementation interface.

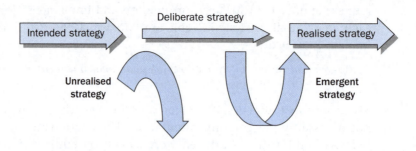

Figure 6.1 **Deliberate and emergent strategy**

According to research carried out by Simkin and Dibb (1998), many UK companies are quite happy to look for short-term returns and very few firms actually use long-term marketing plans. They divided companies into the categories shown in Table 6.2.

Table 6.1 **The planning and implementation interface: literature versus findings**

The literature	*The findings*
The literature frequently depicts marketing planning and implementation as if:	In the context of smaller industrial firms, the study finds that:
marketing planning and implementation are independent, sequential processes, that marketing plans lead to market implementation	*marketing planning and implementation are highly related – their relationship is characterised by responsiveness*
marketing planning is a rational process, based on full market information and deliberate evaluation of alternatives	*marketing plans are often not much more than a set of sales goals and a rough notion about action steps, so strategies are emergent and the nature of the marketing planning–implementation interface and how it is managed, significantly impacts market outcomes*
formal strategies hold clear, well-defined actionable implications for implementation-directed actions	*formal marketing planning is not universally conducted and clear, direct implications for implementation actions are largely absent*
future strategic gains in marketing are likely from improvements in implementation instead of improved strategy content (e.g. Bonoma 1985)	*the relationship between marketing planning and implementation processes is complex and isolating their impact on marketing outcomes is speculative at best*
effective plans lead to effective marketing implementation	*marketing implementation effectiveness is a result of (a) the interaction between planners and implementers, (b) the responsiveness in planning and implementation and (c) direct managerial actions*
marketing's effectiveness is indicated by sales revenues, market share, customer satisfaction and other indicators	*marketing's effectiveness is indicated by both these factors and psychosocial outcomes, such as employee satisfaction, job security and the creation of a good working environment*

Source: Sashittal and Tankersley 1997

Table 6.2 **Diversity of criteria and approaches**

Life is simple	Forward thinking	
How many customers	**Customer fit**	
Where located	*Future potential sales volumes*	
Profit levels	*Customers' needs*	
Sales levels	*Likely differential advantage*	
Short but effective	Analytical	
Brand loyalty	**Weight**	**Variable**
contributions (£)	3	*Market size*
	3	*Margin*
	3	*Market share*
Market growth rates	3	*Differential advantage/business*
Competitive intensity		*strengths*
	2	*Competitive intensity*
	2	*Market size trends*
	2	*Propensity for long-term relationships*
	1	*Quality of customers*

Source: Simkin and Dibb

Simkin and Dibb's findings show that marketers often focus on short-term financial measures of market attractiveness at the expense of longer-term issues and criteria relating to the marketing environment and customer relationships. Subjective measures are thus given greater importance than strategy formulation and implementation.

The analysis seems to indicate a gap between theory and practice regarding the way in which marketers implement strategies. It is possible that well-defined plans and segmentation analyses may be lacking in some instances, being replaced with ad hoc responses to market changes and demands. Increasingly, environmental changes demand rapid and flexible responses, forcing companies to be more flexible, collaborative organisations, leading to a fusion of planning and implementation activities. The Guinness case study illustrates the problems associated with a changing environment, reflecting changing consumer tastes that need to be accounted for when implementing new marketing strategies.

CASE STUDY

Dark days for Guinness *(by Owen Bowcott and Simon Bowers)*

The drinks company behind Guinness is expected to reveal this week that the tally of pints of 'the black stuff' drunk in Ireland has fallen by more than a quarter over the past eight years. The persistent decline, believed to have steepened this year, is expected to resurrect calls for Diageo to put its beer business up for sale. Some investors believe the company should focus on its core spirit and wine brands such as Smirnoff vodka, Blossom Hill wine, Captain Morgan rum and Johnnie Walker whisky. Guinness' local troubles in Ireland are expected to get lost among strong performances elsewhere in the group when Diageo reports full-year results on Thursday. Analysts expect the world's biggest drinks firm to make pre-tax profits of more than £2bn, with good figures from Latin America, Russia and Asia. Worldwide, the amount of Guinness sold is actually expected to rise, as

▶

Diageo introduces the stout in bottles and cans to more markets, most recently Russia. It remains one of the group's eight 'global priority brands'. But the decline in its homeland is seen by many as undermining the brand itself. Ireland is the shop window where Diageo promotes Guinness to visitors from around the world. It also trades off its Irish roots overseas – not least in the US. Diageo's Storehouse visitor centre in the Guinness brewery, on the banks of the Liffey in Dublin, is said to be Ireland's most popular tourist attraction. Tales about the role of the river waters in creating the Guinness flavour have passed into folklore and hordes of tourists seeking the essence of Irish culture pursue a traditional pilgrimage to the place. It is an obligatory stop on open-top bus tours. Beguiled by the historical pageant of brand promotion, visitors are mostly oblivious to the rapid domestic decline in sales of Ireland's most famous liquid export. Bars are closing and a new generation is buying lager, cider and wine, and taking it home to drink. Guinness' response has been to raise prices to defend its profits, and to search out new customers by pumping out fresh variants, while continuing to exploit nostalgia for the traditional draught. Critics suspect it has succeeded only in confusing loyal drinkers' tastebuds.

This month, Irish bars are serving Guinness 'Toucan', a brew which boasts 'triple hops' for a smoother taste. Some describe it as sweeter and less bitter. Other pubs still offer Guinness Extra Cold, a pint that was designed to boost consumption during hot summers when sales usually fall back. Meanwhile few opportunities are missed to trade on the stout's glorious past. On the wall outside the Guinness Storehouse, the public facade of the St James Gate brewery, there are reproductions of classic posters reminding visitors how it was once marketed as nutritious, wholesome and pleasurable. 'Guinness for Strength' was the uplifting caption in one famous campaign drawn by the artist John Gilroy in the 1930s, depicting a man balancing a steel girder above his head. 'My Goodness, My Guinness' was another above a picture of a zookeeper failing to entice a bear down from a post: the animal dismisses the offer of a bun as it cradles a bottle. Inside the Storehouse visitors find a bewildering array of Guinness merchandise. There are Guinness-emblazoned T-shirts, jackets, footballs, rugby balls, golf balls, clocks, socks, oven gloves, pants (in pink and white), playing cards, cufflinks and fridge magnets. There are Guinness slippers (in black and cream fake fur) and Toucan-shaped salt and pepper sets. The piped music is invariably an Irish jig. 'Ten million glasses of Guinness are enjoyed every day worldwide,' the walls proclaim.

But in the bars of Dublin there is rather less euphoria. 'It's not selling as well as it used to years ago,' says the barman at the Auld Dubliner in Temple Bar, a street buzzing with tourists and young Dubliners. 'People say it's an old man's drink. Sales of Murphy's [a rival stout from Cork] are up. I remember 10 years ago, 70 per cent of our draught sales were Guinness. Now it's about 50 per cent. It's €4.50 a pint here, but lager is €5. So it's not the price.' One veteran lunchtime customer, Jimmy Foley, says he has been drinking Guinness since he was 14. 'It used to stick to the counter years ago,' he says. 'It's thinned down a bit. You get a good pint here, but in some pubs it's muck. It's so variable. I keep asking publicans why that is.' Across the street at the Quays Bar, the owner, John McSweeney, says Guinness is still his best seller, but adds: 'The population has changed so much. Pubs in the suburbs have been badly affected by the smoking ban. There may be more people coming to live here but there are fewer going out drinking.'

'People ask for chardonnay'

'A lot of people like cider. It's become very popular. Magners has promoted its Irish cider and increased sales by 30 per cent. Customers are also becoming more demanding about wine. People ask for chardonnay or sauvignon blanc.' Declining bar and overall alcohol sales are blamed on a series of changes: the smoking ban in pubs, stricter drink-driving laws, greater consumption of wine, condemnation of binge drinking and people taking home cut-price lager from supermarkets and off licences. The effect on Guinness has been particularly severe because 90 per cent is sold in Ireland as draught; relatively little in cans or bottles.

In February Diageo revealed Irish Guinness sales had dropped 9 per cent in the first half of its financial year – the steepest fall yet. Andrew Morgan, President of Diageo Europe, had little hope of an imminent reversal. 'Historically, per capita consumption has been very high and we are likely to see a reduction in pints consumed in an evening . . . that is likely to continue.' The group has previously tinkered with marketing but appears to accept consumer trends are running away from Guinness in Ireland. The breweries have been left underused. Two years ago Diageo closed its Park Royal brewery in west London, transferring brewing for Britain back to Dublin. Sales declines in Ireland rather than Britain were behind the move.

At Toner's, a traditional bar around the corner from the Dáil, politicians and civil servants are regulars. Jim Costello is head barman. 'Guinness is still our best seller, but it's mainly for working people in their thirties to fifties,' he says. 'The company messed up the taste putting in the Extra Cold Guinness. Most bars, like us, have had those taps taken out now . . . it was tasteless.' Back outside the Guinness Storehouse, a young Dubliner tries to tempt departing tourists into a horse-drawn trap. Does he drink Guinness? 'No, I drink Budweiser,' he says. 'Guinness may do you a power of good, but it's old-fashioned.'

Backstory

Arthur Guinness started brewing stout at the St James Gate brewery, Dublin, in 1759 after inheriting a dormant brewery in his godfather's will. Little over a century later it was the world's largest brewery and Arthur Guinness & Sons was listed on the London Stock Exchange. In 1990 the so-called 'Guinness Four' – Ernest Saunders, Sir Jack Lyons, Anthony Parnes and Gerald Ronson – were convicted of conspiring to ramp up the share price during a £2.6bn bid for rival firm Distillers. In 1997, Guinness entered into a £24bn merger with another drinks group, Grand Met, and the group was renamed Diageo. The company asserted its dominance of the drinks trade in 2003 by buying Seagram. Today, its newly built headquarters in Park Royal, west London, towers over an empty Guinness brewery, a much-loved 1930s building. Closed two years ago, it was sold to developers last week.

Source: Owen Bowcott and Simon Bowers, *The Guardian*, 29 August 2006. Copyright Guardian News & Media Ltd 2006.

What marketing strategies should be implemented to change Guinness' fortunes in Ireland? It is clear that the implementation of new strategies is vital to the company's market positioning within its home marketplace.

The main factors influencing strategy implementation

The success of the implementation process – or, in other words, the actualisation of more or less formal strategic plans – is determined and influenced by a series of elements located inside and outside the organisation. Figure 6.2. shows the main elements that should be taken into account by managers and marketers in the process of implementing strategic marketing plans.

Technology is both an internal and an external factor that shapes the choice and the implementation of marketing strategies, but also influences all the other factors. Among other important internal factors are the organisational profile, people and competitive advantage. While considering the external factors, it is necessary to take into account the supply chain, competitive situation and customers. In the following subsections, the specific influences of these factors will be discussed and analysed, sometimes using specific illustrations of each one. This chapter ends with a presentation of the complex role of technology in integrating all the elements of the marketing implementation process.

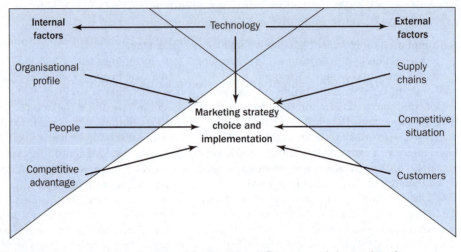

Figure 6.2 The internal and external factors that influence and determine the development and implementation of marketing strategies

Internal factors

Organisational profile

The specific profile of an organisation is likely to determine the way in which marketing strategies are selected and implemented. One of the most obvious elements that will influence the implementation process is the size of the company. There are specific elements that differentiate small firms from large corporations.

In the literature, there is much debate and various opinions about the classification of companies according to their size. The UK ESRC Centre for Business Research uses the following classification:

■ micro firms – fewer than ten employees
■ small firms – 10 to 99 employees
■ medium-sized firms – 100 to 499 employees
■ large firms – more than 500 employees.

However, the Canadian Small Business Research and Policy Unit defines the categories differently:

■ small firms – fewer than 50 employees
■ medium-sized firms – 50 to 299 employees
■ large companies – more than 300 employees.

This variability of definitions is normal because, depending on the sector of activity, there are various elements that can determine the size and profile of a firm. For example, an Internet-based firm will tend to be smaller than traditional companies and, therefore, in the online environment it is better to apply a different classification.

It is widely accepted that small and medium enterprises (SMEs) have characteristics that differ from those of larger companies (Jennings and Beaver 1997). These differences can be summarised in three main features:

- SMEs have limited internal resources
- SMEs are managed in an entrepreneurial style
- SMEs usually have a small influence on the market environment.

SMEs, by definition, are small in size and this situation has a major significance on their management and decision-making capability. Internally, SMEs are severely restricted by their lack of financial resources, which limits their growth potential (Carson et al. 1995). In many cases, they do not have an expert team for managing various business functions professionally, but instead rely on generalist individuals – usually the owner-manager. Externally, the SMEs' small size means that it does not have much control over their competitive environment. Because of this, they are extremely vulnerable to adverse environmental change and competitive threats. In SMEs, efforts are usually concentrated not on predicting and controlling the operating environment, but on adapting as quickly as possible to the changing demands of the business environment and implementing procedures to reduce or eliminate the negative consequences of market threats.

The following case study presents some of the main strategic mistakes made by small firms.

CASE STUDY

'Do your homework', French professor tells small firms *(by John Dunn)*

Small firms rarely find enough time to stop and think about where they are going. Even when they pay to get expert marketing advice from Professor Paul Millier, head of industrial marketing at Lyon Business School in France, he says they still do not do their homework.

'They never sit down for even half an hour to reflect on their situation. When I work with them and tell them to write a marketing plan, they never do it. They are too busy.'

It may seem a paradox, he says, but small firms face exactly the same problems as big ones in getting innovations accepted. 'All companies have to convince someone. In big companies, the laboratory researcher has to convince his small business unit or marketing department. The entrepreneur has to convince his bank manager or his shareholders.

'Carrying out a proper marketing study is a very good way of persuading them. But with small companies it's always the same. A year or two after they have started they have got a list of perhaps

one or two hundred contacts they have made, but they don't have a proper view of their market.'

As a result, Mr Millier says, they spread their energy and resources over hundreds of clients rather than concentrating on a few market niches which are likely to prove successful. 'When you are a small firm you are always very busy. You are more comfortable taking the car to visit a client or picking up the phone to arrange an appointment, rather than stopping to reflect on your marketing strategy.'

The biggest mistake a company can make is to assume the market for a new idea is a homogeneous whole, Mr Millier says. In fact, it consists of several market segments or niches, each different from the others. The trick is to identify them and then concentrate on just one or two that are the easiest to attack.

A big company can spend £25,000 on a marketing study. But a start-up business has not got that sort of money, Mr Millier says. Instead it should sit back after the first year or so and analyse all its sales information to make a proper market segmentation. Then it should concentrate on those areas where it can really bring an added value.

Usually, small firms will have enough data. The problem, he says, is that they never make time to analyse it. 'They really need help from outside.'

In Lyon, the local chamber of commerce has attempted to tackle the problem by subsidising the cost of a consultation with Millier. For around £800 local small firms receive training in analysing their markets and help with drawing up a marketing plan. 'I tell them to work on their case, but they never do it,' he sighs.

With a technological breakthrough, the only way to succeed in marketing is to start from scratch, finding new applications, suggests Mr Millier.

'Use the creativity of your customers. The individual is never clever enough or creative enough to think of all the applications clients will think of,' he warns.

So the first step to success is what he calls expansion – 'let the product go in all directions' – to obtain feedback from customers and contacts. Don't rely on your own ideas of what will sell, he says. 'If you try to guess what a client wants from your product, you're always wrong.'

The second step is market segmentation, says Mr Millier. 'After a year or two, stop for a while and take an overview of your market. Appraise each segment, arranging them in order from the easiest to attack to the hardest and then start by choosing the easiest.'

Finally, he says: 'Focus on the chosen segments and try desperately to solve any problem that occurs until you're the best in that market. Above all, don't give up. Try to take the biggest market share in each niche. The stronger you are in your sector, the longer you will survive.'

Source: John Dunn, *The Guardian*, 8 June 1999. Copyright Guardian News & Media Ltd 1999.

In comparison to small firms, the large corporations usually have a wide range of internal resources and capabilities that allow them to collect data, analyse the market, choose the best strategic approach and implement it systematically according to a predetermined plan. They are capable of influencing the market via intensive marketing communication and modifying the competitive environment by investing in or disinvesting from specific sectors of activity.

However, the small firms also have certain advantages in the implementation process. Their small size and informal structure permits internal communication and decision making processes to be much quicker than is possible in a large firm as there is a more cohesive organisational culture. Therefore, a small firm will be capable of adapting more quickly to the unpredictable changes in the competitive environment and can follow more closely the consumption trends of the most important clients. As their client base is also much smaller than those of large companies, small organisations are capable of developing effective relationships with clients, suppliers and business partners. Finally, the small size of the firm permits the manager-entrepreneur to continuously have a unified vision of the firm, balancing dynamically the organisational strengths and weaknesses.

By contrast, many large corporations have transformed themselves into bureaucratic dinosaurs, with multiple hierarchical levels, formalised communication and a slow, multi-stage, decision making process. The general manager or the CEO usually does not have first-hand experience of the various functions of the organisation because of the sheer volume of data and simultaneous activities. The top manager often relies on the various reports and messages – sometimes these are incomplete and misleading, sent by divisional managers and filtered by the secretarial staff. A decision taken at corporate level may also need to be approved by a scientific/experts committee, the board of directors and major investors.

It is obvious that these significant differences between firms will influence the selection and implementation of marketing strategies. In a small firm, the strategic objectives can be set up and adjusted several times during the implementation process and the initial strategy can be modified flexibly to adapt its focus on new threats/opportunities provided by the market. On the other hand, a large corporation will establish at top level a series of clear strategic objectives, often on a long-term basis, which will be then divided accordingly for each divisional unit of the organisation. The marketing strategy will also be developed on multiple hierarchical and functional levels, the specificity and flexibility of implementation procedures growing significantly at the level of business units and project teams. However, managing the complex interrelationship of various strategic projects, interlocked at different hierarchical levels, can prove to be a complex puzzle, especially when the organisation experiences unexpected competitive situations.

People

Strategic implementation comprises actions made by people in order to achieve the established objectives. From this perspective, no strategy can succeed if people are not willing to act or else act differently from what was expected, either because they do not understand the strategic aims and means or they have their particular set of objectives.

The primary role of people in the implementation process outlines the importance of consensus, understanding and acceptance of strategic objectives and plans. There are various methods for involving the employees in the design and implementation of corporate strategies that are often complemented by various financial and/or non-financial incentives.

Bottom-top and top-bottom planning and implementation

To create a real sense of participation in the selection and implementation of marketing strategies, in some organisations the formulation of strategic plans is initiated at task team (bottom) level and then, progressively, the established strategic aims are integrated and developed further at project, department, business unit and corporate (top) level. As a result of this participatory process, the top management team ends up with a document that synthesises the vision of every person in the organisation.

The implementation process then develops this process in the opposite direction, each implementation action and procedure being detailed as it is passed down from the higher hierarchical levels (top) to various business units and organisational divisions, until every employee (bottom) is provided with a set of activities related to the strategic aims of the organisation. See Figure 6.3 for a summary of this process.

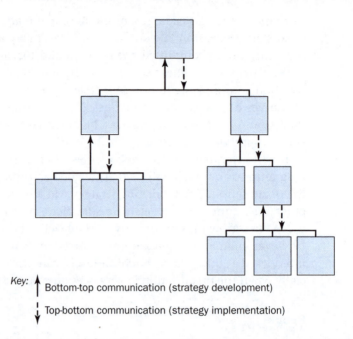

Key:
Bottom-top communication (strategy development)

Top-bottom communication (strategy implementation)

Figure 6.3 **The bottom-top and the top-bottom methods of internal communication**

Two main conditions are necessary for the success of this method.

1 the managers at various levels need to be able to synthesise and translate the ideas and opinions of their subordinates (bottom-top communication) and then transmit clear instructions for implementation actions that suit the skills of every person in their department/team (top-bottom communication)
2 the application of this method should not be only a rhetorical exercise – something that is presented in theory to improve the image of managers internally, but which is hardly applied in reality. Such attempts to mime organisational democracy cannot be sustained on a long-term basis as they create disappointment and alienation among the employees.

Representation

An alternative method of participation in the process of strategy design and implementation is the creation of a work committee composed of representatives from various groups of employees. Often, when using this method, each functional division chooses a representative (such as accounting and finance, manufacturing, supply, marketing, sales, research and development and so on) who brings the expertise, vision and interests of people working in their department to the planning process. The work committee combines and conciliates the various perspectives, creating a common implementation plan that is then developed specifically for every functional department (see Figure 6.4).

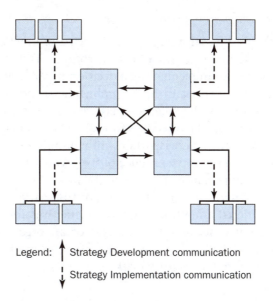

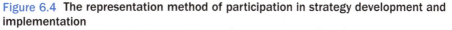

Legend: ↑ Strategy Development communication

          ↕ Strategy Implementation communication

Figure 6.4 The representation method of participation in strategy development and implementation

Direct participation

In small firms, the choice of strategy and the consequent development of an implementation process can be done by means of the direct participation of all the people working in the organisation (see Figure 6.5). This participation can take the form of informal meetings in which various aspects of the strategic process are considered and debated, often using a problem-solving framework. Some manager-entrepreneurs even organise regular general meetings in a relaxed atmosphere in order to facilitate the exchange of opinions between members of staff.

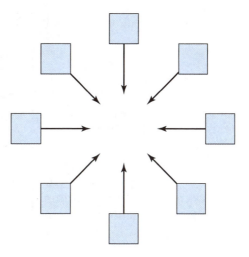

Figure 6.5 The direct participation route to strategy development and implementation

Direct management intervention

Despite their advantages, the participatory methods for strategic planning are not suitable in all the situations. In conditions of market crisis, when the rapidity of making and implementing a decision is paramount for the survival of the firm, the manager or specialist in the problem area should take control and indicate quickly the actions to be taken (see Figure 6.6). In these circumstances, people will fully comply with the directives formulated by managers if they trust their competence and vision. Otherwise, they will willingly or unwillingly create barriers that can jeopardise the very existence of the organisation.

The importance of people to the process of strategy development and implementation increases the complexity of the marketing function. Marketing should be considered a methodology for contacting and satisfying both the external and internal customers (employees) of an organisation. A good balance between inward-orientated and outward-orientated marketing is a prerequisite for success in the twenty-first century marketplace.

Competitive advantage

Regarding the main competitive advantages a firm may have in relation to its competitors, Michael Porter has defined three generic strategies.

- *Cost leadership* The company that is capable of producing and commercialising a product for less than its competitors can adopt a cost leadership strategy. This firm will usually target groups of consumers that have basic, unsophisticated needs, requiring cheap and low-quality products and services.
- *Differentiation* This strategy has much more scope than the previous one. Differentiation can be achieved on the basis of any specific organisational skill or competence that gives a company a competitive advantage when compared

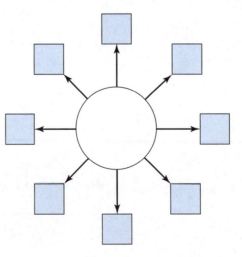

Figure 6.6 Direct management intervention as a way of implementing a strategy

with other firms. Although it can be argued that the cost leadership strategy can also by seen as a differentiation strategy, in this case, the accent is on differentiation in terms of superior quality and service. In fact, while the cost leadership strategy is characterised by successive reductions in the selling price, by differentiating its product or service in terms of quality or service, a firm can charge a premium price, yielding higher profit margins.

■ *Market niche leadership* Sometimes, a company is capable of developing a highly specialised expertise in satisfying a clearly defined group of customers with specific needs and demands. In this situation, the firm will apply a strategy of market niche leadership. Again, this strategy can be viewed as a particular case of differentiation, but, it is argued, market niche leadership is usually adopted by small firms and they lack the resources needed to achieve cost leadership or differentiation advantages.

Porter notes that the worst position for a firm to be in is 'stuck in the middle' – in other words, trying to pursue simultaneously more than one competitive strategy. It can be argued that, in the present market environment, when the competitive pressures have multiplied substantially, this argument is no longer true. Some highly differentiated firms are forced to reduce prices in order to sell their merchandise because of fierce competition that has developed in their strategic group. Porter's classification also fails to integrate the role of the customer relationship into the three alternative strategies.

A possible model of marketing strategy that outlines the strength of the relationship with customers is presented in Figure 6.7.

From this perspective, cost leadership seems the least attractive strategy. This view is further confirmed by the fact that it is difficult to maintain low-cost leadership in a globalised, dynamic market (see the case study on Asda in Chapter 5) in which new competitors can appear at any moment with better-value propositions. Usually, cost leadership is an appropriate strategy for a short time period because this strategic position is likely to be attacked by challengers who attempt to capture the consumer groups interested in one-shot bargains.

The second strategic option given in Figure 6.7 is to differentiate your offer in terms of its quality and the service provided, although the basic concept is highly standardised. This is the strategy adopted by strong, traditional brands that appeal to elitist groups of people. This can be an effective strategy for tribal marketing.

Figure 6.7 **Generic marketing strategies and the strength of the customer relationship associated with them**

In order to further enhance the relationship with its customers, a firm has to consider their needs in more specific detail. For instance, the implementation of a personalised marketing approach, supported by customer relationship management (CRM) procedures and technology, can significantly increase the satisfaction and loyalty of customers.

To take this a stage further, the final strategic option given in Figure 6.7 could be adopted. It is based on recognising that the client is not only a buyer and a consumer but also a valuable partner in the strategic marketing process. The theory of value co-creation presented by Prahalad and Ramaswamy (2004) is that consumers represent important sources of information, ideas and skills that can be creatively channelled and used by companies in order to improve the value of their offer (see Chapter 10 for more details). This argument has been further developed by Vargo and Lusch (2004), who considered that the present market conditions require the development of a new marketing paradigm. They argue that the service paradigm is the most appropriate for explaining the present relationships between companies and customers, including the way in which clients buy, use and consume products and services. From this perspective, customer satisfaction is the result of a long-term collaboration between firms and their customers that goes beyond the moment of a transaction.

The influence of a firm's competitive advantage on which strategy should be chosen and implemented is clear and important. However, the existing framework of strategic analysis has to be adapted to the new realities of the twenty-first century, when a customer-centred approach should be adopted by any company that wishes to be competitive. From this new perspective, the competitive value of an internal skill varies depending on its capacity to enhance (or not enhance), the long-term relationship between a company and its customers.

External factors

The supply chain

The implementation of a strategy has to be supported by the existing suppliers and the very organisation of the supply chain. The suppliers are an essential part of the value-added chain that is centred on a company and they are participants in the value co-creation process.

The Industrial Marketing and Purchasing Group has developed a framework that explains the development of relationships between industrial suppliers and companies. Building on the concept of exchange in marketing (Alderson 1957), Håkansson and Prenkert (2004) have proposed a model of value creation in business exchanges, by distinguishing between two separate, but interdependent, value-creating processes:

- *exchange value* the efficiency of the exchange between the parties
- *the use value* how effectively the parties use each other's resources.

The exchange process can sometimes determine the gradual development of a relationship that transforms the open exchange process into a closed, dyadic system (Engeström 1987). The parties collaborate because they are dependent on each other's resources, which are available only as a result of their cooperation. Borys and Jemison (1989: 241) define value creation in this context as a 'process by which the capabilities of the partners are combined so that the competitive advantage of either the hybrid or one or more of the partners are improved.'

Different types of interdependencies determine specific value-creation possibilities (Håkansson and Persson 2004; Thompson 1967):

- *sequential interdependence* when the input of a partner's activity is the output for the other (Borys and Jemison 1989), the value being created as a result of economies of integration
- *pooled interdependence* when the parties develop a common pool of resources (Borys and Jemison 1989) that are then shared and used to create economies of scale or scope
- *reciprocal interdependence* when the parties both exchange inputs and outputs, progressively learning about each other, the main benefits of this being either improved problem-solving capabilities and/or a more effective use of resources.

No participant in the market environment can be self-sufficient – all companies have to engage in exchanges with other participants as a condition of their survival. However, as various organisations possess heterogeneous resources, it makes a difference which ones you interact with and how you interact with them. Therefore, each actor will try to identify, and interact with, a partner that owns highly valuable resources and is willing to collaborate (see Figure 6.8).

Considering the importance of supply chain relationships, choosing and implementing a strategy will be influenced by the existing suppliers. The impact of that decision will be more significant in a situation of strategic change, when the schedule and the amounts of necessary supplies may be drastically modified.

Depending on the importance of the supplier and the strength of the relationship between the supplier and the firm, a series of alternatives have to be taken into account when implementing strategic change. As presented in Figure 6.9, it is important for the firm to maintain the relationship already developed with suppliers, as the initiation of a new relationship requires time and significant costs. In the case of important suppliers, which the firm cannot afford to lose, the approach to strategic change should take the form of a dyadic system rather than a focus on independent objectives. Close collaboration and communication between the firm and the supplier permits the identification of possible strategic challenges that can be properly addressed simultaneously by the two organisations in order to maintain the cohesion and coherence of the relationship.

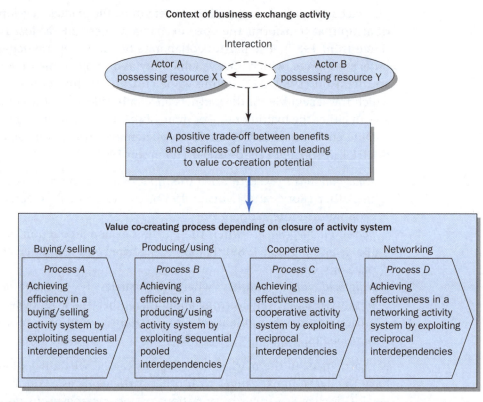

Figure 6.8 Different value-creating processes exploit different types of interdependencies to achieve efficiency or effectiveness

Source: Forsström 2005, p.79

Competitive situation

The competitive situation of a firm within its market will determine which specific strategy and approach will be used in the implementation stage. The competitive situation can be discovered by analysing the structure of the strategic group in which the company competes and defining the firm's position in relation to its competitors.

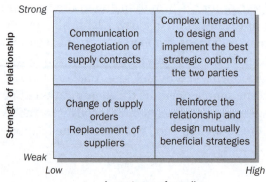

Figure 6.9 Implementation of strategic change in the relationship with suppliers

The structure of the competitive group can be assessed by using the bidimensional matrix presented in Figure 6.10, the two axes representing the number of direct competitors there are within the strategic group and the intensity of the competition.

When the market is characterised by a small number of competitors and a low intensity of competition, it is a *stalemate* situation. This is usually the case when a market is in decline, no specific technological or strategic innovation is possible and a few surviving firms try to stay longer in the market. The firms in this situation should choose either harvesting – selling remaining stocks as quickly as possible, for the best possible price – or managing a decline-stage leadership – staying in the market longer than other firms that apply the harvesting strategy. With the latter option, a company can become a major player in a declining market that few wish to serve.

Being within a group with few competitors and a high level of competitiveness is to be in the *close race*. This is mainly characteristic of markets in development, with products either in the launch or growth stages. The firms in this category should focus on quick reactions to competitors' moves and taking aggressive marketing actions to maximise their market share.

A market in which there are many competitors but a low competitive intensity is usually in the mature stage – the *quiet pond*. The strategic group has reached a position of equilibrium and the companies in it are happy to preserve the status quo. The strategy to choose here will recycle the same procedures that have proven to be successful in the past as the companies in this group will strive to maintain the existing competitive balance.

Finally, a *cyclone* market – one with a large number of competitors and a high level of competitive intensity – often occurs in high-tech areas of the market where the pace of technological innovation and market change is extremely rapid. The strategy to choose for this market would most probably focus on technology and innovation leadership, while the implementation process should be highly flexible in order to allow the firm to respond quickly to any competitive challenge.

The competitive situation a company is in can be considered from two different perspectives:

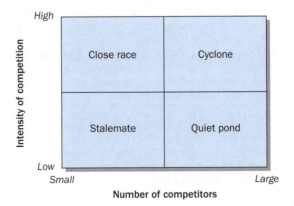

Figure 6.10 **Assessing the competitive situation facing a firm in its market**

- its approach to the introduction of new products
- its competitive position within its strategic group.

A firm's approach to new products being introduced can put it into the category of either pioneers or followers (this is also discussed in the time pentagon in Chapter 1). Both these positions have their specific advantages and disadvantages in terms of strategic position (see Table 6.3).

In absolute terms, there is no 'best' position because the strategic success of specific pioneers or followers will ultimately depend on their capacity to mitigate between existing advantages and disadvantages, enhancing the strength of their position and reducing competitive threats.

Choosing which strategy to use and how to implement it are also influenced by the competitive position of the company within its strategic group. The group leader will have a different impact on the market than a challenger, so this perspective will also influence the strategic approach of the organisation.

The various strategies available to market leaders are presented in Figure 6.11.

- *Direct confrontation* is applied in a situation in which the strategic group leader feels a direct and immediate threat from one or more challengers. The implementation of this strategy can be proactive – when the leader has clear information that another competitor will challenge its position in the near future – or reactive – when the competitive threat is already present. In this particular case, the leader will improve the customer value of the product/service that is directly threatened by the challenger.
- *Flanking attack* is a manoeuvre of differentiation, by means of which the leader attacks a weak side of the challenger. This strategy can, again, be proactive or reactive and takes place when there is a specific possibility of market expansion that is targeted by both the leader and the challenger.

Table 6.3 The advantages and disadvantages of being pioneers and followers

Pioneer position	*Follower position*
Advantages	*Advantages*
• Economies of scale and experience • Create barriers for future market entry • Define the structure of the market • Influence on consumer choice criteria and attitudes • Possibility of pre-empting scarce resources • Occupy the best distribution channels	• Learn from the pioneer strategy and avoid marketing, product and positioning mistakes • Take advantage of a new technological wave • Penetrate an already developed market
Disadvantages	*Disadvantages*
• High investments • High risks • Difficulties in segmenting the market and choosing the strategic position • Unpredictable consumer reaction • Market development efforts	• Consumers' perceptions and attitudes already shaped by the pioneer • Weaker brand reputation • Loss of high profits in the launching phase • Possible market entry barriers created by the pioneer

- *Leapfrog strategy* consists of developing a second generation of product/service using superior resources and new technology. This new offer gives customers improved quality and makes the existing products of competing organisations out of date.
- *Encirclement* is an extremely aggressive manoeuvre that can be applied to either completely eliminate or discipline a threatening challenger. The market leader uses its superior level of resources and capabilities to expand the range of its product/service offering, addressing the needs of various consumer subgroups within the target market, including the existing customers of the challenger.
- *Consolidation* is a more defensive strategy. The leader attempts to take advantage of its superior market reputation and consolidates its position, raising new market entry barriers.
- *Strategic withdrawal* is applied by the leader when its resources are thinly divided between too many projects, weakening its competitive position. The organisation can make an in-depth analysis of its specific strengths and weaknesses in the context of the competitive situation and then decide which projects to abandon and those to keep and develop further.
- *Expansion* is implemented when the market is developing quickly in directions that do not lead to direct confrontation with other competitors. However, by quickly filling the gaps in consumer demand, the leader is eliminating possible expansion opportunities for its challengers.

The strategic options available for challengers are represented in Figure 6.12. Most of them are similar to those for market leaders, such as the frontal attack, flanking attack, leapfrog strategy, encirclement and expansion. The main difference between the leader and the challenger in the implementation of these strategic options is the fact that the leader often takes the initiative even before the market is ready, attempting to develop the demand for a product/service. The challenger, on the other hand, because of its limited resources and weaker market reputation, is more inclined to wait for favourable market circumstances, attempting to identify new competitive opportunities and exploit them quicker than the leader.

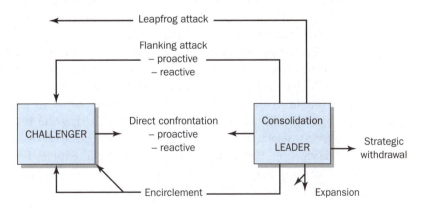

Figure 6.11 **Strategies available to market leaders**

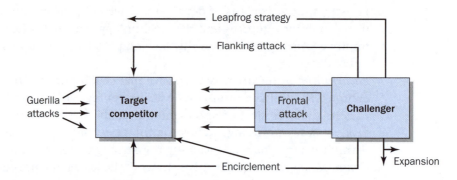

Figure 6.12 **Strategies available to challengers**

An additional strategic option that is specific to challengers is the guerrilla attack. Guerrilla attack operations are launched for a short time period on specific targets, in order to destabilise the position of the competitor. A good example of a guerrilla attack is a price reduction promotion lasting two weeks in a major city for a product that competes directly with the market leader's.

The strategic options presented in Figures 6.11 and 6.12 are derived from classical warfare techniques and their diversity indicates the complexity of strategic choice and implementation in the modern market environment. Of course, there is no general recipe for success. Starting from a good understanding of its position within the strategic group, each firm has to identify the best strategy and implementation method specifically for its organisational profile and objectives. The complexity of the strategic confrontation can be increased even further when a company uses a combination of the strategies presented above.

Customers

Customers are arguably the most important factor that determines which marketing strategy is chosen and how it is implemented. They represent both the trigger for strategic change and a key influence on the way in which the strategy is implemented. As a general rule, the implementation of any marketing strategy must have as its main objectives to increase the value for customers and enhance the relationship with the company's clients.

Recent advances in information and communication technologies (ICT) have empowered customers. The traditional passive role of customers in market transactions has shifted so that now they have a more active stance because of the ready availability of information, globalisation, ability to network and desire to experiment (Prahalad and Ramaswamy 2004). Using the Internet, customers can easily access, select and compare information regarding the available offers of goods and services, globally. More than that, they can express their own views and opinions regarding personal consumption experiences, creating lasting online knowledge that can benefit other consumers.

As a result of enhanced communication and interactive access to information, consumers have become more knowledgeable and active in the way they relate to the market environment.

Lawer (2004) identifies the rise of the 'one minute customer', who has an increased technological ability to find the necessary market information from all different sources and initiates a new type of contact with companies. This new customer is characterised by four main requirements during such interactions.

- *Value for time* The recent technological advances in ICT compress and enrich time and, as a consequence, accelerate and fragment human activity. In these conditions, time rapidly becomes a valuable currency for customers and organisations alike. The new customers perceive saving time and being efficient as important quality dimensions of their interaction with firms (Stalk 1988).
- *Value for attention* The high level of interactivity of the new media channels offer the customer increased control over the information consumed. On the other hand, multiple marketing messages with different contents are competing for consumers' attention. Godin (1999) estimates that consumers in the USA are exposed to roughly 5000 advertising messages every day. To protect themselves, modern customers learn how to use ICT to select and control the number and content of these received messages and, increasingly, are capable of identifying the marketing methods used by companies to step up commercial pressure and manipulate emotions. As a result, the marketing media overload leads to lower levels of consumer attention as people are willing to access only personally meaningful messages.
- *Control of personal data* The implementation of information intensive data-mining techniques and aggressive customer relationship campaigns has increased modern customers' awareness of the value of their personal data. In an increasingly competitive environment, the consumers quickly learn how to leverage the information about their private buying and consumption behaviour that has become a strategic resource for companies.
- *Life-enhancing services* Customers are focusing more and more on services rather than products, looking for life-enhancing experiences (Vargo and Lusch 2004).

As we saw for suppliers, the process of implementing strategies becomes most difficult when given scenarios undergo change. Figure 6.13 presents the implementation measures that have to be considered by a firm in various market situations, depending on the intensity of change and the characteristics of the targeted consumer group.

The existence of a responsive (CRM) system is an invaluable tool for implementing strategies, permitting an in-depth understanding of consumer behaviour and preferences and indicating the performances related to present and past marketing strategy implementation processes. By comparing these two elements, marketers are able to identify the performance gaps in the implementation process and design solutions for their reduction or elimination, depending on the success patterns that are discerned.

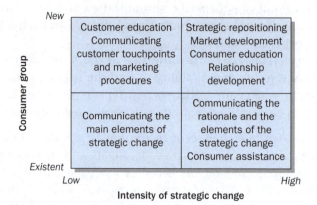

Figure 6.13 The implementation of marketing strategies in various consumer market contexts

The CRM system is a part of the central information system of the organisation and probably the most important element of the marketing knowledge infrastructure. The main parts of the CRM system are represented in Figure 6.14. The interactions between company and customer are registered by real-time data mining tools that collect and transmit data as inputs to a centralised customer database. When a specific department requests information, a specific data processing protocol is selected and applied, resulting in information that it is then transmitted to the department as an input for its process of situation analysis and decision making.

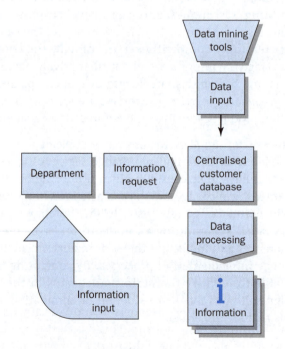

Figure 6.14 The use of an integrated CRM system

The rapid development of new IT applications, often connected with the Internet, have significantly increased the capacity of business organisations to access, collect, store, process and analyse customer information – and in real-time. This is a good example of the impact of technology on the implementation process both directly – acting on which marketing strategies are chosen and how they are implemented – and indirectly – influencing the other elements that impact the choice and implementation of marketing strategies.

The impact of technology on marketing implementation

The success of many marketing strategies depends on the effective utilisation of sophisticated IT (Berthon et al. 1996; Kitchen 1999; Hoffman and Novak 1996; O'Connor and Galvin 1997 and 1998). For example, the rapid growth of the Internet and Internet marketing suggests that IT has an important role to play in the implementation of effective online marketing communications (Kassaye 1999). Internet-based technology can facilitate information dissemination, file transformation, information gathering, as well as searching and browsing activities (Keeler 1995; O'Connor and Galvin 1997). Thus, for the business and marketing, better utilisation of state-of-the-art IT becomes a fundamental task – one that is too important to be exclusively delegated to IT professionals (O'Connor and Galvin 1998).

Technological deployment corresponds to the way in which companies plan and manage IT to benefit from its potential and effectiveness in the implementation of marketing strategies (Croteau and Bergeron 1991, 1998 and 2001). There are six components to deploying technology.

- *Strategic use of IT* IT applications are used to help the organisation gain a competitive advantage, reduce competitive disadvantage or meet other strategic enterprise objectives (Bergeron et al. 1991; Bergeron and Raymond 1995).
- *Management of IT* IT-related activities such as the usage of current and new technologies, the development of specific IT applications and the degree of IT usage practised by the employees are examined (Bergeron and Raymond 1995; Das et al. 1991).
- *Role of the information system/information technology IS/IT* The organisational importance of IT planning, the quality of the alignment of IT with the organisational structure, the effectiveness of software development and the management of communication networks (Bergeron and Raymond 1995) need to be looked at carefully here.
- *Technological infrastructure* The IT architecture and formalised procedures used to guide and control the firm's IT resources (Das et al. 1991) should be considered.
- *Organisational infrastructure* This is the internal functioning of IT/IS development, such as structure, processes, reporting relationships, support groups and skills (Das et al. 1991; Henderson and Venkatraman 1999).
- *Administrative infrastructure* This concerns the managerial policies and actions that influence and guide the work of employees involved with the IT/IS development (Das et al. 1991).

Marketing is, and will continue to be, heavily influenced by IT. Marketers who do not embrace the current technology will not survive in the postmodern marketing environment (Bruce et al. 1996, Komenar 1997).

The following case study illustrates the role of technology in enhancing the flexibility and competitiveness of modern companies.

CASE STUDY

What makes a business more agile?

In order to remain productive and competitive, businesses need to be agile. Staff empowerment, cost efficiency and improved communications are some of the key elements that define business agility.

Over the last few years a huge wave of technological innovation has been unleashed which is rapidly changing society, the nature of work and the ways in which companies are interacting with their customers.

The introduction of text messaging, always-on Internet connectivity and the possibilities of mobile working are prompting companies to fundamentally review their internal processes and the way they operate in order that they can keep up and survive in a more dynamic and demanding society.

Martin Heath, Head of Communications Consultancy for KPMG in the UK, says the biggest test for companies in today's rapidly moving marketplace is learning how to manage the implementation of new technologies that will enable them to respond faster to change. 'Technology is a means to an end. Simply putting in a new broadband link does not create any value in itself. It's only when you change your strategies and automate your processes that technology can bring business benefits. Technology is an enabler and you need to make sure you change your structures to account for that technology.'

Despite the difficulties associated with implementing new technologies, he believes that companies need to embrace new concepts such as mobile working in order for them to remain agile and productive in the marketplace. 'As soon as any of us are away from our desks, our productivity goes down. We no longer have access to our e-mail. We no longer have access to knowledge management systems.'

Heath sees the traditional office eventually extending outwards through networks which staff can tap into. 'The office will be on your laptop, PDA and phone. All the technology you get in the office will be on a mobile device.'

As the world becomes increasingly interconnected through a plethora of fast and pervasive communications platforms and as customers demand service every day of the week, companies are having to introduce flexible working arrangements. The traditional nine-to-five model is no longer adequate in a 24/7 environment and employers also know if they want to retain skilled staff, especially those with children and other family obligations, they are going to have to be open to part-time working and job-sharing arrangements. Otherwise they could severely restrict the resources they can recruit from.

'Organisations can become more agile by deploying infrastructures that support them becoming agile. Your IT structure and networks have to permit flexible job patterns, instant messaging and videoconferencing,' explains Danny McLaughlin, Managing Director of BT Major Business, a division of BT Retail. He argues that businesses need to take full account of the fact that electronic communications are fundamentally changing the nature of work. 'Work is what you do and not where you go. We use Web-based meetings so we can bring together the right specialists who may be based in different parts of the country. But there has to be the right infrastructure in place before you can have an e-enabled workforce.'

McLaughlin adds that the company has plans to provide all of its 5200 home workers with access to ADSL. He argues that if companies can allow individuals to work more on their own terms then they will feel empowered and motivated, which is likely to lead to a rise in productivity levels. 'If you create a satisfied employee base then it is going to impact upon customer satisfaction. If you equip people with the right kind of infrastructure and tools, they are more empowered to do their job and they can make decisions quicker.'

In order to make itself more agile, Virgin Atlantic recently launched a collaborative website for its 18 marketing offices around the world. The site stores product photographs, approved copy, videos of ads, poster campaigns and radio commercials in audio formats. The idea behind this online collaborative tool is that the airline's international marketing teams can upload their work, access material and share ideas in real time with others around the world. There are also contact numbers for external agencies who carried out specific types of work so they can be rehired for future campaigns.

'It's improving internal processes simply because it channels everyone to one specific area. It means we can be more responsive globally, whereas before it might have taken a bit of time for campaigns to kick in,' explains Bill Gosbee, Virgin Atlantic's UK Design Manager. He adds that new collaborative Web-based tools have a unifying effect and he feels they are most relevant for companies with a fragmented workforce.

Christoph Michel, Chief Executive of Hyperwave, which develops collaborative knowledge management systems, has helped advertising agencies to set up sites similar to the one deployed by Virgin Atlantic. He believes it is in the self-interests of companies to disseminate and share information more quickly online. 'Essentially they are after efficiencies for themselves and the business. The advertising gets done a lot quicker and they can have meetings online.' He adds that easily searchable information can make it less expensive for businesses to expand; local offices can easily tap into existing corporate knowledge and call up previous examples of work to help them pitch to new clients without having to pay to fly in executives from other countries to assist them.

Jonas Hjerpe, Marketing Director for Parity Technology, whose clients include Consignia, believes that a flexible IT architecture is crucial to the ability of a company to remain agile.

'Companies that tend to be successful have more strategic views of their information technology.' He points out that it is not just the private sector that is harnessing technology in order to become more agile; local councils across the UK are piloting Web-based technologies so they can, for example, purchase goods and services online in paper-less environments. Leeds City Council has set up a Web-based tendering service so suppliers can log on and see what is being tendered and then download and upload tender information.

'It's giving people who want to apply for the Council's contracts more time to do it. Instead of waiting for material to be published in the newspaper and then contacting us, they can go straight in and download it,' explains the Council's Information Manager Teddi Coutts.

And councils in Cornwall have clubbed together to pilot advanced multifunctional smart cards which can be used by a variety of organisations to make services more accessible to people in rural areas. In the initial roll-out, cards are being made available through schools for registration and meals payments. The cards are being used in libraries (as replacements for standard cards) and for paying for tickets in local car parks and on buses.

'The world outside a company's four walls is quite different from the world about four years ago. Enterprises have to have very fluid structures and must quickly align their skills and knowledge to deliver what a market opportunity wants,' explains Andy Mulholland, Chief Technology Officer for Cap Gemini Ernst and Young. He says the speed at which a company responds has to be dictated by the market and not by the traditional internal structures of the organisation.

He explains how companies such as Dell are now enjoying competitive advantages because they are using Web-based channels to make new computers to order, while car companies such as Audi are enabling customers to configure the car models of their choice online. Tasks that were traditionally performed by a sales team are being supported by Web-based tools that help customers design and swiftly order new products.

The agility of a business depends to a large extent on the ability of management teams to rethink how their companies operate. And many business

▶

consultants believe that UK directors are still a long way off from fully understanding how they can best integrate new technologies into their operations. Take mobile communications, for example. It sounds promising in theory in terms of being able to send marketing information to consumers on the move. But not many businesses appear fully geared up to deliver tailored individual marketing messages to consumers on mobile devices. Many are still mass media orientated.

Mobile working sets executives free from their desks but it has its disadvantages as well, as KPMG points out. Not least is the fact that many companies are extremely worried about the security of their data as it travels out of the physical office and through the air to someone's mobile device which could be lost or stolen. 'There are big concerns over security,' admits Heath. 'I think the security issues are manageable. But the real debate is around the changing work practice issues.'

Finding smart ways to apply technology is not easy. Technology can facilitate home working, for example, and create significant savings as space is not required in traditional office premises. Such practices are open to abuse and require a significant amount of trust. It is by no means clear to companies how you manage home workers effectively and keep them motivated. Nor is home working suited to everyone. Many prefer the social interaction of working with other people.

While there are clearly many new possibilities, there is still some way to go before the concept of business agility is successfully mastered by UK directors. 'I don't think the process has been cracked yet,' says Heath. 'We're just at the stage where we are beginning to learn how to deal with this huge wave of technology innovation.'

Source: Justin Hunt, 'What makes a business more agile', *The Guardian*, 9 May 2002

IT-related organisational benefits

IT can benefit organisations in many ways, but it has to be successfully managed. The sensible use of IT allows the effective design and implementation of creative and innovative strategies that are required in the present complex and dynamic marketplace (Schlegelmilch and Sinkovic 1998). The application of IT helps marketing with automation, information and transformation (Remenyi et al. 1995; Zuboff 1988).

Automation

Traditionally, IT has been primarily used for automating manual systems of recording data. This function is useful for routine and tactical activities, because it can significantly improve efficiency (Peattie and Peters 1998).

Information

This is the next stage of development, in which IT systems are used to translate data into useful information that can be utilised for developing and implementing marketing strategies. At this stage, the data obtained via automation is scrutinised and converted into information.

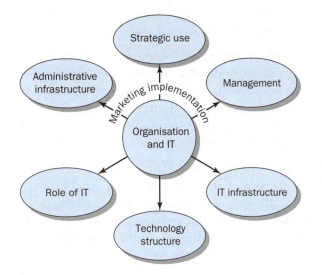

Figure 6.15 **IT strategies**

Transformation

This stage is reached when organisations fully embrace IT and start to 'think out of the box' (Schegelmilch and Sinkovic 1998). Then, companies start to focus on new ideas and concentrate on developing, adapting and using knowledge to transform themselves into effective market-orientated organisations (Brady et al. 1999).

IT is now the key driver in most businesses and many companies are conducting business in cyberspace. Equally, with the growth of the Internet, companies also need to be able to work and undertake transactions on a global basis. Because of this, many companies that do implement effective IT systems to deal with value chains on a global basis show good returns on their investment.

Information and knowledge creation

Specific areas of IT applications in marketing are growing. One area is the systems that provide market intelligence on a global basis. As companies expand their IT infrastructures to a global level, they are increasingly looking to access systems that can provide them with business intelligence. Business intelligence gathering is becoming a complex issue for most companies as the technology develops further. Access to information is now possible via hard-wired systems as well as wireless protocols. Mobile technologies must also be integrated into these intelligence-gathering systems.

Another important area of growth is knowledge management (KM). Knowledge management services include consulting, implementation, operation (outsourcing), maintenance and training. Increasingly, corporations are beginning to realise that implementing a KM system is not merely a technical undertaking but also requires management endorsement, employee acceptance and buy-in. Implementing new systems means transforming people, processes and technology in order to address the specific needs of an organisation. In the twenty-first century, companies increasingly need to:

- build knowledge capital and invest in efforts that create long-term competitive advantage rather than short-term return on investment (ROI)
- link knowledge areas by developing conceptual and transactional areas of knowledge contained internally, which is achieved by connecting planning, research, marketing, e-business and customer relationships
- make sound business decisions based on knowledge.

An IT knowledge repository has many benefits, as shown in Figure 6.16.

This type of model is suitable for most businesses, especially those in telecommunications and financial services markets. In general, linking company data to market information can lead to greater marketing insights and better strategic planning. Better planning, in turn, can lead to better relationships with vendors and customers, and help the organisation to minimise competitive threats.

Digital loyalty networks, e-differentiated supply chain and customer relationship management

In a survey undertaken by Deloitte Hoskins (Deloitte Research 2003), 850 manufacturing executives were interviewed in 35 countries across Asia-Pacific, Europe, North America, Latin America and South Africa. They found that if manufacturers successfully link their supply chain management (SCM) and CRM to create loyalty networks, they can generate significant competitive advantages. Companies that collaborate extensively with their supply chain partners (suppliers, distributors/retailers and customers) and use effective procedures of internal communication and CRM usually exceed their goals for customer loyalty, performing far better than most other companies (see Figure 6.17).

On the vertical axis, companies are classified according to their supply chain collaboration index. This index is based on executives' answers to the question 'How well has your company integrated with suppliers, distributors/retailers, customers

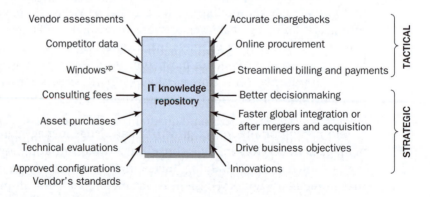

Figure 6.16 The benefits of an IT knowledge repository
Source: Flohr 2000

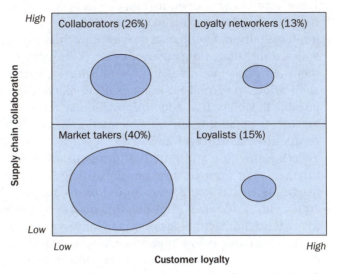

Note: Size of circles represents share of companies interviewed

Figure 6.17 Digital loyalty network quadrant
Source: Deloitte Research 2003, www.dc.com/obx Deloitte Consulting

and internally? – each group measured on a five-point scale. Because four elements were being measured, the index can take on values from 0 to 20, with 0 being the lowest score and 20 the highest. The results were as follows (and graphically represented in Figure 6.17).

- *Loyalty networkers* (in the upper right-hand quadrant) are those companies that scored 4 or 5 on customer loyalty/retention and 14 or higher on the collaboration index. Only 13 per cent of all manufacturers in the survey were classified as loyalty networkers.
- *Collaborators* (upper left-hand quadrant) scored 14 or higher on the collaboration index. However, despite these efforts, they were less successful in terms of building customer loyalty, scoring 3 or less, or did not measure customer loyalty/retention. The result was that 26 per cent of companies were classified as collaborators.
- *Loyalists* (lower right-hand quadrant) excelled in generating loyal customers, scoring 4 or 5 for customer loyalty/retention. However, their supply chains were not well integrated (scoring 13 or below on the integration index). About 14 per cent of companies surveyed were loyalists.
- *Market takers* (lower left-hand quadrant) constituted the remaining 46 per cent of all respondents. These companies neither succeeded in integrating with supply chain partners (scoring 13 or below on the collaboration index) nor achieved much success generating customer loyalty (scoring 3 or less or did not measure customer loyalty/retention).

These results again demonstrate the importance of information networks that straddle the globe and lead to effective customer management and marketing implementation. Companies surveyed in this research tended to be large multinational manufacturing enterprises. As IT investments grow and the technologies themselves become increasingly sophisticated, companies need to understand IT applications' potential for implementing marketing strategies and, especially, the possible flexibility that good information systems offer marketers, helping to fuse together the planning and implementation where they interface. Technology offers competitive advantages and can be used to create linkages between activities, affecting the cost and potential differentiation of products and services. The Internet, apart from creating new institutions, such as online auctions and digital marketplaces, has had a great impact on reconfiguring existing industries (Porter 2001). Therefore, when implementing marketing strategies, attention must be paid to the impact of technology on a company's value chain.

The above discussion illustrates the great impact that technology has on implementing marketing strategies. In addition to this, it is necessary to consider its impact on CRM.

Customer relationships

Kalakota and Robinson (1999) explain the value of integrating processes when building relationships, leading to three phases in CRM. Their argument is that, as intimacy grows over time, a customer relationship can be progressively developed and reinforced. However, companies need to implement such marketing strategies speedily as the competition can 'lock in' potential customers. Customers, too, have a variety of partners with whom they can deal.

There are three phases in CRM, each demanding a different kind of relationship over time (see Figure 6.18).

- *Acquiring new customers* Customers can be acquired by promoting product/service leadership that pushes performance boundaries with respect to convenience and innovation. The value proposition to the customer is the offer of a superior product, backed by excellent service.
- *Enhancing the profitability of existing customers* This relationship can be encouraged by excellence in cross-selling and selling upmarket products and services.
- *Retaining profitable customers for life* Retention focuses on making the service adaptable and ascertaining customers' needs. The value proposition for customers consists of a proactive relationship that works in their best interests. Retaining customers costs less than acquiring new ones.

As all the phases of CRM are interrelated, systems integration and, more importantly, people and process integration are crucial for success. It is always difficult for companies to align all three phases and correctly implement each one. A company should try to excel in implementing one particular area without losing sight of the other two. Much depends on the types of technology that are used.

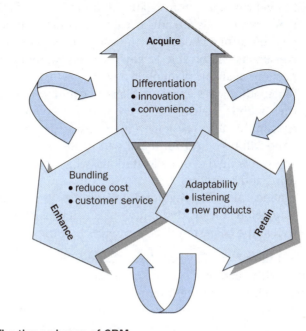

Figure 6.18 **The three phases of CRM**

Source: Adapted from Kalakota and Robinson 1999

Companies need to have the right technology and software to excel in one area and then support this with their strength in the other two. The best companies are able to manage all the facets of CRM.

This whole area is changing as a result of the rise of mobile communications. As greater numbers of individuals shift towards mobile communications, radical and subtle changes in the ways in which marketing strategies are implemented need to be considered by most organisations.

Customer retention is an increasingly important aspect of CRM. The cost of retaining a current customer by using relationship marketing strategies saves a company five times the cost of recruiting a new customer (Rosenberg and Czepiel 1984). Companies are also able to boost their profits by 100 per cent by retaining 5 per cent of their customers (Reichheld and Sasser 1990). One of the intangible aspects of having a good relationship marketing strategy is the ability to test-market new products prior to implementing marketing strategies, which can significantly reduce competitive risks (Shani and Chalasani 1992).

The technology drivers also create the following possibilities:

■ salespeople, on the road, can be updated on customers' requirements as necessary and this information can be used to enhance CRM and logistics operations
■ as mobile devices become more sophisticated, customers will be able to access the inventories of their suppliers, which means that they can place orders and specify delivery times and this can be done via links to an intranet or the Internet

- individuals, apart from talking to others, will also be able to communicate with machines (this is already a reality in some instances, consumers being able to buy soft drinks, chocolates and car parking places via mobile devices)
- consumers will be able to pay for various products and services via secure connections available via mobile devices
- Bluetooth devices enable retailers to communicate special offers to customers on their mobile devices if they are within a 20 metre radius from their shops and, equally, this allows customers to undertake transactions with shops and restaurants)
- radio will become an integral part of the mobile device, allowing an individual access to a myriad of radio stations, which has important implications for advertising and branding
- the incorporation of ground positioning systems (GPS) into mobile devices sent via satellite, means that individuals will be able to easily locate their positions as well as the nearest outlets or services that they need.

As yet, however, IT systems (see Figure 6.19) are not fluid nor dynamic enough to cope with customers who are ubiquitous and can contact companies via mail, mobile phones and the Internet.

As customers become more dynamic and unpredictable in the ways they contact and interact with companies, companies need to be fluid in their market approach. In many organisations, the IT/marketing link is not good. The marketers do not understand what happens in IT regarding to service provision and prices and the information officers are puzzled by the qualitative approach taken by the marketing staff. This is what is behind the cultural gap between marketing and IT. There needs to be a better integration of companies' IT and marketing processes.

It is important for good CRM that IT and marketing work together, with IT being able to understand what the needs of the customers (managers, project teams, functional departments) are. A change of philosophy is required so that IT professionals shift from building solutions, to defining requirements from the front-end with internal and external customers. The ideal is a one-to-one relationship – when a customer is known to and interacts with the enterprise, while the organisation is

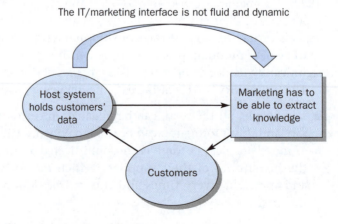

Figure 6.19 **Current systems architecture**

flexibly adapting its activities to respond to the customer's evolving needs. The enterprise needs to have a unified view of each customer across the entire enterprise, which results from integrating various functional and geographical units into a unified marketing approach.

As internal relationships develop across functional boundaries, the firm then truly becomes a learning organisation, while its customers discover that a long-term relationship can offer substantial advantages and so they are less attracted by opportunistic competitive offers. However, relationship building needs to be regarded as a business process rather than the automatic result of buying a new technology suite. Equally, however, technology needs to support and enable this process (see Figure 6.20).

Many companies have previously relied on CRM software to a great extent. However, they are now realising the importance of people and processes. McKean (1999) comments:

> *Most firms cited personnel challenges as being the single biggest obstacle to success. In most cases, there was no specific plan to address the personnel issue. The people issue, which made up roughly 20 per cent of the total transformation challenge, virtually went unaddressed.*

Table 6.4 shows the imbalance between the real needs of an organisation and the structure of its investments. Modern organisations should understand that IT cannot develop their competitive advantage on its own and an effective technological improvement must be combined with important investments in people and processes.

Therefore, to implement marketing strategies successfully, organisations must take into account not only their profile and cultural attributes, but also their technological prowess and their integration into the processes delivering value to customers. In order to integrate these three key aspects of implementing marketing strategies – technology, people and processes – a questionnaire has been designed

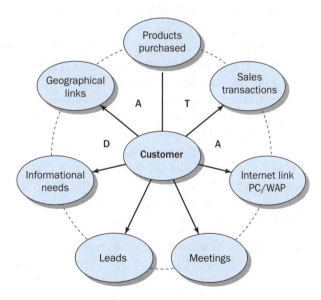

Figure 6.20 **Creating a relationship web**

Table 6.4 **Investments and determinants**

	Historical customer information investments (%)	Customer information competency determinants (%)
People	2	20
Processes	2	15
Organisation	2	10
Culture	1	20
Leadership	1	10
Information	10	15
Technology	82	10

Source: McKean 1999

to test how capable an organisation is of being flexible and adaptive to customers' needs (see Figure 6.21).

Once the scores to all the questions have been totalled, for the IT and organisational context sections, they can be plotted on a bidimensional implementation matrix, as shown in Figure 6.22. The implications of being positioned in each of the four quadrants are as follows.

- *Integrated marketing implementation* Companies in this quadrant have a well-balanced process for implementing marketing strategies based on good IT systems and a dynamic, flexible organisation. People, processes and the technology work in unison. The company is likely to have a highly efficient and responsive information system and its resources are shared dynamically by all the departments in the organisation.
- *Fragmented marketing implementation* Companies located in this quadrant have excellent capabilities in terms of people and processes. However, their technological resources are poor and not very well integrated. They require extra investment in IT infrastructure and closer integration of marketing procedures and information systems.
- *Technologically driven marketing implementation* In this quadrant, companies tend to rely to a greater extent on technology than the other two elements – people and processes. The management of these last two elements tends to be poor, determining the prevalence of a mechanistic approach. This often makes the employees feel alienated and poorly informed, reducing the efficiency of the entire organisation.
- *Poor marketing implementation* Companies finding themselves in this quadrant tend to have outdated organisational practices and possess poor technology systems. These companies need to bring about both organisational change and investment in technology to update their capabilities to deal effectively with an increasingly dynamic marketplace.

The implementation matrix provides a useful measure of a company's ability to implement marketing strategies within an environment that is increasingly driven by technology. However, this tool is only the starting point for a complex process of improvement of all the aspects of IT and marketing interactions within the organisation.

IT context	Strongly agree	Agree	Neutral	Disagree	Strongly disagree
	1	2	3	4	5
1 We utilise Web-enabled customer management systems	☐	☐	☐	☐	☐
2 We incorporate mobile protocols within our systems	☐	☐	☐	☐	☐
3 We have the systems to disseminate information internally	☐	☐	☐	☐	☐
4 We can easily relay information to our suppliers	☐	☐	☐	☐	☐
5 We have a clear idea of our customers' requirements	☐	☐	☐	☐	☐
6 Customers can easily contact us	☐	☐	☐	☐	☐
7 We can easily keep track of all customer contact	☐	☐	☐	☐	☐
8 Our field service managers can easily keep in touch with our systems	☐	☐	☐	☐	☐
9 Our systems are global, integrated supply chains	☐	☐	☐	☐	☐
10 Our data warehouse allows customer segmentation	☐	☐	☐	☐	☐
11 We have effective competitor intelligence data	☐	☐	☐	☐	☐
12 The marketing/IT interface is good	☐	☐	☐	☐	☐

Total points ☐

Organisational context	Strongly agree	Agree	Neutral	Disagree	Strongly disagree
	1	2	3	4	5
1 There are few blockages in information flow between functional areas	☐	☐	☐	☐	☐
2 The organisation is flexible and can reconfigure itself in a short time	☐	☐	☐	☐	☐
3 The people find it easy to implement information systems	☐	☐	☐	☐	☐
4 Change is readily embraced by staff	☐	☐	☐	☐	☐
5 There are good links between marketing strategy formulation and execution	☐	☐	☐	☐	☐
6 Customer requirements take priority	☐	☐	☐	☐	☐
7 It is easy to disseminate information formally and informally	☐	☐	☐	☐	☐
8 Creativity is accepted and rewarded	☐	☐	☐	☐	☐
9 The organisation is innovative	☐	☐	☐	☐	☐
10 There is an accepted vision for the development of marketing strategies	☐	☐	☐	☐	☐
11 Marketing and IT work together	☐	☐	☐	☐	☐
12 Competitors' actions are monitored and acted on	☐	☐	☐	☐	☐

Total points ☐

Figure 6.21 Questions to determine key organisational and IT success factors

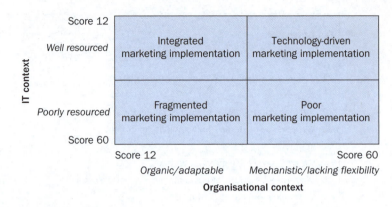

Figure 6.22 **Implementation matrix**

Summary

A good strategic plan can hardly guarantee market success if there is not also a flex-ible process of implementation. Often the strategic objectives can only indicate the general direction for market development, while all the other elements of the strat-egy are emergent, being implemented as creative solutions to the combination of competitive threats and opportunities encountered in the market. In this context, a multidimensional approach to the strategic implementation process, taking into account various internal and external factors that influence a company's opera-tions, is the only path to success.

In a market environment that is continuously evolving, the capacity of the firm to quickly identify, collect, process and interpret information about consumer behaviour, can significantly enhance the profitability of the firm. The creation of powerful and responsive knowledge management systems is the basis for enhanc-ing competitiveness and customer loyalty. However, this objective can only be reached when there is close collaboration between the IT and marketing specialists within an organisation. A good balance between IT systems, people and processes will allow the company to adapt effectively to various market challenges while quickly exploiting the existing competitive opportunities.

Chapter questions

1 What factors determine the use of emergent marketing strategies in the modern marketplace?

2 How is technology influencing the implementation of competitive marketing strategies?

3 Why is knowledge management important and what are the main factors that can influence its development and use in modern organisations?

7 Understanding and creating effective marketing cultures

Introduction

Organising for marketing is a multifaceted phenomenon. For the implementation of successful marketing strategies it is important to recognise and understand the visible and invisible elements composing and surrounding organisations. The visible element of an organisation is often recognised as its structure, or organisational chart, and is characterised by centralisation, formalisation and departmentalisation. For example, Figure 7.1 shows the visible elements of the marketing function within an organisation.

The invisible elements consist of informal functions, actual communication flows, current cultural norms and behaviour patterns. These are much more subtle than the visible elements and are expressed via cultural patterns and norms (see Figure 7.2). The challenge of developing a successful cultural pattern, therefore, does not necessarily lie in organising the marketing department, but in structuring the whole firm in such a way that marketing functions efficiently within it. At the same time, effective interaction procedures must be set up between organisations to facilitate transactions and the continuous exchange of assets and capabilities.

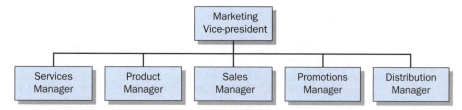

Figure 7.1 Organisational chart of the marketing function

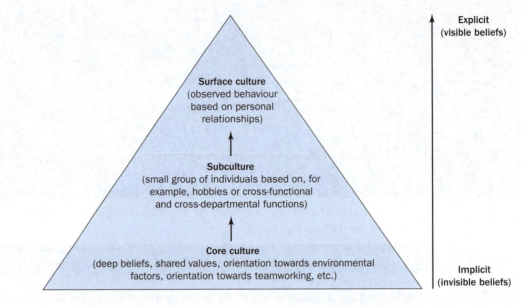

Figure 7.2 **The visible and invisible elements of an organisation's culture**

The visible and invisible parts of an organisation

We first explicitly describe below what constitutes the visible and invisible parts of the organisation. This is followed by a discussion of the basic concepts of organisational analysis and their implications for marketing practice. The ways in which an organisation can develop a marketing culture that takes into account the invisible elements are then presented, complementing the more formal organisational approaches.

The visible parts of an organisation

Organisations are concerned with the way in which tasks are distributed, understood and executed by individuals. This encompasses several aspects (Desreumaux, 1998; Helfer, Kalika and Orsoni, 1998; Mintzberg 1990 (see Figure 7.3):

- departmentalisation
- specialisation
- standardisation
- coordination
- formalisation
- decentralisation/centralisation
- control
- differentiation/integration.

Figure 7.3 **Organising: a multifaceted phenomenon**

- *Departmentalisation* refers to the principles according to which a firm is organised – that is, departmentalisation by functions (marketing, accounting, HR and so on), markets or products.
- *Specialisation* concerns the extent to which tasks are defined and allocated to a specific person. One can distinguish two types of specialisation: vertical specialisation, which corresponds to the number of hierarchical levels, and horizontal specialisation, corresponding to the number of different functions identified.
- *Standardisation* refers to the degree to which there are procedures explaining how tasks should be accomplished. This dimension can be either conceptualised as a characteristic of structure (Kalika 1995) or as a possible coordinating mechanism (see Mintzberg 1990). According to Mintzberg, *coordination* – that is, the regulation of all organisational components – can be achieved in a variety of ways: mutual adjustment on a one-to-one basis, direct supervision that applies hierarchical authority and, finally, *standardisation* of procedures, results, qualifications, or norms. Here again it should be noted that the coordinating process could be considered to be part of the *integration* process (Lawrence and Lorsch 1986), together with the concept of *differentiation*.
- *Formalisation* corresponds to the use of written documents in communication and information processes. The *decentralisation/centralisation* axis relates to the levels at which decisions are made. The decentralisation of an organisation implies lowering of the decision level.
- *Control* refers to the evaluative process by means of which tasks are judged. Results or the implementation of control can be evaluated.

Differentiation and integration can and may overlap (Lawrence and Lorsch 1986). Differentiation reflects the degree to which each department develops its own way of functioning and accomplishing tasks. For instance, a marketing department may develop skills in marketing communications as opposed to accounting skills, which are likely to be developed by the financial department. However, to develop coherent strategies, an organisation needs mechanisms for integration. These involve mutual adjustment, hierarchy (direct supervision), standardisation of procedures, committees, task groups, coordinating agents, project managers, product managers, common objectives, common norms and values, training and so on. This is illustrated in Figure 7.4.

The overall structure of an organisation is often represented in a chart that shows areas of function and responsibility. The chart shown in Figure 7.5 illustrates the structure of a small biotechnology firm that is essentially hierarchical in nature.

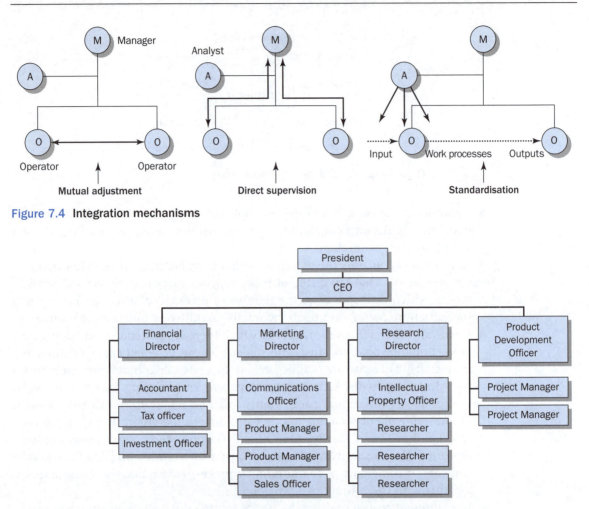

Figure 7.4 **Integration mechanisms**

Figure 7.5 **Organisational chart of a small biotechnology firm**

Organisational structures and marketing

Organisations are complex entities that exhibit varying degrees of centralisation, formalisation and specialisation and require different degrees of coordination. As markets become increasingly complex and global in nature, the utilisation of marketing knowledge (Menon and Varadarajan 1992) is seen as an increasingly important managerial area generally and one of the most important activities undertaken by the marketing department.

The three main uses of marketing knowledge have been identified as:

- *instrumental* when market information is used directly to solve a problem
- *conceptual* when employees/managers reflect on an issue, the marketing knowledge serving to define priorities
- *symbolic* when information is not used directly for a specific task – usually, then the marketing knowledge involves a political dimension, the information being used (or misused) with a specific intent.

The way in which marketing knowledge is used by employees and managers has implications for its form, content and structure within the organisation. For instance, in organisations using marketing knowledge symbolically, centralisation and formalisation can either stimulate or impede the transmission and use of this information. A high degree of formalisation can result in a clear organisation of internal information flows, but can also impede it as a result of rigidity in the internal communication system.

In most market-led organisations, roles and responsibilities are often highly formalised so as to enable them to respond quickly and efficiently to the market's needs. This is illustrated, as we saw, in Figure 7.1 and also in Figures 7.6 and 7.7.

After reading the following case study consider how market analysis and the notion of adding value changed the visible and invisible parts of the LGB organisation. Also, consider the symbolic, instrumental and conceptual use of marketing knowledge.

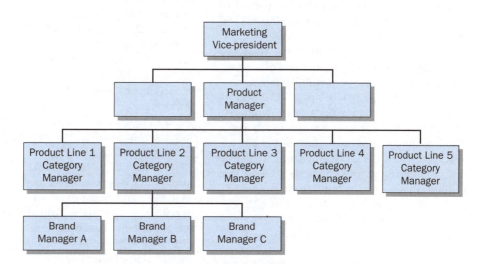

Figure 7.6 **The product-based marketing organisation**

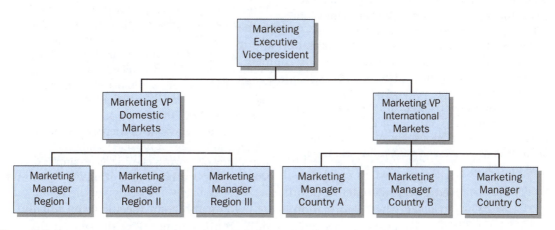

Figure 7.7 **The geographically based marketing organisation**

CASE STUDY

Setting off a chain reaction

This company relied on identifying value-adding, non-value-adding and wasteful activities to strengthen the chain of processes and people. L.G. Balakrishnan & Brothers had been through a recent business process restructuring (BPR) exercise. Speaking to a senior official at LGB, *eWorld* got the feeling that managing change – which is a natural fallout of any BPR initiative – must have come easily to LGB. The first promoters of the company could sense imminent change well enough. They managed to see the coming of nationalisation of bus services and prepared to exit the business of running a fleet of buses and enter into manufacturing components for buses. Then, changing ever so slightly for the sake of a teeny-weeny BPR must have been child's play.

Satyam Computer Services helped LGB with the BPR, with the redesign of the order-generation process and of the product-engineering process. These components of the project took about six years from April 1995. BPR alone took some three years to implement with satisfaction. LGB is in a business that it calls the transmissions business. It derives its revenues predominantly from chains required for automotives while it is also in the business of supplying industrial chains. With 14 lines of business, a group turnover of Rs 200 crore (of which the chains business contributed Rs 120 crore) and with manufacturing bases at five locations in South India and three regional offices across the country reporting to HQ at Coimbatore, LGB's BPR must have been quite a job.

Why did the company launch the BPR drive? Says S. Ramesh Kumar, Senior Consultant at Satyam, 'It had very little margins in its markets, the original equipment segment and in the replacement segment. Competition was gearing up for expansion and its own productivity levels had to go up to become price competitive.' So it set about making up a vision plan, calling it the P4 plan for BPR:

- a 270 per cent increase in productivity
- 100 per cent increase in production capacity in three years' time

- reduce elongation of chains by 10 per cent (performance)
- make the pricing ratio conducive to improving the marketability of the product.

A business process map helped define the whole business in six processes. Of these, the one that looked most like it could do with a change was the order fulfilment process. Says Kumar, 'Low overall equipment effectiveness was a concern. The long set-up time too was a concern. Employee involvement and skills had to be upgraded.' Adds the official, 'The quality of products was not a concern at all. But other parameters such as inventory turn ratio and other productivity norms had to be addressed.'

Satyam recommended the cellular design for the factory set-up. In other words, a factory within a factory model helped LGB improve in the areas causing concern. Here, IT played a role in setting up a Kanban manufacturing system, order management system that integrated with the order fulfilment process, the equipment effectiveness monitoring system and the measures of a performance monitoring system. The highlight of the project was the input–output analysis of the process. This helped define the activities of the organisation into three types: value-adding (VA), non-value-adding (NVA) and wasteful. Satyam helped LGB look at the number of activities making up a process and the man-hours required for those activities. He then divided these activities into those that worked for the customer (VA), those that worked for the company but did not directly affect the customer and those that worked for nobody (wasteful). Says Kumar, 'The idea here was to make sure that one maximised VA by removing obstacles to performance to minimise NVA and to eliminate waste.'

It is easy to see what VA processes are. But NVA?

Kumar just jumps at the query and says, 'Expediting or progress chasing are examples of NVA. Storing, warehousing, moving material in and out of the company, preparation of checks and controls documents and inspection also form part of the NVA.'

And waste? Pat comes the reply: 'Searching for a part or tool and reconciliation among documents is a classic case of wasteful activities. They add value to nobody.'

In the case of the OFP, it was found that VA contributed to about 68.2 per cent of the activities and NVA contributed to 31.7 per cent while the rest was wasteful. The official says that most of the objectives were met. The redesign of the order generation process for industrial chains was as follows: the objective was to substantially increase the efficiency of the process. Satyam took up a market analysis to illustrate the actual position of LGB, to identify market needs, demands and customer expectations of LGB and to spot and analyse the gaps between customer expectation and delivery.

Satyam's analysis of the existing gaps indicated that there was no true standard operating procedure, several customer interfaces, not enough market intelligence, need for active business development, incorrect understanding of customer specifications and poor brand visibility.

Satyam came up with the following positioning strategy: based on market surveys, LGB had to have a solutions provider image that would help it best in the circumstances. The highlights of these were to have a single window for all chain-related requirements, strategic partnerships with customers and just-in-time deliveries. Action on these fronts resulted in a 184 per cent increase in the number of enquiries received, 169 per cent increase in enquiries quoted, 300 per cent increase in number of samples submitted and a 460 per cent increase in the number of approved samples.

For obvious reasons with regard to competition, neither the company nor the consultant was willing to reveal absolute figures. The highlight of the redesign of the product engineering process (PEP) was the recommendation for concurrent engineering. The objective of the PEP redesign was to reduce the cycle-time of the enquiry process and to reduce new product development time each by half.

One of the issues the consultant cited as unproductive was the back and forth shunting of drawings from the sales force to the R&D for want of clear specifications.

The formation of a cross-functional team helped prevent unsuitable specifications creeping into the design at the concept stage itself. Industry-specific project leaders now came into the picture, thus helping the client himself decide what he wanted.

The product data management component of the redesign used technology to reduce new product development time. LGB created a repository of design and related data that came in handy for re-use for future designs. A system that aided the online release of documents was also put in place. The company achieved its objectives on this front. Further, application engineers were brought in to ensure that accurate information was passed on between the customer and the vendor.

Would LGB do this differently now? What were the lessons it learnt? Says the official, 'We would do it faster now, because of the learning that has accrued. Further, our priorities would be different now. For instance, we would look at new product development because that is crucial.'

Finally, why an external consultant? Would you do this again all by yourself?

The official feels, 'Satyam helped accelerate our progress. We might have been doing things on our own. Some were adequate, others not so. Further, bringing in Satyam helped us keep in touch with modern management and manufacturing trends. It is easy being in a state capital. But in a place like Coimbatore, we have to consistently keep deputing people to attend seminars or conferences where new issues are discussed, at state capitals or the national capital. Having an external consultant helps.'

Source: Bharat Kumar, 'Setting off a chain reaction', *The Hindu Business Line*, 2 October 2002

The roles of the invisible parts of an organisation

The invisible parts of the organisation include the corporate culture as well as its differentiation and integration mechanisms. As mentioned earlier in this chapter, differentiation is the degree to which each department has its own way of functioning and accomplishing tasks. Thus the structure of a marketing department can be very different from that of a purchasing or accounting department. For instance, the UK based organisation WHSmith, a company that specialises in newspapers, stationery and books, divides the marketing areas into branding and customer offers (see Figure 7.8). However, under branding, there are heads of design, instore marketing management and advertising, whereas under customer offers emphasis is placed on market intelligence. The design area looks at both store design and packaging design. The instore managers handle book events and promotion, while the head of advertising manages both local and national advertising.

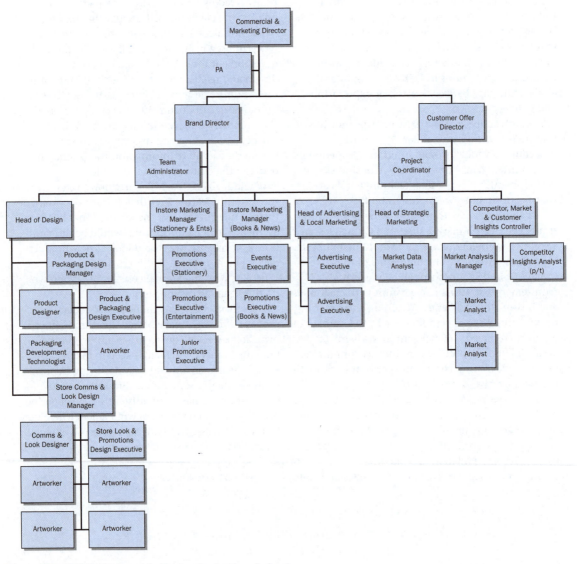

Figure 7.8 **WHSmith's marketing organisational chart**
Source: WHSmith

For other types of organisations, departments can be organised according to brand types, different marketing functions (such as sales, promotion and new product development) or can be based on geographical locations. Sometimes, when a department is formally structured (as shown in Figures 7.1, 7.6 and 7.7) possibilities of misunderstanding and misdirected communication with other functional departments can ensue. The inner structure of each department can be different, as well as the degree of standardisation, formalisation and decentralisation. Ultimately, this can generate interdepartmental conflicts, leading to inefficiency and suboptimal performance. However, as organisations grow, size is often a critical factor, leading to differentiation (Kalika 1995).

Culture as an invisible dimension

Culture is a problematic but extremely powerful integrating mechanism for organisations. Organisations function coherently as a result of the 'glue' provided by their culture (Ouchi 1980). Weick (1987) argues that culture is a source of reliability. Cultures develop over time and become stable, responding in specific ways to given stimuli.

Schein (1992) distinguishes three layers of organisational culture. The first one is called 'basic assumptions'. It pertains to the main beliefs that are shared within the organisation. For instance, is man good or evil, what is the right way to compete, what is reality? The basic assumptions behind the answers to these questions influence values – which are the second cultural layer.

Values are the principles that guide social interactions and constitute a goal in themselves because of their intrinsic value.

The third layer is represented by historical documents – the most tangible or visible manifestation of previous situations. They can correspond to rituals, practices and discourses. Corporate culture can be understood by deciphering such historical artefacts and linking them with values and basic assumptions. Culture's layers can be represented shown in Figure 7.9 (see also Figure 7.2).

Culture and marketing culture – defining organisational culture

Although the scope of organisational culture has not been completely established by organisational theorists, several common features have emerged, which are encompassed by Schein's central work (1992). The pivotal idea is that culture serves

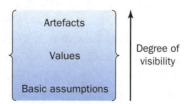

Figure 7.9 Components of culture, according to Schein
Source: Schein 1992

as a framework for organisational actions, enhancing external adaptation and internal coordination. Schein (1993) defines organisational culture as:

> *a pattern of basic assumptions that a given group has invented, discovered, or developed in learning to cope with its problems of external adaptation and internal integration, a pattern of assumptions that has worked well enough to be considered valid and, therefore, to be taught to new members as the correct way to perceive, think, and feel in relation to those problems.*

Understanding culture is not easy and many authors have different views regarding its meaning and effectiveness in the organisational context. From a marketing perspective, it is important to understand the articulation and functioning of a marketing culture within the general culture of an organisation.

From general organisational culture to marketing culture

Although many different authors have attempted to look at organisational culture and define it (Hofstede 1980; O'Reilly et al. 1989, 1991a, 1991b), very few have considered this concept in a marketing context. Working within IBM, Hofstede initially identified four dimensions that can be used to analyse a culture:

- distance from power
- risk avoidance
- individualism versus collectivism
- masculinity versus femininity.

In a second study (1990), however, he developed the following framework defining three types of values:

- need for security
- centrality of work
- need for authority.

Hofstede held that these values shape the beliefs of an employee and the functioning of an organisation. For instance, a typical statement representing the 'need for security' value is, 'working in a well-defined job situation is important'; for the 'centrality of work' dimension, 'work is more important than leisure time' and for the 'need for authority' value, 'it is not appropriate that management authority can be questioned'.

From this framework, six types of practices emerge, each reflecting a specific type of value (see Table 7.1).

Table 7.1 Cultural practices

Dimension	Typical statement
Process-orientated v. results orientated	Employees are told when a good job has been done
Employee-orientated v. job-orientated	Organisation is only interested In the work people do
Parochial v. professional	People's private lives are their own business
Open system v. closed system	Only very special people fit into the organisation
Loose control v. tight control	Everybody is cost-conscious
Normative v. pragmatic	Pragmatic, not dogmatic, in matters of ethics

Source: Hofstede et al. 1990

O'Reilly et al. (1989, 1991a, 1991b), on the other hand, analysed the fit between individuals and organisations from a cultural standpoint. He developed an analytical tool called the organisational culture profile – OCP. Various dimensions are used to describe organisational culture:

- innovative
- attention to detail
- results-orientated
- aggressive
- supportive
- reward emphasis
- team-orientated
- decisive.

The advantage of this tool is that it provides a list of adjectives that can be used to assess the fit between a potential candidate and the proposed firm. However, there is absolutely no mention of the customer nor the market.

An analytical framework developed by Quinn and Rohrbaugh (1981) was initially dedicated to understanding organisational performance, but was also found to be useful for describing the corporate culture. This analytical framework functions on three axes:

- axis 1 – flexibility v. control
- axis 2 – people v. organisation
- axis 3 – means v. goals.

On this basis, the competing values model (CVM) establishes four organisational types:

- clan culture
- adhocracy culture
- hierarchical culture
- market culture.

Cameron and Freeman (1991) state: 'Because cultures are defined by the values, assumptions and interpretations of organisation members, and because a common set of dimensions organises these factors on both psychological and organisational levels, a model of culture types can be derived.'

The four classifications of culture shown in Figure 7.10 imply varying degrees of differences in approach to a competitive marketplace. The figure shows the y-axis as a continuum from organic to mechanistic processes. This shows whether an organisation's emphasis is more on flexibility, spontaneity and individuality or control, stability and action. The x-axis, on the other hand, concentrates whether there is an emphasis on internal maintenance (smoothing activities, integration) or external positioning (competition, environmental differentiation). The culture types that result from such classifying parameters are clan, hierarchy, adhocracy, and market. These labels are broadly similar to those discussed and explained by Mintzberg (1979) and Ouchi (1980). They also match the leadership typologies and

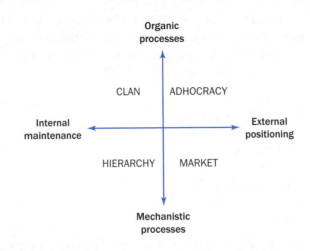

Figure 7.10 Organisational culture types
Source: Adapted from Deshpande et al. 1993

culture outlined in writings on organisational lifecycles (Quinn and Cameron, 1983). Figure 7.10 shows the relative positionings of organisations, based on their dominant attributes. The key types are as follows.

- *Adhocracy* Exhibiting entrepreneurship, creativity and adaptability, supported by a risk-taking leadership style, which in turn creates the climate for bonding. This type emphasises strategies that spur a company on to growth, innovation and searching for new resources.
- *Clan* Exhibiting cohesiveness, participation, teamwork and a sense of family, supported by a mentoring type of leadership, creating loyalty, tradition and interpersonal cohesion. The strategies that are emphasised are mainly internal, focused on developing human resources, commitment and morale.
- *Hierarchy* Exhibiting order, rules, regulations and uniformity, supported by a coordinating, administrative type of leadership, creating bonds by means of rules and policies. The strategic emphasis is aiming towards stability, predictability and smooth operations.
- *Market* Exhibiting competitiveness and goal achievement with a decisive, achievement-orientated leadership, creating bonds via goal orientation, production and competition. The strategies adopted are aimed at competitive advantage and market superiority.

Even though various SBUs within an organisation may have different cultures, there is often one dominant corporate culture – one predominates over the others. These cultural types are regarded as modal or dominant ones rather than mutually exclusive. Over time, it is expected that one type of culture emerges as the dominant one.

Figure 7.11 contains a questionnaire that organisations can use with employees when they want to understand their organisational culture and find ways to implement best practices.

Another interesting analytical model incorporating culture within an organisational framework has been formulated by Calori and Sarnin (1993). This model differentiates between cultural values and practices (see Figure 7.12).

Organisational culture

The following questions relate to what type of culture your marketing operation is closest to. Each box contains four descriptions of organisations. Please distribute 10 points among the 4 descriptions, depending on how similar, or not, the description is to your business – that is, give *most* points to the description that is most like your organisation. None of the descriptions is any better than the others; they are just different manifestations of a culture. You may divide the points in any way you wish. Most businesses wil be a mixture of the various descriptions. It is important that each box's total is 10.

Kind of organisation (Please distribute 10 points)

My organisation is a very personal place. It is like a family. People seem to share a lot of themselves.	My organisation has a very formal and extended structure. Established procedures generally govern what people do
My organisation is a very dynamic and entrepreneurial place. People are willing to stick their necks out and take risks.	My organisation is very production-orientated. A major concern is with getting the job done, without much personal involvement.

Leadership (Please distribute 10 points)

The head of my organisation is generally considered to be a mentor, sage – a father/mother figure.	The head of my organisation is generally considered to be a coordinator, an organiser or an administrator.
The head of my organisation is generally considered to be an entrepreneur, innovator or risk-taker.	The head of my organisation is generally considered to be a producer, technician or a hard driver of the business.

What holds the organisation together (Please distribute 10 points)

The glue that holds my organisation together is loyalty and tradition. Commitment to this firm runs high.	The glue that holds my organisation together is formal rules and policies. Maintaining a smooth-running business is a priority.
The glue that holds my organisation together is a commitment to innovation and development. There is an emphasis on being first in many areas.	The glue that holds my organisation together is the emphasis on task and goal achievement. A production orientation is commonly shared.

What is important (Please distribute 10 points)

My organisation emphasises human resources. High cohesion and morale in the firm are important.	My organisation emphasises performance and stability. Efficient, smooth operation is important.
My organisation emphasises growth and acquiring new resources. Readiness to meet new challenges is important.	My organisation emphasise competitive actions and achievement: measurable goals are of key importance.

Figure 7.11 **Determining what your organisation's culture is**

In order to find out what your organisation's typology is, first add together all the scores for the statements in the top left-hand corner of each box. For instance:

My organisation is a very personal place...	6 points
The head of my organisation is generally considered to be a mentor...	6 points
The glue that holds the organisation together is loyalty...	5 points
My organisation emphasises human resources...	7 points
Total (out of 40)	24 points

Then repeat for the bottom left-hand corners and so on until you have four totals.

The total in the example above indicates that the organisation is veering towards a clan type as its dominant culture. The other points will have been distributed among the other types, but these are not the dominant one.

Thus, the corner that receives the highest score indicates your organisation's dominant culture, as follows:

- descriptions in the top left-hand corners of the boxes reflect a clan culture
- descriptions in the bottom left-hand corners indicate an adhocracy culture
- descriptions in the top right-hand corners indicate a hierarchy culture
- descriptions in the bottom right-hand corners indicate a market culture.

It is quite possible to have a score that is not clear-cut, having 25 points for an adhocracy culture and 25 points for a market culture, for example, with no points allocated to any of the other culture types. Equally, you may obtain a general low spread across three types with one culture dominating.

Figure 7.11 **Continued**

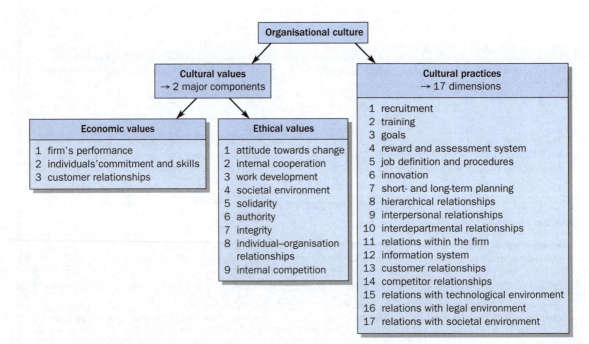

Figure 7.12 **Describing organisational culture – Calori and Sarnin's framework**

Source: Calori and Sarnin 1993

Calori and Sarnin's model is the only one that integrates market-orientated values *and* a cultural diagnosis. Given the complexities surrounding the notion of market and customer orientation, it is difficult to develop any formulaic stances for a market-led organisation. However, in marketing, as the emphasis changes from products and markets to *relationships* and *relationship-building*, a different focus is required for the future. In the existing competitive conditions, organisations need to adopt a stronger marketing approach and build their organisational culture around nurturing customer relationships.

The transition from focusing on products to a customer orientation

There are several reasons companies need to consider a customer-focused approach when designing their organisation.

■ Production technologies allow 'mass customisation', resulting in a greater ability to service smaller segments with product features more appropriate to their needs. It is therefore no longer necessary to spend large sums on developing organisations that focus on *products* to the detriment of *customers* (see Figure 7.13).

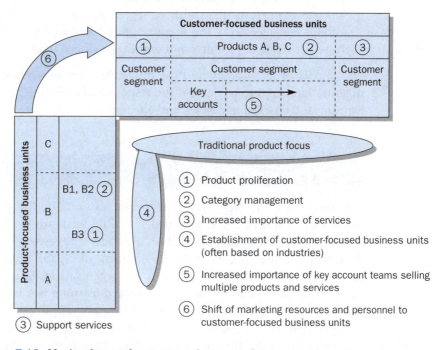

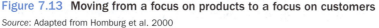

Figure 7.13 Moving from a focus on products to a focus on customers

Source: Adapted from Homburg et al. 2000

- Customer data warehouses and datamining techniques make it possible to uncover previously unknown patterns of customer behaviour. These IT-based tools help marketers to make better decisions regarding relationships with customers. The growing importance of IT means that marketers can concentrate more on developing a better knowledge of customers and of their spending habits than was possible before.
- Increasing amounts of products mean that resellers want product category-level assistance. Companies are therefore appointing product category managers. If a customer is regarded as a complex individual, then his or her needs and wants are likely to vary and retailers selling to them need to have a very good understanding of the categories of goods (such as electronics or haircare) they are offering to customers. Companies manufacturing these goods therefore need to implement a *category* specialisation as opposed to *product* specialisation.
- Services are becoming more and more important, with many major firms now receiving more profits from services than from products. Many organisations realise the importance of building relationships with customers on a long-term basis. The development of these relationships often also entails better service-level agreements. Better relationships lead to greater profitability. It is cheaper to retain customers than it is to find new ones.
- Many firms are beginning to reorganise their salesforces around customer groups (often industry-based) to develop coherent solutions out of the products and services coming from multiple divisions.
- Following on from this industry segmentation, many firms then assign key account managers to be the single points of contact with major accounts, selling the entire range of products and services produced by their firms.

The impact of technology and the movement towards relationships means that organisations need to be flexible and responsive to customers' needs and capable of learning and changeing quickly and efficiently.

The learning organisation

Organisational learning can be defined as, essentially, the process of improving actions by means of better knowledge and understanding (Fiol and Lyles 1985). Several other descriptions of it have also been suggested, including adaptation, information processing patterns, development of organisational theory-in-use and institutionalisation of experience in the organisation (Shrivastava 1983). These descriptions demonstrate that organisational learning is a multifaceted phenomenon, covering different degrees of learning and application. From a marketing point of view, the benefits of organisational learning can be reflected in faster and more efficient marketing processes. Indeed, several marketing authors (Day 1994; Sinkula 1994) suggest that positive synergistic effects occur, such as that:

- organisational learning is the development of new knowledge or insights that have the potential to influence behaviour
- learning facilitates behaviour changes that lead to improved performance
- dynamic and turbulent environments demand learning and behaviour changes and these lead to improved performance.

What are learning processes?

As suggested by Shrivastava (1983), organisational learning can have different meanings. In some instances, it can mean the ease with which an organisation can adapt to its environment. In others, it can mean the efficient utilisation of information (information processing patterns). In both instances, learning takes place, but it is either a *reactive* process (adaptation) or a *static* process (information processing).

More recently, the learning organisation has been viewed as a continuously creative, innovative organisation (Senge 1990) and a coherent, cohesive structure where each member is willingly active (Nonaka 1991). If an organisation is to be continuously creative and innovative and each member willingly active, then we need to understand the learning processes that are involved.

To improve this understanding, two types of learning have been defined. The first is a type of lower-level learning, also called single-loop learning (Argyris and Schön 1978) or behavioural development. The second one is a type of higher-level learning, also known as double-loop learning or cognitive learning.

Single-loop learning

The first level of learning is usually limited to a section of an organisation. Often this section will be given a defined set of behaviours, designed to cope with particular problems. These are routine patterns, triggered by particular stimuli within the environment. For instance, for a brewing company, if beer sales are low, it will launch its current advertisements. Any short-term problems are also efficiently dealt with. This type of behaviour can also be described as reactive learning. Hence, single-loop learning is similar to mere behavioural adaptation. This process does not stretch to questioning the phenomena that create the response (asking why the beer sales are low but) it merely sets in motion conditioned responses to external stimuli.

Single-loop, or adaptive, learning often contains a 'learning boundary'. The way in which the business is conceptualised guides what the core capabilities need to be, but, in many instances, what exists are 'core rigidities' concentrated on the served market, fostering quite a narrow perspective. Therefore, an adaptive approach (single-loop) is usually sequential, incremental and focused on issues or opportunities within the traditional scope of the organisation's activities (see Figure 7.14).

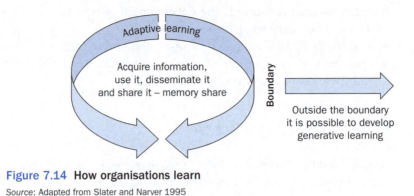

Figure 7.14 **How organisations learn**
Source: Adapted from Slater and Narver 1995

Double-loop learning

This higher-level of learning affects the whole organisation and is rarely contained within functional areas. It entails a deeper challenge to routine practices and rules. This type of generative learning shows a willingness to question long-held assumptions about mission, customers, capabilities or strategy. Often, this is based on systems thinking and works through existing relationships, linking key issues and events.

When an organisation begins to embrace 'double-loop' learning, interrelationships and dynamic processes of change are important. Often, a learning organisation adept at double-loop learning can take advantage of windows of opportunity that may be available to companies. Slower-moving organisations, however, that have fixed views of markets and their role within them, may fail to take advantage of these opportunities.

Higher-level learning usually occurs during some type of crisis, such as the adoption of a new strategy, apointment of a new leader and/or significant changes in the market. It corresponds to the development of a new frame of reference(s). One of the consequences of being a double-loop learning organisation is that it is then necessary to 'unlearn' old processes as old frames are no longer effective in coping with the new reality.

The impacts of single-loop and double-loop learning are summarised in Figure 7.15.

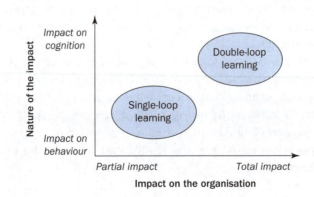

Figure 7.15 **The impacts of single- and double-loop learning**

Which approach is best?

The ability to learn is obviously necessary for any organisation. However, trying to place lower- and higher-level forms of learning in a hierarchy is short-sighted. Single-loop learning, with its smaller reactive change, is necessary for everyday operational tasks. Some authors (Fiol and Lyles 1985) suggest defining lower-level learning as *adaptation* and higher-level learning as *learning*, which means 'the development of insights, knowledge, and associations between past actions, the effectiveness of those actions, and future actions'. Although adaptation and learning are both important to managerial performance, there can sometimes be a conflict between them, with adaptation routines preventing an organisation from engaging in comprehensive learning. This is why the articulation between the different types of learning is important. A key aspect of this is to consider the impact of learning systems.

Learning systems

Shrivastava (1983) distinguishes six types of learning systems. These systems represent different ways of generating learning, which is another way of classifying learning processes. First, the 'one-man institution' corresponds to the scenario where only one person knows everything about the competitive situation. The learning process here is reduced to an individual learning, who then diffuses that knowledge to other members of the organisation.

The second approach, the 'mythological learning system', functions by means of the exchange of stories and myths between members of an organisation. In these two learning systems, the knowledge is mainly, if not totally, subjective.

The third system is the 'information-seeking culture', where each member of the organisation is encouraged to be curious about the business and its environment. The diffusion of knowledge is mainly by word-of-mouth mode. Informality is the main characteristic of this learning system.

The 'participative learning system' pertains to one in which ad hoc committees and working groups are formed in order to solve certain managerial problems. Hence, knowledge is produced on a very specific basis. The formalisation of knowledge is for the purpose of sharing it and the associated expertise of the different participants in the ad hoc groups. It is decision-orientated.

The 'formal management system' is the organisational solution for perpetuating the learning process. It corresponds to the planning, control and sharing of information. Virtually any organisational subsystem can take this approach – strategic planning, information system management, financial/budgetary control systems and so on.

Last in the list is the 'bureaucratic learning system', which goes one step further than the previous one. It is the most formal way in which to organise knowledge, entailing procedures and regulations. It aims at producing absolute, objective, impersonalised knowledge. One major danger of this type of system is that it concentrates on formal knowledge and is unable to deal with tacit knowledge.

From this review of learning systems, we can see that learning can be initiated, developed and framed in different ways (see Figure 7.16).

One step further: deutero-learning

Theorists have identified another type of learning more recently: *deutero-learning*. This process enables a firm to understand how knowledge is created and how learning happens. While double-loop learning is the ability to create new solutions (cognitive frame + behaviour), deutero-learning is the process of learning itself. This is not an abstract way of thinking about learning but a contextualised, firm-specific audit of how learning is achieved in the firm.

The deutero-learning idea suggests that the firm, when reflecting on its current learning process (by carrying out a learning audits, for example, such as in Figure 7.17), can foster its learning results. This reflexive process can speed up learning. For instance, Moingeon and Edmondson (1996) show how Intel developed its 'carbon copy' learning system. This offered Intel the opportunity to quickly transpose its new R&D technologies from one factory to another. Hence, once the firm has understood its own learning processes, it can select, systematise and replicate the most powerful learning processes in various departments and business units.

From individual to organisational learning

One big problem with organisational learning is the question of how it is to be developed. The term 'learning' suggests that it begins at an individual level.

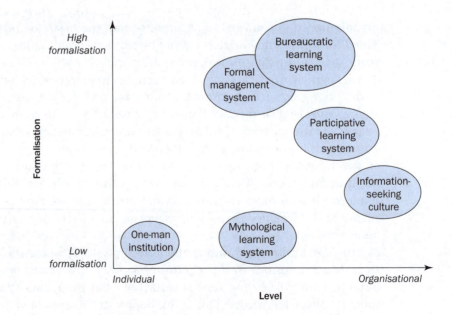

Figure 7.16 Different types of learning systems

Source: Adapted from Shrivastava 1983

Learning audit

First glance

1 Do we give the impression of learning from our business, activity, role, market and environment?

2 Do we feel that there are changes in the environment? Do we respond to these changes? Do we anticipate them?

3 At what rate do we generate new ideas (products, new managerial tools, etc.)?

More in-depth analysis

1 Over the past five years, *how many* things did you learn?

2 What is *the scope* of the learning (better operations, new procedures, new ways of thinking, etc.)?

3 What *type of knowledge* was developed (subjective, mythological, objective, general, problem-specific, task- or area-specific)?

4 Is this learning *shared* (at top management level, at middle-management level, at employee level, in every department, in every SBU)?

5 Is this learning *stored?* (Specify degree of development of the information system, interactivity, utilisation, writs, notes, memos, internal newsletter, reports, word of mouth.)

6 Do you engage in formal meetings for *diffusing, sharing and discussing* the new things you discovered?

7 *Why* did you engage in the learning process (crisis, problems, periodic requirement, specific decision, ongoing process)?

8 *Who* initiates the learning process (individual or top management, informal network, department, task group)?

9 Do you *evaluate* the benefits of your learning process (in terms of economic performance, efficiency, organisational climate, members' motivation and satisfaction with their jobs)?

Figure 7.17 **Example of a learning audit**

Indeed, one could question how can an *organisation learn*. Is organisational learning more or less than the sum of *individual* learning? Several authors have worked on this complex matter.

From individual learning …

The knowledge base regarding individual learning has evolved from learning being considered within a stimulus–response paradigm to notions such as memorising and forgetting (Shrivastava 1983). Later, Kim (1993) explained that individual learning corresponds to both the acquisition of skills, or know-how, and know-why. This, in turn, corresponds to two levels of learning: operational and conceptual. He suggests that learning is acquired via a four-step process, set out in Figure 7.18.

Kim observes that there is a missing link between individual and organisational learning. The main question is how (and is it possible) to convert individual learning into organisational learning? This is the product of the learning – knowledge. We could reformulate the question in the following way: how can the organisation integrate and share knowledge that has been produced on an individual basis? However, another question remains to be answered – that is, is it possible to generate knowledge that is not individual-based? This is especially important in

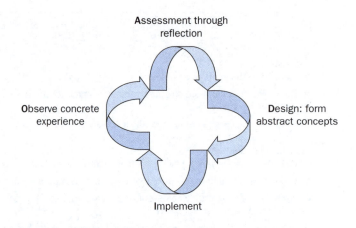

Assessment through
reflection

Observe concrete
experience

Design: form
abstract concepts

Implement

Figure 7.18 The OADI process of individual learning
Source: Adapted from Kofman, in Kim 1993

marketing as much of a marketing concept relies on disseminating intelligence and developing knowledge bases.

Shrivastava (1983) remarks that, while it was individual learning that was originally studied by psychologists, several disciplines have tried to understand organisational learning. What is known about organisational learning is thus more fragmented, which helps to explain the difficulty of building a comprehensive view of how organisational learning occurs.

... to organisational learning?

Kim (1993) states that 'An organisation can learn only through its members, but learning is not dependent on any specific member'. Several models assume that organisational learning functions like individual learning. However, this premise is fraught with difficulty, as individuals may learn in different ways.

Kim indicates that one needs to understand the transfer mechanism from individual to organisational learning. The transfer lies in shared mental models. To him, mental models are the structure of the organisational memory. The organisational learning cycle can thus be illustrated in the following way:

- it starts at the individual level as individual learning is achieved by means of the OADI process (shown in Figure 7.18)
- the result of learning is a change in individual mental models
- at this stage, organisational learning can occur if there is a change to shared mental models
- this leads to new organisational actions
- organisational actions are then assessed via individual actions and further learning occurs.

This process is illustrated in Figure 7.19.

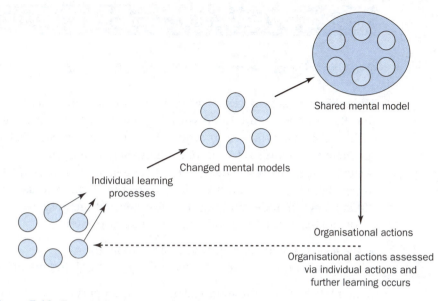

Shared mental model

Changed mental models

Individual learning
processes

Organisational actions

Organisational actions assessed
via individual actions and
further learning occurs

Figure 7.19 **From individual to organisational learning**

Nonaka and Takeuchi (1995) suggest that other types of processes also exist by means of which knowledge creation can occur. This can also assist in linking individual and organisational learning. They identify two types of knowledge:

■ tacit
■ explicit.

Tacit knowledge is acquired by a process of diffusion resulting from social interaction. In this instance, a worker learns unconsciously from the experiences of others. Tacit knowledge can be made explicit by using analogies, metaphors, models and concepts. For instance, the now widely used BCG model was initially utilised by the Boston Consulting Group, which made the knowledge available to others by publishing it. Similarly, organisations can express ideas using models or analogies. In some instances, organisations resort to storytelling and metaphors. At its most basic level, tacit knowledge is shared in the form of written rules and procedures.

Learning is not solely dependent on sharing and diffusing tacit knowledge. Learning processes involve *explicit* knowledge. It is possible for several pieces of explicit knowledge to be combined to create new explicit knowledge. This occurs when written models and procedures that exist in different parts of an organisation are brought together and suddenly new patterns or ideas emerge. The next section considers ways in which to trap the benefits of a learning organisation.

Keeping the benefits of a learning orientation

Organisational memory and mental models

The role of memory is viewed as prevalent in learning processes. Kim (1993) states that 'learning has more to do with acquisition, whereas memory has more to do with retention of whatever is acquired'. Mental models are structures that organise the memory and this is true of both individuals and organisations. As noted before, the challenge is to build shared mental models so that individual learning is stored in people's memories and becomes part of the organisational memory. Part of the difficulty lies in understanding the subsystems of memory.

Memory subsystems are organised around two axes:

- the level (individual, collective and centralised)
- the nature of the memory (declarative, procedural, judgmental).

Taking into account these subsystems is very important in order to be able to audit the learning capabilities of the firm. This is also crucial to developing the utmost learning capability – the capacity for deutero-learning.

Girod (1995) is a French researcher who was identified nine subsystems of organisational memory (see Table 7.2).

Table 7.2 Organisational memory subsystems

	Nature		
Level	Declarative (knowledge)	Procedural (know-how)	Judgmental (know-why)
Individual	1 Individual knowledge (brain and documents) used within the organisation	4 Individual skills used within the organisation	7 Individual prospective memory, ability to interpret based on individual experience
Collective, non-centralised	2 Acquisition of knowledge from others or knowledge creation via interaction	5 Skills creation via collective action	8 Creation of a shared interpretation
Centralised	3 Knowledge in centralised database	6 Procedures described in manuals	9 Official culture, formalised in documents

Source: Girod 1995

The culture of learning

Although it is possible to give general guidelines concerning the development of learning, it is clear that, for organisations, learning is not only a matter of formalisation and the creation of a framework for learning. In fact, many organisations are aware that the culture and climate that exists within their environment can either facilitate or hinder learning, as illustrated by the case study that follows.

CASE STUDY

Adapt or die...

Just as evolutionary history tells us that the fittest species survived because they were able to adapt to change, so should corporations in a changing business environment.

In Darwin's theory, evolution was characterised as a gradual process in which all species went through changes at regular intervals. On examination of fossils, though, it was found that in reality evolution is punctuated. That is, crises in the environment, natural or self-imposed, demanded that species adapt or die.

Today, we are facing similar crises in business. Billions of dollars are being spent on change management, yet most successful organisations cannot keep pace with their more nimble competitors. That which is targeted to change, remains unchanged. More is required by less. Organisations are required to cannibalise or be eaten . . .

These and several other paradoxes indicate that the business environment is demanding that corporations change their way of operating. Through evolutionary history, those species that did survive did so because they were able to adapt to their environment. They proved to be complex adaptive systems. They thrived on disequilibrium and chaos and changed themselves to enter a new relationship with the environment. There are lessons to be learned from behaving as complex adaptive systems.

If an organisation operates as a 'material' level complex adaptive system, then it is tied to the past, and to what may have once made it successful. Its world consists of known customers, known products, known markets, known processes and structure and known strategies. Innovation is about 'tweaking' and about moving within the boundaries that have already established what it is. An organisation centred at this level has a limited number of options to choose from when confronted with change. Change itself is engineered as though the world is fixed, and therefore any efforts are only incremental, within the confines of the described world. To the degree that an organisation centred at this level can call on attitudes and strategies that are centred at the higher levels, it will likely be able to function far more successfully than an organisation that perceives and acts in the world solely from a material perspective.

An organisation operating as a 'financial' level complex adaptive system has more degrees of freedom. Being centred in financial results, whether ROI, sales or market share, it is not necessarily bound to the world that has made it successful. It is not necessarily bound by past markets, customers, products, processes, structures or strategies. It has the added flexibility of changing any of these to ensure that it meets its specified financial goals. Yet, if it were required to go through a quantum change, as is being required by many organisations today, it runs the risk of becoming extinct so long as it remains insistently focused on meeting its imposed financial goals. It is to be noted that organisations operating at this level do embody all the positive capacities of the previous, material, level. At the same time, to the degree that an organisation centred at this level can call on attitudes and strategies that are centred at the conceptual level, it will likely be able to function far more successfully than an organisation that

▶

perceives and acts in the world solely from a financial or a financial–material perspective.

An organisation operating as a 'conceptual' level complex adaptive system is not bound by its past. It has more degrees of freedom and is in essence more fluid and adaptive than any form that precedes it. It seizes on ideas and will change its customers, products, markets, processes, structures and/or strategies to ensure that these ideas can be fulfilled. It, too, has the know-how and capability of all the previous levels embedded into it. Thus, material and financial capabilities are deeply embedded or easily available to it.

An organisation operating as an 'intuitional' level complex adaptive system is perhaps fulfilling some deep need, possibly far beyond what it might even imagine. As such, it has opened to deep forces of formation and is bound only by its ability to give the receiving intuition a form. At such a level of operation, old, accepted ways of organising may prove inadequate or incomplete and the organisation may have to conduct its operations in new, virgin forms. Such an organisation is deeply creative and perhaps becomes the model by which many other organisations develop. Examples of organisations at each of these levels follow.

- An example of focused material-level operation, to the point where it becomes restrictive, is that as exercised by the US rail industry. They wanted to continue to provide rail services, even though others had begun to provide transport services, and therefore signed their own death warrant.

- Another example of the material-level operation is that of a company in the typewriter business. Computers now provide all the capabilities provided by a typewriter, and a lot more. Any company that insists on providing typewriters will soon be wiped out.

- An example of financial-level operation is that of Barnes & Noble. When Amazon.com actually began following through on its vision of becoming the largest bookstore on the planet, Barnes & Noble, threatened by its diminishing market share, spun off barnesandnoble.com. Their motivation was simply to regain lost market share. If, instead, they had moved to an ambition at the concept-based level, they may have been able to reinvent the retailing industry by being the first truly click-and-mortar type company.

- Another example of an enterprise operating at the financial level is Covisint, the e-marketplace joint effort between General Motors, Ford, and DaimlerChrysler. While Covisint had the possibility of being a concept-led play, in reality it has been motivated by a vision that is at a less empowering financial level. Thus, to avoid the continuing costs of ongoing battles and pains associated with continuing to support their own auto parts marketplaces against the efforts of other competitors in the same space, the Covisint principals decided to join forces to come up with a joint auto parts marketplace. Since their motivation has been driven by the financial level, they have been unable to step up to the broader concept-led leadership required to bring such a venture to successful fruition. Thus, from the word 'Go', they have been attended by a host of problems, starting from the inability to come up with a mutually acceptable name for the project, to the ongoing difficulty in selecting the right technology platform, to the potentially crippling inability to really bring their suppliers along. These leadership problems have been further compounded by the Federal Trade Commission's concern that the combined purchasing power of the automakers could be anti-competitive for suppliers.

- An example of a concept-led company is that of Amazon.com. At its inception it sought to create the world's largest virtual bookstore. It sought to allow the user to browse titles in the comfort of their home, while allowing users to view online reviews by other readers. They shipped books to buyers at prices compatible with or less than those available at its competitors. Its concept for selling books was so different from existing sellers of books that investors allowed it to continue in operation for five years before it had even begun to show a profit. Further, it drew investors to its unique concepts and through the funds that became available to them was able to quickly mobilise capabilities at the previous level – material and financial.

- Another example of a concept-led organisation is that of Aravind Eye Care System. Note that this is not a business organisation and therefore the inclusion on this scale is tenuous, but done, nonetheless, to provide a rough indication of what different levels of operation may mean. Aravind Eye Care System has grown organically, without upfront planning, and has assumed a unique practical shape, with a reach into the village level unparalleled by any other organisation. This reach has assisted it in creating a unique culture through the young village girls who join Aravind to become its nurses and the backbone of the organisation. This reach also allows Aravind to provide service to numerous blind throughout Southern India. It is driven by the vision and idea of its founder and there is an adhesion to this vision, even though circumstance and time go on. In this sense it remains concept-led. To the best of the author's knowledge companies at the intuitive level do not exist, though several may be in formation, driven by the vision of their leaders.

An organisation should, thus, be centred at the higher levels. This then provides it with the flexibility and living-quality to become an effective organisation constantly fulfilling real needs. It thus becomes imperative to create a culture whereby there is always a push to the higher levels. As such, proactive actions and reactive measures need to be taken at every instance to ensure that every part of the organisation is operating with the highest degrees of freedom available to it.

Source: Pravir Malik, 'Adapt or die', *The Hindu Business Line*, 3 October 2002

How can the typology of organisations discussed in the case study help or hinder the formation of a learning organisation? As culture has an important part to play in learning, it is useful to understand why this is (Baumard 1995).

- an informed organisation is not necessarily more competitive – it is what the organisation makes out of the information that really counts
- one observes that, usually, individual learning is dispersed into the organisation, with no real benefit at the collective level
- learning from other managerial systems (for example, the USA trying to learn from Japanese management) is very difficult because one misses the details.

All of these observations indicate that the deeper capabilities of a firm are very dependent on its culture. Surface-level learning without the required cultural dimension can lead to poor implementation of strategies.

Thus, it is important to re-emphasise that culture cannot be managed in the same ways as other organisational elements because it is complex, socially constructed and always evolving. As Barney (1986) demonstrated, culture is, by definition, unique, which means that each firm has to find its own way. Often, mergers and acquisitions occur in the hope that the more successful culture will dominate, but the performance level after most mergers and acquisitions is poorer than that of the freestanding companies.

It is clear that top management has a lot of influence on the culture of an organisation (Schein 1983, 1992, 1993) and that this can stimulate development. However, it is also clear that the expansion and integration of the changes initiated or desired by the management will depend on every member of the organisation buying in to the changes. Hence, the ability of a firm to develop a learning culture will depend on its existing abilities and characteristics (see Figure 7.21). A particular organisation's potential is quite unique and cannot easily be compared with that of another firm – each has to develop its own capacities.

While developing a learning culture, the firm has to keep an eye on its environment (competitors, market, customers, suppliers and other salient stakeholders) because learning also occurs via interactions with external contacts. In such instances, benchmarking studies can be useful to assess competitors' strengths and weaknesses. This learning can then be translated into specific actions that correspond to the firm's strengths and its particular culture.

Developing a learning culture can be a problem for certain firms that are not aware of their existing culture. In such cases, a cultural diagnosis can help the organisation to rethink and redefine its learning process, as the organisational culture is like the nervous system of the firm (see Figure 7.20).

Learning is not straightforward

All the preceding considerations suggest that learning is not necessarily straightforward – that either it is not part of the initial culture or it is difficult to maintain as inertia impedes continuous learning. In line with this, at least three aspects require attention. First, several authors indicate that unlearning is critical. Second, learning and culture evolution require time. Last, the learning perspective can stand as a new approach to the change process and its management.

The question of *unlearning* is a very important issue. It is linked to the different shortcomings of the learning process itself. Indeed, in their famous article 'The myopia of learning', Levinthal and March (1993) have identified three types of pitfalls that can catch people out. These are the tendencies to:

■ ignore the long term, especially in the first level of reactive learning
■ ignore the bigger picture – the firms' cognitive resources are limited by a strict specialisation of learning activities
■ overlook failures as they are considered irrelevant.

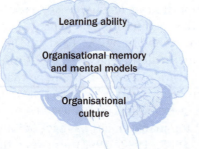

Learning ability

Organisational memory
and mental models

Organisational
culture

Figure 7.20 **The brain as a metaphor for the links between culture, memory and learning**

By unlearning, the organisation puts into question present and past knowledge that has been generated by learning. In fact, researchers (Spender and Baumard 1995) have witnessed the phenomenon of firms that made considerable efforts to learn being unwilling to change the core of their learning, which they had gained from the hard learning phase. Hence, while learning should be an ongoing process, it can lead to learning rigidities because the process itself is so resource-hungry (in terms of time, people, money) that the firm is no longer in a position to reinvest in such efforts.

This is linked to what has been called the 'exploitation/exploration balance' by Levinthal and March (1993). The idea is that higher-level learning consists of two phases: the *exploration phase* and the *exploitation phase*. A poor balance between exploration and exploitation can be described as follows. A learning organisation has sunk a lot of resources into exploring a specific issue, but it does not have enough resources to go further and elaborate on this, so the result is weak knowledge exploitation and incomplete learning (see Figure 7.21).

Firms can encounter two different kinds of problems: either an excess of exploration or an excess of exploitation. In both cases, unlearning past behaviour patterns can contribute to a better balance between the two. For instance, a company may be very good at market research and continually pride itself on this. However, when it comes to getting the goods to market and on to the shelves, it invariably fails. In this instance, this firm has to 'unlearn' the previous behaviour pattern of predominant market research and balance this with a better learning of production capabilities.

In addition to this, a company must be able to assimilate learning over a long period of time. Often, key individuals within a company are so absorbed in day-to-day requirements, that they fail to leave time for learning or reflection. Many researchers are (Baumard 1995; Levinthal and March 1993), finding that the time spent on reflection yields competitive advantage. Too much emphasis is often placed on speed of operations – especially by external agencies – yet time spent on reflection and understanding the company and market dynamics can lead to a distinctive competitive advantage being discovered.

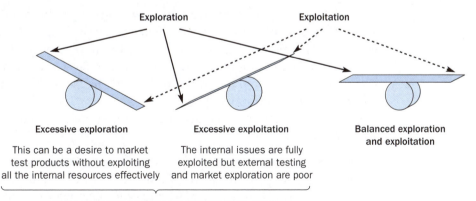

Excessive exploration

This can be a desire to market test products without exploiting all the internal resources effectively

Excessive exploitation

The internal issues are fully exploited but external testing and market exploration are poor

Balanced exploration and exploitation

Learning and unlearning are important in these cases

Figure 7.21 **Exploration and exploitation of knowledge**

Companies then, can be seen as managing a time paradox. They have to be efficient in their marketing, R&D and production operations, necessitating a great deal of interdepartmental coordination and even overlap in matrix organisations. However, they also have to take the time to integrate, digest and exploit the knowledge that they have just produced as a result of their learning. In the long run, this paradox should be overcome as the learning process will, *in time*, help to speed up operations.

An organisation can stimulate balanced learning in a variety of ways (Levinthal and March 1993). First, it can develop a whole range of incentives. Classic economic responses can be considered to stimulate innovation (patents, intellectual property rights and so on). However, human resource management tools should also be used – notably career advancement – as a way of rewarding innovative people. Recruitment and the resulting selection process are also an important tool for integrating 'newness' into the organisation.

In order to avoid inertia, the organisational structure can also be used to keep exploration ongoing. Instead of relying heavily on integration and socialisation, the firm can try to maintain diversity and individuality. Preserving individual 'deviance' can stimulate individual learning, which is the first step towards organisational learning. At the same time, top management can encourage risktaking and creativity, improving a firm's ability to innovate (Kohli and Jaworski 1990). Learning also needs to be exploited and it is the top management's role to integrate, digest, conceptualise and diffuse the results of learning within the organisation.

Developing a learning, market-orientated organisation

In order to understand how marketing can benefit from a learning orientation, different types of marketing knowledge, generated as a result of various levels of learning, need to be harnessed.

Levels of learning and marketing knowledge

One of the most important issues in management practice (and consequently in academic research) is to use the knowledge that has been created as a result of either learning processes or information gathering. Firms often accumulate huge amounts of data without exploiting them. In other words, data is not in-formed (Latin: *in – formare*, to put into form). Creating marketing knowledge means using collected data and information.

Menon and Varadarajan (1992) point out that there are different ways in which to use knowledge.

■ *Instrumental* use of knowledge is the direct application of findings in order to solve a problem. For instance, when the decision to launch a new product is made, the instrumental use of information obtained from market research will be reflected in packaging, the date of introduction, the communication campaign and so on. In this situation, knowledge is generated in direct relation to a marketing problem ('How should we package the product?', 'When should we launch it, ideally?', 'What should the communication mix be?') (Koenig 1990).

■ The *conceptual* use of marketing knowledge is when it is not directly applied to a specific problem. Rather, it is used to enhance the existing knowledge base of the firm and its managers. This usage helps to modify the vision, add new concepts and create new perspectives for viewing traditional problems. For instance, studying the development of Internet technologies and the possibilities they offer can not only be used directly when proposing a new product or service offering but also indirectly to rethink the process of product innovation. The generation of knowledge can be either problem-specific or the result of strategic scanning (Koenig 1990).

■ The *symbolic* use of knowledge is when there is a distortion of the meaning of information in order to serve managerial purposes. This amounts to the political use of information. Here, although knowledge was initially generated for a specific issue, its use is far removed from the initial intention. As already mentioned, Menon and Varadarajan (1992) suggest that the organisation of a firm influences the way and intensity with which marketing knowledge is used.

While Menon and Varadarajan focus their analysis on the use of marketing knowledge generated as a result of research and studies, Sinkula (1994) provides a more comprehensive view by proposing to link marketing information processes. He considers the use of marketing information in terms of acquiring, distributing, interpreting and storing this information in order to create and apply a specific learning orientation. Based on these assumptions, he has proposed a model of a market-based organisational learning process.

Market-based learning

In Sinkulas' view, market-based learning (MBL) is fundamentally different from classic organisational learning in four respects:

■ the external focus that underlies MBL leads to a more open perspective – it can also be considered as a prerequisite of internal-orientated learning, because learning has to be nurtured by new, mainly external, data

■ it is a source of competitive advantage as the focus on the environment naturally leads to a learning that will have an important impact on the competitiveness of the firm

■ it infers that the observation of other firms is not necessarily a fruitful exercise

■ marketing information that resides within organisations is sometimes difficult to access because each individual has his or her own method of storing this information but it is much more important than other types of information (financial data, productivity results and so on), so, even if it might be more difficult, firms that seek to gain a competitive advantage from their learning processes should focus particularly on MBL.

Focusing on MBL supposes that one understands the different types of marketing knowledge and how they can be generated as a result of learning. Sinkula proposes the framework shown in Table 7.3 (1994: 39).

Table 7.3 Levels of MBL – manifestations and examples

Types of knowledge and learning process	Manifestations	Examples
Dictionary	Labelling and descriptions of things	Descriptions of market segments, product movements
Episodic	Development of historical databases	Description of past sales, past phenomena and cause–effect relationships
Endorsed	Development of a system of norms and strategies	Development of an 'espoused' way of doing market research
Procedural	Actual practices that may deviate from the endorsed knowledge	Actual practices and tacit rules that are involved in market research
Axiomatic	Development of fundamental organisational beliefs	The fundamental reason for conducting market research, the way it is and continues to be this way
Augmented	Response to gaps detected between espoused and actual ways of doing things	Renewed ways of organising market information acquisition
Deutero	Development of consciousness about how to learn	Understanding of how marketing information is developed and used within the firm and of its impacts

Source: Adapted from Sinkula 1994

For organisations, a formal framework such as this opens up opportunities to assess its own MBL processes. Initially, the analysis should focus on the amount and nature of marketing knowledge that is gathered in the firm. Second, further attention should be given to the progress of each type of marketing information within the firm. Who produces or gathers it? What is done with this information? Who are the other people who access it? What is the sequence of dissemination? Do the people affected by the information use it and in what ways? This can assist in understanding what is done with marketing information and what are the potential discrepancies between a firm's knowledge needs and the internal learning process.

Day (1994) was one of the first authors to underline the potential virtuous circle of learning and market orientation. For him, learning corresponds to the ability to ask the right question at the right time. Firms that are market-orientated share assumptions about how their markets behave and evolve. To support their views and keep contact with their customers, they have to implement market-driven learning.

Developing continuous learning about markets supposes that the following skills have to be acquired:

- scanning with peripheral vision
- ensuring sensible decisions are made by using market research
- activating the sensors at the point of customer contact
- learning from benchmarking
- continuously experimenting.

Creativeness and innovation are clearly developed by a learning process that entails peripheral vision and experimentation. In order to foster this within individuals, top management needs to be open and not fazed by risktaking. In other words, managers must have the ability to create an environment that facilitates learning and the sharing of information. If this is achieved, it can have a profound impact on developing an organisation that is market-orientated (Baker and Sinkula 1999). In general, firms that have a definite learning orientation are also strongly market-orientated and perform well in the marketplace. Knight (2002) discusses the importance of network learning by a group of organisations within any context. Learning can take place at individual or at interorganisational levels, or within a dyadic relationship. A model such as this brings both individuals and organisations together (see Table 7.4) and much emphasis is placed on sharing knowledge.

Communication is increasingly important for organisational learning, especially in the digital age. Information and ideas can now be shared as never before via intranets and the Internet, especially by means of blogs. Peters and Fletcher (2004) highlight the importance of linking an organisation's internal communications (between employees) to its external communications (with partners, suppliers and customers). They argue that, by adopting a network perspective and placing communication behaviour within a larger context, more can be understood about communication influences beyond the confines of the individual team members. In effect, the communication processes need to be plotted on Table 7.4. As digital technology improves, learning processes will evolve and change as the marketplace changes.

Table 7.4 Cross-tabulation of the levels of learner with context of learning

Level of learner	*Context of learning*				
	Individual *I*	*Group* *G*	*Organisation* *O*	*Dyad* *D*	*Interorganisational* *I/O*
Individual **I**	Individual learns alone	Individual learns within a group	Individual learns within an organisation	Individual learns within a dyad	Individual learns within a network
Group **G**	Group's learning is influenced by an individual	Group learns through intragroup interaction	Group learns within an organisation	Group learns within a dyad	Group learns within a network
Organisation **O**	Organisation's learning is influenced by an individual	Organisation's learning is influenced by a group	Organisation learns through intraorganisational interaction	Organisation learns through a dyad	Organisation learns within a network
Dyad **D**	Dyad's learning is influenced by an individual	Dyad's learning is influenced by a group	Dyad's learning is influenced by an organisation	Dyad learns through intradyad interaction	Dyad learns within a network
Network **N**	Network's learning is influenced by an individual	Network's learning is influenced by a group	Network's learning is influenced by an organisation	Network's learning is influenced by a dyad	Network learns through intranetwork interaction

Source: Knight 2002

Hypertext organisation – a way forward for market-orientated learning organisations?

Based on the idea that learning is of foremost importance to the organisation and for effective marketing development, a market-orientated learning organisation could be designed according to the observations of organisational learning (OL) theorists.

Ingham (in Nonaka and Takeuchi 1995), notes that certain types of structures seem to favour learning:

■ decentralised structures
■ participative structures
■ flat structures
■ group project or taskforce structures
■ flexible structures.

Nonaka and Takeuchi (1995) propose an amalgamation of the effective elements of previous structures while suggesting a new way of seeing and designing the organisational structure. This new model is the *hypertext organisation*. This type of organisation is made of multiple, interconnected layers. Interdepartmental connections are key to achieving effective market orientation.

The central layer consists of the core activities of the firm, with this part of the organisation concentrating on its routine functions. In this scenario, a hierarchical organisation is adequate.

The top layer consists of multiple group projects where employees are expected to work creatively. Members of the group projects come from different departments and are dedicated to their specific group until the project is achieved.

Finally, a third, invisible layer – called the *knowledge base* – consists of sharing and recontextualising knowledge and this is created by the first two layers. Strategic vision and organisational culture mainly guide it. Nonaka and Konno (1993) proposed the structure for the hypertext organisation can be seen in Figure 7.22.

This organisational design appears to have a lot of the features that we know are required for good market orientation. A market-orientated firm needs a smooth and responsive organisational structure together with a large measure of innovation. The hypertext organisation takes advantage of traditional structure types, such as bureaucracies, hierarchies, taskforces, matrix structures and so on, and superimposes the desired elements. An organisational design of this kind is not necessarily easy to describe and explain in annual reports, even though it may be one of the most effective ways to stimulate market orientation, learning and innovation, and may perhaps be the key to developing competitive advantage. The linking up of core systems, knowledge systems and groups working in unison is perhaps the best way to develop customercentric organisations capable of building good relationships.

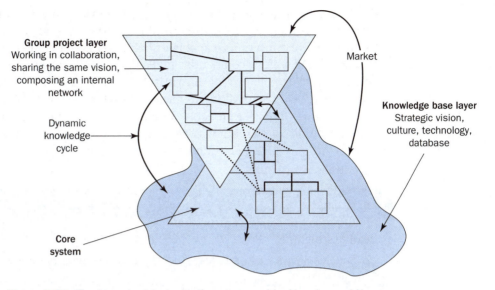

Figure 7.22 The hypertext organisation proposed by Nonaka and Konno
Source: Nonaka and Konno 1993

Summary

Designing the structure of an organisation appropriately is an important component in developing competitive advantage. The right structure helps to influence the functioning and adaptability of a firm. There are eight traditional forms, which are departmentalisation, specialisation, standardisation, coordination, formalisation, decentralisation/centralisation, control and differentiation/integration. Assessing the degrees to which an organisation incorporates these aspects helps to determine its tangible elements, although its, differentiating and integrating mechanisms constitute the less tangible aspects.

Culture is also an important intangible aspect of organisations that needs to be considered.

In an era where the acquisition, transmission and use of knowledge determine competitive advantage, it is important to consider how organisations can effectively and efficiently build customer relationships. At the same time, it is important that organisations develop learning capacities as these enhance their ability to become market-orientated. Essentially, organisational learning can be defined as the process of improving action as a result of better knowledge and understanding. Two main types of learning levels can be distinguished: *single-loop learning*, which is a reactive type of learning, and *double-loop learning*, which is a more profound conceptual and proactive type of learning. A third type can also be identified: *deutero-learning*, which is understanding how knowledge is created and what enables learners to learn.

Different types of organisational systems will generate different types of learning. For example, a one-man institution will generate individual-based knowledge, whereas a bureaucratic system will generate organised formalised knowledge. The development of shared mental models helps to form the link between organisational and individual learning. At the same time, the top management's ability to foster an environment conducive to creative thinking and risktaking, appears to develop better learning organisations, capable of being market-orientated and better positioned in the increasingly competitive marketplace of the twenty-first century.

In the future, it is likely that organisations will develop different layers that function effectively and cogently to meet and exceed customers' expectations.

These organisations will probably develop along the hypertext model described at the end of this chapter. Knowledge creation and dissemination will be dynamic, creating a virtuous circle of customer–firm interactions.

Chapter questions

1   What is organisational learning? What are the consequences of it?

2   Traditionally, what types of learning have been identified? Is there a better type of learning?

3   How can individual learning be transferred at organisational level?

4   What is the role of organisational culture in the learning processes?

5   How is organisational memory organised? What is its role in organisational learning?

6   Why is unlearning so important?

7   Why is learning not straightforward?

8   What distinguishes market-based learning from organisational learning?

9   What are the links between organisational learning and market orientation (refer also to Chapter 1)?

10 To what extent can we distinguish standardisation from coordination?

11 Does the organisational chart represent the whole structure of a company? Why?

12 How can the role of differentiation mechanisms be conceptualised from a market-orientated point of view?

13 What is the instrumental use of market information?

14 According to Schein (1992), how many components can be identified in organisational culture? What are the links between these components?

15 What types of changes towards market-orientated culture can be identified? What are their respective benefits and drawbacks?

16 Is there a link between structure and the level of market orientation? Is it a strong, established link?

17 Does a firm's size matter when trying to create a market-orientated culture?

18 Outline the design of a hypertext organisation.

19 What are the benefits of the hypertext organisation with regard to market orientation?

8 Globalising marketing efforts

Introduction

In the last 50 years, the world has experienced globalisation, but in the last 15 it has accelerated phenomenally. Globalisation has occurred as a result of a series of factors, such as the rapid advances in transportation and communication technologies and the exponential increase in international trade after 1950. The interplay of all these factors has transformed the mentality of people, changed the structure and functioning of world markets, and created new opportunities and challenges for companies.

Table 8.1 The impacts of internationalisation, globalisation and Internetisation

	Internationalisation	*Globalisation*	*Internetisation*
Consumers	Increased awareness and demand for foreign brands, products and services	Standardisation of demand on a transnational basis	The possibility of accessing and exchanging information, products and services in cyberspace without restrictions of time or space
Markets	Increase in transnational trade of goods and services	The development of transnational segments of consumers with similar demands. Complex interactions between the elements of the international business environment	Development of online markets and virtual communities
Companies	Increased exchange of inputs and outputs across national borders	Rationalisation of companies' structures in relation to the cost of production in various locations and profits in specific markets	Quick access to online suppliers and consumers localised worldwide

The globalisation of world markets is an ongoing process of internationalisation that began as soon as man traversed continents. Globalisation has accelerated in the last 15 years, especially since the development of the Internet. The Internetisation of business transactions has created a parallel world market with certain characteristics. The Internet is more than just a communication channel because, in comparison with other media, it offers increased possibilities for inter-action and is capable of not only transmitting information but also storing and processing it.

Internationalisation, globalisation and Internetisation have different effects, meanings and consequences at the levels of consumers, markets and companies (see Table 8.1). The stage of internationalisation is reached when firms start to sell their products across borders and the trade flows increase at the international level. Globalisation is the next stage on, when there is not only an increase in the volume and value of goods and services exchanged internationally but also the emergence of transnational segments of consumers with similar demands, the development of global brands that are actively known and promoted worldwide, as well as an increased interdependence of various elements of the international busi-ness environment at the global level.

The main factors influencing international marketing operations

International marketing operations are influenced by many different factors in the international business environment. A good knowledge and understanding of the critical factors for a company's international strategy is paramount for marketing success in foreign markets. Many failures in international marketing operations can be explained by the lack of knowledge of strategic decision makers regarding the international business environment and its evolution. As the elements of the inter-national business environment are, usually, outside the influence of most companies, the firms engaged in international operations must use their internal resources (money, physical assets, experience) to adjust and adapt their strategies to the dynamic changes in international markets. Therefore, success in international marketing operation is built on:

- a good knowledge of the evolution of the international business environment
- the existing assets of the firm
- the capacity of managers to rapidly adapt the firm's strategies to the continuous changes in international markets.

Figure 8.1 The three main conditions for success in international marketing operations

The internationalisation of firms

Globalisation has increased the importance of internationalisation theories for both academics and practitioners. Academic research has developed three main categories of models to describe the process of internationalisation:

- experiential learning models
- systematic planning models
- contingency models.

There are two experiential learning models:

- Uppsala model, developed by Johanson and Wiedersheim-Paul (1975)
- Management Innovation model, described in the work of Bilkey and Tesar (1977).

The systemic approaches of these last two models are nearly the same. Both describe the internationalisation process as a gradual evolution of the firm through a series of stages that correspond to the increasing involvement of the company in business with other countries (see Figure 8.2).

The *Uppsala model* explains the internationalisation process by considering two main strategic dimensions:

- the market knowledge possessed by the firm about different foreign markets
- the commitment of the firm's resources to those markets.

The evolution of the company from a mainly domestic activity to a fully international profile is described as a slow, incremental process that involves the gradual acquisition, integration and use of knowledge about the characteristics of foreign markets, as well as an increasing commitment of the company's resources to international activities. The model also predicts that a firm will first target the markets that are most familiar in terms of language, culture, business practice and industrial development, in order to reduce the perceived risk of international operations and increase the efficiency of information flows between the firm and its target market (Johanson and Vahlne 1977 and 1990).

Figure 8.2 The successive stages of a firm's internationalisation, according to the Uppsala model

The *Management Innovation model* tends instead to explain the initiation of the internationalisation process as being the result of a series of management innovations implemented within the firm. The original model created by Bilkey and Tesar (1977) emphasises the evolution of a firm's internationalisation occurring in the process of successive learning stages.

The classical models of internationalisation have been extensively challenged over the years, with numerous scholars advancing various criticisms of their validity and assumptions. Some authors have questioned the deterministic nature of the Uppsala and Management Innovation models, saying that many firms do not follow a consistent path to internationalisation (Andersen 1993; Rosson 2004; Turnbull 1987). Many studies have found that the management of an internationalising firm considers a variety of strategic approaches (Root 1987; Welch and Luostarinen 1988), the internationalisation process representing a strategic answer to the evolving market conditions (Reid 1981 and 1983).

Other critics have demonstrated that the first step in the internationalisation process may not be exporting, but one of several alternative international activities, such as licensing, franchising, joint venture or network relationships (Håkansson 1982; Nordstrom 1991; Root 1987).

These criticisms show that it is difficult and even dangerous to draw a unique recipe for the internationalisation process (Buckley et al. 1975; Root 1987 Varaldo 1987) and the firm's stage of internationalisation is largely determined by the operating environment, industry structure and its own marketing strategy (Turnbull 1987).

These criticisms have been crystallised in two additional orientations:

- the strategic planning models, based on the research published by Root (1987), Miller (1993) and Yip et al. (2000), which claim that systematic planning founded on a careful analysis of competitive factors and circumstantial conditions can significantly increase the success of the internationalisation process

■ the contingency perspective, developed by Turnbull (1987) and then refined by Boter and Holmquist (1996) and Roberts (1999).

However, there are important differences between the internationalisation process in small and medium size firms (SMEs) and large corporations. Traditionally, the big companies had important advantages in their international competition with SMEs: financial and human resources, as well as previous experience and the possibility of accessing external expertise by counselling. However, in the last 20 years, a series of studies have outlined the existence of 'born global' firms – SMEs that succeed in achieving internationalisation quickly, exporting a large percentage of their output in the first years of their activity.

The following case study presents the challenges encountered by small firms when entering foreign markets.

CASE STUDY

Sabon cleans up in America

The small Israeli chain of natural bath-product boutiques is making inroads into the upscale US beauty business.

Sabon, a small but growing Israeli-based chain of handmade, natural bath-product boutiques, quickly attracted a loyal customer following when it landed in New York City three years ago. The flagship store's unique environment of apothecary-style luxury – with its centrepiece sink made of a large stone water well from the ancient city of Jericho, chandeliers, world music mixes, rows of soap blocks sold by the slice, aromatic oils, rose petal mineral balls and loofah sponges dipped in glycerine – immediately distinguished it from the growing flutter of beauty lotion-and-potion emporiums.

Sabon, which means soap in Hebrew, got its start nine years ago after entrepreneur Avi Piatok discovered a store that sold old-fashioned soap by the pound while travelling in New Zealand. When he returned to Israel, he found a man who could make natural soap using minerals from the Dead Sea and decided to open a store based on the concept. The outfit's brand of bath products, made using a 70-year-old process and produced on a kibbutz with natural ingredients like olive oil, sea salts and lavender, became a hit. Soon, Sabon grew

into a chain of 22 shops across Israel, including trendy places like Tel Aviv's Sheinkin Street.

But Israel, with its population of nearly 7 million, has a small domestic market. And as a result of regional hostilities, the country is all but closed off economically from its Arab neighbours. However, Piatok wanted to grow his business. To do so meant launching Sabon internationally. So, in 2003 he tapped his childhood friend Sharon Hasson, a Tel Aviv retailer, to open a New York flagship store.

Celebrity following

It was a pilot venture for the partners. If Sabon could work in Manhattan, they believed that they could replicate the concept globally. So confident were they, says Hasson, who moved to New York full-time that same year, that they didn't even bother to create a business plan (see BusinessWeek.com, 2/24/03, 'Burn your business plan!'). 'I just knew I had to find a location,' he says. 'There wasn't really anything like us here, and I knew the reaction of our clients.'

Hasson's instincts were on the money. Although the pair did not advertise, Sabon quickly became popular with celebrities like Julia Roberts and Susan Sarandon, who fell for what *Women's Wear Daily* called the company's 'rough-hewn luxury' – giving the fledgling store star cachet. Relying only on word of mouth and sales clerks who offer product samples to passers by, Sabon earned several nods in beauty and fashion magazines like *Vogue* and *Elle*, whose editors did not fail to notice Sabon's celebrity attraction.

According to Hasson, within ten months, Sabon's American flagship surpassed its sales goals (the private firm would not disclose numbers) and rolled out a second location. Currently, Sabon has six shops in New York, two in Chicago and one in Boston. The company opened a shop in Toronto last year and another in Rome in May. The partners are now considering opening boutiques in London and Tokyo.

Niche growth

'I like the atmosphere, it's really linked to the product for me,' says Leila Djemal, an organisational development consultant, who originally shopped at Sabon on trips to Israel and then noticed one in Manhattan. 'I like the whole package of the store, the way they display things, the rich creams. It's always kind of luxurious.'

Sabon's entry into the beauty market comes at a time when luxury niche brands is the fastest-growing segment in the industry. Spurred in part by the wildly successful Body Shop that began in England in 1976 and has expanded to include 2100 stores in 55 countries (see BusinessWeek.com, 3/17/06, 'L'Oréal's latest leap'), brands like America's Kiehl's and France's L'Occitane have attracted rabidly loyal customers who are flocking to natural skin and beauty care products. According to Karen Grant, a senior beauty industry analyst at the NPD Group, a Port Chester (NY) consultancy, this particular area of niche brands has been growing in the double digits since 2002, without slowing down. Last year, it contributed $265 million of the total $2.2 billion prestige skin care category. 'The one thing that is important,' says Grant, 'is that customers want product efficacy, service, a product that is different from something else.'

Despite Sabon's nearly overnight success, Hasson concedes that as a foreign entrepreneur coming to America, he faced a number of challenges. Although Sabon had already proved successful in its native

Israel, the company had to make some adjustments in order to duplicate that achievement in this country. 'Being an entrepreneur in the US was difficult initially,' says Hasson. 'I needed to figure out the system first as it's so different from Israel.'

Love of lavender

For starters, he couldn't just arrive and hang a shingle. He needed to get a business visa and a Social Security number. As well, according to Hasson, it costs about $50,000 to open a new location in Israel, compared to $300,000 here. There were cultural differences, too. Hasson found that his American customers were much more interested in knowing how the products are made and what their ingredients are. He also notes differing tastes, like lavender-infused products being more popular in the US than back in Israel.

But Hasson says he also discovered that in running a business here, 'Americans work hard. The competition is enormous, and people know they have to give their all if they want to succeed. The work ethic here is unique – people don't complain about long hours and, especially in New York, I think they expect to give 100 per cent.'

He also had to learn to adhere to America's more formal business procedures. 'If you don't know the formula,' he explains, 'you will struggle. But once you learn it, you can get it to work well for you. There are also so many rules and regulations to take into account, which can be frustrating initially. But now that Sabon is growing rapidly, I appreciate that control. The standards here are extraordinarily high, which is impressive – maybe because there's so much competition. In Israel things take longer. It's a small country and a lot of business ventures are between friends and family. So, the trust is there, which is nice. But sometimes people are less professional.'

Starting from scratch

Now that Sabon has a significant toehold in America, it is looking to expand its footprint. In September it opened a new store in Paramus, NJ, and is considering Miami and Los Angeles locations. Hasson says his ultimate goal is to roll out 100 shops across the country by 2012. And while Sabon has been approached by some department and speciality stores, Hasson says, at least for now, they don't want to dilute the personality of the store by opening mini-boutiques inside larger stores.

In hindsight, Hasson says: 'Being a foreigner in the States is hard, obviously. There is nothing easy about it. There is a different language to learn, the culture is different, and in a way you need to start from scratch. I was fortunate in that I had some good Israeli friends and connections in New York from Day One. But looking back, it was one of the hardest things I've ever done.'

Source: Stacy Perman, 'Sabon cleans up America', *BusinessWeek*, 28 September 2006

A study by Knight and Cavusgil (1996) regarding the widespread emergence of the 'born global' companies in different areas of the world economy represents another important challenge to experiential learning models. Based on a study conducted in Australia, the born global companies were defined by the following specific characteristics (Knight and Cavusgil 1996):

- management views the world as its marketplace from the outset of the firm's founding, so, unlike traditional companies, they do not see foreign markets as simple adjuncts to the domestic market
- born globals begin exporting one or several products within two years of their establishment and tend to export at least a quarter of their total production
- they tend to be small manufacturers with average annual sales usually not exceeding $100 million
- the majority of born globals are formed by active entrepreneurs and tend to emerge as a result of a significant breakthrough in some process or technology
- they may apply cutting-edge technology to developing a unique product idea or a new way of doing business
- the products that born globals sell typically involve adding substantial value – the majority of such products may be intended for industrial uses.

Knight and Cavusgil (1996) argued that this phenomenon was facilitated by a series of more recent trends that have increased the capacity of many companies to initiate international activities early on:

- the increasing role of niche markets, especially in the countries of the developed world, determined by increased demand for specialised or customised products
- the advances in process technology that have created the possibility of flexible, low-scale and low-cost production
- the advances in communications technologies have reduced the costs of information transmission with distant markets
- the inherent advantages of small companies, such as quicker response time, flexibility, adaptability and direct customer relations, facilitate the international operations of born global companies and offer them an important competitive edge compared with the larger multinationals
- the means of internationalisation, such as knowledge, technology, tools and facilitating institutions, have become more accessible to all firms, regardless of their size or activity sector
- the emergence of complex transnational networks of strategic alliances.

The born global model is supported by numerous studies that show these types of companies emerging in many national economies. The born global phenomenon is not limited to high-tech companies alone, as the case study demonstrates. The internationalisation of world business has created new opportunities for small firms that pursue rapid globalisation because the virtual market eliminates many of the time, space and cost barriers specific to physical trade, as this case study illustrates.

CASE STUDY

Success for Tasmanian 'born global'

Tasmanian-based Beauty and the Bees, a leading producer of organic skincare products, is a typical 'born global' exporter. From the day it was established as a mail order business in 1992, its customer base has had no geographical boundaries, with orders coming from all corners of the world.

Twelve years on, mail order still remains the company's key distribution system, however its customer list has changed from predominantly small buyers to include larger international distributors. This has led to a significant increase in company revenue as well as an obvious strain on the company's resources.

Founder and CEO of Beauty and the Bees, Jill Saunders, said the business had developed sophisticated logistics and transport systems to cope with large influxes in demand.

'We've learnt a lot in terms of sourcing the necessary raw materials and establishing good distribution systems to meet surges in demand. After many years of struggling with transport and freight problems we've now found an ideal partner in Toll Ipec', Ms Saunders said.

Ms Saunders said the focus on attracting large international buyers and marketing the products globally over the Internet had encouraged her to approach Austrade for assistance. 'Austrade has been extremely helpful in providing assistance through their overseas posts, particularly in the UK and Japan, which are our two largest export markets,' she said. 'We recently signed a $25,000 deal with a major Japanese distributor, which is something we never could have achieved on our own. This deal was possible due to our participation in Austrade's New Exporter Development Program and if it weren't for Haruhiko-Ban (Austrade's Business Development Manager – Nagoya), the deal would not have gone ahead. We are very, very grateful for his help.'

Ms Saunders grew up in England in a family where natural herbal remedies were part of everyday life. After researching ancient herb and honey recipes and developing her own range of natural skin care products she immigrated to Tasmania in 1992 to seek out the island's abundant and natural ingredients.

Beauty and the Bees began harvesting and making natural skincare products in Australia in 1993 using fresh, local ingredients – focusing on our rainforest island's unique, aromatic leatherwood honey and beeswax. Ms Saunders first established a mail order business then opened her first retail outlet, a fresh skincare deli in the historic waterfront village, Bellerive, in 1997. More recently the company opened a store in Hobart, where it offers the full range of lip balms, bath salts, body oils, creams, butters, powders and natural soaps. 'We will continue with both the retail and mail order sides of the business because this is a strategy working well for us at the moment,' she said. 'In terms of export we have quite a few overseas markets in mind, and we will continue to explore these with the help of Austrade.'

Source: Australian Government, Austrade (available at: www.austrade.gov.au/corporate/layout/0,,0_S1-1_-2_-3_PWB110464128-4_-5_-6_-7_,00.html)

Considering the impact of knowledge on the internationalisation process, it can be considered the most important resource in terms of achieving success in international ventures. The necessary knowledge about globalisation can come from different sources.

■ *Internal knowledge* The firm develops the necessary knowledge about foreign markets and the procedures required for international operations within its own organisational boundaries. Internal knowledge can be developed by means of individual and organisational learning, external recruitment or internal transfer of expertise between the various business units of the same organisation.

■ *Shared knowledge* The firm initiates and achieves stable joint ventures or strategic alliances with one or more business partners in order to obtain, and offer, specific knowledge and expertise necessary for international operations.

■ *Outsourced knowledge* This is obtained from governmental agencies or consulting firms that specialise in support services for the initiation and development of international activities. Often, the firm has to pay for this knowledge, although in some cases the government might support the international expansion of international firms by subsidising such programmes.

This classification indicates the kinds of business organisations that are possible sources of the kind of knowledge required for the internationalisation process, offering firms the opportunity to assess their internal capabilities and decide what source, or combination of sources, should be used (see Figure 8.3).

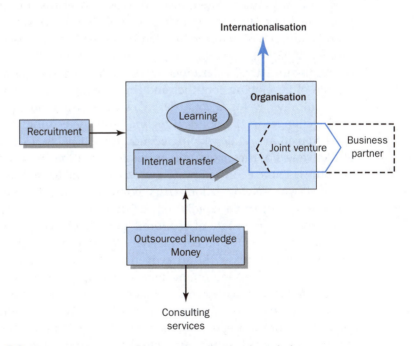

Figure 8.3 **The main sources of internationalisation knowledge**

Offshoring and globalisation of suppliers

Globalisation affects not only the cross-border trade in products and services for final consumption but also the elements transferred between firms as inputs for future production processes, such as raw materials, installations, fuel, information, technology or services. From this perspective, it can be seen that not only have consumer markets become more global, but so have supplier markets.

The globalisation of suppliers has been favoured by the large-scale liberalisation of international trade and the increased standardisation of technical specifications (such as the ISO international norms). This trend has influenced the practice of international marketing and even the theoretical definition and classification of global firms. A study published by the Organisation for Economic Co-operation and Development (OECD) in 1997, concerning the international activities of SMEs, published the classification shown in Table 8.2, which includes multiple elements.

The technical and competitive advances in transportation and communication have significantly reduced logistics costs and the quality of industrial supplies has become more uniform across various producers located in different countries. As a consequence, production costs constitute an important differentiating dimension, determining which long-term suppliers are chosen. These factors have caused changes not only in the locations of companies' suppliers but also, in some cases, led to a complex restructuring of corporate activities and organisation. This is all due to the phenomenon of offshoring.

Even if offshoring – the transfer of jobs to overseas countries – is a well-known phenomenon related to the increased globalisation of world business, the debate on this subject has increased in intensity in the last five years or so (Rutherford and Mobley 2005). The possible cause of this renewed interest is the development of offshoring initiatives determined by the political and economic changes realised in a series of developing countries and the structural transformations experienced by economically developed countries in a series of traditional industries.

The changes in the political regimes and the economic reforms introduced in most transition and developing economies in the last 15 years have increased the attractiveness of these countries as possible locations for offshoring or outsourcing activities. These economies are generally characterised by a large pool of well-qualified workers, low labour costs (compared with those in economically developed countries) and a rapidly improving infrastructure. Many such countries are experiencing a high rate of economic growth and are gradually being integrated into larger economic and commercial organisations, such as the EU, NAFTA and ASEAN, which increases the attractiveness of their markets.

Offshoring has an important impact on employment levels, the structure of the labour market and management of global business operations (Baily and Lawrence 2004). The first wave of offshoring was linked to labour-intensive industries. At present, the offshoring development is determined by advances in IT and telecommunications, which permit the relocation or outsourcing of information-related services in other countries with low labour costs.

Table 8.2 **The dimensions of SME globalisation**

Description	Traded inputs and outputs	Establishments and affiliations	Market opportunities and competition
No globalisation 'Domestic'	All inputs sourced from local area, all outputs sold in local area	Single establishment, no establishments or affiliations outside local area	No market outside local area, no potential competition from outside local area
Limited globalisation 'Mainly domestic'	< 10% of inputs sourced across borders, and < 10% revenue from across borders, usually within a limited span of nations	At least one establishment or affiliate outside local area or outside national area	Barriers to entry to outside markets and to local market (for competitors) are significant and amount to more than 50% of costs
Major globalisation 'Internationalised'	> 10% but < 40% of inputs sourced internationally, and > 10% but < 40% of revenue from across borders, usually across two major international regions	Establishments or close affiliates in at least four different nations and in two major international regions	Barriers to entry are noticeable, make up to 10% of cost disadvantage, but can be overcome fairly easily
Extensive globalisation 'Globalised'	> 40% of inputs sourced internationally, > 40% of revenue from outputs traded across borders, across all major international regions	Establishments or close affiliates in at least one country in all three major international regions	Barriers to entry to international markets are not significant impediment for firm or competitors, make up less than 5% cost disadvantage
Complete globalisation 'Fully globalised'	Majority of inputs of any establishment sourced across borders, large majority of outputs traded across borders	Multiple establishments or affiliates in many countries and in all major international regions	Markets in all major international regions, competition likely to be present or come from any international region

Source: OECD 1997, p.23

The scale of offshoring activities is difficult to assess. Research so far has provided contradictory findings, most probably due to the lack of common definitions and measurement tools. A study published by Bronfenbrenner and Luce (2004) in *Multinational Monitor*, indicates that 255 organisations in the USA had reported or announced job shifts from the USA to foreign countries in the period January–March 2004. The most common destinations for these offshoring operations were Mexico (69 shifts), China (58 shifts) and India (31 shifts). The intensity of offshoring varies from one industry to another. First place goes to ICT (7756 jobs shifted abroad), followed by the auto parts industry (6490 jobs), food processing (6265 jobs), electronics and electrical equipment (5871 jobs), appliances (5371 jobs), industrial equipment and machinery (3508 jobs), household goods (2956 jobs), metal fabrication and production (2836 jobs), and chemicals and petroleum (2245 jobs).

Despite this obvious trend towards an increase in the number of offshoring operations (Bronfenbrenner and Luce 2004), other research studies have indicated a different picture (Vogel and Connelly 2005). According to an annual study published by Diamond Cluster International, a Chicago-based management consulting firm, the level of satisfaction among the clients of outsourced services is decreasing (McEachern 2005). The 2005 Global IT Outsourcing Study surveyed 210 senior IT executives at 100 global companies and 242 senior executives at outsourcing service providers in the USA, India and other countries. The results of the survey were that 51 per cent of respondents indicated that they have terminated an outsourcing contract during the last year and only 62 per cent of respondents said that they were satisfied with their outsourcing relationships – this figure was 79 per cent the previous year.

Despite the interest demonstrated by researchers and professionals in the offshoring phenomenon, there is still a lack of common understanding about what offshoring is and how it can be measured. Most definitions do not differentiate between various forms of offshoring and do not consider how these operations relate to the global strategy of the firm. Here, we develop a framework that takes all these issues into account, in order to clarify the conceptual and the practical bases of offshoring operations.

The most common definition of offshoring is the shift of production and employment from a national basis to overseas locations in order to satisfy the demand of national consumers (Colquhoun et al. 2004). Other authors expand the scope of offshoring, stating that it represents any move of a company's operations into another country – that is, not only production but also finance and accounting, human resources, customer service, IT, sales and marketing, operations, engineering and development, procurement, real estate and facilities management, environment and health and safety operations (Williams 2003). This form of operation is facilitated and supported by the new organisational model of centralising data and decentralising corporate functions (Rutherford and Mobley 2005).

The specialists outline two main forms of offshoring:

■ *relocation* when the firm moves some of its operations in a foreign country
■ *outsourcing* when the firm subcontracts some functions or operations to companies located in foreign countries (Schultze 2004).

The advantages presented by these two forms vary depending on the industry and the specific competitive conditions experienced by the company (Preston 2004). However, other studies include a more complete classification of various inter-organisational forms of offshoring (Innovation Insight 2004):

■ *captive direct* when a firm establishes its own fully owned subsidiary overseas
■ *joint venture* when the firm creates a partnership with a foreign organisation to develop a new operational unit overseas
■ *direct third party* when the firm outsources some of its operations using a foreign supplier
■ *indirect third party* when the firm makes a contract with a domestic firm, which then subcontracts a part of the operation to a foreign supplier.

Although comprehensive, this classification is not necessarily logical. The inclusion of the category of an indirect third party (or intermediated outsourcing) as a form of offshoring increases confusion about this concept. This group can be reclassified under direct third party offshoring, if one considers only the relationship between the domestic contractor and the foreign supplier.

In order to develop a more clearly defined framework, it is important to identify the main elements that characterise specifically the phenomenon of offshoring. The two main elements that can define the profile of a business operation are the place of production and the place of consumption. From this perspective, we can identify four main types of companies (see Table 8.3):

- *domestic firm*, which produces in the country of origin to satisfy the demands of its domestic consumers
- *exporting company*, which produces in the country of origin, exporting a part or the totality of its output
- *conquering company*, which produces abroad in order to satisfy the demand of its foreign consumers
- *offshoring company*, which produces abroad in order to satisfy the demand of consumers from its country of origin.

These categories are not fully exclusive. The complexity of the modern business environment and the strategies of modern multinational companies often mean that a mix of these possible situations is used. For example, a conquering company that produces abroad to satisfy the demand of that foreign market may also export its products to other overseas countries – as is the case with Renault's production units for Logan, located in Romania.

The evolution of these firms usually starts with a domestic orientation, then, after a while, the firm starts to export the products manufactured for the local market to countries with a similar profile of demand. If that is successful, the firm will set up manufacturing units in the targeted foreign markets in order to reduce the international transportation costs. Finally, the cost advantages may mean that the firm manufactures its products abroad to sell in its domestic market (offshoring).

We can distinguish three forms of interorganisational offshoring:

- *fully captive offshoring* when the company creates a fully owned subsidiary overseas in order to produce items for its market of origin

Table 8.3 The offshoring phenomenon considered from the perspectives of place of production and place of consumption

	Domestic consumption	Foreign consumption
Domestic production	Domestic firm ⟶	Exporting firm
Foreign production	Offshoring firm ⟵	Conquering firm

Source: Adapted from Villemus 2005

- *joint venture offshoring* when the company creates a partnership with a foreign company in order to satisfy demand from its country of origin
- *outsourcing* when the company outsources one or more of its business operations from a foreign supplier.

A macroeconomic restructuring scenario is probably the best explanation of the present offshoring phenomenon, especially if we take an entire industrial sector or the entire global economy as the unit of analysis. The sectorial competitive advantage is evolving at global level. Developing countries can offer a specific competitive advantage in that the manufacture of labour-intensive products can be achieved with low labour costs and good standards of quality. However, the developed countries evolve as well and develop competitive advantages in other areas that are beyond the reach of developing countries, such as personalised services, research and development, innovation, design, high-tech industries and education. The balance of employment should be considered at macroeconomic level and if, on a long-term basis, this balance evolves positively towards high-value/high-tech sectors, the offshoring phenomenon can be considered beneficial, indicating that the macroeconomic profile should be developed further. On the other hand, firms need to bear in mind that changes in the sectorial distribution of jobs are painful and challenging for individuals and organisations as they need to quickly adapt to the new macroenvironmental conditions. The only logical answer in such cases is to ensure that there is an increase in adaptability and flexibility as the introduction of protectionist measures will only determine higher prices for domestic consumers and a stagnation of the economy will result if the realities of a globalised world are ignored. This has happened in the former communist countries, many of which were highly structured with rigid economic systems built on ideological bases rather than market realities. The problems experienced by countries in transition as they restructure their economies on competitive bases are representative of the kinds of dangers of long-term protectionism and insulation that can be suffered at a company level.

International marketing orientations

An international marketing strategy can be any one of three possible orientations:

- domestic market extension
- multinational
- global.

The firms following a *domestic market extension model*, usually have one or more products or services that are highly successful in their domestic market, but no international activity. Following this domestic success, sometimes the managers actively consider the opportunity to sell the same products or service in foreign markets that are very similar to their domestic market. In these conditions, the company does not have to make complex modifications to its basic offer in order to adapt it to the foreign demand and, therefore, the cost of international expansion is minimised. It is possible that the idea to sell abroad comes about as a result of spontaneous demands from foreign customers, without the firm having made any efforts to promote its product or service abroad. In this case, the firm follows a *reactive* strategy of internationalisation rather than an *active* one.

The *multinational* orientation in international marketing is characterised by the presence of a firm in many different countries, with products specifically adapted to the consumers' demands in each of these foreign markets. For this type of firm, each market is considered as a national operation and all international operations represent a diversified portfolio of independent products/markets. The firms having a multinational marketing orientation adapt the same products or services concepts to the existing conditions in every target market and manage their international operations as independent business units in these foreign markets.

The *global* orientation in international marketing requires the identification of a transnational segment of consumers located in different foreign countries, but having similar needs and wants. Sometimes the total number of these consumers in each of the foreign countries, when considered separately, is quite small and the segment only reaches the required critical mass to move into profit when considered at transnational level. This is the case, for example, with luxury products or drugs for rare diseases. The firm that succeeds in identifying the existence of such transnational consumer segments can develop a product or service that satisfies this global demand, creating an opportunity to sell it in various countries, targeting these specific consumers. The global orientation is usually accompanied by a high level of standardisation of the offered product or service, with a strong, globally known brand name – such as Coca-Cola, McDonald's, Cartier, Mercedes and so on. However, in particular cases, the marketing mix is slightly adapted to the specificities of a particular country if it means that consumers will then adopt the product or service and it will quickly increase the volume of sales. Coca-Cola does this by slightly changing its soft drinks to suit the tastes of different countries.

Standardisation versus adaptation

One of the most difficult areas of international marketing strategy is the debate on standardisation versus adaptation theories. In 1983, Levitt published a seminal paper in the *Harvard Business Review*, in which he argued that, as world markets are highly globalised and consumers needs and wants show a high degree of convergence and similarity, the best international strategy is the creation of a high-quality, low-priced product concept, that can be produced using significant economies of scale and then distributed on a global basis as a highly standardised, value offer.

Many authors have criticised Levitt, arguing that, although globalisation is an important pattern in international business, the standardisation of consumers' needs and wants is not clear in all sectors and markets. If, in the industrial markets, the degree of standardisation is very high and this is even endorsed by the introduction of various technological and quality standards, in more volatile markets, such as consumer goods or services, local cultures still shape the preferences of national consumers to a significant degree. In these types of markets, the global approach has little chance of succeeding, so the marketing mix strategy needs to be adapted to meet the local market's requirements.

Related to this, there are several changes taking place at international level, that incline the balance towards one or the other of the two poles in the debate:

- the international movements of immigrants to different countries create multi-cultural markets and provide opportunities for a transnational marketing that focuses on these ethnic communities
- the antiglobalisation movements and attitudes in some countries create barriers for the commercialisation of foreign or global brands
- the Internet has created a parallel digital market in which people are coagulating their activities around specific centres of interest, providing opportunities for a transnational tribal marketing
- the fragmentation of market segments requires companies to take an increasingly personalised approach, using one-to-one marketing techniques.

The best answer to the question of how to choose between these two extreme – standardisation or adaptation – depends on the specific characteristics of the market served by any one firm. A company should try to identify both the common and disparate elements of consumer demand and behaviour, as well as the degree of similarity between different local markets, and decide, in every particular situation, what elements of the marketing mix should be standardised and what should be adapted. For example, Coca-Cola is using a global brand name, but the price, the container, and even the taste of its drinks is adapted to suit local market characteristics. Such combinations of standardised and adapted elements within the same marketing mix is called a *glocal marketing strategy*. McDonald's – another successful global firm – applies this same theory to its operations by changing its menus in different countries. In the UK it has beef, pork and chicken hamburgers, in France it offers a choice of salads and in China it has introduced rice, fish and sushi to the menu.

Selecting which foreign markets to target

The process of selecting foreign markets to target is paramount to the success of any firm's international marketing operations. Making the wrong decision at this stage can mean important losses of the firm's resources and profits and provide other companies with a precious competitive advantage.

In order to select the best foreign markets for future international operations, the management team has to apply a five-stage process of research, analysis and decision (see Figure 8.4):

1 evaluate and understand the assets and strategic objectives of the firm
2 define the main criteria for selecting a country

3 apply the selection criteria and select the country or countries
4 study the profile of the selected foreign market(s)
5 develop the strategic marketing plan.

The selection of the most appropriate foreign target markets represents a complex process of matching the company's assets and objectives with the foreign market profile, considering also the restrictions imposed by the firm's existing domestic market. These restrictions can be financial, economic or political, such as the interdiction of the US government limiting American companies working in defence-related sectors to selling products (such as encryption programs) only to specifically nominated countries. This complex process of selection requires, in the first instance, a good understanding of the company's assets, capabilities and objectives.

Evaluate and understand the assets and strategic objectives of the firm

The success of a firm in its international marketing operations will be determined by the level and quality of its resources, as well as its capacity to use them efficiently. The decision makers must consider that, usually, international marketing projects are more difficult and complex than domestic marketing operations, requiring the investment of various resources on a long-term basis. In many cases, international marketing operations do not bring any profit in the first two to five years of the project, so the firm has to continually invest resources during this time

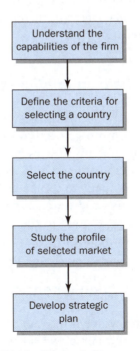

Figure 8.4 The process of selecting target markets

in order to build and stabilise its presence in the foreign market. From this perspective, before initiating any new international business operations, it is vital that managers evaluate correctly the required resources and how long it will take before they will return any profit.

Some of the resources required for international marketing operations are similar to those required for domestic marketing – money, production and distribution facilities, human resources and management capabilities, for example. However, international expansion requires a series of specific resources in addition to these, such as:

- managers with international experience – that is, they can collect, process, analyse and understand foreign business data
- a marketing strategy that is capable of being adapted to the conditions within the foreign market and their continuous evolution
- the strategic assets required to successfully initiate and develop international marketing operations – these need to be identified, listed and evaluated by the managers because the lack of such resources can represent specific limitations that have to be taken into account when defining the selection criteria for foreign markets.

The new international marketing operations must also correspond to the general strategic objectives of the firm. The decision makers should make predictions of the marketing objectives of the firm at international level and select target foreign markets that will increase the firm's chances of achieving these objectives. So, for example, if a firm desires to increase the volume of its international sales, it should only take an interest in markets that promise future growth.

On the basis of the above internal analysis of assets, capabilities and strategic objectives, the managers will then need to identify the most appropriate criteria for selecting a foreign market.

Define the main criteria for selecting a country

There are probably hundreds or even thousands of possible foreign market selection criteria, but no organisation has the time and resources to use such a large number. Because of this, it is essential that the company's management identify and apply only those criteria most important to them. The number of these criteria can vary from company to company, but usually they should be limited to between 10 and 15. If this procedure is applied and then it is found that the countries selected do not correspond to the capabilities and objectives of the firm, it means that the criteria were not well selected.

Apply the selection criteria and select the country or countries

In order to narrow down the choice of the foreign target market quickly, the firm must establish and apply two types of criteria. First, an absolute incompatibility criteria should be identified – in other words, a highly discriminating characteristic of a foreign market that would make it completely unattractive or inaccessible for the firm, such as the lack of a convertible currency.

Second, after the first criteria has been applied, the remaining countries will need to be evaluated by using a series of criteria of relative attractiveness – market size, market growth rate, spending power, political stability, quality of infrastructure, intensity of competition and so on.

On the basis of data collected via market research, any remaining country will be evaluated against these selection criteria again using a value scale – say, from 1 to 10, where 1 can be considered as the least attractive, and 10 the most attractive. After every criteria of relative attractiveness has been evaluated and allocated a value, these values can be added up, the final totals indicating which is the most attractive foreign target market for the firm and which is the least promising.

Often, however, not all the criteria are of equal importance to the firm. The managers may, for example, consider that the market's size and growth are more important than the quality of the country's infrastructure. In this situation, these key selection criteria should be adjusted with an additional value that indicates their greater level of importance for the firm. The evaluations made for each of these key selection criteria are then multiplied by these additional values, the resulting figures being added up for each country in order to indicate the market with the highest relative attractiveness for the firm.

Considering the complexity of this process, it is crucial that highly discriminating absolute incompatibility criteria are chosen in order to reduce the total number of countries remaining after the second stage to just a few to save time and effort effectively.

The practicalities of applying the selection criteria are illustrated in the following case study.

CASE STUDY

Establishing countries' attractiveness for exporting opportunities

A UK firm specialising in selling mobile phone accessories decides to pursue a future expansion in continental Europe. Therefore, the foreign countries considered for future operations are: Germany, France, Italy, Spain, Russia, the Netherlands, Belgium, Switzerland, Sweden, Turkey, Austria, Poland, Norway, Denmark, Greece, Ireland, Finland, Portugal, the Czech Republic, Hungary, Ukraine, Romania, Kazakhstan, Croatia, Slovakia, Luxembourg, Slovenia, Belarus, Serbia, Montenegro, Bulgaria, Bosnia and Herzegovina, Lithuania, Cyprus, Iceland, Latvia, Estonia, Azerbaijan, Albania, Malta, Macedonia, Georgia, Armenia, Moldova, Andorra, Liechtenstein, Monaco, San Marino, Vatican City.

In the first stage of the selection process, the firm will produce an in-depth internal analysis, evaluating the existing resources and the strategic objectives established for the international expansion. On the basis of this analysis, the firm will establish, in the second stage of the selection process, two categories of selection criteria: the criteria of absolute incompatibility and the set of criteria measuring the relative attractiveness of various countries.

▶

Taking into account the cultural expertise of the manager responsible for this international expansion, the firm has established the lack of use of the English language for business transactions as the criteria of absolute incompatibility. Applying this selection criteria to the list of countries presented above, the decision makers have retained the following possible targets: the Netherlands (Ned), Sweden (Swe), Norway (Nrw), Denmark (Dnm), Ireland (Irl), Finland (Fld), Cyprus (Cyp) and Iceland (Icd).

The criteria of relative attractiveness of the countries established by the decision makers are market size (MS), market growth (MG), intensity of competition (IC), financial infrastructure (FI), compatibility of technical standards (TS) and geographical distance (GD). The first three criteria are considered two times more important than the last three. Applying an adjusted evaluation of the countries' attractiveness on these six criteria, using a value scale from 1 to 10, in which 10 is allocated for maximum attractiveness and 1 for minimum attractiveness, the managers develop the following evaluation table (Table CS 8.1).

Considering the sums of the values allocated for every criteria, the most attractive foreign target market for the UK firm appears to be Ireland (75 points), followed at quite a long distance by Sweden and Finland (62 points).

After selecting the most attractive foreign country, in stage four, the UK firm will have to collect detailed information about the target market, followed, in stage five of the process, by the development of a strategic marketing plan for international expansion.

Source: Gurău 2006, written for this chapter

Table CS 8.1 **The evaluation on various countries using specific foreign market selection criteria**

	Ned	Swe	Nrw	Dnm	Irl	Fld	Cyp	Icd
MS	2 x 6	2 x 7	2 x 6	2 x 6	2 x 8	2 x 5	2 x 4	2 x 3
MG	2 x 5	2 x 6	2 x 7	2 x 7	2 x 9	2 x 7	2 x 4	2 x 5
IC	2 x 5	2 x 8	2 x 7	2 x 7	2 x 7	2 x 8	2 x 6	2 x 5
FI	8	7	7	7	8	8	6	6
TS	7	6	6	7	9	7	5	8
GD	9	7	8	7	10	7	5	6
Total	56	62	61	61	75	62	36	46

The dynamic dimension of the international business environment increases the complexity of this evaluation and selection process. Considering the fact that the situation in a given country or region can change dramatically in a very short time (months or even weeks) and the international operations of the firm will not start until some point in the future, it is important to assess not only the present situation in various countries but also predict, as accurately as possible, their future profile and performance.

The application of these criteria will have, as a final result, the identification of the foreign country or countries that have the highest relative attractiveness for the firm.

Study the profile of the selected foreign market(s)

Even if the selection process has been finalised, the firm still has to fully analyse, study and understand the profile of the foreign target market. In the second and third stages, the need for efficiency has meant that the number of aspects of each country analysed by the firm has been limited. However, there is an important difference in terms of objectives between the previous stages and this one. The multi-country analysis was made for selection purposes, while the aim of the in-depth analysis of the target market is to develop a successful strategic marketing plan.

The profile of the target market must be studied and analysed as completely as possible by the manager responsible for the future international operations and his or her team. On the one hand, the elements considered during the selection process should be considered in more detail, but, on the other hand, additional elements should be considered, too, so that a complete understanding of the target country's economic, social, legal, financial and cultural system can be achieved. If, during this in-depth analysis, the management team discovers additional elements that reduce the overall attractiveness of the country or even indicate its absolute incompatibility with the company's resources and objectives, the market selection process (second and third stages) should be applied again.

Develop the strategic marketing plan

On the basis of the information analysed in the fourth stage, the firm should now be capable of developing a strategic marketing plan for its future operations in the targeted market. This plan will provide a roadmap for the main strategic operations, listing the marketing objectives of the firm, the resources allocated for penetrating the market and developing its presence, the specific operational stages and the staff responsible for their realisation, as well as a provisional schedule.

One of the most important elements included in the marketing plan is the market entry strategy, which often shapes the organisational structure and market positioning of the firm in the targeted country.

The foreign country selection procedure can be standardised only at procedural level. The unique situation of each firm and the specific conditions of the international business environment require a personalisation of the selection criteria and process. However, the selection process presented above can be considered to be a 'rational' method. Sometimes, despite clear results being produced by this systematic procedure, the final decision is taken on the basis of the personal experience and intuition of the general or international manager – a method largely used by many SMEs that do not have the necessary resources to collect and analyse complex data about a series of foreign countries. Although the intuitive method has many merits, it is not advisable to eliminate completely the rational approach to foreign market selection. Ultimately, a balanced combination of these two approaches provides the best chance for success in international ventures.

Market entry strategies

The classical market entry strategies in foreign markets are:

- exporting
- licensing
- franchising
- strategic alliances and joint ventures
- wholly owned subsidiaries, either developed or acquired.

Each of these market entry modes has specific advantages and disadvantages that have to be properly considered by firms before initiating an international venture. Usually, the strategy that is best for a specific competitive situation can be found by analysing the firm's resources and expertise, the specific circumstances of the foreign business environment and the strategic objectives of the firm – especially the ones relating to profitability, market share and degree of operational control (see Figure 8.5).

Exporting

This is the traditional internationalisation method and it is still extremely popular because of its simplicity and low level of risk.

Exporting has for a long time been considered the best way to initiate the internationalisation process because of its low involvement with the foreign market and its capacity to provide quick revenues to the company. The classical models of internationalisation suggest initiating exporting activities in countries that are very similar to the firm's domestic market. Today, exporting activities can be developed using various alternative methods, requiring differing levels of involvement of the firm – that is, direct exporting, exporting via specialised agencies or confirming houses and piggybacking.

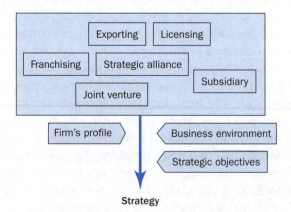

Figure 8.5 Market entry strategies and factors influencing the choice of strategy

Exporting is favoured by national governments because it not only confirms the international competitiveness of its national firms, but also brings direct and quick value inputs into the country. Because of this, many countries actively support the development of exporting activities, supporting national firms by means of counselling, market information and even subsidies.

Despite its advantages, exporting does not allow for a very good control of the product and company's image in the foreign country. Some companies also use it for the opportunistic exploitation of foreign markets during crisis periods.

Licensing

Licensing allows a company to exploit the financial value of its intellectual property portfolio by selling the use of patents or technology to foreign customers.

Traditionally, licensing has been used mainly in industrial markets, where innovative companies sell the use of their discoveries to other firms. More recently, however, the use of licensing has been dramatically expanded in the consumer goods markets, covering products such as software programs.

The contract that regulates a licensing agreement can contain specific clauses related to confidentiality, competition and grant-back conventions – that is, the obligation of the licensee to communicate to the licensor any development made on the initial licensing object.

Licensing can be used in countries where the competition is too intense to create a subsidiary. In this case, a business client is allowed to apply the protected innovation under specifically defined rules. The client pays royalties for the right to use the innovation, making regular payments.

Franchising

Franchising combines the advantage of a reputable brand name with the transfer of specific know-how. Famous examples of franchising firms are found in the fast food market, such as McDonald's or Pizza Hut, fashion retailing, such as Benetton, services, such as financial counselling and property dealers Century21, and consumer goods, such as Coca-Cola.

Franchising is based on a legal agreement between the franchisor – the company owning the brand name and the know-how – and the franchisee – a firm or individual having a good knowledge of the local, regional or national market environment. This combination of complementary knowledge allows the franchisor to expand internationally at rapid pace, in conditions of low investment and risk.

Franchising has been used by many of the US companies mentioned above, in order to quickly expand into a huge internal market. The success achieved has provided a platform for international expansion.

A network of franchisees is developed progressively, in the markets or areas in which the brand is known and there is a growing demand for its products or services. However, the franchisor has to make sure that the quality of the franchised establishment is in line with the brand's image. A large variation in quality levels of various franchisees will send conflicting messages to consumers, who could then become alienated.

Another danger is the threat of competitors, which can copy the style and know-how of the franchise. Only a part of the elements transmitted to the franchisee can be protected by intellectual property laws, such as the brand name, logo and text of adverts. However, the success of a franchise can inspire local competitors to copy it and use the same elements, with small modifications, for much lower prices. In these conditions, a strong brand image and a constant level of quality represent the best weapons in maintaining popularity and market share.

Franchising is a commercial method that is based on many globalisation trends:

- the facility to communicate to distant markets and consumers allows the reputation of a brand to spread globally
- the movement of people across borders creates a transnational group of consumers that will look for a familiar brand even when they are abroad
- the convergence of many national legislations on fair competition and intellectual property protection laws allows for similar levels of brand and business protection to be maintained in different countries.

Strategic alliances

These are formal or informal agreements between two or more companies from different countries that enable them to coordinate their business operations, exchange information, knowledge or technology, or collaborate on specific projects. Each firm involved in the agreement still keeps its organisational identity and no other business structure will be created as a result of the strategic alliance.

The reasons for creating strategic alliances are many and varied.

- In an oligopolistic market, large competitors might decide to create informal agreements in order to stabilise market shares. These agreements are usually illegal because, in many countries, they are considered to restrain competition. A good example of this type of strategic alliance was the agreement on the level of pricing in the French market, concluded in 2005 by three telecommunications companies: Orange, SFR and Bouygues Telecom.
- Two or more multinational firms may decide to create strategic alliances in order to reduce costs and risks or create economies of scale. A good example of this is the large number of strategic alliances developed in high-tech sectors, such as biotechnology and pharmaceuticals, to share the costs of the research and development process between the partners. Another is when Sony and Ericsson jointly produced a mobile phone, linking together their respective strengths. Many car manufacturers create strategic alliances in order to use the same technology platform for various car models, such as the Fiat-GM partnership.

■ Companies from different countries can decide to initiate strategic alliances with the purpose of using the facilities and knowledge of their overseas partners to penetrate the foreign market.

Strategic alliances are usually flexible and limited to a specific number of objectives. Sometimes, two competing companies create a strategic alliance in order to enhance a specific area of their business operations, whether it be R&D, manufacturing or distribution, while continuing to compete in global markets. This mix of competition and collaboration has become an interesting feature of the present global business environment. Companies are looking for advantages and synergies from all the possible sources, including competitors.

Joint ventures

Joint ventures are agreements realised between two or more companies to pursue common strategic objectives for a specific period of time by creating an independent structure in which the partners share responsibilities, management and profits. The existence of a new organisational entity means that joint ventures have less flexibility than strategic alliances, requiring an increased commitment from the partners.

Many joint ventures are short-lived because of the potential conflicts that can develop between partners. These problems are even more complex in an international context as the relationship between companies from different countries is often marked by clashes of national and organisational cultures.

Joint venture agreements are based on complex contracts, which may include licensing, the transfer of technology, and a specific definition of the rights and obligations of each party.

Besides the importance of a clearly written contract, the following elements have to be taken into account in order to maximise the chances of success of a joint venture:

■ the strategic objectives of the joint venture should be well understood and commonly shared by the business partners
■ the contribution of the two firms to the joint venture should be based on complementarity
■ the decision making process and the division of profits should be based on the risks taken by each partner and the levels of resources allocated to the joint venture
■ a good understanding of the organisational and national culture of the foreign partners can facilitate understanding and collaboration
■ the partners should maintain, during the entire life of the joint venture, a strong commitment towards flexibility and open communication.

Often, even when the strategic objectives of the joint venture have not been fully achieved at the end of the established period, the partners can continue and extend their collaborations, considering the benefits of mutual understanding and the synergies between the two organisations. In this context, the economic and profitability objectives are not always the most important ones – the partners also need to take into account benefits such as collaboration, mutual understanding and organisational synergies.

Subsidiaries

These are used to expand the activity of a firm in overseas countries by establishing a direct presence in the target market.

Compared with the previous forms of market entry, subsidiaries allow a greater degree of control and coordination, but this strategy may require more investment and carries considerable risks. Foreign subsidiaries can fulfil various objectives such as the following.

- *Sales and marketing subsidiaries* When the firm tries to control closely its commercial operations in a foreign market.
- *Manufacturing subsidiaries* When a firm wants to take advantage of low-cost manufacturing in a foreign location or reduce the costs of transportation between its headquarters and large foreign markets.
- *R&D subsidiaries* Although, traditionally, the R&D function has been concentrated at firms' headquarters, the development of specific scientific competencies in some countries or world regions provides incentives for corporations to relocate some of their R&D activities overseas. A good example of this is the creation of a centre of excellence for software development in India, with many software companies relocating all or a part of their research and development activities there.
- *Service subsidiaries* Some companies have taken advantage of developments in ICT to relocate their customer service call centres to overseas markets where labour costs are lower. This strategy has been used by many British firms that moved their call centres to India, although, in some cases, customers complained about a reduction in the quality of the services provided. Traditionally, the creation of overseas subsidiaries has been used as the main method of international expansion for service companies. As, in order to provide services, the employees and firm need to be in direct and close contact with local customers, the creation of new overseas units was the only possible way for hotels, banks, universities or consulting services to expand overseas. However, today, the existence of the Internet has changed this limited perspective. It is now possible to provide global services to customers from different locations using advanced ICT applications, such as telephone, e-mail, discussion forums and video-conferencing.
- *Cloned headquarters* These subsidiaries have, in their organisational structure, all the functions of the firm's headquarters, representing complete copies of the mother firm, but have a high level of strategic, financial and operational autonomy. These subsidiaries are characteristic of a multi-domestic approach to international markets.

Subsidiaries can be either newly created or integrated into the company's structure as a result of the acquisition of local firms. Both these methods provide specific advantages and challenges:

- newly created units require large investments in terms of money and effort to organise and build a coherent corporate culture
- acquired units need to be transformed to be integrated into the corporate culture of the mother company, requiring restructuring at various levels – personnel, departments, functions, processes and communication methods, for example – and it may be the case that an acquired unit needs to function according to the cultural context of the country rather than its parent's cultural context.

Although it is not considered to be a pure method of foreign market entry, *mergers* between two or more companies can serve the same purpose. In a merger, two or more organisations decide to combine their organisational structures and capabilities, creating a legal entity that will use either the combined names of the merged firms, the name of one of the merging organisations or an entirely new name.

Besides allowing access to foreign markets and local market knowledge, mergers can achieve other objectives, such as:

- reducing the number of global competitors
- creating economies of scale and experience
- achieving complementary skills and assets in order to expand the business in other economic areas
- capturing and internalising the sources of rare, strategic resources, such as raw materials, human resources, information and technology.

The following case study demonstrates that, sometimes, it is not only tangible assets that multinational corporations are after when acquiring other firms but also intangible elements, such as reputation and an ethical image.

CASE STUDY

When big business bites

Can niche firms keep their fans when snapped up by the multinationals?

(by Fiona Walsh)

You start the day with a refreshing shower – taking care to conserve water, of course – but still enjoying the aroma of Body Shop's satsuma shower gel. A quick brush with Tom's of Maine toothpaste, then it's a pot of Rachel's Organic vanilla yogurt for breakfast.

For lunch, grab a sandwich at Pret A Manger, followed by a mini-tub of Ben & Jerry's ice-cream. In need of an afternoon sugar rush? Then a treat-sized bar of Green & Black's organic chocolate should do the trick.

So far, so ethical – or is it? From Body Shop to Green & Black's, smaller companies known for their ethical principles and counter-culture approach are being taken over by multinationals keen to establish credentials in the booming ethical market.

Body Shop has just become part of the French cosmetics giant L'Oréal; Tom's of Maine fell to Colgate-Palmolive last month; Wales-based Rachel's Organic is a subsidiary of the American conglomerate Dean Foods, which has come under fire in the US over its industrial-scale organic dairies and factory-farm milk production.

Pret A Manger is one-third owned by McDonald's; Ben & Jerry's has been under Unilever's ownership for six years and Green & Black's belongs to Cadbury-Schweppes, the world's biggest confectionery company.

▶

For consumers, those multinational names don't have quite the same ethical ring to them, although many shoppers remain unaware of the ultimate ownership of some of their favourite brands. For those who are, does the change of ownership really matter? And can a smaller company built on a different set of values really operate comfortably within a global corporation?

At Ben & Jerry's in the US, the relationship with Unilever remains an uneasy one. Ben & Jerry's most recent social audit highlighted a 'disappointing' lack of social initiatives at the company and poor morale among employees. It questioned whether the company was 'simply a Unilever marketing operation using the brand's reputation for social responsibility to promote sales.'

That charge is vehemently denied by Helen Jones, who has run Ben & Jerry's in the UK for 11 years. 'We are fully supported by Unilever and we've doubled our charitable donations under them,' she says. But, clearly, there are tensions within the larger Ben & Jerry's operation.

Battering

At Body Shop, despite a chorus of protest at Dame Anita Roddick's decision to sell out to L'Oréal, the company says sales have not been affected by the deal. But its ethical reputation has certainly taken a battering, as have all niche players taken over by multinationals.

Ethical Consumer magazine runs an online shoppers' guide, at www.ethiscore.org, which rates companies and their products on their ethical credentials. Body Shop's rating has plunged from 11 out of 20 to just 2.5 since the L'Oréal deal and the magazine has urged a boycott of its products in protest not only at the French cosmetics group's ownership, but also its links with Nestlé, which owns 26 per cent of L'Oréal. Nestlé has faced boycott campaigns over issues from animal testing to the marketing of baby milk substitutes.

Last month's takeover of Tom's of Maine by Colgate-Palmolive sent its ethical rating tumbling from 16 to just 5, as it paid the penalty for Colgate-Palmolive's rock-bottom rating on environmental reporting and animal testing.

Best-known for its toothpaste, Tom's of Maine started more than 30 years ago making phosphate-free washing powder. Like Anita Roddick, who has made repeated jibes at companies such as L'Oréal over the years, Tom's of Maine founder Tom Chappell has in the past been critical of major brands such as Colgate and their use of artificial additives.

But, like other founders who have handed over their businesses, he was convinced by assurances from the new owners that it would continue to operate as an independent entity and its principles would remain intact.

Those assurances have held firm at the organic chocolate maker Green & Black's, according to Mark Palmer, its marketing director. Its sales had rocketed from £4m to £40m in the past five years, but financial support from Cadbury, which took over last year, will help it make a big push into the US this year.

'We've just had the first anniversary of the takeover and the amazing thing is that nothing has changed at all,' Mr Palmer says. 'In one sense, it was a bit of an anticlimax because absolutely nothing happened.'

He accepts that customers were suspicious, but says: 'Cadbury's understands that Green & Black's is a special case. And they are astute enough to realise that you don't pile in and mess about with credentials like that.'

Like most of the niche businesses bought by multinationals, Green & Black's is run as an entirely separate operation within the Cadbury empire. 'It's a case of how they can help us, not telling us what to do,' Mr Palmer says.

One advantage of Cadbury's coffers is that Green & Black's is now pursuing international expansion, something Mr Palmer admits the company 'has always been a little scared of.'

It exports just 10 per cent of its turnover, but has just set up a US subsidiary in Connecticut and is in the process of hiring a team out there. 'We're not being put into the situation where we're managed by Cadbury in the States,' Mr Palmer says. 'But it's up to us to be a bit grown-up about it too. We are independent – and we're also fortunate that we can call on Cadbury's expertise and experience.'

Mr Palmer accepts there is scepticism when big companies move in on niche brands. But, he says, 'it's worked for Green & Black's.'

He adds: 'You can be fiercely independent and not have any funds to grow. But does that help the cocoa growers in Belize?'

As to whether Green & Black's is less ethical under Cadbury, that depends on the individual consumer, says Ruth Rosselson of *Ethical Consumer* magazine. Many consumers simply don't know who owns their favourite brands, and others don't care: 'It really depends on what your reasons for buying ethical are,' she says. 'If you mind where the money ultimately goes, then giving it to a company that tests on animals or uses child labour is a contradiction. If you're just looking at the product, then ownership doesn't really matter.'

Swallowed

Ms Rosselson believes there will be longer-term damage to brands swallowed by multinationals, despite the hopes of entrepreneurs like Dame Anita that they will be able to force changes within the larger organisations.

'The real "deep green" consumer does feel betrayed,' she says. 'We hear the big optimistic speeches from people like Craig Sams [founder of Green & Black's] and Anita Roddick about the influence they can wield on the new owners, but it

hasn't happened yet. Ben & Jerry's was bought up in 2000 and Unilever hasn't suddenly gone organic.'

Dr Tim Lang, Professor of Food Policy at City University, also urges caution. 'There's no doubt it's a win for the big company because they are buying a ready-made package of values and history of trust.' But, he says, there will always be 'a tension and contradiction' between the small ethical firms and their multinational masters. 'The former owners argue that they can change from within. In the short term, that may well be the case but over the longer term values get dissipated and weakened.'

'My own argument with the ethical trading world – of which I am a supporter – is that it is pursuing a risky strategy. Everything is dependent on how the relationship with the movement is retained by these companies. And if Fair Trade, animal welfare or the ethical movement do their homework, they will make sure customers are reminded who owns these companies.'

'For big business, the key is how careful they are with the values they have bought. For the movement that gave birth to those values, eternal vigilance is required.'

Source: Fiona Walsh, *The Guardian*, 8 June 2006. Copyright Guardian News & Media Ltd 2006.

The increased popularity of mergers in the last 20 years witnesses to an accelerated trend of concentrating strategic assets across companies and global regions. Despite the advantages offered by this strategy, the accommodation of the two merging corporate structures can take a long time and effort, requiring the resolution of various cultural conflicts.

Sometimes a corporation will use two or more market entry strategies for the same market, often in a precise time succession. For example, in some Eastern European countries, Coca-Cola initiated its operations by creating subsidiaries and, then, when the company succeeded in better understanding the local market conditions as a result of trust built up with local entrepreneurs, it switched its overseas operations to franchising agreements.

Managing international operations

The organisation and management of overseas activities require the implementation of specific corporate structures and procedures. Depending on the specific corporate culture of every company, and taking into account the characteristics of the foreign markets serviced by the firm, the organisation can adopt various management models.

Bartlett and Goshal (1989) have identified, on the basis of extensive research, four main types of corporate structures.

- multinational
- international
- global
- transnational.

Multinational

The multinational firm usually has a number of highly independent business units located in various countries. Many assets, resources and responsibilities are decentralised to local level and the marketing strategy, designed and implemented by local subsidiaries, is highly adapted to the specific needs and wants of local customers. Although the name of the firm can be adopted by all business units, headquarters perceives the foreign subsidiaries as a portfolio of independent activities, not as an integrated structure at global level (see Figure 8.6).

International

In an international firm, many assets, resources and responsibilities are also decentralised, but the internal business processes are more closely controlled by the top management of the mother company. The marketing strategy of every subsidiary is adapted to the local market conditions, but has a series of common elements that are central to the corporate culture of the company, such as the same product concept, same brand name or same technology platform. The managers of foreign subsidiaries are usually trained at headquarter level and then sent to coordinate the activities of foreign markets in the spirit of clearly defined corporate values. Top management considers the foreign business units as appendices of a central organisation (see Figure 8.7).

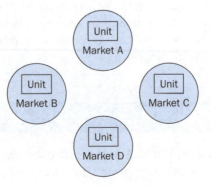

Figure 8.6 **The multinational's organisational structure**

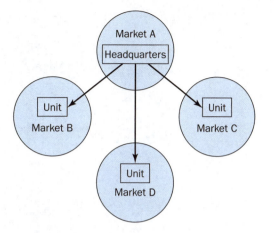

Figure 8.7 **The international firm's organisational structure**

Global

A global organisation is characterised by its highly centralised management of strategic assets and resources. Based on a strong corporate culture and a highly standardised product concept, the company attempts to increase efficiency and profitability at global level, serving a transnational segment of consumers with very similar needs and wants. Having a global perspective of the sources of competitive advantage offered by various countries, the managers will decide to locate various departments of the firm in the overseas areas that can maximise the efficiency of the firm. The top management considers the local operations as distribution pipelines for delivering a highly standardised product concept to the group of transnational consumers located in various geographical areas (see Figure 8.8).

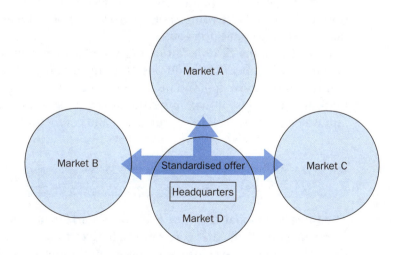

Figure 8.8 **The global firm's organisational structure**

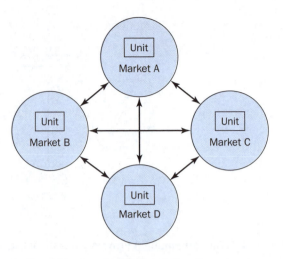

Figure 8.9   The transnational firm's organisational structure

Transnational

The transnational organisation is based on the flexible mixing and matching of resources located in various overseas locations in order to maximise the efficiency of specific business projects. Compared to the global firm's structure, the localisation of resources is not rigid and static, but dynamic and flexible. The management should be able to quickly combine the necessary assets and capabilities in order to effectively answer the threats and opportunities manifested in various geographical locations. Often, the organisation of the transnational firm applies the model of an integrated network of highly competitive business units. The structure of the firm is bidimensional, using both products and markets as centres for responsibility and decisionmaking. Therefore, for the effective realisation of a business project in a specific overseas market, a product manager and a market manager have to join resources, capabilities and responsibilities, in order to manage the situation and make the best possible decisions.

Considering the flexible nature of present-day markets and the unpredictable evolution of competitive conditions, this organisational structure (see Figure 8.9) is considered the most appropriate for companies in the twenty-first century global marketplace because it maximises the flexibility and responsiveness of the corporate structure to changes in consumption and competitive patterns.

Summary

The increased globalisation of the world markets influences both international companies and firms that consider themselves to be local. The competitive environment of many developed and developing countries is becoming multicultural and international in terms of competition, product offerings and consumer demand. All these elements force businesses to adopt the principles and methods of international marketing and consider the possibility of initiating overseas marketing operations.

The complexity of the international marketing approach is greater than that of domestic marketing activities because many foreign elements are unknown and unfamiliar as they are difficult to understand and predict. This situation requires firms engaged in international marketing activities to make an increased commitment to their overseas markets, in terms of investment, costs, effort and strategic horizon.

The variety of markets and the sometimes conflicting tendencies at international level means that firms are increasingly relying on a range of ways to enter and develop overseas markets. The diversity of market conditions necessitates the selection and combination of various strategic approaches in order to maximise efficiency and reduce risk. In the postmodern environment of the twenty-first century, the strategic approach to overseas market expansion is characterised by hybrid procedures and methods, crisscrossing the specific competitive advantages of various business units and different geographical locations.

Chapter questions

1 How do you explain the complexity of the modern-day global business environment?

2 Do you think that two or more market entry strategies can be combined to penetrate the same overseas market? Provide examples and discuss the advantages and challenges of this approach.

3 Provide examples of companies active today that are using the four different types of organisational structure and management. Which model is most effective in the present market conditions. Why? Is it possible to combine two or more of these organisational models within the same corporation?

9 Measuring for effectiveness in marketing

Introduction

Currently, there is a great debate in marketing regarding the measurement of performance. Marketers are increasingly pressurised by top management to become more accountable for their expenditures and activities. Accountancy has always taken pride of place in assessing company performance, using well-developed and well-used financial performance measures. It is now becoming increasingly important that marketers develop measures of effectiveness that will sit side by side with financial performance measures. Some authors, such as Doyle (2000) and Highson et al. (2001), are beginning to address this growing area of concern for marketers and businesses in general.

Measuring marketing performance

One of the most controversial areas in marketing is that of understanding how marketing actions affect performance. Traditionally, as noted, measures have been financial in nature and the accounting profession dominates much of the debate surrounding performance measurement. With the opening of the debate on measuring levels of market orientation in the last two decades, the focus on the effects of such an orientation on a company's performance has sharpened. Unlike accounting, marketing does not have standardised techniques for measuring performance. For this reason, in many companies, marketing expenditure and budgets tend to be allocated arbitrarily, relegating the importance of marketing to a lower level. Often, marketing expenditures may not lead in a linear way to results that can be measured within a short period of time. For example, an advertising campaign may result in better sales performance after a ten-month time lag. However, company accounts are presented yearly and generally fail to capture the link because of such time lags.

Utilising appropriate performance measures helps to gauge the level of commercial success that a company is experiencing: what you measure is what you get. Thus, a company's measurement system has a strong impact on the behaviour of managers and employees (Kaplan and Norton 2003). From this it is clear that objectives set by a company need to be supported by appropriate measures that can be used to continually monitor the company's performance against those objectives (Foulks Lynch 2004). Ideally, performance measures would meet the requirements of parsimony, predictive ability, pervasiveness, stability and applicability to compensation (Meyer 2002).

- *Parsimony* means that relatively few measures would be used because information would actually be lost by using too many measures.
- *Predictive ability* means that non-financial measures would predict subsequent financial performance.
- *Pervasiveness* means that the same measures would apply everywhere in the organisation.
- *Stability* means that the measurement system would be stable over time.
- *Applicability* to compensation means that people would be rewarded for performance on these measures.

In a company, the business areas can be divided into sales/marketing, credit control, production, personnel, accounting, and purchasing and stores (Foulks Lynch 2004). Different areas of a business will have different requirements for operational planning and control and, thus, will use different performance measurements.

At present, the marketing measures most intensely used are market share, return on investment and brand equity. However, companies define and apply many more measures. These new indicators vary according to the sectors in which a company is operating. This chapter will begin by looking at the role of financial analysis and then the role of marketing metrics. As the area of marketing metrics is wide and not fully developed, there are likely to be more questions than answers. However, some comprehensive measurement models are presented and discussed.

The role of financial analysis

For the purposes of disseminating information to shareholders and stakeholders, companies produce annual accounts explaining financial flows, profits and losses and balance sheets. Many accounts also contain information on market shares, geographical segmentation and regional segmentation. More recently, there has been considerable interest generated in understanding the use of particular sets of data pertaining to marketing. These can be measurements of brand equity, customer satisfaction, loyalty/retention, share of voice and marketing spend. Interestingly, not many companies actually utilise the full range of marketing metrics for measuring their marketing performance. Often, we are only left with the age-old financial measures. These do help in understanding the position of a company. Senior managers can use previous years' data to project possible trends (especially if the results are available in the same format). In most cases, the analyses are based on financial ratios. These accounting ratios are used in the interpretation of financial statements. Usually, these ratios are at their most useful when compared to ratios for different time periods. This can be helpful in identifying trends and understanding strengths and weaknesses. If, for instance, looking at a balance sheet, the inventory levels are high, does that imply there is a peak and the company is anticipating a surge in demand for products or does it imply falling sales? Financial ratios are often the backbone of company reporting and have been used for a very long time.

Profit ratios

Profit ratios measure management's overall effectiveness in generating profits from the available resources. If a company is highly efficient in its markets, then it should exhibit a high level of profitability. It is useful to compare a company's profitability with that of its major competitors in its industry. Such a comparison tells whether the company is operating more or less efficiently than its rivals. Over a period of time, any changes in profit ratios will indicate whether a company is improving its performance or not.

Gross profit margin

The gross profit margin is obtained by deducting variable production expenses from the general sales. The amount remaining can then be allocated to cover general and administrative expenses and other operating costs. This can be defined as follows:

$$\text{Gross profit margin} = \frac{\text{Sales revenue} - \text{cost of goods sold}}{\text{Sales revenue}}$$

Net profit margin

This is calculated by dividing the net profit by the sales revenue. Net profit is the profit after production costs and overheads have been deducted, but before the deduction of tax. (Note that this is normally known as profit before interest and tax (PBIT) and some companies may calculate this as profit after interest and taxes (PAIT)).

Net profits are important because companies need to make profits to survive and also invest in the future to develop and grow markets. They need profits to pay dividends to shareholders who support the company, too.

$$\text{Net profit margin} = \frac{\text{Net profit}}{\text{Sales revenue}}$$

Return on total assets

This ratio measures the profit earned on the employment of assets. It is defined as follows:

$$\text{Return on total assets} = \frac{\text{Net income}}{\text{Total assets}}$$

Net income

Net income is the profit after preferred dividends (those set by contract) have been paid. Total assets include both current and fixed assets.

Return on shareholders' equity

This ratio measures the percentage of profit earned on the shares held within the company. Companies attractive to shareholders are those that can maximise this ratio. The greater the return, the greater the amount of money that can be distributed to individual shareholders. It is defined as follows:

$$\text{Return on shareholders' equity} = \frac{\text{Profits after taxes}}{\text{Total equity}}$$

Liquidity ratios

The amount of liquidity refers to cash and realisable assets that are available to an organisation for immediate use. The lower the liquidity, the greater the danger of a company not being able to meet its immediate cash commitments or tactical marketing requirements. It is important to note that the quick ratio is useful for determining the readily realisable assets and cash available to a company as, quite often, it is difficult for a company to speedily dispose of stocks (these are included in the current ratio).

$$\text{Current ratio} = \frac{\text{Current assets}}{\text{Current liabilities}}$$

$$\text{Quick ratio} = \frac{\text{Current assets} - \text{Stock}}{\text{Current liabilities}}$$

$$\text{Inventory to net working capital} = \frac{\text{Inventory}}{\text{Current assets} - \text{Current liabilities}}$$

Leverage ratios

Leverage ratios – also known as *gearing* – show the level of an organisation's debt in relation to its assets. This ratio is of interest to shareholders and potential investors as the level of gearing affects shareholders' returns.

Efficient use of debt can often enhance returns whereas inefficient use of loans and debt can seriously reduce shareholders' returns. An example of this was the demise of Enron.

If a company has borrowed little money, then it is possible to increase the amount of money it can raise in the marketplace, either through loans or share issues. The money can enable further investments in marketing or new product development.

$$\text{Debt to assets ratio} = \frac{\text{Total debt}}{\text{Total assets}}$$

$$\text{Long-term debt to equity ratio} = \frac{\text{Long-term debt}}{\text{Total equity}}$$

Activity ratios

This reflects the efficiency with which the company is operating in the market place. High inventory levels could signify flagging sales, indicating poor distribution, lack of advertising or sales efforts.

$$\text{Inventory turnover} = \frac{\text{Sales}}{\text{Inventory}}$$

$$\text{Fixed asset turnover} = \frac{\text{Sales}}{\text{Fixed assets}}$$

$$\text{Average collection period} = \frac{\text{Accounts receivable}}{\text{Average daily sales}}$$

As you will notice, many of the measures outlined so far incorporate sales data, so that some degree of marketing performance may be carried out. Measures related to marketing are complex and varied and so the next section looks at some of the likely measures that can be used for assessing marketing performance.

Marketing metrics

As the marketplace becomes more turbulent and competitive, companies are forced to balance their books and, therefore, marketing expenditure tends to grow and shrink depending on revenue streams (McCullough 2000). Such decisions are based on perceptions that marketing is an expense and it is difficult to assess its impact on profitability. If accounting measures alone are used to measure performance, there are several caveats to what the figures seem to indicate:

- accounts can be difficult to interpret, even if accurate financial data are reported
- the absolute ratios of performance (as given above) are affected by industry-related factors (Miller and Toulouse 1986)
- accounting measures can vary from company to company, depending on the protocols adopted
- companies can and do either overestimate or underestimate earnings for tax and other reasons
- there may be a fine line between honest and dishonest reporting of accounts and even the large accounting firms are not immune from such practices.

Financial performance measures are clearly important for firms, but they tend to tap only the economic dimensions of performance, perhaps neglecting other more important goals that a firm may have (Venkatramen and Ramanujam 1986).

An organisation's performance measurement system strongly affects the behaviour of people both inside and outside it. Organisations need to use measures derived from their strategies and capabilities. Unfortunately, many organisations espouse strategies that are all about customer relationships, core competencies, and organisational capabilities, yet measure performance using only financial measures. Such measures are valuable for summarising the readily measurable economic consequences of actions already taken, but should not be thought of as the last word.

Performance measures indicate whether or not a company's strategy, implementation and execution are contributing to an improvement in the bottom line. Moreover, performance measurements provide managers with better insights into planning, control and improving the organisational's performance than financial measures do. Not all companies are able to translate improvement in customer satisfaction or quality, for example, into bottom-line financial results, however.

This means that, although financial measures have shortcomings, they are still important for all stakeholders (Kaplan and Norton 2003). Among the most commonly used performance measures are financial measures such as return on investment, net profit, liquidity and leverage ratio, gross and net contribution margin, as well as market share, sales growth, turnover and other financial measures.

There are three major marketing attributes that performance measures should include:

- adaptability or innovativeness
- effectiveness
- efficiency.

Adaptability or innovativeness

The *adaptability or innovativeness* of a firm should be included as a performance measure (Bhargava et al. 1994; Walker and Ruekert 1987). Measuring adaptability helps firms to understand the changing environment and their ability to create and market new products or innovations and registers the importance of this (as discussed when considering market-driving strategies in Chapter 1).

Effectiveness

The *effectiveness* of particular marketing strategies needs to be measured. The analysis of strategic effectiveness helps to foster a clearer understanding of competitive stances adopted by a firm. Effectiveness measures the extent to which organisational goals and objectives are achieved (Ambler 1997; Walker and Ruekert 1987, for example). The management team whose performance meets or exceeds the organisation's goals is considered effective. These goals are the reference points for measuring effectiveness against (Clark 2000).

The marketing audit is the first systematic attempt (Dunn et al. 1994; Kotler et al. 1977) and the best-known, most frequently cited instrument (Webster 1995) for assessing the effectivenes of marketing strategies.

The marketing audit was introduced to the marketing literature in 1959 in an American Management Association (AMA) report entitled 'Analyzing and Improving Marketing Performances' (Rothe et al. 1997). Since then, it has been defined and redefined several times (Oxenfeldt 1966). Kotler is regarded as one of the most authoritative writers on the subject of the marketing audit and his definition of it still remains popular (Kotler et al. 1977).

A marketing audit is a comprehensive, systematic, independent, and periodic examination of a company's – or business unit's – marketing environment, objectives, strategies, and activities with a view to determining problem areas and opportunities and recommending a plan of action to improve the company's marketing performance.

Another major contribution Kotler made, in the 1970s, was the identification of six fundamental components of the marketing audit (Morgan et al. 2002; Rothe et al. 1997):

- *marketing environment audit* concerned with markets, customers, competitors, distributors and the forces and factors that influence a company's future
- *marketing strategy audit* assesses the consistency of the marketing strategy with environmental opportunities and threats
- *marketing organisation audit* assesses the effectiveness and quality of the interactions between the marketing and sales functions.
- *marketing systems audit* examines the procedures currently being used to gather information, plan and control the marketing operation
- *marketing productivity audit* assesses key accounting data to determine optimal sources of profits, as well as potential cost savings
- *marketing function audit* examines key marketing functions in depth, based on prior audits' findings.

The primary purpose of the marketing audit is to identify underutilised marketing resources and generate recommendations for ways in which more effective use could be made of these resources. However, Morgan et al. (2002) have summarised some significant problems with the marketing audit.

- The lack of implementation of the marketing audit process in companies (Taghian and Shaw 1998) due to:
  - the lack of suitably qualified independent auditors (Kotler et al. 1977)
  - the information is not available (Rothe et al. 1997)
  - the lack of sufficient communication with top managers to ensure access to and understanding of information (Bonoma 1985).
- The audit is disconnected from the overall control system. The marketing audit should be concerned not only with how effectively marketing performs its assigned functions in the areas of promotion and distribution but also may want to – and should be able to – question the organisation's choice of positioning in its market, which will be dictated by the corporate strategy (Brownlie 1993).
- There are periodic, rather than ongoing, assessments of marketing performance. The marketing audit should be conducted regularly, not only when some aspects of marketing activities are thought to be out of control (Kotler et al. 1977).
- The audit measurement approaches have been primarily qualitative checklists, with little empirical validation (Rothe et al. 1997).

Efficiency

Finally, firms need to be *efficient* in their execution of particular strategies. The efficiency of marketing strategies needs to be understood and measured (Bonoma and Clark 1988; Drucker 1974; Walker and Ruekert 1987). To check a firm's efficiency, marketing outputs need to be compared to marketing inputs, with the intention of maximising the former in relation to the latter (Bonoma and Clark 1988). Productivity analyses assess the efficiency of the transforming process where inputs and outputs are linked (Sink 1985).

There is a wide variety of inputs, such as money, skills, time and management effort. These could be measured by looking at marketing expenses and investments, quality (such as the quality of employees), effort and the allocation of overheads. The inputs most commonly measured to this end are marketing expenses, investments and numbers of employees (Bonoma and Clark 1988).

Methods that are used to measure the outputs include profitability analysis (Sevin 1965), marginal revenues and marginal costs (Feder 1965), and discounted cash flows (Day and Fahey 1988). The most frequently used measurements of output are profits, sales (unit and value), market share, and cash flow (Bonoma and Clark 1988).

Morgan et al. (2002) report that there are many related problems with the application of marketing productivity analyses. For instance, they assume that marketing inputs and outputs can be assessed economically and accurately and that such measures will be stable over time. However, relevant inputs and outputs are difficult to define. For example, should the relevant output be the number of units sold, number of satisfied customers, number of loyal customers or some other measures? Can the amount that is spent on marketing in the present or the previous year be considered a relevant input? Should it include costs other than marketing (Selnes 1992)? Moreover, in order to allocate marketing costs, organisations need to analyse how much time and effort they expend on different products and customers. It is difficult to obtain accurate measurements in these areas (Selnes 1992). Also, the accuracy and stability of such measurements can be problematic when marketing inputs and outputs do not have common denominators. For instance, they could be modified periodically or when the strategic emphasis of the organisation changes following a new appointment.

Efficiency analyses rely on the knowledge of cause-and-effect relationships, linking inputs and outputs. However, productivity analyses largely ignore time lags between marketing inputs and their effects on outputs and the impact of cumulative effects is also impossible to discern. Productivity focuses on the amount, not the quality, of marketing inputs and outputs.

Measuring the major marketing attributes

In order to make sense of the discussion above, we propose the model shown in Figure 9.1 to bring the key components of a variety of performance measures together so that organisations can at least classify them according to whether they measure adaptability, effectiveness or efficiency.

Figure 9.1 Key performance measures

Note that marketing measures will vary from one industry sector to another. Also, it is clear that performance measures will differ for the services and manufacturing sectors.

Each of the key areas introduced above is now explored in some detail.

Adaptability

For a company to be continually successful in the marketplace, it has to demonstrate that it can adapt to the changing environment. The kinds of changes a company needs to respond to include those relating to:

- customer preferences and tastes
- demographic shifts
- new offerings from competitors
- cultural and social dimensions
- technology
- service expectations.

In order to cater for such changes, a company needs to measure its successes in the following areas:

- new product success rates
- new service delivery success rates
- the number of patents registered
- the number of trademarks registered
- percentage of income derived from new products or services in the last five years
- success of new products and services compared to those from the competition
- the number of R&D projects underway
- the number of acquisitions of new brands
- assessment of changing pricing levels.

Efficiency

The efficiency measures in marketing reflect a company's ability to utilise its asset base to the best of its ability. For different companies, efficiency may have different meanings. A fast food restaurant, for instance, may find that it measures its efficiency in terms of service levels and the rapid turnover of clients, whereas a manufacturing company may look at its R&D and capacity utilisation. The range of measures for this attribute, therefore, is quite wide:

- capacity utilisation
- R&D productivity
- percentage employee turnover
- turnover per employee
- distribution efficiency and levels
- inventory levels
- speed of service delivery

- IT efficiency
- productivity per employee
- return on investment (ROI)
- product availability (in different geographic locations).

Effectiveness

Every organisation needs to assess the effectiveness of its marketing strategies. Measures of effectiveness, again, vary from industry to industry and from company to company. However, some broad measures can be put forward. These are:

- unit sales
- market shares by unit and volume
- market share by segment
- number of customers
- customer loyalty
- customer complaints
- relative quality
- relative value.

In addition to these measures of effectiveness, it is also important to understand the brand equity measures such as:

- customer preferences
- purchase intent
- brand value
- brand strength
- level of trust in the brand
- brand image.

Brand equity

Brand equity is the 'added value endowed by the brand to the product' (Farquhar 1989). The quality of information about a brand, its perceived value and its general standing within a local or global marketplace help to determine its strength (see Chapter 5).

If a particular brand is a success, this endows the company with profits and then the possibility of gaining future profits, thereby creating an asset, which has a value. It is possible to assess how successful a product can be if there is an understanding of the level of brand equity that is has achieved so far, taking into consideration the effects of advertising (Ambler 2003). It should be noted, however, that advertising rarely has an immediate effect, so advertising expenditure may show up as achieving a poor performance level in terms of sales, but the marketing activity could have boosted the brand equity, resulting in a *future* growth in sales and profits. These future profits could arise from the memory and positive image created in the minds of consumers by this present advertising campaign.

This area of building equity has been further complicated by the growth of the Internet and mobile communications. The level of trust associated with a brand is also important and could be considered (Boulding et al. 1993) to be:

- part of the brand–consumer relationship and therefore brand equity
- dynamic and non-linear – slow to build and fast to destroy
- an antecedent *and* a consequence of success (this needs to be considered carefully when assessing performance levels)
- a consumption habit.

Towards an integrated model

All these measures are useful when analysing a company's performance. Companies may be better or poorer than their counterparts in some areas of their performance.

The changing nature of what and how performance is measured and the factors that influence it as a result of the development of the Internet and mobile technologies also need to be taken into account. The Internet often also augments the effects of the marketing strategies adopted by a company. Specific measures include *customer retention*, which is closely associated with customer satisfaction; *sales improvement*, which is closely associated with the profitability of the development of online marketing; and *image enhancement*, which is the focus of developments in Internet marketing. These measures are built on the understanding that effective marketing activities are characterised by a service orientation, a drive towards innovation, a focus on quality, and a reasonable achievement in terms of return on investment (ROI). If a company's Web presence is effective, it will encourage consumers to visit and explore its website until they find what they need. Website visits and repeat visits can be achieved in a number of ways, including sponsoring Web contests, offering free sample products and providing value-added Internet-based customer services.

Given the fact that measuring marketing performance is generally fraught with difficulties and there are few general standards to adhere to, it may be useful to try and integrate financial and non-financial measures. This will eventually lead to a greater understanding of what generates a good ROI (Lenskold 2002). The general argument underlying the model shown in Figure 9.2 is that the ROI measure can account for all costs and the complete customer value, prioritising marketing investments and maximising profits. These can be broken down into the tiers shown in the Figure 9.2.

It is important that organisations can assess the returns that marketing investments can provide and this is put in terms of profit. 'Marketing investments' could be those made in customer retention or public relations as well as advertising.

The three key measures presented in Figure 9.2 are as follows.

- *Customer lifetime value (CLV)* CLV (see Figure 9.3) indicates the profits that flow from customer transactions. These transactions are a result of marketing investments. As future numbes of transactions grow, they will have a positive impact on the ROI. This measure also helps the company to allocate resources for target markets effectively and develop customer retention and new customer attraction strategies. The use of technology and CRM software helps to determine the value of each customer, currently and in the future.

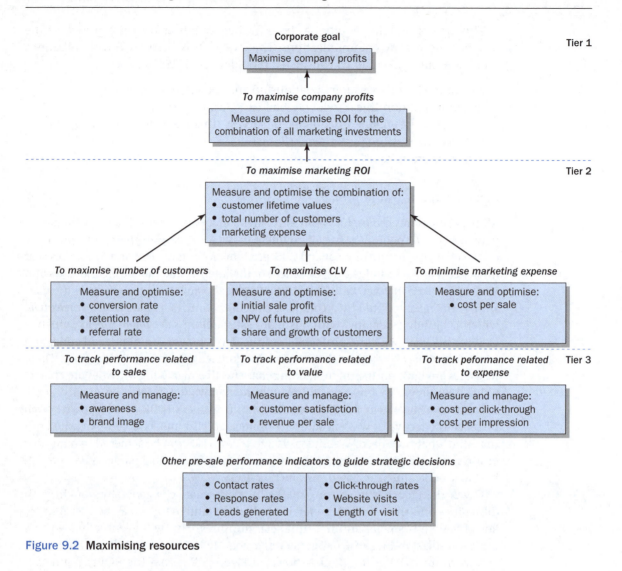

Figure 9.2 **Maximising resources**

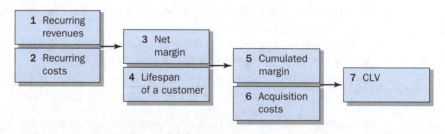

Figure 9.3 **Seven-step process for measuring CLV**

Source: Bacuvier et al. 2001

- *The total number of customers generated as a result of marketing investments.* The ROI will continue to improve unless the cost of generating new customers exceeds the cost of retaining old ones.
- *The marketing expense undertaken in order to generate returns.* As profits grow and the expenditure ratio lessens, the ROI will improve.

Three-tier performance indicators

These indicators have been discussed at length in the section above and the list can be quite varied, depending on the sector in which a company is operating. By monitoring how these indicators eventually lead to greater sales, the links between the third and first tiers shown in Figure 9.2 can be ascertained. It is important to note that measures such as customer satisfaction or the number of hits on a website do not automatically translate themselves into profit. Marketing managers therefore need to utilise these measures cautiously and apply them in ways that improve and modify their marketing strategies rather than see them as performance indicators per se.

A clear example of the incorrect use of indicators is the meteoric rise of dot.com businesses. Online web measures, such as hits and click-through rates, were the justification for pushing up the share prices of many of these companies, which then failed to provide adequate returns on investment and so the bubble burst. For this reason, whenever marketing measures are utilised, they should be carefully evaluated to see how effectively they contribute to the company goal of generating profits.

For not-for-profit organisations and NGOs, it may be perfectly acceptable to use the model given in Figure 9.2, but replace certain measures, as shown in Figure 9.4.

What we have learned

The above discussion shows that the use of marketing measures is becoming an essential component in understanding the effectiveness of marketing strategies. However, it is always difficult to separate out causes and effects in marketing, as marketing strategies often have effects in the longer term. It is also difficult to devise a composite set of measures for any company. The measures depend on the sector in which the company operates as well as its particular characteristics in terms of operations management and customer retention strategies. Often, companies utilise different types of software for gauging customer contact. As technology develops, it is likely that the use of marketing measures will become *more* complex rather than simpler.

Research into consumers' perceptions of e-service quality (Yang and Jun 2002) showed that Internet purchasers valued (in order), reliability, access, ease of use, personalisation, security and credibility. On the other hand, Internet non-purchasers valued (again in order), security, responsiveness, ease of use, reliability, availability and personalisation. This demonstrates the need to interweave technology-based measures with the standard measures used by organisations. Measures may also need to be tailored to the customer segments being addressed.

The key to properly understanding the lifetime value of a specific customer and applying the most appropriate customer management strategy is segmentation

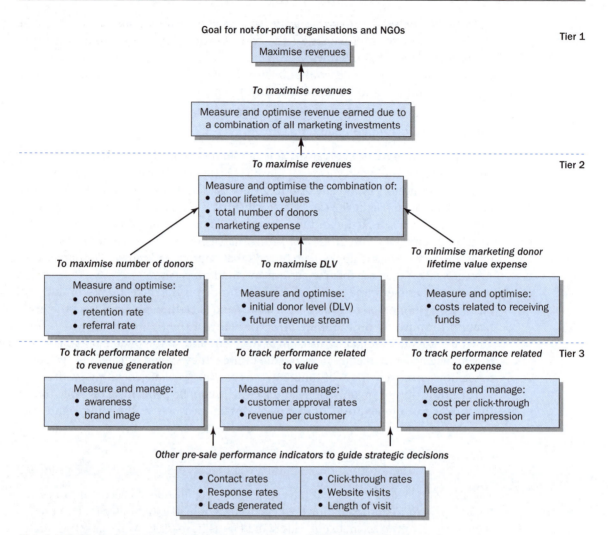

Figure 9.4 **Maximising revenues for not-for-profit organisations and NGOs**

(Bacuvier et al. 2001). Business organisations should aim at adopting a simple and operational segmentation methodology that can be readily used by operational managers and discriminate sufficiently by customer value (Doyle 2000). The selected segmentation dimensions should discriminate either on the revenue side (by usage intensity and behaviour, for instance), or on the cost side (by products purchased, channel used, intensity of customer care usage and service levels, for example). That way, the company can have a complete map of the 'wells' of value *creation* and 'pits' of value *destruction* of the business and an understanding of why they are such.

Making clear connections between customers' behaviour and their demographic profiles is critical to companies interested in keeping customers and increasing their profitability. The implementation of an efficient profiling/segmentation methodology has to address the following issues (Thearling 1999; Wundermann 2001).

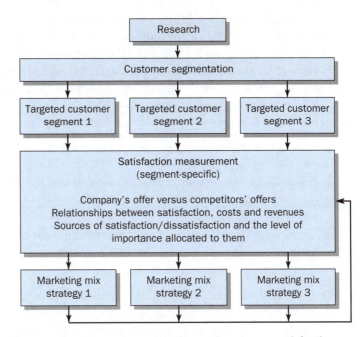

Figure 9.5 **The use of customer segmentation and customer satisfaction measurement for designing and implementing targeted marketing mix strategies**

- robust transaction data, properly collected and updated
- data warehousing capabilities for capturing and storing the data (databases)
- associated retrieval and data delivery system
- datamining tools that reflect the unique nature of the business
- detailed costing information, including the process costs, as well as the physical product or service costs
- a meaningful business model that represents clearly the company–customer interaction and the fluctuation of customers' and business' lifecycle.

The measurement of customer satisfaction has to be specific for each customer segment being targeted by the company. The needs and wants of the various customer segments are usually different, as well as the quality standards regarding the offered products and services.

Not only do organisations need to benchmark their results after the completion of a customer survey but they also have to evaluate the process they used to obtain these results. Such data must be as accurate as possible, especially if staff bonuses or other incentives are triggered by achieving satisfaction improvement targets (Chambers 2000). It is also important to disseminate the results of measurements of customer satisfaction to all organisational levels. Little action will be taken to improve customer satisfaction if employees do not know enough about these results or their implications (Hill et al. 2001). The extent of the feedback provided to employees sends messages to them about how important the customer survey is to the organisation.

Thorough research into the specific sources of customer satisfaction/dissatisfaction and the importance they allocate to each will indicate the areas of excellence and those needing improvement in the company's strategy (see Figure 9.2).

On the basis of this research, a marketing mix strategy targeting specific customer segments can be designed and implemented. You will recall that the issue of customer value and equity (Rust et al. 2000) has already been discussed in Chapter 2, but the key components are:

- *value equity* the customers' perception of value based on how the quality, price and convenience are viewed
- *brand equity* the customers' perceptions of a brand, especially the ones that are not fully explained by a firm's objectives – these perceptions could be emotional, subjective and irrational
- *retention equity* customer equity results from customers choosing to do business with a company – retention-building activities and repeat purchasing patterns help to build retention equity.

The essential elements that should be taken into account are the various components driving customer equity. However, it is clear that each component has cost elements associated with it. The creation of value, development of a brand, as well as creating customer retention, all have associated costs and these have to be amortised within the customer base. In essence, all these elements contribute to customer satisfaction levels for a product or service.

Understanding measurement within the global context

Companies operating globally have to be aware of a range of measurements with regard to their product or service offering. They often measure their levels of success in different countries by looking at their relative market shares in each country or the levels of distribution achieved. In some cases, the measures may include profit levels per product or service category. There is a good argument for companies looking at their global market share as a performance measure (Usunier 1999), so that competition is seen as being global right from the outset, as discussed in the previous chapter. This helps to prevent companies from being too absorbed in their own markets and makes them more aware of there position in relation to the competition.

Performance measures can also be improved as a result of experience effects. In this instance, effective measures of performance could be one or more of the following.

- *Scale effects* Large-scale production on a global basis means that costs can come down and the savings measured. The increasing profits could be spent on R&D. An example of this is the rapid growth of the Samsung brand on a global basis.
- *A building up of brand equity* A brand's image can be measured using a very wide range of variables and these can vary according to the type of research carried out. For instance, when Philips began its campaign 'Let's Make things Better', it relied on measuring the impact of the advertisement on the 'share of voice' it had

gained in various countries around the world. The 'share of voice' is how easily the slogan can be recalled and, at the same time, customers' perceptions vis-à-vis Philips' main competitor, Sony, are recorded. The measure of success in this instance is the growth of brand awareness and a strong association of the slogan with the brand. The use of a standard brand slogan is being utilised by Philips to create a global brand and one that is easily recognised. In the middle of the 1990s, Philips had a disparate brand image in different countries. The brand was associated with products ranging from lightbulbs to televisions. The slogan is now being used to promote a coherent image of innovation and quality.

Chupa Chups is a company that has global ambitions, but it also needs to measure its performance. The case study on this company illustrates the challenges it faces.

CASE STUDY   FT

Sweet ambitions to tempt more takers

Branding a boiled sugar sweet on a stick takes an unusual amount of marketing imagination. The makers of Chupa Chups, the world's best-selling lollipop, have responded to the challenge recently by packaging the product in toys, in plastic dynamite sticks and hand grenades, in make-up kits and paint cans and in something called 'Jaws Pop' – described by the company magazine as a collection of 'cranky crocodiles and shady sharks that reveal a Chupa Chups lollipop when the lever on their backs is moved'.

The family-owned Catalan company has had merchandising deals with Barbie dolls, the Simpsons, Pokémon and the Spice Girls. It has become adept at cheeky publicity stunts, such as sending 'the first lollipop into space' with Russian astronauts in 1995.

Its efforts have helped the brand spread to 170 countries. Now the company's goal is to transform Chupa Chups into 'the Coca-Cola of lollipops' – as ubiquitous, and as ingrained in the dietary habits of teenagers, as the sugary, carbonated drink.

For a while, a strategy built around a flawless distribution system, international expansion and zany marketing seemed to work: Chupa Chups' consolidated sales during the 1990s grew at an annual compound rate of 27 per cent, to €424m (¥271m) in 2000, when the sugar confectionery industry as a whole was growing at a mere 2–3 per cent a year.

Last year, however, sales fell for the first time in more than a decade, to €414m. The company's vertiginous expansion came to a halt after a merchandising deal with Pokémon went sour. Children tired of the Japanese cartoons, leaving Chupa Chups with a lot of unsold Pokémon lollies.

Some executives also believe that the prolific marketing department was out of control. 'Lollipops in [plastic] hand grenades was completely over the top,' one executive confides.

Had Chupa Chups, a household name in Spain, with its flowery, red and yellow logo designed by Salvador Dali, mistaken its impressive sales abroad for the belief that it had established a powerful international brand?

David Hensley, a consultant with Futurebrand in the UK, says companies that are expanding rapidly often confuse strong sales with brand recognition. 'Chupa Chups has a great distribution network. It has been the key to its international success. But what youngsters are buying are lollipops. They are not necessarily choosing Chupa Chups over other lollipops. It takes a lot of time and advertising to elevate a commodity into a brand.'

Xavier Bernat, the current Chairman, whose father founded Chupa Chups 44 years ago, rejects this judgment. Mr Bernat believes he has built Chupa Chups into an internationally recognised brand. By marketing in the club scene and in clothes stores, he says, he has expanded his 'target

▶

market' of 7-to-12-year-olds in the past three years to include teenagers, who now buy more than half of his lollipops. In Russia, where Chupa Chups set up a factory ten years ago, the company sells 1bn lollipops a year.

Mr Bernat is also stretching the brand through licensing agreements with Unilever, which is producing Chupa Chups toothpaste and ice-cream, and with perfume and clothes manufacturers. 'Chupa Chups is not a passing fad,' he says. 'It is a growing business.' Nevertheless, Mr Bernat concedes that most of his efforts have been devoted to building the distribution network and expanding overseas. Licensing deals bring in only marginal income. Distribution, he says, must precede brand recognition. 'Chupa Chups has to be everywhere. In clubs, petrol stations, cinemas, kiosks and all kinds of stores. It must be instantly available, like Coca-Cola, always an arm's length away from desire.'

The question is whether Mr Bernat will succeed in making Chupa Chups as desirable as Coke. Breakthroughs come from the most unexpected quarters. When Johan Cruyff, former coach of Barcelona football club, was told to stop smoking after a heart attack, Chupa Chups sent him lollipops to help combat his craving for cigarettes. Photos of Mr Cruyff sucking lollies on the trainer's bench sent Chupa Chups sales soaring in Catalonia. Since then, they have become popular among football players. Zinedine Zidane likes to chew them after training sessions. David Beckham was spotted with one during last month's World Cup in Japan.

'Celebrity suckers', as Chupa Chups likes to call them, have made it acceptable for adults to buy lollipops. But Chupa Chups' main customers remain children and teenagers, whose fickleness poses a particular challenge for a company intent on building an enduring brand.

Mary Peterkin, a brand consultant at Enterprise IG in London, says the key to success is to remain relevant to your customers. 'Competition from other confectioners and changes in fashion trends pose particular difficulties for companies that market to teenagers. Levi Strauss is an example of a company that lost sight of its customers' needs. Drinks and cosmetics companies are constantly reinventing themselves to keep abreast of fashion trends. Chupa Chups will also have to reinvent its product to remain relevant to each new generation of teenagers.'

She thinks that Chupa Chups has a fighting chance. 'The company is in tune with the way young people think,' Ms Peterkin says. 'That is a good platform to build on.'

Source: Leslie Crawford, Sweet ambitions to tempt more takers' Financial Times, 16 July 2002

Identify and discuss the key measures of performance that could be considered useful for Chupa Chups as it becomes a global brand.

Organisations such as Chupa Chups also rely on short-term promotions and the success generated is often measured along the following lines.

■ *Measuring the impact of promotions* Shorter-term performance measures depend on understanding the impact of promotions on customers. Promotions can be based on:

– *price differentiation* either raising or lowering prices and considering their impact on sales

– *buy one, get one free offers* this has now become a common strategy for promoting products, ranging from magazines to vitamin tablets

– *trial and sampling* small samples of a product are distributed so that consumers can try them – this type of promotion is usually simplest for items such as perfumes and food

– *competitions* promotions can be offered in the form of quizzes and other types of competitions and, increasingly, on the Internet in the form of pop-ups and via banner advertising.

Table 9.1 **Objectives by types of promotion**

Consumer promotions	Commercial promotions
Trial	Visit to new outlets
First purchase	Customer retention
Repurchase	Visit frequency increase
Loyalty	First purchase growth
Reduced prices	Increases in average price basket
Increase of quantity consumed	
Purchase frequency increase	
Trial of a new variety	

Distribution promotions	Network promotions
List of new products	Increase in quantity sold
Stock	Gain in distribution presence
Facing increase	Introduction of new products
Point of purchase display	Increase in size or range
Participation to advertising	Reselling actions

Source: Ingold 1995

The impacts of these promotional activities and the types of measures that can be used to assess their effects are shown in Table 9.1.

The above discussions show the range and scope of measures that can be adopted in marketing. As technology evolves and even smaller companies begin to compete in world markets, the range and complexity of measures can seem quite complex and bewildering. The following section therefore sets out the best types of measures for different businesses.

Measuring environmental effectiveness

Many organisations, either through choice or coercion, as a result of legislation, are now beginning to measure their environmental performance and use this in their marketing strategies. The way that they measure this is by using environmental performance indicators (EPI). In many cases, companies go through crisis orientation, move towards process orientation and then chain orientation (Scherpereel et al. 2001). During the crisis orientation stage, companies tend to be compliant with legislation, considering a system of fines and penalties. By avoiding legal penalties, they try to demonstrate improvement in environmental compliance to their shareholders. In the process-orientated stage, control of environmental risks and cost-efficient reduction of pollution and waste goes beyond legislative requirements. Companies at this stage have comprehensive and systematic environmental management systems, which are measured and reported in the company accounts. Finally, in the chain-orientated stage, environmental performance measures are extended along the value chain and social performance measures are also included. Some of these are (Spencer-Cooke 1998):

- human rights
- labour conditions (including forced and child labour, collective bargaining)
- supply chain and overseas suppliers (including fair trade and factory monitoring)
- technology transfer and investments in emerging economies
- trade with oppressive regimes
- defence and weapons
- alcohol, tobacco, gambling, pornography
- animal testing
- philanthropy and volunteerism
- downsizing and restructuring.

Comprehensive guidelines for adopting measures are shown in Table 9.2 and, in Tables 9.3a and b, indicators of performance are listed that are used by the World Council for Sustainable Development.

Tables 9.3a and b show the indicators of performance that have been used by the World Business Council for Sustainable Development (WBCSD) (Lehni 1998). The seven elements defining eco-efficient improvement are:

- reduced material intensity
- reduced energy intensity
- reduced dispersion of toxic substances
- enhanced recyclability
- maximised use of renewables
- extended product life
- increased service intensity.

Eco-efficiency calls for businesses to achieve more value from lower inputs of materials and energy and with reduced emissions. It applies throughout the entire business system – to marketing and product development just as much as to manufacturing or distribution. The range of possibilities outlined here demonstrates the pervasive nature of eco-efficiency. The WBCSD also recommends that the indicators should:

- be relevant and meaningful with respect to protecting the environment and human health and/or improving the quality of life
- inform decisionmaking to improve the performance of the organisation
- recognise the inherent diversity of business
- support benchmarking and monitoring over time
- be clearly defined, measurable, transparent and verifiable
- be understandable and meaningful to identified stakeholders
- be based on an overall evaluation of a company's operations, products and services, especially focusing on all those areas that are under direct control of management
- recognise relevant and meaningful issues related to upstream (suppliers) and downstream (product use) aspects of a company's activities.

Table 9.2 **Measuring environmental effects**

Environmental orientation	Related EPIs	Examples of indicators
Crisis-orientated stage	Output indicators directed at compliance	Environmental discharges to air and water, efficiency of pollution treatment equipment, quantity and disposal conditions of waste per type
	Environmental management indicators directed at compliance	Number and frequency of complaints, fines and penalties, their nature and impact intensity, extent and effectiveness of corresponding corrective programmes
Process-orientated stage	Eco-efficiency indicators at the company level for inputs (resource conservation)	Energy, water, material (raw material/packaging) consumption efficiency related to product volume, number of employees or financial returns per category
	Eco-efficiency indicators at the company level for outputs (impact minimisation, pollution prevention, valorisation)	Emissions per substance/effect/media concerned, waste by type/originating activity/production quantity
	Environmental accounting indicators directed at the environmental management system	Environmental expenditures, costs resulting from environmental non-compliance and litigation, environmental costs and savings avoidance of the current year and previous years
		Degree of specific codes, internal policies or standards, number of training programmes and participants, improvements achieved, return on investment for environmental improvement projects, number of levels of management with specific environmental responsibilities, community relations (complaints, negative press reports, formal reports)
Chain-orientated stage	Output indicators on a product chain level	Environmentally harmful substances in the product chain (toxic dispersion) using lifecycle assessment (LCA)
	Input indicators on a product chain level	Materials intensity with the idea of closing material loops through re-use, recycling, product durability, resource conservation and energy intensity along the chain (including extraction/supply and use phases)
	Social performance indicators	Employment generated, labour productivity (value added to the national GDP/number of employees), relationship between employee and company (personnel fluctuation rate, average duration of contract), education to build and maintain human capital (time invested for education and training), disabling illness, income level and distribution, investments made outside the company in benefit for the community, sustainable metrics

Source: Scherpereel et al. 2001 and Lehni 1998

Table 9.3a   Indicators of performance used by the World Business Council for sustainable development

Indicators	Units	Measurement methods	Potential data sources
Greenhouse gas (GHG) emissions Amount of GHG emissions to air from fuel combustion, process reactions and treatment processes including CO_2, CH_4, N_2O, HFCs, PFCs and SF_6 (excluding GHG emissions released in generation of purchased electricity)	Metric tons of CO_2 equivalents	List of greenhouse gases: Kyoto Protocol, Annex A Global Warming Potentials: IPCC, Climate Change 1995, Second Assessment Report. Transformation factors for fuels: from fuel carbon content, e.g. Responsible Care: Health Safety and Environmental Reporting Guidelines, CEFIC November 1998, page 31ff. GHG emissions from process reactions and treatment processes are calculated/estimated using specific knowledge of processes, waste composition and treatment efficiency	Cost reports Fuel invoices Plant surveys EHS records Estimation or calculation

Note: Businesses and their stakeholders may find it useful to provide additional information for some generally applicable indicators (e.g. energy consumption indicator for total energy consumption and energy consumption by specific sources, such as electricity, fuel-based, and non-fuel-based consumption, greenhouse gas emissions in total CO_2 equivalents and specific CO_2, CH_4, N_2O, HFCs, PFCs and SF_6 emissions).

Table 9.3b   Potential generally applicable indicators

In this table we list those indicators that might soon become generally applicable if current efforts to develop common global agreement on measurement methods are successful.

Indicators	Units	Potential measurement methods	Potential data sources
Value indicators **Net profit/earnings/income**	US$, euro, yen or company's usual reporting currency	Net sales minus all expenses for the period including cost of goods sold, selling, general and administrative expenses, technology expenses, R&D costs, amortisation and adjustment of intangible assets, restructuring and special charges, interest expenses, other expenses, income tax International Accounting Standards Committee (IASC) Generally Accepted Accounting Principles (GAAP)	Financial reports
Environmental influence indicators **Acidification emissions to air** Amount of acid gases and acid mists emitted to air (including NH_3, HCl, HF, NO_2, SO_2 and sulphuric acid mists) from fuel combustion, process reactions and treatment processes	Metric tons SO_2 equivalents	List of acids: ICI: Environmental Burden The ICI Approach 1997 Acidification Potentials: Heijungs et al. 1992, Hauschild and Wenzel, 1997	Plant surveys EHS reports Estimation or calculation
Total waste Total amount of substances or objects destined for disposal	Metric tons	Definitions of waste and disposal: Basel Convention, 1992: Definitions and Annex IV	Plant surveys EHS reports Estimation or calculation

Source: (9.3a and b) Lehni 1998

The case study on the Co-operative Bank provides an interesting example of how different types of marketing and other metrics are utilised to gauge the company's performance along ethical and sustainable lines. The notable feature of this case is the recognition this has received from external agencies, which awarded the company with a prize.

CASE STUDY

The Co-operative Bank

Awards for Excellence 2004 Big Tick winner, the Impact on Society Award in association with Tomorrow's Company

As a business with its roots in the cooperative movement, the bank is part of a tradition that inherently recognises that business has a purpose beyond profit. Its current commitment to sustainable and ethical business stems from the bank's customer-mandated Ethical Policy, which was first launched, following consultation with customers, in 1992. The bank launched its Partnership Approach to sustainable development in 1997, identifying seven groups, or Partners, upon whom its continued success was dependent and pledging to deliver value to these groups in a socially responsible and ecologically sustainable manner. Commitment to transparent reporting was first demonstrated in 1998 with publication of the bank's first triple bottom line independently verified Partnership Report. Both its Ethical Policy and its Partnership Reports have received numerous plaudits over the years.

Processes

The bank's Chief Executive, Mervyn Pedelty, is a powerful advocate of sustainable development; his external commitments include Chair of the FTSE4Good Advisory Committee, Deputy Chair of the North West Business Leadership Team and Board Member of Business in the Community. Furthermore, leadership and accountability are integrated through the bank. For example, the 2002 Partnership Report sets out some 77 targets, alongside which appears the name of the individual who is charged with responsibility for its achievement.

The bank is involved in, and in many cases leads, a number of social, ethical and environmental standards. For example, it has played a key role in the development of the world's first social assurance standard (AA1000) and in the development of GRI's [Global Reporting Initiative] first sector supplement for financial services.

Committed to tackling financial exclusion, it is the UK's biggest provider of financial services to the UK Credit Union movement, and lends more money to businesses in disadvantaged areas than the industry average with data for 2003 showing a significant increase in this support. The bank has played a key role – contributing £500,000 – in Co-operative Action, a new fund that was established to assist communities to develop cooperative, mutual or social enterprises through the provision of grants and loans.

The bank's community investment, at 2.7 per cent of pre-tax profit, is among the best in the UK, and right up at the top of the financial services sector. Additionally, during 2002, the bank issued affinity credit cards for 13 national charities/non-governmental organisations, which received a total of nearly £1.2 million as a result. And the bank's campaigns regularly mobilise customers to have their say on pressing international issues. For example, a 2003 campaign asked customers to sign up to a 'Diamond Pledge' to help stamp out the illicit trade in conflict diamonds – a source of finance that has fuelled civil wars and human rights abuses in Africa.

In addition to the campaign on cluster bombs, which was identified as the national Example of Excellence in Business in the Community's Cause Related Marketing Award 2003, the bank has won numerous other awards for its environmental and social programmes, including a Big Tick in the

▶

Case study *continued*

Awards for Excellence 2004 for its education programme organised by staff in Skelmersdale.

Impact

- A 2002 New Economics Foundation survey found it to be the most trusted business by UK influencers and 2002 research by the BPRI Group placed it best at demonstrating Corporate Social Responsibility.
- 2002 also saw a Queen's Award for Enterprise in the Sustainable Development category being conferred on the bank in recognition of its partnership approach to management.
- In the past two years, the bank has been rated as best Sustainability Reporter in the world by UNEP, and in Europe and UK by ACCA.
- In 2004, the bank was ranked in the 'Premier League' of the 2004 Business in the Environment Index and was ranked seventh in the second Business in the Community Corporate.

Source: 'The Co-operative Bank', Business in the Community, 2004

There has been much discussion about the triple bottom line approach – that is, organisations should judge their success in the marketplace on the basis of their financial, social and environmental impacts. An example of this is provided by the following Novo Nordisk case study.

CASE STUDY

Novo Nordisk: TakeAction! – make the triple bottom line your business

Sustainable development is about preserving the planet while improving the quality of life for its current and future inhabitants. Novo Nordisk uses the term 'triple bottom line' (TBL) to indicate sustainability in terms of financial, social and environmental responsibility. It is an important part of Novo Nordisk's guidelines for all company planning and decisionmaking processes as it builds its business in a way that is financially profitable, environmentally sound and socially responsible. This involves being clear about its purpose and taking into consideration the needs of all its stakeholders – shareholders, customers, employees, business partners, governments, local communities and the public.

Throughout its history, Novo Nordisk has initiated a large number of activities that reflect the triple bottom line. To build on these initiatives, the company aims to integrate and embed TBL far more into the business than ever before. The TakeAction! programme is one way to enhance this integration – and in the long run – create a TBL mindset or culture. The many local initiatives made by employees should make them reflect on how they can do their daily work in a more responsible way. To that effect, Novo Nordisk wishes to obtain a much larger outcome than it would obtain from individual activities.

Essentially, TakeAction! informs, inspires and supports employees to initiate and drive social and environmental activities and allows employees to spend time doing these activities. It further serves as a platform for sharing best practices. As most activities under the TakeAction! umbrella are driven by employees, the task of the TakeAction! team is to serve as a clearing house and resource for all of Novo Nordisk's employee-driven social and environmental initiatives.

Novo Nordisk is a focused healthcare company and a world leader in diabetes care with the broadest product portfolio in the industry, including the most advanced products within the area of insulin delivery systems. In addition, Novo Nordisk has a leading position in areas such as haemostasis management, growth hormone therapy and hormone replacement therapy. Novo Nordisk employs more than 18,000 people in 68 countries and markets its products in 179 countries.

Starting blocks

TakeAction! was launched in January 2003 at Novo Nordisk's yearly International Meeting (IM) for top managers. Two hundred and ten of the 300 participants signed a TakeAction! commitment sheet and agreed to seek ways to make their actions reflect the triple bottom line. Lars Rebien Sørensen, CEO, encouraged them to present TakeAction! to their employees and inspire them to get involved.

All participating managers were supplied with TakeAction! posters, brochures, pins and a presentation to help them inform their colleagues about the programme. They were urged to encourage others to sign the commitment sheet. Each employee signing the sheet receives a TakeAction! pin and when all employees in a department sign the commitment sheet the department receives a TakeAction! plaque as a symbol of their commitment. In January 2004 the TakeAction! team had received signatures from 7 per cent of all employees worldwide.

To further support its activities, the TakeAction! website was launched in January 2003 and aims to communicate general information about the programme and share best practices.

Employees are encouraged to send in their ideas to TakeAction! and report on already implemented activities.

The targets for the first year were: to have a successful launch with positive feedback, launch a sponsor programme and volunteer opportunity, receive 100 applications for the volunteer opportunity, inspire employees to initiate at least 10 new initiatives and to share at least 10 already implemented initiatives.

Four targets have been identified for 2004. The first target was to present an award for the best TakeAction! activity for 2003 at the International Meeting 2004. Additionally, a 'TakeAction! – the year in review film' was presented to all participants at the meeting showing them the past year's activities.

Another target is to conduct TakeAction! workshops in four selected affiliates. The purpose is

to give the employees additional tools to engage in TakeAction! and to get their feedback and ideas to the further development. Finally, a status report is planned for all VPs in December 2004.

Hitting the ground running

The activities offered by the employees through the TakeAction! programme are as numerous as they are varied. Activities are communicated through the company intranet, the TakeAction! website, a calendar highlighting a different project every month, as well as the annual TakeAction! Award which recognises initiatives based on their outcome, business relevance and innovation. As employees share their experiences, they help others learn and take initiatives of their own.

Novo Nordisk concentrates its corporate TakeAction! initiatives on two main programmes – the sponsor program and the volunteer opportunity in Tanzania.

The sponsor programme

Since May 2003, Novo Nordisk employees in Denmark may sponsor two different diabetes programmes in developing countries through automatic monthly donations from their pay cheques. Employees can choose between supporting children with diabetes in Bangladesh or people with diabetes in El Salvador directly through the TakeAction! website's sponsor programme section. The national diabetes associations in Bangladesh and El Salvador are working to raise awareness about diabetes care and prevention, but their resources are limited. By supporting one of these programmes Novo Nordisk employees can help the associations reach even further in their fight against diabetes. The World Diabetes Foundation, founded by Novo Nordisk, administers the programme. In 2003 150 employees raised nearly US$ 9000 for the programme in Bangladesh and US$ 5000 for the one in El Salvador. The sponsors receive regular updates on how their contributions make a difference.

The sponsor programme contributes to the TBL by raising awareness about diabetes in Bangladesh and El Salvador while contributing to employee satisfaction and motivation at home. This is because Denmark does not have a long tradition for

▶

individual contributions to charity due to its welfare system. The country is one of the largest public contributors of financial aid to developing countries (measured per BNP) and many have thereby felt that they pay their share via public taxes. However, this is slowly changing as charity organisations experience more individual contributions than ever. It is the aim of the sponsor programme to meet this increasing interest by giving the employees the possibility to support a cause that they – via their job – have a special interest in.

Volunteer opportunity (Tanzania)

In April 2003, Novo Nordisk launched a TakeAction! volunteer opportunity where employees worldwide can apply to become volunteers for three weeks at a local diabetes centre in Dar es Salaam, Tanzania. Volunteers are invited to use their competencies to help develop the centre's processes and expertise in close collaboration with local staff. The clinic's staff determines the specific qualifications they need at a specific time and the job offers are posted on both the TakeAction! website and the internal Novo Nordisk job site. In 2003, the TakeAction! team received more than 100 applications and more than 200 enquiries from interested employees. This initiative contributes to the TBL by:

- raising awareness about diabetes in Tanzania
- helping employees broaden their understanding of diabetes in developing countries (which is an increasing problem that the company aims to address)
- giving a broader understanding of customers' needs
- promoting employee satisfaction, motivation and loyalty as volunteers are proud to work for a company that provides them with such an opportunity and which acts on its responsibilities
- helping attract new employees as they tend to look further into a company's CSR [corporate social responsibility] programmes before committing to employment
- supporting the perception of Novo Nordisk as leading the fight against diabetes
- building stakeholder trust among employees and partners in Tanzania.

The volunteer opportunity gives the volunteer (and their colleagues who hear about it) a unique insight into the severe diabetes situation in Tanzania. The volunteers have all been deeply affected by their experiences and many of them have stated that they look at their daily life from a whole new perspective after their return.

In addition to these two large programmes, Novo Nordisk subsidiaries around the world also organise events of their own. These initiatives have common bottom line motivations including improving employee satisfaction and motivation, as well as the company's reputation, positively influencing stakeholder trust (employees and partners where the activites take place), supporting the perception of Novo Nordisk as socially responsible, supporting the perception that the company is leading the fight against diabetes and increasing awareness about diabetes through articles etc. leading up to the event.

- In China, 75 employees and their families planted more than 100 trees at the foot of Miyun reservoir to increase afforestation to avoid sand storms.
- Employees in Denmark collected 9 tons of clothes, linen and toys for a diabetes centre in Tanzania.
- South African employees held a walk-a-thon to raise money for the establishment of a local diabetes clinic.
- Indian IT department employees donated used computers to a facility for poor children and now plan to teach them to use them.
- Russian employees collected money for flu vaccine, toys, food and clothing for children in a Moscow orphanage.
- In the Ukraine, employees held the 'beware of diabetes' public awareness campaign where they produced a leaflet about disease and its complications and distributed on the streets of Bila Tserkva (winner of TakeAciton! Award 2003).

Measurements of success

Following the launch of the programme the TakeAction! team has received positive feedback from employees. To follow up on employee demands, employees have enhanced access to information on how to take action through news stories about future, current and past activities as well as guidelines describing how to carry out various activities. A TakeAction! idea list was developed providing concrete ideas (both team and individual) on how to take action.

TakeAction! poll

In October 2003, Novo Nordisk's official IntraWeb site, People+, ran a poll asking employees if they had participated in a TakeAction! activity. Sixty-five per cent of the 657 respondents answered either 'Yes' or 'No, but I plan to'. Twenty-one per cent responded that they didn't have the time, 2 per cent that they were not interested and finally 5 per cent that they had never heard about TakeAction! The TakeAction! team will address the 21 per cent who answered that they do not have the time by providing more concrete examples as to how TakeAction! can be incorporated in their existing work programme.

TakeAction! Guide

In June 2003 managers received a TakeAction! Guide with practical information on the programme and a summary of the programme's status. The purpose of the guide is to provide an overview of the programme and some practical tools to get started on or continue their work with TakeAction! The questionnaire, which 11 per cent of the managers returned, measured how well integrated the programme was and asked for ideas for improvements. Overall the answers were positive and the respondents all saw the value of TakeAction! However, the answers also identified some barriers standing in the way of TakeAction!, including lack of time and resources and lack of support to daily business focus. The TakeAction! team will discuss how to overcome these barriers during 2004 and has commissioned a benchmark on this matter. Before the team makes any decisions it will investigate how other companies address the issue.

It is difficult to measure whether or not there has been a change of mindset – especially as the programme has only been running for one year. However, over the last year the TakeAction Team has identified an increasing interest in diabetes in developing countries. Employees who have ideas on how their department can contribute to TakeAction! are continuously approaching the team. This often involves a break from old procedures, which can be seen as an indication of a change of mindset.

Living the values

The annual employee survey, eVoice, consisting of more than 100 questions, has been the benchmark by which the TakeAction! programme knows its initiatives are making a difference to the TBL. The tool assesses the working climate, and particular attention is given to measuring how well management is translated into daily business practice. Each unit reviews its own data and takes action on low performance scores. At Novo Nordisk, 'living the values' is one of the ten core global leadership competencies and a key indicator of performance.

Values as attraction factor

Changing demographics, an expected skills shortage and changing employee expectations are stretching companies' ability to attract and retain talented people. Novo Nordisk believes its commitment to sustainable development gives the company an advantage in a competitive labour market. Several studies show the importance of alignment between corporate and personal values. In 2003, for the second year in a row, Novo Nordisk was ranked the number one preferred employer among young professionals and business, engineering and science graduates in a survey by the international consulting firm Universum Communications. Eighty-five per cent associated Novo Nordisk with a good reputation and 53 per cent named high ethical standards as one of the three most important characteristics that they associate with the company.

Sustainability approach as retention factor

When Novo Nordisk employees were asked in the 2003 eVoice survey how they feel about the vision and the values of the company, three out of four consider Novo Nordisk's results within the social and environmental area to be important for the future of the company. To many Novo Nordisk employees the translating of corporate values into triple bottom line approach contributes to their job satisfaction and supports their decision to remain with the company.

Source: WBCSD, 'Novo Nordisk: TakeAction! – make the triple bottom line your business', 1 April 2004 www.wbcsd.ch/templates/TemplateWBCSD5/layout.asp?MenuID=1

Developing individual measures

Given the different ways in which performance measures could be adopted by organisations, it is important that some general framework is put in place (see Figure 9.6) so that individual companies can develop measures that may be suitable for them.

When choosing suitable measures for an organisation, they should be assigned to the following categories.

Strategic

These are the measures that are eventually used to ascertain the overall performance of an organisation. They could be key measures, such as market share and return on investment (ROI). They could also include market share in geographic regions and the overall effectiveness of branding strategies. They should also include the eco-efficiency of the products made, as this is becoming increasingly important in advertising the green aspects of a company.

Tactical

These measures could include short-term strategies to improve customer satisfaction, loyalty rates and promotional effects.

The range of measures adopted for each area could vary according to the type of business activity that is undertaken. For choosing and developing measures, it is

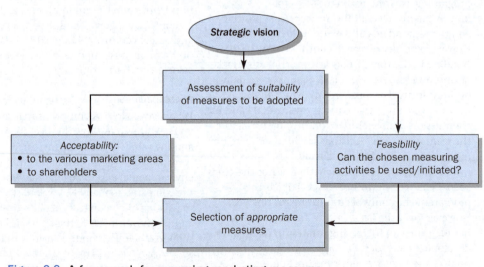

Figure 9.6 A framework for screening marketing measures

Source: Adapted from Johnson and Scholes 2002

useful to adopt a screening procedure to try and understand the acceptability, suitability and feasibility of the measures being considered (adapted from Johnson and Scholes 2002).

Suitability

This provides an assessment of the most suitable measures that could be adopted for a particular company. This is likely to depend on the following:

- industry sector
- service or product orientation of the organisation
- if it is a not-for-profit organisation or NGO
- the level of technology used for automatic measurement – for instance, on the Internet, transactions can be recorded automatically, when loyalty cards are used, the customer transactions are recorded on a database – these records subsequently being used for datamining
- the strategic vision of the company – for some companies, there may be an emphasis on rates of return, for others, such as NGOs, the emphasis could be on the rates of consumer awareness or the levels of funds generated
- whether or not the measure chosen is likely to be valuable in the long run and trends can be ascertained
- whether or not the measures chosen can be used as benchmarks regarding the competition.

The measures chosen as a result of considering these factors can then be screened by looking at the following two criteria.

Acceptability

Are the measures acceptable to the various stakeholders? Do they make sense and do they actually measure the right areas/issues? There are instances where measures have been adopted, but have really not been acceptable to the individuals developing the strategies. This then results in fudged or anomalous results. The measures would also have to demonstrate something tangible to the various stakeholders and be in line with their expectations. Measures such as brand equity are often undertaken by advertising agencies and, as such, they need to be acceptable and meaningful to marketing personnel.

Feasibility

This tests whether or not the chosen measures can be usefully adopted. For instance, does the organisation have the correct software to automatically measure customer contact information, especially if it is introducing CRM strategies? Has the company enough resources to carry out brand equity research via an agency? Does it have procedures that are implemented in collaboration with retailers to obtain details of revenues generated at point of sale via electronic point of sale (EPDS) systems?

Using the measures and the TBL (Triple Bottom Line)

When making the final selection of measures, it is useful to carry out the following exercise. Consider the model presented in Figure 9.7, which categorises the measures according to their social, environmental and financial impacts – the TBL – and complete the grid accordingly.

This grid can be used by any type of company in order to combine various performance measurements to form a complex image of their results. The competitive conditions of today's markets and the multidimensional perspectives of many organisations require just such a combination of these various elements in order to assess their performance.

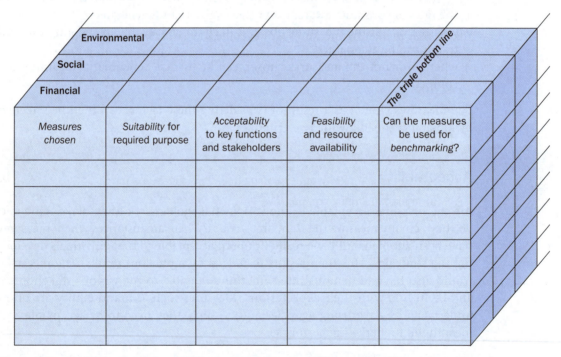

Figure 9.7 Grid for measuring suitability, acceptability, feasibility and the TBL

Summary

This chapter has outlined some of the key measures that can be used in marketing. The use of measures is as much an art as it is science. Some measures, such as financial ones, are those that a company is obliged to publish according to the rules laid out by accounting authorities and the standards required within each nation. Companies are not, as yet, obliged to publish marketing measures of performance, but many are now beginning to show these in their company reports.

This chapter has offered some practical guidelines on adopting measures and assessing their possible effectiveness by enabling a better return on investment. However, for NGOs and not-for-profit entities, other measures may be more appropriate.

It is impossible to list all the potential measures that could be adopted, as each company has its own systems and idiosyncrasies. Companies now also need to be aware of their ecological efficiency and its impact on lowering costs and promoting sustainable development. Given the fact that measures are likely to vary from company to company, some systematic appraisal is necessary to determine the best possible outcomes for each organisation and the ways in which they can be realised. These measures are important aids in determining strategy development and the vision for the organisation. As the twenty-first century progresses, it is likely that marketing measures will become increasingly important in determining company performance and its strategic, ethical and environmental health.

Chapter questions

1 Why are marketing measures now considered to be an important aspect of a company's performance?

2 Assess the complexity of developing marketing measures for:

   (a) a manufacturing company
   (b) a financial services company.

3 Why should marketers be concerned about using environmental measures of performance?

10 New perspectives in marketing and the way forward

Introduction

Over the last century, marketing has undergone many changes and is now a more complex discipline than in the past, involving many other areas, as discussed in Chapter 1. When all the issues discussed in the previous chapters are taken into account, it is clear that marketing in the twenty-first century is likely to incorporate many more changes resulting from the evolution in demographics, values, technology, ethics and a more globalised society.

Many marketing managers have to be able to deal with uncertainty and are finding that the old paradigm of working through the marketing mix and the 4 Ps, although helpful when developing strategies, is no longer a sufficient framework with which to address the new challenges posed by changing markets and innovative technologies.

This chapter consolidates the material discussed in previous chapters and offers some new perspectives on marketing that ought to be considered by marketing strategists.

Moving away from the 4 Ps

The product, price, promotion and place concept has helped and continues to help marketers develop appropriate strategies for their products, taking into account the various elements in the marketing mix. However, with the changes in society, often determined by the evolution of technology, it is becoming apparent that this is a somewhat limited view of the scope and nature of marketing. There is a strong argument that marketing needs to have a much higher profile in companies and must embrace a much more holistic view than before. In order to do this successfully, companies have to integrate and apply the marketing concept more thoroughly and become more 'customercentric' (Deshpande 1999; see Figure 10.1).

Being customer-orientated has never been as easy or as difficult as now. On the one hand, the growth of better information systems and the rapidity of data transfer means that the range and breadth of customer information can be made available at any place, any time, within a split second. On the other hand, even given the availability of this information, for many companies, being customer-orientated is posing many difficulties. These are usually related to the development of better processes and organisational structures (discussed in Chapters 5, 6, 7 and 8). The marketing mix is no longer static and 'place' is no longer a fixed location. Similarly, a promotion is no longer confined to a product but goes beyond it to the brand that is being communicated. Pricing structures may vary according to time (seasonal and other factors) and global locations. There is even the potential to tailor products to suit individuals. Given these factors, the 4 Ps seem to offer a straitjacket from which marketing needs break out in order to move forward.

The advent of the Internet and wireless communications technologies offer a different perspective on the 4 Ps. One of the key features of the new electronic communication media is the ability of consumers to control both contact and content (Kitchen 1999; Peters 1998). Early research into the willingness of consumers to utilise technology in shopping behaviour revealed that their ability to control the presentation of product information has a strong influence on their involvement in computer mediated environment (CME) activities (Carson et al. 1996). This development emphasises the need for marketers to develop a proper online environment to allow their consumers to interface with their online presence. Within the virtual environment, both experiential (such as surfing) and goal-directed (such as searching) behaviour compete for consumers' attention (Hoffman and Novak 1996). Consumers' surfing behaviour is normally based on different information needs than their searching behaviour. Moreover, they tend to follow different navigation routes that reflect the different online behaviour patterns associated with each mode. Marketers need to possess some core competencies in understanding these new patterns of consumer behaviour so that online marketing activities result in a degree of success.

Owing to these new technological features, normal marketing practices need to be revisited and revised effectively (Hoffman and Novak 1996; Kitchen 1999). Information-intensive activities are transforming marketing and handing more power to consumers (Clark 1997; Griffith 1998). The possible impact on the 4 Ps is assessed below.

Price

Unlike conventional marketing development (Davenport 1995), Internet marketing can no longer focus solely on previous *pricing* mechanisms as the transparent nature of the Internet makes price comparisons simple. It could be argued that, instead of the conventional strategies, competition should be based on the 'speciality axis' online pricing reflecting the degree of *added value* to online consumers (Hoffman and Novak 1996). It should not be based on a 'cost plus' attitude to pricing.

Product

In the digital marketing environment, consumers can be intimately involved in online marketing processes (Clark 1997). In other words, the conventional concept of *product* development is no longer appropriate in the new environment. Instead, marketers should focus on developing *capabilities* to allow customers to mediate with online marketing processes (Bishop 1996). An example of this is the site for MySki Inc., where customers can interact with the company and provide size details and requests for specific styles or other requirements in their ski design. Other companies provide a virtual dressing option, where a customer's avatar is used to try on clothes and design modifications can be requested. This allows customers to interact with companies on a global, not just on a localised, basis. This further augments the idea of co-creation in marketing (Sheth et al. 2000). Co-creation marketing involves both the marketer and the customer, who interact in aspects of design, production and consumption of the product and service.

Place

As shown, the constraints of geographic *location* no longer exist on the Internet (Kitchen 1999). Rather, Internet marketers should focus on building a user-friendly online environment to enhance the customers' *experience* on the Internet (Peters 1998).

Promotion

With the advances in telecommunications, large quantities of information can be transmitted inexpensively, multimedia objects can be transported efficiently and isolated computers can be networked globally. Consequently, marketing communications need to change from a traditional, information-poor, emotion-rich focus, to an information-rich, multidimensional focus. The educational, personal and entertainment aspects of marketing communications become useful catalysts to enable this transformation (Rohner 1998).

Such developments are all leading towards a more relational, less transactional approach to marketing. The customer is part of the transactional process, not an idle recipient of a product augmented by promotion, price and directed to a place to purchase it. There is now considerable interest in trying to understand how companies can become customercentric. Every organisation, whether it is profit-orientated or not, has to be able to satisfy its customers. Figure 10.1, shows the gradual evolution that has taken place in marketing towards this customer-orientated approach. In order to be customercentric, marketers need to be able to assess each customer individually and satisfy their needs, either directly or via a third party.

In order to develop a customercentric focus within organisations (see Figure 10.2) , many issues have to be taken into account.

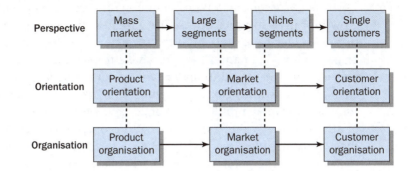

Figure 10.1 The growth in customercentric marketing
Source: Sheth at al. 2000

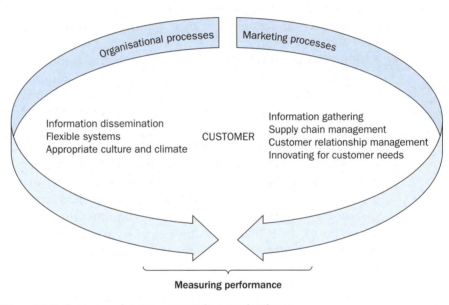

Figure 10.2 Features of customercentric organisations
Source: Adapted from Deshpande 1999

Consumer behaviour

How do consumers really behave, given the fact that, at any one moment, they are faced with a huge range of services and products. These services and products are not only available globally and locally but also on the Internet. Marketing is moving from a process involving transactions with consumers to relationship-building with them.

Relationship-building has implications for understanding brand loyalty and consumer behaviour. Are customers loyal or not? What are their behaviour patterns and how can consumer groups be categorised? How are segments really behaving globally and locally?

The lifecycle concept has been built on understanding the gradual evolution and growth of mass markets, but markets are now increasingly fragmented and those fragments may have similarities that stretch across the globe rather than regionally or nationally. Companies therefore have to be aware, when carrying out market research, that they need to understand consumer behaviour and product diffusion characteristics within globally fragmented markets. Each customer is not a simple static demographic profile, but changes and evolves over time, exhibiting a range of attitudes, behaviour, experiences and economic factors (Wyner 2002). Each of these variables offers marketers a chance to ascertain market behaviour that may translate into the purchasing of a particular product or service. In order to track this behaviour and understand the product or service purchasing propensity of a customer, a company has to develop relationship marketing skills and needs to become customercentric. This can be done by developing comprehensive databases and tracking the changing behaviour patterns. At the same time, companies need to be effective and efficient in their approaches to customers, ensuring increased sales and better profits. Marketing productivity depends on efficiency (doing the right things) and effectiveness (doing things right), as shown in Figure 10.3.

The marketing function needs to create loyal and committed customers for a low cost. If loyal customers are created at unacceptably high costs via loyalty programmes or promotional offers, companies could create expensive and ineffective customer bases (Sheth et al. 2000). Family norms are changing (one-parent families, extended families, second families, same gender families, singles and so on.) and gender roles are evolving in society, making the segmentation process evermore complex. To add to the complexity, individuals may straddle different professions. Lawyers in patenting law may also be biochemists and a doctor could specialise in medical law. Individuals, too, find that the distinction between home life and work life is blurring as the use of technology becomes prevalent. All this demands flexibility and a dynamic view of segmentation (Karin and Preiss 2002; see Figure 10.4)

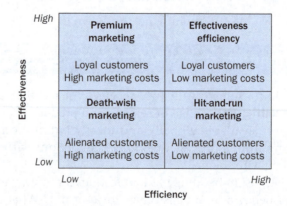

Figure 10.3 Achieving marketing efficiency and effectiveness

Source: Sheth and Sisodia 1995

TRADITIONAL APPROACH (Discrete variables)	NEW APPROACH (Continuous variables)
Geographic	
Density (urban, suburban, rural)	Intensity and nature of activity
Climate (northern, southern)	Natural and artificial conditions
Demographic	
Chronological age (young/old)	Psychological age
Marital status (single/married)	Household arrangement
Gender (male/female)	Sexual self-image
Income (all major currencies)	Buying ability
Profession	Capability
Nationality	Community affiliation
Religious affiliation	Level of orthodoxy
Home–work separation	Home–work combination
Psychographic	
Choice of lifestyle (hippy, swinger, straight)	Spectrum of lifestyle preferences
Pigeonhole definition of personality (compulsive, gregarious, authoritarian, ambitious)	Apparent personality changes with circumstances
Behavioural	
Occasions (regular or special)	Perception of the occasion
Benefit (quality, service, economy, speed)	Benefit mix
User status (non, ex, potential, first time, regular)	Degree of user experience
Usage rate (light, medium, heavy)	Degree of usage rate
Loyalty status (non, medium, strong, absolute)	Satisfaction level
Readiness stage (unaware...intending to buy)	Ripeness level
Attitude towards product (enthusiastic...hostile)	Degree of openness towards offer

Figure 10.4 **Modified segmentation model**
Source: Karin and Preiss 2002

Understanding consumers is a complex process, especially when cultural aspects are thrown into the melting pot, as shown in the following case study.

CASE STUDY

The cultural melting pot

As first-generation immigrants are nearing retirement, subsequent generations are living in a multicultural and diverse environment. These second- and third-generation immigrants cannot be neatly categorised as clear cut segments, but, instead, possess a wide range of beliefs, values and interests that have been influenced by both an Eastern and Western upbringing, with a predominately Western backdrop.

So how do marketers segment to these groups or even individuals? These are people who are native-born British Asian or Asian British (depending on how patriotic one feels), who may be second-, third- or even fourth-generation and have been raised within a British culture but have both Eastern and Western mindsets. Their affiliations can be strongly linked with mainstream Britain, unlike those who have emigrated from their same country of origin more recently.

Their views and beliefs are often a mixture of host and home country loyalties. Peers, family, work colleagues and other relevant groups can also influence their purchasing decisions. However, a confusion/conflict may arise for marketers as they realise that the concept of 'situational identity' is very relevant to these segments.

This chameleon behaviour of British Asians, being able to switch back and forth between roles in an ethnic culture and British mainstream culture, leads marketers to either reassess their generic marketing communications strategies or completely ignore these groups, due to the perceived complications of the segment.

Thus, marketing activity is often targeted in a somewhat stereotypical way that makes a mockery of the segment and doesn't really relate to the group's 'needs and wants' as marketing purports to do. Individuals who find their social identities at the intersections of at least two salient subcultures use their bicultural skills to bridge those worlds.

So where does the future lie for marketers? Can they continue merely to pay lip-service to this group's needs by segmenting in a manner that doesn't scratch the surface of the cultural diversity within the group? Alternatively, can they move away from the 'generic marketing and cultural melting pot' and dig deeper to find differences and similarities and perhaps even an element of 'man-made culture' to develop more relevant segmentation systems that will foster truly customer-orientated marketing activities?

Source: Adapted from Sekhon, personal communication, 2002

In addition to the cultural aspects of market segmentation briefly explored in the case study, there is much interest in ascertaining the role of emotions in marketing. Research on emotions and its role in consumer behaviour is in its infancy, yet emotions govern the way in which advertising content is developed and then perceived, as well as the motivations behind purchasing decisions made by consumers. Questions that arise concern the role of emotions in marketing exchanges and relationships and developing, maintaining or severing marketing relationships (Bagozzi et al. 1999). There are even bigger questions regarding the role of emotions in all areas of marketing that concern satisfaction levels and customer loyalty. In the twenty-first century, real progress will be made by customercentric organisations that can truly understand how and why consumers behave in the ways that they do. At the same time, an exploration of how better-performing companies behave is also likely to be crucial in developing successful marketing strategies.

Following on from the discussion above, the next section will explore the area of value co-creation that is becoming an important area of study in marketing.

Value co-creation

Modern markets are characterised by their dynamism, unpredictability, intense competition and increased consumer power, evolving towards an increased fragmentation of targeted segments. In this context, creating and delivering customer value is increasingly considered to be the next source of competitive advantage. Many leading scholars have argued that this process can be enhanced by emphasising marketing relationships as opposed to transaction-based exchanges (Grönroos 1997; Kotler 2000; Parvatiyar and Sheth 1997; Webster 1992).

In their book *The Future of Competition*, Prahalad and Ramaswamy (2004) suggest that value is co-created by companies working together with their customers and, therefore, marketing should adopt a relational approach. From this perspective, value is embedded directly in the co-creation experience and does not stem from products, services or the expertise of marketers and service providers. This orientation leads to a service-dominant logic in marketing, according to which the firm concentrates on operant rather than operand resources in order to develop valuable experiences for its customers (Vargo and Lusch 2004).

The service-dominant logic in marketing

A clear shift in marketing logic occurred with the statement that consumers do not buy products and services, but, rather, life-enhancing experiences (Vargo and Lusch 2004). This new approach has eliminated most of the differences between product and service marketing and extended the value-delivering process from transactions to relationships – both ante- and post-purchase.

For centuries, the excessive focusing of theorists and practitioners on exchange value created an important conceptual bias in firms' marketing orientation (Vargo and Lusch 2004). In the context of the service-dominant logic, it is now seen, instead, that the value in use to the consumer determines the level of his or her satisfaction (Grönroos 2000; Gummesson 2002; Normann 2001; Normann and Ramírez 1993). Compared to the exchange value, which was standardised and rigid, the value in use is relative, depending on the specific needs, wants, perceptions, attitudes and circumstances of every customer. Satisfaction can therefore be defined as the affective response of the customer to the consumption experience of a product or a service, being always personal and subjective (Giese and Cote 2000; Westbrook 1987).

Compared to previous marketing paradigms, the service-dominant logic modifies the source of competitive advantage from operand to operant resources. Constantin and Lusch (1994) define operand resources as physical, tangible assets on which operant resources, such as skills, knowledge and know-how, are applied in order to produce specific effects. If consumer satisfaction is personal and subjective, determined by a dynamic relationship rather than an impersonal transaction, the creative use of operant resources is the key to developing and delivering personalised experiences to customers.

This conclusion supports the service-dominant paradigm in marketing, showing that the role of the firm is not confined to manufacturing and commercialisation but extends also to facilitating consumption during the entire period of customer–object or consumer–service interaction. On the other hand, this new paradigm drastically redefines the role of the customer and his or her responsibilities. Customers cannot be considered any more as passive elements in the transaction process – the new orientation implies active customers, participating in the design, development and choosing of elements that permit the fulfilment of their needs and wants. The customers become partners in the value-creation process (Deighton and Narayandas 2004).

In the classical marketing paradigm, a company researched the market, collecting data about consumers' needs and wants, which was then used as a basis for developing, manufacturing and commercialising standardised products and services, targeted towards specific groups of consumers (see Figure 10.5). The dynamism of present day markets makes this model highly ineffective:

■ the preferences expressed by consumers may change by the time a new product is launched in the market
■ modern consumers are not happy to spend time and provide personal information for a plethora of hypothetical projects without seeing a direct and immediate impact of their intervention on the value proposition.

In today's conditions, companies have to find new solutions to create customer-centric value. Only by fully accepting the new role of the modern consumer in the market equation can the firm build mutual trust and shared knowledge, sustained by the principles of partnership and reciprocity, and underwritten by a common purpose and meaning.

The customers' involvement in all the stages of the value chain (Mascarenhas et al. 2004) enhances the significance of the marketing offer because customers have been through a process of co-creating value with the company (Prahalad and Ramaswamy

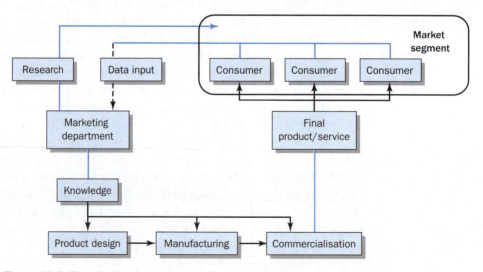

Figure 10.5 The circuit of value in the classical model of marketing

2004), and the experience of co-producing and co-owning the final product (Lengnick-Hall 1996), determining the responsibility for purchasing and repurchasing it, and supporting the firm with positive referrals (Schneider and Bowden 1999).

Involving customers in this complex value co-creation partnership requires a restructuring of organisational processes, frameworks and procedures and a change in strategic focus. The elements of the value added chain must become more flexible in order to accommodate the willingness and capacity of various customers to participate in the value co-creation process (see Figure 10.6).

Marketing flexibility

The direct result of applying the theoretical and practical elements of a service-dominant marketing paradigm is an increase in the flexibility of marketing structures and processes. The opportunity to receive real-time information from consumers who expect immediate value benefits can be used only if the organisational value chain allows flexible participation, interaction and implementation.

Flexibility regarding customers' participation

Customers should be capable of deciding if, and in what measure, they want to participate in the value co-creation process. When consumers' needs are simple and the value of the purchase is low, they may prefer to purchase a highly standardised product that is of a reasonable level of quality. Other possible elements that can determine the degree of customers' involvement in the co-creation process is their

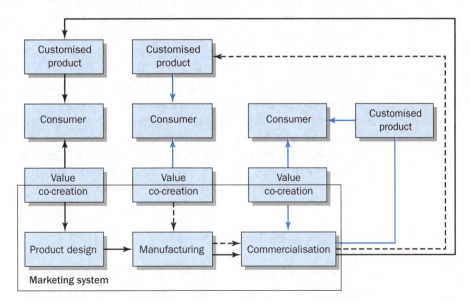

Figure 10.6 The interactions between customers and the corporate marketing system that lead to value co-creation

degree of technical competence, the subjective satisfaction they derive from their co-creation process and the sacrifices/costs required for a meaningful participation.

The flexibility companies need to have regarding customers' participation in the co-creation process requires that they maintain a combination of classical and modern marketing systems and use them according to each specific situation where there is customer involvement:

- when consumers decide *not* to participate, a standardised version of a product should be available on demand – in this situation, all marketing systems act by default, using the data collected from market and consumer research to produce a standardised consumer offer – that is, standardised marketing
- when consumers decide not to participate, but are willing to explore alternative offers, the marketing system should use the inputs provided by other customers with similar demographic profiles to make new value propositions – that is, tribal marketing
- when consumers are active participants in one or more phases of the co-creation process, their contributions should be integrated into the final value proposition, resulting in customisation – that is, personalised marketing.

Flexibility of interaction

When customers decide to get involved in the value co-creation process, it must be possibile for them to interact with the organisation at different levels and via various systems. The main challenges of interaction flexibility are:

- adapting the interaction process to fit the specific levels of consumers' competence – consumers involved in the value co-creation process will present individual variations in terms of communication skills, level of technical competence and cooperation patterns, so the interactive systems must incorporate a sufficient level of flexibility to make it possible for them to adapt to specific consumer profiles and approaches and usually, this is achieved by structuring them as a combination of operand (technical elements) and operant (human elements) resources, the human factors allowing a higher level of adaptability
- efficiently centralising the information provided by customers
- making this information readily available to any department that can customise the marketing offer – considering all the possible communication formats and channels that can be used today by consumers, this problem can be solved mainly by using an integrated marketing communication/information system.

Flexibility of implementation

If customers' contributions are received but not implemented, it is not possible to speak of this being a real value co-creation system. The organisational value chain should be capable of both absorbing *and* implementing customers' requirements and thus creating the basis of a personalised marketing offer.

A personalised marketing approach might not be profitable or desirable for every organisation, however. Because of this, in reality, any organisation will need to define the level of marketing flexibility that it can profitably sustain and, on this basis, develop a series of implementation points at which consumers contributions can be absorbed and used to customise the offer to add the value. The sooner consumers' contributions are implemented in the value added chain, the more customised will be the marketing approach.

- *Flexibility of product design* This will determine a made-to-order marketing approach. The project will be expensive, for both the firm and the customer, and the firm's internal resources will often limit the production output to a specific number of projects per year. This is commonly the case with public construction projects that are developed as a result of a close collaboration between architects, construction firms and beneficiaries.
- *Flexibility of production* This will determine a modular marketing approach. In such a situation, consumers are capable of selecting from and combining a number of the pre-existing modular components of the final product. This is the case with online car configurators, which are now available on the websites of most car manufacturers, or of Dell, which allows customers to configure online or by phone the computers they order.
- *Flexibility of supporting service* This will determine a customised service approach. Here, the level and specificity of supporting services, is adapted to each customer's requirements. As, in the service marketing model, consumers are actively participating in the creation and consumption of services, not only the type of service but also the service scenario has to be flexible and customisable. This case is exemplified by the post-purchase assistance provided to firms by suppliers of electronic equipment, such as computers or telecommunication systems.

The level of marketing flexibility in the value co-creation process will be influenced significantly by the predominance of operand and operant resources in the value added chain. As operant resources are, by their nature, more flexible and adaptable than operand ones they will allow a higher level of marketing flexibility. On the other hand, consumers' contributions often represent an operant resource that has to be flexibly absorbed and integrated in the process of value creation.

The new theories of value advocate an extension of marketing analysis and scope from a purely customercentric model to a multi-centred approach that takes into account the interests of companies' employees and stakeholders (Payne and Holt 2001). From this perspective, the flexibility of the marketing structure and processes during the participation, interaction and implementation stages should be considered within an extended model of value co-creation that addresses the creation and management of dynamic value constellations comprising employees, customers and other categories of stakeholders. The flexibility of marketing systems has to be applied to all the processes of participation, interaction and implementation in order to develop complex value constellation systems that are capable of maximising the satisfaction and the benefits of all parties involved (see Figure 10.7).

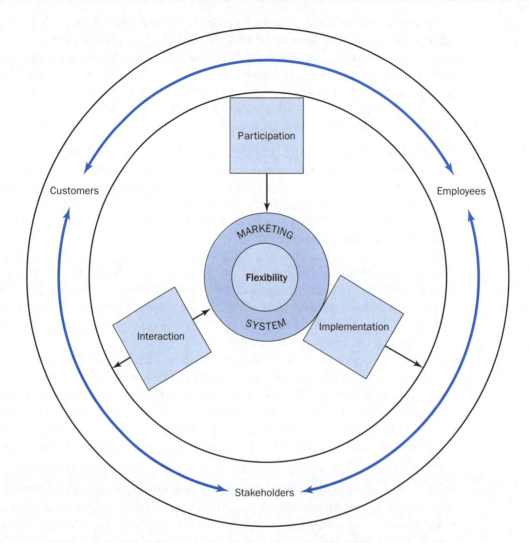

Figure 10.7 **An integrated model of marketing system flexibility for effectively managing participation, interaction and implementation processes with employees, consumers and stakeholders**

Open innovation

Another direct application of the value co-creation model extends to the process of research and development outside the boundaries of the organisation. This is especially important for companies from sectors experiencing an accelerated pace of innovation and change.

The classical model of closed innovation was based on the need to closely control the innovation process and its outputs. Nowadays, this model has been challenged by the evolution of the market structure (Chesbrough 2003). The focus of market exchanges has shifted from transactions to relationships and the value chain model advocated by Porter is often replaced by a value constellation, which implies a process of value co-creation that includes all the various actors in the commercial environment. In this context, often the model of open innovation becomes a necessity for sustaining the competitiveness of the firm in the face of rapid and unpredictable market evolutions.

All these transformations of the competitive environment have had a strong impact on the innovation model, determining a gradual transition from a closed, highly centralised innovation system (see Figure 10.8) to an openly managed innovation framework with multiple sources of scientific competencies, technological assets and resources (see Figure 10.9).

As customers and other stakeholders are the ones who benefit from the introduction of new products, services and processes, it is logical to attract and use their competencies and opinions in order to improve and accelerate the research and development process. In these circumstances, companies must now manage the process of innovation outsourcing actively and effectively.

The managerial approach to the open innovation system has been analysed and described from the point of view of a large corporation by Fetterhoff and Voelkel (2006), directors of technology management at Roche Diagnostics. The model presented has the objective of maximising the value and efficiency of the open innovation system by concentrating on five key operational stages:

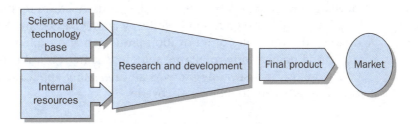

Figure 10.8 The centrally controlled innovation model
Source: Adapted from Chesbrough 2003, Figure i-2

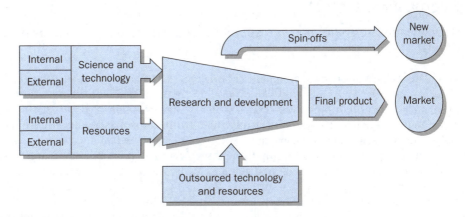

Figure 10.9 The open innovation model
Source: Adapted from Chesbrough 2003, Figure i-4

1 seeking opportunities
2 evaluating the market potential and inventiveness of a given opportunity
3 recruiting potential partners by building a convincing argument
4 capturing value by means of commercialisation
5 extending the innovation offering.

The two authors also discuss a 'six C' framework, which is used to assess the potential of external technology:

1 customer utility
2 competition or uniqueness of the opportunity
3 commerce or the market size
4 capital or the cost of the opportunity
5 copyright or intellectual property
6 company fit or strategy.

The process of evaluating opportunities for open innovation is considered within the context of the company strategy, taking into account market needs and competition – aspects that accompany any well-developed strategic analysis. By using this multifaceted process, firms are capable of accelerating significantly their research and development activity, reducing the risks and costs of innovation.

The open innovation activity is changing the way in which companies create and develop new products because the shared use of resources for innovation often implies a shared exploitation of profits by all the parties involved. This requirement changes the very rules of innovation protection and exploitation and requires creativity to find new forms of partnerships for sharing and using pooled knowledge.

The following case study presents an interesting application of the open source innovation system to biotech discoveries.

CASE STUDY

Open-source biotech

Borrowing the software model to spur innovation in life sciences finds common ground with IT

Australian Richard A. Jefferson, an American-born molecular biologist, is out to increase innovation in the life sciences by applying software's open source model to biotechnology. His goal is to change the global patent system and how people use intellectual property, and break the grip that the big multinationals hold on the tools of innovation.

Supporters and critics alike believe he has a decent shot at succeeding. But just how far and fast he can push the open source biotech movement is still an open question.

Mr Jefferson, the man credited with inventing one of the main tools used in plant genetic engineering, started his campaign in 1987 by doing what the big companies that dominate agricultural biotech rarely do: he shared his discovery of beta-glucuronidase gene (GUS), an indicator that tells where a gene is, how much it expresses and when it acts.

GUS is widely credited for enabling many breakthroughs in plant biotech, including the development of one of Monsanto's first and most profitable agricultural products, Roundup Ready soybeans. Mr Jefferson first provided GUS and all the know-how to use it for free to hundreds of labs around the world. When he secured his patents, he charged only what people could afford: Monsanto, he says, paid a substantial amount; academics and companies in the developing world, including those who wanted to use his work for commercial purposes, received it free of charge. One small company in California got to use his invention in exchange for enough cash for Mr Jefferson to buy an old Martin guitar.

Plan of attack

Mr Jefferson invested the money earned from GUS in Cambia, a non-profit institute in Canberra, Australia. The Australian capital became his base for shaking up the biotech sector and making waves in innovation and patent policy. The lesson Mr Jefferson learned from GUS is that freeing the basic tools of biotech – the keys to inventions affecting human and plant – is crucial to spurring innovation.

Had Monsanto or DuPont invented GUS, Mr Jefferson reckons it would have been a different story. 'When big companies invent, discover or acquire these technologies they rarely use patents to generate and share the next generation of technology.'

'If multinationals are allowed to hold patents on basic tools and gene sequences that are the very operating systems of life, promising new sectors will be left undeveloped and society will lose out', says Mr Jefferson. He is convinced that the open source movement in software should be applied to agriculture and to drug discovery.

In agricultural biotech, for example, fewer than a half dozen big companies in the United States and Europe own more than 70 per cent of the patent rights, including basic tools. 'The fragmentation of the remaining patent rights then invites patent trolls and overvaluing, further stalling an already moribund industry', says Mr Jefferson.

As much as 20 per cent of the human genome is controlled by patents, of which about two-thirds are owned by private firms.

Taking a collaborative open source approach could speed efforts to reduce hunger and disease. 'It is not about paternalistically saving the third world, it is about changing the practical and normative realties of how innovation is done, is coalesced, and

is shared,' says Mr Jefferson. 'That is what will make the difference.'

Sir John Sulston, who won the Nobel Prize in Physiology or Medicine in 2002 for his work on human genome sequencing, says he supports Cambia's approach to a science commons because he shares Mr Jefferson's views that advances are being stunted by the current patent system. Universities, for example, are increasingly looking to make money by patenting technologies that might otherwise have been placed in the public domain for society's free use, says Sir John. That skews their own research and prevents others from building on their work.

Gain ground

Many scientists see the need for open source biotech, 'so hopefully the idea will catch on,' says long-time Cambia supporter Richard Jorgensen, Editor-in-Chief of scientific journal *The Plant Cell* and the discoverer of a breakthrough technology now known as RNAi.

However, some believe that if the open source biotech movement is to gain credibility and mass appeal, a Monsanto or a pharma company like Merck will have to take a giant leap, as IBM did when it embraced open source software, deciding to make money on higher-level applications rather than from basic tools. But it is not clear that drug companies and agriculture product makers are ready to play.

'The problem is dislodging the incumbents who are rich and powerful', says Columbia University Law School Professor Eben Moglen, General Counsel of the Free Software Foundation and Director of a non-profit group called the Public Patent Foundation, which mounts court challenges against questionable patents in pharmaceuticals and other sectors.

Hugh Grant, the CEO of agricultural biotech giant Monsanto, declined to be interviewed. In an e-mailed statement to *Red Herring*, Monsanto spokeswoman Lori Fisher says, 'We think the concept [of open source biotech] is interesting from an intellectual point of view and reflects the growing consensus that biotechnology has much to offer developing country agriculture.' But, she adds, 'Our experience is that intellectual property issues

▶

are not the major obstacles to transferring technology, but rather . . . things like lack of science-based regulatory policy and practices, lack of capacity, infrastructure and funding to convert good ideas into finished products farmers can plant.'

Treading lightly

DuPont is taking a wait-and-see approach, says Ganesh Kishore, DuPont's Vice-president of Science and Technology and Chief Biotechnology Officer.

'I think this kind of open source approach could well transform the landscape and advance the rate of progress of innovation, but due to understandable reluctance from established players, I don't know if it will be in as explosive and transforming of a manner as I think Richard would hope,' says L. Val Giddings, until recently Vice-president for Food and Agriculture of the Washington DC-based Biotechnology Industry Organisation (BIO), which represents agricultural biotech giants Dow, Bayer, DuPont, Monsanto and Syngenta, as well as the major pharma companies.

Cambia has already launched a technology development and sharing initiative called Biological Innovation for Open Society (BIOS). The programme is a protected commons in which scientists can collaborate and contribute via the Internet. Mr Jefferson says BIOS is not trying to do away with intellectual property, just proposing a way to share the tools and 'operating systems' of innovation. This will allow innovation at the application layer, he argues, but with fair and open competition.

Mr Jefferson and his staff of 35 at Cambia kick-started BIOS by making all of their technologies freely available under the terms of the group's Biological Open Source licence. These include a version of GUS called GUSPLUS and Transbacter, which bypasses the established and heavily patented transformation process for transferring genes into plants.

As it grows, the online BIOS tool kit should allow ag-bio startups to make genetic improvements to neglected crops or solve low-margin problems without signing early stage licensing or partnering agreements with multinationals currently controlling the genes and the means to transfer plants.

That is important because, for example, a number of patent constraints are preventing the results of research that the Rockefeller Foundation is funding from being developed and disseminated to small-scale farmers, says Gary Toenniessen, Director of Food Security at the New York City-based non-profit organisation. The Rockefeller Foundation is the largest financial supporter of Mr Jefferson's Cambia initiative.

In many cases big companies, through patents, gain control of the basic tools of doing plant biotech, says Mr Toenniessen, although the tools were developed at universities or public-sector institutions.

While scientists are still allowed to use those tools for research to, say, make an improved strain of rice, they cannot transfer their invention to public-sector institutions in countries like Vietnam or Bangladesh without first obtaining a licence from the patent holder. Often the multinationals have no interest in granting the licence because liabilities are high in small-margin innovations and profits are small or non-existent.

One of the more prominent examples is golden rice, a variety of rice that was engineered to provide dietary vitamin A to populations in need. Lack of vitamin A causes roughly 500,000 cases of blindness and contributes to more than 2 million deaths annually. But in translating the research into deliverable plants, the developers encountered more than 70 patents in several countries and 6 material transfer agreements that delayed the work substantially, Yale professor Yochai Benkler, a proponent of 'open innovation,' explains in his latest book, *The Wealth of Networks: How Social Production Transforms Markets and Freedom*, due out this month.

While this problem was solved by licensing and concessions from the private-sector players because of golden rice's prominence as a public relations poster child, it did not provide solutions to the industrywide problem, says Mr Jefferson.

Cambia is tackling the issue by giving free access to its discoveries, but there's a catch: anyone using the technology has to contribute the improvements to the core tool kit – a model similar to the general public licence (GPL) used in open source software. Mr Jefferson, in fact, thinks the better analogy is licensing for open source Apache servers, which accommodate downstream private use, a necessary step for securing investment for the lengthy and expensive development process.

Software v. biotech

Brian Behlendorf, founder and Chief Technology Officer of Collabnet, a for profit open source company in Brisbane, California, and the driving force behind the Apache web server and the foundation that guides it, says that despite important differences he is convinced that the open source model can work in life sciences. 'It just might be harder and take a bit longer,' he says.

Collabnet, Mr Behlendorf's company, hosted one of Cambia's services for six months as part of an experiment exploring parallels between the open source approaches to life sciences and software. Life sciences are different because patents are more of an obstacle, innovation cycles take longer (a new plant variety or new drug will often not be ready until ten years after its inception) and the costs of innovations are higher.

And critics say the approach won't work in life sciences because of the expense and specialised equipment needed. Mr Jefferson argues that there is excessive capacity in the public sector that, when aggregated and focused, can be mobilised for collaborative delivery of outcomes that will help combat malnutrition and major diseases.

Mr Jefferson, Cambia's Deputy Director Marie Connett and scientists at major cancer research centres are now discussing collaboration on an open source approach to cancer diagnosis and therapeutics. Cambia will start things off with its patents on telomerase, an enzyme that restores DNA at the ends of chromosomes called telomeres. Without telomeres, cells cannot divide and they die. Unlike regular cells, cancer cells keep making telomerase so that they are kept intact. The hypothesis is that blocking telomeres with drugs should destroy cancer cells.

It's a good example of marshalling efforts to solve a problem. More people die from cancer than infectious disease in both the developing and developed world, yet 4 million die every year because they can't afford medications offered by big pharma, according to Mr Jefferson. 'Imagine it is

your mother with advanced breast cancer and she's too poor to pay the $50,000 for a course of Avastin or Herceptin that Genentech says it deserves, so you watch her die painfully,' he says. 'Now tell me it is not time for some new approaches.'

Opening up the data

Creative Commons, which, with the help of Stanford University law professor Lawrence Lessig, has developed an alternative copyright system to make literature, music, film and scholarship freely available online, supports the idea of applying new approaches to scientific processes. Last year saw the creation of Science Commons, which is trying to expand Creative Commons' work in the sciences by developing alternative mechanisms to allow universities and industry to share data and intellectual property in a more open manner. Its first adherent, Uniprot.org, which claims to have the world's most comprehensive catalogue of information on proteins, is now using Creative Commons' licensing.

And, not surprisingly, IBM, which has embraced open source software and incorporated it into its business model, is supporting the idea of porting the model to basic tools in life sciences.

'Discoveries yet to come will be extraordinary but they won't happen if people lock up intellectual property,' says Carol Kovac, IBM's General Manager for Health Care and Life Sciences.

Just as Richard Stallman, founder of the free software movement, campaigns against software patents and extensions of copyright law, Mr Jefferson is making it his life's mission to break the grip that big companies have on advances in agricultural biotech and biomedicine.

Besides opening access to diagnostic tools, Mr Jefferson is out to reform the global patent system so that innovation can flourish and myriad small- and medium-sized companies can also make money from their inventions. Mr Jefferson claims to be a descendent of Thomas Jefferson, who reluctantly created the US patent system as a means of ensuring advances for the public good.

Cambia has created Patent Lens, the world's largest free full-text database of patents. It will soon allow third-party observations when patents are filed anywhere in the world, giving industry and

▶

citizens alike the opportunity to alert patent offices to prior art and warn them when patents are too broad or just absurd. The database, originally limited to life sciences, has just been extended to patents in all sectors. In time, its reach will include Asia as well as the US and Europe.

Teamwork

Mr Jefferson says Cambia is in discussions with US and European Union patent offices and the World Intellectual Property Organisation on ways to work together. He is also talking with the Open Source Development Lab about improving his organisation's database by leveraging that group's expertise in software with Cambia's expertise in patents.

All open-source initiatives – in any sector – depend on total transparency and understanding of patents, he argues. 'We can wish they'd just go away as some in the Free and Open Source Software community do, but one patent right withheld can destroy an entire initiative and the confidence of innovators and investors,' Mr Jefferson says. 'Patent transparency is the lifeblood of the new open source and patent reform is a logical consequence of total public transparency and engagement.'

Cambia's moves come at a time when pressure is growing to change the patent system. Research in Motion's recent court battle over its popular BlackBerry wireless e-mail service is just one example. A case argued before the US Supreme Court last month questioned whether the patent for a blood test for a vitamin deficiency was so broadly construed that it included a natural process of the human body, possibly preventing other inventors from developing new and better tests. Another US Supreme Court case argued in March involved claims that eBay's 'Buy It Now' features infringe on two patents held by a company called MercExchange.

While IT companies complain that they can be held to ransom by owners of questionable patents, Mr Jefferson and others argue that many lines of research and development are blocked by misuse of intellectual property before work even begins.

Some, like Mr Moglen, General Counsel of the Free Software Foundation, are less optimistic than Mr Jefferson about the odds that the US patent offices or others will formally incorporate third-party observations.

It doesn't matter, says Mr Jefferson. Cambia's Patent Lens doesn't need the immediate buy-in of the world's patent offices. The data sets are in hand or can be bought. Once patents are harmonised, annotated, properly commented and linked to prior art, pressure will be brought to bear from the public to only grant valid ones, helping all patent offices to make better and more transparent decisions, he says.

His distant uncle, Thomas Jefferson, would approve, says Mr Jefferson. The historical Mr Jefferson established patents solely to further the public good. For the modern-day Mr Jefferson, ensuring that principle is kept is a matter of unfinished family business.

Source: 'Open-source biotech', *Red Herring*, 17 April 2006

The case study illustrates the ways in which the co-creation model works. Added to the complexity of the ways in which consumers' interactions are changing is the way in which market dynamics are changing as a result of innovation, research and development.

The dynamic environment

The marketplace has never been as dynamic and muddled as it is in the twenty-first century. This dynamism is a result of great changes:

- *in the structure of markets* markets are becoming global and, as a result of deregulation and technological changes, there is a blurring of sectors and the boundaries defining them
- *in the mobility of many individuals in the world and the great increase in global travel* with global travel come global offerings and familiarity and, at the same time, markets are also beginning to fragment into different mosaics and niches
- *in the growth of IT and its impact on marketing* the Internet heralded great changes in the globalisation of information exchange in the 1990s, which is embedding itself into company systems and procedures, and, hot on the heels of the Internet, is the growth of wireless communications, leading to faster customer communications on both a local and global scale
- *in the changing nature of marketing segments* market segments are not static as before as there have been fundamental shifts in family structures, ethnic mixes and segments that straddle global boundaries
- *in the growth of strategic alliances and networks between companies* many companies now work on a collaborative basis, sharing R&D and new product development, and this collaboration leads to a greater emphasis on branding.

Structure of markets

In the twenty-first century, firms collaborate, compete or even act as customers. Every firm enacts these multiple roles. The term *cooptition* is now often used in marketing. This is illustrated by the rise in the number of alliances globally. The new economy is moving towards networks, partnerships and joint ventures.

According to one study (Fountain and Atkinson 1998), social capital (networks, shared norms and trust), as fostered in collaboration and alliances, may be as important as physical capital (plant, equipment and technology) and human capital (intellect, character, education and training) in driving innovation and growth. These relationships can not only create value but also drive innovation.

As competition intensifies and the markets become more complex, firms are beginning to embrace partnerships with suppliers, customers, universities, government sources, research laboratories and other competitors in order to access new technologies and innovate. The USA has led the way in this with a rapid growth in networks of organisations that are the result of the creation of partnerships or consortiums. This has determined significant revolutions within the economy, in the USA resulting from the creation and application of technological innovations. While Europe and the USA had approximately the same numbers of industry technology alliances in 1985 (Fountain and Atkinson 1998), alliances in the USA have since boomed, especially in the 1990s, as can be seen in Figure 10.10. Without the impact of the USA-led initiatives, the level of alliances generally appears to be quite low.

As discussed, consumer segmentation patterns are changing and consumers' choices are increasing. An important indicator of consumer choice is the number of trademarks that are patented. In the USA especially, patent applications soared to their highest ever levels. In general, the public in the USA is informed of an

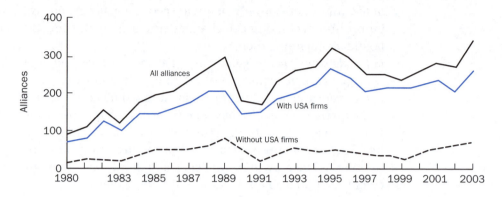

Note: Includes business alliances with joint R&D or technology development agreements, contracts or equity joint ventures

Figure 10.10 Industry technology alliances in the USA, 1980–2003

Source: Courtesy National Science Board, *Science and Engineering Indicators 2006*, Volume 1

estimated 50,000 new products annually (McKenna 1997). Table 10.1 illustrates patent applications in the USA by country and the size of growth over 13 years.

There are also discernible trends in the global marketplace, with high-tech manu-facturing industries becoming the key contributors to economic growth in the USA and around the world. In essence, according to the National Science Board (2006):

Table 10.1 US patents (in thousands) granted to foreign inventors by country/economy of origin, 1990–2003

Year	Japan	Germany	France	Taiwan	United Kingdom	South Korea
1990	19.53	7.61	2.87	0.73	2.79	0.23
1991	21.03	7.68	3.03	0.91	2.80	0.41
1992	21.93	7.31	3.03	1.00	2.43	0.54
1993	22.29	6.89	2.91	1.19	2.30	0.78
1994	22.38	6.73	2.78	1.44	2.23	0.94
1995	21.76	6.60	2.82	1.62	2.48	1.16
1996	23.05	6.82	2.79	1.90	2.45	1.49
1997	23.18	7.01	2.96	2.06	2.68	1.89
1998	30.84	9.10	3.67	3.10	3.46	3.26
1999	31.10	9.34	3.82	3.69	3.57	3.56
2000	31.30	10.24	3.82	4.67	3.67	3.31
2001	33.22	11.26	4.04	5.37	3.97	3.54
2002	34.86	11.28	4.04	5.43	3.84	3.79
2003	35.52	11.44	3.87	5.30	3.63	3.94

Note: Selected countries/economies are top six recipients of US patents during 2003. Country of origin is determined by residence of first-named inventor.

Source: US Patent and Trademark Office, Office of Electronic Information Products, Patent Technology Monitoring Division, special tabulations, 2004, National Science Board 2006

- the global market for high-tech goods is growing faster than that for other manufactured goods
- over the past 24 years (1980–2003), world output by high-tech manufacturing industries grew at an inflation-adjusted average annual rate of 6.4 per cent, while output by other manufacturing industries grew at just 2.4 per cent
- the EU had the world's largest high-tech manufacturing sector between 1980 and 1995
- beginning in 1996 and for each year thereafter, the USA's high-tech manufacturers generated more domestic production (value added) than the EU or any other single country, while estimates for 2003 show the USA's high-tech industry accounting for more than 40 per cent of the global value added, the EU for about 18 per cent, and Japan for about 12 per cent.

This growth is fuelled by the new products that not only industry but also consumers are utilising in their daily life. For instance, iPods are now common and there are millions of mobile telephones in the world. Laptops and computers are continuously evolving and being upgraded. Added to this, there are new advances in medicine as a result of biotech breakthroughs. In time, the new technologies will also embrace areas such as cleaning up pollution, more biotech products and hydrogen-powered vehicles.

Speed

Intense competition means that technology-based products and services face shorter product cycles, as new and better products come on stream regularly. The accelerated speed of information transmission, as well as global competition, have led to compressed product development cycles. According to one study, new products in the USA now take 23 months to produce, on average, compared to 35.5 months in 1990. This is the much-heralded productivity revolution, shortening product development cycles. IT is a great driver of increasing efficiency, customisation of products and services and speeding business procedures. At the same time, there is a blurring of industry sectors and services. Examples of this are shown in Table 10.2.

Table 10.2 The blurring of industry boundaries

Old sectors	New sectors
Publishing (print)	Print/media/Internet/digital/information/TV
Telephony (land lines)	Wireless applications/Internet/digital downloads/data transmission
Education (fixed locations)	Globalisation/Web-based/interactive
Brewing	Leisure/entertainment/inns/food

The future impact of technology

As the price of data transmission drops to very low levels, it is likely that most products will soon contain data transmission devices. Fridges will be able to transmit faults directly to the company that manufactured them or has a service agreement for them, so that repairs can be made with the minimum of inconvenience to the consumer. Figure 10.11, illustrates how the price of data transmission is dropping dramatically as the price of transmission devices falls to a fraction of a cent (Figure 10.12). For instance, what it cost to transmit 1 bit of data over 1 kilometre of fibre-optic cable declined by three orders of magnitude between the mid 1970s and the beginning of the 1990s, allowing more data to be transmitted over longer distances for less. This trend facilitates instantaneous global communica-

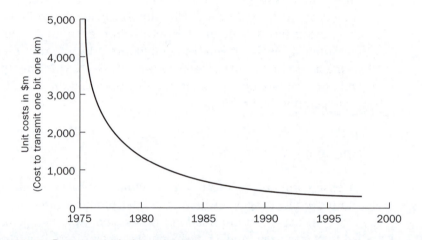

Figure 10.11 **Data transmission cost curve**

Source: Fountain and Atkinson 1998

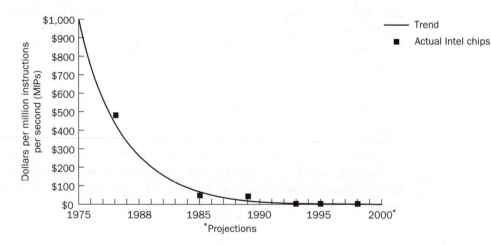

Figure 10.12 **Microprocessor price curve**

Source: Fountain and Atkinson 1998

tion. Strangely, it also means that companies can track consumers and understand how and why they purchase certain goods. Companies such as Gillette have begun experimenting by creating 'smart shelves' in supermarkets and 'smart tags' on razors. The purpose of this is to speed up supply chains and prevent theft.

The other benefits centre on customers, offering them better warranties, returned goods services and enhanced customer relationships. In the end, the success of such developments (which would have been inconceivable even a short time ago) will depend on consumers' acceptance of an intrusion into their privacy (*The Economist* 2003). In anticipation of this, Gillette will offer the option to 'kill' the tags at the checkout counter. Current costs of smart tags for goods are estimated to cost between 20 and 10 cents. If larger volumes are produced, then the cost could drop to around 5 cents. This is a small additional cost on most items, ranging from luxury handbags to razor blades.

The rapidity with which mobile communications have been embraced by populations all over the world indicate that humans wish to communicate continuously. This also creates many new opportunities for marketers. As consumers are able to access information from anywhere at any time, the ubiquitous consumer is beginning to emerge. Where technology was once the preserve of sophisticated consumers and businesspeople, it is now firmly in the general public domain. This change has major repercussions for marketers, as speed of communications and agility in providing goods and services at different locations becomes important. Thus, the next section is devoted to Digital Marketing and the new technological developments in this area,

Digital marketing

Introduction

Marketing is entering a new age in terms of the different avenues that are open to organisations in the way that they promote and deliver products and services to the marketplace. In the last five years, many new methods of communication have been developed, aided and abetted by new innovative software and changes in Internet-based technology. Customers have been very quick to embrace the new possibilities that are available to them, often creating and developing areas in cyberspace that they inhabit and in which or they communicate with or to a networked audience around the world. Many individuals have access to a range of devices, such as mobiles, laptops, standalone PCs, networked computers and PDAs, not to mention GPS systems. This means that they can be contacted, and possibly even tracked as to where they are located, where they may be socialising, working, playing sport and so on.

What is happening to the individual?

According to a report by Ofcom (2006), more and more individuals are spending time texting and using the Internet to the detriment of mainline television channels. The effect of broadband, where individuals are hooked up to the Internet for 24 hours, has been the creation of virtual communities and social networking via sites such as Myspace, Friends Reunited, Bebo and Second Life. These sites are used to establish and renew social contacts and communication with online communities. In fact, lately, more people were clicking on MySpace than on Google. Individuals are creating blogs for networking and communicating. A blog is typically a website where users can post entries in chronological order and these are viewable either by the public or within private forums. It appears, according to Technorati, a blog service, that there are over 175,000 new blogs everyday (www.technorati.com). The sites on MySpace, for instance, can be used for filesharing, MP3 downloads, movie downloads and video clips. According to an article in the *New Scientist* (Gefter 2006),

> If the Web was once an enormous library, it is now a vast conversation. Transmitting information from one person to another has never been easier. Everyone can participate. Young people now communicate more through social networking websites than through e-mail. Instead of keeping diaries, they keep blogs; instead of photo albums, they have Flickr. While older adults go online to find information, the younger crowd go online to live. The boundaries beween offline and online are blurring, and there is a widening generation gap between adolescents growing up with social technology and adults who find it foreign and unsettling. Welcome to the MySpace generation.

Ofcom's (2006) report supports this statement as its research has indicated (see Figure 10.13) that:

- 70 per cent of Internet users between 16 and 24 have used social networking websites (compared to 41 per cent of the general population), with over half doing so on a weekly basis
- 37 per cent of 18 to 24-year-olds have posted material online compared to 14 per cent across all age groups
- 1 in 5 has his or her own website or blog.

Individuals in this same group also use mobile phones as their primary telecommunications platform, with 85 per cent saying that they would use a mobile text or call as the preferred method of arranging to meet a friend, compared to 48 per cent across all age groups. What is interesting is the remarkable speed with which the social networking sites have grown, having first been created just three years ago. However, before these sites came about, it is important to remember that there were sites such as Tripod and Geocities that had chat rooms and discussion groups. What is particularly interesting is that blogs and sites such as MySpace have become part of daily life for many individuals.

This amazing growth has many implications for marketing. For instance, Bebo, launched in July 2005, now has 25 million members and is the number one social

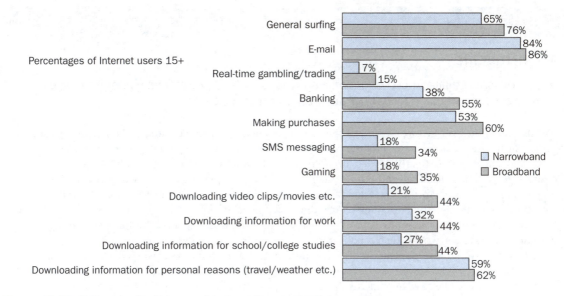

Figure 10.13 Online applications used by broadband and dial-up users
Source: Ofcom 2006, Ofcom research, Q1 2006

networking site in the UK. It is clear that the Internet is becoming more important for socialising, not used just for information gathering (see Figure 10.14).

In addition to this, there is serious growth in the numbers of individuals that are willing to embrace alter egos and create new identities, or avatars, within virtual worlds. One of the fastest-growing virtual worlds (as discussed in Chapter 1) is Second Life and the following case study explores what it is like and some of its implications.

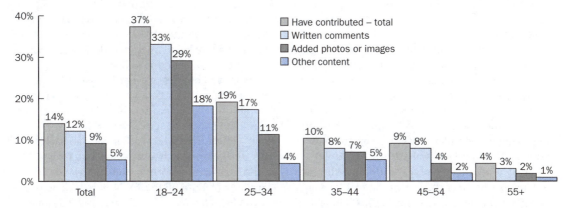

Figure 10.14 Percentages of adult Internet users contributing to websites and/or blogs, by age group
Source: Ofcom 2006, Ofcom ad hoc survey, fieldwork conducted by ICM, June 2006

CASE STUDY

My virtual life

A journey into a place in cyberspace where thousands of people have imaginary lives, some even make a good living; big advertisers are taking notice

As I step on to the polished wood floor of the peaceful Chinese country house, a fountain gurgles softly and a light breeze stirs the scarlet curtain in a doorway. Clad in a stylish blue-and-purple dress, Anshe Chung waves me to a low seat at a table set with bowls of white rice and cups of green tea. I'm here to ask her about her booming land development business, which she has built from nothing two years ago to an operation of 17 people around the world today. As we chat, her story sounds like a classic tale of entrepreneurship.

Except I've left out one small detail: Chung's land, her beautifully appointed home, the steam rising from the teacups – they don't exist. Or rather, they exist only as pixels dancing on the computer screens of people who inhabit the online virtual world called Second Life. Anshe Chung is an avatar, or onscreen graphic character, created by a Chinese-born language teacher living near Frankfurt, Germany. And the sitting room in which Chung and my avatar exchange text messages is just one scene in a vast online diorama operated by Second Life's creator, Linden Lab of San Francisco. Participants launch Second Life's software on their personal computers, log in, and then use their mice and keyboards to roam endless landscapes and cityscapes, chat with friends, create virtual homes on plots of imaginary land, and conduct real business.

Real bucks

The avatar named Anshe Chung may be a computerised chimera, but the company she represents is far from imaginary. Second Life participants pay 'Linden dollars,' the game's currency, to rent or buy virtual homesteads from Chung so they have a place to build and show off their creations. But players can convert that play money into US dollars, at about 300 to the real dollar, by using their credit card at online currency exchanges. Chung's firm now has virtual land and currency holdings worth about $250,000 in real US greenbacks. To handle rampant growth, she just

opened a 10-person studio and office in Wuhan, China. Says Chung's owner, who prefers to keep her real name private to deter real-life intrusions: 'This virtual role-playing economy is so strong that it now has to import skill and services from the real-world economy.'

Oh yes, this is seriously weird. Even Chung sometimes thinks she tumbled down the rabbit hole. But by the time I visited her simulated abode in late February, I already knew that something a lot stranger than fiction was unfolding, some unholy offspring of the movie *The Matrix*, the social networking site MySpace, and the online marketplace eBAY. And it was growing like crazy, from 20,000 people a year ago to 170,000 today. I knew I had to dive in myself to understand what was going on here.

As it turns out, Second Life is one of the many so-called massively multiplayer online games that are booming in popularity these days. Because thousands of people can play at once, they're fundamentally different from traditional computer games in which one or two people play on one PC. In these games, typified by the current No. 1 seller, World of Warcraft, from Vivendi Universal's Blizzard Entertainment unit, players are actors such as warriors, miners, or hunters in an endless medieval-style quest for virtual gold and power.

All told, at least 10 million people pay $15 and take up to a month to play these games, and maybe 20 million more log in once in a while. Some players call World of Warcraft 'the new golf', as young colleagues and business partners gather online to slay orcs instead of gathering on the green to hack away at little white balls. Says eBay Inc. founder and Chairman Pierre M. Omidyar, whose investing group, Omidyar Network, is a Linden Lab backer: 'This generation that grew up on video games is blurring the lines between games and real life.'

Second Life hurls all this to the extreme end of the playing field. In fact, it's a stretch to call it a game because the residents, as players prefer to be called, create everything. Unlike in other virtual worlds, Second Life's technology lets people create objects like clothes or storefronts from scratch, Lego-style, rather than simply pluck avatar outfits or ready-made buildings from a menu. That means residents can build anything they can imagine, from notary services to candles that burn down to pools of wax.

Property rights

You might wonder, as I did at first, what's the point? Well, for one, it's no less real a form of entertainment or personal fulfilment than, say, playing a video game, collecting matchbook covers, or building a life list of birds you've seen. The growing appeal also reflects a new model for media entertainment that the Web first kicked off: don't just watch – do something. 'They all feel like they're creating a new world, which they are', says Linden Lab Chief Executive Philip Rosedale.

Besides, in one important way, this virtual stuff isn't imaginary at all. In November, 2003, Linden Lab made a policy change unprecedented in online games: it allowed Second Life residents to retain full ownership of their virtual creations. The inception of property rights in the virtual world made for a thriving market economy. Programmer Nathan Keir in Australia, for example, created a game played by avatars inside Second Life that's so popular he licensed it to a publisher, who'll soon release it on video game players and cell phones. All that has caught real-world investors' attention, too. On March 28, Linden Lab raised a second, $11 million round of private financing, including new investor Jeff Bezos, CEO of Amazon.com Inc.

Virtual worlds may end up playing an even more sweeping role – as far more intuitive portals into the vast resources of the entire Internet than today's World Wide Web. Some tech thinkers suggest Second Life could even challenge Microsoft Corp.'s Windows operating system as a way to more easily create entertainment and business software and services. 'This is why I think Microsoft needs to pay deep attention to it', Robert Scoble, Microsoft's best-known blogger, recently wrote.

Weak spot

A lot of other real-world businesses are paying attention. That's because virtual worlds could transform the way they operate by providing a new template for getting work done, from training and collaboration to product design and marketing. The British branding firm Rivers Run Red is working with real-world fashion firms and media companies inside Second Life, where they're creating designs that can be viewed in all their 3D glory by colleagues anywhere in the world. A consortium of corporate training folks from Wal-Mart Stores, American Express, Intel and more than 200 other companies, organised by learning and technology think tank The MASIE Center in Saratoga Springs, NY, is experimenting inside Second Life with ways for companies to foster more collaborative learning methods. Says Intel Corp. learning consultant Brent T. Schlenker: 'We're trying to get in on the front end of this new workforce that will be coming.'

The more I kept hearing about all this, the more I knew this was wa-a-a-ay more than fun and games. So early this year I signed up at www.secondlife.com, downloaded the software, logged on, and created my persona. As reporter 'Rob Cranes', I embarked on my journey.

And promptly got lost in the vast, uncharted terrain.

Click: I land at the Angry Ant, a nightclub holding a 'Naked Hour' where avatars are in various stages of undress, dancing lasciviously. Is it getting warm in here?

Click: I stumble upon someone teaching a class on how to buy and sell virtual land to a motley crew of avatars sitting attentively on chairs watching PowerPoint slides. Do we get a toaster when we're done?

Click: Suddenly, I'm underwater at Cave Rua, watching a school of fish swim by. Cool, but what do I do here?

Click: Here's a virtual doctor's office, where a researcher runs a simulation of what it's like to be a hallucinatory schizophrenic. A menacing British voice from a TV urges: 'Shoot yourself. Shoot them all. Get the gun out of the holster and shoot yourself, you !@#&!' Yikes, where's that teleport button?

My disorientation points up one of the big challenges of these virtual worlds, especially one so open-ended as Second Life: with nothing to shoot and no quest to fulfil, it's hard for newbies to know what to do. Virtual worlds require personal

▶

computers with fairly advanced graphics and broadband connections and users with some skill at software. 'The tools are the weak spot,' says Will Wright, legendary creator of The Sims video game, who nonetheless admires Second Life. For now, he says, 'That limits its appeal to a fairly hardcore group'.

Still, there's no denying the explosion of media, products, and services produced by users of these virtual worlds. IGE Ltd, an independent online gaming services firm, estimates that players spent about $1 billion in real money last year on virtual goods and services at all these games combined, and predicts that could rise to $1.5 billion this year. One brave (or crazy) player in the online game Project Entropia last fall paid $100,000 in real money for a virtual space station, from which he hopes to earn money charging other players rent and taxes. In January inside Second Life alone, people spent nearly $5 million in some 4.2 million transactions buying or selling clothes, buildings, and the like.

That can add up to serious change. Some 3100 residents each earn a net profit on an average of $20,000 in annual revenues, and that's in real US dollars. Consider the story of Chris Mead, AKA 'Craig Altman', on Second Life. We exchange text messages via our keyboards at his shop inside Second Life, where he hawks ready-made animation programs for avatars. It's a bit awkward, all the more so because as we chat, his avatar exchanges tender caresses with another avatar named 'The Redoubtable Yoshimi Muromachi'. Turns out she's merely an alter ego he uses to test his creations. Still, I can't help but make Rob Cranes look away.

Shopping spree

Mead is a 35-year-old former factory worker in Norwich, England, who chose to stay home when he and his working wife had their third child. He got on Second Life for fun and soon began creating animations for couples: when two avatars click on a little ball in which he embeds the automated animation program, they dance or cuddle together. They take up to a month to create. But they're so popular, especially with women, that every day he sells more than 300 copies of them at $1 or less apiece. He hopes the $1900 a week that he clears will help pay off his mortgage. 'It's a

dream come true, really', he says. 'I still find it so hard to believe.'

His story makes me want to venture further into this economy. Besides, my photo editor is nagging me to get a shot of my avatar, which needs an extreme makeover. Time to go shopping! First I pick out a Hawaiian shirt from a shop, clicking on the image to buy it for about 300 Lindens, or about a dollar. Nice design but too tight for my taste, so I prowl another men's shop for a jacket. I find something I like, along with a dark grey blazer and pants. As a fitting finishing touch for a reporter, I add a snazzy black fedora, though I'm bummed that it can't be modified to add a press card.

I'm also feeling neglectful leaving my avatar homeless every time I log out. It's time to buy some land, which will give me a place to put my purchases, like a cool spinning globe that one merchant offered cheap. And maybe I'll build a house there to show off to friends. I briefly consider buying a whole island, but I have a feeling our T&E [testing and evaluation] folks would frown on a $1250 bill for imaginary land. Instead, I purchase a 512-square-metre plot with ocean view, a steal for less than two bucks. Plopping my globe on to my plot, I take a seat on it and slowly circle, surveying my domain. My Second Life is good.

I soon discover that Second Life's economy has also begun to attract second-order businesses like financial types. One enterprising character, whose avatar is 'Shaun Altman', has set up the Metaverse Stock Exchange inside Second Life. He (at least I think it's a he) hopes it will serve as a place where residents can invest in developers of big projects like virtual golf courses. In a text chat session in his slick Second Life office, Altman concedes that the market is 'a bit ahead of its time. I'm sure it will take quite some time to build up a solid reputation as an institution.' No doubt, I'm thinking, especially when the CEO is a furry avatar whose creator refuses to reveal his real name.

Premature or not, such efforts are raising tough questions. Virtual worlds may be games at their core, but what happens when they get linked with real money? (For one, people such as Chung's owner start to take changes to their world very seriously. She recently threatened to create her own currency inside Second Life after the Linden dollar's value fell.) Ultimately, who regulates their financial activities? And doesn't this all look like a great way for crooks or terrorists to launder money?

Beyond business, virtual worlds raise sticky social issues. Linden Lab has rules against offensive behaviour in public, such as racial slurs or overtly sexual antics. But for better or worse, consenting adults in private areas can engage in sexual role-playing that, if performed in real life, would land them in jail. Will that draw fire from law enforcement or, at least, publicity-seeking politicians? Ultimately, what are the societal implications of spending so many hours playing, or even working, inside imaginary worlds? Nobody really has good answers yet.

My head hurts. I just want to have some fun now. It's time to try Second Life's most popular game. Tringo is a combination of bingo and the puzzle-like PC game Tetris, where you quickly try to fit various shapes that appear on a screen into squares, leaving as few empty squares as you can. I settle in on a floating seat, joining a dozen other competing avatars at an event called Tringo Money Madness @Icedragon's Playpen – and proceed to lose every game. Badly. I start to get the hang of it and briefly consider waiting for the next Tringo event until I see the bonus feature: a movie screen showing the band Black Sabbath's 1998 reunion tour.

Instead, I seek out Tringo's creator, Nathan Keir, a 31-year-old programmer in Australia whose avatar is a green-and-purple gecko, 'Kermitt Quirk'. It turns out Keir's game is so popular, with 226 selling so far at 15,000 Lindens a pop, or about $50, that a real-world company called Donnerwood Media ponied up a licensing fee in the low five figures, plus royalties. Tringo soon will grace Nintendo Co.'s Game Boy Advance and cell phones. 'I never expected it at all,' Keir tells me, his awe evident even in a text chat clear across the world. He's working on new games now, wondering if he can carve out a living. That would be even cooler than the main benefit so far: making his mum proud.

Talent bank

After all my travels around Second Life, it's becoming apparent that virtual worlds, most of all this one, tap into something very powerful: the talent and hard work of everyone inside. Residents spend a quarter of the time they're logged in, a total of nearly 23,000 hours a day, creating things that become part of the world, available to everyone else. It would take a paid 4100-person software team to do all that, says Linden Lab. Assuming those programmers make about $100,000 a year, that would be $410 million worth of free work over a year. Think of it: the company charges customers anywhere from $6 to thousands of dollars a month for the privilege of doing most of the work. And make no mistake, this would be real work were it not such fun. In Star Wars Galaxies, some players take on the role of running a pharmaceutical business in which they manage factory schedules, devise ad campaigns, and hire other players to find raw materials – all imaginary, of course.

All this has some companies mulling a wild idea: why not use gaming's psychology, incentive systems, and social appeal to get real jobs done better and faster? 'People are willing to do tedious, complex tasks within games,' notes Nick Yee, a Stanford University graduate student in communications who has extensively studied online games. 'What if we could tap into that brainpower?'

In other words, your next cubicle could well be inside a virtual world. That's the mission of a secretive Palo Alto (California) startup, Seriosity, backed by venture firm Alloy Ventures Inc. Seriosity is exploring whether routine real-world responsibilities might be assigned to a custom online game. Workers having fun, after all, likely will be more productive. 'We want to use the power of these games to transform information work,' says Seriosity CEO Byron B. Reeves, a Stanford professor of communications.

Building boom

Whether or not their more fantastic possibilities pan out, it seems abundantly clear that virtual worlds offer a way of testing new ideas like this more freely than ever. 'We can and should view synthetic worlds as essentially unregulated playgrounds for economic organisation,' notes Edward Castronova, an associate professor in telecommunications at Indiana University at Bloomington and author of the 2005 book *Synthetic*

▶

Worlds: The business and culture of online games [University of Chicago Press, 2006].

I get a taste of the lack of regulation just as we're about to go to press. Logging in to Second Life after a few days off, I see that someone has erected a bunch of buildings on my avatar Rob Cranes' land, which is located in a region called Saeneul. The area was nearly empty when I arrived, but now I'm surrounded by Greek temples under construction. So much for my ocean view. Online notes left by one 'Amy Stork' explain that the 'Saeneul Residents Association' is building an amphitheatre complex, and 'your plot is smack bang in the middle.' She's 'confident that we can find a *much* better plot for you than this one ... Love, Amy xx.'

Oh, really? For some reason, this causes Rob Cranes to blow a gasket. He resists my editor's advice to 'head to the virtual gun store,' but he fires off angry e-mail complaints to Ms Stork and Linden Lab and deletes the trespassing buildings, planting some trees in their place. Then he reconsiders: maybe a ramshackle cabin with a stained sofa and a sun-bleached Chevy up on blocks would be a great addition to his plot.

At first, I wonder why I (or my avatar) has such a visceral reaction to this perceived intrusion. Then a flush of parental pride washes over me: my avatar, which so far has acted much like me, hanging back from crowds and minding his punctuation in text chats, suddenly is taking on a life of his own. Who will my alter ego turn out to be? I don't know yet. And maybe that's the best thing about virtual worlds. Unlike in the corporeal world, we can make of our second lives whatever we choose.

Source: 'My virtual life', *BusinessWeek*, 1 May 2006

It is clear from the case study that the digital evolution is having far-reaching consequences for marketers. In fact, most marketers are not even keeping up with the changes. Many entrepreneurs are embracing the changes more quickly than established professionals and creating new marketing propositions and services, as discussed in the case study. In countries such as Korea, which has an established games culture, avatars are common. Most young South Koreans embrace the virtual world with alacrity and, in many ways, lead the world. Cyworld has become very popular by offering personal blogs with 'avatars' that represent their users. Users have avatars that visit and can link to each other's 'minihompy' – a miniature home page that's actually a 3D room containing a user's blog, photos and virtual items for sale. Cyworld's digital garage sales include music, ringtones, clothes for your avatar and furnishings for your own minihompy (Taylor 2006).

Delving deeper into some of the new marketing tools that are being applied, it is useful for marketers to understand the importance of digital possibilities such as blogging, mobile marketing and search advertising.

Blog marketing

Blogs are now being used by businesses, individuals, individuals within businesses, broadcasters such as the BBC, newspapers and, in the future, possibly even politicians. So, what are blogs and what purpose do they really serve?

Blogging, essentially, is a communications vehicle that can be used for marketing to and listening to customers that may be spread globally. It is also a way of interacting directly with individual customers on a one-to-one basis. In many ways, it is a marketing communications tool, listening device, conversational vehicle and log of events all rolled into one. As anyone can set up a blog at any time and network it to any site, both supporters and detractors of a particular company's products and services can make their feelings known quite openly within the public sphere of the Internet. Some companies have discovered, to their chagrin, that customers, if they have a bad experience of a particular product or service, can actually damage the brand as a result of their online protests. For instance, an article by Andrew Clark in *The Guardian* (2006) explained how Dell learned about the growing power of the blogosphere when it recalled 4.1 million laptop batteries after a video that showed one of its computers bursting into flames was posted on the Internet. The brief clip zig-zagged through cyberspace and went from cult viewing to national television. As a result of this, Dell started to keep a closer eye on blogs and the impact they could have on the company brand.

The article also pointed out areas where bloggers now have the power to bring about changes in company policies. Among the examples given were the following.

- *Apple* Nick Ciarelli, barely 20 years old, has become a thorn in Apple's side. His website (www.thinksecret.com) has a reputation for being a reliable source of information about planned launches. The site broke the news about the iPod ahead of its launch in 2001, as well as giving details of the Mac mini ahead of time. The site's latest rumour was that a touch-screen iPod was on its way and, sure enough the iPhone was introduced at the Macworld Conference Expo in San Francisco in January 2007.
- *Wal-Mart* People love to hate Wal-Mart. One of the best-known sites dishing the dirt on America's biggest retailer is Wal-Mart Watch (www.walmartwatch.com). It culls stories from across the USA on issues such as alleged low pay and healthcare and its impact on local firms, as well as providing tools such as Battle-Mart – a guide to keeping the retailer out of your town. See also AsdaWatch (asdawatch.org), which keeps an eye on Wal-Mart's British operations.

Ofcom's report (2006) indicates the extent of the penetration of blogging (see Figure 10.15).

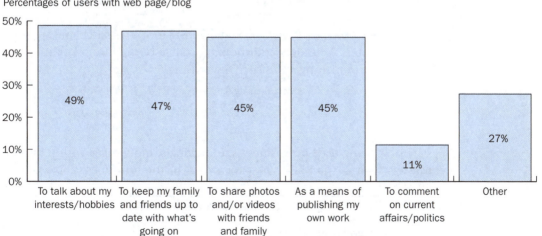

Percentages of users with web page/blog

Figure **10.15** **Users of web pages/blogs**

Source: Ofcom 2006, Ofcom research, fieldwork conducted by ICM, June 2006

Thus, blogging can expose a company's corporate social responsibility (CSR) policy to the general public. Equally, however, companies can benefit from embracing blogging and utilising it as a marketing tool. For busy executives, instead of responding to all e-mails, they could simply set up a blog on their company's website, reaching a very wide audience. This type of communication can often pre-empt malicious bloggers as well. According to Wright (2006), for companies, blogging is about three things:

- *information* telling your customers what you're doing and finding out what they are thinking
- *relationships* building a solid base of positive experiences with your customers that changes them from plain old consumers for evangelists for your company and products
- *knowledge management* having the vast stores of knowledge within your company available to the right people at the right time.

Over time, much can be gleaned about the types of customers that are buying into a company's product/market mix. These can be classified as shown in Figure 10.16.

Customers can either be a company's best friend or worst enemy. In many ways, in an ideal world, most customers would be in the right-hand quadrant of the matrix in Figure 10.16. However, in the real world, the customer base is more likely to include all or most of the categories shown in the matrix.

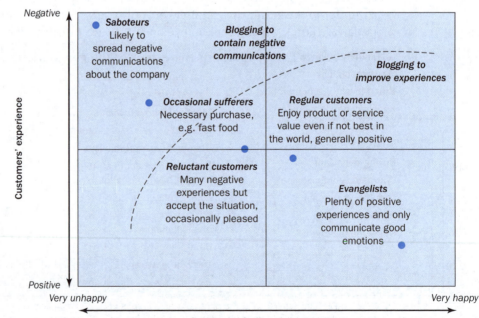

Figure 10.16 Categories of customers

Source: Based on categories mentioned in Wright 2006

For companies, it is important to be proactive regarding communications and a key element of this is blog monitoring and usage if saboteurs are to be contained. Of course, positive blogs from evangelists can go a long way towards enhancing the company brand. Thus, creating customer evangelists should be a priority for all companies. Further uses for blogs are listed in Table 10.3 (Wright 2006).

Table 10.3 **Using blogs**

External	*Internal*
Communication	Knowledge management and sharing
Marketing	Administrative tool
E-mail newsletter support	Internal document review
FAQ section	Collaboration
Industry news opinion	Idea archiving
Service updates	Internal dialogue
Learning	Dynamic archiving – not stale, like e-mail
Interactive journalism	Corporate intelligence – knowing what your employees are
Public feedback	saying and thinking, noting patterns
Customers' queries/watchlists	Loyalty – creating identification with the company via such
Aggregation of news sources	interaction
Self-expression	Status reports – what we work on and with whom, all tracked
Storytelling	on the employee's aggregator
Customer service	Top-down ideas/goal setting
Public relations	Bottom-up ideas generation and interaction
Viral marketing	Creation of a corporate culture of expression, collectivity,
Campaigning/social reform	knowledge sharing
Community building	Getting the information out faster: have an idea?
Sales mechanism	Frustrated with the chain of getting someone to listen?
Brand loyalty – a human face	Post and it will get noticed, supported and heard
Knowledge management	Calendar sharing
Trending	Meeting announcements
CRM	Meeting notes v. e-mail broadcast notices
Buying behaviour	Sharing of market intelligence
Competitive intelligence	Brainstorming about strategy, feature sets and processes –
Thought leadership	sharing customer notes
Product changes	Asking others for help
Crisis management	Ability to segment blogs by individual or department for easy
	blog subscription
	Best practices
	Thought leadership
	Team creation – match up those passionate about an item or people with differing ideas so that they can work out optimal solutions
	Organised links – categorise links within the blog to most frequently requested/used information, strategies, technical manuals, sales material, online learning, etc.

Source: Arieanna Foley in Wright 2006. Reproduced with permission of The McGraw-Hill Companies.

As Table 10.3 shows, blogs can be used for both internal and external marketing within companies, laying the foundations for an integrated approach to product and brand management. Compared to lengthy market research exercises, blogs can provide instant qualitative information from customers, including new ideas that they may offer to improve products or services. Many companies are beginning to use blogs for these purposes. It is likely that this system will be transferred (in fact, it is already happening) to mobiles. As mobiles become more versatile, being able to transmit voice messages, texts, videos, photographs to other individuals and websites, they will increasingly become part of the blogging landscape.

Mobile marketing

As technologies converge and more companies are using different methods to attract and retain customers, one important addition is mobile marketing. Mobile marketing is coming of age and many companies are using different techniques to build relationships and brands with customers. According to Dupree and Bosarge (2006):

> With the advent of wireless technologies, all bets are off regarding media touch points; the home-based tether has been severed and media consumption locations are virtually anywhere. Hand-held and portable devices from smart phones to PDAs redefine the relationship with media, making it an increasingly personal choice.

Many leading industry brands are committing themselves to interactive digital marketing to the tune of 5 to 25 per cent of their advertising budgets. Currently, the budget for mobile advertising stands at $1 billion and is set to grow to $10 billion in 2010 (The Shosteck Group 2006). However, for mobile marketing to succeed, both technological and legal hurdles have to be understood and overcome. One element described by Becker (2006) is the Common Short Code (CSC or short code). This code, which is generally an abbreviated five- to six-digit number, can be used as an 'address' for text and multimedia messages. In addition to the short messaging service (SMS) and Internet protocol (IP) mobile data network routing, CSCs can command premium billing capabilities. The USA's Short Code Administration (CSCA) defines the common short code as:

> Short numeric codes (e.g. 47647, 63459) to which text messages can be sent from a mobile phone. Wireless subscribers send text messages to short codes with relevant keywords to access a wide variety of mobile content. Common Short Codes (CSCs) are compatible across all participating carriers and easy to remember. CSCs are either five-digit or six-digit numbers.
>
> In the United Kingdom the Mobile Data Association calls it UK Code of Practice for Common Mobile Short Codes (CMSC), the concept being the same as in the USA.

According to the MDA, mobile technology is being used extensively in partnership with broadcasters, owing to the growth in popularity of TV reality shows, along with daytime popular programmes that are often developed in a 'magazine' style, together with live debates. Audiences are now used to voting for their favourite stars on programmes such as *Pop Idol* and *Big Brother* and, at the same time, they regularly participate in competitions. The UK's mobile content providers can now establish their services with ease across all networks and, at the same time, subscribers are quick to embrace mobile technology as a means of receiving digital information. Competition in the marketplace continues to rise along with the emergence of new short code services incorporating voice, images and video content.

So why are CSCs so powerful as marketing tools? Why are they much more powerful than a URL or e-mail address? It is for the following reasons.

- *Bi-directional (and interactive)* This can create two-way permission-based interactive traffic between the customer and the marketer's mobile or mobile-enhanced traditional media initiative (such as videos, ad ringtones and so on). Customers have the ability to opt in or out of messages. The communication can be independent of location and time. A consumer can opt in to a call for action if he or she so desires. Often it is something like 'Text MGP to 7743 for the latest 5 updates on Monaco Grand Prix and for free Grand Prix wallpapers'. People can also take part in sweepstakes and bids.
- *Enabled to work across interoperable carriers (service providers)* As a CSC allows a standardised addressing format, a message can be sent across all mobile carriers. This avoids wastage and means that large audiences can be targeted with a single message. Currently this is possible in the USA, UK, Canada, France and China. However there is no intercountry code at present, so global initiatives are not possible yet.
- *Personal (consumers can have their own profile and vanity codes)* As soon as customers opt in to particular marketing initiatives, marketers can capture a lot of data, such as the number, make and model of phone, and the mobile operator used by the customer. Particular messages can then be sent to individual customers and offers can be tailored to individual needs by using well-developed CRM systems. Companies can also buy or lease CSCs that spell their name, such as Sprite 777183 (these are vanity short codes). However, there are legal conventions that need to be followed so that this type of marketing does not become intrusive.
- *Billing engines (premium SMS)* These short codes can be effective vehicles for billing customers who decide to participate in mobile initiatives or for the purchase of mobile content.
- *Effective mechanism for permissions marketing (opt in and opt out)* This type of system can be utilised for marketing initiatives of any kind and permission can be obtained quite quickly.
- *Useful for a wide range of marketing campaigns and services.*

An example of digital marketing is given in the following case study (from *Mediaweek* 2006). As mobile services become easily accessible and much simpler, more marketing campaigns will shift to this medium. In time, with more phones having integrated GPS systems, customers' behaviour could also be tracked.

CASE STUDY

Digital marketing – flying higher and higher via mobile platforms

To enter the biggest sweepstakes in mobile marketing history earlier this year, all you had to do was buy some chicken fries at Burger King and find the text code on the box. The next step, sending a text message with the code, produced a landmark response rate among Sprint subscribers to win a Super Bowl Sweepstakes prizes of an expenses paid trip to the game and special access to the Rolling Stones' half-time gig. Sports and rock and roll have gained particular emphasis in Sprint's digital marketing game plans, which is a clear indication of today's prime market demographic of young, upscale early adopters attuned to wireless technology. 'It starts with the youth market and if the US follows what's happened in Europe and Asia, then you would expect that would prompt penetration on all age scales,' says John Styers, Sprint's Director of Data Communication Services.

Source: Anonymous, Flying higher and higher via mobile platforms', *MediaWeek*, 5 June 2006, 16(23), 54.

Marketing on the Internet

In 1998, Sergey Brin and Larry Page initiated their university project to turn a search engine into a viable business, which they called Google (Milstein and Dornfest 2004). The difference then between Google and other search engines on the Internet was that Google did not use the number of keywords on a web page to rank web pages in its results list. Instead, Google 'evaluated a site primarily on how many other sites linked to it, and ranked search results accordingly.' (Milstein and Dornfest 2004). The more web pages that linked to a particular website or web page, the higher up the results list the particular website or web page would be. 'Google's philosophy of delivering results is based on popularity,' (Milstein and Dornfest, 2004), which is essentially a form of online word of mouth. A link from 'Website A' to 'Website B' is a way of recommending the user to take a look at 'Website B'. The more websites that link to 'Website B', the greater the credibility of 'Website B', so it will be higher up the results list than websites with fewer links.

The Google way of ranking web pages meant that web developers were unable to manipulate web pages in an attempt to push their websites up the search results lists (Milstein and Dornfest 2004). The only ways to creep up the Google results lists were to either pay Google for using certain keywords or increase the numbers of links on other websites that direct online users to that website.

Google's revenue comes from a combination of website publishers paying to be registered on Google's database of web pages and via Google's own advertising mediums. In fact, 99 per cent of Google's revenue comes from advertising, (Coy 2006), although Google remain guarded over disclosing exactly how much revenue the various elements of advertising generate (Battelle 2005). Google's clients, whether they are small or large businesses, attempt to maximise traffic to their sites by using Google adwords. These can then be tracked to see how optimal they are and companies can then try to adjust their promotional mix accordingly. All the statistics that follow are provided by Google. Figure 10.17 illustrates the possibilities for a courier company wishing to use different words.

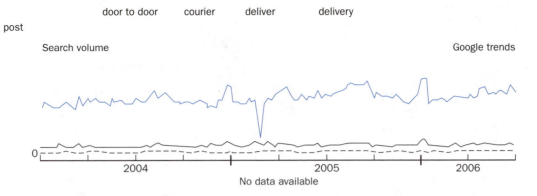

Figure 10.17 **Search engine optimisation**

In Figure 10.17, the word 'deliver' seems to be more effective in the long run than the others. The word usage is a direct result of consumer search preferences. This area is continually developing and many marketers are training to become Google Ad Professionals (GAPs). Through this kind of marketing, companies can keep track of customers, while also measuring their popularity and performance on the Net. Of course, from time to time this can be open to abuse as rivals may just click on the sites of their opposition in order to inflate the number of visitors and, hence, the cost to the company. This has resulted in large sums of compensation for some companies that have convincingly proven that this type of practice has been detrimental to their business.

What next in the digital age?

Over the next year, it is likely that there will be a convergence of technology. This is already happening, but there is currently only one provider in the UK (NTL) that can realise this kind of convergence, which means links between a home PC (broadband), mobile telephone, digital television and landline telephones (see Figure 10.18).

- *Tight segmentation* As companies learn more about their customers from mobile campaigns, segmentation criteria can be tightened and more one-to-one marketing will take place.
- *Use of multimedia* Most mobile operators are now providing multimedia facilities and so are all broadband operators. The use of this media is likely to grow exponentially with podcasts.
- *Range of channels* The range of channels is growing and audiences are gravitating to their favourite channels and often even listening or watching programmes at different times as they are now stored digitally on the Internet.
- *The growth of hyperreality* In the postmodern age, hyperreality is well and truly taking off, as shown in the case study on Second Life. This will become ever more sophisticated and the crossover beween the real and the hyperreal worlds will be increasingly blurred as a new generation grows up embracing the virtual world.

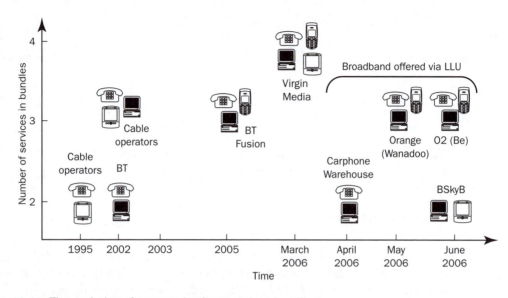

Figure 10.18 **The evolution of communications services bundling**

Note: Chart refers to time when bundles were first announced. LLU = local loop unbundling

Source: Ofcom 2006

- *Speed* In time, marketing offers and communications will be not only instantaneous in nature but also have a global reach. It is likely that campaigns will be shorter and specific.
- *Community building* Community networks have proved to be hugely popular, as already discussed, and this can only grow, with many different community configurations appearing across national boundaries. In the long run, many different possibilities will open up and much will depend on the imagination of marketers. However, they will have to be ethical in the way that they engage with customers.

Ethics as a source of competitive advantage

As marketing practice is now busy integrating the potential of ICT by using databases and Internet marketing, new issues arise about how this data is used and manipulated. Billions of potential consumers can now be reached this way. The discussion above on the use of smart tags also indicates the way customers could be located wherever they live. A brief observation of the practices of marketing on the Internet shows that some firms implement aggressive actions, such as pop-ups, deceptive banners (banners offering prizes, but really directing surfers to particular sites), hyperlinks and other forms of intrusive mechanisms that impinge on personal privacy. As technology moves from desk-based PC applications to mobile communications, there is the potential to become even more intrusive, with the possibility of local tracking (within a 50-metre radius of a food or retail outlet with GPS technology, for example).

Given the fact that such powerful devices are already available, we advocate that firms wishing to differentiate themselves from their competitors will have to turn to marketing ethics in order to gain and keep consumers. Short-termist thinking will push firms towards ever shorter campaigns and advertising plans, directing many companies towards an unethical stance. This danger can be averted by firms that adopt a proactive ethical attitude towards consumers within their e-marketing strategies. In order to adopt such a proactive stance, companies need to develop a model of ethical interactivity with consumers. Figure 10.19 illustrates the problems associated with intrusiveness, when using different communication mediums.

Gathering information – the issue of consumer information privacy

Internet technology provides opportunities to gather consumer information on an unprecedented scale (Kelly 2000). However, some aspects of information gathering are visible (such as self-divulgence of information for making a purchase, when accessing a website, to be sent free samples) and some are less so (such as anonymous profile data, IP, cookies). Owing to these possible uses and abuses of information, many consumers remain hesitant about buying things on the Internet. The development of software allowing a 'private Internet experience' and 'completely undetected surfing' is an indication of the level of consumers' concern regarding the invasion of privacy.

A survey (Culnan 1999a and b) of the top 100 commercial websites shows that only 20 per cent apply a full ethical policy. This shows that there is room for the development of competitive advantage (Culnan 1999a and b). The reports on Internet privacy policies show that five aspects can be used to describe a website's position concerning privacy:

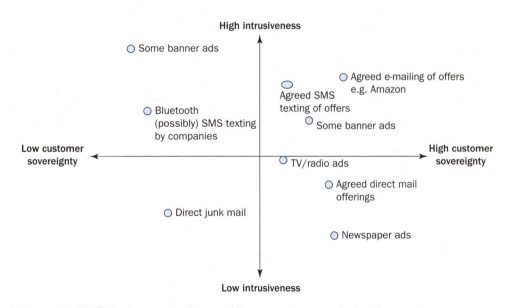

Figure 10.19 **Ethical perceptual map of the current range of advertisements**
Source: Gauzente and Ranchhod 2001 (© Academy of Marketing Science)

- *notice* that is, an indication to consumers about what information is collected, how it will be used, whether or not it will be disclosed to third parties and whether cookies are used or not
- *choice* give consumers' the choice to agree with aspects of information gathering or not
- *access* consumers can be given access to the information gathered and the possibility of reviewing and correcting that information
- *security* this concerns the protection given to information transferred and its subsequent storage
- *contact* consumers can be given details of a contact person or address should they need to ask questions or register complaints regarding privacy.

As Internet software becomes more sophisticated, it will be increasingly possible to tailor sites to suit individuals' ethical preferences. The seven criteria shown in Figure 10.20 could form the basis for creating and sustaining online competitive advantages.

Figure 10.20 clearly illustrates that ethical marketing is critically associated with a firm's long-term orientation. Advantages such as image, trust, relationship quality, database reliability and database updates are typically representative of the goals of long-term, market-orientated firms. A firm that has a short-term orientation is likely to lose its competitive advantages in the long run against firms that develop ethics as a marketing weapon for the consumers' benefit (Gauzente and Ranchhod 2001).

Another important area that has to be explored explored is social marketing, as this a major contemporary issue within global societies, fuelled by better and more scientific information.

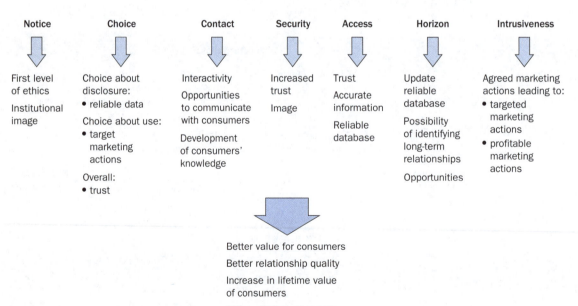

Figure 10.20 **Ethical marketing criteria and competitive advantage**

Source: Gauzente and Ranchhod 2001 (© Academy of Marketing Science)

Social marketing

Social marketing means social change-management mechanisms that involve the design, implementation and control of marketing communications technology aimed at increasing the acceptability of a social idea or practice in one or more groups of target adopters. It utilises concepts of market segmentation, consumer research, product concept development and testing, directed communication, facilitation, incentives and exchange theory to maximise the target adopters' response. These target groups may need to be advised about healthy living or the importance of being active in saving the environment, for example. In the long run, this type of marketing communication needs to create a change of behaviour in individuals (Andreasen 2002). The social marketing approach should therefore entail:

- behaviour change in the individuals who are targeted, such as them stopping smoking
- continuous market research, with market testing of intervention strategies and the monitoring of the success of these interventions
- careful segmentation of target audiences to ensure maximum efficiency and effectiveness in the use of scarce resources
- the creation of attractive and motivational exchanges with target audiences
- an attempt to use all 4 Ps of the traditional marketing mix, so, for example, it is not just advertising or communications but also creates attractive benefit packages (products) while minimising costs (price) wherever possible, making the exchange convenient and easy (place) and communicating powerful messages via media relevant to and preferred by the target audiences (promotion)
- careful attention being paid to the competition faced by the desired behaviour, so, for instance, healthy eating may be challenged by fast and processed foods or the social behaviour of a particular group (see Table 10.4).

Marketers are also becoming aware of the positive impacts that marketing actions with a social dimension can have on organisations (Handelman and Arnold 1999). Increasingly, companies such as the Body Shop engage in 'enlightened capitalism' as it promotes social causes via its brand, enhancing its brand image in the process (Richards 1995).

Social marketing campaigns represent a new field of marketing application, in both industrialised and developing countries. They are often prompted by the perception that some situation represents a social problem and so merits social action.

The Social Marketing Institute defines social marketing as:

the planning and implementation of programmes designed to bring about social change using concepts from commercial marketing.

The main objective of social marketing campaigns is to influence behaviour. It is considered that the public will change its behaviour if the benefits of this change are perceived as more important than the costs associated with making that change. The role of social marketing, therefore, is to maximise the perception of

Table 10.4 Possible collaboration of approaches to social marketing given the sources acting as barriers to action

Problem	Barrier	Role for social marketing	Role for community mobilisation	Role for structured change approaches
Motivation	Individual	Creating awareness; promoting great benefits at a low cost	Urging media cooperation	Building web links to hard-to-reach individuals
	Community	Urging opinion leaders to motivate others	Creating awareness, raising public concern	Creating incentives for group organisation
	Structural	Urging change in structural rewards/penalties (e.g. taxes)	Holding briefings	Changing structural rewards penalties (e.g. taxes)
Opportunity	Individual	Creating awareness of behavioural opportunities	Urging business and political cooperation	Changing economic barriers to individual action
	Community	Urging businesses to provide access to change agents	Changing repressive social norms	Eliminating antitrust restriction on business cooperation
	Structural	Urging use of government facilities for programmes	Bringing pressure to bear on legislators	Providing government subsidies, changing physical environments
Ability	Individual	Providing modelling of ideal behaviour	Pointing group members to individualised change tools	Allowing government agencies to provide training
	Community	Providing communication tools for outreach	Conducting group training	Allowing government premises (e.g. schools) to be used for group training
	Structural	Urging removal of public disincentives	Changing community structures	Removing public disincentives

Source: Andreasen 2002

change benefits, while at the same time reducing the costs of the change. This action is based, as in the case of classical marketing, on a marketing mix concept:

- *product* the benefits associated with the desired change in behaviour
- *price* minimising the price of change – the sacrifices that have to be made by people in order to change their existing behaviour
- *place* creating the opportunities for change in specific places that correspond to the target audience's lifestyle
- *communication* communicating the benefits of change to the targeted public, as well as the way in which the behaviour change can be realised.

It is more than this, however, as, for many individuals, change such as this is not merely a marketing issue but also something that has to be set and endorsed by particular peer groups and the communities in which they reside. As social problems are complex and interrelated, solutions need to be developed in light of the specific socio-economic, historical, religious and cultural frameworks concerned (Gray 1996). Often, segments of society that are particularly vulnerable or exposed need to be identified in order to be able to develop a targeted campaign.

Some social campaigns are designed merely to help bring problem areas out into the open and draw attention to their causes, which can often be taboo subjects. Although increasing the social awareness of a problem is indeed necessary, it is by no means sufficient for determining changes in societal attitudes and behaviour as these are shaped by habits, interests, feelings and beliefs, among other factors (Novartis 2001). For these reasons, social campaigns conceived only to educate or admonish often turn out to be relatively ineffective.

These limitations and the success of advertising techniques used in the commercial world have provided the impetus for the development of social marketing. Introduced by Philip Kotler and Gerald Zalitrian in 1971, this concept combines traditional approaches to social change with commercial marketing and advertising techniques (Kotler and Andreasen 1991; Kotler and Zalitrian 1971). Its originators define social marketing as the design, implementation and control of programmes aimed at increasing the acceptability of a social idea or practice in one or more groups of target adopters (Kotler 1979; Kotler and Zalitrian 1971).

Previous studies

In the last ten years, social marketing has become an important field of action and research (Lefebvre and Flora 1988). The number of non-profit organisations and governmental agencies applying social marketing techniques has increased substantially and their operational effectiveness has been refined.

Specialists and practitioners have researched the organisation and ethics of strategic alliances in social marketing (Andreasen 2000a), the transfer of knowledge concepts and tools from commercial to social marketing (Andreasen 1984 and 2000b) and organisation of specific social marketing campaigns (Andreasen 2000b; Bang 2000). There is also an extensive body of literature available on theories and models of behaviour change, which have direct applications in social marketing (Cooper 1979; Frederiksen et al. 1984; Glanz et al. 1990; Kotler and Clarke 1986; Rothschild 1999).

Robinson (1998) has developed a model describing the main stages of a social marketing campaign:

1 *knowledge* being or becoming informed about the existing problem and possible solutions
2 *desire* inspiring the targeted public to imagine a better future and develop the desire to experience it
3 *skills* providing the public with the necessary skills to realise the desired change
4 *optimism* developing a positive attitude that change can be realised and that it is beneficial
5 *facilitation* providing support to the public, facilitating the change process
6 *stimulation* the public often needs encouragement in order to initiate the change process, especially when the change concerns behavioural routines developed and stabilised in time

7 *feedback and reinforcement* the social marketing campaign has to be permanently reinforced with new messages in order to maintain the momentum of the behaviour change and, at the same time, the people engaged in the behaviour change should be provided with feedback that helps them to identify the various stages of the change process and the relationship between partial changes and the final objective.

Theories and models of social change

A correct understanding of social change theories is paramount when designing and implementing any social programme if it is to be a success (Frederiksen et al. 1984; Glanz et al. 1990). Social marketing campaigns are no exception to this. Theories and models explain people's behaviour and suggest ways to change its undesirable aspects. They can also provide methods that can be used to identify and define the main target audiences and the most effective means to reach them.

Adopting an ecological perspective on social marketing

The ecological perspective provides two key ideas for identifying the individual and environmental leverage points for social marketing campaigns.

First, behaviour is viewed as being affected by, and affecting, multiple levels of influence. Five levels of influence for health-related behaviour and conditions have been identified. They are:

1 intra-personal or individual factors
2 interpersonal factors
3 institutional or organisational factors
4 community factors
5 public policy factors (McLeroy et al. 1988 and see Table 10.5).

Table 10.5 An ecological perspective: levels of influence

Concept	Definition
Intra-personal factors	Individual characteristics that influence behaviour, such as knowledge, attitudes, beliefs and personality traits
Interpersonal factors	Interpersonal processes and primary groups, including family, friends and peers, that provide social identity, support and role definition.
Institutional factors	Rules, regulations, policies and informal structures that may constrain or promote recommended behaviours
Community factors	Social networks and norms, or standards, that exist in formal or informal forms among individuals, groups and organisations
Public policy	Local and national policies and laws that regulate or support healthy actions and practices for disease prevention, early detection, control and management

Source: Adapted from National Cancer Institute 1995

The second key idea relates to the possibility of reciprocal causation between individuals and their environments – that is, behaviour both influencing and being influenced by the social environment. Regarding the Internet, this principle has an important consequence. This multilevel, interactive medium clearly shows the advantages of interventions that combine behavioural and environmental components.

Cognitive-behavioural models

Contemporary behaviour models at the individual and interpersonal levels usually fall within the broad category of cognitive-behavioural theories (Bandura 1977 and 1986; Fishbein and Azjen 1975). Two main concepts are common to these theories (National Cancer Institute 1995):

- behaviour is mediated by cognitions – that is, what we know and think affects how we act
- knowledge is necessary, but not sufficient, to produce behaviour change – perceptions, motivation, skills and factors in the social environment also play important roles.

The 'stages of change' model

The 'stages of change' model explains behaviour changes of individuals. The basic premise of this model, introduced by Prochaska et al. (1992), is that behaviour change is a process and not an event, and that individuals have different levels of motivation, or readiness, to change. People at different points in the process of change can benefit from different interventions, matched to the stage they are in at that time.

Five distinct stages are identified in the 'stages of change' model (see Table 10.6):

- precontemplation
- contemplation
- decision/determination
- action
- maintenance.

It is important to understand that this is a circular, not linear, model. People do not go through the stages rigidly – they can enter and exit at any point and often recycle. Also, there appear to be differences between how the stages fit the situation when the individual is dealing with different problem areas. For example, for a problem that involves overt, easily recognised behaviour and includes a physical addiction component (such as alcoholism), the stages might have a different meaning than they would for a problem where target goals are not easily identified and undesirable habits may have been formed without physiological addiction (such as following a diet with no more than 30 per cent of the calories coming from fat).

The 'stages of change' model can be used both to understand (explain) why people are sensitive to different methods that are used to effect behaviour change and develop social marketing campaigns that are targeted effectively.

Table 10.6 **The 'stages of change' model.**

Concept	Definition	Application
Precontemplation	Unaware of problem, hasn't thought about change	Increase awareness of need for change, personalise information on risks and benefits
Contemplation	Thinking about change in the near future	Motivate, encourage to make specific plans
Decision/determination	Making a plan to change	Assist in developing concrete action plans, setting gradual goals
Action	Implementation of specific action plans	Assist with feedback, problem-solving, social support, reinforcement
Maintenance	Continuation of desirable actions or repeating periodic recommended step(s)	Assist in coping, reminders, finding alternatives, avoiding slips/relapses

Source: Adapted from National Cancer Institute (1995)

The 'health belief' model

The 'health belief' model (HBM) can be useful when analysing people's inaction or non-compliance regarding their health. It was one of the first models that adapted theory from the behavioural sciences to health problems and remains one of the most widely recognised conceptual frameworks for health behaviour (National Cancer Institute 1995). It was originally introduced in the 1950s by psychologists working in the US Public Health Service (Hochbaum et al. 1992). They assumed that people feared diseases and action taken regarding health was motivated in relation to the degree of fear (perceived threat) and expected fear-reduction potential of those actions – as long as that potential outweighed practical and psychological obstacles to taking action (net benefits).

The HBM can be summarised in terms of four constructs that represent the perceived threat and net benefits (see Table 10.7):

■ perceived susceptibility
■ perceived severity
■ perceived benefits
■ perceived barriers (National Cancer Institute 1995).

These concepts were proposed as accounting for people's 'readiness to act.' An added concept is cues to action, which are those factors that activate that readiness and stimulate overt behaviour. A more recent further addition to the HBM is the concept of self-efficacy, or your confidence in your ability to successfully perform an action. This concept was added by Rosenstock et al. (1988) to help the HBM better fit the challenges of changing habitual unhealthy behaviour, such as being sedentary, smoking or overeating.

As in the case of the 'stages of change' model, the HBM can be used to explain people's behaviour and enable improved social marketing strategies for behaviour change to be designed.

Table 10.7 The 'health belief model'

Concept	Definition	Application
Perceived susceptibility	One's opinion of chances of getting a condition	Define population(s) at risk, risk levels, personalise risk based on a person's features or behaviour, heighten perceived susceptibility if too low
Perceived severity	One's opinion of how serious a condition and its consequences are	Specify consequences of the risk and the condition
Perceived benefits	One's opinion of the efficacy of the advised action to reduce risk or seriousness of impact	Define action to take, how, where, when, clarify the positive effects to be expected
Perceived barriers	One's opinion of the tangible and psychological costs of the advised action	Identify and reduce barriers by means of reassurance, incentives, assistance
Cues to action	Strategies to activate 'readiness'	Provide 'how to' information, promote awareness, reminders
Self-efficacy	Confidence in one's ability to take action	Provide training, guidance in performing action

Source: Adapted from National Cancer Institute 1995

The role of social marketing campaigns

Social marketing campaigns attempt to change the behaviour of individuals and groups of people within a society. The benefits of this change are two-fold:

- at the individual level, the person who succeeds in eliminating a behaviour or a habit that has negative consequences will most likely experience an improvement in his or her standard of living and better health
- at the social level, society benefits from the reduced costs of treating some diseases or accidents that are caused by negative social behaviour and habits and then these resources are freed up to be redirected towards other social needs.

Although changes regarding a negative habit can be triggered by a social marketing campaign, whether or not it will be completely realised will depend on the effects of the influences of various social layers and structures. There are many other factors that contribute to the success or failure of such endeavours. For example, the attitudes of other people and the influences of close social groups can significantly affect the pace and achievement of change. In some cases, a person's membership of a group can represent a barrier to behaviour change. For example, a teenager whose friends are all smoking heavily will not be able to quit smoking because this very habit facilitates his or her social inclusion.

This last example illustrates that, in reality, social marketing campaigns are not based on short-term actions, but should be planned and implemented as a permanent activity aimed at educating people, preventing the adoption of negative behaviour and questioning the utility of negative habits for personal health and happiness. The social marketing mix, therefore, comprises, besides the 4 Ps of the classical marketing model, two more Ps:

- *publics* all groups of people who can influence the social change process and be targeted by social marketing messages
- *politics* the general vision and plan of governmental agencies and NGOs for positive social change, on a long-term basis.

Figure 10.21 presents the various layers that need to be taken account of in social marketing campaigns.

In many cases, the application of commercial advertising principles to social marketing campaigns significantly increases their attractiveness and efficiency. For example, the use of popular role models can significantly enhance the success of social marketing campaigns, as the case study opposite demonstrates.

Online social marketing

Social marketing is distinguished by its emphasis on so-called non-tangible products, ideas and practices, as opposed to the tangible products and services that are often the focus of commercial marketing (Andreasen 1995). Considering this, the Internet should be considered as an attractive communication channel for social marketing. As most social marketing activities focus on changing beliefs, perceptions and attitudes, the ubiquity, flexibility and interactiveness of the Internet can offer important advantages for effective social marketing campaigns.

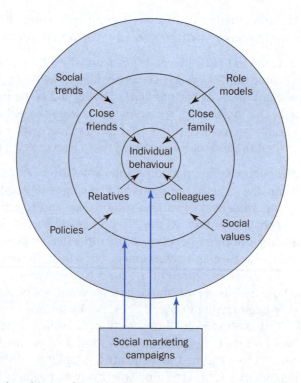

Figure 10.21 Various layers of social influence affecting an individual's decision to change his or her behaviour

Jamie Oliver in talks over campaign for family meals *(D Brindle, J Maley)*

The Department of Health is negotiating with Sainsbury's about a joint campaign, to be fronted by the celebrity chef Jamie Oliver, to encourage families to make time to eat together more often as a key means of improving the nation's diet.

The move would mark a controversial departure for government public health campaigns in its tie-up with a commercial brand. A report commissioned by the health department and published yesterday argues that such partnerships should be encouraged, provided appropriate ethical guidelines are put in place.

It comes as research showed that over the past year spending on frozen foods had fallen almost 3 per cent, with sales of frozen ready meals and meat products – including the Turkey Twizzlers ridiculed by Oliver during his influential TV series on school meals – down more than 8 per cent.

The family meal has been highlighted as a prominent factor in social cohesion, as well as nutritional wellbeing. Surveys suggest that as few as three in 10 families now sit down to eat together more than once a week, with most of those

watching television at the same time. This year, the dining table was dropped from the official basket of goods said to reflect the country's buying habits.

Dr Fiona Adshead, the deputy chief medical officer for England, told public health experts yesterday: 'Over the coming weeks, we are going to be working with Sainsbury's and Jamie Oliver about how we get families back eating together by thinking about basic recipes.'

Sainsbury's pays the TV chef an estimated £1m a year to star in its advertisements. The proposed relationship reflects a growing trend for companies to get involved in promotion of healthy living.

Some public health campaigners may question whether the health department is allowing its messages to be hijacked by commercial interests. But Jeff French, co-author of yesterday's report on use of social marketing techniques in public health work, said: 'They can be part of the problem, but there is no solution that doesn't involve them . . . in terms of reach.'

Source: David Brindle and Jacqueline Maley, *The Guardian*, 27 June 2006. Copyright Guardian News & Media Ltd 2006.

However, if the Internet is ever to be used effectively for such campaigns, the requirements and elements of social change theories have to be incorporated into the design, structure and content of the website used. It is also important that the online social marketing campaign is not perceived as distant by targeted audiences. For this, it is often necessary to establish clear links between online social marketing messages and information, and real-life social marketing groups and activities. Table 10.8 presents the most important elements that have to be incorporated into social marketing campaigns websites.

A study of the websites (Gurău 2005) used for social marketing campaigns indicates a number of shortcomings concerning the integration of online messages with real-life activities.

- The online social marketing campaigns are usually integrated with other marketing operations, but indirectly, such as in lists of online messages about social marketing events. The connection is not clearly specified and the website is often limited to the function of an advertising channel.
- The information presented by the websites addresses the social problems from different perspectives, including individual (online messages relevant for individual behaviour/situations), interpersonal (the effects of undesirable behaviour

Table 10.8 The most important elements of websites and their corresponding functions for social marketing campaigns

Elements	Function
Online information about site's integration with the physical world of the social marketing campaign	Integration with other social marketing policies
Online messages addressing individual, interpersonal, institutional, community and public policy problems and factors	Capacity of the website to present different aspects of the same problem
Possibilities for online interaction between users, organisation and community: ■ interaction with the organisation via telephone, e-mail ■ interaction with the site via search and personalisation tools ■ interaction with the community via discussion forums	Capacity of the website to provide personalised interactive possibilities and build a dynamic communication pattern
Time passed since last update	Flexibility and relevance of content
Educational messages	Capacity of the website to educate its users
Site's content, structure and design in relation to the subject presented	Capacity of the website to adapt to the social marketing topic
Online messages targeted at users in different stages of the behaviour change process: ■ pre-contemplation ■ contemplation ■ decision ■ action ■ maintenance	Capacity of the website to segment and target different audiences

Online messages that:
■ emphasise:
  – disadvantages of undesirable behaviour
  – positive aspects of behaviour change
■ minimise – barriers to change
■ provide solution for overcoming the barriers to change
	Strategic approach of the online social marketing campaign

on friends, relatives and so on), institutional (organisations that support behaviour change and their specific policies), community (community events, social statistics, discussion forums) and social policy (regulations/legislation/initiatives relevant to the social problem addressed, the official opinion of government and other non-profit organisations) elements. It is important to note that the messages addressing various issues are also influenced by the characteristics of the social problem being addressed and the strategic approach of the website.

■ The interactive possibilities generated by the websites that were studied were very different in nature. Usually, websites offer a very clear means of connecting with the organisation concerned, providing a physical address, telephone numbers, e-mail connections or standardised feedback forms.

The second most frequent interactive feature found in the study was the existence of virtual communities, connected via bulletin boards or discussion forums. The use intensity of these discussion forums varies a lot, ranging from fewer than 10 messages per month to more than 100 messages per month. The identification of factors that determine and influence the use intensity of discussion forums on social topics is a good subject for future research as the capacity to provide social interaction and a sense of community between distant people is one of the major advantages offered by the Internet.

Another interesting feature of online discussion forums is their rather limited geographical reach. Most of the users are located within a region or nation. Although this is understandable considering the local, regional or national character of the sponsor organisations, it does not take advantage of the international dimension of the Internet network.

The capacity of websites to become personalised was found to be quite low. Some sites offer rudimentary personalisation options, asking the user to select a specific topic of interest. Usually these are the sites that offer connections to multiple and various subjects.

- One of the main purposes of social marketing websites is to educate their users. This function is evident from the large number of reports, social statistics, documents explaining the consequences of undesirable behaviour and the benefits of change, that are available online. The editing of these texts and their specified purposes also demonstrates the strategic approach being taken by online marketing campaigns and the circumstantial adaptations to the problems addressed. In some cases, children are directly targeted by educational messages displayed on social marketing websites and there are attempts to create virtual communities of children (for example, the Children's Traffic Club on Road Safety Scotland's site: www.srsc.org.uk/).

Often, the sites provide lists of links to other similar sites created by international or foreign organisations, enhancing the scale of interconnectedness and adding an international dimension to the social marketing campaigns' educational sources.

- The social marketing websites show a high degree of circumstantial adaptation to the problems addressed. The content is highly relevant and, in most cases, frequently updated. The structure is complex as most sites present a large amount of information. However, the existence of site maps and general contents lists provides a clear picture of information categories and eases the web navigation. The design was frequently found to be both appropriate to the subjects of the websites and the profiles of their main users:
  - the sites targeting younger users (children, teenagers) are colourful, dynamic, direct, surprising, involving
  - the sites targeting older users are sober and structured, the accent being put on increased accessibility and ease of navigation
  - the health-related sites focus mainly on scientific facts, using these as powerful arguments for change, and these are supported by practical advice/procedures for health improvement or maintenance.

■ The capacity of social marketing websites to segment and target the users belonging to different stages of the behaviour change process is not very evident. The sites rely on the capacity of users to segment themselves by choosing from the information available and the topics of main interest. In many cases, the users are supported by mini search engines active within the sites. This strategy can be justified by the great diversity of people accessing the sites and the limitations of personalisation tools available. However, considering the common characteristics of the users at different stages of the behaviour change process, the online marketing sites should implement more active methods to segment them and differentiate their information offerings. This is a necessary premise for increasing the effectiveness of online social campaigns and saving the Internet users' time.

■ Most sites adopt a strategic approach. The information provided addresses both the negative aspects of the undesired behaviour and the possible benefits of behaviour change. In many cases, the barriers to change are identified, explained via reports, FAQs, personalised communications, discussion forums) and practical solutions are provided for their resolution or avoidance (see, for example, Ash's website at: www.ash.org.uk).

A theoretical framework for online social marketing

The theoretical principles of online social marketing derived from the research findings can be considered on two different levels:

■ content
■ function.

This classification corresponds to the specific characteristics of a website that can be defined by the categories of contents hosted and multiple functionalities provided.

At the *content* level, there is a close connection between the message categories, strategic approach and circumstantial adaptation of the website. However, these three dimensions seem to lack a similarly close connection with a segmentation of the different categories of its audience (see Figure 10.22).

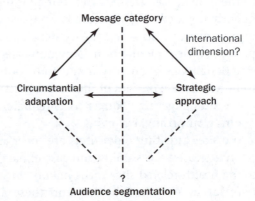

Figure 10.22 **The diamond of dimensions of the content of a social marketing website**

The implementation of a better segmentation approach in the early stages of users accessing the website would provide the basis for better targeting and customisation of online information. For example, a number of alternatives can be designed to target the specific needs of users in the precontemplation, contemplation, decision, action and maintenance stages, and these can be connected to a practical means of characterising each individual user (such as a short online questionnaire). Once the new user has completed the questionnaire, the software can automatically identify his or her needs and connect that person to the most appropriate alternative website.

Most social marketing websites do not adapt their information to accommodate an international perspective. The context of the problems debated, organisations involved and contact numbers given are usually local, regional or national and therefore they lack a true international reach. However, this in part reflects the fact that some social problems may be regionally based. For instance, obesity is becoming an increasing problem in the USA and UK, but may be less of a problem in France and Italy.

At the *functional* level, online social marketing campaign websites need to have the following:

- interactiveness
- education
- flexibility.

Unfortunately, in many cases, the integration of the online campaign with other social marketing operations is vague and indirect – when it exists. Every function should be integrated within a complex network of digital and physical events and processes that enhance the overall effectiveness of the campaign. For example, the education provided on the Web can be connected with open days and seminars organised within local communities, when the representatives of the organisation can meet, discuss and interact with the website's users.

The improvement of these connections at the content and functional levels can significantly enhance the success of social marketing campaigns. In fact, the improvement of these two levels are interrelated as a better segmentation of the website's users helps the integration of the online campaign with the appropriate social marketing events. In this way, specially targeted environments can be designed to address the specific needs of people, in both digital and physical universes. The effectiveness of the campaign will be further enhanced by the application of lifecycle theories of behaviour change and the complex combination of Internet information and social events (see Figure 10.23).

The integration of all these dimensions can also improve the development of an international dimension to an online social marketing campaign. Connections with global institutions and events can increase the scope of the campaign and the reach of its influence. The article reproduced in the following case study illustrates how some social issues do have a global reach.

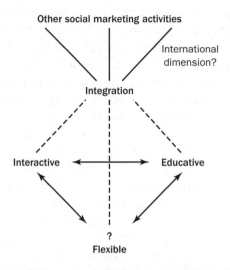

Figure 10.23 The diamond of dimensions of the functions of a social marketing website

CASE STUDY

Diet industry will be winner in battle of the bulge as Europe goes to fat *(by John Carvel)*

A tide of obesity will sweep Europe over the next four years and cause a boom in the diet industry as consumers try to get back into shape, market analysts said yesterday. The most serious weight problems will be seen in Germany where the proportion of people who are overweight or obese will increase from 57 per cent last year to 71 per cent in 2006. Problems of excess weight will affect 69 per cent of adults in Spain and the Netherlands, 60 per cent of Swedes and 59 per cent of Italians. Although Britain and France will have weight problems, they will have more people who are underweight than obese. In Britain the proportion who are overweight or obese will increase from 48 per cent last year to 52 per cent in 2006. In France it will rise from 37 per cent to 50 per cent.

The forecasts were prepared by the market analysts Datamonitor on the basis of trends since 1996. Obesity was measured using a body mass index to measure excess fat. The index divides the person's weight in kilograms by their height in metres squared. A BMI of 20–25 is normal, 25–30 is

overweight and more than 30 is obese. Andrew Russell, the company's consumer market analyst, said the trend to excess weight followed 20 years of convenience foods and unconventional mealtimes. 'Modern diets are more calorific, yet people expend less energy during the day . . . Those who find themselves overweight and those who are keen to avoid being in that position are increasingly interested in using both exercise and diet to manage their shape,' he said.

The diet food and drinks market would increase from £51bn in 1996 to £61bn in 2006. The underweight were the least likely to take exercise, but people of normal weight were 'a good market segment as they display a strong desire to manage their shape and more willpower to apply the necessary changes to their lifestyle,' he said.

The overweight were the second most profitable group. They would continually try to make small changes to their lifestyle and diet without ever removing the underlying need to do so. This made them 'potentially lifelong customers'. 'While both the normal weight and overweight consumer can oscillate between a desire for health and a desire for indulgence, the overweight consumer will do so with greater frequency – possibly even between lunchtime and dinner.' Mr Russell said people abstaining from alcohol because they were concerned about their weight or shape would cost the European drinks industry £3.2bn by 2006.

Children are 'eating themselves sick' with poor diets and unhealthy lifestyles, nutritionists warned

yesterday during a conference at the Royal College of Paediatrics and Child Health in London. They suggested that postwar rationing was better for children than the twenty-first century snack culture. Youngsters today were experiencing the nutritional equivalent of the Victorian age when rickets and scurvy were commonplace.

Source: John Carvel, *The Guardian*, 31 May 2002. Copyright Guardian News & Media Ltd 2002.

Allied to the interest in social marketing, in the twenty-first century rural marketing is also likely to play an important role, developing rural markets for the benefit of rural communities. A major proportion of the world lives in rural areas, but, with the advent of satellites, both mobile communications and television, it is now possible to market goods and services to rural locations. At the same time, it is possible for individuals within rural communities to market their own products and services more easily than ever before.

Rural marketing

As populations increase around the globe, more consumers will be entering the marketplace. A large proportion of these individuals will be living in isolated rural locations throughout the world. This market is generally regarded as being invisible and not very profitable according to traditional marketing views (Mahajan et al. 2000). However, the rural markets in countries such as India and China are huge and, as Table 10.9 shows, they are set to become even greater by 2025 as roughly 70 per cent of the population will then be rural.

These hitherto invisible markets are becoming increasingly significant to both small and large companies. In spite of very low per capita income in large swathes of rural Asia, South America and Africa, the large numbers represent growing

Table 10. 9 Population breakdown by continent/region, in millions

Continent	1999	2025
Asia	3588	4725
Africa	778	1454
Europe	729	701
USA and Canada	304	369
Australasia, South Pacific	29	41
Latin America, Caribbean	449	690

Source: Data obtained from the United Nations Population Division, http://esa.un.org/unpp/

buying power, especially when families or groups of people team together to purchase large items such as televisions or computers. At the same time, many individuals from rural locations may have also successfully emigrated to cities and other countries, looking for work. These individuals often bring new ideas and new consumption patterns back to their original rural locations. As the world shrinks further, in terms of communications, more and more products can be sold universally. At the same time, films set in rural China or Bollywood films set in India are important catalysts for change.

Many multinationals are thus beginning to see that the major growth area for consumption lies within the rural regions of the main continents. They are therefore developing different and more localised branding strategies for their products. In creating such strategies, it is useful to consider different approaches to marketing.

Develop products that meet market needs

Many rural markets need products that improve their efficiency. For instance, simple vehicles or scooters may be more appropriate in rural locations than cars and so on as they can help to speed up the transport of goods or services. Equally, a rotovator may work more effectively than a tractor.

Understand the informal economy

Many rural transactions are undertaken informally and do not register on many countries' GDPs. This method of making transactions and the amounts involved need to be understood by marketers attempting to sell to rural markets. For instance, economist Friedrich Schneider estimates that the 'shadow', or informal, economy may account for one-seventh of the output of the world's wealthiest nations and a much higher proportion of that of developing nations. According to these estimates, the shadow economy has been growing three times as fast as the formal economy since the 1960s. In India, in 1998, only 12,000 of the nation's roughly 900 million citizens admitted to earning an income of more than $28,000 per year and only 1 in 77 people filed a tax return at all. Others estimate that India's unofficial economy may be as large as its national income (Mahajan et al. 2000).

Understand the role of second-generation émigrés to countries in Europe, the USA, Canada and Japan

In many countries in the world there are large proportions of émigrés from the major rural economies of the world. Figure 10.24 and Table 10.10 shows the differing population mixes in some of the major economies of the world. It does not give a breakdown by country of origin.

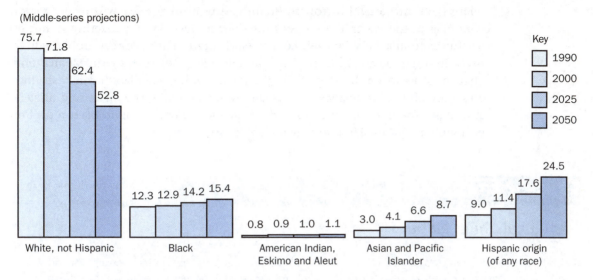

Figure 10.24 Percentages of the population of the USA by race and Hispanic origin

Source: US Bureau of the Census 1997, www.census.gov/prod/3/98pubs/p23-194.pdf

Table 10.10 Population of the UK, France and Germany by ethnic group

UK	Population (July 2000 estimate)		59,778,000
	Ethnic groups %	English	81.5
		Scottish	9.6
		Irish	2.4
		Welsh	1.9
		Ulster	1.8
		West Indian, Indian, Pakistani and other	2.8
France	*Population (July 2000 estimate)*		*59,766,000*
	Ethnic groups	Celtic and Latin with Teutonic, Slavic, North African, Indochinese, Basque minorities	
Germany	*Population (July 2000 estimate)*		*83,251,000*
	Ethnic groups %	German	91.5
		Turkish	2.4
		Other, made up largely of Serbo-Croation, Italian Russian, Greek, Polish, Spanish	6.1

Source: Based on Central Intelligence Agency figures, 2002

This data indicates the growing significance of other races within the major economies of the West. It also opens the door to developing marketing strategies for ethnic populations for their countries of origin. For instance, individuals of Hispanic origin in the USA are very likely to have close links with Mexico and other countries in South America. Similarly, the Chinese population will have close links with China. Companies such as Unilever, featured in the case study, already understand the importance of rural markets and are beginning to blaze a trail in the adoption of these kinds of new marketing strategies.

CASE STUDY

Act local, think global

Hindustan Lever's strategic and marketing innovations have the potential to transform its business in India and to improve the quality of life of the country's rural citizens. Now the company is exporting those ideas to other parts of the world – from Indonesia to the Congo.

'Necessity is the mother invention.' That may be the most basic lesson behind Hindustan Lever's remarkable track record of innovation in rural India. When a giant company with a 30-year track record of growth suddenly confronts flat sales, it has two choices: cut costs to stay profitable or work harder to discover new ways to grow. The leaders at Hindustan Lever have opted for the second choice – and have identified India's hundreds of millions of rural consumers as a high-priority market. That's why every management trainee at Hindustan Lever begins his or her career by spending six to eight weeks in a rural village, eating, sleeping, and talking with the locals. Marketing executives make frequent two-day visits to low-income and rural areas. Managers at every level are trained in techniques for talking and listening to consumers. And scientists apply time and energy figuring out how to do more with less.

'We need to apply top-class science to solve simple problems at a reduced cost for the consumer,' says Dr V.M. Naik, Deputy head of Hindustan Lever's Research Laboratory in Bangalore, India. Naik, who spends about 70 per cent of his time in the lab, was the primary scientist behind recent mass-market products, such as low-cost ice-creams and low-cost soaps. The success of the soap process and others – like Hindustan Lever's marketing campaigns – started

with a fundamental insight into consumers. Both researchers and marketers recognised that Indian women who wash clothes at a public tap or river often use the same laundry soap to wash their body. But the laundry soaps were typically too harsh for both skin and water. So researchers developed a lightweight laundry soap to double as a personal soap. Behind the product-concept innovation are manufacturing innovations. Lever labs and pilot plants are replete with manufacturing machines that its scientists built themselves – either because existing machines cost too much or because the technology didn't exist to make products in the cost-efficient way that Hindustan Lever had designed. The new laundry soap, for example, uses a simple process to cast the soap immediately in the shape of a plastic package. The manufacturing process is an energy saver, too, because it doesn't convert the soap as many times – from liquid to tablet to bar – as other soap-making processes do. Lever built a machine for less, saved energy costs, and plans to pass on the savings to consumers.

Because Naik identified a different consumer need, he was able to develop a different process to meet that need. 'Technology that once liberated consumers can be a constraint for new innovation,' says Naik. 'New products require new principles.' His new principle: reduce the load on the environment. That means using less detergent and fewer hydrogenated oils. The result? The company uses less than half of the current agricultural land usually required to raise oil seeds to produce soap. And fewer active ingredients mean less harm to the water supply. What's next on the innovation agenda, both for Hindustan Lever and its global parent, Unilever? To export the ideas and techniques that are unleashing growth in rural India to other parts of the world with similar strategic hurdles: language barriers, limited water and electricity, political instability, financial upheaval, barely motorable roads. Here are some examples of Lever's ongoing strategic ingenuity from around the world.

Nice product, but can you get it to market?

In the Philippines, a country composed of more than 7000 islands, physical distribution can get expensive – when it's possible at all. And Unilever faces an additional market hurdle in that country, a former US colony: a historical preference for buying American (read: Procter & Gamble). Unilever's response? Change the game. To lower the overhead cost of Surf laundry detergent, compared to P&G's Tide, sachets of Surf were distributed in jute rice sacks. The sacks were cheaper than cardboard and were more flexible for storage, and they kept the product dry. The company's local affiliate then focused on bicycle brigades as an inexpensive method of distribution. It designed a bicycle that could carry the heavy load of the bags and still be lightweight enough for someone to pedal to remote areas.

In tumultuous times, focus on fundamentals

The Congo is not anyone's idea of a stable, comfortable place to do business. But even in the midst of political upheaval in the Congo, 'people still need to wash their clothes and eat staple foods,' says John Miller, Senior Vice-president for Home and Personal Care for Unilever South Africa. Of course, people may eat only once every two days instead of every day, and they may well use detergent bars for both their clothes and their dishes. So instead of trying to move consumers into new or higher-margin products, Miller and his colleagues in the Congo focused on the fundamentals with radio ads that featured pitches for the most basic elements in Unilever's product line.

Want profits? Sell lots of small things

Nihal Kaviratne, the Chairman of Unilever Indonesia who cut his teeth in India with Hindustan Lever, wasn't shocked to find that 63 per cent of Indonesia's 204 million people live in rural areas. So he borrowed from the company's prior success with sachets. 'Our whole business is built on low-dose sizes,' he says. But how could the company keep the sachets profitable? Although it's expensive to produce so many small units, the sachet material used in Indonesia is less expensive than elsewhere. That means Indonesia gets the same profit margin on a plastic 6-millilitre sachet of shampoo as it does from a 50-millilitre bottle.

Source: Rekha Balu, 'act local, think global', *Fast Company*, June 2001 (available at: www.fastcompany.com/articles/2001/05/lever_sidebar.html)

Companies such as Coca-Cola are also embracing rural markets with verve by developing and selling smaller-sized bottles (Kripalani 2002). Apart from consumer goods, services such as mobile phones and insurance are growing, too. Mobile phone operators such as Escotel Mobile Communications Ltd, a joint venture between Hong Kong investment firm First Pacific and New Delhi-based Escorts Ltd, are finding new customers all over rural India. Fishermen in coastal Kerala, in the south, use the phone service to find the best prices for their catch – a practice that can earn them up to 50 per cent more. Escotel now controls 14 per cent of India's non-metro mobile market, providing services to 500,000 subscribers in 3240 towns and villages. This enables local producers to market goods locally, adding to the growth of rural economies.

In the twenty-first century, rural marketing is going to play an important role in the development of the world's poor communities. However, marketers will be walking a thin line between meeting real local marketing needs and the marketing needs of large multinationals wishing to expand their market base. The

Alternatives Committe of the International Forum on Globalization (2007) underlines the position quite clearly:

> it bears repeating that roughly half of the world's people still live directly on the land, grow-
> ing their own staple foods, feeding families and communities. They are indigenous seed
> varieties developed over centuries. They have protected their own organic fertilisers, crop
> rotation and natural pesticide management. Their communities have traditionally shared all
> elements of the local commons, including water, labour and seeds. They have been exem-
> plary in preserving the biodiversity necessary for community survival, and have fed the local
> communities for centuries. But they are all under assault from the corporate industrial agri-
> cultural system.

In this respect, companies such as Hindustan Lever have tried to work to benefit both
the communities and corporate profits by collaborating closely with rural self- help
groups (SHGs). With the help of their Project Shakti, the SHGs have the option of distributing the firm's relevant products as a sustainable, income-generating activity.
The model hinges on a win–win relationship, with the SHGs engaging in an activity
that brings sustainable income, while Hindustan Lever gets an interface by means of
which it can interact with its customers (Kaul and Lobo 2002).

An alternative to this is the marketing model developed by Vandana Shiva (Mehta
2002). She has formed an organisation called Navdanya (Nine Seeds), based in Delhi.
This organisation encourages farmers to produce hardy, native varieties of crops that
can be grown organically without the help of fertilisers and chemicals. The produce
is then marketed via the farmers' own network. In this manner, local needs are met
and the marketing of the produce takes place via the network. In the end, the consumers benefit from a greater variety of locally produced goods than was available
previously. This initiative reflects one solution to the continuing battle between the
globalisation and the localisation of products and services in marketing.

Towards a new strategic marketing model

As explained in Chapter 1, there is a range of marketing models that can be
adopted by companies. In the course of reading this book, you will have come to
understand some of the key drivers of marketing in the twenty-first century.
Bringing all of these together, we now propose a new marketing model, taking
account of the new realities (see Figure 10.25).

This model takes into account the various points discussed in the preceding
chapters. It includes each of the aspects presented in the book that need to be considered before developing company-specific strategies. The key issues to think
about, as discussed in the various chapters, are the following.

■ Understanding the role of strategic planning in delivering the marketing concept and the need to adopt a wider view of marketing strategy, as discussed in
  Chapter 1. Companies also need to consider all the various stakeholders and the
  key issues when developing mission statements.

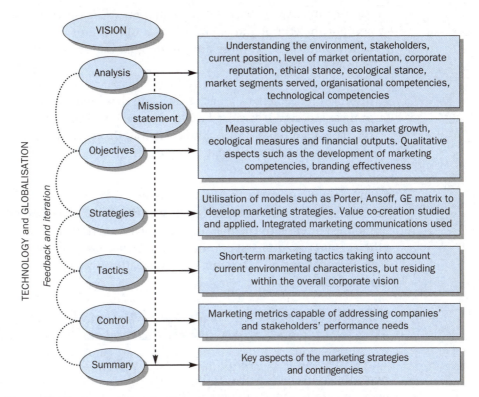

Figure 10.25 **Strategic marketing model for the twenty-first century**

- No strategies can be developed without a strategic analysis of a company's current position. In this respect, Chapters 2 and 5 contain important elements that need to be taken into account – Chapter 2 gives a comprehensive account of analytical techniques and Chapter 5 discusses the importance of brands and advertising strategies.
- In developing the overall strategy, a company needs to understand the nature of its stakeholders and its own approach towards them. Ethical and environmental issues must also be taken into account. These matters are discussed in Chapters 3 and 4.
- Communicating products and services relies on integrating branding messages and this is covered in Chapter 5.
- The values and the learning abilities of organisations determine their ability to deliver customer-orientated strategies. In the twenty-first century, competitive ability is often determined by the speed at which organisations can learn and implement strategies. Many of these aspects are developed in detail in Chapters 6 and 7.
- Globalisation is now part and parcel of many companies' strategies and this has to be understood and nurtured, as discussed in Chapter 8.
- For most companies, strategic success depends very much on the ability to measure performance in many different directions. As there are differences from company to company, it is important that these measures are tailor-made for

each company, as discussed in Chapter 9. Measures should also take into account the ethical and environmental dimensions of marketing, linking back to Chapters 3 and 4. More and more organisations are urged to use the triple bottom line approach.

■ As technology changes and evolves, all marketers need to be able to make informed judgements about the new and developing areas in marketing. Many of these aspects are discussed under the heading 'Digital marketing' in this chapter. This chapter has also looked in depth at value co-creation and social marketing – something that many organisations are now having to integrate into their marketing plans.

Each of these aspects is covered in the boxes as shown in the model in Figure 10.25. It is not entirely prescriptive, as different companies will have different emphases in terms of the markets they serve and target. It also incorporates the ethical and ecological stances that ought to become important aspects of a company's reputation and marketing communications strategy.

Summary and final observations

This chapter and the preceding ones lay the groundwork for understanding how marketing is likely to evolve as the twenty-first century moves forward. The general environment is undergoing many changes and marketing strategies need to reflect the evolution in competition and consumption patterns that is taking place around the world. Technology is playing a crucial role in bringing markets closer (via the Internet), while mobile communications are making it easier for distant communities and individuals to communicate easily. Transparency in managing companies means that a greater emphasis needs to be placed on corporate governance and the role of stakeholders. Organisations need to become increasingly concerned about the fragility of the planet and its eco-systems by developing products and services that minimise pollution and conserve energy. At the same time, the profiles of consumers are changing. In the richer nations, consumers are becoming more sophisticated and also concerned about global issues; in poorer countries, consumers still have to be reached, but their marketing needs are now evolving rapidly, as illustrated in this chapter. Companies also have to consider how they develop relationships with their consumers and how they organise themselves effectively internally. In marketing terms, companies should not be judged by their returns on investment alone but also by a wide range of measures, including their ecological performance.

The old models of marketing need to be revisited and adapted to meet the needs of this century. Marketers today need to work with the fact that pushing consumption is only one aspect of marketing and meeting social and ecological needs is becoming more important as resources dwindle. New products and services with new localised marketing strategies are likely to benefit consumers more than global standardisation.

The era of responsible, customer-orientated marketing is dawning and marketers need to embrace this with vigour. Marketers now have a range of tools that are available to them as a result of the technological advances that have taken place. There is also a great concern that consumers have about the degradation of the environment and ethical stances taken by companies. NGOs and consumers themselves are increasingly voicing these concerns openly. In order to enable you to work within this new order and truly become customer-orientated, this book has shown the wider context in which marketing operates today and the ways in which a customer orientation can be implemented.

References and further reading

Chapter 1

Abell, D. F. (1978) 'Strategic windows', *Journal of Marketing*. 42(3), 21–27.

Ackoff, R. L. (1981) *Creating the Corporate Future*. London: Wiley.

American Marketing Association (1985) 'The definition of marketing', *Marketing News*. 1 March, 2.

American Marketing Association (2005) 'AMA adopts new definition of marketing'. www.marketingpower.com/content24159.php

Andreasen, A. R. and Drumwright, M. E. (2001) 'Alliances and ethics in social marketing', in Andreasen, A. R. (ed.), *Ethics in Social Marketing*. Washington, DC: Georgetown University Press.

Barney, J. B. (1996) *Gaining and sustaining competitive advantage*. Reading, MA: Addison-Wesley.

Bart, C. and Baetz, M. (1998) 'The relationship between mission statements and firm performance: an exploratory study', *Journal of Management Studies*. 35(6), 823–52.

Boeker, W. (1989) 'Strategic change: the effects of founding and history', *Academy of Management Journal*. 32(3), 489–515.

Boulding, W. and Christen, M. (2003) 'Sustainable pioneering advantage? Profit implications of market entry order', *Marketing Science*. 22(3), 371–92.

Carrillat, F. A., Jaramillo, F. and Locander, W. B. (2004) 'Market-driving organizations: a framework', *Academy of Marketing Science Review*. 5, 1–14.

Cova, B. (1996) 'What postmodernism means to marketing managers', *European Management Journal*. 14(5), 494–9.

Cronin, M. J. (1996) *Global Advantage on the Internet*. New York: Van Nostrand Reinhold.

David, F. R. and David, F. R. (2003) 'It's time to redraft your mission statement', *Journal of Business Strategy*. 24(1), 11–16.

Davis, D., Morris, M. and Allen, J. (1991) 'Perceived environmental turbulence and its effects on selected entrepreneurship and organisational characteristics in industrial firms', *Journal of Academy of Marketing Science*. 19, 43–91.

Deng, S. and Dart, J. (1994) 'Measuring market orientation: a multi-factor, multi-item approach', *Journal of Marketing Management*, 10, 725–42.

Dibrell, C., Davis, S. P. and Danskin, P. (2005) 'The influence of internationalization on time-based competition', *Management International Review*. 45(2), 173–95.

Fields, G. (2006) 'Innovation, time and territory: space and the business organization of Dell Computer', *Economic Geography*. 82(2), 119–47.

Grant, R. M. (2002) *Contemporary Strategy Analysis: Concepts, techniques, applications* (4th edition). Malden, MA: Blackwell.

Hamel, G. and Prahalad, C. K. (1989) 'Strategic intent', *Harvard Business Review*. 67(3), 63–77.

Hamel, G. and Prahalad, C. K. (1994) *Competing for the Future*. Cambridge, MA: Harvard University Press.

Hannan, M. T. and Freeman, J. (1984) 'Structural inertia and organizational change', *American Sociological Review*, 49, 149–64.

Jaworski, B. J. and Kohli, A. K. (1993) 'Market orientation: antecedents and consequences', *Journal of Marketing*. 57 (July) 53–70.

Jaworski, B. J., Kohli, A. K. and Sahay, A. (2000) 'Market-driven versus driving markets', *Journal of the Academy of Marketing Science*. 28, 45–54.

Johnson, G. and Scholes, K. (2000) *Exploring Corporate Strategy* (5th edition). London: Prentice Hall.

Johnston, L. L., Lee R. P.-W., Sani A. and Grohmann, B. (2003) 'Market-focused strategic flexibility: conceptual advances and an integrative model', *Journal of the Academy of Marketing Science*. 31(1), 74–89.

Kaufman-Scarborough, C. and Lindquist, J. D. (1999), 'Time management and polychronicity: comparisons, contrasts, and Insights for the workplace', *Journal of Managerial Psychology*. Special issue on polychronicity. 14(3/4), 288–312.

Kohli, A. K. and Jaworski, B. J. (1990) 'Marketing orientation: the construct, research and managerial implication', *Journal of Marketing*. 54 (April), 1–18.

Kotler, P. (1996) *Leading Change*. Boston, MA: Harvard Business School Press.

Kotler, P. (1997) *Marketing Management: Analysis, planning, implementation, and control* (9th edition). Englewood Cliffs, NJ: Prentice Hall.

Kotler, P. (2000) *Marketing Management* (10th edition). Englewood Cliffs, NJ: Prentice Hall.

Kumar, N., Scheer, L. and Kotler, P. (2000) 'From market-driven to market driving', *European Management Journal*. 18(2), 129–42.

Levitt, T. (1960) 'Marketing myopia', *Harvard Business Review*. 38(4), 45–56.

Lindstrom, M. (2006) 'Reinvention', *AME Info* (available at: www.ameinfo.com/65664.html).

McDonald, M. H. B. (1993) *'Strategic marketing planning'*. London: Kogan Page.

Mintzberg, H. (1987) 'The strategic concept 1: five Ps for strategy', *California Management Review*. 30 (fall), 11–24.

Mintzberg, H. (1994). *The Rise and Fall of Strategic Planning*. New York: Free Press.

Narver, J. C. and Slater, S. N. (1990) 'The effect of market orientation on business profitability', *Journal of Marketing*. Oct, 20–35.

Oliver, R. L. and Swan, J. E. (1989) 'Equity and disconfirmation perceptions as influences on merchant and product satisfaction', *Journal of Consumer Research*. 16, 372–83.

Patron, M. (1996) 'The future of marketing databases', *Journal of Database Marketing*. 4(1), 6–10.

Pearce, J. and David, F. (1987) 'Corporate mission statements: the bottom line', *Academy of Management Executive*. 1(2), 109–14.

Porter, M. E. (1985) *Competitive Advantage*. New York: Free Press.

Power, C. Driscoll, L. and Bomn, E. (1992) 'Smart selling', *Business Week*. 3 (August), 46–8.

Ranchhod, A. and Hackney, R. A. (1997) *Marketing through Information Technology: From potential to virtual reality* (vol. 1). Helensburgh, Argyl: Academy of Marketing.

Reichheld, F. and Sasser, W. (1990) 'Zero defections comes to services', *Harvard Business Review*. September/October, 105–11.

Ruekert, R. W. (1992) Developing a market orientation: an organisational strategy perspective, *International Journal of Marketing*. 9, 225–45.

Schein, E. H. (1983) *Organisational Culture and Leadership: A dynamic view*. San Francisco, CA: Jossey Bass.

Schein, E. H. (1992) 'Organisational culture', *American Psychologist*. 45, 109–19.

Stinchcombe, A. L. (1965) 'Social structure and organizations', in March, J. G. (ed.), *Handbook of Organizations*. Chicago, IL: Rand McNally. 153–93.

Szymanski, D. M., Troy, L. C. and Bharadwaj, S. G. (1995) 'Order of entry and business performance: an empirical dynthesis and re-examination', *Journal of Marketing*. 59(4), 17–34.

Tanner, J. F. (1996) 'Re-engineering using the theory of constraints', *Industrial Marketing Management*. 25(4), 311–20.

Tedlow. R. (1993) 'The fourth phase of marketing', in Tedlow, R. S. amd Jones, G. (eds) *The Rise and Fall of Marketing*. London: Routledge.

Tellis, G. J. and Golder, P. N. (1996) 'First to market, first to fail?, Real causes of enduring market leadership', *Sloan Management Review*. 37(2), 65–76.

Webster, F. E. (1997) 'The future role of marketing in the organisation', in Lehmann, D. R. and Jocz, K. E. (eds), *Reflections on the Future of Marketing*. Cambridge, MA: Marketing Science Institute.

Wilkie, W. (1990) *Consumer Behaviour* (2nd edition). New York: John Wiley.

Yasumuro, K. (1993) 'Conceptualising an adaptable marketing system', in Tedlow, R. S. and Jones, G. (eds), *The Rise and Fall of Marketing*. London: Routledge.

Yeung, S. and Campbell, A. (1991) 'Creating a sense of mission', *Long Range Planging*. 24(4), 10–20.

Chapter 2

Abell, D. F. and Hammond, J. S. (1979) *Strategic Market Planning: Problems and analytical approaches*. Englewood Cliffs, NJ, and London: Prentice Hall.

Armstrong, A. and Hagel, J. (1996) 'The real value of online communities', *Harvard Business Review*. 74(3), 134–41.

Andreasen, A. R. (1984) 'Life status change and changes in consumer preferences and satisfaction', *Journal of Consumer Research*. 2 (December), 784–94.

Cahill, D. J. (1997) *How Consumers Pick a Hotel: Strategic segmentation and target marketing*. Binghampton, New York: Haworth Press.

Clegg, S. R. (1991) Modern Organisations: *Organisation studies in the post modern world*. London: Sage.

Coffey, J. J. and Palm, G. (1999) 'Fixing it in the measurement mix', *Bank Marketing*. 31(6), 24–9.

Cova, B. (1996) 'What postmodernism means to marketing managers?' *European Management Journal*. 14(5), 494–9.

Day, S. G. (1986) 'The evolving role of strategy analysis methods', in King, W. R. and Cleland, D. I. (eds), *Strategic Planning and Management Handbook*. New York: Van Nostrand-Reinhold.

Day, S. G. (1990) *Market Driven Strategy*. New York: Free Press.

Firat, A. F. and Schultz II, C. J. (1997) 'From segmentation to fragmentation', *European Journal of Marketing*. 31(3/4), 183–207.

Frank, R. E., Massy, W. F. and Wind, Y. (1972) Market Segmentation. Englewood Cliffs, NJ: Prentice Hall.

Grant, R. M. (2002) *Contemporary Strategy Analysis: Concepts, techniques, applications* (4nd edition). Malden, MA: Blackwell.

Gunter, B. and Furnham, A. (1992) *Consumer Profiles: An introduction to psychographics*. London: International Thomson Business Press.

Gurău, C. and Ranchhod, A. (2002), 'How to calculate the vale of a customer', *Journal of Targeting, Measurement and Analysis for Marketing*. 10(3), 20–220.

Gurău, C. and Ranchhod, A. (2002) 'Measuring customer satisfaction: a platform for calculating, predicting and increasing customer profitability', *Journal of Targeting, Measurement and Analysis for Marketing*. 10(3), 203–19.

Hawkins, Del I., Best, Roger J. and Coney, Kenneth A. (2004) *Consumer Behavior* (9th edition). Boston, MA: McGraw-Hill Irwin.

Hax, A. C. and Majluf, N. S. (1984) *Strategic Management: an integrative perspective*. Englewood Cliffs, NJ: Prentice Hall.

Hof, D. R., Browder, S. and Elstrom, P. (1997) 'Internet communities', *Business Week*. 5 May, 38–45.

Hughes, G. D. (1981) *Marketing Management: A planning approach*, Reading, MA: Addison-Wesley.

Kerin, R.A., Mahajan, V. and Varadarajan, P. R. (1990) *Contemporary Perspectives on Strategic Market Planning*. Boston, MA: Allyn and Bacon.

Kotler, P. (1988) *Marketing Management: Analysis, planning, implementation and control* (6th edition). Englewood Cliffs, NJ: Prentice Hall.

Kotler, P., Armstrong, G. Saunders, J. and Wong, V. (2001) *Principles of Marketing* (3rd European edition). Harlow: Prentice Hall.

Lunn, A. (1982) 'Some basic principles and recent development', Seminar on Classifying Consumers: A need to rethink. Brugge, Belgium: ESOMAR.

Meuller-Heumann, G. (1992) 'Market and technology shifts in the 1990s: Market fragmentation and mass customisation', *Journal of Marketing Management*. 8, 303–14.

Palmer, R. and Lucas, M. (1994) 'Formulating retail strategy', in McGoldrick, P. J. and Greenland, S. J. (eds), *The Retailing of Financial Services*. London: McGraw-Hill.

Porter, M. (1985) *Competitive Advantage*. New York: The Free Press.

Robinson, S. J. Q., Hitchen, R. E. and Wade, D. P. (1978) 'The directional policy matrix: tools for strategic planning', *Long Range Planning*. 11, 8–15.

Rogers, E.M. (1995) *Diffusion of Innovations* (4th edition). New York: Free Press.

Rowe, A.J., Mason, R.O. and Dickel, K.E. (1986) *Strategic Management*. Reading, MA: Addison Wesley.

Usunier, J.-C. (1999) *Marketing Across Cultures*. London: Prentice Hall.

Van Raaij, W. F. (1982) 'Consumer classification based on behavioural measures', Seminar on Classifying Consumers: A need to rethink. Brugge, Belgium: ESOMAR.

Vargo, S. L., and Lusch, R. F. (2004) 'Evolving a services dominant logic', *Journal of Marketing*. 68, 1–17.

Venkatesh, A., Sherry Jr, J. F. and Firat, A. F. (1993) 'Postmodernism and the marketing imaginary', *International Journal of Research in Marketing*. 10, 215–23.

Weiss, M. J. (1994) *Latitudes and Attitudes: An atlas of American tastes, trends, politics and passions from Abilene, Texas, to Zanesville, Ohio*. Boston, MA: Little Brown and Company.

Wells, W. D. (1975) 'Psychographics: a critical review', *Journal of Marketing Research*. 12 (May), 196–213.

Wells, W. and Gubar, G. (1966) 'Life cycle concept in marketing research', *Journal of Marketing Research*. 3, November, 355–63.

Wensley, R. (1981) 'Strategic marketing: betas, boxes, or basics', *Journal of Marketing*. 45 (summer), 173–82.

Wind Y., Mahajan V. and Gunther R. E. (2001) *Convergence Marketing*. London: Financial Times Prentice Hall.

Wilkie, W. L. and Cohen, J. B. (1976) 'An overview of market segmentation: behavioural concepts and research approaches', *Marketing Science Report*. Cambridge, MA. 77–105.

Ziff, R. (1971) 'Psychographics for market segmentation', *Journal of Advertising Research*. 11(2), 3–9.

Chapter 3

Bailey, D. and Clancey, J. (1997) 'Stakeholder capitalism via socialism', *Renewal*. 5(2), 49–60.

Bannerjee, H. (2000) *The Dark Side of the Nation: Essays on multiculturism, nationalism and gender*. Toronto: Canadian Scholaris Press.

Berman, S. L., Wicks, A. C., Kotha, S. and Jones, T. M. (1999) 'Does stakeholder orientation matter? The relationship between stakeholder management models and firm financial performance', *Academy of Management Journal*. 42, 488–506.

Bower, J. (1970) *Managing the Resource Allocation Process*. Homewood, IL: Irwin.

Burgelman, R. A. (1983) 'Corporate entrepreneurship and strategic management: insights from a process Study', *Management Science*. 29(12), 1349–64.

Burgelman, R. A. (1991) 'Intraorganisational ecology of strategy making and organisational adaptation: theory and field research', *Organisational Science*. 2, 239–62.

Clarkson, M. B. E. (1995) 'A stakeholder framework for analyzing and evaluating corporate social performance', *Academy of Management Review*. 20(1), 92–117.

Conti, T. (2004) 'Making stakeholders a strategic asset', *Quality Progress*. 37(2), 53–9.

Donaldson, T. and Preston, L. E. (1995) 'The stakeholder theory of the corporation: concepts, evidence and implications', *Academy of Management Review*. 20(1), 65–91.

Doyle, P. (2000) *Value-based Marketing: Marketing strategies for corporate growth and shareholder value*. Chichester: Wiley.

Dyer, J. H. and Singh, H. (1998) 'The rational view: cooperative strategy and sources of interorganisational competitive advantage', *Academy of Management Review*. 23(4), 660–80.

Fama, E. F. and Jensen, M. C. (1983) 'Separation of ownership and control', *Journal of Law and Economics*. 26(2), 301–25.

Freeman, E. (1984) *Strategic Management: A stakeholder approach*. London: Pitman.

Friedman, M. (170) 'The social responsibility of business is to increase its profits', *New York Times Magazine*. 13 September.

Frooman, J. (1999) 'Stakeholder influence strategies', *Academy of Management Review*. 24, 191–205.

Greenley, E. G. and Foxall, G. R. (1997) 'Multiple stakeholder orientation in UK companies and the implications for company performance', *Journal of Management Studies*. 34(2), 259–84.

Groenewegen, J. (2000) 'European integration and changing corporate governance structures: the case of France', *Journal of Economic Issues*. 34(2), 471–9.

Hamel, G. (2000) *Leading the Revolution*. Boston, MA: Harvard Business School Press.

Hutton, W. (1996) 'The 30/30/40 society: the economic and fiscal implications', Third Cantor Lecture on the Future of Work, *RSA Journal*. March, 32–6.

Jawahar, I. M. and McLaughlin, G. L. (2001) 'Toward a descriptive stakeholder theory: an organisational life cycle approach', *Academy of Management*. 26(3), 397–414.

Jones, T. M. (1995) 'Instrumental stakeholder theory: a synthesis of ethics and economics', *Academy of Management Review*. 20(2), 404–37.

Jones, T. M. and Wicks, A. C. (1999) 'Convergent stakeholder theory', *Academy of Management Review*. 24, 206–21.

Jonker, J. and Foster, D. (2002) 'Stakeholder excellence? Framing the evolution and complexity of a stakeholder perspective of the firm', *Corporate Social Responsibility and Environmental Management*. 9(4), 187–95, John Wiley & Sons Limited.

Kelly, P. (1997) 'From blueprint to reality: the quest for resources', in Birley, S. and Muzyka, D. F. (eds), *Mastering Enterprise*. London: Pitman. 72–5.

Kirchgaessner, S. (2006) 'US lobby groups aim to weaken CFius bill further', *Financial Times*. 31 March.

Krantz, M. (1999) 'Online workers' windfall could flatten investors', *USA Today*. 26 October.

Kreiner, P. and Bhambri, A. (1991) 'Influence and information in organisation–stakeholder relationships', in Preston, L.E. (ed.), *Research in Corporate Social Performance and Policy* (Vol. 12). Greenwich, CT: JAI Press. 3–36.

Lannoo, K. (1995) 'Corporate governance in Europe', Centre for European Policy Studies, Working Party Report No. 14.

MacDougall, A. (1995) 'Tomorrow's company? Feedback', *Renewal*. 3(2).

Miller, R. L and Lewis, W. F. (1991) 'A stakeholder approach to marketing management using the value exchange models', *European Journal of Marketing*. 25(8), 55–68.

Milner, M. (2006) 'Arcelor green light for Mittal merger', *The Guardian*. 26 June.

Mitchell, R. K., Agle, B. R. and Wood, D. J. (1997) 'Toward a theory of stakeholder identification and salience: defining the principles of who and what really counts', *Academy of Management Review*. 22, 853–86.

O'Neal, D. and Thomas, H. (1995) 'Director networks/director selection: the board's strategic role', *European Management Journal*. March, 79–90.

O'Neal, D. and Thomas, H. (1996) 'Developing the strategic board', *Long Range Planning: International Journal of Strategic Management*. 29(3), 314–27.

Pettigrew, A. M. and McNulty, T. (1995) 'Power and influence in and around the boardroom', *Human Relations*. 48(8), 845–73.

Pfeffer, J. (1972) 'The size and composition of corporate boards of directors: The organisation and its environment', *Administrative Science Quarterly*. 17, 218–28.

Pfeffer, J. and Salancik, G. R. (1978) *The External Control of Organisations: A resource dependence view*. New York: Harper & Row.

Porter, M. E. (1985) *Competitive Advantage*. New York: Free Press.

Posner, R. (1995) *Overcoming Law*. Cambridge: Cambridge University Press.

Preston, L. E. and Donaldson, T. (1999) 'Stakeholder management and organisational wealth', *Academy of Management Review*. 24(4), 619.

Ranchhod, A. and Gurău, C. (1999) 'Looking good: public relations strategies for biotechnology', *Nature Biotechnology*. Summer Supplement (Europroduct Focus). 5–7.

Ranchhod, A. and Park, P. 'Market positioning and corporate social responsibility', *International Journal of Business Governance and Corporate Social Responsibility*. 1(2–3), 175–91.

Rowley, T. (1997) 'Moving beyond dyadic ties: a network theory of stakeholder influences', *Academy of Management review*. 22(4), 887–910.

Rust, R. T., Zeithaml, V. A. and Lemon, K. N. (2000) *Driving Customer Equity: How customer lifetime value is reshaping corporate strategy*. NY: Free Press.

Simpson, P. (1998) 'County open air "genetic testing site"', *The Daily Echo* (Southampton). 14 April, 9.

Steger, U. (1998) 'A mental map of managers: an empirical investigation into managers' perceptions of stakeholder issues', *Business & the Contemporary World*. 10(4), 579–609.

Stiles, P. (2001) 'The impact of the board on strategy: an empirical examination', *Journal of Management Studies*. 38(5), 627–50.

Watkins, D. (1997) 'Criteria for board construction in the entrepreneurial firm'. Paper presented to RENT XI Conference – Research in Entrepreneurship and Small Business, Mannheim. 26–29 November.

Weise, E. (2006) 'California stem cell research goes forward as judge rejects lawsuits', *USA Today*. 23 August.

Wicks, A. C., Berman, S. L. and Jones, T. M. (1999) 'The structure of optimal trust: moral and strategic implications', *Academy of Management Review*. 24, 99–131.

Williamson, O. E. (1984) 'The economics of governance: framework and implication', *Journal of Institutional and Theoretical Economics*. 140, 195–223.

Wright, M. and Robbie, K. (1997) 'Entrepreneurial spirit propels buy-outs', in Birley, S. and Muzyka, D. F. (eds), *Mastering Enterprise*. London: Pitman. 270–9.

Zajac, E. J. (1988) 'Interlocking directorates as an interorganisational strategy: a test of critical assumptions', *Academy of Management Journal*. 31, 428–38.

Chapter 4

Allenby, B. (1994) 'Industrial ecology gets down to earth', *IEEE Circuits and Devices*. 10(1), 20–4.

Anderson, S. and Cavanagh, J. (1996) *Top 200: The rise of global corporate power*. Washington, DC: Institute for Policy Studies.

Anonymous (2000) *The State of the World*. Worldwatch Institute.

Anonymous (2001) 'Clean me a river', *New Scientist*. 171(2303), 17.

Bennet, M. and James, P. (1999) *Sustainable Measures: Evaluating and reporting of environment and social performance*. Sheffield, UK: Greenleaf.

Bien, M. (2001) 'Ethical investing: even a blue chip share can be green', *The Independent*. 25 February (foreign edition).

Business in the Community (ND) 'Coca-Cola Great Britain, responsible marketing', availabile at: www.bitc.org.uk/resources/case_studies/coca_cola_market.html

Charter, M. and Polonsky, M. J. (1999) *Greener Marketing: A global perspective on greening marketing practice*. Sheffield, UK: Greenleaf.

Clift, R. (1995) 'Clean technology: an introduction', *Journal of Chemical Technology and Biotechnology*. 62, 321–6.

Cottrill, K. (1998) 'Out of the lab and on to the table', *Journal of Business Strategy*. 19(2), 38–9.

Crosbie, L. and Knight, K. (1995) *Strategy for Sustainable Business: Environmental opportunity and strategic choice*. Maidenhead: McGraw-Hill.

Datamonitor (1999) '1999 US Organics', Organic Trade Association and Datamonitor.

EPA (1992) *Life Cycle Design Guidance Manual*, EPA 600 1R–92/226. Cincinnati, OH: EPA. (available at www.epa.gov)

Fomburn, C. (1996) *Reputation: Realising value from the corporate image*. Boston, MA: Harvard Business School Press.

French, H. (2000) 'Coping with ecological globalization', in Brown, L. R. *State of the World: 2000*. Worldwatch Institute. New York and London: W.W. Norton.

Fuller, D. A. (1999) *Sustainable Marketing: Managerial–ecological issues*, Industrial Examples. London: Sage.

GEMI (1993) *Total Quality Environmental Management*. Washington, DC: GEMI.

Hart, S. L. (2000) *Beyond Greening: Strategies for a sustainable world*, Business and the Environment. Boston, MA: Harvard Business School Press.

Jenkinson, A. (2001) 'APRIL takes a leaf out of the green book', *Pulp and Paper International*. 42(8), 19–21.

Lawrence, F. (2006) 'Sales of organic produce up to 30% in years', *The Guardian*. 2 September.

MacMillan, A. (2000) 'Genetically modified foods: the British debate', available at: http://cbc.ca/news/viewpoint/correspondents/mamillan_gmf.html

Makower, J. (1994) *Beyond the Bottom Line: putting social responsibility to work for your business and the world*. London: Simon & Schuster.

Makower, J. (2005) 'Green marketing: lessons from the leaders', available at: www.worldchanging.com/archives/003502.html

McKenzie-Mohr, D. and Smith, W. (1999) *Fostering Sustainable Behavior: An introduction to community-based social marketing*. Gabriola Island, British Columbia, Canada: New Society.

MORI (2003) 'Green choice is still a middle-class affair', available at: www.ipsos-mori.com/polls/2003/ ncc.shtml

National Science Board (1998) 'Science and engineering indicators 1998', National Science Foundation.

NEETF/Roper (2000) 'The ninth annual national report card on environmental attitudes, knowledge and behaviours', NEETF/Roper.

Ottman, J. (1993) *Green Marketing: Challenges & opportunities for the new marketing age*. Lincolnwood, IL: NTC Books.

Oyewole, P. (2001) 'Social costs of environmental justice associated with the practice of green marketing', *Journal of Business Ethics*. 29, 239–51.

Pearce (2006) 'Earth: the parched planet', *New Scientist*. 25 February.

Peattie, K. (1995) *Environmental Marketing Management*. London: Pitman.

Peattie, K. and Charter, M. (1997) 'Green marketing', in McDonagh, P. and Prothero. A. (eds), *Green Management: A reader*. London: Dryden Press.

Piasecki, W. B., Fletcher, K. A. and Mendelson, F. J. (1999) *Environmental Management and Business Management: Leadership skills for the 21st century*. London: John Wiley.

Procter & Gamble (2003) 'Sustainability report: linking opportunity with responsibility', available at: www.pg.com/content/pdf/01_about_pg/corporate_citizenship/sustainability/reports/sustainability_report_2003.pdf

Ranchhod (2001) figures prepared for first edition.

Rand Corporation (2000) 'Consumer power', section entitled 'Green consumption', available at: www.rand.org/scitech/stpi/ourfuture/Consumer/section6.html

Sauven, J. (2006) 'The odd couple', *The Guardian*, 2 August.

SETAC (1998) 'Evolution and development of the conceptual framework and methodology of life-cycle impact assessment', available at http://setac.org/files/addendum.pdf

SPOLD (1995) 'Synthesis report on the social value of LCA workshop', SPOLD/IMSA, available from Proctor & Gamble Services Company, Temsalaan 100, 1853 Strombeek-Bever, Belgium (Fax +32 2 568 4812). (Note that SPOLD terminated its activities at the end of 2001. Its history may be obtained by visiting: www.spold.org/whatis.html)

Stauber, J. and Rampton, S. (1995) *Toxic Sludge is Good for You: Lies, damn lies and the public relations industry*. Monore, ME: Common Courage Press.

UNEP (2002) *GEO-3: Global Environment Outlook 3*. UNEP. (Available at: www.unep.org/geo/geo3)

UNEP (2005a) 'Talk the walk: advancing sustainable lifestyles through marketing and communications', available at: www.uneptie.org/pc/sustain/reports/advertising/Talk_the_Walk.pdf

UNEP (2005b) 'UNEP annual report', available at: www.unep.org/Documents.multilingual/Default.asp?DocumentID=67&ArticleID=5125&l=en

UNEP (2005c) 'E-waste: the hidden side of IT equipment's manufacturing and use', 'Early warnings on emerging environmental threats' No. 5, UNEP.

Vogel, D. (2006) *The Market for Virtue: The potential and limits of corporate social responsibility*. Washington: DC. The Bookings Institution.

Wagner, S. A. (1997) *Understanding Green Consumer Behaviour*. London and New York: Routledge.

Wasik, J. F. (1996) *Green Marketing and Management: A global perspective*. Cambridge, MA: Blackwell.

Wirthlin Institute (2000) 'Environmental update', 10(8), available at: http://209.204.197.52/publicns/Twr1100.pdf

Wong, V., Turner, W. and Stoneman, P. (1996) 'Marketing strategies and market prospects for environmentally friendly consumer products', *British Journal of Management*. 7(3), 263–81.

Worcester, R. (1997) 'Public opinion and the environment', in Jacobs, M. (ed.), *Greening the Millennium? The New Politics of the Environment*. Oxford: Blackwell.

Chapter 5

Ackerman, L. D. (1990) 'Identity in action', *IABC Communication World*. 33–50.

ACNielsen (2001) 'ACNielsen finds 43 brands have a billion dollar global presence', available at: http://acneilson.com/news/european/2001/20011031.htm

Alba, J. W. and Hutchinson, J. W. (1987) 'Dimensions of consumer expertise', *Journal of Consumer Research*. 13(1), 411–54.

Alvesson, M. (1990) 'Organization: from substance to image?', *Organization Studies*. 11(3), 373–94.

Ambler, T. (1998) Advertising and profit growth', *Admap*. 384, May, 20–3.

Armstrong, A. and Hagel III, J. (1996) 'The real value of online communities', *Harvard Business Review*. 74(3), 134–41.

Berry, L. L. (2000) 'Cultivating service brand equity', *Academy of Marketing Science Journal*. 28(1) 128–37.

Beverland, M. and Luxton, S. (2005) 'Managing integrated marketing communication (IMC) through strategic decoupling: how luxury wine firms retain brand leadership while appearing to be wedded to the past', *Journal of Advertising*. 34(4), 1–15.

Blattberg, R. C., and Deighton, J. (1996) 'Manage marketing by the customer equity test', *Harvard Business Review*. 74(4), 136–44.

Blattberg, R. C., Glazer, R. and Little, J. D. C. (eds) (1994) 'Introduction', in *The Marketing Information Revolution*, Boston, MA: Harvard Business School Press.

Bridges, S., Lane, K. K. and Sood, S. (2000) 'Communication strategies for brand extensions: enhancing perceived fit by establishing explanatory links', *Journal of Advertising*. 29(4), 1–11.

Carlivati, P. A. (1990) 'Measuring your image', *Association Management*. 42, 49–52.

Cleland, K. (1995) 'Few wed marketing communications', in Pickton, D. and Broderick, A. (2001) *Integrated Marketing Communications*. Harlow: Pearson Education.

Dillon, W. R., Madden, T. M., Kirmani, A. and Mukherjee, S. (2001) 'Understanding what's in a brand rating: a model for assessing brand and attribute effects and their relationship to brand equity', *Journal of Marketing Research*. 38(4) 415–29.

Dru, J. M. (1997) *Disruption: Overturning conventions and shaking up the market place*. New York: Wiley.

Duncan, T. R. (2002) *IMC: Using advertising and promotion to build brands*. New York: McGraw-Hill.

Duncan, T. and Caywood, C. (1996) 'The concept, process and evolution of integrated marketing communications', in Thorson, E. and Moore, J. (eds), *Integrated Communications: Synergy of persuasive voices*. Hillside, NJ: Erlbaum Associates.

Duncan, T. and Moriarty, S. (1997) *Driving Brand Value: Using integrated marketing to manage profitable stakeholder relationships*. New York: McGraw-Hill.

Durkin, M. and Lawlor, M.-A. (2001) 'The implications of the Internet on the advertising agency–client relationship', *The Services Industries Journal*. 21(2), 175–90.

Eagle, L. and Kitchen, P. J. (2000) 'IMC: brand communications and corporate cultures', *European Journal of Marketing*. 34(5), 667–86.

Fombrun, C. and Shanley, M. (1990) 'What's in a name? Reputation building and corporate strategy', *Academy of Management Journal*. 33, 233–58.

Griffin, R. W. (ed.) (1999) *Management*. Boston, MA: Houghton Mifflin.

Gronstedt, A. (2000) *The Customer Century: Lessons from world-class companies in integrating marketing and communications*. New York: Routledge.

Hackley, C. and Kitchen, P. J. (1998) 'IMC: a consumer psychological perspective', *Marketing Intelligence & Planning*. 16(3), 229–35.

Hoffman, D. L. and Novak, T. P. (1996) 'Marketing in hypermedia computer-mediated environments: conceptual foundations', *Journal of Marketing*. 80(4), 50–68.

Kazoleas, D., Kim, Y. and Moffitt, M. A. (2001) 'Institutional image: a case study', *Corporate Communications: An International Journal*. 6(4), 205–16.

Keegan, W., Moriarty, S. and Duncan, T. (1992) *Marketing*. Englewood Cliffs, NJ: Prentice Hall.

Kiani, R. G. (1998) 'Marketing opportunities in the digital world', *Internet Research: Networking Applications and Policy*. 8(2), 185–94.

Kitchen, P. J. (1999) *Marketing Communications: principles and practice*. London: International Thomson Business Press.

Kitchen, P. J. and Proctor, T. (2002) 'Communication in postmodern integrated marketing', *Corporate communications: An International Journal*. 7(3), 144–54.

Kitchen, P. J. and Schultz, D. E. (1999) 'A multi-country comparison of the drive for IMC', *Journal of Advertising Research*. 39(1), 21–38.

Kitchen, P. J., Brignell, J., Li, T. and Jones, G. S. (2004), 'The emergence of IMC: a theoretical perspective', *Journal of Advertising Research*. 44(1), 19–31.

Knapp, D. E. (1999) 'Brand equity', *Risk Management*. 46(9), 71–4.

Knoll, H. E. and Tankersley, C. B. (1991) 'Building a better image', *Sales and Marketing Management*. 143, 70–8.

Kotler, P. and Mindak, W. (1978) 'Marketing and public relations', *Journal of Marketing*. 42(4), 13–20.

Martin, J. (1996) *Cybercorp: The new business revolution*. New York: AMACOM.

Mazur, L. (2000) 'Meddling with a brand does not help manage it', *Marketing*. 24 February, 20–1.

McKenna, R. (1995) 'Real-time marketing', *Harvard Business Review*. 73(4), 87–96.

McKim, B. (2002) 'The difference between CRM and database marketing', *Journal of Database Marketing*. 9(4), 371–5.

Niemann, I. (2005) 'Strategic integrated communication implementation: towards a South African conceptual model', Pretoria: University of Pretoria. (Available at: http://upetd.up.ac.za/thesis/available/etd-10062005-100746)

Percy, L. (1997) *Strategies for Implementing Integrated Marketing Communication*. Chicago, IL: NTC Business Books.

Pickton, D. and Broderick, A. (2001) *Integrated Marketing Communications*. Harlow: Pearson Education.

Pratt, M. G. and Foreman, P. O. (2000) 'Classifying managerial responses to multiple organizational identities', *Academy of Management Review*. 25(1), 18–42.

Proctor, T. and Kitchen, P. J. (2002) 'Communication in postmodern integrated marketing', *Corporate Communications: An International Journal*. 7(3), 144–54.

Ranchhod A., Gurău, C. and Lace, J. (2002) 'On-line messages: developing an integrated communications model for biotechnology companies', *Qualitative Market Research Journal: An International Journal.* 5(1), 6–18.

Rayport, J. F. and Sviokla, J. J. (1995) 'Exploiting the virtual value chain', *Harvard Business Review.* 73(6), 75–85.

Schultz, D. E. (1993) 'How to overcome barriers to integration', *Marketing News.* 27(15), 16–17.

Schultz, D. E. (1999) 'Integrated marketing communications and how it relates to traditional media advertising', in Jones, J. P. (eds), *The Advertising Business: Operations, creativity, media planning.* London: Sage.

Schultz, D. E. and Kitchen, P. J. (2000) *Communicating Globally: An integrated marketing approach.* Chicago: McGraw Hill.

Schultz, D. E., Tannenbaum, S. I. and Lauterborn, R. F. (1993) *Integrated Marketing Communications: Pulling it together and making it work.* Chicago, IL: NTC Business Books.

Shimp, T. A. (2000) *Advertising Promotion: Supplemental aspects of integrated marketing communications* (5th edition). Fort Worth, TX: Dryden Press.

Smith, Paul R., Berry, C. and Pulford, A. (1997) *Strategic Marketing Communications: New ways to build and integrate communication.* London: Kogan Page.

Tomkins, R. (2000) 'Fallen icons: Coca-Cola and McDonald's seemed ready to take over the world, but global branding has lost its appeal', *Financial Times.* 1 February.

Williams, S. L. and Moffitt, M. A. (1997) 'Corporate image as an impression formation process: prioritizing personal, organizational, and environmental audience factors', *Journal of Public Relations Research.* 9(4), 237–58.

Chapter 6

Alderson, W. (1957) *Marketing Behavior and Executive Action.* Homewood, IL: Richard D. Irwin.

Bergeron, F., Buteau, C. and Raymond, L. (1991) 'Identification of strategic information systems opportunities: applying and comparing two methodologies', *MIS Quarterly.* 15(1), 89–103.

Bergeron, F. and Raymond, L. (1995) 'The contribution of information technology to the bottom line: a contingency perspective of strategic dimensions', *Proceedings of the International Conference on Information Systems*, Amsterdam. 167–81.

Berthon, P., Pitt, L. and Watson, R. (1996) 'The World Wide Web as an advertising medium', *Journal of Advertising Research.* 36(1), 43–54.

Bonoma, T. V. (1984) *Managing Marketing.* New York: Free Press.

Bonoma, T. V. (1985) *The Marketing Edge: Making strategies work.* New York: Free Press.

Borys, B. and Jemison, D. B. (1989) 'Hybrid arrangements as strategic alliances: theoretical issues in organizational combinations', *Academy of Management Review.* 14(2) 234–49.

Brady, M., Saren, M. and Tzokas, N. (1999) 'The impact of IT on marketing: an evaluation', *Management Decision.* 37(10), 758–66.

Bruce, M., Leverick, F., Little, D. and Wilson, D. (1996) 'The changing scope and substance of marketing: the impact of IT', in Beracs, J., Bauer, A. and Simon, S. (eds), *Proceedings of the European Academy of Marketing Conference: Marketing for an Expanding Europe*, Vol. 1. Budapest University of Economic Science, Budapest. 185–204.

Carson, D., Cromie, S., McGowan, P. and Hill, J. (1995) *Marketing and Entrepreneurship in SMEs: An innovative approach.* Harlow: Pearson Education.

Cespedes, F. V. (1991) *Organizing and Implementing the Marketing Effort.* Reading, MA: Addison-Wesley.

Crittenden, V. L. and Bonoma, T. V. (1988) 'Managing marketing implementation', *Sloan Management Review.* 29(Winter), 7–14.

Croteau, A. and Bergeron, F. (1991/1998/2001) 'An information technology trilogy: business strategy, technological deployment and organisational performance', *Journal of Strategic Information Systems.* 10, 77–99.

Das, S. R., Warkentin, M. E. and Zahra, S. A. (1991) 'Integrating the content and process of strategic MIS planning with competitive strategy', *Decision Sciences.* 22, 953–84.

Deloitte Research (2003) 'Creating digital loyalty networks', Deloitte.

Engeström, Y. (1987) 'Learning by expanding: an activity-theoretical approach to developmental research', Orienta-Konsultit Oy, Helsinki.

Flohr, T. (2000) 'IT: know thyself', *Intelligent Enterprise*, 3(8). (Available at: www.intelligententerprise.com/ 000515/feat2.shtml)

Forsström, B. (2005) *Value Co-creation in Industrial Buyer–Seller Partnerships: Creating and Exploiting Interdependencies*, Doctoral Thesis, Åbo Akademi University Press.

Godin, S. (1999) *Permission Marketing: Turning strangers into friends and friends into customers.* London: Simon & Schuster.

Håkansson, H. (1982) *International Marketing and Purchasing of Industrial Goods: An interaction approach.* New York: John Wiley.

Håkansson, H. and Persson G. (2004) 'Supply chain management: The logic of supply chains and networks', *International Journal of Logistics Management*.15(1), 11–26.

Håkansson, H. and Prenkert, F. (2004) 'Exploring the exchange concept in marketing', in Håkansson, H., Harrison, D. and Waluszewski, A. (eds), *Rethinking Marketing*. New York: John Wiley. 75–97.

Henderson, J. C. and Venkatraman, N. (1999) 'Strategic alignment: leveraging information technology for transforming organizations', *IBM Systems Journal*. 38(2/3), 472–84.

Hoffman, D. L. and Novak, T. P. (1996) 'Marketing in a hypermedia computer-mediated environment: conceptual foundations', *Journal of Marketing*. July, 50–68.

Jennings, P. and Beaver, G. (1997) 'The performance and competitive advantage of small firms: a management perspective', *International Small Business Journal*. 15(2), 63–75.

Kalakota, R. and Robinson, M. (1999) *e-Business Roadmap for Success*. Canada: Addison-Wesley Longman.

Kassaye, N. (1999) 'Sorting out the practical concerns in World Wide Web advertising', *International Journal of Advertising*. 18, 339–61.

Keeler, L. (1995) *Cybermarketing*. New York: Amacall.

Kitchen, P. J. (1999) *Marketing Communications: Principles and practice*. London: International Thomson Business Press.

Komenar, M. (1997) *Electronic Marketing*. New York: Wiley.

Lawer, C. (2004) 'Changing the long-playing marketing record', OMC White Paper, The OMC Group.

McKean, J. (1999) *Information Masters: Secrets of the customer race*. New York: John Wiley.

Mintzberg, H. and Waters, J. A. (1985) 'Of strategies, deliberate and emergent', *Strategic Management Journal*. 6, 257–72.

Noble, C. H. and Mokwa, M. P. (1999) 'Implementing marketing strategies: developing and testing a managerial theory', *Journal of Marketing*. 63(4), 57–73.

O'Connor, J. and Galvin, E. (1997) *Marketing and Information Technology*. London: Pitman.

O'Connor, J. and Galvin, E. (1998) *Creating Value Through e-Commerce*. London: Financial Times.

Peattie, K. and Peters, L. (1998) 'The marketing mix in the 3rd age of computing', *Marketing Intelligence and Planning*. 15(2/3), 142–50.

Piercy, N. (1989) 'Marketing concepts and actions: implementing marketing-led strategic change', *European Journal of Marketing*. 24(2), 24–42.

Porter, M. (1985) *Competitive Advantage*. New York: Free Press.

Porter, M. E. (2001) 'Strategy and the Internet', *Harvard Business Review*. 79(3), 62–78.

Prahalad, C. and Ramaswamy, V. (2004) *The Future of Competition*. Boston, MA: Harvard Business School Press.

Reichheld, F. and Sasser, W. (1990) 'Zero defection comes to services', *Harvard Business Review*. 68(5), 105–11.

Remenyi, D., Money, A. and Twite, A. (1995) *Effective Measurement and Management of IT Costs and Benefits*. Oxford: Butterworth Heinemann.

Rosenberg, L. J. and Czepiel, J. A. (1984) 'A marketing approach to customer retention', *Journal of Consumer Marketing*. 1, 45–51.

Sashittal, H. C. and Tankersley, C. (1997) 'The strategic market planning – implementation interface in small and midsized industrial firms: an exploratory study', *Journal of Marketing*. 5 (Summer), 77–92.

Schlegelmilch, B. B. and Sinkovic, R. R. (1998) 'Marketing into the information age: can incoming goods plan for an unpredictable future?', *International Marketing Review*. 15(3), 162–70.

Shani, D. and Chalasani, S. (1992) 'Exploiting niches using relationship marketing', *Journal of Services Marketing*. 6(4), 43–52.

Simkin, L. and Dibb, S. (1998) 'Prioritising target markets', *Marketing Intelligence & Planning*. 16(7), 407–17.

Stalk, G. (1988) 'Time: the next source of competitive advantage', *Harvard Business Review*. July/August.

Thompson, J. D. (1967) *Organizations in action*. New York: McGraw-Hill.

Vargo, S. L. and Lusch, R. F. (2004) 'Evolving a services-dominant logic', *Journal of Marketing*. 68, 1–17.

Zuboff, S. (1988) *In the Age of the Smart Machine*. London: Heinemann.

Chapter 7

Argyris, C. and Schön, D. A. (1978) *Organizational Learning*. Reading, MA: Addison-Wesley.

Baker, W. E. and Sinkula, J. M. (1999) 'The synergistic effect of market orientation and learning orientation on organizational performance', *Academy of Marketing Science Journal*. 27(4), 411–27.

Barney, J. B. (1986) 'Organizational culture: can it be a source of sustained competitive advantage?', *Academy of Management Review*. 11(3), 656–65.

Baumard, P. (1995) 'Des organisations apprenantes? Les dangers de la "consensualité"', *Revue Française de Gestion*. September–October, 49–57.

Calori, R. and Sarnin, P. (1993) 'Les facteurs de complexité des schémas cognitifs des dirigeants', *Revue Française de Gestion*. March–May, 86–93.

Cameron, K. and Freeman, S. (1991) 'Cultural congruence, strength and types: relationship to effectiveness', *Research in Organisational Change and Development*. 5, 23–58.

Day, G. S. (1994) 'Continuous learning about markets', *California Management Review*. 36(4), 9–31.

Deshpande, R., Farley, J. and Webster, F. (1993) 'Corporate culture, customer orientation, and innovativeness in japanese firms: a quadrad analysis', *Journal of Marketing*. 57(1), 23–34.

Desreumaux, A. (1998) *Théorie des organisations*. Caen: Editions Management et Societé Editions.

Fiol, C. M. and Lyles, M. A. (1985) 'Organizational learning', *Academy of Management Review*. 10, 803–13.

Girod, M. (1995) 'La mémoire organisationnelle', *Revue Française de Gestion*. September–October, 30–42.

Helfer, J. P., Kalika, M. and Orsoni, J. (1998) *Management, Stratégie et Organisation* (2nd edition). Paris: Vuibert Gestion.

Hofstede, G. (1980) *Culture's Consequences*. Beverley Hills, CA: Sage.

Hofstede, G., Neuijen, B., Ohayv, D.D. and Sanders, G. (1990) 'Measuring organizational cultures: a qualitative and quantitative study across twenty cases', *Administrative Science Quarterly*. 35, 286–316.

Homburg, C., Workman Jr, J. P. and Jensell, O. (2000) 'Fundamental changes in marketing organization: the movement toward a customer-focused organizational structure', *Academy of Marketing Science Journal*. 28(4), 459–78.

Kalika, M. (1995) *Structure d'entreprise: Réalités, déterminants, performance*. Paris: Economica.

Kim, D. H. (1993) 'The link between individual and organizational learning', *Sloan Management Review*. 35(1), 37–51.

Knight, L. (2002) 'Network learning: exploring learning by interorganizational networks', *Human Relations*. 55(4), 427–54.

Koenig, G. (1990) *Management Stratégique: Vision, manceuvres et tactiques*. Paris: Nathan.

Kohli, A. K. and Jaworski, B. J. (1990) 'Market orientation: the construct, research propositions, and managerial implications', *Journal of Marketing*. 54, 1–18.

Lawrence, P. R. et Lorsch, J. W. (1986) *Organization and Environment*. Boston, MA: Harvard Business School Press.

Levinthal, D. A. and March, J. G. (1993) 'The myopia of learning', *Strategic Management Journal*. 14, 95–112.

Menon, A. and Varadarajan P. R. (1992) 'A model of marketing knowledge use within firms', *Journal of Marketing*. 56(4), 53–71.

Mintzberg, H. (1979) 'Patterns in strategy formation', *Management Science*. 24, 934–48.

Mintzberg, H. (1990) *Le Management*. Paris: Les Editions d'Organisation.

Moingeon, B. and Edmondson, A. (eds) (1996) *Organizational Learning and Competitive Advantage*. London: Sage.

Nonaka, I. (1991) 'The knowledge-creating company, *Harvard Business Review*. 69(6), 96–104.

Nonaka, I. and Takeuchi, H. (1995) *The Knowledge-creating Company*. Oxford: Oxford University Press.

Nonaka, I. and Konno, N. (1993) 'Knowledge-based organization', *Harvard Business Review*. 41(1), 59–73.

O'Reilly, C. A. (1989) 'Corporations, culture and commitment: motivation and social control in organizations', *California Management Review*. 31(4), 9–25.

O'Reilly, C. A., Chatman, J. and Caldwell, D. F. (1991a) 'People and organizational culture: a profile comparison approach to assessing person–organization fit', *Academy of Management Journal*. 34(3), 487–516.

O'Reilly, C., Chatman, J. and Caldwell, D. (1991b) 'People and Organizational Culture: a Q-sort approach to assessing person–organization fit', *Academy of Management Journal*. 34(3), 487–516.

Ouchi, W. (1980) 'Markets, bureaucracy and clans', *Administrative Science Quarterly*. 25 (March), 129–41.

Peters, L. D. and Fletcher, K. P. (2004) 'Communication strategies and marketing performance: an application of the Mohr and Nevin framework to intra-organisational cross-functional teams', *Journal of Marketing Management*. 20(7/8), 741–70.

Quinn, R. E. and Cameron, K. (1983) 'Organisational lifecycles and shifting criteria of effectiveness: some preliminary evidence', *Management Science*. 29(1), 33–51.

Quinn, R. and Rohrbaugh, J. (1981) 'A competing values approach to organizational effectiveness', *Public Productivity Review*. 5, 122–40.

Remenyi, D., Money, A. and Twite, A. (1995) *Effective Measurement and Management of IT Costs and Benefits*. Oxford: Butterworth Heinemann.

Schein, E. H. (1983) 'The role of the founder in creating organizational culture', *Organizational Dynamics*. 12, 13–28.

Schein, E. H. (1992) *Organizational Culture and Leadership* (2nd edition). San Francisco, CA: Jossey-Bass.

Schein, E. H. (1993) 'On dialogue, culture and organizational learning', *Organizational Dynamics*. 22(2), 40–51.

Senge, P. M. (1990) 'The leader's new work: building learning organizations', *Strategic Management Review*. 32(1), 7–23.

Shrivastava, P. (1983) 'A typology of organizational learning systems', *Journal of Management Studies*. 20(1), pp. 7–28.

Sinkula, J. M. (1994) 'Market information processing and organizational learning', *Journal of Marketing*. 58(1), 35–45.

Slater, S. F. and Narver, J. C. (1995) 'Market orientation and the learning organization', *Journal of Marketing*. 59(3), 63–74.

Spender, J. C. and Baumard, P. (1995) 'Turning troubled firms around: case evidence for a Penrosian view of strategic recovery', Academy of Management Annual Meeting, Vancouver.

Weick, K. E. (1987) 'Organizational culture as a source of high reliability', *California Management Review*. 29(2), 112–27.

Chapter 8

Anderson, O. (1993) 'On the internationalization process of firms: a critical analysis', *Journal of International Business Studies*. 24(2), 209–31

Baily, M. N. and Lawrence, R. Z. (2004) 'What happened to the great US job machine? The role of trade and electronic offshoring', *Brookings Papers on Economic Activity*. 2, 211–84.

Bartlett, C. A. and Ghoshal, S. (1989) *Managing Across Border: The transnational solution*. London: Century Business.

Bilkey, W. J. and Tesar, G. (1977) 'The export behavior of smaller Wisconsin manufacturing firms', *Journal of International Business Studies*. 8(1), 93–8.

Boter, H. and Holmquist, C. (1996) 'Industry, characteristics and internationalization processes in small firms', *Journal of Business Venturing*. 11(6), 471–87.

Bronfenbrenner, K. and Luce, S. (2004) 'Offshoring', *Multinational Monitor*. 25(12), 26–9.

Buckley, P. J., Newbould, G. D. and Thurwell, J. (1979) 'Going international: the foreign direct investment behaviour of smaller UK firms', in Mattsson, L. G. and Wiedersheim-Paul, F. (eds), *Recent Research on the Internationalization of Business. Proceedings of the Annual Meeting of the European International Business Association*, Uppsala.

Colquhoun, G., Edmonds, K. and Goodger, D. (2004) 'Offshoring: how big an issue?', *Economic Outlook*. 28(3), 9–15.

Håkansson, H. (1982) *International Marketing and Purchasing of Industrial Goods*. Chichester: Wiley.

Innovation Insight (2004) 'Baseline analysis of offshoring in the Tampa Bay region', available at: www.cas.usf.edu/GlobalResearch/PDFs/2004_Offshoring_Report_Briefing.pdf

Johanson, J. and Vahlne, J. (1977) 'The internationalization process of the firm – a model of knowledge development and increasing foreign market commitments', *Journal of International Business Studies*. 8(1), 23–32.

Johanson, J. and Vahlne, J. (1990) 'The mechanism of internationalization', *International Marketing Review*. 7(4), 11–24.

Johanson, J. and Wiedersheim-Paul, F. (1975) 'The internationalization of the firm: four Swedish cases', *Journal of Management Studies*. 12(3), 305–22.

Knight, G. and Cavusgil, S. T. (1996) 'The born global firm: a challenge to traditional internationalization theory', in Cavusgil, S. T. (series ed.) and Madsen, T. K. (volume ed.), *Advances in International Marketing* (Vol. 8). JAI Press: London. 11–26.

Levitt, T. (1983) 'The globalization of markets', *Harvard Business Review*. 61, 92–102.

McEachern, C. (2005) 'A look inside offshoring', *VARBusiness*. 21(17), 50.

Miller, M. M. (1993) 'Executive insights: the 10 step roadmap to success in foreign markets', *Journal of International Marketing*. 1(2), 89–100.

Nordstrom, K. A. (1991) 'The internationalization process of the firm', doctoral dissertation, Institute of International Business, Stockholm School of Economics.

OECD (1997) 'Globalization and small- and medium-sized enterprises (SMEs)', *Principles of Corporate Governance*. OECD, Paris.

Preston, S. (2004) 'Lost in migration: offshore need not mean outsourced', *Strategy & Leadership*. 32(6), 32–6.

Reid, S. (1981) 'The decision-maker and export entry and expansion', *Journal of International Business Studies*. 12(2), 101–12.

Reid, S. (1983) 'Firm internationalization, transaction costs and strategic choice', *International Marketing Review*. 1(2), 44–56.

Roberts, J. (1999) 'The internationalization of business service firms: a stages approach', *The Service Industries Journal*. 19(4), 68–88.

Root, F. (1987) *Entry Strategies for International Markets*. Lexington, MA: Lexington Books.

Rosson, P. (2004) 'The Internet and SME exporting: Canadian success stories', in Etemad, H. (ed.), *International Entrepreneurship in Small and Medium-sized Enterprises: Orientation, environment and strategy*. London: Edward Elgar. 145–77.

Rutherford, B. and Mobley, S. (2005) 'The next wave: refining the future of offshoring', *Journal of Corporate Real Estate*. 7(1), 87–95.

Schultze, C. L. (2004) 'Offshoring, import competition, and the jobless recovery', available at: www.brookings.edu/views/papers/schultze/20040622.pdf

Turnbull, P. (1987) 'A challenge to the stages theory of the internationalization process', in Rosson, P. and Reid, S. (eds), *Managing Export Entry and Expansion*. New York: Praeger. 21–40.

Varaldo, R. (1987) 'The internationalization of small- and medium-sized Italian manufacturing firms', in Rosson, P. and Reid, S. (eds), *Managing Export Entry and Expansion*. New York: Praeger. 203–22.

Villemus, P. (2005) *Délocalisations: Aurons-nous Encore des Emplois Demain?* Paris: Seuil.

Vogel, D. A. and Connelly, J. E. (2005) 'Best practices for dealing with offshore software development', *Handbook of Business Strategy*. 6(1), 281–6.

Welch, L. and Luostarinen, R. (1988) 'Internationalization: evolution of a concept', *Journal of General Management*. 14(2), 34–55.

Williams, K. (2003) 'Is offshoring for you?' *Strategic Finance*. 85(1), 19.

Yip, G. S., Biscarri, G. and Monti, J. A. (2000) 'The role of the internationalization process in the performance of newly internationalizing firms', *Journal of International Marketing*. 8(3), 10–35.

Chapter 9

Ambler, T. (1997) 'How much of brand equity is explained by trust?', *Management Decision*. 35(3/4), 283–92.

Ambler, T. (2003) *Marketing and the Bottom Line*. London: FT Prentice Hall. 505.

Bacuvier, G., Peladeau, P., Trichet, A. and Zerbib, P. (2001) 'Customer lifetime value: powerful insights into a company's business and activities', Booz Allen-Hamilton.

Bhargava, M., Dubelaar, C. and Ramaswami, S. (1994) 'Reconciling diverse measures of performance: a conceptual framework and test of a methodology', *Journal of Business Research*. 31, 235–46.

Bonoma, T. V. (1985) *The Marketing Edge: Making strategies work*. New York: Free Press.

Bonoma, T. V. and Clark, B. H. (1988) *Marketing Performance Assessment*. Boston, MA: Harvard Business School Press.

Boulding, W., Kalra, A., Staelin, R. and Zeithaml, V. (1993) 'A dynamic process model of service quality: from expectations to behavioural intentions', *Journal of Marketing Research*. 30 (February), 7–27.

Brownlie, D. (1993) *Rethinking Marketing: New perspectives on the discipline and the profession*. Coventry: Warwick Business School Research Bureau.

Chambers, J. (2000) 'Customer satisfaction at Cisco Systems', available at: www.tdmktg.com/resources.html#cisco.

Clark, H. B. (2000) 'Managerial perceptions of marketing performance: efficiency, adaptability, effectiveness and satisfaction', *Journal of Strategic Marketing*. 8(1), 3–25.

Day, G. S. and Fahey, L. (1988) 'Valuing market strategies', *Journal of Marketing*. 52, 45–57.

Doyle, P. (2000) *Value-based Marketing: Marketing strategies for corporate growth and shareholder value*. Chichester: John Wiley.

Drucker, P. (1974) *Management: Tasks, responsibilities, practices*. New York: Harper & Row.

Dunn, M. G., Norburn, D. and Birley, S. (1994) 'The impact of organizational values, goals, and climate on marketing effectiveness', *Journal of Business Research*. 30(2), 131–41.

Farquhar, P. H. (1989) 'Managing brand equity', *Marketing Research*. 1 (September), 24–33.

Feder, R. A. (1965) 'How to measure marketing performance', *Harvard Business Review*. 43(May–June), 132–42.

Foulks Lynch (2004) *Management Accounting Performance*. Kaplan Publishing Foulks Lynch.

Highson, C. J., Ambler, T. and Barwise, T. P. (2001) 'Marketing metrics: what should we tell shareholders?' *Market Leader*. Winter, 10–11.

Hill, N., Roche, G. and Self, B. (2001) *Customer satisfaction measurement for ISO 9000:2000*. Oxford: Butterworth Heinnemann.

Ingold, P. (1995) *Promotion des Ventes et Action Commerciale*. Paris: Vuibert.

Johnson, G. and Scholes, K. (2002) *Exploring Corporate Strategy: Text and cases*. London: Prentice Hall.

Kaplan, R. S. and Norton, D. P. (2003), The Strategy-focused Organization. Boston, MA: Harvard Business School Press.

Kotler, P., Gregor, W. T. and Rogers, W. H. (1977) 'From sales obsession to marketing effectiveness', *Harvard Business Review*. 55, 67–75.

Lenskold, J. D. (2002) 'Marketing ROI: playing to win', *Marketing Management*. 11(3), 30–4.

Lehni, M. (1998) 'WBCSD project on eco-efficiency metrics and reporting: state-of-play report'. Geneva: World Business Council for Sustainable Development.

McCullough, R. (2000) 'Marketing metrics', *Marketing Management*. 9(1), 64–5.

Meyer, W. M. (2002) *Rethinking Performance Measurement: Beyond the balanced scorecard*. Cambridge, UK: Cambridge University Press.

Miller, D. and Toulouse, J. M. (1986) 'Chief executive personality and corporate structure in small firms', *Management Science*. 32(11), 1389–1409.

Morgan N. A., Clark B. H. and Gooner R. (2002) 'Marketing productivity: integrating multiple perspectives', *Journal of Business Research*. 55(5) 363–75.

Oxenfeldt, A. R. (1966) *Executive Action in Marketing*. Belmont, CA: Wadsworth.

Quinn, R. E. and Cameron, K. (1983) 'Organization lifecycles and shifting criteria of effectiveness: some preliminary evidence', *Management Science*. 29(1), 33–51.

Rothe, J. T., Harvey, M. G. and Jackson, C. E. (1997) 'The marketing audit: five decades later', *Journal of Marketing, Theory and Practice*. 5(3), 1–16.

Rust, R. T., Zeithaml, V. A. and Lemon, K. N. (2000) *Driving Customer Equity: How customer lifetime value is reshaping corporate strategy*. New York: Free Press.

Scherpereel, C., Koppen, V. and Heering, G. B. F. (2001) 'Selecting environmental performance indicators', *Greener Management International*. 33 (spring), 97–114.

Selnes, F. (1992) 'Analyzing marketing profitability: sales are a dangerous cost-driver', *European Journal of Marketing*. 26(2), 15–26.

Sevin, C. H. (1965) *Marketing Productivity Analysis*. New York: McGraw-Hill.

Sink, D. S. (1985) *Productivity Management: Planning, measurement and evaluation, control and improvement*', New York: John Wiley.

Spencer-Cooke, A. (1998) 'The true asset of the social bottom line', *The Tomorrow Exchange* (interactive video conference programme). Stockholm: Tomorrow Publishing.

Taghian, M. and Shaw, R. (1998) 'The marketing audit and business performance: a review and research agenda', *Proceedings of the Australian and New Zealand Marketing Academy Conference*. University of Otago, Dunedin, New Zealand. 2557–71.

Thearling, K. (1999) 'Increasing customer value by integrating data mining and campaign management software', *Direct Marketing Magazine*. February.

Usunier, J-C. (1999) *Marketing Across Cultures*. London: Prentice Hall.

Venkatramen, N. and Ramanujam, V. (1986) 'Measurement of business performance in strategy research: a comparison of approaches', *Academy of Management Review*. 11(4), 801–14.

Walker, O. C. and Ruekert, R. W. (1987) 'Marketing's role in the implementation of business strategies: a critical review and conceptual framework', *Journal of Marketing*. 51, 15–33.

Webster, C. (1995) 'Marketing culture and marketing effectiveness in service firms', *Journal of Services Marketing*. 9(2), 6–21.

Wundermann, C. J. (2001) 'Unlocking the true value of customer relationship management', CRM-Forum. (Available at: www.geocities.com/consumidorcl/pbl/Unlocking TheTrue.pdf)

Yang, Z. and Jun, M. (2002) 'Consumer perception of e-service quality: from Internet purchaser and non-purchaser perspectives', *Journal of Business Strategies*, 19(1), 19–41.

Chapter 10

Alternatives Committee of the Institutional Forum on Globalization (2002) 'Report summary: A better world is possible! Alternatives to economic globalization', *International Forum on Globalization*. (Available at: www.ifg.org/alf–eng.pdf)

Andreasen, A. R. (1984) 'A power potential approach to middlemen strategies in social marketing', *European Journal of Marketing*. 18(4), 56–71.

Andreasen, A. R. (1995) *Marketing Social Change*. San Francisco, CA: Jossey-Bass.

Andreasen, A. R. (2000a) 'Alliances and ethics in social marketing', in Andreasen, A. R. (ed.), *Ethics in Social Marketing*. Washington, DC: Georgetown University Press.

Andreasen, A. R. (2000b) 'Intersector transfer of marketing knowledge', in Bloom, P. N. and Gundlach, G. T. (eds), *Handbook of Marketing and Society*. Thousand Oaks, CA: Sage.

Andreasen, A. R. (2002) 'Marketing social marketing in the social change marketplace', *Journal of Public Policy and Marketing*. 21(1), 3–13.

Bagozzi, R. P., Gopinath, M. and Nyer, P. U. (1999) 'The role of emotions in marketing', *Journal of the Academy of Marketing Science*. 27(2), 184–206.

Balu, R. (2001) 'Act local, think global', *Fast company*. June. (Available at: www.fastcompany.com/articles/2001/05/lever_sidebar.html)

Bandura, A. (1977) *Social Learning Theory*. Englewood Cliffs, NJ: Prentice Hall.

Bandura, A. (1986) *Social Foundations of Thought and Action*. Englewood Cliffs, NJ, Prentice Hall.

Bang, H.-K. (2000) 'Misplaced marketing', *Journal of Consumer Marketing*. 17(6), 479–80.

Battelle, J. (2005) 'The birth of google', *Wired Magazine*. 13 August. (Available at: www.wired.com/wired/archive/13.08/battelle.html)

Becker, M. with contribution from Vile, R. (2006) *Understanding the Common Short Code: Its use, administration, and tactical elements*, Academic Review. Mobile Marketing Association (restricted 691 communication).

Bishop, B. (1996) *Strategic Marketing for the Digital Age.* Toronto: Harper Business.

Brindle, D. and Maley, J. (2006) 'Jamie Oliver in talks over campaign for family meals', *The Guardian.* 27 June.

Carson, C. and Ogle, V. E. (1996) 'Storage and retrieval of feature data for a very large online image collection', *Data Engineering Bulletin.* 19(4), 19–27.

Chesbrough, H. (2003) *Open Innovation: The New Imperative for Creating and Capturing Value,* Boston, MA: Harvard Business School Press.

Chesbrough, H. W. (2003) 'The era of open innovation', *Sloan Management Review.* 44(3), 35–41.

Clark, A. (2006) 'Companies wake up to blogs' barking', *The Guardian.* 19 September.

Clark, B. H. (1997) 'Welcome to my parlor', *Marketing Management.* Winter, 11–25.

Constantin, J. A. and Lusch, R. F. (1994) 'Understanding resource management', The Planning Forum. Oxford, OH.

Cooper, P. D. (1979) 'Health care marketing: issues and trends', Aspen Systems Corporation, Germantown, MD.

Coy, P. (2006) 'The secret to Google's success: its innovative auction system has ad revenues soaring', *Business Week.* 6 March.

Culnan, M. J. (1999a) 'Privacy and the top 100 websites: report to the Federal Trade Commission', Georgetown University, Washington, DC. June.

Culnan, M. J. (1999b) 'The Georgetown Internet privacy policy survey: report to the Federal Trade Commission', Georgetown University, Washington, DC. June.

Davenport, T. H. (1995) 'Marketing on the Internet', *Journal of Targeting, Measurement and Analysis for Marketing.* 261–69.

Deighton, J. and Narayandas, D. (2004) 'Service provision calls for partners instead of parties', in 'Invited commentaries on "Evolving to a new dominant logic for marketing"', *Journal of Marketing.* 68(1), 18–27.

Deshpande, R. (1999) '"Foreseeing" marketing', *Journal of Marketing.* 63, 164–70.

Dupree, L. and Bosarge, J. (2006) 'Media on the move: how to measure in- and out-of-home media consumption', ACNielsen. Available at: http://us.acnielsen.com/pubs/2004_q4_ci_media.shtml)

Fetterhoff, T. J. and Voelkel, D. (2006) 'Managing open innovation in biotechnology', *Research – Technology Management.* 49(3), 14–18.

Fishbein, M. and Azjen, I. (1975) *Belief, Attitude, Intention, and Behavior: An introduction to theory and research.* Reading, MA: Addison-Wesley.

Fountain, J. E. and Atkinson, R. D. (1998) 'Innovation, social capital, and the new economy: new federal policies to support collaborative research', PPI briefing. Progressive Policy Institute, Washington, DC: 1 July. (Available at www.ppionline.org/ppi_ci.cfm?knlgArealD=140&subsecID=293&contentID=1371)

Frederiksen, L. W., Solomon, L. J. and Brehony, K. A. (1984) *Marketing Health Behavior: Principles, techniques, and applications.* New York: Plenum.

Gauzente, C. and Ranchhod, A. (2001) 'Ethical marketing for competitive advantage on the Internet', *Academy of Marketing Science Review.* 10, The Academy of Marketing Science, University of Miami.

Gefter, A. (2006) 'Living online: this is your space', *New Scientist.* 16 September.

Giese, J. L. and Cote, J. A. (2000) 'Defining consumer satisfaction', *Academy of Marketing Science Review.* (Available at: http://oxygen.vancouver.wsu.edu/amsrev/theory/giese01-00.html)

Glanz, K., Lewis, F. M. and Rimer, B. K. (1990) *Health Behavior and Health Education Theory, Research and Practice.* San Francisco, CA: Jossey-Bass.

Gray, R. (1996) 'Making an impact on society', *Marketing.* 15 August, 26–8.

Griffith, D. A. (1998) 'Making the Web strategically accountable', *Marketing Management.* 13(3), 113–36.

Grönroos, C. (1997) 'Value-driven relational marketing: from products to resources and competencies', *Journal of Marketing Management.* 13(5), 407–19.

Grönroos, C. (2000) *Service Management and Marketing: A customer relationship management approach.* Chichester: Wiley.

Gummesson, E. (2002) 'Relationship marketing and a new economy: it's time for deprogramming', *Journal of Services Marketing.* 16(7), 585–89.

Gurău, C. (2005) 'The principles of online social marketing communication campaigns', Proceedings of the 10th Conference on Corporate and Marketing communications, Nicosia, Cyprus, 8–9 April. 76–91.

Handelman, J. M. and Arnold, S. J. (1999) 'The role of marketing actions with a social dimension: appeals to the institutional environment', *Journal of Marketing.* 63(3), 33–48.

Hochbaum, G. M., Sorenson, J. R. and Loring, K. (1992) 'Theory in health education practice', *Health Education Quarterly.* 19(3, fall), 295–313.

Hoffman, D. L. and Novak, T. P. (1996) 'Marketing in hypermedia computer-mediated environments: conceptual foundations', *Journal of Marketing.* 60(3), 50–68.

Karin, I. and Preiss, K. (2002) 'Strategic marketing models for a dynamic competitive environment', *Journal of General Management.* 24(4), 63–78.

Kaul, S. and Lobo, A. (2002) 'Rural thrust: sluggish sales push FMCG firms to take new initiatives', *Business India*. (2–15 September), 88–9.

Kelly, E. P. (2000) 'Ethical and online privacy in electronic commerce', *Business Horizons*. 43(3), 3–12.

Kitchen, P. J. (1999) *Marketing Communications: Principles and practice*. London: International Thomson Business Press.

Kotler, P. (1979) 'Strategies for introducing marketing in to non-profit organizations', *Journal of Marketing*. 43(1), 37–44.

Kotler, P. (2000) *Marketing Management* (The Millennium Edition). Englewood Cliffs, NJ: Prentice Hall.

Kotler, P. and Andreasen, A. R. (1991) *Strategic Marketing for Non-profit Organizations* (fourth edition). Englewood Cliffs, NJ: Prentice-Hall.

Kotler, P. and Clarke, R. N. (1986) *Marketing for Health Care Organizations*. Englewood Cliffs, NJ: Prentice-Hall.

Kotler, P. and Zalitrian, G. (1971) 'Social marketing: an approach to planned social change', *Journal of Marketing*. 35, 3–12.

Kripalani, M. (2002) 'Battling for pennies in India's villages: Coke and Pepsi struggle to control market', *BusinessWeek*. 3786, (10 June), 18.

Lefebvre, R. C. and Flora, J. A. (1988) 'Social marketing and public health intervention', *Health Education Quarterly*. 15(3), 299–315.

Lengnick-Hall, C. A. (1996) 'Customer contributions to quality: a different view of the customer-oriented firm', *The Academy of Management Review*. 21(3), 791–824.

Mahajan, V., Pratini De Moraes and Wind, J. (2000) 'The invisible global market', *Marketing Management*. 9(4, winter), 30.

Malhotra, S. and Mangrulkar, S. (2001) 'Branding in the last of unsaturated markets', *Design Management Journal*. 12(4, fall), 53–8.

Mascarenhas, O. A., Kesavan, R. and Bernacchi, M. (2004) 'Customer value chain involvement for co-creating customer delight', *Journal of Consumer Marketing*. 21(7), 486–96.

McKenna, R. (1997) *Real Time: Preparing for the age of the never satisfied customer*. Boston, MA: Harvard Business School Press.

McLeroy, K. R., Bibeau, D., Steckler, A. and Glanz, K. (1988) 'An ecological perspective on health promotion programs', *Health Education Quarterly*. 15, 351–77.

Mediaweek (2006) 'Flying higher and higher via mobile platforms', *Mediaweek*. 16(23), 4–6.

Mehta, D. (2002) 'Heroes: Vandana Shiva – seeds of self-reliance', *Time*. 60(10, September), 32.

Milstein, S. and Dornfest, R. (2004) *Google: The missing manual*. Cambridge, MA: Pogue Press and O'Reilly.

National Cancer Institute (1995) 'Theory at a glance: a guide for health promotion practice', US department of Health and Human Services, National Institutes of Health. (Available at: www.cancer.gov/PDF/481f5d53-63df-41bc-bfaf-5aa48ee1da4d/TAAG3.pdf)

National Science Board (2006) 'Science and engineering indicators 2006', National Science Foundation. (Available at: www.nsf.gov/statistics/seind06)

Normann, R. (2001) *Reframing Business: When the map changes the landscape*. Chichester: John Wiley.

Normann, R. and Ramírez, R. (1993) 'From value chain to value constellation: designing interactive strategy', *Harvard Business Review*. 71(4), 65–77.

Novartis (2001) 'A short course in social marketing', Novartis.

Ofcom (2006) 'The communications market 2006: 3 telecommunications, Ofcom. 10 August. (Available at: www.ofcom.org.uk/research/cm/cm06/telec.pdf)

Parvatiyar, A. and Sheth, J. N. (1997) 'Paradigm shift in interfirm marketing relationships', in Sheth, J. N. and Parvatiyar, A. (eds), *Research in Marketing* (Vol. 13). Greenwich, CT: Jai Press, 233–55.

Payne, A. and Holt, S. (2001) 'Diagnosing customer value: integrating the value process and relationship marketing', *British Journal of Management*. 12(2), 159–82.

Peters, L. (1998) 'The new interactive media: one-to-one, but who to whom?' *Marketing Intelligence & Planning*. 16(1), 22–30.

Prahalad, C. K. and Ramaswamy, V. (2003) 'The new frontier of experience innovation', *Sloan Management Review*. 44(4), 11–18.

Prahalad, C. K. and Ramaswamy, V. (2004) *The Future of Competition: Co-creating unique value with customers*. Boston, MA: Harvard Business School Press.

Prochaska, J. O., DiClemente, C. C. and Norcross, J. C. (1992) 'In search of how people change: applications to addictive behaviors', *American Psychologist*. 47(9), 1102–12.

Richards, A. (1995) 'Does charity pay?', *Marketing*. (21 September), 24–5.

Robinson, L. (1998) 'A 7 step social marketing approach', paper presented during the Waste Education Conference, Sydney, 20 November.

Rohner, K. (1998) *Marketing in the Cyber Age: The why, the what, and the how*. Chichester: John Wiley.

Rosenstock, I. M., Strecher, V. J. and Becker M. H. (1988) 'Social learning theory and the health belief model', *Health Education Quarterly*. 15, 175–83.

Rothschild, M. L. (1999) 'Carrots, sticks and promises: a conceptual framework for the management of public health and social issues behaviors', *Journal of Marketing*. 63, 24–37.

Schneider, B. and Bowden, D. E. (1999) 'Understanding customer delight and outrage', *Sloan Management Review*. 41(1), 35–45.

Sheth, J. and Sisodia, R. S. (1995) 'Feeling the heat: making marketing more productive', *Marketing Management*. 4(2), 8–23.

Sheth, J. N. and Sisodia, R. S. (1999) 'Revisiting marketing's lawlike generalisations', *Academy of Marketing Science Journal*. 27(1), 71–87.

Sheth, J. N., Sisodia, R. S. and Sharma, A. (2000) 'The antecedents and consequences of customer-centric marketing', *Journal of the Academy of Marketing Science*. 28(1), 55–66.

Taylor, Chris (2006) 'The future is in South Korea', *Business 2.0 Magazine* 14 June. (Available at: http://money.cnn.com)

The Economist (2003) 'The IT revolution: the best thing since the bar code', *The Economist*. 366(8310), 71–2.

The Shosteck Group (2006) 'Two sides to every story: is mobile advertising good for Mobile?' The Shosteck Group. June.

US Bureau of the Census (1997) 'Population profile of the United States: 1997', Series P23–194, Washington, DC, US Bureau of the Census.

Vargo, S. L. and Lusch, R. F. (2004) 'Evolving to a new dominant logic for marketing', *Journal of Marketing*. 68(1), 1–17.

Webster Jr, F. E. (1992) 'The changing role of marketing in the corporation', *Journal of Marketing*. 56(4), 1–17.

Westbrook, A. R. (1987) 'Product/consumption-based affective responses and postpurchase processes', *Journal of Marketing Research*. 24(3), 258–70.

Wright, J. (2006) *Blog marketing: The revolutionary new way to increase sales, profits and growth*. New York: McGraw Hill.

Wyner, G. A. (2002) 'Tracking an expanding universe', *Marketing Research*. 14(1), 4–8.

Index

accommodating stakeholder relationships 107
accounting 296, 301
'Achilles heels' 32
ACORN approach to segmentation 56–7
activity ratios 300
adaptability of firms 302, 305
added value 306
'adhocracies' 8, 238
adoption of a product 36–7
Adshead, Fiona 377
advertising 153–5, 306; 'obsolescence' of 76
AEG 94–5
ageing industries 34
airline industry 42–3, 62–5
alliances of companies 286–7, 371
Amazon 19, 23, 252
Ambler, T. 188
American Association of Advertising Agents (AAAA) 157
American Marketing Association (AMA) 4–5
Amnesty International 24
Andreasen, A.R. 60
Anheuser-Busch 135
annual reports and accounts 90, 297
Ansoff matrix 50
Apple Computers 9–11, 359
Aravind Eye Care System 252–3
arbitration 103
Arcelor 106
Arlov, Laura 62
Armani 187
Armstrong, A. 77
Asda 176–7
Ashridge mission model 15–16
Asia Pacific Resources International (APRIL) 129–32
Atkinson, R.D. 347
attractiveness of an industry 41, 48–9
Audi 215
audit committees 90
Austria 120
automation 216

average collection period 300

Baconguis, Beau 93
Baenen, Sean 45
Baetz, M. 16
Balu, Rekha 387
banking services 25
Barbut, Monique 114
Barnes & Noble 252
Barney, J.B. 253
Bart, C. 16
Bartlett, C.A. 292
BCG matrix 34–5
Beauty and the Bees 270
Bebo 76, 352–3
Becker, M. 362
Beckham, David 314
behaviour models 373
behavioural attributes, segmentation by 56
Behlendorf, Brian 345
Ben & Jerry's 289–91
benchmarking studies 254
Benetton 285
Benkler, Yochai 344
Berman, Steve 45
Bernat, Xavier 313–14
Bevan, Judi 79
Beverland, M. 159
Bhatia v. *Sterlite Industries* 100
Bilkey, W.J. 265–6
Biocatalyst 46
biotechnology industry 23, 47, 108–9
Blair, Tony 186–7
blogs 77, 352, 358–62
Bluetooth devices 222
boards of directors 83–6
body mass index 382
The Body Shop 134, 268, 289–90, 369
Boeker, W. 18
Bond, Archy 177
'born global' companies 267–70
Borys, B. 205
Bosarge, J. 362

Boston Consulting Group (BCG) 34, 249
boundaries between industries, blurring of 349
Bracy, Michael 45
Bradesco 25–6
brand equity 158–9, 180, 188–9, 297, 306–7, 312–13, 325
brand image 42, 95–6, 111–12, 135
brand management 180–1, 189
brand names 175, 177, 188–9
brand relationships 168
brand salient attributes (BSAs) 187
brand strategies 178–80
brand values 184, 188–9
Branson, Richard 22
Brazil 125
Brin, Sergey 364
British Biotechnology 108–10
broadband technology 154, 171, 214, 352–3
Broderick, A. 157, 161
Bronfenbrenner, K. 273
budgeting 161
Budweiser beer 180
bureaucratic learning systems 245, 261
Bush, George W. 88, 103
Business in the Community 146
business intelligence 217
Business Week 185
buyer power 46–7, 99

Cadbury-Schweppes 289–91
Calori, R. 238–40
Calvin Klein 187
Cameron, K. 237
Campbell's brand 180
capacity utilisation 46
Cappi, Luiz Carlos Trabuco 25
car manufacturers 46
Carat UK 154
carbon dioxide emissions 94, 116, 119, 121
Carrillat, F.A. 8
cartels 44

Cartier 277
'cash cows' 34–5
Castronova, Edward 357–8
Cavusgil, S.T. 269
Caywood, C. 163–5
census data 56
Century21 285
CFCs (chlorofluorocarbons) 139–40
challengers in a market, strategies available to 209–10
change, organisational, fear of 162
Chappell, Tom 290
charities 4–5, 92
chemicals, use of 117, 127
chief executive officers (CEOs) 83–4, 88, 91–2, 103, 198
chief financial officers 88
China 116, 119, 129, 273
Chowdhury, Jitubhai 123
Christian Aid 92
Chupa Chups 313–14
Ciarelli, Nick 359
Cisco Systems 42
clan culture 238
Clark, Andrew 359
Clarkson, Jeremy 186–7
clean technology 133
Clegg, S.R. 76
Cleland, K. 161
climate change 94–5, 116–17, 122
cloned headquarters for firms operating abroad 288
'close race' markets 207
closed-loop planning 166–9
Coca-Cola 19, 42–3, 47, 146, 154, 180, 183, 277–8, 285, 291, 387
Coco Pops 188–9
co-creation marketing 330, 335–42
cognitive-behavioural models 373–5
Cohen, J.B. 55
Colgate-Palmolive 42, 187, 289–90
collaborator companies 219
Committee for Foreign Investment in the United States (CFIUS) 105
Common Short Code (CSC) 362–3
communications technology 2–3; see also information and communication technology
communicative action, theory of 105
communist countries 103, 276
community networks 366
company law, harmonisation of 90
competition factors contributing to market attractiveness 49
competitive advantage 7, 38, 100–1,

136, 142, 202–5, 257, 261, 276, 335; and ethics 366–8; and mission 39–40; sustainability of 115
competitive industries 42–3
competitive marketing strategies 101–8
competitive position 34, 206–10
competitive strength 48–9
competitors: differentiation from 71, 73, 367; range and diversity of 43–4
complementary resources 39
complex adaptive systems 251–2
computer games 41, 59
computer hardware industry 46
computer-mediated environment (CME) 329
computer software industry 43
concentration, industrial 43
concept-led organisations 252–3
conceptual use of knowledge 257
Connett, Marie 345
consolidation 209
Constantin, J.A. 335
consumer behaviour 331–3, 347; see also under customer(s)
consumption patterns, multiple influences on 145
contact points and contact preferences 158–9, 168
Conti, T. 102, 112
Cooper, Alan 62
Co-operative Bank 16, 319–20
cooptition in marketing 347
coordination within companies 229
corporate governance 82–90; government and global pressures on 86–7
corporate identity 156, 171–2
corporate reputation, measurement of 91–2
corporate social responsibility (CSR) 87–8, 100, 181, 360; and the law 88–9
cost advantages or disadvantages 42, 46
cost leadership strategy 202–3
Costello, Jim195
Coutts, Teddi215
Cova, B.75–6
Covisint252
Crest187
Cruyff, Johan314
Culnan, M.J.367
cultural creative (CC) consumers 141
cultural model of meaning 156
cultural patterns and norms 227

cultural practices 236
culture, organisational 162, 235–41; definition of 236; questionnaire on 239–40; types of 237–8; uniqueness of 253–4; visible and invisible aspects of 228; see also marketing culture
current ratio 299
customer equity 96
customer lifetime value (CLV) 66–9, 307–10
customer loyalty 11, 96, 219, 332–4
customer orientation and customercentric approaches 7, 241–2, 328–36, 391
customer power 47, 95
customer relationship management (CRM) 204, 211–12, 218–23, 331; three phases of 221
customer relationships 261; in different markets 68; duration of 69
customer retention 96, 220–1, 307, 312
customer satisfaction 11–12, 96, 204, 215, 307, 311–12, 335
customers: acquisition of 220; characteristics 55; definition of 68; enhancement of profitability of 220; information on 211–13, 367; and marketing strategy 210–13; types of 141, 360
'cyclone' markets 207
Cyworld 358

Darwin, Charles 251
databases, use of 53, 161, 168, 174, 332
data-mining 211, 242
Datamonitor 382
David, F. 16–17
Day, S.G. 33, 258
Dean Foods 289
debt-to-assets ratio 300
decentralisation of decision-making 160
defensive stakeholder relationships 107
Dell Computers 19–20, 215, 359
Deloitte Hoskins 218
demographic segmentation 57–8
departmentalisation 229
design of products, flexibility in 339
deutero-learning 246, 250, 261
developing countries 272, 276
Diageo 193–5

Diamond Cluster International 274
Diaz, Cameron 144
Dibb, S. 191–3
Dibrell, C. 20
dieting 382–3
differentiation 202–3; between
        departments within a firm 29,
        234; from competitors 71, 73,
        367
diffusion of products 36–7
digital cameras 23
digital divide 4
digital loyalty networks 218–19
digital marketing 351–3, 364
Dillon, W.R. 187
'direct confrontation' situations 208
'direct response' advertising 154
directional policy matrix (DPM) 50
directors of companies 83–6;
        disqualification of 90;
        non-executive 89–90
Disneyworld 181
distribution channels 42
Dixons Group 17
Djemal, Leila 268
'dogs' 34–5
Doha round of trade talks 119
dominant competitive position 34
Dornfest, R. 364
dot.com businesses 309
double-loop learning 246, 253–4,
        261
Doyle, P. 101, 296
Duncan, A. 154
Duncan, T. 158, 161–5
DuPont 344
Dupree, L. 362
dynamic marketplaces 346–51
Dyson, James 73
Dyson vacuum cleaner 36, 73

early adopter consumers 36–7
early majority consumers 37
easyJet and easyGroup 22, 42
e-Bay 7–8, 23, 352
eco-efficiency 316
ecological footprint 114, 123–4
ecological perspectives 372–3; *see
        also* industrial ecology
economic factors contributing to
        market attractiveness 49
Edmondson, A. 246
Edsjö, Karl 143
efficiency and effectiveness 302–6
Electrolux 143
electronics industry 127–8
Elle 268
embryo cloning 103

embryonic industries 34
émigrés 384–6
Eminem 44–5
emotions and marketing 334
employees: conflict with 103; roles
        of 100
'encirclement' strategy 209
energy consumption 94–5
Enron 87, 90–1, 300
entry barriers 42–3
environment, definition of 13–14
environmental concerns 77–8
environmental effectiveness,
        measurement of 315–19
environmental factors affecting
        strategy 14–15
environmental justice 116
environmental marketing 115–25
Environmental Protection Agency,
        US 115, 133
Ericsson 286
Escotel 387
ESRC Centre for Business Research
        196
Ethical Consumer magazine 290–1
ethical investment 16, 118, 136
ethical issues 116, 138, 149, 289
ethical marketing 24, 368
ethical stance matrix 136–7
ethics as a source of competitive
        advantage 366–8
ethnic minority communities 278
euro currency 91
European Agency for the Evaluation
        of Medicinal Products (EMEA)
        108–9
European Commission 133
European Single Market 91
European Union 90, 95, 103, 349
evolution, theory of 251
exit barriers 46
expansionary marketing strategy
        209
expectations of customers 11–12
experience effects 312
experiential advantages 22
experiential learning 19
explicit knowledge 249
exploitation/exploration balance
        255
exporting 284–5
external analysis by companies 40–5

fairtrade policies 81
'family lifecycle' concept 60
favourable competitive position 34
fear of change 162
feedback analysis 174

Fetterhoff, T.J. 341
Fiat 286
Financial Accounting Standards
        Board 87
financial analysis 297–8
financial factors contributing to
        market attractiveness 49
financial measures of performance
        301
Financial Reporting Council 90
Financial Research Survey (FRS) 61
Financial Times 108
FINPIN coding 61
Fiol, C.M. 245
Firat, A.F. 77
first mover advantages and
        disadvantages 19
Fisher, Lori 343–4
five-forces model of industry analysis
        43–4
fixed asset turnover ratio 300
'flanking attacks' 208
Fletcher, K.P. 259
flexibility of marketing structures
        and processes 337–40
flexible working arrangements 214
Flora 154
follower firms, advantages and
        disadvantages of 208
Food and Drug Administration 109
food safety 98
Ford Motors 77, 135
foreign markets, selection of 278–81
forest sustenance 131
formalisation of communication
        processes 229, 231
Foster, D. 104, 106
founders of companies 18
Fountain, J.E. 347
4:40 effect 113–14
'Four Ps' concept (product, price,
        promotion and place) 328–9
Foxall, G.R. 104
fragmentation: of markets 2–3, 76,
        150, 172, 278, 332, 335; of
        society 3, 75
France 87
franchising to foreign countries
        285–6
Frank, R.E. 55
Franklin Associates 140
Freeman, E. 82
Freeman, J. 18
Freeman, S. 237
Freeserve 17
French, Jeff 377
Friedman, Milton 88
Friends of the Earth 92–3

Fuller, D.A. 140
functional specialisation within
    firms 160–1

Gallup Polls 139
Gap Inc. 115, 187
GardenWeb 77
Gates, Bill 25
gearing 300
Geels, Scott 186
general brand impressions (GBIs)
    187
General Electric 48, 114–15
General Motors 135, 286
genetic engineering 342
genetically-modified (GM) foods
    92–4, 97–8
Geocities 76–7
geodemographic segmentation 61
geographic segmentation 56–7
Germany 87–9, 94, 113, 120, 382
Ghoshal, S. 292
Giddings, L. Val 344
Gillette 351
Girod, M. 250
global marketing 277–8
global organisations 293
globalisation 86–7, 91, 96, 116, 118,
    263–5, 271–3, 277, 294, 347,
    388; impact on small and
    medium-size companies 273;
    knowledge about 271
Godin, S. 211
Goldmacher, Steve 143–4
Goodman, Michael 45
Google 7–8, 23, 154, 364
Google ad professionals (GAPs) 365
Gosbee, Bill 215
government regulation 42
Grant, Hugh 343
Grant, Karen 268
Grant, R.M. 17
Green & Black's 289, 292
green consumers 139–42, 147
green management 138
green marketing 123–5, 142, 146
green products 115, 122, 125, 149
Greenbury, Richard 80
greenhouse gases 119
Greenley, E.G. 104
Greenpeace 92–4, 97–8, 125–8, 135,
    146
'greenwashing' 134, 137, 141
'grey' market 58
Griffin, R.W. 162
The Grocer 176
Gronstedt, A. 165–6
gross profit margin 298

ground positioning systems (GPS)
    222
growth industries 34
growth vector analysis 50–1
'guerilla attacks' 210
Guinness 193–5
Gurau, C. 282
GUS (beta-glucuronidase gene)
    342–3
GUS (Great Universal Stores) 80

Habermas, Jürgen 105
Hagel, J. 77
Haji-Ioannou, Stelios 22
Hamel, G. 15, 100
Hannan, M.T. 18
Hardiyanti, Anny 130
Harrison, Nick 176
Hart, S.L. 136
'harvesting' strategy 207
Harvey-Jones, Sir John 181
Hassell, Chris 155
Hasson, Sharon 267–9
health belief model (HBM) 374–5
Heath, Martin 214, 217
hedonic benefits from products 187
Heinzer, Bruno 93
Hensley, David 313
Heseltine, Michael 80
HFCs (hydrofluorocarbons) 95
hierarchical culture 238
Higgs Report (2003) 88–90
Highson, C.J. 296
high-tech goods 348–9
Hindustan Lever 386–8
Hjerpe, Jonas 215
Hodgkinson, Tom 21
Hofstede, G. 236
holistic approaches 328
Homburg, C. 241
home working 215–16
Honore, Carl 21
horizontal communication 160
Human Genome Project 23
human resource management 256
Hunt, Justin 216
hyperreality 3, 76, 365
hypertext organisations 260–2
Hyundai 33

IBM 62, 65, 236, 343, 345
identity, sense of 15–17
image, corporate 155–6, 171–4
image marketing 76
implementation of marketing
    strategies 6, 190–202, 220;
    bottom-up or top-down
    199–200; impact of tech-

nology on 213–14; main
    influences on 195–7;
    management intervention in
    202; planned or emergent
    190–3; role of people in 199,
    202
implementation matrix 224, 226
India 116, 119, 123, 129, 273
individualism 3, 76
industrial ecology 134
Industrial Marketing and Purchasing
    Group 204
industrial sectors, definition of 41
industry analysis 47–8
industry attractiveness/business
    competitive strength matrix
    48–9
inertia, organisational 18
informal economy 384
information and communication
    technology (ICT) 151,
    210–11
information-seeking culture 245
information systems 52–3, 174, 212,
    220, 329
information technology (IT)
    213–15, 347
information transmission, speed and
    cost of 349–51
infrastructure, technological,
    organisational and
    administrative 213
innovation models 340–1
innovativeness of a particular firm
    302
innovator consumers 36
inputs to marketing 303–4
institutional investors 86–7, 109
instrumental use of knowledge 256–7
intangible resources 29–30
integrated marketing
    communications (IMC)
    150–75, 189; advantages of
    158–9; definition of 157–8;
    implementation of the
    concept 159–70; in an online
    environment 170–5
integrated online marketing
    communications (IOMC)
    170–5
Intel 183, 246
interdependencies of partner firms
    205–6
internal analysis by companies
    29–40
internal resources of companies
    30–2; and corporate
    objectives 39–40

international firms 292–3
International Forum on
    Globalisation 388
international marketing operations
    264–5, 276–80, 284–5
internationalisation 263–4; of firms
    265–7; knowledge about 271
Internet banking 25
Internet companies 100
Internet resources 2, 23, 44, 47, 76,
    96, 151–5, 170–3, 210, 213,
    217, 220, 278, 307–9, 329–30,
    352–3, 367–8, 376; conflicting
    tendencies created by 172
Internetisation 263–4
inventory: in relation to net working
    capital 299; turn-over ratio
    300
invisible parts of an organisation
    233–41
iPods 9–11, 349, 359
Italy 113

Jabulika Uranium Mine 105
Jefferson, Richard A. 342–6
Jeffery, Will 155
Jemison, D.B. 205
Jobs, Steve 9–11
Johnson, G. 13–14
joint ventures 287–8
Jones, Helen 290
Jones, Neil 154
Jonker, J. 104, 106
Jorgensen, Richard 343

Kalakota, R. 220
Kaufman-Scarborough, C. 20
Kaviratne, Nihal 387
Keegan, W. 157
Keir, Nathan 355, 357
Kellogg's 135, 188–9
Kentucky Fried Chicken (KFC) 154
Kim, D.H. 247–50
King County Commission 147
Kishore, Ganesh 344
Kitchen, P.J. 158, 166–70
Kleisterlee, Gerard 185–6
Knight, G. 269
Knight, L. 259
know-how 42, 246
know-why 246
knowledge, uses of 256–7
knowledge management (KM) 217
Kodak 23
Konno, N. 260
Kotler, Philip 171, 302, 371
Kovac, Carol 345
KPMG 216

Kumar, Bharat 232–3
Kumar, S. Ramesh 232
Kyoto Protocol 119

labour-saving devices 20
laggard adopters of new products 37
Lang, Tim 291
La Roque, Ed 144
late majority consumers 37
Lawer, C. 211
leapfrog strategy 209
learning: contexts of 259; culture of
    251–4; *lower level* and *higher*
    level of 243–5, 255;
    organisational (and learning
    organisations) 223, 242–3,
    246–9, 255–61; *see also*
    market-based learning
learning audits 246–7
learning orientation, benefits of 250
learning processes 243–6
learning systems 245–6
Leeds City Council 216
legitimacy 105
Lego 23
Leroy, Phillipe 25
Lessig, Lawrence 345
leverage 15, 17, 22, 24; by
    customers 211
leverage ratios 300
Levinthal, D.A. 254–5
Levis 19, 184–7
Levitt, T. 277
Lewis, W.F. 104
L.G. Balakrishnan & Brothers (LGB)
    232–3
liberalisation 118, 272
licensing agreements 285
lifecycle analysis (LCA) 126, 140
lifecycle concept 332
lifecycle design (LCD) 133
life-enhancing experiences and
    services 211, 335
life-stage segmentation 60
'lifestyle snapshots' 62–5
lifestyles of health and sustainability
    (LOHAS) 141–2, 145
lifetime relationships with customers
    96
lifetime value of customers 66–9
Lindquist, J.D. 20
Lindstrom, M. 23
liquidity ratios 299
long-term debt to equity ratio 300
loyalty networker companies 219
Luce, S. 273
Lunn, A. 56
Lusch, R.F. 30, 204, 335

Luxton, S. 159
Lyles, M.A. 245
Lyons, Sir Jack 195

McDonald, M.H.B. 12–13
McDonald's 124–5, 181, 277–9, 285
McKean, J. 223
McKinsey Consulting Group 48
McLaughlin, Danny 214–15
McLoughlin, Coleen 176
McSweeney, John 194
Makower, J. 142
Malik, Pravir 253
management innovation model of
    experiential learning 265–6
March, J.G. 254–5
Marismastat 108–9
market-based learning (MBL) 257–8
market-driven and *market-driving*
    strategies 7–8
market entry strategies 284–9
market factors contributing to
    industry attractiveness 49
market leaders 19; strategies
    available to 208–9
market-led organisations 231
market orientation and *market-*
    orientated organisations 6–9,
    258–62, 296–7
market orientation scales 6
market quality and *market position*,
    assessment of 51
market research 72–3, 332, 336
market shares 35, 297, 312
market strategies, *efficiency* and
    effectiveness of 302–6
market structures 347–8
market takers 219
marketing, definition of 4–5
marketing audits 302–3
marketing concept 4–5; strategic
    planning for delivery of
    12–14
marketing culture 236, 238
marketing information systems
    52–3
marketing knowledge 256; uses of
    230–1
'marketing myopia' 41
marketing process 5–6
markets, definition of 69
Marks, Michael 79
Marks, Simon 80
Marks & Spencer (M&S) 79–81, 84,
    99, 103
Marlboro band 180
Martin International 99
mass communication 76, 150

mass customisation 241
mass marketing 2
mature industries 34
Mazur, L. 184
Mead, Chris 356
Menon, A. 256–7
mental models 248–50, 261–2
Mercedes 277
mergers of companies 289
metrics of marketing 297, 301
Mexico 273
Michel, Christoph 215
microprocessor prices 350
Microsoft 7, 36, 41, 43, 77, 355
Miller, John 387
Miller, R.L. 104
Millier, Paul 197–8
Milstein, S. 364
Mindak, W. 171
Mintzberg, H. 12–13, 229, 237
mission, corporate 15–16, 39–40
mission statements 16–17
Mitsubishi 135
Mittal Steel 106
mobile marketing 362–3
mobile phones 37
mobile working 214, 216
mobility of labour 347
modern consumers 141
Moglen, Eben 343
Moingeon, B. 246
Mokwa, M.P. 191
money as a resource 30
monochromic consumers 20
Monsanto 92, 343
Mooney, Paul 93
Morgan, Andrew 194–5
Morgan, Charles 182
Morgan, N.A. 303
Morgan Motor Company 55, 181
MORI 113, 145
Moriarty, S. 161–5
Morrison's 177
MOSAIC coding 61
Mulholland, Andy 215
multiculturalism 278, 294–5
multinational corporations 96, 124,
      220, 286, 289–92, 384
multinational marketing orientation
      274
Munoz, Canesio P. 129–30
MySki Inc. 330
MySpace 76–7, 155, 352, 354
mythological learning systems 245

Naik, V.M. 386
nappies, *disposable* and *reusable* 140
Narver, J.C. 6

National (US) Environmental
      Education and Training
      Foundation 139
National (US) Science Board 348–9
National (US) Science Foundation
      139
Natural Marketing Institute 141
Navdanya 388
NBC 155
Nestlé 97–8, 290
net income 299
net profit margin 298
Netherlands, the 87
network learning 259
networked environment 152–3
new entrants, threat from 41–2
new products: firms' approaches to
      208; users of 36–7
News Corp. 155
Next 81
niche firms and niche markets 55,
      203, 289
Niemann, I. 168–9
Nike 24, 125–6
Nintendo 23, 43
Noble, C.H. 191
Nokia 128
Nonaka, I. 249, 260,
non-executive directors (NEDs)
      89–90
non-governmental organisations
      (NGOs) 92–4, 309–10, 391
not-for-profit organisations 309–10
Novartis 93
Novo Nordisk 320–1
NTL 365
nuclear power 95

Oates, Keith 80
obesity 381–3
objectives, corporate 39, 297
observability of products 36
Ofcom 154, 352, 359
offshoring 272–6
oligopoly 43, 286
Oliver, Jamie 377
Omidyar, Pierre M. 354
'one minute customers' 211
one-to-one marketing 76
online communities 77
online games 354–6
online marketing 41, 213, 307,
      329–30, 376–7, 380–2
OPEC (Organisation of Petroleum
      Exporting Countries) 44
'open innovation' model 340–2
operant and *operand* resources 30–1,
      335, 338–9

opportunities: in stakeholder
      management 107; in target
      markets 40–1; *see also* SWOT
      analysis
Orange 286
L'Oréal 289–90
O'Reilly, C. 237
organic products 148–9
Organisation for Economic
      Cooperation and
      Development (OECD) 82–3,
      272
organisational charts of the
      marketing function 227–8
organisational culture profile (OCP)
      237; *see also* culture,
      organisational
organisational learning *see* learning:
      organisational
organisational memory 250
organisational structures of firms
      159–63, 229–31, 256
Oucchi, W. 237
outputs of marketing 303–4
outsourcing 274–6
Oxfam 92, 115
ozone depletion 95

Page, Larry 364
Palmer, Mark 290–1
Parkin, Matthew 182
Parnes, Anthony 195
parsimony in measurement 297
participative learning systems 245
participative strategic planning
      200–1
patent protection 19, 22–3, 42, 285,
      345–8
PCBs (polychlorinated biphenyls)
      114–16
PDCA (plan-do-check-act) cycle 134
Pearce, J. 16
Pedelty, Mervyn 319
Pepsi-Cola 43, 47, 180
perceptual maps 72–5, 187, 367
Percy, L. 160–2
performance measurement 296–7,
      301–4, 312; for individual
      companies 324–6; three tiers
      of indicators for 309
Perman, Stacy 269
personal data on customers 211
personal video recorders (PVRs) 154
personalised marketing 2–3, 150,
      204, 338–9
personality characteristics 61
personas (Cooper) 62–5
Peterkin, Mary 314

Peters, L.D. 259
Petrini, Carlo 21
pharmaceutical companies 42, 44, 47
Philippines, the 93
Philips group 22, 143–4, 185–6, 313
Piatok, Avi 267
Pickton, D. 157, 161
Piergallini, Al 93
Piet a Manger 289
PinPoint analysis 61
pioneer firms, advantages and disadvantages of 208
Pizza Hut 285
PlayStation games platform 23, 58–9
pollution 116
polychromic attitude index (PAI) 20
pooled interdependence of partner firms 205
Porsche 89
Porter, M. 38, 41–6, 202–3, 340
portfolio matrices 52
positioning 29, 71–3, 109–12: of brands 187; *horizontal* and *vertical* 39
postcodes 57
postmodernism and the postmodern marketing environment 3, 75–7, 150, 214
Prahalad, C.K. 15, 204, 335
precautionary principle 127–8
price reductions 210
pricing mechanisms 329
privacy 351, 367
proactive stakeholder relationships 107
'problem children' 34–5
Prochaska, J.O. 373
Procter & Gamble 11, 55, 154, 183, 387
Proctor, T. 158
product development process 38–9, 330, 349
product differentiation 46
product lifecycle (PLC) model 33–7
product portfolio analysis 33–5
production, flexibility in 339
productivity analysis for marketing 303
profiles of priority consumer segments 71
profit impact of marketing strategies (PIMS) 46
profit margins 298
profit ratios 298–9
promotions for marketing, impact of 314–15
psychographic segmentation 61, 65

Public Interest Disclosure Act 100
PVC (polyvinyl chloride) 128

qualitative variables for segmentation 56
quick ratio 299
'quiet pond' markets 207
Quinn, R. 237

Rachel's Organic 289
Raebe, Felix 93
Ramaswamy, V. 204, 335
Rampton, S. 137
rational market planning 12–13
rationality 105–6
ratios, financial 298–300
Ray, Paul 141
reactive stakeholder relationships 107
reciprocal interdependence of partner firms 205
recycling 124–5
Reebok 24
Reeves, Byron B. 357
reflection, need for 255
regionalisation of marketing programmes 56
regulation 88–90
relationship marketing 96, 330
relationship webs 223
relocation of operations abroad 274
Renault 275
representation as a method of participation 200–1
research and development 340
resource-based strategy 17
resources, *tangible* and *intangible* 29–30
responsible marketing 145–6
return on customer investment (ROCI) 169
return on investment (ROI) 297, 307–9
return on shareholders' equity 299
return on total assets 299
Riau Andalan Pulp and Paper (RAPP) 129–32
rivalry, industrial 42–3
Rivers Run Red 355
Roberts, Julia 267
Robinson, L. 371–2
Robinson, M. 220
Roddick, Anita 290–1
Rogers, E.M. 36
Rohrbaugh, J. 237
Ronson, Gerald 195
Rooney, Wayne 176
Roper-Starch Worldwide 140

Rose, Stuart 81
Rosedale, Philip 355
Rosenstock, I.M. 374
Rosselson, Ruth 291
Rowley, T. 104
rural marketing 383–6
Russell, Andrew 382
Russia 116
Ryanair 42

Sabon 267–9
Sadler, David 99
Safeway 80
Sainsbury's 176–7, 377
salient features of products 72–4
Salsbury, Peter 80
Sams, Craig 291
Sarandon, Susan 267
Sarbanes-Oxley Act 88–9
Sarnin, P. 238–40
Sashittal, H.C. 191
Saunders, Ernest 195
Saunders, Jill 270
scale effects 312
Schein, E.H. 18, 235–6
Schlenker, Brent T. 355
Schneider, Friedrich 384
Scholes, K. 13–14
Schultz, C.J. 77
Schultz, D.E. 166–70
Scoble, Robert 355
search engines 364–5
Second Life 3–4, 76, 352–8, 365
second mover marketing strategy 19
Securities and Exchange Commission 87
segmentation 5, 50–5, 150, 198, 309–11, 332, 347, 380–1; constant evolution of 77; criteria for 55–7, 69–71; by customer lifetime value 66–9; demographic 57–8; geodemographic 61; geographic 56–7; by life-stage 60; modified model of 333; process of 69–71; psychographic 61, 65; by sex 57–8
self-efficacy concept 374
sequential interdependence of partner firms 205
service-dominant logic in marketing 335–7
sex segmentation 57–8
shadow economy 384
Shalett, Mike 45
'share of voice' 313
shareholder value principle 101

shareholders 86–91; and corporate social responsibility 87–8; protection of 87; rights of 101; roles of 90–1
Shell Chemicals 50
Shiva, Vandana 388
Shrivastava, P. 243, 245, 248
Siegle, Lucy 21
Simkin, L. 191–3
Singer, Stephen 94–5
single-loop learning 243–5, 261
size of firms 186–7
Slater, S.N. 6
'sleeper' resources 32
slogans for brands 313
slow food movement 20–2
small and medium-size firms (SMEs) 196–9, 267, 272, 283; and globalisation 273
Smith, Digby 182
Smith, Sir Robert 90
social attitudes 144
social capital 347
social class, concept of 57–8
social marketing 147–9, 368–82; definition of 369; ecological perspectives on 372–3; online 376–7, 380–2; role of campaigns in 281, 375–7; websites for 377–82
social networking 352
social relationships within organisations 162
social responsibility 92; see also corporate social responsibility
Society for the Promotion of Lifecycle Development (SPOLD) 132–3
sociopolitical factors contributing to market attractiveness 49
Sony 8, 23, 43, 59, 77, 286, 313
Sørensen, Lars Rebien 321
Spain 113
specialisation within companies 229
'stages of change' model 373–4
stakeholder influence, network theory of 104
stakeholder interactions 82–6
stakeholder management 101–12
stakeholder power 105, 109–10
stakeholder theory 82–101
stakeholders 5, 17, 114, 153, 158, 165–6; definition of 79, 82, 103–4
stalemate situations 207
Stallman, Richard 345
standardisation: of company procedures 229; of products 277–8, 338

'star' products 34–6
Starbucks 7
Stauber, J. 137
Stefani, Martin 93
stem cell research 103, 105
Sterlite Industries 100
Stiles, P. 84
Stock Exchange Commission, US 89
stockmarket pressure 102
strategic alliances 286–7, 371
Strategic Compensation Research Associates 100
strategic co-ordination 157
strategic groups 206–10
strategic marketing 1, 5–6, 77; abroad 283; new model of 388–90
strategic marketing planning 24–7
strategic planning 104, 160–1, 388; key components of 27–8; of marketing 12–14
strategic withdrawal from a market 209
strategy/power matrix 110–11
strengths, organisational 30–2; see also SWOT analysis
strong competitive position 34
Styers, John 364
subcontracting to foreign firms 274
subsidiary companies 288–9, 292
substitutes 47
Sulston, Sir John 343
Sunny Delight 183
supermarkets 177
supplier power 47, 98–9
supply chain collaboration index 218–19
supply chain relationships 204–6, 218
surface-level learning 253
sustainability 113–15, 119–20, 149; of marketing 126
sustainable lifestyle marketing model 145–6
Swiss watches 47
Swissair 42, 62–5
SWOT analysis 12, 24, 163, 165
symbolic use of knowledge 257
synergy 112, 157, 159, 170–1, 242, 287–8

tacit knowledge 249
tactical performance measures 324–5
Takeuchi, H. 249, 260
tangible resources 29–30
Tankersley, C. 191
technological advances 2–4, 17, 22–4
technological deployment 213

technological factors contributing to market attractiveness 49
technology: convergence of 365; likely future impact of 350–1
Technorati 352
television 153–5
tenable competitive position 34
Tesar, G. 265–6
Tesco 2, 176–7
text messaging 352
Thatcher, Margaret 80
Thompson, John M. 62
threats: in stakeholder management 107; in target markets 40–2; see also SWOT analysis
time: perceptions of 20; as an issue in planning 18–20; value of 211
time pentagon 18
TNS Worldpanel 176–7
Toenniessen, Gary 344
Tom's of Maine 289–90
Tombraider game 36
total quality environment management (TQEM) 134
toxic substances 116
Toyota 135, 144
traditional consumers 141
transactional marketing 278
transnational organisations 294
trialability of products 36
tribal marketing 203, 338
triple bottom line (TBL) 320, 326
Tripod 76–7
turbulence, environmental 14, 112
24-hour shopping 2

Unilever 154, 289–91, 386–7
United Nations Environment Programme (UNEP) 118, 120, 144–5
United States 88, 116, 119, 211, 347–9; Supreme Court 346
unlearning 254–5
Uppsala model of experiential learning 265–6
'usage scenarios' 63–5
'use cases' 63
Usunier, J.-C. 56

value-added 146, 204
value added chain, concept of 38–9
value co-creation, theory of 204
value constellations 340–1
value in use 335
value-creating processes 4, 204–6
value-defining, value-developing and value-delivering processes 5–6
values 235–6

Vandevelde, Luc 80
Varadarajan, P.R. 256–7
Vargo, S.L. 30, 204
Virgin Atlantic and Virgin group 22, 215
virtual communities 77, 379
virtual environments 3, 329, 355–8
Visa 24, 77
visible parts of an organisation 228–33
Voelkel, D. 341
Vogel, D. 115
Vogue 268
Volkswagen 155

Waitrose 177
Wal-Mart 176–7, 359
Walsh, Fiona 291
WAP technology 65

Warner index of social classification 58
waste, electronic 128–9
water, use of 123
weak competitive position 34
weaknesses, organisational 30–2; *see also* SWOT analysis
websites 377–82
Weiss, M.J. 61
WH Smith 234
Wilkie, W.L. 55
windows of opportunity 25
Windows operating system 36, 43
Winter Report (2002) 90
win-win attitudes 112
Wirthlin Institute 139
Women's Wear Daily 267–8
work committee system 200
World Business Council for Sustainable Development (WBCSD) 316

World Wide Web 8, 355
World Wildlife Fund (WWF) 94–5
Worldcom 89–90
worldviews, *old* and *new* 139
Worldwatch Institute 116
Wright, J. 360
Wright, Will 356
wrongful trading 90

Xbox 41, 43
Xerox 175

Yee, Nick 357

Zalitrian, Gerald 371
'zero-based' thinking 157, 159, 169
Zhu Yanling, Eileen 97–8
Zidane, Zinedine 314
Ziff, R. 61